DATE DUE

FE 26 '93		
JE 22 '93		
JA 28 '94		
JE 23 '98		
FE 17 '98		

DEMCO 38-296

THE APPLAUSE / BEST PLAYS

THEATER YEARBOOK OF 1990-1991

FEATURING

THE TEN BEST PLAYS

OF THE SEASON

THE APPLAUSE / BEST PLAYS
THEATER YEARBOOK
OF 1990-1991
featuring the Ten Best Plays of the Season

EDITED BY OTIS L. GUERNSEY JR.
AND JEFFREY SWEET

Illustrated with photographs and
with drawings by HIRSCHFELD

APPLAUSE
THEATRE BOOK PUBLISHERS
211 WEST 71 STREET • NEW YORK NY • 10023

Copyright © 1992 by Applause Theatre Book Publishers

~~55783-106-8 (cloth)~~

~~5783-107-6 (paper)~~

~~N: 1063-620X~~

~~United States of America~~

Copyright © 1990 by John Guare. Reprinted by permis-
House, Inc. See CAUTION notice below. All inquiries
ision of Random House, Inc. 201 East 50th Street, New
York, NY 10022.

"Falsettoland": by William Finn and James Lapine. Music and lyrics by William Finn. Copyright ©
1990 by WB Music Corporation and William Finn. Reprinted by permission of the author's representatives, Rosenstone/Wender and International Creative Management. See CAUTION notice below.
All inquiries should be addressed to the author's representatives: Rosenstone/Wender, 3 East 48th
Street, New York, NY 10017 (for William Finn) and International Creative Management, 40 West
57th Street, New York, NY 10019 (for James Lapine).

"The Sum of Us": by David Stevens. Copyright © 1990 by David Stevens. Reprinted by permission of
the author's representative, Barrett, Benson, McCartt & Weston. All rights reserved. See CAUTION
notice below. All inquiries concerning Stock and Amateur rights should be addressed to: Samuel
French, Inc., 45 West 25th Street, New York, NY 10010. All other inquiries should be addressed to:
Barrett, Benson, McCartt & Weston, 9320 Wilshire Boulevard, Suite 300, Beverly Hills, CA 90212,
Attention: Irv Schwartz.

"Shadowlands": by William Nicholson. Copyright © 1990 by William Nicholson. Reprinted by permission of David Higham Associates Limited. See CAUTION notice below. All inquiries concerning
North American amateur and stock rights should be addressed to: Samuel French, Inc., 45 West 25th
Street, New York, NY 10010; rights elsewhere are controlled by Samuel French Ltd., 52 Fitzroy
Street, London W1P 6JR, England. All inquiries concerning other rights, including but not limited to
professional and first class production rights, and motion picture, television, radio and the right of
translation, should be addressed to: David Higham Associates Limited, 5-8 Lower John Street,
London W1R 4HA, England.

"The American Plan": by Richard Greenberg. Copyright © 1991 by Richard Greenberg. All rights
reserved. Reprinted by permission of Helen Merrill, Ltd. See CAUTION notice below. All inquiries
concerning stock and amateur performing rights should be addressed to: Dramatists Play Service, Inc.,
440 Park Avenue South, New York, NY 10016. All other inquiries should be addressed to: Helen
Merrill, Ltd., 435 West 23rd Street, #1A, New York, NY 10011.

"Lost in Yonkers": by Neil Simon. Copyright © 1991 by Neil Simon. Reprinted by permission of the
author's representative, Gary N. DaSilva. All rights reserved. See CAUTION notice below. The complete play published by Random House, Inc. All inquiries concerning stock and amateur performing
rights should be addressed to: Samuel French, Inc., 45 West 25th Street, New York, NY 10010. All
other inquiries should be addressed to: Gary N. DaSilva, 10100 Santa Monica Boulevard, Suite 400,
Los Angeles, CA 90067.

"The Substance of Fire": by Jon Robin Baitz, Copyright © 1991 by Available Light, Inc. All rights
reserved. Reprinted by permission of the author's representative, William Morris Agency, Inc. See
CAUTION notice below. Playwrights Horizons, Inc., New York City, produced "The Substance of
Fire" off Broadway in 1991. World Premier Presented at The Long Wharf Theatre, M. Edgar
Rosenblum, Executive Director, Arvin Brown, Artistic Director, 1990. All inquiries should be
addressed to: William Morris Agency, Inc., 1350 Avenue of the Americas, new York, NY 10010,
Attention: George Lane.

EDITOR'S NOTE

THE THEATER was wrestling with destiny and hard times in 1990-91, putting old and new policies to the test, as is explained in detail in the Offstage section of Jeffrey Sweet's review of the New York season. Onstage events, however, preoccupy most of our extensive coverage in this 1990-91 edition of *Best Plays*. Continuity is our game in this 72d volume in our series of yearbooks—continuity of the record and review of the American theater year, with its continuity of special excitements onstage, through thick and thin of offstage turbulence. In 1990-91, for example, Broadway glittered with the best new verse play in years (*La Bête*) with Neil Simon's 27th production, 14th Best Play and first Pulitzer Prize winner (*Lost in Yonkers*); with a helicopter (in *Miss Saigon*) and a parade of long-stemmed American beauties (in *The Will Rogers Follies*) descending to the stage. Off Broadway wore a crown of six Best Plays, including our pick for the year's best play (*Six Degrees of Separation*) and musical (*Falsettoland*). Elsewhere, doubly cited as an outstanding script was *Sincerity Forever*, a play by Mac Wellman, 1) by the American Theater Critics Association in a Berkshire Festival staging and 2) by Mel Gussow in an off-off-Broadway production. (Can the Wellman play go on to get a hat trick, a third citation in commercial theater? Stay tuned.) And Mr. Continuity himself, August Wilson, must make room among his three Critics Award and two Pulitzers for still another accolade, the 1990-91 New Play Award from the ATCA committee chaired by T.H. McCulloh of the Los Angeles *Times*, for his new script *Two Trains Running*.

Continuity is the name of our game in publication, with the baton passed from Dodd, Mead, originator of the *Best Plays* yearbook series in 1919-20, and now firmly in the grasp of Glenn Young and his Applause Theater Books; in supervision by the meticulously attentive Jonathan Dodd; in editing by the undersigned and his persistently helpful wife; in reviewing by Jeffrey Sweet—playwright, screen writer, teacher and 21st-century version of the *Best Plays* critics who have preceded him from the age of O'Neill to the age of Sondheim—and Mel Gussow, distinguished drama critic of the New York *Times*, who annually surveys the OOB scene for this yearbook. Camille Croce continues to build a rock-solid factual report from the shifting sands of each OOB season, while Sheridan Sellers does the same for new plays and musicals presented in the regional theaters across America.

We'll keep publishing every available Al Hirschfeld drawing of the theater's personalities, in the certain knowledge that his incomparably colorful and revealing caricatures are as much a delight to our readers as they have always been to the subjects. Our yearbook also continues to enjoy the indispensable services of Rue E. Canvin (play publications and necrology), Sally Dixon Wiener (Best Play synopses), William Schelble (Tony Awards listing), Thomas T. Foose (historical foot-notes), Henry Hewes (a former *Best Plays* editor and present help in every kind of need), Michael Kuchwara (Critics Circle voting) and Ralph Newman of the Drama Book Shop—and of course the indefatigable and willing men and women in the press offices who provide Broadway, off-Broadway, off-off-Broadway and cross-country information services that make our coverage of the theater possible in its expanded, comprehensive 1990s form.

The creators of costumes for the New York theater have again made available for *Best Plays* reproduction samples of the year's best designs in the form of original working drawings. We thank Richard Hudson and Willa Kim for helping us to maintain this perception between the observers and the work observed. And we are proud to include the graphic reality of the theater's "look" in the form of the photos which grace our pages, created by New York and cross-country stage photographers including Martha Swope and her associates (Carol Rosegg and Blanche Mackey); Michael LePoer Trench/Joan Marcus for the photos synopsizing *Miss Saigon*); and Richard Anderson, Fred Andrews, Susan Cook, Peter Cunningham, T. Charles Erickson, Gregory M. Fota, Ron Franklin, Gerry Goodstein, Terry deRoy Gruber, Will Gullette, Gary Gunderson, Mark Koslowski, Brigitte Lacombe, Anthony Loew, Bob Marshak, Roger Mastroianni, Jim Moore, Miguel Pagliere, Walter H. Scott, Richard C. Trigg and Michael Vaughn.

And when we think of continuity, we must always remember that the theater in 1990-91, as in every year since long before Aeschylus, lives by the talent of its playwrights and their dedication to what is certainly one of the worthiest of artistic causes. We're also reminded that, rough-hew our continuum as we will, we can't avoid the ravages of time. Ossia Trilling's incapacitating illness has taken from us support from London which we have greatly appreciated. And the death this year of Stanley Green, the theater historian who compiled our Cast Replacements section for more than two decades, has cost us a friend and colleague affectionately admired throughout the profession. His work for us, as in his published volumes on aspects of the musical stage, is a firm foundation on which we will continue to build.

OTIS L. GUERNSEY Jr.
Editor

September 1, 1991

CONTENTS

THE APPLAUSE / BEST PLAYS
THEATER YEARBOOK OF 1990-1991

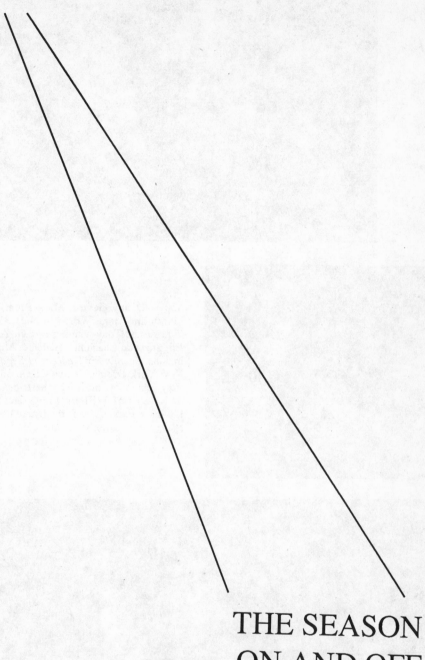

THE SEASON
ON AND OFF
BROADWAY

1990-91
Best
of
Bests

Above, Danny Gerard, Mark Blum, Jamie
Marsh and Irene Worth in Neil Simon's
Pulitzer and Tony-winning *Lost in Yonkers*,
left, Stockard Channing and James McDaniel
in John Guare's *Six Degrees of Separation*,
New York Drama Critics Circle and *Best*
Plays choice as the year's best; *below*, the
entire cast of William Finn's and James
Lapine's *Falsettoland*, designated by *Best*
Plays as the season's best musical

BROADWAY AND OFF BROADWAY

By Jeffrey Sweet

OK, LET'S get it out of the way right at the beginning: *Miss Saigon*. Mind you, its quality is far from undisputed. (In the *Village Voice*, critic Michael Feingold expressed his belief that its production signalled the end of Western civilization and prescribed a number of Swiftian responses, including the razing of the theater district and the mass execution of cultural czars.) One thing that *is* undisputed is that it was there—the year's single most discussed enterprise, the most expensive production in Broadway history ($10 million), generating the largest advance sale in Broadway history (a reported $37 million) and commanding the highest ticket price for a single evening's entertainment in Broadway history (a staggering $100 for a seat in the front mezzanine). In addition, the pre-production wrangling dominated the theater pages for months and stimulated debate in the national media.

1990-91 was also a year in which an unusually large number of offerings drew their inspiration from real-life figures. Broadway saw shows about Buddy Holly, Will Rogers, C.S. Lewis, Isak Dinesen, John Barrymore and Florence Aadland (who? mother of an Errol Flynn companion). Off Broadway, the ghosts of Virginia Woolf, Huey Long, Lyndon Baines Johnson, Amelia Earhart and an ensemble of Presidential assassins were summoned by talented actors. And Spalding Gray, Rick Reynolds and Tom Mardirosian were praised for playing themselves.

Another distinguishing characteristic of the season was the prevalence of works in which homosexuality was an important element. Gay characters were prominent figures in the Best Plays *Six Degrees of Separation, The Sum of Us, The American Plan, Falsettoland* and *The Substance of Fire* as well as such other plays as *Walking the Dead, A Bright Room Called Day, Dead Mother, or Shirley Not All in Vain, Prin, Indecent Materials, Advice From a Caterpiller, The Old Boy* and *Casanova.*

Falsettoland, an off-Broadway collaboration between William Finn and James Lapine, proved to be the season's strongest musical. Though it had its fervent supporters, Stephen Sondheim and John Weidman's *Assassins* was generally counted to be an intriguing disappointment. These two works both originated at Playwrights Horizons, as did the year's best Broadway musical, Lynn Ahrens and Stephen Flaherty's *Once on This Island* (which was named a Best Play last season on the basis of its spring 1990 run at that valuable theater). The Alain Boublil-Claude-Michel Schönberg-Richard Maltby Jr. collaboration *Miss Saigon* is cited as a Best Play for reasons discussed later. The Tony Award for best musical,

The 1990–91 Season on Broadway

PLAYS (9)

Stand-Up Tragedy
Lincoln Center:
*SIX DEGREES OF
SEPARATION*
(transfer)
Mule Bone
LA BÊTE
LOST IN YONKERS
The Speed of Darkness
The Big Love
(one-actor perf.)
Lucifer's Child
(one-actor perf.)
I Hate Hamlet

MUSICALS (6)

Once on This Island
(transfer)
Buddy: The Buddy
Holly Story
Shogun: The Musical
MISS SAIGON
The Secret Garden
The Will Rogers Follies

FOREIGN PLAYS IN ENGLISH (3)

SHADOWLANDS
Taking Steps
*OUR COUNTRY'S
GOOD*

HOLDOVERS WHICH BECAME HITS IN 1990-91 (4)

Gypsy
City of Angels
Lettice & Lovage
The Piano Lesson

REVIVALS (5)

The Miser
Oh, Kay!
Fiddler on the Roof
Peter Pan
Gypsy
(return engagement)

SPECIALTIES (3)

*Jackie Mason: Brand
New*
Christmas Spectacular
*Penn & Teller: The
Refrigerator Tour*

REVUE (1)

Those Were the Days

Categorized above are all the new productions listed in the Plays Produced on Broadway section of this volume.
Plays listed in CAPITAL LETTERS have been designated Best Plays of 1990-91.
Plays listed in *italics* were still running June 1, 1991.
Plays listed in **bold face type** were classified as hits in *Variety*'s annual estimate published June 10, 1991.

however, was given to *The Will Rogers Follies*, which was the teamwork of veterans Peter Stone, Cy Coleman, Betty Comden, Adolph Green and Tommy Tune. *The Secret Garden*, the most significant American attempt at a book musical, fell short despite a libretto by Marsha Norman and music by promising Broadway neophyte Lucy Simon.

If the season was short on solid accomplishment in musical theater, it was long on genuinely strong straight plays. The Pulitzer Prize went to one of Neil Simon's hardier efforts, *Lost in Yonkers*; but, for many, the clear giant was John Guare's deeply unsettling comedy, *Six Degrees of Separation*. Creditable cases for Pulitzer worthiness might also have been made for Richard Greenberg's *The American Plan* and Jon Robin Baitz's *The Substance of Fire*. Of the plays originating in foreign theaters, the most impressive were Timberlake Wertenbaker's drama of convicts transported to 18th century Australia, *Our Country's Good,* and *Shadowlands*, William Nicholson's play about C.S. Lewis's bittersweet marriage to poet Joy Davidman.

As has been the rule for the better part of the past two decades, most Broadway offerings originated outside the commercial Broadway economy. In addition to *Our Country's Good, Shadowlands* and *Miss Saigon*, Britain supplied us with Alan Ayckbourn's *Taking Steps* and *Buddy: The Buddy Holly Story*. The all-black version of the Gershwin musical *Oh, Kay!* began at the Goodspeed Opera House, *The Speed of Darkness* at Chicago's Goodman Theater, *The Big Love* in an off-off-Broadway staging at the Perry Street Theater, *The Secret Garden* at the Virginia Stage Company, *I Hate Hamlet* at Albany's Capital Rep, *Stand-Up Tragedy* at the Mark Taper Forum and the Hartford Stage Company and, as mentioned before, *Once on This Island* at Playwrights Horizons. Non-profit production on Broadway included Circle in the Square's two offerings, *Taking Steps* and *The Miser* and two sponsored by Lincoln Center, *Six Degrees of Separation* and *Mule Bone*.

Off Broadway, other plays originated or were developed at Actors Theater of Louisville, City Lit Theater Company, Crossroads Theater Company, Duke University, the Eureka Theater, Ford's Theater, the George Street Playhouse, the Goodman Theater, La Jolla Playhouse, the Long Wharf Theater, Los Angeles Theater Center, the Manbites Dog Theater Company, the Old Globe Theater, River Arts Rep, South Coast Repertory, Stages Repertory Theater, the Williamstown Theater Festival, the Playhouse in London and the Market Theater of Johannesburg.

The season was shy of the array of movie-star power on display in the 1989-1990 season, which is not to imply there was any shortage of superb performances. Among the actors who made indelible marks on theatergoers' memories were Stockard Channing, Courtney B. Vance, Ron Rifkin, Jane Alexander, Nigel Hawthorne, Mercedes Ruehl, Irene Worth, Cathy Rigby, Jonathan Pryce, Eileen Atkins, Audra Lindley, Wendy Makkena, Joan Copeland, Nicol Williamson, Paul Hipp, Lindsay Crouse, Maureen Moore, Bruce Adler, Len Cariou, Kathryn Erbe, Amelia Campbell, Tracey Ellis, Cherry Jones, Ron McLarty and J. Smith-Cameron.

Jerry Zaks won a well-deserved Tony for staging *Six Degrees of Separation* and was also represented by *Assassins*. The most exciting musical theater direction was James Lapine's hyperkinetic work on *Falsettoland*. Other directors who

Among the year's best costume designs were those of Richard
Hudson for *La Bête*. A selection of them is pictured here

achieved particular distinction include Mark Brokaw (*The Good Times Are Killing
Me*), Scott Ellis (*And the World Goes 'Round* and the New York City Opera
Company's revival of *A Little Night Music*), Nicholas Hytner (*Miss Saigon*), Mark
Lamos (*Our Country's Good*), Michael Schultz (*Mule Bone*), Evan Yionoulis (*The
American Plan*) and Tommy Tune (*The Will Rogers Follies*). In addition to direct-
ing, Tommy Tune choreographed a phalanx of scantily-clad ladies of the chorus to
stirring effect. Susan Stroman worked similiar wonders with the versatile cast of
five in *And the World Goes 'Round*.

The musicals displayed the most elaborate designers' conceits, set designer
Heidi Landesman and lighting designer Tharon Musser triumphing with their evo-
cation of Victoriana in *The Secret Garden*, Tony Walton and Jules Fisher celebrat-
ing show biz conventions in *The Will Rogers Follies,* and John Napier and David
Hersey summoning up nightmares of Southeast Asia in *Miss Saigon.* Among the
less flashy but artful designs for straight plays, special praise is due Christopher
Barreca for *Our Country's Good* (lighting by Mimi Jordan Sherin) and Santo
Loquasto for his beautifully-detailed work on *Lost in Yonkers.*

The particular franchise of this book is to celebrate the best playwriting efforts
which gave employment to other theater artists. To quote Otis L. Guernsey Jr. in
past volumes, "The choice is made without any regard whatever to the play's
type—musical, comedy or drama—or origin on or off Broadway, or popularity at
the box office or lack of same. We don't take the scripts of bygone eras into consideration for Best Play citation in this one, whatever their technical status as
American or New York 'premieres' which didn't have a previous production of

record. We draw the line between adaptations and revivals, the former eligible for Best Play selection but the latter not, on a case-by-case basis. If a script influences the character of a season, or by some function of consensus wins the Critics, Pulitzer or Tony Awards, we take into account its future historical as well as present esthetic importance. This is the only special consideration we give, and we don't always tilt in its direction, as the record shows."

Our choices for the Best Plays of 1990-91 are listed below in the order in which they opened in New York (a plus sign + with the performance number signifies that the play was still running on June 1, 1991).

Six Degrees of Separation
   (Off B'way, 155 perfs.;
   B'way, 234+ perfs.)

Falsettoland
   (Off B'way, 215 perfs.)

The Sum of Us
   (Off B'way, 259 perfs.)

Shadowlands
   (B'way, 169 perfs.)

The American Plan
   (Off B'way, 37 perfs.)

Lost in Yonkers
   (B'way, 114+ perfs.)

The Substance of Fire
   (Off B'way, 84+ perfs.)

Miss Saigon
   (B'way, 58+ perfs.)

Our Country's Good
   (Off B'way, 38+ perfs.)

The Good Times Are Killing Me
   (Off Off B'way, 37 perfs.)
   (Off B'way, 12+ perfs.)

La Bête (special citation)
(B'way, 25 perfs.)

ELLIOT LOVES—Christine Baranski
and David Pierce in Jules Feiffer's play

New Plays

One evening, a well-spoken, well-dressed young black man named Paul appears on the doorstep of art speculator Flan Kittredge and his wife Ouisa. Bloodstains on his shirt, Paul tells them he has been stabbed during a mugging and that he turned to them for help because their children at Harvard are friends of his. The Kittredges patch him up and give him a new shirt. In thanks, the young man whips up a dinner for them and the business friend they are entertaining and tells them of a paper he's written on *Catcher in the Rye*. Beguiled, the Kittredges offer him their son's room for the night and lend him money to tide him over until his father—who happens to be Sidney Poitier—gets into town the next day. Early the next morning, they are shocked to find Paul has invited a hustler off the street into their apartment to share his bed. Pleading that they not tell his father of his homosexuality, Paul beats a hasty retreat.

The Kittredges are in for more shocks. Investigation proves that everything Paul has told them is a lie—he does not know their children, he does not attend

Harvard, and he most definitely is not Sidney Poitier's son. They further discover that they are not alone in having been conned by him; but, as John Guare's *Six Degrees of Separation* unfolds, we realize that Paul is less a calculating scoundrel than a pathetic young man at the mercy of an out-of-control fantasy life and a hunger to storm the walls of a society closed to him. Guare has set up a kind of dramatic cyclotron, with Paul bashing up against a variety of characters and relationships and, in destabilizing them, revealing aspects previously unquestioned and unexamined. The collision which most concerns Guare is with Ouisa.

When we first meet her, Ouisa impresses as a clever, superficial, materialistic woman—a satiric creation. But the encounter with Paul changes her profoundly. In trying to understand why she swallowed Paul's fabrications so readily, she comes to grips with the underlying self to which he instinctively appealed, ultimately recognizing the unsettling bond of commonality which ties her to this disturbed young man.

Guare enhances his tale with a deftly-sketched gallery of supporting characters and a constant stream of pointed observations about the moral underpinnings and internal contradicitions of upper middle class life. Particularly poignant is the observation that one reason so many of Paul's victims have been eager to believe him is that he showed them respect which is in scant supply from their own children.

Guare's script was brilliantly served by Jerry Zaks's staging. Zaks and designer Tony Walton added a row of seats ringing the downstage playing area. During the course of the performance, one discovered with a happy shock that the people seated there were not fellow audience members but much of the supporting cast who, as needed, would rise in place for a quick observation and enter into the ongoing action. By having actors emerge from the audience, Zaks created a sense of community akin to a campfire gathering at which an urban folk tale is being shared.

Guare was blessed, too, in the casting. Actor after actor created a vivid impression, sometimes with only a handful of lines. I was particularly taken with the hilariously miserable father-son relationship between Stephen Pearlman's and Evan Handler's characters. John Cunningham made an eerily contained Flan Kittredge. James McDaniel originated the role of Paul, emphasizing the character's mystery. By the time the production moved upstairs from Lincoln Center's "off-Broadway" space, the Mitzi Newhouse, to a Broadway contract in the Vivian Beaumont, McDaniel had left the show for a Hollywood opportunity and was succeeded by Courtney B. Vance. Vance's take on Paul was more seductive and accomplished the unusual feat of making the con man paradoxically guileless. In one of the season's most highly-praised performances, as Ouisa, Stockard Channing made the journey from a *New Yorker*-like cartoon figure to a fully invested, three-dimensional woman with nary a perceptible effort.

Though Guare doesn't tub-thump the racial issues inherent in the story, the line dividing black and white was very much present on his stage. *The Good Times Are Killing Me*, which Lynda Barry adapted from her own novel, dramatizes the time in the life of her young protagonist when that line is first drawn explicitly. Growing up in an integrated working-class neighborhood in the 1960s, Edna makes friends

The 1990–91 Season Off Broadway

PLAYS (41)

Elliot Loves
Price of Fame
SIX DEGREES OF SEPARATION
Quiet on the Set (transfer)
Public Theater:
Indecent Materials
The Big Funk
A Bright Room Called Day
Dead Mother
Casanova
Money Talks
Playwrights Horizons:
Young Playwrights Festival
Subfertile
THE SUBSTANCE OF FIRE
The Old Boy
About Time
Circle Repertory:
The Colorado Catechism
Love Diatribe
Road to Nirvana
Walking the Dead
Handy Dandy
Manhattan Theater Club:
The Wash
Abundance
THE AMERICAN PLAN

Manhattan T.C. (con't):
Life During Wartime
Black Eagles
The Stick Wife
Life on the Third Rail
American Place:
Struck Dumb & The War in Heaven
States of Shock
Chelsea Stage:
The March on Russia
The Voice of the Prairie
Lyndon (one-actor perf.)
A Room of One's Own (one-actor perf.)
The Little Tommy Parker Celebrated Colored Minstrel Show
Pvt. Wars
The Kingfish (one-actor perf.)
Advice From a Caterpillar (transfer)
Ivy Rowe (one-actor perf.)
Breaking Legs
THE GOOD TIMES ARE KILLING ME

MUSICALS (12)

Jekyll and Hyde
Playwrights Horizons:
FALSETTOLAND
Assassins
Smoke on the Mountain (transfer)
Pretty Faces
Yiddle With a Fiddle
Catch Me If I Fall
Township Fever
The Gifts of the Magi
An Unfinished Song
Pageant
Song of Singapore

REVUES (2)

Broadway Jukebox
And the World Goes 'Round

REVIVALS (15)

Roundabout :
Light Up the Sky
King Lear
The Country Girl
Pygmalion
The Subject Was Roses
Shakespeare Marathon:
The Taming of the Shrew
Richard III
Henry IV, Part 1
Henry IV, Part 2
Public Theatre:
Through the Leaves
Machinal
Gonza the Lancer
The Caucasian Chalk Circle
The Way of The World
The Haunted Host & Pouf
Positive

SPECIALTIES (5)

Mambo Mouth
(one-actor perf.)
Monster in a Box
(one-actor perf.)
Sex, Drugs, Rock & Roll
(one-actor perf.)
(return engagement)
The Fever
(one-actor perf.)
The Wizard of Hip
(one-actor perf.)

FOREIGN PLAYS IN ENGLISH (4)

Manhattan Theater Club:
Prin
Absent Friends
THE SUM OF US
Mump & Smoot in "Caged"
With Wog

Categorized above are all the new productions listed in the Plays Produced Off Broadway section of this volume.
Plays listed in CAPITAL LETTERS have been designated Best Plays of 1990-91.
Plays listed in italics were still running June 1, 1991.

with Bonna, a black girl of the same age from across the street. Inevitably this introduces the two girls to each other's worlds. Edna attends foot-stomping Baptist services with Bonna's family, Bonna goes with Edna and her tightass aunt's family on a camping trip. Ultimately, though, the closer the two get to the adult world, the more they are divided, until, finally, they find themselves more defined by the pressures of their tribes than their feelings for each other.

The play does not limit itself to race relations. It is a play about socialization in general—the process by which society shapes the values of its young and the hard experience it can dish out in teaching these lessons. Some of the lessons have to do with loss—in addition to the destruction of a friendship, Edna must cope with abandonment by a parent and witness the shock of the accidental death of a young neighbor. Other lessons have to do with the pressure to mold oneself into a form acceptable to peers—to embrace what is currently endorsed as the hip music and be invited to hang with the cool (that is, most affluent) crowd. Part of Barry's achievement is to restore childhood crises to the scale they had in our lives when we were children. At the same time we laugh with indulgent affection at Edna's awkwardness and naivete, we can't help being reminded of the seriousness with which we viewed similar events in our own lives. As an adult, we can look back and smile, but when we were young, the pain and anxiety didn't feel at all cute.

Under Mark Brokaw's direction, the production fluidly shifted gears between Edna's intimate confidences to the audience to exuberant set pieces featuring the entire company of 14. Though the cast as a whole was admirable, the primary responsibilities of the enterprise necessarily rest on the actress playing Edna. Young Angela Goethals was simply superb, performing with a subtlety and precision that would be the envy of more seasoned performers. Opened as a limited off-off-Broadway engagement, *The Good Times Are Killing Me* had shifted to the continuous run it so richly deserved before the end of the season.

Shadowlands, one of the year's dramas, began life in another medium, having first been seen as an award-winning British television movie. Based on true events, William Nicholson's play begins by introducing author C.S. Lewis as he lectures on why God permits suffering. Lewis has got it all figured out from a theoretical perspective, and indeed it *sounds* wise—something about suffering being God's instrument to awaken compassion in man. But Lewis's view of suffering is the view of one who has lived life on the sheltered sidelines—specifically, the clubby, all-male world of Oxford academia. The action of the play consists of how American poet Joy Davidman, a divorcee who begins as a pen pal and becomes a friend, yanks him off those sidelines. Lewis marries her in order to help her and her son stay in England. It is only when she is stricken with cancer that Lewis begins to realize that he has fallen deeply in love with his wife. As he tries to cope with her imminent death, Lewis is brought face to face with the profound inadequacy of his theoretical ideas on suffering.

There have been both gains and losses from the television version. The play has more leisure to explore the philosophical issues than did the film, but the added length also makes much of the second act—particularly the scenes in which Lewis

BREAKING LEGS—Vincent Gardenia and Philip Bosco in Tom Dulack's comedy

articulates his love for her during her illness—seem padded and repetitious. Nigel Hawthorne, the brilliantly funny character actor familiar as the Machiavellian civil servant on the satiric TV series *Yes, Minister*, showed a side hitherto unseen by American audiences, here playing a profoundly decent man whose mild manner is a cover for feelings the depth of which surprises even him. As Joy Davidman, Jane Alexander projected an American brashness which had eluded Claire Bloom in her otherwise lovely performance in the film. For the richness of its characterization and the grace with which it deals with the philosophical issues, *Shadowlands* merits citation as one of the season's Best Plays.

The Sum of Us, a Best Play by Australian David Stevens, proved particularly popular among gay audiences, presenting as it did the rare dramatic image of a father who not only accepts his son's homosexuality but tries to encourage the shy young man in his romantic life. The script is laid out somewhat schematically: in the first act, the presence of the father thwarts a relationship between the son and a young man he brings home; in the second act, the son's homosexuality is the barrier between Dad and a divorcee. Though the craft is crude, the script is heartfelt, and it offered a splendid cast—Tony Goldwyn as the son, Richard Venture as the father, Phyllis Somerville as the divorcee and Neil Maffin as the young man the son brings home—rich opportunities for sensitive and frequently funny work under Kevin Dowling's direction. Though its appeal understandably is greater to those who identify most directly with the characters, it is a play that obviously moves straight audiences as well.

In contrast to the accommodating father in *The Sum of Us* is the mother portrayed in A.R. Gurney's *The Old Boy* who attempts to deny her son's homosexuality. The central figure of the play is a politician named Sam who has returned to the private boarding school he had attended to give a speech. When a student there, Sam had been the "old boy" or informal advisor to a younger student named Perry. A genuine friendship had developed. When Perry had revealed to Sam his homosexual leanings, Sam had persuaded him to try to deny these feelings and pushed him into a marriage with his (Sam's) inconvenient girl friend. After several years in the marriage, Perry had come out of the closet, left his wife, taken a male lover, and subsequently died of AIDS. Learning of his friend's death, Sam puts aside the appropriate speech planned for him and talks instead of the need for America to acknowledge all the "different" people who contribute to the culture. Unfortunately, the play's payoff is contingent upon our believing that some discontent is already stewing in Sam when he arrives at the school. Stephen Collins gave an assured performance as both the mature man and, in flashbacks, the callow youth, but he couldn't act what Gurney didn't give him—some inkling in the first act of a man in serious turmoil. John Rubinstein directed the smooth production, getting a particularly scary performance out of Nan Martin as the aforementioned mother, but the play was a bit too neatly tailored to pack the intended emotional punch.

Set mostly during a summer in the Fifties, *The American Plan*, Richard Greenberg's second Best Play (his first was *Eastern Standard*) offers another dark view of a parent-child relationship. Eva Adler, a wealthy Jewish refugee from Hitler's Germany, has brought with her from the nightmare of Europe a well-earned but destructive cynicism. She has created an enclave by a lake in the Catskills where her daughter, Lili, summers with her in a Rapunzel-like existence. What first appear to be Lili's eccentric charm and animation are masks for deep psychological problems which Greenberg implies are the product of her mother's bleak worldview. The action of the play is framed by Lili's courtship by what appears to be a prosperous-looking, clean-cut young WASP named Nick Lockridge. Nick turns out not to be all he seems. He is, in fact, a fortune hunter not unlike the suitor in Henry James's *Washington Square*. Indeed, much of the action is reminiscent of Ruth and Augustus Goetz's fine adaptation of the James novel, *The Heiress*, with a ruthless parent pitted against the young man who seeks her daughter's hand for reasons other than love. But this is no derivative construction. Greenberg's characters are rooted in the specifics of 20th century history, and he artfully manages to convey the idea that his characters' personal conflicts are reflections of the world's larger griefs. Under director Evan Yionoulis, a fine cast gave vivid life to Greenberg's tortured trio, Wendy Makkena achingly vulnerable as Lili, D.W. Moffett confirming his reputation as one of our best young actors as Nick, and Joan Copeland both terrifying and pitiable as the monstrous Eva.

Another Best Play, Neil Simon's *Lost in Yonkers*, focuses on the painful relationship between another monstrous mother and her fragile daughter. Like Eva Adler, Grandmother Kurnitz has been emotionally scarred by her experiences as a Jew in Europe. Unlike Eva, she has no wealth to buy a sheltering enclave, but instead barricades herself against the world in her candy store and the apartment above it she shares with the slightly retarded 35-year-old Bella. At the play's beginning, one of her other children, Eddie, persuades Grandmother Kurnitz to take in his two young boys so he can go on the road and raise the money to pay off the debts incurred during his late wife's illness. The boys' stay there provides the shape of the play.

The question would seem to be whether this bitter, unhappy woman, who has so damaged her own children, is going to wreak similar emotional havoc on her grandchildren while they are in her charge. But this question is never seriously explored—throughout, the two kids remain admirably plucky, coping with instances of the old lady's tyranny with well-articulated defiance. Another promising possibility—that the boys' presence might be the catalyst for Bella's rebellion—is also barely engaged. Instead of involving the kids in some ongoing dramatic action, Simon uses them as Aunt Bella's confederates and straight men to Louie, the swaggering gangster uncle who hides out for a time in his mother's apartment.

Though *Lost in Yonkers* is susceptible to criticism on structural grounds, it still earns its place among the year's best because of the vividness of the characters. Even as one may carp about the awkward exposition, Simon's inability to refrain from some easy gags and the sentimentality which threatens to overwhelm credibility, it is impossible to deny the richness of the best of the humor and the emotional impact of the confrontations between Bella and her mother.

Simon has given most of the actors in his company a wealth of opportunity to register strongly. With the exception of the throwaway part of Aunt Gert (played by Lauren Klein, an actress too fine to be thrown away), all of the roles are strong ones, and, under Gene Saks's direction, the cast responded with memorable performances. Mercedes Ruehl, in her first New York stage role since the feisty and sexy attorney in *Other People's Money*, played Bella with the wide-eyed enthusiasm of a child combined with the pain of a lonely adult to heartbreaking effect. Irene Worth, in a startling transformation from her series of elegant roles, was a formidable Grandmother Kurnitz, growling out cruelties she justified as character-building and trying to tamp down the pain of her emotional isolation. Kevin Spacey shared the great fun he had playing both the charming and the bullying sides of Louie. Danny Gerard was suitably adorable as Arty, the younger boy; Jamie Marsh was particularly impressive as older brother Jay, meeting the assorted challenges of his various daunting relatives and trying to cope with the onslaught of adolescence. Performances this good are no accident; they are possible because of the gifts of a playwright who has more than earned his position as Broadway's most popular dramatist.

Still a third Jewish refugee monster-parent—this time a father— is the focus of Jon Robin Baitz's Best Play, *The Substance of Fire*. When we first meet Isaac Geldhart, he is struggling with his children over the control of the publishing company he heads. Resolutely anti-commercial, he refuses to issue a trashy novel which might restore the company to financial health, preferring instead to release a six-volume account of Nazi medical atrocities which will surely doom it to bankruptcy. His three children—vice president son Aaron, landscaping professor Martin and TV actress Sarah—propose compromises; but, dripping contempt for all of them, Isaac refuses to budge from his fixed position and brings about his own downfall. The second act, set more than three years later, is a portrait of Isaac in decline—completely cut off from two of his children, on strained terms with the third, and having increasingly tenuous relations with such details of reality as the day of the week and the identity of people with whom he is speaking. A social worker has been dispatched to make an initial evaluation of his competency, and the bulk of the balance of the play concerns their confrontation in his book-lined tomb of an apartment. During the course of this scene, we learn the details of his survival of the Holocaust, which claimed the lives of most of his family, and his resulting sense of mission to publish accounts of the horror. We understand, too, how his inflexibility has made a desert of his life.

Despite some awkward exposition, the first act is thrilling. Baitz has written no patsies or easy foils. All four—father and children—are impassioned and articulate, and their battle is fought on a high intellectual level. Baitz is particularly good at implying how the children's philosophies have been formed in reaction to their parent's moral absolutism. The second act is more problematic; the author has given the social worker a secret, and the exchange of tales of suffering strikes me as too neat and symmetrical and the resulting solution unearned. Still, on balance, *The Substance of Fire* is a substantial accomplishment. There was fine work from the entire cast under Daniel Sullivan's direction, headed by Ron Rifkin's stunning performance as the haunted and hurtful Isaac.

Surely *La Bête*, specially cited as a Best Play for its versified dialogue, was among the oddest of this season's Broadway entries, set in 17th century provincial France and concerning a narcissistic vulgarian being imposed by a titled patron on a theatrical troupe run by a principled actor-manager named Elomire (an anagram of Molière). Author David Hirson apparently means to dramatize the perpetual war between artistic integrity and sheer vital crassness; but in execution, his theme appears to be less important to him than the opportunity to flaunt an undeniable ability to compose cascades of clever rhyming couplets. The leading role, that of the vulgarian Valere, was played by Tom McGowan with great bounce and flair, and he was justly applauded for sustaining an extraordinary 25-minute monologue in the first act. The most striking aspect of the production was Richard Hudson's scenic design, which portrayed an elegant chamber with a violently distorted perspective dominated by a huge chandelier set at an extreme angle.

Timberlake Wertenbaker's *Our Country's Good*, a Best Play based on Thomas Keneally's novel *The Playmaker*, also engages a theatrical subject in an historical context. Set in the early days of Britain's use of Australia as a penal colony, the plot deals with a young officer's assignment to mount a production of Farquhar's *The Recruiting Officer* with a cast made up of convicts. During the course of the evening, we watch as a group of brutalized and debased prisoners finds a measure of hope, dignity and purpose through a communal artistic effort. Art, Wertenbaker is saying, is not just for diversion, it is in itself a social good. In production, what undercut the play's drift toward preachiness was the vividness of many of its nearly two dozen characters as played by a versatile ensemble of 13 under the direction of Mark Lamos. The script gave particularly strong opportunities to four of the company's women—Cherry Jones, Tracey Ellis, J. Smith-Cameron and Amelia Campbell—doubling as abused and desperate female prisoners and four of their male captors. Ron McLarty also distinguished himself as Harry Brewer, the Provost Marshal haunted by the memory of a man he hanged. Christopher Barreca designed the impressive unit set which employed the tilted deck of the transporting ship as a central image; Mimi Jordan Sherin supplied the equally impresive lighting.

The Big Love brings us back to the theme of destructive motherhood. A one-woman show, it concerns Florence Aadland, whose sole and dubious claim to fame was to be the mother of the underage girl who was Errol Flynn's companion in the last years of his life. Co-written (with her daughter Brooke) and directed by Jay Presson Allen, who did such an impressive job with Tru, last season's solo show on Truman Capote, the piece is meant as an examination of the way in which the obsessions with celebrity and show business may corrupt basic human values. The chief problem was that, even given Tracey Ullman's scrupulously detailed performance, Florence was not interesting enough to sustain a full evening.

Neither, surprisingly, was Isak Dinesen, at least in Lucifer's Child, William Luce's solo play about the writer, commissioned for Julie Harris. Miss Harris is always welcome company, but if one had only the evidence of this piece, it would be hard to make a case for Dinesen as a figure of consequence. Eileen Atkins fared better as Virginia Woolf in a piece adapted by director Patrick Garland from Woolf's book, A Room of One's Own. Instead of the autobiography of Lucifer's Child, which calls for the actress to putter through her wardrobe as she spills intimacies, A Room of One's Own puts its central figure into the realistic context of a lecture. The lecture's thesis—that male domination accounts for the small number of women who have distinguished themselves in literature—though eloquently articulated, suffered from repetition, but Miss Atkins served it up bracingly.

Two politicians were also portrayed in solo shows, Laurence Luckinbill playing a sympathetic Lyndon Baines Johnson in Lyndon and John McConnell offering a boisterously convincing Huey Long in Larry L. King and Ben Z. Grant's The Kingfish. Material adapted from playwright-activist Larry Kramer's book Reports From the Holocaust: The Making of an AIDS Activist was the basis of a solo piece portraying Kramer's impassioned response to the AIDS epidemic; it was paired with a piece adapted from the public statements of Senator Jesse Helms in which the North Carolina senator took aim at federal arts funding. Two performers—one man, one woman—took turns interpreting Helms while a dancer (presumably representing the Artistic Spirit) performed in counterpoint. The program, presented under the joint title Indecent Materials, was further proof that "correct" politics are not in themselves sufficient for compelling theater.

Not all of the solo enterprises were biographical. Mambo Mouth, written by and starring John Leguizamo, offered a gallery of theatrical snapshots of various characters, male and female, from the Latino community. The best-written moments were sharply observed in the clear-eyed, unsentimental tradition of Eric Bogosian. But Leguizamo is not yet as disciplined a writer as Bogosian, and he tended to let pieces go on too long after he had made his points. Also, it is some-what disconcerting that in all of his characters he couldn't summon up the image of one vaguely admirable Latino figure; there is little in these portraits to challenge stereotypes. This is not to deny Leguizamo's considerable promise as a writer, or his versatility and dynamism as a performer.

In his solo outing, *The Fever*, Wallace Shawn played a single character—a nameless American violently ill in the bathroom of a hotel in a third-world country. The fever in question is a fever of moral clarity. Shawn's thesis is that Americans are blithely indifferent to the fact that their privileged lives are based on the exploitation of the poor and powerless. The profession of liberal sympathies is not a sufficient response to our moral complicity in accepting the benefits of such a murderous system, Shawn insists, as, with unsparing logic, he knocks down the illusions with which much of his audience presumably comfort themselves. The critical reaction was largely negative, concentrating on Shawn's political naivete and the irony of his challenging the alleged social benefits of art while performing in the Public Theater, an institution largely based upon the assumption of these ben-efits. I will not make great claims for it as a piece of dramatic writing—Shawn tends to bludgeon rather than imply—but the questions it raises are raised all too rarely in today's theater, and it seems to me that its ability to disturb and compel the audience to examine their values make this a piece not to be dismissed lightly.

No such clarity of purpose was evident in another of the Public Theater's offer-ings, *The Big Funk*, which John Patrick Shanley wrote and directed. Filled with sentimental absurdities and moralizing reminiscent of William Saroyan, the script seems to lurch arbitrarily from one effect to another. The most discussed scene depicts a young woman having her head covered in Vaseline by a bizarre man. This is followed by a sequence in which another man invites her home and, onstage, gives her a bath and shampoo and pats her dry. In performance, some pro-fessed to see this as a metaphor for being cleansed of crippling psychological bag-gage. I must confess that all that I saw was a very attractive and talented actress named Jeanne Tripplehorn demonstrate considerable poise through a potentially embarrassing nude scene. Later, the actor playing the young man who cleans her had the even less enviable task of walking on stage naked carrying a mirror and, with house lights on, telling the audience that what the times demand is a naked man carrying a mirror. My hunch is that times don't demand it but John Patrick Shanley did. And I have no idea why.

Jules Feiffer's *Elliot Loves* is a dramatic investigation of ambivalence in mod-ern romance. After an extended monologue in which the title character reveals to the audience both his desire for a serious relationship and his terror of it, the action begins with a scene in which he tries to persuade Joanna, the woman with whom he's involved, up to the apartment where some of his friends wait to meet her. Her terror at having to audition for them keeps her from getting into the elevator, and he ends up going up alone to hash out his feelings with his friends. To his surprise, Joanna appears later and makes a success, which paradoxically sends Elliot over the edge. In a final scene, Elliot and Joanna manage to talk their way from a probable breakup to the brink of a reaffirmation.

As is usual in a Feiffer play, there is much wit at the expense of the torturous syllogisms his characters construct to rationalize their behavior. The problem with *Elliot Loves* is that, in order for it to work, Feiffer has to make the audience feel a stake in seeing Elliot and Joanna get together; and, with me at least, he failed. As interesting as I found them—and, portrayed by the gifted Anthony Heald and Christine Baranski, it would be hard not to find them interesting—I never felt that their union was a desirable thing. Having no rooting interest in their reconciliation, I remained emotionally unengaged during what was evidently intended to be its most wrenching scenes.

Mike Nichols, who directed *Elliot Loves,* previously collaborated with Feiffer on the film *Carnal Knowledge.* This season, a stage version of *Carnal Knowledge* (it was in fact originally written as a stage play) was presented off Broadway under the direction of Martin Charnin. I am mystified by the largely negative reaction it received. The first act, a self-contained tale of a romantic triangle between one female and two male college students in the late 1940s, struck me as being very nearly perfect, particularly moving in its depiction of a smart, sensitive young woman with insufficient defenses against the emotional blackmail practiced by the two boys competing for her favors. The second act, which covered the sexual and romantic misfortunes of the two as men over the next two decades, felt more disjointed and archly constructed, and the task of convincingly playing their aging was just outside the reach of the actors, Judd Nelson and Jon Cryer. Their performances in the first act, however, and that of Justine Bateman as the object of their attentions, were all that could be desired. In the intimacy of a tiny off-off-Broadway theater, they achieved an exquisite balance, finding even more in the material than had their justly-celebrated predecessors in the film version.

The sole black play on Broadway was *Mule Bone,* a piece adapted from an attempted 1930 collaboration between two leading figures from the Harlem Renaissance, Zora Neale Hurston and Langston Hughes, supplemented by material by George Houston Bass. Such story as there is revolves around a rivalry between a pair of best friends over an attractive young woman. The real subject of the play, however, is the rural Southern community in which these characters live. Most of the playing time is devoted to story-telling, speechifying, bickering and joking among more than two dozen colorfully-costumed, oversized characters. (If white writers had created this piece, they might well have been accused of condescension and stereotyping.) In production the result resembled nothing so much as a nonstop party. Michael Schultz did wonders with the constant roil of activity, and Taj Mahal contributed music for several engaging songs. Off Broadway, the Manhattan Theater Club produced the season's other notable black play, *Black Eagles,* Leslie Lee's earnest and informative depiction of the Tuskegee Airmen, the World War II flyers who were the first black fighter pilots.

MULE BONE—In foreground, Allie Woods Jr. (holding hat), Marilyn Coleman, Mansoor Najeeullah and Kenny Neal in a scene from the musical play by Zora Neale Hurston and Langston Hughes.

Both Steve Tesich's *The Speed of Darkness* and Sam Shepard's *States of Shock* deal with the aftereffects of combat. Tesich's play focuses on Joe, a Vietnam vet who, after a difficult transition back to civilian life, has become one of the town's leading citizens. But underneath the public image is a secret which threatens to destroy his family. The contradictions between his public image and his private world are exacerbated by the arrival of Lou, a fellow vet with a dubious hold on sanity who knows what Joe is running from. Tesich has tried to cram so many weighty matters into one play—Vietnam, homelessness, environmental problems— that it threatens to burst its sides, at times verging on silliness. As might be expected from this erratic gifted writer, however, there are some vivid passages; under the direction of Robert Falls, the cast seized their opportunities. Len Cariou invested Joe with beefy power, Stephen Lang made Lou a pathetic, funny and unsettling presence, Robert Sean Leonard conveyed idealism and naivete without simpering, and, most impressively, Kathryn Erbe found a delicate balance between vulnerability and independence as Joe's sensitive daughter Mary.

Shepard's play, his first in several years, concerns an unstable veteran of an unnamed war and his attempt to buy a dessert in a "family restaurant" for a crippled companion who may be his son. Needless to say, the restaurant ends up a shambles. So, unfortunately, does the play. Shepard seems to be saying something about the violence of war being brought home to America by the warriors scarred by it, but I can offer no further theories with any conviction. Ultimately, the piece slips into muddy symbolism and incoherence. The production had the benefit of a characteristically eccentric performance by John Malkovich as the unstable veteran, most threatening when going to greatest pains to make his confused intentions clear.

British dramatist Alan Ayckbourn was represented by two of his older works. Dating from 1975, *Absent Friends* introduces Colin, a man who a month or two before the curtain rises lost his fiancee to drowning. A group of sympathetic friends (most of whom don't actually *like* Colin much) decide to rally around him with emotional support and condolences. The central irony of the play is that it is the friends who emerge from the session much the worse. Colin has mythologized his brief relationship into a great love, and his raptures about the joy their marriage would have been profoundly depress his friends, all trapped in joyless, soul-killing unions. Unfortunately, Ayckbourn hasn't been able to spin two full acts out of the situation; the central irony is stated and restated, as if the playwright had confused reiteration with development. Still, it was fascinating to see in this work the hints of more successful Ayckbourn to come. Lynne Meadow staged the strong production at the Manhattan Theater Club, particularly notable for Brenda Blethyn's performance as Diana, the most sensitive and consequently most miserable character in the piece.

A handful of blocks away, the uptown Circle in the Square offered the Broadway premiere of Ayckbourn's *Taking Steps*, whose central conceit places all three floors of a rambling house onto the same playing level so that actors playing characters understood to be in different rooms pass within inches of each other. Many of the resulting space-warp physical gags are fun, but it rarely builds up enough dizzying speed to succeed as a farce, and the characters have insufficient depth for it to make much of an impression as a comedy. Despite these two disappointments, the news that the Manhattan Theater Club intends to maintain a continuing relationship with Ayckbourn is welcome indeed. At his best, he has few serious challengers as a writer of serious comedy.

As was commonly observed, Andrew Davis's *Prin* bears a more than casual resemblance to Simon Gray's *Butley*. Like *Butley*, *Prin* is a British play about a gay teacher with a withering wit who, during the course of a day, sees both personal and professional lives disintegrate. The key difference between them is that Butley is male and Prin female. As *Butley* provided Alan Bates with a tour de force role, so did *Prin* give Eileen Atkins (again) a chance to stride the stage with authority, batting out barbed comments with aplomb. The most original character of the play is a somewhat dim teacher named Walker who, in the face of similar ruin, can only laugh at his haplessness; in this role, John Christopher Jones contributed one of the season's perfect cameos.

Bill Cain's *Stand-Up Tragedy* was set in quite a different school, a parochial institution in the inner city where, over the objections of the battle-scarred priest who is his superior, an idealistic young teacher attempts to save a talented young student from a destructive home life. The play does not manage to avoid many of the obvious sentimental and melodramatic traps inherent in its premise, but I think it merited a better reception than it received, if only for its chilling concept that evil has its own ecology which, if disturbed by the well-intentioned, will unleash even more evil. Stylistically, the play was extraordinarily theatrical—at times almost numbingly so. Under Ron Link's direction, the company was in ceaseless motion—jiving, dancing, colliding, often playing several characters at once. Marcus Chong gave a flashily accomplished performance as the doomed student *and* his family, and Charles Cioffi gave the hard-bitten superior a specificity that elevated the character from stock character status. As flawed as the play and production were, my hunch is that, had the producers offered it off Broadway and not had to contend with so fiercely negative a review in the *Times*, the show might well have stimulated and unsettled audiences for months.

James Whitmore and Audra Lindley appeared in repertory in two-handed plays about elderly characters. In Tom Cole's *About Time*, they were a long-married couple sparring and reconciling and attempting to cope with the fast-approaching ends of their lives. William Gibson's *Handy Dandy* pits an activist nun against a conservative judge in a series of ideological debates which draw them closer together personally. In concert with much of the press, I have to agree that both plays had potent moments but felt attenuated as full-length pieces. Whitmore gave the roles his usual solid crusty imprint. Previously unfamiliar to me, Lindley was a marvel in both assignments. Their bios made mention of the two having once played the Tyrones in *Long Day's Journey Into Night*, and one could easily imagine how extraordinary they would be in those roles.

My first encounter with Keith Curran was at Circle Rep—a production a few years back of his unsuccessful *Dalton's Back*, which concerned a man whose emotional problems had their sources in a troubled relationship with his mother. Curran returned to Circle Rep this season with *Walking the Dead*, whose central character, a young woman named Veronica Tass, also has a mother problem. Specifically, Veronica's mother Dottie refuses to accommodate her daughter's gay identity. The situation is further complicated when Veronica, without informing Dottie, undergoes a sex change operation; then, in order to attend her mother's remarriage, cross-dresses as a woman, in which condition she/he is accosted and murdered by gay-bashers. The form Curran has chosen to tell this story is a memorial by Veronica's friends, during which they summon up scenes from their encounters with their late friend. The device is clumsy, but the evening gives ample evidence of Curran's growth as a writer. Whereas *Dalton's Back* was tediously obvious, *Walking the Dead* crackles with surprises and unexpected insights into a stratum of contemporary gay life. Curran was well-served by a strong cast, with Myra Taylor and Cotter Smith especially memorable as, respectively, a black lesbian performance artist and an acerbic, alcoholic gay copywriter.

This was the high point of Circle's Rep's season. Vincent J. Cardinal's *The Colorado Catechism*, concerning a painter and his relationship with a woman who is a fellow patient at an institution designed to help people kick their addictions, demonstrated again how difficult it is to write a play for only two characters without lapsing into coy strategies to stretch the length. Harry Kondoleon's *Love Diatribe* began interestingly as a story of adult children who scamper back to the shelter of their parents' house, but got sidetracked into labored fantasy. *Road to*

Nirvana, Arthur Kopit's attack on the wretched values of Hollywood (has a play-wright ever written a *defense* of Hollywood?) was too self-consciously gross to score as satire.

Most of the other plays concerned with aspects of contemporary show business came to similar grief. Despite Sue Giosa's accomplished turn as a man-hungry Mafia princess and Philip Bosco's surprising transformation into a godfather, Tom Dulack's *Breaking Legs* did little justice to the promising premise of gangsters dab-bling in play producing, contenting itself mostly to make obvious jokes on the hoods' illiteracy. Charles Grodin wrote himself a leading role in *Price of Fame*, the tale of a beleaguered movie star's flirtation with an interviewer. Grodin and his co-star, Lizbeth Mackay, played with grace and assurance, but the play misfired in its attempt to muster poignancy out of the star's emotional isolation. More successful was Paul Rudnick's *I Hate Hamlet*, in which the ghost of John Barrymore returned from beyond to assist a terrified young TV star in his attempt at Shakespeare's most challenging role. There were plenty of the usual dog-eared jokes about the shallow-ness of Hollywood and the crassness of agents, but Nicole Williamson gave a mas-terful comedic performance as Barrymore. (At any rate, he did the night I saw him. Reportedly, those in other audiences were not always so lucky; I heard several accounts of his half-heartedly stumbling his way through other performances.)

The most successful of the plays given at the Manhattan Theater Club's Stage II was Philip Kan Gotanda's *The Wash*, the story of the disillusion of a Japanese-American marriage in an understated style reminiscent of Horton Foote. Keith Reddin's *Life During Wartime*, a black comedy concerning corrupt home security specialists, couldn't reconcile Reddin's tendency toward glibness with his desire to stir a deeper emotional response out of the murder of its most engaging character, a middle-aged mother named Gale played with great warmth and vitality by Leslie Lyles. Darrah Cloud's *The Stick Wife* suffered from a profusion of inconsistent images and poetic devices, but it must be thanked for bringing the remarkable Lindsay Crouse back to the New York stage in a standout performance as the bru-talized wife of a Klansman.

I have knowledgeable friends who insist that David Greenspan's *Dead Mother, or Shirley Not All in Vain* is a startling and remarkable play. In perfor-mance at the Public Theater, I was taken with the script's central conceit—that in impersonating his dead mother, a gay man suddenly finds himself possessed by her spirit—but much of the rest of the piece struck me as arbitrarily outrageous. The Public generally had little luck with the plays it premiered. Tony Kushner's *A Bright Room Called Day* depicted a circle of left-leaning friends in Berlin making futile efforts to counter Hitler's increasing influence in Germany. Kushner's overt message is that there are parallels between prewar Germany and contemporary America. Michael Greif's direction drove every point home with thuds—literally; the sound design for this was oppressively obvious in its punctuation. Greif did stronger work with Constance Congdon's peripatetic *Casanova*, tumbling out one arresting image after another, almost obscuring the obviousness of the author's feminist take on the legendary rake.

Beth Henley's *Abundance* offered another feminist slant on history in an attempt to present the anti-romantic chronicle of two mail-order brides brutalized over 25 years by life in the male dominated Old West. Amanda Plummer and Tess Harper gave the material their best effort; but despite the occasional telling passage, Henley's script ultimately seemed overlong and underwritten.

Among the season's other offerings, John Olive's *The Voice of the Prairie*, a tale of early radio broadcasters, lacked a strong narrative, but the moment-by-moment warmth and humor of the work, plus the pleasure of seeing its talented three-person cast (Wendy Barrie-Wilson, Jack Cirillo and Kevin Geer) double adroitly as sharply different characters demonstrated why this script has achieved

THE STICK WIFE—Lindsay Crouse and Julie White in a scene from the play by Darrah Cloud

such popularity in regional productions. Tom Mardirosian's *Subfertile* featured the author playing himself as he dealt with his attempts to get his sperm count up in quest of fatherhood; the result was both funny and touching. Graham Reid's *Remembrance* depicted a romance in Northern Ireland between an aging couple— he Protestant, she Catholic—and the problems it occasions with their children; the writing was frequently clumsy and predictable, but every now and then scenes took life, particularly those between the mother and her daughters, played with special passion by Aideen O'Kelly, Ann Dowd and Terry Donnely. David Storey's *The March on Russia* focused on more generational conflict in a manner reminiscent of his *In Celebration*. Susan Browning provided a good deal of life as the child most determined not to let herself be dragged down by old emotional baggage, but the script is nowhere near the level of Storey's most accomplished work.

Even the presence of the spirited and sassy Helen Gallagher couldn't redeem *Money Talks*, Edwin Schloss's attempt at social comedy about a group of women dabbling in investments; similarly, Douglas Carter Beane's *Advice From a Caterpillar*, a wan tale of bed-hopping in the downtown art world, offered the plucky movie actress Ally Sheedy scant opportunity to show what she might be capable of onstage.

Here's where we list the Best Plays choices for the outstanding straight play achievements of 1990-91 in New York, on and off Broadway. In the acting categories, clear distinction among "starring," "featured" or "supporting" players can't be made on the basis of official billing, which is as much a matter of contracts as of esthetics. Here in these volumes we divide acting into "primary" or "secondary" roles, a primary role being one which might some day cause a star to inspire a revival in order to appear in that character. All others, be they vivid as Mercutio, are classed as secondary. Furthermore, our list of individual standouts makes room for more than a single choice when appropriate. We believe that no useful purpose is served by forcing ourselves into an arbitrary selection of a single best when we come upon multiple examples of equal distinction.

PLAYS

BEST PLAY: *Six Degrees of Separation* by John Guare

BEST FOREIGN PLAY: *Our Country's Good* by Timberlake Wertenbaker

BEST REVIVAL: *Pygmalion*

BEST ACTOR IN A PRIMARY ROLE: Nigel Hawthorne as C.S. Lewis in *Shadowlands;* Ron Rifkin as Isaac Geldhart in *The Substance of Fire*

BEST ACTRESS IN A PRIMARY ROLE: Stockard Channing as Ouisa Kittredge in *Six Degrees of Separation;* Angela Goethals as Edna Arkins in *The Good Times Are Killing Me;* Wendy Makkena as Lili Adler in *The American Plan*

ASSASSINS—Jonathan Hadary as Charles Guiteau, Victor Garber as John Wilkes Booth and Terrence Mann as Leon Czolgosz in the musical with book by John Weidman and score by Stephen Sondheim

BEST ACTOR IN A SECONDARY ROLE: John Christopher Jones as Walker in *Prin;* Cotter Smith as Bobby Braz in *Walking the Dead*

BEST ACTRESS IN A SECONDARY ROLE: Kathryn Erbe as Mary in *The Speed of Darkness;* Carole Shelley as Frosine in *The Miser*

BEST DIRECTOR: Mark Brokaw for *The Good Times Are Killing Me;* Jerry Zaks for *Six Degrees of Separation*

BEST SCENERY: Christopher Barreca for *Our Country's Good;* Richard Hudson for *La Bête;* Santo Loquasto for *Lost in Yonkers*

BEST COSTUMES: Lewis Brown for *Mule Bone;* Richard Hudson for *La Bête*

BEST LIGHTING: Paul Gallo for *Six Degrees of Separation;* Mimi Jordan Sherin for *Our Country's Good*

Musicals, Revues and Special Presentations

To be a female lead of color in a Broadway musical this season was to have a slim chance of surviving till the curtain call. In *Miss Saigon*, *Shogun: The Musical* and the Broadway transfer of last year's Best Play *Once on This Island*, the leading ladies all followed their hearts to death.

As the world knows, *Miss Saigon* transplants the story of *Madama Butterfly* to Vietnam and its aftermath. Chris, an American marine, falls in love with Kim, a Saigon prostitute. They are separated during the chaos of the fall of Saigon in 1975. Three years later, now married to an American woman, Chris learns that Kim is still alive, has borne him a son named Tam and is sustaining herself as a B-girl in Bangkok. His trip with his wife to Bangkok, in an attempt to reconcile his new life with his responsibilities to Kim and Tam, triggers Kim's self-sacrificing suicide. The power of the basic story is undeniable; obviously it served Puccini well. And obviously, the success *Miss Saigon* has met both here and in London speaks to the effectiveness of this incarnation for a lot of people, in deference to which it is selected as a Best Play. This is one of the cases in which a work is so cited because it both helps define a season and has a sizable critical and popular following. Mine, then, is hardly an undisputed opinion; for the record, I find it an almost complete artistic failure.

I don't doubt the sincerity of the desire of collaborators Claude-Michel Schönberg, Alain Boublil and Richard Maltby Jr. to use the musical theater form to explore the American responsibility for the tragedy in Vietnam. But the methods used consistently trivialize the theme. Nowhere is the dichotomy of good intentions and cheesy realization more blatant then in the song "Bui-Doi," an appeal on behalf of the outcast, half-breed illegitimate offspring Americans left behind in Southeast Asia. As Hinton Battle and a chorus sing with great showbiz fervor, above them on a large screen documentary footage of these children is projected. The wrenching views of their genuine suffering makes the contrasting synthetic gushing on the stage appear all the more exploitative and objectionable.

Schönberg's music is a mix of bombast and syrup similar to that which he employed in *Les Misérables,* with a few Oriental grace notes as garnish. As for the lyrics, most of the underlying ideas of the songs—which might be called the points of attack—strike me as being thumpingly obvious; but line by line, the technical level of the *execution* of these ideas is frequently expert. The program credits the original French drafts to Alain Boublil and the English adaptation to Richard Maltby Jr. and Boublil with additional material by Maltby. Between these credits and familiarity with their past work, my hunch is that the ideas were mostly Boublil's and the most technically felicitous parts of the English versions are Maltby's handiwork.

Wherever the responsibilities lie, the results left me frustratingly unmoved, despite earnest and impassioned work by Lea Salonga and Willy Falk as Kim and Chris. Not being saddled with the responsibility to sell sentimentality, Jonathan Pryce as Kim's Eurasian pimp nicknamed "the Engineer" fared better. To him was assigned the bulk of the most cynically-phrased material. If the anti-American anthem "The American Dream" rested on attacking such tired symbols of Western decadence as white Cadillacs and 42nd Street, Pryce put these used goods over with a wonderfully nasty flair (though nobody with functioning eyes would mistake him for the offspring of French and Vietnamese parents).

For that matter, a nasty flair was evident in much of the production. John Napier, the master designer of the sets for several epic British productions of the past, provided another flash-and-dazzle design, most effective in conveying the seedy corners of Saigon and Bangkok; David Hersey contributed correspondingly virtuosic lighting. The huge machinery of the show—both technical and dramatic —moved with dispatch under Nicholas Hytner's direction. No doubt about it, the physical production was as impressive as it intended to be; too bad the material supporting it wasn't worth the effort. But, as I said, the show has some articulate and sincere defenders.

Shogun, based on James Clavell's bestselling novel, was the season's other musical epic about a Western man tragically involved with an Eastern woman. Set in Samurai-dominated Japan, John Driver's script is so convoluted as to render much of the story unfathomable, and his lyrics frequently give rise to unintended chuckles. Though much of the music is pompous and overblown, composer Paul Chihara's ballads offer evidence that the right project might stimulate him to write a distinguished score in the future. The actors essayed valiantly through the hokum, June Angela doing especially well with the resourceful and sexy Lady Mariko, and Francis Ruivivar suitably imposing as a warlord.

The best way to enjoy *Shogun* was to concentrate on the work by set designer Loren Sherman, costumer Patricia Zipprodt and lighting designer Natasha Katz which served up a series of arresting visions of feudal Japan. Their collaboration provided the season with its most breathtaking image—an army on horseback in a slow motion charge toward the audience through the smoke of battle. For those 20 or 30 seconds, one had the illusion of a Kurosawa samurai epic come to life.

These two Western attempts at Asian themes couldn't help bringing to mind *Pacific Overtures*, the stunning Stephen Sondheim-John Weidman musical portraying the American opening of Japan from the point of view of the Japanese. Sondheim and Weidman collaborated again this season on another musical based on historical themes, an off-Broadway offering called *Assassins*. One approaches any Sondheim show with heightened expectations; a large percentage of the best musicals of the past 30-odd years have employed one or both of his enormous talents as a composer and lyricist. This project, however, was a let-down. The central conceit of the show is a kind of convention of various misfits and lunatics who once attempted to kill—sometimes with success—the President of the United States. Sondheim and Weidman are trying to demonstrate that disappointment in various aspects of the American dream sowed the seeds of the madness which possessed these murderous souls. Intellectually, the idea is intriguing. Dramatically, despite the variety of tones and musical styles marshaled, the show becomes monotonous; each sequence is about the same thing—the investigation of yet another figure with

THE WILL ROGERS FOLLIES—*Above*, Keith Carradine as the stage and screen humorist, surrounded by a bevy of chorines in the Peter Stone-Cy Coleman-Betty Comden-Adolph Green musical. *Below*, selections from Willa Kim's outstanding costume designs for the show

access to a gun sufficiently addled to try to seek redress for his/her frustrations by popping the chief executive. Sondheim has distinguished himself in the past by his refusal to repeat himself, but here he seems to be returning to the themes of *Sweeney Todd*. In fact, if one did not know the dates of their composition, one might well believe that *Assassins* was a dry run for that masterwork.

Still, any Sondheim offers satisfactions. Here the fascination lies in his commentaries on various strains of American popular music—vaudeville turns, folk songs, pop ballads, traditional Broadway. In the small off-Broadway space of Playwrights Horizons, the accompaniment was limited to keyboards, guitar and percussion.

Playwrights Horizons also produced the season's best musical. *Falsettoland*, a Best Play, is the third of three musicals following the tale of Marvin, a New Yorker who, in previous instalments, discovered he was gay and was divorced from his wife. In this instalment, set in the early 1980s, Marvin copes with his unorthodox constellation of intimates and friends—his lover Whizzer, his ex-wife Trina, his son Jason, his ex-wife's new husband Mendel (who also happens to be Marvin's former psychiatrist) and a couple of warm-hearted lesbians. The task of maintaining equilibrium is challenged by two new developments—Jason's approaching bar mitzvah and a strange new illness sapping Whizzer's strength (of course, we in the audience in the 1990s know what that illness is and how many others will be devastated by it). *Falsettoland* is similar to *The Sum of Us* in that it presents the picture of straights in profound sympathy with gays. It is all the more poignant for the audience's knowledge that this bittersweet portrait of a bickering but loving extended family reflects little of actual behavior during the early years of the AIDS epidemic. William Finn, who stumbled with two disappointing shows last season, rebounded triumphantly as the composer-lyricist of *Falsettoland*. In the Playwrights Horizons program there was no credit for the book; in the published edition, Finn shares authorship with James Lapine, who directed the dazzling production.

On Broadway the most enjoyable new show was a curious enterpise called *The Will Rogers Follies*. Ostensibly a bio-musical about the humorist, the show is virtually devoid of drama. Rogers may have been a funny man, but from the evidence of Peter Stone's script he seems to have faced no hard choices or moral crossroads; there is no story here that is crying out to be told. As a result, the show's focus is not so much on telling us much about Rogers's life and times as on using him as the excuse for a series of vaudeville turns and lavish production numbers. There is an ingenuousness about the enterprise I couldn't help finding ingratiating. Keith Carradine was too boyishly handsome to invoke much of Rogers's personality, but he was a constantly agreeable presence. As his wife, Dee Hoty projected wifely gumption and made the most of her big ballad.

The main reason to see the show was Tommy Tune's staging with its bounty of choreographic inventions on cowboy imagery. One routine, which might have been offensive if it hadn't been so deliciously silly, called for a line of young women costumed as steers twirling their rope-tails, the noise of the tails slapping the floor in perfect synchronized rhythm. This, plus a dog act starring "the Mad Cap Mutts" and a number featuring lariat tricks in black light typified the show's aspirations—to embrace any means necessary (no matter how shamelessly cornball) to coax a smile out of the audience. It's a long way from the power of Tune's last show, the haunting *Grand Hotel*, but perhaps that was the point. Tony Walton provided his usual scenic magic, evoking the kitsch of Ziegfeldiana with the assistance of lighting designer Jules Fisher, and Willa Kim obviously had great fun dressing the bevy (am I *really* writing the word "bevy"?) of beautiful chorus girls. The score, with music by Cy Coleman and lyrics by Betty Comden and Adolph Green, is amiable but must be counted as a minor addition to the catalogues of these writers, who have contributed so much to musical theater in the past.

I never read Frances Hodgson Burnett's novel *The Secret Garden*, but I suspect if I ever want to know what happens in the story I will have to, for I found the musical version to be long on arresting stage pictures and short on clarity. Between Marsha Norman's book and Susan H. Schulman's direction, I frequently didn't know whether a scene was meant to be interpreted as reality or dream. More successful was composer Lucy Simon, who drew imaginatively on English folk influences (though someone should have done her the favor of pointing out that the melody "Come to My Garden" bore a distracting resemblance to the main theme from *Gone With the Wind*). The most successful aspect of the production was the scene design by Heidi Landesman, a cornucopia of Victorian dollhouse imagery. Daisy Eagan was the requisite combination of charm and pluck as Mary Lennox, the orphan whose quest for the restorative garden in question is the focus of the show, and Alison Fraser gave another of her galvanizing performances as a supportive chambermaid. As Mary's mysterious Uncle Archibald, Mandy Patinkin sang beautifully, as usual, but he played at such an unmodulated and overwrought pitch that his performance grew monotonous.

Mbongeni Ngema, who a few seasons back was responsible for *Sarafina*, the hit musical about black youth in South Africa, returned with a new musical, *Township Fever*. The story centers on how an idealistically-motivated strike by black members of the South African Transport Services got away from the strikers to the point of the gruesome murder of blacks who had violated the picket lines. Ngema's intention was to dramatize how, under pressure-cooker circumstances, good people can do bad things. The show built to a plea for sympathy and understanding for those charged with the deaths. The moral waters struck me as being rather muddy here. One doubts that Ngema would argue as passionately for sympathy and understanding for black policemen who, under pressure-cooker circumstances, had brutually murdered strikers. If Ngema's book was problematic, there was ample compensation in the stirring choral music he composed and arranged for his large and gifted cast.

The chief attractions of *Buddy: The Buddy Holly Story* were recreations of Holly's cheerful rock songs and Paul Hipp's startling incarnation of the title character. The first act consisted of a fairly pedestrian account of Holly's rise. The bulk of the second act was a recreation of his final appearance on February 2, 1959 and also included impersonations of rock stars Ritchie Valens and the Big Bopper singing their biggest hits (Holly, Valens and the Bopper died later that night in a plane crash). There was nothing subtle or profound about the enterprise, but only a confirmed grump could fail to find the performance rousing.

The remaining new Broadway musical attraction was *Those Were the Days*, a beguiling revue made up of material from the Yiddish theater, tracing Jewish migration from Europe to America. No massive stage pyrotechnics overwhelmed here; the show rested firmly on the charm and abilities of its cast of five as they

AND THE WORLD GOES 'ROUND—Karen Ziemba and Bob Cuccioli in a scene from the musical revue featuring songs by composer John Kander and lyricist Fred Ebb

sailed through a series of songs and sketches. One of the five, Eleanor Reissa, also directed, earning a well-deserved if surprising Tony nomination for her work. Bruce Adler, the show's nimble and utterly engaging song-and-dance man, also was rewarded with a Tony nomination.

Another revue, *And the World Goes 'Round*, proved to be one of off Broadway's most appealing offerings. Directed by Scott Ellis and choreographed by Susan Stroman, the cast—Bob Cuccioli, Karen Mason, Brenda Pressley, Jim Walton and Karen Ziemba—offered two hours of beautifully sung and imaginatively staged material from the catalogue of John Kander and Fred Ebb. While short on the psychologically precise portraits found in the Sondheim school of musical theater writing, *And the World Goes 'Round* makes a persuasive case for Kander and Ebb being today's foremost practitioners of the flat-out "we're-gonna-entertain-you-if-it-kills-us" Broadway tradition. Yet another revue, *Broadway Jukebox*, was made up of songs from mostly-forgotten shows, reminding one that even such transitory enterprises as *Come Summer* and *All American* had redeeming aspects. If *Broadway Jukebox*'s guiding spirit Ed Linderman ever gets around to putting together an off-Broadway edition, he might well choose "The Beach House," an appealing song from *Catch Me If I Fall*, Barbara Schottenfeld's short-lived musical about a green card marriage.

The season also saw three shows which were the musical equivalents of theme restaurants. Each broke down the fourth wall by creating the illusion of events in which the audience found themselves cast in roles. In *Smoke on the Mountain*, the audience was told they were members of a Baptist congregation being entertained by a musical family specializing in bluegrass and gospel music interspersed with spiritual homilies. *Pageant* made the audience the spectators at a beauty pageant sponsored by a cosmetics firm; the central joke of the very silly evening was that all of the ladies in competition were played by men, a conceit underscored when their chorus of baritone and tenor voices belted out a song in which they claimed to be "natural-born females." Best of this genre was *Song of Singapore*, in which playgoers were seated at tables and served drinks in a Singapore nightclub in 1941 on the eve of Pearl Harbor. As the club's band, fronted by an amnesiac chanteuse named Rose, knocks its happy way through a series of original songs making gentle fun of the songwriting conventions of Tin Pan Alley, various colorful characters rush about in pursuit of stolen treasure and the answer to the Amelia Earhart mystery. Donna Murphy as Rose was the element who made this amiable nonsense a must-see evening. A sensationally versatile singer and a comedienne blessed with perfect timing, Miss Murphy gave this season's most memorable musical theater performance.

Among the non-musical specialty entertainments, the emphasis was on comedy. Jackie Mason returned with *Brand New*, somehow managing the trick of being personally off-putting and still riotously funny as he caricatured cultural stereotypes. Spalding Gray's latest piece, *Monster in a Box*, concerned his struggles to fulfill a contract for an autobiographical novel. As in previous ventures, Gray offered a rueful stream of satiric observations on his struggles with a relentlessly absurd (when not downright hostile) world. My pleasure was undercut somewhat by the impression he conveyed that, while he wanted the approval of the audience, he wouldn't care to associate with any of us under other circumstances. For hip entertainment without a trace of socially redeeming value, there was the team of Penn & Teller whose show, entitled *The Refrigerator Tour*, recycled bits from their first show along with new routines, simultaneously pulling off dazzling feats of daring and prestidigitation while mocking the hokey trappings of standard magic acts.

To end on the most positive note, here's where we list the *Best Plays* choices for the musical and revue bests of 1990-91.

MUSICALS AND REVUES

BEST MUSICAL OR REVUE: *Falsettoland*

BEST REVIVAL: *Fiddler on the Roof*

BEST BOOK: William Finn and James Lapine for *Falsettoland*

BEST MUSIC: Stephen Sondheim for *Assassins*

BEST LYRICS: William Finn for *Falsettoland*

BEST ACTOR IN A PRIMARY ROLE: Paul Hipp as Buddy Holly in *Buddy: The Buddy Holly Story;* Jonathan Pryce as the Engineer in *Miss Saigon*

BEST ACTRESS IN A PRIMARY ROLE: Donna Murphy as Rose in *Song of Singapore*

BEST ACTOR IN A SECONDARY ROLE: Bruce Adler in *Those Were the Days*

BEST ACTRESS IN A SECONDARY ROLE: Alison Fraser as Martha in *The Secret Garden*

BEST DIRECTOR: Scott Ellis for *And the World Goes 'Round;* Tommy Tune for *The Will Rogers Follies*

BEST CHOREOGRAPHY: Susan Stroman for *And the World Goes 'Round;* Tommy Tune for *The Will Rogers Follies*

BEST SCENERY: Heidi Landesman for *The Secret Garden*

BEST LIGHTING: David Hersey for *Miss Saigon*

BEST COSTUMES: Willa Kim for *The Will Rogers Follies*

SPECIAL CITATION: The ensemble of *And the World Goes 'Round*

PYGMALION—Charles Keating (Alfred Doolittle), Madeleine Potter (Eliza), Anthony Heald (Henry Higgins), Earle Hyman (Col. Pickering) and Anne Pitoniak (Mrs. Higgins) in the Roundabout Theater Company revival of the George Bernard Shaw classic

Revivals

This was not a year with an abundance of distinguished revivals. Denzel Washington made a fair stab at *Richard III* in Central Park, but the production offered little of the guilty pleasure a good *Richard III* should—that of relishing the title character's villainy. (In contrast, the Folger Theater's version in Washington featured Stacy Keach in a gloriously oversized performance that seemed to be modeled on *Fantasia*'s tyrannosaurus.) Tracey Ullman played Kate, and Morgan Freeman was Petruchio in the other Central Park production, *The Taming of the Shrew*. In order to neutralize objections to sexism, the play was set in the old West, giving rise to a fair amount of slapstick with ropes and six-shooters. Little of the script's emotional life was sounded, but the show had the redeeming virtue of triggering more than a few belly laughs.

I must admit to having had trepidations approaching JoAnne Akalaitis's *Henry IV, Parts I* and *II*, having been less than thrilled by her attempt on *Cymbeline* a couple of seasons back. I can't pretend that I thought the *Henry*s came within shouting distance of total success—she ruined most of the Eastcheap scenes with a lot of noisy farting, puking and coupling—but, working with an ingenious retractable two-tiered set by George Tsypin, she pulled off some fine sequences. The robbery in the first part, making good use of apples as weapons, was both credible and funny; and, in the second, Hal's renunciation of Falstaff made a breathtaking stage picture, Hal aloof and out of reach on a traveling elevated platform. Larry Bryggman seemed a touch too refined for Henry IV (what a Richard II he would make!), but Thomas Gibson was a vital Hal and Louis Zorich a very strong Falstaff. Jared Harris achieved the distinction of being an admirably lusty Hotspur in Part 1 and a dismayingly over-the-top Pistol in Part 2. The most encouraging aspect of these productions were the signs that Akalaitis actually cared to tell the story rather than impose on the text showy but irrelevant effects.

All the above productions were courtesy the New York Shakespeare Festival. A non-Festival Shakespeare, the Roundabout's *King Lear*, featuring Hal Holbrook in the title role, was curiously flat and unaffecting. This is especially surprising given that it was staged by Gerald Freedman, who has proved himself to be among the most consistently successful directors of Shakespeare (witness his first-rate productions of *Love's Labor's Lost* and *Much Ado About Nothing* in recent seasons).

The Shakespeare Festival sponsored some non-Shakespeare revivals. David Greenspan took on William Congreve's *The Way of the World* and *Gonza the Lancer* by Chikamatsu, a Japanese playwright who lived in the late 17th and early 18th centuries. Both were staged with glaringly anachronistic costumes, the point of which escaped me. Worse, for all the wit in the text, the Congreve rarely raised a laugh. As for the Chikamatsu, I must assume that it has more tragic force when it is not staged with props and costumes reminiscent of *I Love Lucy*.

Michael Greif did better by another of the Festival's revivals, a fiercely expressionistic staging of *Machinal*. The problem here was the play. Sophie Treadwell's 1928 drama about a woman crushed by male-dominated society merits credit as pioneering work, but the characters exist only as types (Treadwell gives none of them proper names; the female lead is denoted simply as "Young Woman"), with the result that it was difficult to make an emotional investment in their fates. George C. Wolfe, who had such a notable success last season with *Spunk*, his adaptation of Zora Neale Hurston stories, stumbled with Thulani Davis's version of Brecht's *The Caucasion Chalk Circle*. One had to go to Washington's Arena Stage in the fall to see a *Chalk Circle* with the requisite sense of high adventure in act one and satiric panache in act two. (For the record, the versatile Loy Arcenas did admirable work designing both productions.)

The news wasn't much better at the uptown Circle in the Square, which presented Stephen Porter's surprisingly tame staging of Molière's *The Miser* with the usually splendid Philip Bosco in the title role. Only when Carole Shelley entered as the matchmaker Frosine did the evening rise above the merely amusing; the scene in which Frosine tries to dislodge Harpagon's stinginess through an appeal to his unjustified vanity was a model of energy and specificity. If the rest of the evening had met this level, this would have been a fine production.

The most impressive revival of a straight play was the Roundabout's *Pygmalion*, directed by Paul Weidner. John Conklin's unconventional set design made no pretense of supplying realistic environments for the action. Elements suggesting the various locations were simply lined up in a row above the action; where the current action was taking place was indicated by lights directed at the appropriate elements. The rest of the design consisted of chairs rearranged from scene to scene. Having grown accustomed to ornate settings from other stagings of this work, I was pleasurably surprised to see how little the play's success depends on them. Madeleine Potter was a bracingly unsentimental Eliza, and she was partnered with Anthony Heald, one of the youngest actors to play Higgins in recent memory. Some critics complained that there was no sexual chemistry between the two, but it seemed to me they were criticizing *Pygmalion* for not being *My Fair Lady*; the latter is a love story, the former can be played as one or not, depending on the director's choice. Here, quite plainly, director Weidner chose not. In any case, Heald made Higgins a gifted but emotionally immature tyrant, precisely the sort of character initially to inspire awe in a student and then to be fled as soon as instruction is over. Most memorably, this *Pygmalion* featured Charles Keating, who fused raw intelligence with vulgarity into the definitive Alfred Doolittle.

Among the musicals, a recreation of the Jerome Robbins production of *Fiddler on the Roof*, featuring Topol in the role he had previously played with distinction in the film and in London, testified to its place among the pantheon of great American musicals, though the Gershwin Theater was much too large to afford the necessary intimacy. Another piece originally directed by Robbins returned, the musical version of *Peter Pan*, this time with Cathy Rigby in the title role. Miss Rigby gained her fame as an athlete, winning international medals for gymnastics, and her Peter flew with special vigor. But this was no gimmick casting; she sang and acted with authority. In the passage in which Peter explains to Wendy that whenever a child disclaims belief in fairies, somewhere a fairy falls down dead, she subtly invested the word "dead" with the little thrill that children betray when they have license to talk about grownup matters. Miss Rigby has expressed a wish to play the lead in *Annie Get Your Gun*. I hope someone takes her up on it soon.

David Merrick returned to the production scene with a revival of *Oh, Kay!*. Well, sort of a revival. The score was still by the Gershwins, and the book was credited to Guy Bolton and P.G. Wodehouse, but James Racheff was listed for his "adaptation," which consisted of shifting the action from its original Long Island setting to Harlem and making white characters black. There is no way of knowing who among Racheff, Merrick and director-choreographer Dan Siretta are to blame, but the script is hobbled with basic mistakes, not the least of which is delaying the entrance of the title character until halfway through the first act so that she seems to be an afterthought in the proceedings. Angela Teek, whom Mr. Merrick hired as Kay after a much-publicized talent search, was widely shellacked for her performance, which struck me as unfair. It is hard to register strongly in a part so ill-defined in the writing. The most notable aspect of the production was the musical performing of four of the supporting players cast as nightclub entertainers—Gregg Burge, Stanley Wayne Mathis, Kevin Ramsey and Kyme. Not burdened to carry much of the book, they could concentrate their considerable singing and dancing abilities on putting over such infectious songs as "Slap That Bass," "You've Got What Gets Me," "Heaven on Earth" and (the highpoint of the evening) "Clap Yo' Hands."

The New York City Opera doesn't belong strictly within our Broadway-off-Broadway legitimate stage venue, but it's worth footnoting that it continued its practice of reviving pieces which originally premiered on Broadway. *Street Scene*, adapted from the Elmer Rice play by composer Kurt Weill and librettist Langston Hughes, was more interesting for Weill's jazz-influenced music than for its drama. But Scott Ellis's staging of *A Little Night Music*, featuring Stephen Sondheim's most romantic score and a Chekhovian book by Hugh Wheeler (adapted from Bergman's film *Smiles of a Summer Night*) was a pure treat musically and dramatically. Fortunately the Ellis production (which, to give credit where it's due, drew many of its devices from Hal Prince's original staging) was broadcast on PBS, giving VCR-equipped musical theater enthusiasts the happy option of seeing a worthy version of this classic at will. This is an especially appealing option, given that it

OH, KAY!—Gregg Burge and Kyme *(center)* with members of the cast of David Merrick's revival of the George and Ira Gershwin musical

offers the opportunity to relish again Maureen Moore's tart and immensely touching performance as Charlotte, the acerbic countess with the bad luck to be in love with a vain and faithless husband.

Also outside our perimeter but worthy of a memory-lane footnote closing this chapter was what our consulting historian, Thomas T. Foose, called "the big event of 1990-91," a total of five New York productions of *Romeo and Juliet* in various peripheral circumstances including college stagings and a Mexican company at the Festival Latino playing in a mixture of Spanish and Mayan. "Going back to 1930," continued Mr. Foose, "There have been a very few 'star' productions of this play: Olivia De Havilland and Douglas Watson for 49 performances in 1950-51, Laurence Olivier and Vivien Leigh for 36 performances in 1939-40, and in 1934 and 1935 the Katharine Cornell stagings. The fact that Miss Cornell was then in her mid-30s did not seem to bother anyone in those days. She always surrounded herself with the best people. For instance, her choreography for these productions was by Martha Graham. In 1934 (77 performances) her Romeo was Basil Rathbone, Mercutio was Brian Aherne and the Nurse was Edith Evans. An actor by the name of Orson Welles was Tybalt. She took this production on tour with a somewhat different cast, and she brought the tour cast back to the Martin Beck for Christmas of 1935 for 15 performances. Her Romeo was now Maurice Evans. Ralph Richardson was the Mercutio, and Florence Reed was the Nurse. The Benvolio was played by a young actor still in the shadow of his father—Tyrone Power Jr."

Offstage

The press release from the League of American Theaters and Producers was phrased in a determinedly up-beat mode, announcing that, in spite of the distraction of the Gulf War and the decline in hotel bookings, Broadway's gross of $267 million for the season was the second highest in history. Still, Broadway is primarily a commercial arena, and any commercial arena prefers that the lines on its graphs go up. This season two of the lines went down. The $267 million gross represents a 6 percent decline from last season's $283 million, and attendance slumped 9 percent to 8.03 million from 8.14 million. One commercial line did go up, though—income from tours rose 22 percent from last year's $367 million to $449 million.

As mentioned before, at $10 million, *Miss Saigon* had the highest capitalization in Broadway history, topping the previous record, the $8.8 million required for *Jerome Robbins' Broadway*. In contrast, the more modestly-scaled musical *Once on This Island* managed to transfer to Broadway for about $1.2 million. The year's most expensive straight play, *La Bête,* was capitalized at a staggering $2 million. Off Broadway, the elaborate production of *Elliot Loves* lost its capitalization of $600,000, among the largest losses for a straight play in the history of that arena.

The high cost of New York capitalization, of course, is one of the reasons why so many plays are tried out first in less expensive venues outside of New York, many of these venues being affiliated with the League of Resident Theaters (LORT). Recognizing the increased importance of these companies, last season the Dramatists Guild designed a contract intended to offer its more than 7,500 members minimum protections and guarantees when produced by LORT houses. As reported in last year's edition of this series, the LORT theaters refused to acknowledge the validity of the contract. This season, the Guild urged its membership to withhold permission for the production of *any* of their works—new or old—by theaters which would not commit to employing the contract in all subsequent production agreements with dramatists. The hope was that being cut off from the vast majority of contemporary American plays (as well as quite a few foreign ones) would nudge the LORT theaters into a less obdurate posture.

Shortly after this plan was announced, the membership was surprised to learn that A.R. Gurney, one of the prime movers behind the contract's composition, had resigned from the Guild (giving up his office as the organization's secretary) so as to accept a contract not approved by the Guild for the production of his new play, *The Snow Ball*. Despite Gurney's action, the Guild membership in general maintained their resolve. By the end of the season, the organization could claim success with eight LORT managements — the Actors Theater of Louisville, the George Street Playhouse, the Huntington Theater Company, McCarter Theater Center for the Performing Arts, the Roundabout Theater, the Seattle Repertory Theater, Theater Three and the Walnut Street Theater. The Guild was optimistic that other companies would join their ranks soon.

To continue with labor matters, the United Scenic Artists, representing Broadway designers, negotiated their first new contract in a dozen years with the League of

American Theaters and Producers. Under the new terms, union members will receive 5 percent pay increases each year for the next three years, as well as participate in royalties for the designs at a higher rate and from the first paid performance.

Labor cooperation made possible one of the more hopeful developments of the season, an experimental program called the Broadway Alliance. In order to encourage the production of plays in three of the less-used Broadway houses by lowering production costs, the unions and guilds agreed to cuts of about 25 percent in minimums and royalties. Shows under the plan must be capitalized for under $400,000, plus a 15 percent overcall, and must charge no higher than $24 for tickets. Should a show make its way into the black, those working for cut wages would share in 10 percent of the profits. The plan became effective on Sept. 1, 1990, and this season saw the first two offerings under the formula, Steve Tesich's *The Speed of Darkness* and Timberlake Wertenbaker's *Our Country's Good*. Unfortunately, neither show prospered financially, but no serious commentator suggested that their failures were caused by the plan. For now, the mechanism of Broadway Alliance remains in place, and there are rumblings that other adventurous souls will attempt to employ it.

Two of the most-discussed theatrical stories of the year revolved around the issue of artistic choice. One concerned the reauthorization of the National Endowment for the Arts, the federal agency whose grants support nonprofit theaters and other arts organizations. The debate centered on two questions: first, whether Congress should reauthorize the N.E.A. at all; second, if it did, whether the relevant legislation should include language to preclude the use of federal funds in support of art which might be deemed offensive or obscene by some taxpayers.

Some immediately cried censorship. Others countered that censorship was not involved; after all, they claimed, Congress wasn't talking about *banning* controversial works, just questioning whether it was appropriate for public monies to be used to support them. This argument struck many in the arts community as disingenuous. As they saw it, threatening the withholding of funds would tend to discourage organizations chronically strapped for money from considering risky projects; the result, many felt, inevitably would have the same effect as censorship.

Ultimately, Congress reauthorized the N.E.A., and a federal judge ruled that requiring N.E.A.-funded artists to sign an "anti-obscenity" pledge was unconstitutional. The N.E.A. subsequently withdrew the pledge, though the agency itself is now bound by legal language mandating it to insure that grant recipients will observe "general standards of decency and respect for the diverse beliefs of the American public." Arts advocates sighed in collective relief and went back to the battle to have the agency funded at effective levels, noting that appropriations for the Endowment have not kept pace with inflation. (In a related story, the new budget for the financially-strapped State of New York included a proposed cut of 56 percent for the New York State Council on the Arts in 1992, a cut which would hit New York City's many nonprofit theaters and associated artists particularly hard. Arts advocates mobilized in protest.)

The theatrical community rallied with impressive solidarity around the principle of freedom of expression in relation to the N.E.A.; but the same artistic-choice principle in a different context stirred a virtual civil war. At issue was producer Cameron Mackintosh's right to freedom of expression in casting the Broadway production of *Miss Saigon*. Mackintosh wanted to bring over the stars of the original London production, Jonathan Pryce and Lea Salonga. Some members of Actors' Equity opposed both, though on different grounds.

In order to promote opportunity for American talent, Equity rules forbid the employment of a non-American actor in the United States except under certain specific conditions. Among these conditions: that the performer in question be recognized as an international star or possess unique abilities for a given role that no American performer could duplicate. Filipino Lea Salonga could make little claim of being a star of international reknown, so Mackintosh pressed to have her qualified for admission as a unique talent. The matter was submitted to arbitrators, who ruled in Mackintosh's favor, though his claims for her unique ability to play Kim would seem to be undercut by the fact that he hired another actress, Kam Cheng, to alternate with Salonga in the demanding role.

The Salonga controversy raises again the question of whether American artists (as members of Actors' Equity presumably see themselves) should have the right to block foreign artists from appearing on American stages (or, for that matter, whether foreign artists should have the right to ban Americans from appearing in their countries, as is the policy of British Equity regarding our actors). Surely one of the functions of art is to help transcend the boundaries of nationality and culture and so identify with humanity at large. I submit this ideal is compromised when protectionist policies keep audiences from being exposed to the theatrical glories of other societies and cultures.

The larger controversy in which *Miss Saigon* figured was generated by the casting of Pryce. A past winner of the Tony Award, as well as many British honors (including the Olivier Award for *Miss Saigon*), he was obviously entitled to work in New York as a recognized international star. But many members of the theatrical community were offended by the idea of a Caucasian actor playing the part of the Engineer. If, as generally agreed, it is unacceptable for white actors to use blackface in playing black characters, then, they reasoned, it similarly should be unacceptable for whites to "yellow up" and play Asian characters.

Given the paucity of opportunities for Asian-American actors, the question was worth raising. I must concur, however, with those who believe that the specific case in which it was raised was shaky at best. The Engineer is not Asian but Eurasian—half Asian, half European. By what reason does anybody claim that only an Asian should have the right to play a character of mixed race?

The issue of race in casting in general has prompted many progressive members of the theatrical community to endorse ideals that, upon considered examination, are contradictory. On the one hand, there is popular support for race-specific casting—that is to say, a policy that would require the hiring of, say, Asian performers for Asian roles. At the same time, many of the people who support this concept endorse a policy of "non-traditional" casting, which would encourage the placing of actors of color in roles which, in previous days, would have gone to whites. The two concepts are not consistent. The producer who embraces color-blind casting might well offer the role of Big Daddy in *Cat on a Hot Tin Roof* to James Earl Jones. The ideal of race-specific casting would move to reject Jones, a black actor, from consideration for a character whose whiteness is as much a part of his identity as his gender.

What people who give support to both ideals seem to be talking about in reality is affirmative-action casting—on a case-by-case basis coming down on the side of whatever casting choice would give advantage to actors who, because of minority status, have been underemployed in the past. That efforts should be made to include more representation of these actors is something few would challenge pub-licly. But if affirmative action has proven to be difficult to implement in public policy legislation, proposing mechanisms to mandate quotas for minority employ-ment in the arts—however well-intentioned—strikes me as an invitation to disaster. In the name of redressing a social ill, another one would be perpetrated—limiting writers, directors and producers to "approved" casting choices. Sounds like a form of censorship to me. In any case, when the dust settled, Pryce had his part, and a great deal of attention had been paid to an important issue—both palpably good things. Producer Mackintosh claimed vindication when both Pryce and Salonga

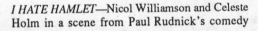

I HATE HAMLET—Nicol Williamson and Celeste Holm in a scene from Paul Rudnick's comedy

were awarded Tonys for their performances.

Vanessa Redgrave found herself at the center of another controversy. Scheduled to head a Shubert Organization-sponsored tour of Peter Shaffer's *Lettice & Lovage*, she was given to understand that comments she made criticizing America's action against Iraq this year critically damaged the producers' ability to sell the show to the American public. She took out a large ad in the New York *Times* to support her assertion that her comments had been reported out of context, but to no avail; the tour was cancelled. Redgrave called upon Actors' Equity to take action on her behalf. The union filed a formal grievance with the League of American Theaters and Producers charging that the Shuberts' action constituted blacklisting, a violation of the agreement between Equity and the League.

Another British star, Nicol Williamson, proved to be a handful. Over the objections of *I Hate Hamlet*'s writer and director, Williamson interpolated passages from *Hamlet* and felt free to wander away whenever he judged his presence unnecessary to the play's action. The climax of his rambunctious behavior came when, in the middle of a stage duel with co-star Evan Handler, he improvised a swipe of his foil at Handler's rear. Protesting Williamson's unprofessional and potentially dangerous behavior, Handler immediately walked out of the scene, the theater and the production. This is not the first time Williamson has got into trouble with a fellow cast member. When playing Henry VIII in the musical *Rex*, he was brought up on Equity charges for striking a member of the chorus.

The waning months of this season brought the announcement of changes which will affect next season. Gregory Mosher, under whose leadership the Lincoln Center Theater Company has flourished, announced his intention to step down from administrative duties so as to concentrate on his directing career. Shortly thereafter, Playwrights Horizons' artistic director Andre Bishop was tapped to succeed Mosher. Shortly after this, Don Scardino, the well-regarded director of *A Few Good Men*, was announced as Bishop's successor.

Another story involved another move—off-Broadway's Roundabout Theater Company announced it would shift its home from the Christian C. Yegen Theater, with its unfortunate acoustics, to the 499-seat Criterion Center/Stage Right, thus becoming a Broadway company and so eligible for Tony Awards. Producing director Todd Haimes spelled out the advantages of the new venue: "Because of the Tony Award eligibility, we will have a tremendous advantage when it comes to obtaining the rights to plays, securing directors and attracting distinguished actors." Not everybody was thrilled with the prospect of this advantage. Some producers on the Tony Administration Commitee, miffed that another non-profit theater company (in addition to Lincoln Center and the uptown Circle in the Square) would compete with their commercial productions for awards, tried (unsuccessfully) to have the company disqualified for eligibility.

This brings us to the subject of awards. The face-off for musical theater honors essentially came down to the camps for *Miss Saigon* and *The Will Rogers Follies* with *The Secret Garden* as a spoiler. *Will Rogers* won most of the "best musical" citations—including the Tony, the Drama Desk and the Critics Circle; there was some speculation that all the hooplah around *Miss Saigon* and the fact that there was a viable American alternative to it may have been factors in the disposition of these honors beyond the quality of the respective works.

The "best play" award amounted to a choice between *Lost in Yonkers* and *Six Degrees of Separation*. *Yonkers* won the high-profiled Pulitzer Prize and the Tony; *Six Degrees* the New York Drama Critics Circle Award and the Hull-Warriner (the only prize given by playwrights *to* a playwright). That *Yonkers* is the more accessible and sentimental work certainly didn't hurt it any in the balloting. There was also the widely-held perception that the awards for *Yonkers* were as much awards for Simon's extraordinary career and history of contributions to the American theater as for this specific script.

When the award season was over, the Tonys were again placed at the center of controversy. Members of the Administration Committee, reportedly upset by some of the nominations produced by the Nominating Committee as well as by the amount of debate and reballoting that went into the deliberations, purged the Nominating Committee of eight of its 13 members. One member of the Administration Committee, speaking from the courageous position of anonymity, was quoted by *Times* columnist Alex Witchel as saying this was intended "to send a message that the purpose of being a nominator is to make the best nominations possible, not to go on extended ego trips about personal favorites." Speaking with the indisputable objectivity of one of the purged, I feel that what this action communicates instead is the desire of some of the entrenched powers of the Administration Committee—particularly certain producers who were disappointed that their projects didn't receive certain nominations—to manipulate the Nominating Committee's make-up so as to be able to exert undue control over that Committee's deliberations—all in all, not behavior to inspire much faith in the integrity of the Tonys.

But, happily, the Tonys are only one part of the New York theater scene. The season may have produced an unusual amount of conflict, but it also produced *Six Degrees of Separation*. Even if there had been no other works of value—and plainly there were many—Guare's acomplishment marks this as a year of special significance.

A GRAPHIC GLANCE

Annie Golden, Victor Garber, Terrence Mann, Jonathan Hadary and Debra Monk in *Assassins*

Madeleine Potter, Anthony Heald and Earle Hyman in *Pygmalion*

Mercedes Ruehl, Kevin Spacey and Irene Worth in *Lost in Yonkers*

Reggie Montgomery in *Spunk*

Alison Fraser, Robert Westenberg, Rebecca Luker, Mandy Patinkin, Daisy Eagan, John Babcock and John Cameron Mitchell in *The Secret Garden*

Jonathan Pryce, Lea Salonga and Willy Falk in *Miss Saigon*

John Herrera, Francis Ruivivar, Philip Casnoff and June Angela in *Shogun: The Musical*

Morgan Freeman and Tracey Ullman in *The Taming of the Shrew*

Keith Carradine in *The Will Rogers Follies*

Stephen Bogardus in *Falsettoland*

Robert Westenberg in *Les Misérables*

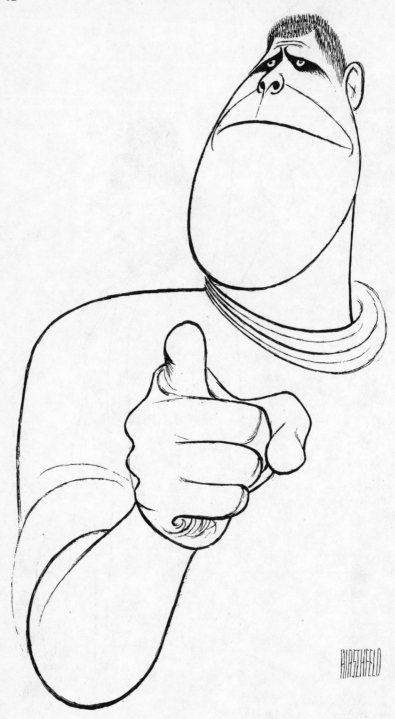

Ron Perlman in *A Few Good Men*

Margaret Tyzack in *Lettice & Lovage*

Charles S. Dutton in *The Piano Lesson*

Eileen Atkins in *Prin*

Gary Sinise in *The Grapes of Wrath*

Lois Smith in *The Grapes of Wrath*

Loni Ackerman in *Cats*

Stephen Hanan in *Peter Pan*

Robert Cea in *Tony 'n' Tina's Wedding*

Michael Greif, director of *Machinal*

Julie Harris in *Lucifer's Child*

Eileen Atkins in *A Room of One's Own*

Vernel Bagneris in *Further Mo'*

Reathel Bean in *Smoke on the Mountain*

Timothy Hutton in *Prelude to a Kiss*

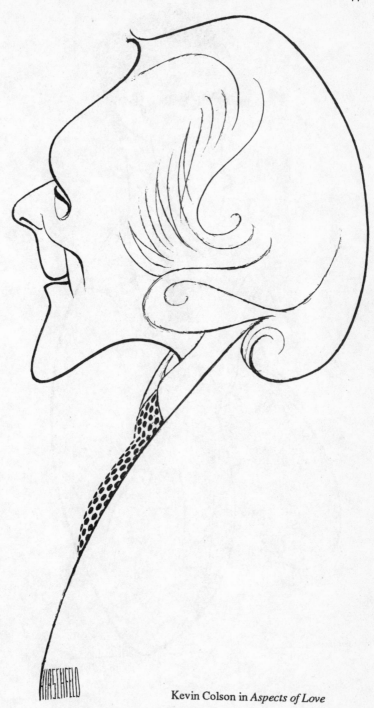

Kevin Colson in *Aspects of Love*

Patrick Fitzgerald in *Philadelphia, Here I Come!*

(*Clockwise from top*) Jason Graae, David Engel,
Guy Stroman, and Stan Chandler in *Forever Plaid*

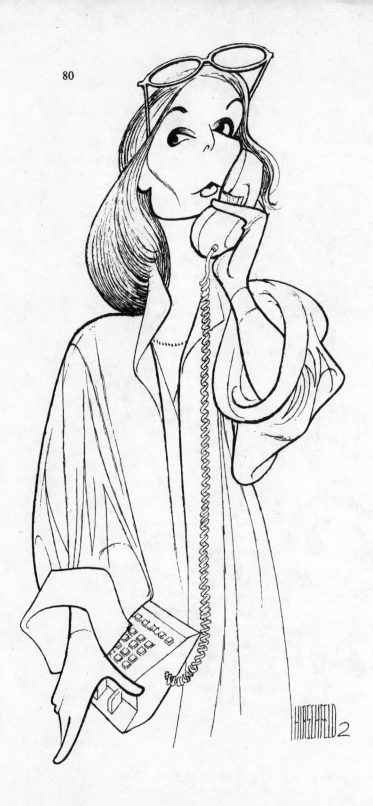

Catherine Russell in *Perfect Crime*

Sam Stoneburner in *Six Degrees of Separation*

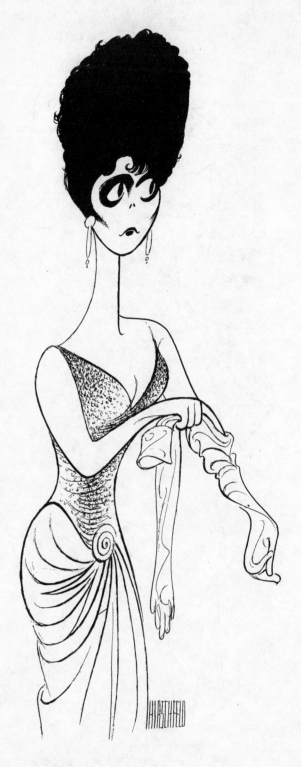

Crista Moore in *Gypsy*

Topol in *Fiddler on the Roof*

Nigel Hawthorne and Jane Alexander in *Shadowlands*

Charles Durning in *Cat on a Hot Tin Roof*

Cole Porter

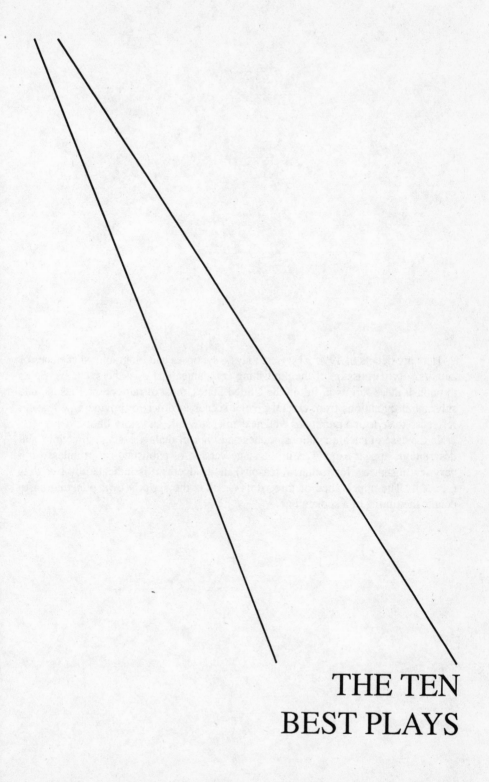

THE TEN
BEST PLAYS

Here are details of 1990-91's Best Plays—synopses and biographical sketches of authors. By permission of the publishing companies that own the exclusive rights to publish these scripts in full in the United States, most of our continuities include substantial quotations from crucial pivotal scenes in order to provide a permanent reference to style and quality as well as theme, structure and story line.

In the case of such quotations, scenes and lines of dialogue, stage directions and descriptions appear exactly as in the stage version or published script unless (in a very few instances, for technical reasons) an abridgement is indicated by five dots (. . . . .). The appearance of three dots (. . .) is the script's own punctuation to denote the timing of a spoken line.

SIX DEGREES OF SEPARATION

A Full-Length Play in One Act

BY JOHN GUARE

Cast and credits appear on pages 309 & 330-331

JOHN GUARE was born Feb. 5, 1938 in New York City. His father was a Wall Streeter and his uncle was Billy Grady, the erstwhile M-G-M casting director. Guare attended Roman Catholic schools and Georgetown University, graduating in 1960, and went on to get his M.F.A. in 1963 at Yale Drama School, where his one-acter Did You Write Your Name on the Snow? *was staged. He kept on writing plays and in 1966 began working on his* The House of Blue Leaves *and had finished a draft of it when his* The Loveliest Afternoon of the Year *and* A Day of Surprises *were staged off off Broadway at Caffe Cino. His professional stage career began April 28, 1968 with the off-Broadway production of* Muzeeka, *which won the Obie Award on a double bill with Sam Shepard's* Red Cross. *Guare's playwriting career continued with a short-lived Broadway production of his* Cop-Out *which nevertheless won him the Variety poll's "most promising playwright" citation. That promise was dramatically fulfilled with the off-Broadway production Feb. 10, 1971 of* The House of Blue Leaves *for 337 performances during which it was named a Best Play and won the New York Drama Critics Circle, Obie and Outer Critics Circle citations.*

The summer of that year, 1971, saw the production of the musical version of Two Gentlemen of Verona *(co-adapted by John Guare and Mel Shapiro, music by Galt MacDermot, lyrics by John Guare) in Central Park by Joseph Papp, who moved it to Broadway Dec. 1 for 627 performances, winning the Drama Critics best musical and the Tony best musical and best book awards. Guare's New York productions in the 1970s and 1980s have included* Two Gentlemen of Verona *(revived in Central Park, 1973)*, Rich and Famous *(1976 off Broadway, 78 performances)*, Marco Polo Sings a Solo *(1977 off Broadway, 64 performances)*, Landscape of the Body *(1977 off Broadway, 64 performances)*, Bosoms and Neglect *(1979 on Broadway, 4 performances)*, In Fireworks Lie Secret Codes *(1981 in Lincoln Center's One-Act Play Festival, 37 performances)*, Gardenia *(1982 off Broadway, 48 performances)*, Lydie Breeze *(1982 off Broadway, 29 performances)*, The House of Blue Leaves *(1986, its Broadway debut in a 398-performance Lincoln Center revival nominated for the best-play Tony) and* The Talking Dog *(1986 off Broadway, a one-act adaptation of Anton Chekhov's story* Joke*)*.

Six Degrees of Separation *is Guare's second Best Play, having opened at Lincoln Center early this season, on June 14, for a 155-performance off-Broadway run at the Mitzi E. Newhouse Theater, followed by its transfer upstairs Nov. 8 to the larger Vivian Beaumont Theater for a continuing Broadway run, winning the Critics Award for best play.*

Other notable Guare works are the plays Women and Water *and* Moon Over Miami *and the screen play* Atlantic City, *the 1981 New York Film Critics, Los Angeles Film Critics and National Film Critics awards and Venice Film Festival Grand Prize winner, and an Academy Award nominee. As a Yale college fellow and an N.Y.U. adjunct professor and lecturer, he has shared his expertise with students. As a mainstay of the modern theater, Guare has actively shouldered many and varied responsibilities as a fellow of the New York Institute of Humanities and a member of the Dramatists Guild Council, the Authors League, the board of directors of the Municipal Arts Society, the former vice president of the Theater Communications Group and the co-editor of the Lincoln Center New Theater Review. He was elected to the American Academy and Institute of Arts and Letters in 1989. He is married and lives in Manhattan.*

Time: Today

Place: New York City

SYNOPSIS: As the play begins, *"A painting revolves slowly, high over the stage. The painting is by Kandinsky. He has painted on either side of the canvas in two different styles. One side is geometric and somber. The other side is wild and vivid. The painting stops its revolve and opts for the geometric side."*

Flanders ("Flan") and Louisa ("Ouisa") Kittredge are on stage in a state of extreme agitation, obviously because they've had an unwelcome visit from an intruder. As Flan voices his worry that something may have been stolen, actors appear momentarily, holding up a Victorian inkwell and then a framed portrait of a dog. Ouisa's concern is, "We could have been killed . . . . . slashed—our throats slashed."

Flan and Ouisa are dressed for dinner under their robes, which they pull off as they address the audience to recount what happened here the evening before. They were entertaining a visiting friend from South Africa, the "King Midas rich" owner of a gold mine there. Flan is an art dealer, and the friend's visit at this time was a happy coincidence.

FLAN: When he called it was like a bolt from the blue, as I had a deal coming up and was short by. . .

OUISA: . . . two million.

FLAN: The figure is superfluous.

OUISA: I hate when you use the word "superfluous." I mean, he needed two million and we hadn't seen Geoffrey in a long time and while Geoffrey might not have the price of a dinner he easily might have two million dollars.

FLAN: The currents last night were very churny.

OUISA: We weren't sucking up. We like Geoffrey.

FLAN: It's that awful thing of having truly rich folk for friends.

OUISA: Face it. The money does get in the—

FLAN: Only if you let it . . . . .

Flan adds that when Geoffrey called and asked to be taken for dinner, "He made a sudden pattern in life's little tea leaves because who wants to go to banks? Geoffrey called and our tempests settled into showers and life was manageable. What more can you want?"

And now Geoffrey ("an elegant, impeccably British South African, slightly older than Ouisa and Flan") is with them, explaining over drinks that he keeps on living in South Africa to help the blacks in their struggle against apartheid: "We'll know we've been successful when they kill us." In brittle, superficial conversational style they bring up some of the world's trouble spots, then glide smoothly into the subject of New York restaurants. All the while (Ouisa and Flan confide to the audience) they can't get the thought of the two million dollars out of their minds.

The doorbell rings, and while Ouisa goes to answer it, Flan describes a certain Cezanne painting to Geoffrey. He is interrupted by the entrance of a young black man, Paul ("in his early 20s, very handsome, very preppy . . . . . blood seeps through his white Brooks Brothers shirt"), supported by the doorman and followed by Ouisa. Paul tells them he has been mugged and robbed in Central Park and has come here for help, presenting himself as a friend of Flan's and Ouisa's children at Harvard.

As the doorman departs, Geoffrey makes a move to go, but Ouisa, obsessed by the thought of the two million dollars, maneuvers him into staying and continuing to discuss Cezanne. Meanwhile, Flan has taken Paul out to dress his wound and lend him a clean pink shirt over which he dons his blazer when he and Flan come

John Cunningham as Flan, Stockard Channing as Ouisa and
Sam Stoneburner as Geoffrey in *Six Degrees of Separation*

back. Paul tells them, "Your children said you were kind. All the kids were sitting around the dorm one night dishing the shit out of their parents. But your kids were silent and said, No, not our parents. Not Flan and Ouisa. Not the Kittredges. The Kittredges are kind. So after the muggers left, I looked up and saw these Fifth Avenue apartments. Mrs. Onassis lives there. I know the Babcocks live over there. The Auchinclosses live there. But you lived here. I came here."

Paul's good friends and college mates Tess and Woody Kittredge have described this apartment in detail, including the reversible Kandinsky. Geoffrey breaks his silence by asking Paul abruptly, "Did you bitch your parents?" No, Paul, like the Kittredge children, loves his parents. Ouisa urges Paul to tell them more about the children (Flan informs us in an aside that they have three, two at Harvard and another girl at Groton), and Paul sums up the Harvard experience as "luxurious despair and constant discovery and paralysis." Paul's parents are divorced, he tells them, and his father, a Hollywood actor-director, is working on a movie version of *Cats* and will be auditioning here soon.

PAUL: He's going to use people.
OUISA: What a courageous stand!
PAUL: They thought of lots of ways to go. Animation.
FLAN: Animation would be nice.
PAUL: But he found a better way. As a matter of fact, he turned it down at first. He went to tell the producers—as a courtesy—all the reasons why you couldn't make a movie of *Cats* and in going through all the reasons why you couldn't make

a movie of *Cats*, he suddenly saw how you could make a movie of *Cats*—

OUISA: Eureka in the bathtub. How wonderful.

FLAN: May we ask who—

OUISA *(to us):* And it was here we pulled up—ever so slightly—pulled up closer—

FLAN *(to us):* And he told us.

OUISA *(to us):* He named the greatest black star in movies. Sidney—

FLAN: Don't say it. We're trying to keep this abstract. Plus libel laws.

OUISA: Sidney Poitier! There. I don't care. We have to have truth. *(To us.)* He started out as a lawyer and is terrified of libel. I'm not.

Paul recites to the audience a brief biography of his father, who came from a family "so poor they didn't even own dirt" and found his destiny as "the future Jackie Robinson of films." Ouisa invites Paul to join them for dinner but suddenly realizes that this interruption has probably lost them their reservation at the restaurant. Paul offers to cook them a dinner here as homage to their hospitality. The fact that he knew all three of their children's names has disarmed the Kittredges. Geoffrey too is impressed—"Your father means a great deal in South Africa"—and Paul agrees that he too admires his father, though he admits he can't bring himself to look at the film *The Lost Man* in which Poitier appeared with a white actress who became his second wife after he and Paul's mother split up.

In the kitchen, Paul does wonders with leftovers. He learns that Geoffrey is from Johannesburg. Paul remembers the time his father took him there and he was struck by the contrast between the elegant whites and the rioting blacks. "What about being black in America?" Geoffrey inquires bluntly. Paul was insulated from this condition by living and being educated abroad, he says. "I never knew I was black in that racist way till I was sixteen and came back here," Paul tells the others. "Very protected. White servants. After the divorce we moved to Switzerland, my mother, brother and I. I don't feel American. I don't even feel black."

Ouisa's heart goes out to the young man. Flan asks about Paul's thesis, which was lost to the muggers, and Paul replies with a dissertation on the subject of *Catcher in the Rye*, its impact on him and on society, particularly on certain unstable individuals like the murderer of John Lennon or the would-be assassin of President Reagan. What alarmed Paul most, he says, was the book's aura of paralysis.

PAUL: . . . . . It mirrors like a fun house mirror and amplifies like a distorted speaker one of the great tragedies of our times—the death of the imagination. Because what else is paralysis? The imagination has been so debased that imagination—being imaginative—rather than being the lynch-pin of our existence now stands as a synonym for something outside ourselves like science fiction or some new use for tangerine slices on raw pork chops—what an imaginative summer recipe—and *Star Wars*! So imaginative! And *Star Trek*— so imaginative! And *Lord of the Rings*—all those dwarves—so *imaginative*—The imagination has

moved out of the realm of being our link, our most personal link, with our inner lives and the world outside that world—this world we share. What is schizophrenia but a horrifying state where what's in here doesn't match up with what's out there? Why has imagination become a synonym for style? I believe that the imagination is the passport we create to take us into the real world. I believe the imagination is another phrase for what is most uniquely *us* . . . . . To face ourselves. That's the hard thing. The imagination. That's God's gift to make the act of self-examination bearable.
>   *Pause.*
OUISA: Well, indeed.
>   *Pause.*
FLAN: I hope your muggers read every word.
OUISA: Darling.
GEOFFREY: I'm going to buy a copy of *Catcher in the Rye* at the airport and read it.
OUISA: Cover to cover.

Paul expects to meet his father at the Sherry Netherland the next morning at 7 o'clock, and the Kittredges insist that he stay here with them overnight. Before Geoffrey leaves, Paul promises that they can all be in *Cats* as extras—human, not feline. Noting that they haven't done any business this evening, Geoffrey asks Flan to walk to the elevator with him, and the men go out. Somewhat to Ouisa's embarrassment, Paul insists on doing the washing up.

"Flan returns, amazed"—Geoffrey will put up the two million, expecting that they can buy the Cezanne for six million and sell it to a Japanese buyer for ten. Flan and Ouisa explain to Paul that Flan is a private dealer catering to those who want a particular painting but for some reason—"A divorce. Taxes. Publicity"—don't want anyone to know about it. Tonight was "a very nervous very casual very big thing," and the Kittredges are grateful to Paul for his help. Flan gives Paul $50 for walking around money the next day, and they say their goodbyes now because Paul will get up early and leave to meet his father.

>   *Paul goes. Flan and Ouisa get ready for bed, pulling on their robes.*
FLAN: I want to get on my knees and thank God—money—
OUISA: Who said when artists dream they dream of money? I must be such an artist. Bravo. Bravo.
FLAN: I don't want to lose our life here. I don't want all the debt to pile up and crush us.
OUISA: It won't. We're safe.
FLAN: For a while. We almost lost it. If I didn't get this money, Ouisa, I would've lost the Cezanne. It would've gone. I had nowhere to get it.
OUISA: Why don't you tell me how much these things mean? You wait until the last minute—

FLAN: I don't want to worry you.
OUISA: Not worry me? I'm your partner.
      They embrace.
FLAN: There is a God.
OUISA: And his name is—
FLAN: Geoffrey?
OUISA: Sidney.

Asleep, Ouisa dreams (she tells the audience) that Sidney Poitier (envisioned as Paul dressed in dinner clothes) explains to her his concept of the movie version of *Cats*. Flan dreams of paintings, and of how some artists "lose" their paintings by working on them past the point at which they should stop; a point after which the artist "loses the structure—loses the sense" of the work. That evening he himself was "a painter losing a painting" until his South African friend came to rescue it.

Ouisa awakens at 6 a.m. and goes to make sure Paul is awake early enough to meet his father. She stops in front of Paul's door and after calling his name hears him moaning inside. Ouisa opens the bedroom door and turns on the light.

OUISA *(screams)*: Flan!!!
      The stage is blindingly bright. Paul, startled, sits up in bed. A naked
      guy stands up on the bed.
HUSTLER: What the fuck is going on here? Who the fuck are you?!
OUISA: Flan!
FLAN: What is it?
      Flan appears from the dark, tying his robe around him. The hustler,
      naked but for white socks, comes into the room.
HUSTLER: Hey! How ya doin'?
FLAN: Oh my God!
OUISA *(a scream)*: Ahhh!
HUSTLER *(stretches out on the sofa)*: I gotta get some sleep—
PAUL *(runs into the room pulling on his clothes)*: I can explain.
      Paul tosses the hustler's clothes onto the sofa.
OUISA: You went out after we went to sleep and picked up this thing?
PAUL: I am so sorry.
FLAN: You brought this thing into our house! Thing! Thing! Get out! Get out of my house!

Flan turns the sofa over, spilling the hustler onto the floor. The hustler gets up and menaces both Flan and Ouisa (but Flan remembers to ask Paul to return his $50; Paul has already spent it). Flan throws the hustler's clothes into the hall and orders him out. He leaves, with a parting "Fuck you!" thrown at Flan. Paul begs, "Please. Don't tell my father. I don't want him to know. I haven't told him. He doesn't know. I got so lonely. I got so afraid. My dad coming. I had the money.

I went out after we went to sleep and I brought him back. I couldn't be alone. You had so much. I couldn't be alone. I was so afraid." Ouisa's reply to Paul is "Just go," and he does.

"And that's that," Ouisa tells the audience, ending their recollection of the extraordinary events of the previous evening. Flan is still worried that some of their valuables might have been stolen, while Ouisa is still appalled at the thought that they might have been killed.

There was no answer when they phoned to check with their children, and when their own phone rings they're almost afraid to pick it up. But it's only Geoffrey, calling from the airport with the offer of an additional $250,000 if they find they need it. And Geoffrey also thinks it might be a good idea to put on a Black American Film Festival in South Africa with Sidney Poitier as president of the jury. The Kittredges promise to get in touch with Poitier at his hotel.

A couple in their 40s, Kitty and Larkin, parents of one of the Kittredge children's Harvard classmates, enters with a story to tell (Flan and Ouisa doff their robes and are dressed in daytime clothing). Kitty and Larkin have received a similar visit from Paul. As Larkin tells it, "In the middle of the night we heard somebody screaming Burglar! Burglar! We came out in the hall. Paul is chasing this naked blond thief down the corridor. The blond thief runs out, the alarm goes off. The kid saved our lives." Nothing was stolen, but Larkin gave Paul $25. He phones his son at Harvard but can't reach him.

After comparing notes, the two couples decide to check with Sidney Poitier himself at the hotel, but he doesn't seem to be registered there, and Celebrity Service won't give out any information about him. Meanwhile, the doorbell rings, Flan goes to answer it and returns with an arrangement of flowers and a pot of jam from Paul. This convinces them that they must call the police, but when a detective arrives and hears that nothing has been stolen from either couple, he's not much concerned and advises them, "Come up with charges. Then I'll do something."

The children—Woody and Tess Kittredge and Larkin's son Ben—come down from Harvard and disclaim any knowledge of Paul. When the others depart and Ouisa is alone, she stretches out on the sofa. Paul appears in her mind's eye, still talking about the imagination: "The imagination is the noon voice that sees clearly and says yes, this is what I want for my life." The imagined Paul takes out a switchblade, stabs himself and vanishes as Ouisa *sits up and screams.*

The detective phones to tell them about another of Paul's exploits, which is acted out. It seems that Paul came to a Dr. Fine with the same story. The doctor treated Paul's wound, while he remembers how "I had this sense of self-hatred, of fear" which was relieved by the bravery of this lad's father's movies. When Dr. Fine was called away to treat a patient, he gave Paul the keys to his house. When Dr. Fine thought of his son Doug later, he phoned him at college to tell him about befriending the black lad.

DR. FINE: Amazingly, he was in his room. Doing *what* I hate to ask.

Doug, 20, appears.

So you accuse me of having no interest in your life, not doing for friends, being a rotten father. Well you should be very happy.

DOUG: The son of who? Dad, I never heard of him. Dad, as usual, you are a real cretin. You gave him the keys? You gave a complete stranger who happens to mention my name the keys to our house? Dad, sometimes it is so obvious to me why Mom left. I am so embarrassed to know you. You gave the keys to a stranger who shows up at your office? Mother told me you beat her! Mom told me you were a rotten lover and drank so much your body smelled of cheap white wine. Mom said sleeping with you was like sleeping with a salad made of bad dressing. Why you had to bring me into the world!

DR. FINE: There are two sides to every story—

DOUG: You're an idiot. You're an idiot!

Doug goes into the dark, screaming.

DR. FINE: I went home—courageously—with a policeman.

A policeman accompanies Dr. Fine. Paul appears wearing a silk robe, carrying a snifter of brandy.

Arrest him!

PAUL: Pardon?

DR. FINE: Breaking and entering.

PAUL: Breaking and entering?

DR. FINE: You're an impostor.

PAUL: Officer, your honor, your eminence, Dr. Fine *gave* me the keys to his brownstone. Isn't that so?

DR. FINE: My son doesn't know you.

PAUL: This man gave me the keys to his house. Isn't that so?

POLICEMAN *(screams):* Did you give him the key to the house?

DR. FINE: Yes! But under false pretenses. This fucking black kid crack addict came into my office lying—

PAUL: I have taken this much brandy but can pour the rest back into the bottle. And I've used electricity listening to the music, but I think you'll find that nothing's taken from the house.

Dr. Fine asks that Paul be arrested, but the policeman ignores him and leaves without further ado, as does Paul. Meanwhile, Ouisa has obtained an autobiography of Sidney Poitier and reads, "Back in New York with Juanita and the children, I began to become aware that our marriage, while working on some levels, was falling apart in other fundamental areas." The book contains a photo of the actor with his four daughters—no sons. Paul's adult victims—Flan, Ouisa, Kitty, Larkin and Dr. Fine—summon their children, who are *"groaning,"* for interrogation.

FLAN: It's obvious. It's somebody you went to high school with, since you each go to different colleges.

OUISA: He knows the details about our lives.

FLAN: Who in your high school, part of your gang, has become homosexual or is deep into drugs?

TESS: That's, like, about fifteen people.

LARKIN: I don't want to know.

TESS: I find it really insulting that you would assume that it has to be a guy. This movie star's son could have had a relationship with a girl in high school—

BEN: That's your problem in a nutshell. You're so limited.

TESS: That's why I'm going to Afghanistan. To climb mountains.

OUISA: You are not climbing mountains.

FLAN: We have not invested all this money in you to scale the face of K-2.

TESS: Is that all I am? An investment?

OUISA: All right. Track down everybody in your high school class. Male. Female. Whatever. Not just homosexuals. Drug addicts. The kid might be a drug dealer.

DOUG: Why do you look at me when you say that? Do you think I'm an addict? A drug pusher? I really resent the accusations.

DR. FINE: No one is accusing you of anything.

LARKIN: I don't want to know. I don't want to know. I don't want to know.

The children accuse their parents of racism, McCarthyism, KGB-ism, and Woody is angry particularly about Flan's having given Paul his favorite pink shirt. But they do look through their high school yearbooks and hit upon one Trent Conway who is now at MIT. Tess takes a tape recorder to an interview with Trent, who admits, yes, he knew Paul. In fact, Trent coached Paul for his masquerade when not making love to him. Trent taught Paul to speak correctly and say "sofa" instead of "couch," "bottle" instead of "bodd-il," coached Paul in the names, lifestyles and idiosyncrasies (i.e., all rich people like getting a pot of jam as a gift) of people in his address book.

TRENT *(to Tess):* Paul stayed with me for three months. We went through the address book letter by letter. Paul vanished by the L's. He took the address book with him. Well, he's already been in all your houses. Maybe I will meet him again. I sure would like to.

TESS: His past? His real name?

TRENT: I don't know anything about him. It was a rainy night in Boston. He was in a doorway. That's all.

TESS: He took stuff from you?

TRENT: Besides the address book? He took my stereo and sport jacket and my word processor and my laser printer. And my skis. And my TV.

TESS: Will you press charges?

TRENT: No.

TESS: It's a felony.

TRENT: Why do they want to find him?

TESS: They say to help him. If there's a crime, the cops will get involved.

James McDaniel (*rear,* as Paul), Stockard Channing and
John Cunningham in a scene from John Guare's play

TRENT: Look, we must keep in touch. We were friends for a brief bit in school.
I mean we were really good friends.
TESS: Won't you press charges?
TRENT: Please.

They go. Ouisa appears.

OUISA: Tess played me the tapes . . . . . Can you believe it? Paul learned all that in three months. Three months! Who would have thought of it? Trent Conway, the Henry Higgins of our time. Paul looked at those names and said I am Columbus, I am Magellan. I will sail into this new world. I read somewhere that everybody on this planet is separated by only six other people. Six degrees of separation. Between us and everybody else on this planet. The President of the United States. A gondolier in Venice. Fill in the names. I find that a) tremendously comforting that we're so close and b) like Chinese water torture that we're so close. Because you have to find the right six people to make the connection. It's not just big names. It's *anyone*. A native in a rain forest. A Terra del Fuegan. An Eskimo. I am bound to everyone on this planet by a trail of six people. It's a profound thought. How Paul found us. How to find the man whose son he pretends to be. Or perhaps *is* his son, although I doubt it. How every person is a new door, opening up into other worlds. Six degrees of separation between me and everyone else on this planet. But to find the right six people.

The Kittredges go on with their lives. One day their doorman spits at them and accuses them of rejecting and disowning their secret black son. And then Paul is seen making friends with two young people in Central Park, telling them that his white father, who lives in one of the nearby apartment buildings, married his black mother during a freedom march down South but abandoned her when Paul was born; now Paul is still an outcast while his half-siblings attend the best schools. Paul has tried to get in touch with his father (he tells the two young people, Rick and Elizabeth) but hasn't been able to do so and is forced to live out here in the park.

Rick and Elizabeth have come to New York from Utah aspiring to acting jobs, and of course they invite Paul to share their tenement accommodations. They urge Paul to keep on trying to see his father, and one day he runs in, joyously announcing that his father is going to give him a thousand dollars and make up for past neglect—the only thing is, Paul needs transportation expenses to meet his father in Maine. Rick is ready to lend Paul his and Elizabeth's savings, but Elizabeth puts her foot down: "No. We worked too hard to save that. I'm sorry. I'll meet you both after work. If your father loves you, he'll get you a ticket up there."

But in Elizabeth's absence Rick gives Paul their money. Paul, supposedly with money of his own but really with Rick's loan, takes Rick dancing at the Rainbow Room (they are asked to leave), accompanies him home, kisses him and vanishes, leaving him to confront Elizabeth.

Meanwhile, Larkin and Kitty are having adventures of their own.

LARKIN: Kitty and I were at a roller disco two clients opened.
KITTY: And it was Valentine's Day.
LARKIN: And we came out and saw a body on the street.

KITTY: My legs were still shaky from the roller skating which I have not done in I hate to tell you how many years and we knew the body had just landed there in that clump.

LARKIN: Because the blood seeping out had not reached the gutter yet.

KITTY: You could see the blood just oozing out slowly toward the curb.

LARKIN: The boy had jumped from above.

KITTY: The next day we walked through the park by Gracie Mansion.

LARKIN: And it was cold and we saw police putting a jacket on a man sitting on a bench.

KITTY: Only we got closer and it wasn't a sweater.

LARKIN: It was a body bag. A homeless person had frozen during the night.

KITTY: Was it that cold?

LARKIN: Sometimes there are periods where you see death everywhere.

     Darkness. Ouisa and Flan appear in their robes with the detective and Elizabeth.

DETECTIVE: This young girl came forward with the story. She told me the black kid was your son, lived here. It all seemed to come into place. What I'm saying is, she'll press charges.

ELIZABETH: I want him dead. He took all our money. He took my life. Rick's dead! You bet your life I'll press charges.

OUISA: We haven't seen him since that night.

DETECTIVE: Find him. We have a case.

Flan decides to call friends on the *Times* and ask them to run the story about the smart but soft-hearted New Yorkers being taken in by a con man. The *Times* runs it. They never hear from Sidney Poitier, but one evening when the Kittredges are dressing to go to an art auction, two calls come in on Ouisa's phone lines, one from Tess announcing she's getting married and moving to Afghanistan, and one from Paul.

PAUL: I saw that story in the paper. I didn't know the boy killed himself. He gave me the money.

OUISA: Let me put you on hold. I'm talking to my child—

PAUL: If you put me on hold, I'll be gone and you'll never hear from me again.

     Ouisa pauses. Tess fades into black.

OUISA: You have to turn yourself in. The boy committed suicide. You stole the money. The girl is pressing charges. They're going to get you. Why not turn yourself in and you can get off easier. You can strike a bargain. Learn when you're trapped. You're so brilliant. You have such promise. You need help.

PAUL: Would you help me?

OUISA: What would you want me to do?

PAUL: Stay with you.

OUISA: That's impossible.

PAUL: Why?

OUISA: My husband feels you betrayed him.

PAUL: Do you?

OUISA: You were lunatic! And picking that drek off the street. Are you suicidal? Do you have AIDS? Are you infected?

PAUL: I do not have it. It's a miracle. But I don't. Do you feel I betrayed you? If you do, I'll hang up and never bother you again.

OUISA: Where have you been?

PAUL: Travelling.

OUISA: You're not in trouble? I mean, more trouble?

PAUL: No, I only visited you. I didn't like the first people so much. They went out and just left me alone. I didn't like the doctor. He was too eager to please. And he left me alone. But you. You and your husband. We all stayed together.

OUISA: What did you want from us?

PAUL: Everlasting friendship.

OUISA: Nobody has that.

PAUL: You do.

OUISA: What do you think we are?

PAUL: You're going to tell me secrets? You're not what you appear to be? You have no secrets. Trent Conway told me what your kids have told him over the years.

OUISA: What have the kids told him about us?

PAUL: I don't tell that. I save that for blackmail.

OUISA: Then perhaps I'd better hang up.

Panicked lest Ouisa cut him off, Paul blurts out an account of his recent art gallery-going and book-reading (*The Andy Warhol Diaries* and *The Agony and the Ecstasy*). Ouisa tells Paul about visiting the Sistine Chapel, watching them clean the paintings with Q-tips and water to restore their vivid colors, and climbing the scaffolding to touch the hand of God. But when Paul asks, "Take me to see it," Ouisa replies, "Take you to see it? Paul, they think you might have murdered someone! You stole money!"

Flan comes in, realizes what is happening and picks up the other phone to call the police. But Tess is on the line, having called back after being cut off. Flan asks Tess to get off the line, and she does, but not before exclaiming, "I'm going to ruin my life and get married and throw away everything you want me to be because it's the only way to hurt you!"

Flan reaches the detective and signals to Ouisa to find out where Paul is. Ouisa asks Paul to come to the apartment, but he tells her, "I come there and you'll have the cops waiting." Ouisa asks Paul to trust her, Paul offers to come and cook another meal for the Kittredges. But they're going out this evening to an auction at Sotheby's.

PAUL: That's wonderful! I'll come!
OUISA: You can't.
PAUL: Why? I was helpful last time—
FLAN: Thank him—he was very help—
> *Ouisa hands Flan the phone.*

Paul? You were helpful getting me this contract—
PAUL: Really! I was thinking maybe that what I should do is what you do—in art but making money out of art and meeting people and not working in an office—
FLAN: You only see the glam side of it. There's a whole grotty side that—
PAUL: I could learn the grotty—
FLAN: You have to have art history. You have to have language. You have to have economics—
PAUL: I'm fast. I could do it. Do your kids want to—
FLAN: No, it's not really a profession you hand down from generation to gen— what the hell am I talking career counselling to you! You embarrassed me in my building! You stole money. There is a warrant out for your arrest!

Ouisa grabs the phone lest Paul hang up on Flan. He's still on the line, telling Ouisa that his night with the Kittredges was his happiest ever. Paul ignores her request for his real name but listens to her reproaches for not using his intelligence to make the most of himself.

PAUL: What could I be?
OUISA: So much.
PAUL: With you behind me?
OUISA: Perhaps. You liked that night? I've thought since that you spent all your time laughing at us.
PAUL: No.
OUISA: That you had brought that awful hustling thing back to show us your contempt—
PAUL: I was so happy. I wanted to add sex to it. Don't you do that?
> *Pause.*

OUISA: No.
PAUL: I'll tell you my name.
OUISA: Please?
PAUL: It's Paul Poitier-Kittredge. It's a hyphenated name.
> *Pause.*

OUISA: Paul, you need help. Go to the police. Turn youself in. You'll be over it all the sooner. You can start.
PAUL: Start what?
OUISA: Your life.
PAUL: Will you help me?

Ouisa pauses and makes a decision.

OUISA: I will help you. But you have to go to the police and go to jail . . . . .

Ouisa promises to visit Paul in prison and give him a job when he gets out and help him to educate himself and give him furniture to set up his own place. Paul fears that the police would brutalize a black suspect if he just gave himself up, unescorted, so Ouisa agrees to take him there—tomorrow, because they're going to cocktails this evening before the auction. Flan comes in, dressed, and sees that Ouisa is still on the phone and tells her, "Oh fuck. We have drinks with the Japanese at six-fifteen—Get off that fucking phone. Is it that kid? Get him out of our life! Get off that phone or I'll rip it out of the wall!"

Ouisa looks at her husband for a moment, then tells Paul they'll meet him right now. Paul tells her he's in the lobby of the Waverly movie theater, and they exchange assurances of affection before Ouisa hangs up. Ouisa and Flan phone the detective to meet them at the Waverly, and Ouisa insists, "He's special. Remember that he's special. Honor our promise." Then Ouisa tells the audience there was a lot of traffic, and by the time they got to the Waverly the police had come and gone after arresting a young black man and carrying him off "kicking, screaming."

Ouisa made every effort to find Paul but couldn't; they didn't know his name or even what precinct had arrested him. "Why does it mean so much to you?" Flan wonders, and Ouisa explains, "He wanted to be us. Everything we are in the world, this paltry thing—our life—he wanted it. He stabbed himself to get in here. He envied us. We're not enough to be envied." Flan remembers only that the intruder might have killed them, but Ouisa remembers that "He did more for us in a few hours than our children ever did" and needed help but they couldn't find a way to help him. Ouisa is disgusted that they have made Paul's escapade into "an anecdote to dine out on."

FLAN *(to us):* Cezanne would leave blank spaces in his canvases if he couldn't account for the brush stroke, give a reason for the color.

OUISA: Then I am a collage of unaccounted-for brush strokes. I am all random. God, Flan, how much of your life can you account for?

FLAN: Are you drunk? The Cezanne sale went through. We are rich. Geoffrey's rich. Tonight there's a Matisse we'll get, and next month there's a Bonnard, and after that—

She considers him.

OUISA: These are the times I would take a knife and dig out your heart. Answer me? How much of your—

FLAN: —life can I account for! *All!* I am a gambler!

Pause.

OUISA: We're a terrible match. *(To us.)* Time passes. *(To Flan.)* I read today that a young man committed suicide in Riker's Island. Tied a shirt around his neck and hanged himself. Was it the pink shirt? This burst of color? The pink shirt.

Was it Paul? Who are you? We never found out who you are.

FLAN: I'm sure it's not him. He'll be back. We haven't heard the last of him. The imagination. He'll find a way. *(To us.)* We have to go. An auction. *(To Ouisa.)* I'll get the elevator.

> *Flan goes.*

OUISA *(to us):* But if it was the pink shirt. Pink. A burst of pink. The Sistine Chapel. They've cleaned it, and it's all these colors.

FLAN'S VOICE: Darling—

> *Ouisa starts to go. She looks up. Paul is there, wearing the pink shirt.*

PAUL: The Kandinsky. It's painted on two sides.

> *He glows for a moment and is gone. She considers. She smiles. The Kandinsky begins its slow revolve. Curtain.*

FALSETTOLAND

A Full-Length Musical in One Act

BY WILLIAM FINN AND JAMES LAPINE

MUSIC AND LYRICS BY WILLIAM FINN

Cast and credits appear on pages 334-335

WILLIAM FINN (music and lyrics) was born in Boston in 1952. His father ran a family paper business and sent his son to Williams College, where Finn won the Hutchinson Fellowship for musical composition and graduated in 1974, going on to the University of California at Berkeley for additional studies. But his path was already set straight before him. As a freshman at Williams he so enjoyed acting in a revue that he determined to write scores of his own, at first in collaboration with a classmate. In the next three student years he came up with three shows entitled Sizzle, Rape *and* Scrambled Eggs, *and a distinguished career in musical theater had begun.*

Finn's first New York City credit of record was the music for Paul Leaven's Benny Leonard and the Brooklyn Bridge *off off Broadway at the Open Space in Soho March 30, 1977. His all-music* In Trousers, *music and lyrics by William Finn, made a 28-performance debut at Playwrights Horizons Dec. 8, 1978, when that group was an OOB company, but the work didn't receive a full-fledged but short-lived (16 performance) off-Broadway production until March 26, 1985, after Finn's* March of the Falsettos *had already made its indelible mark on the New York stage. Playwrights Horizons opened the also all-sung* March of the Falsettos *as an OOB production April 9, 1981 and moved it up to full off-Broadway status May 20, 1981 for a run of 268 performances and the Outer Critics Circle citation as the best off-Broadway show of the year. Later it was honored by two Los Angeles Drama Critics Awards. Finn's first Best Play,* Falsettoland, *was also produced by Playwrights Horizons, early this season on June 28. It's opening-night Playbill listed Finn as the sole author of the musical, but Finn insisted on including James Lapine's name in the authors' credits, acknowledging the director's creative contribution. With* In Trousers *and* March of the Falsettos, Falsettoland *rounds out an all-musical trilogy about a central character, Marvin, with friends and family in emotional orbit around him.*

The roster of Finn's New York productions includes America Kicks Up Its Heels *(book by Charles Rubin, music and lyrics by Finn) in workshop at Playwrights Horizons;* Tango Apasionado *(conceived by Graciela Daniele, music by Astor Piazzolla, lyrics by Finn) OOB at INTAR and then on Broadway in 1989 on the program* Dangerous Games *with Orfeo (same credits, lyrics by Finn); James Lapine's staging of* The Winter's Tale *with music by Finn March 21, 1989 in the Public Theater's Shakespeare Marathon; and* Romance in Hard Times *(book, music and lyrics by Finn) at the Public Theater Dec. 28, 1989.*

In addition to his other honors, Finn has been awarded a Guggenheim Fellowship in playwriting. He lives in Manhattan.

JAMES LAPINE was born in 1949 in Mansfield, Ohio where his father was a sales representative. He was educated at Franklin and Marshall (B.A. in history, 1971) and the California Institute of the Arts (M.F.A. in design, 1973). After a year in New York he landed a job in 1975 as a graphics designer for Yale Drama School and their magazine, Yale Theater. For some years he had been interested in writing, and while at Yale he adapted Gertrude Stein's three-page poem Photograph *for the stage, directing it in New Haven and in its Obie Award-winning production in 1977 off off Broadway at The Open Space in Soho.*

The following year Lapine wrote and directed Twelve Dreams *for production OOB by Lyn Austin's Music-Theater Performing Group. His* Table Settings *was produced OOB in 1979 under its author's direction in workshop at Playwrights Horizons, which then presented it in a full-scale, 264-performance off-Broadway production Jan. 14, 1980, its author's first Best Play. The following season he directed William Finn's musical* March of the Falsettos, *launching it into a 268-performance off-Broadway run. In late 1981 he directed his own* Twelve Dreams *off Broadway at New York Shakespeare Festival and staged that group's* A Midsummer Night's Dream *in Central Park the following summer.*

The felicitous Lapine-Sondheim collaboration surfaced when Lapine directed a production of Sunday in the Park With George *(book, James Lapine; music and lyrics, Stephen Sondheim) in workshop at Playwrights Horizons and opening on Broadway May 2, 1984 for 604 performances—Lapine's second Best Play and Sondheim's sixth, winning its authors the 1983-84 Critics Award as the season's best musical and the 1984-85 Pulitzer Prize. The collaboration continued with Lapine's direction of a regional theater revival of Sondheim's 1981 musical* Merrily We Roll Along *at the La Jolla, Calif. Playhouse with great distinction; and with the book and direction of the Broadway musical* Into the Woods, *Nov. 12, 1987 at the Martin Beck Theater (Lapine's third Best Play and the Critics Award winner). His collaboration this season with William Finn as co-author and director of* Falsettoland *brings him his fourth Best Play citation.*

Among Lapine's other recent activities was the staging of The Winter's Tale *at the Public Theater in 1989. He acknowledges the support of the Millay Colony and the Albee Foundation in furthering his career. He lives in New York City.*

Because Falsettoland *is virtually an all-singing show, in the following synopsis we eliminate the usual stage direction "sings" to denote lyrics in the Best Plays style and instead identify the few spoken lines with the direction "spoken"—all else is sung.* Falsettoland *is constructed as a series of scenes, each with its own title; and these titles also serve to identify specific pieces of music, in the absence of any other form of song title in this show.*

Time: 1981-82

Opening

SYNOPSIS: The inhabitants of Falsettoland are onstage to introduce themselves and—some of them—pick up where they left off after the two previous musicals in the Marvin trilogy *In Trousers* and *March of the Falsettos*, expressing themselves in lyrics and music. They are Marvin (a husband and father whose affair with a male lover broke up his marriage but is itself now broken up), Whizzer (the lover), Trina (Marvin's former wife), Jason (Marvin and Trina's son), Mendel (Marvin's psychiatrist, who won Trina away from Marvin and is now married to her) and a lesbian couple from next door, Dr. Charlotte and Cordelia, a caterer. Mendel, singing, sets the scene.

MENDEL:
Homosexuals.
Women with children.
Short insomniacs.
And a teeny tiny band.
Come right in,
The welcome mat is on the floor.
Let's begin:
This story needs an ending.

Homosexual
Father with children.

One bar mitzvah that is scrupulously planned.

ALL:

Separate the wheat from the chaff.
We're so weird you gotta laugh.
Save the funny, kill the bland.
Welcome to Falsettoland.

JASON & TRINA:

Spiky families.

DR. CHARLOTTE:

Women internists.

CORDELIA:

Kosher caterers. . .

ALL FOUR:

Who are trying to expand.

ALL:

Everybody on your mark.

WOMEN:

Congregate in Central Park.

MEN:

Pretty boys are in demand.

ALL:

Welcome to Falsettoland.
Hey.
Ho.
What a world we live in.
Hey.

MARVIN:

It's about time—don't you think?
It's about time to grow up—don't you think?
It's about time to grow up
And face the music—
It's about time.

Marvin continues, explaining what has happened in the past—his marriage, his lover, his wife running off with his psychiatrist.

The Year of the Child

Trina and Mendel are at Marvin's (come to pick up Trina and Marvin's twelve-and-a-half-year-old son Jason), and discussing Jason's upcoming bar mitzvah. Marvin wants his friend Cordelia to cater the party. Mendel derides the whole idea with "Religion's just a trap/That ensnares the weak and the dumb." Trina and Marvin react to Mendel's comments.

TRINA:	MARVIN:	MENDEL:
	Isn't he annoying?	My own bar mitzvah was

Yes he is.

Yes but so
Are you really
Kiddo, so are you

Where's my hug?

Isn't he too much?

Jesus, he's annoying

Jason, where's my hug?

Where's my . . .

A miserable occasion
The cause for such
Abrasion in my family
It still gives
Me
Hives.

Cordelia (who lives next door to Marvin with her lover Dr. Charlotte) enters with samples of food for the bar mitzvah. Jason finally remarks that the grown-ups seem to be "more excited than they should be" over plans for this occasion.

Miracle of Judaism

Jason practices swinging a baseball bat while going over a list of girls he might invite to his bar mitzvah. He likes the sexy, cheap kind, hoping that they won't laugh at his father and his father's friends. In his view, "Selecting girls for one's bar mitzvah/God, that's the miracle of Judaism."

Sitting Watching Jason

MARVIN, MENDEL, TRINA, CORDELIA & DR. CHARLOTTE *(sitting together on the bleachers)*:
> We're sitting
> And watching Jason play baseball.
> We're watching Jason play baseball.
> We're watching Jewish boys
> Who cannot play baseball
> Play baseball . . . . .

All five are advising, "Slide Jason, slide Jason, slide," when Whizzer—Marvin's former lover—enters and sits with them.

MARVIN:
> What is he doing here?

TRINA:
> What are you doing here?

WHIZZER:
> Jason asked me to come.
> Since he asked me to come I came.

TRINA:
> Just what I wanted at a Little League game.
> My husband's ex-lover.
> Isn't that what every mother

Dreams about having
At a Little League Game?

MENDEL:

Looking at Whizzer
Is like seeing treyf.

CORDELIA:

The kid was out.

DR. CHARLOTTE:

The kid was safe.

CORDELIA:

The kid was out.

WHIZZER:

Hey, I love baseball.
I love baseball,
That's what I'm doing here.

MARVIN:

Look who's here.
Say hello.
You're looking sweeter than a donut.

WHIZZER *(spoken, while shaking hands):* Marvin.

MARVIN *(spoken):* Whizzer.

WHIZZER *(To Trina):*

He still queer?

MARVIN *(overhears):*

Am I queer?

TRINA:

I don't know.

MENDEL:

Does it matter?

MARVIN:

It's been so long since I could tell.
(To Whizzer.) Sit in front of me
I wanna see the bald spot.
C'mon, c'mon, move in front of me.
It gives me pleasure to see the bald spot.
Since it's the only physical imperfection that you got.
I wanna see it,
I wanna touch it,
I wanna run my hands through it.

MENDEL & WOMEN:

We're sitting and watch the kid as he misses.
We're watching Marvin throw kisses.
We're watching sixty-seven pounders,
Watching Jewish boys miss grounders,

> Watching boys field, boys bat,
> Boys this, boys that. Watching.
> Jason on deck
> Swinging the bat.

Whizzer rises from his seat in the bleachers and comes down to show hapless Jason how to hit.

> WHIZZER *(giving Jason a batting lesson)*:
> Keep your head in the box,
> Don't think of a thing.
> Keep your head in the box,
> Your eye on the ball,
> Take a breath,
> Then let it out and swing . . . . .
> MARVIN:
> Even bald he looks good.
> WHIZZER:
> Just remember he's an asshole.
> MARVIN:
> He looks damn good
> But he's cheap as dirt.
> WHIZZER:
> Even maniacs can charm
> Which he does
> So beware.
> MARVIN:
> And just be careful. *(Looking studiously at the ball game.)*
> WHIZZER:
> When he smiles that smile, avoid him, or else sound the alert . . . . .
> BOTH:
> How could I know
> Without him
> My life would be
> Boring as shit.
> MARVIN:
> But it is . . .
> WHIZZER *(yells)*:
> Jason, move closer to the plate.
> MARVIN:
> Yes it is . . .
> *(Says to Lesbians):* He's gonna be hit by the ball.
> WHIZZER & MARVIN:
> Please God, don't let me make the same mistake.

MENDEL *(spoken):* Heads up!
ALL:

> We're sitting and watching Jason the batter.
> We know our cheering won't matter
> It's the very final inning
> And the other team is winning.
> And there's two outs, two strikes—
> But the bases are loaded, and . . .

MARVIN:

> Could it be possible to see you
> Or to kiss you
> Or to give you a call.

ALL:

> Anything's possible.
> Jason hit the ball.

(To Jason, who is not moving.) Run!

Michael Rupert as Marvin and Stephen Bogardus as Whizzer
in a scene from *Falsettoland* by William Finn and James Lapine

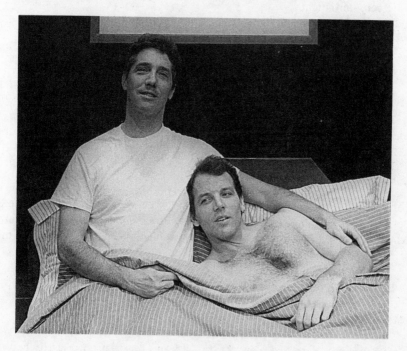

A Day in Falsettoland

At work in his office, Mendel is thinking to himself how deplorable the world has become since the warm-hearted 1960s. Most of his patients today are "Yuppie pagans/Modeled on the/Ronald Reagans" and thinking of nothing but themselves and their careers. At the end of the day he's almost too tired to enjoy Trina's caresses.

At home, Trina wonders why the news that Marvin and Whizzer are back together again should upset her.

In their apartment, Dr. Charlotte has had a hard day at the hospital but she feels unbelievably competent. She can cure anything. Cordelia the caterer doesn't feel so sanguine: "You save lives and I save chicken fat/I can't fucking deal with that."

When Mendel comes home, he sees that Trina is upset and advises her to forget about Marvin and Whizzer. Trina will be all right, she says, after the bar mitzvah is over.

MENDEL:
　　Isn't it enough
　　I want you every night?
TRINA (*spoken*): Ha!
MENDEL:
　　Every other night.
　　Every third night.
　　Everything will be all right.
TRINA: Everything will be all right.

How Was Your Day—Racquetball

Whizzer is beating a lackadaisical Marvin at racquetball *("No ball is used. Rather, when they make a shot, the racquet scrapes the floor and sounds like a ball ricocheting off a racquet.")* The sport acquires sexual overtones. "All I want is you," they both decide, and "Everything will be all right."

The Fight

Trina and Marvin are arguing about the forthcoming bar mitzvah and upsetting Jason, who begs them, "Please stop shrecking" over unimportant things. But the pitch of their quarrel goes higher. Jason decides finally he doesn't want a bar mitzvah. Trina and Marvin are appalled.

MENDEL *(who has been quietly and disgustedly watching)*:
　　Don't disregard the young man you both love.
MARVIN *(to Trina)*:
　　Your husband's out of place!
JASON *(spoken)*: Stop! I don't want a bar mitzvah! Okay? I don't want a bar mitzvah!

MARVIN & TRINA:
> Whaddya mean you don't want a bar mitzvah?
> Whaddya mean you don't want a bar mitzvah?
> How do you think we
> How do you think we
> How do you think we feel about that?

Everyone Hates His Parents

Trying to help Jason through this crisis, Mendel tells the lad, "Everyone hates his parents/Don't be ashamed/You'll grow up/You'll come through/You'll have kids/And they'll hate you too." Jason still insists he doesn't want a bar mitzvah.

MENDEL:
> Everyone hates his parents
> That's in the Torah.
> It's what
> History shows;
> In fact, God
> Said to Moses:
> "Moses, everyone hates his parents.
> That's how it is."
> And God knew
> Because God hated his.

MARVIN *(pulling Jason aside and being joined by Trina)*:
> You are gonna kill your mother.
> Don't feel guilty, kill your mother.
> Rather than humiliate her,
> Killing your mother is the merciful thing to do.

TRINA *(trying to calm herself)*:
> Jason, darling, don't get nervous.
> I'm right here and at your service.
> Look I'm calm and self-deluded.
> Grateful 'cause I hope you'll do
> What I pray you'll do. . . . .

MARVIN & TRINA:
> Jason, please see a psychiatrist.

MENDEL:
> I'm a psychiatrist.
> Get lost.

Mendel reassures Jason that he'll grow up some day and at least hate his parents less. They end in a quirky vaudeville soft show.

What More Can I Say

The lights rise on Marvin and Whizzer naked in bed, Whizzer twisting under the sheets. Marvin is afraid to say how great things are going, for fear of jinxing their increasingly loving relationship. But finally he admits, "It's been more than words can tell."

MARVIN:
..... It's hot,
Just like you read about.
And also caring,
And never too uncouth.
That's the simple truth.

Can you tell
I have been revised?
It's so swell,
Dammit, even I'm surprised.
We laugh, we fumble,
We take it day by day.
What more can I say?

Something Bad Is Happening

DR. CHARLOTTE *(reading medical journals):*
..... Just call me Doc.
Don't call me Lady.
I don't like to talk
When I'm losing the game.
Bachelors arrive sick and frightened.
They leave weeks later, unenlightened.
We see a trend, but the trend has no name.
Something bad is happening.
Something very bad is happening.
Something stinks
Something immoral
Something so bad that words
Have lost their meaning.
Seems a virus has been found
Stories echo underground.
Something bad is spreading
Spreading
Spreading round.

Cordelia asks Dr. Charlotte to taste one of her concoctions, and Dr. Charlotte refuses so sharply that Cordelia thinks it may have been her cooking that has upset her friend. Cordelia tells herself, "She's my doctor, and I love her." Dr. Charlotte tries to distract herself with a copy of *Vogue* ("The men dressed in drag/Next to their moms/Fashion and passion and filler/But not a word about the killer"), but she is too uneasy to enjoy it.

2d Racquetball

Marvin and Whizzer again play racquetball. Whizzer loses and is furious; Marvin begs his pardon for having finally won a game. After Marvin wins again, Whizzer can't catch his breath. Marvin practically carries Whizzer to the hospital, where we see Dr. Charlotte examining him.

Holding to the Ground

Trina is reflecting on her life, which didn't turn out to be as she had hoped. She expected: "I was sure growing up I would live the life/My mother assumed I'd live/Very Jewish/Very middle class/And very straight/Where healthy men/Stayed healthy men/And marriages were long and great." Instead, the ground keeps shifting beneath her, and all she's trying to do is hold on tight. Whizzer, she realizes, is as much a part of her family as Jason and Marvin and Mendel. Incredible.

Days Like This I Almost Believe in God

Whizzer is in the hospital. Marvin approaches the bed tentatively, apprehensively, but is relieved to see that Whizzer looks better than the last time he saw him.

Cordelia brings a sample of possible bar mitzvah fare: "Rugelach. Gefilte fish. It's so good you'd think it's Italian."

Trina enters chattering; Mendel ditto, having had trouble parking the car. Jason comes in bringing a chess board, and Dr. Charlotte follows.

JASON (*going to the bed*):
    Gee, you look awful.
    I think you need to play some chess.
WHIZZER:
    Jason, sit down and begin.
JASON:
    I'll let you win, Whizzer.
    I'll let you win.

The grownups agree that with Whizzer looking so much better, "It's days like this we almost believe in God."

Cancelling the Bar Mitzvah

Everything is ready for the bar mitzvah, except that Jason won't tell Trina and

Mendel whether he wants to go through with it. "Can't we wait till Whizzer gets better?" Jason asks. Finally he tells them "No," he doesn't want them to go ahead with it, and "No," he doesn't want them to cancel it, then storms out.

Unlikely Lovers

In Whizzer's hospital room, Whizzer's reaction to Marvin's affectionate concern is "Don't get morbid . . . . . I haven't died yet."

MARVIN:
   I'm staying here in this spot
   Whether you want me to or not,
   I'm staying.
   Here I am
   By your side
   One old horny lover.
WHIZZER:
      Please go home and don't be scared.
MARVIN:
   What's the fuss?
   I'm not scared.
   What good is a lover
   Who's scared?
   Hit me if you need to.
   Slap my face, or
   Hold me till winter.
   Oh, baby, please do.
   I love you too,
   My lover.
WHIZZER:
   Marvin, just go home and
   Turn on TV.
   Drink a little something till you're dead.
   Think of me around
   Sleeping sound-
   Ly in our bed.
   Marvin, did you hear what I said?
MARVIN:
   Shut your mouth.
   Go to sleep.
   Time I met a sailor.
   Are you sleeping yet or
   What is what?

Whizzer, but
I can't help but feeling I've failed.
Let's be scared together.
Let's pretend that nothing is awful.

Dr. Charlotte and Cordelia come to visit Whizzer. The four of them recognize both the affection and the distress that abounds in this hospital room by talking of everything else. Marvin characterizes the group: "Look at us/Four old friends/Four unlikely lovers."

ALL:
     . . . . . And we vow that we will buy the farm
Arm in arm.
Four unlikely lovers
With heart.
Let's be scared together.
Let's pretend that nothing is awful.
There's nothing to fear
Just stay right here;
I love you . . . . .

Another Miracle of Judaism

Jason addresses God and offers him a deal: make Whizzer better, and Jason will go through with the bar mitzvah. Jason explains, "My dad would laugh/My mom stop crying/It would only take/One man not dying . . . . . That'd be the miracle of Judaism."

Something Bad Is Happening (Reprise)

Dr. Charlotte describes the "something bad" to Marvin. It is "Something that kills/Something contagious/Something that spreads/From one man to another."

You Gotta Die Sometime

Whizzer bravely confronts his prognosis.

WHIZZER:
     . . . . . Let's get on with living while we can
And not play dumb.
Death's gonna come.
When it does, screw the nerves,
I'll be eating hors d'oeuvres,
It's the roll of the dice and no crime;
You gotta die sometime.

Death is not a friend
But I hope in the end, he
Takes me in his arms and lets me hold his face.
He holds me in his arms and whispers something funny.
He lifts me in his arms and tells me to embrace his attack.
Then the scene goes to black.

Life sucks.
People always hate a loser
And they hate lame ducks . . . . .
I would cry if I could
But it does no damn good
To explain I'm a man in my prime.
You gotta die sometime.

Death's a funny pal
With a weird sort of talent.

He puts his arms around my neck and walks me to the bed.
He pins me up against the wall and kisses me like crazy.
The many stupid things I thought about with dread
Now delight.
And the scene turns to white.

Give me the balls to orchestrate
A graceful leave.
That's my reprieve.
To go out
Without care,
My head high
In the air.
It's the last little mountain I'll climb,
I'll climb.
You gotta die sometime. . . . . .

But Whizzer is obviously frightened and making a great effort to keep his emotions under control.

Jason's Bar Mitzvah

Jason comes into Whizzer's hospital room to tell him they are going to hold his bar mitzvah here and now. The others come in with champagne, flowers, decorations, etc.—Cordelia with the food she has prepared. Whizzer dons a robe and gets out of bed to make a toast. When everybody judges that "Everything is lovely," Jason, who has gone to change his clothes, re-enters *in a black suit and colorful tie.*

The cast of *Falsettoland:* Michael Rupert (Marvin), Janet Metz (Cordelia), Heather MacRae (Dr. Charlotte), Danny Gerard (Jason), Chip Zien (Mendel), Faith Prince (Trina), Stephen Bogardus (Whizzer)

MENDEL:
    Trina, try
    To make him smile more.
ALL *(except Marvin):*
    Don't know why
    But he looks like Marvin.
MENDEL:
    Son of Abraham, Isaac and Jacob.
    Son of Marvin, son of Trina, son of Whizzer, son of Mendel.
ALL:
    And godchild to the lesbians next door.

Jason goes into the ritual chant as Marvin draws the hospital curtain.

What Would I Do . . . .

    Alone in front of the curtain, Marvin wonders what would have become of him if he hadn't met and loved Whizzer.

MARVIN:

     . . . . . You're the only one
One out of a thousand others
Only one my child would allow.
When I'm having fun,
You're the one I wanna talk to.
Where have you been?
Where are you now?

Who would I be
If I had not loved you?
How would I know what love is?
God only knows,
Too soon I'll remember your faults.
Meanwhile, though, it's tears and schmaltz.
There are no answers
But what would I do
If you had not been my friend.

Whizzer enters dressed in regular clothes, telling Marvin, "All your life you wanted men/And when you got it up to have them/Who knew it could end your life?" Marvin remembers that he left wife and child to be with Whizzer and declares he'd do it again.

MARVIN:

     . . . . . What more can I say?

WHIZZER:

    What more can I say?

MARVIN:

    How am I to face tomorrow?

BOTH:

    After being screwed out of today
Tell me what's in store

MARVIN:

    Yes, I'd beg or steal or borrow
If I could hold you for
One hour more . . . . .

BOTH:

    Who would I feast my eyes on
Once I was told
That good men get better with age?

MARVIN:

    We're just gonna skip that stage.
There are no answers
But what would I do

If you hadn't been my friend . . .
MENDEL:
   Homosexuals.
   Women with children.
   Short insomniacs.
   We're a teeny tiny band
   Lovers come and lovers go.
   Lovers live and die fortissimo.
   This is where we take a stand.
   Welcome to Falsettoland.

THE SUM OF US

A Play in Two Acts

BY DAVID STEVENS

Cast and credits appear on pages 344-345

DAVID STEVENS was born in Palestine in 1940 of Anglo-Dutch parents. He topped off his education at Terra Sancta College in Jordan and proceeded to make himself at home all around the globe and in a number of occupations, including bartender and barker for a strip club. In England, he settled on the dramatic arts as his profession but didn't settle down. Africa, New Zealand and Australia saw a lot of him, and in 1987 he moved on to California, where he now resides and is working on a new play, Unknown Countries, *(about another world traveler, Sir Richard Burton, and his wife, Lady Isobel), and a TV miniseries based on Alec Haley's new novel* Queen.*

Stevens's various credits include the direction of the TV series A Town Like Alice *and the feature films* The Clinic, Undercover *and* Kansas; *the co-authorship of the Oscar-nominated* Breaker Morant; *and the writing and/or direction of more than 200 hours of TV drama on international screens. His* The Sum of Us *has been called an "Australian" play, set in Footscray, an industrial suburb of Melbourne, and concerning the affectionate relationship between an Australian father and his homosexual son. But it didn't appear down under prior to its developmental staging here in the U.S. at A Director's Theater, Los Angeles, the Williamstown, Mass. Festival and finally its production off Broadway this season on Oct. 16, Stevens's*

New York stage debut and first Best Play—in fact the first and only Stevens playscript on the record so far.

Time: The present

Place: The sitting room of a house in Footscray, an industrial suburb of Melbourne, Australia, and later in the local park.

ACT I

Scene 1

SYNOPSIS: Jeff, an athletic young man scantily dressed in jogging clothes, comes into the modestly-furnished room and collapses on the sofa, mopping his brow. His father comes in and asks how it went in football (soccer) practice. It seems the star kicker for the Footscray team has pulled a hamstring, but the next game isn't a crucial one.

Jeff's dad has dinner almost ready—frozen lasagna, because he had a busy day at work and didn't have time for anything more elaborate. Jeff wants to take a shower and change first. He exits but soon returns wrapped in a towel, complaining that his father has left the tap dripping again, to save the washers (which Jeff, a plumber, could easily replace) but wasting water, which is much more expensive. Dad promises to try not to do it again.

Jeff leaves the room. Dad starts dishing up.

DAD *(to the audience):* He's very wrought up, he only ever mentions that when he's wrought up. He must be meeting someone special. We'll know soon enough. If it's someone he's really keen on, if it's someone really special, he won't eat his pudding. I've got a Sara Lee Blueberry Cheese Cake in the fridge, it's his favorite, but if he thinks he's meeting Mr. Right tonight, he won't eat any, and make some crack about breaking out in spots. He's never been bothered by acne in his life, and I don't think it's going to start now, at twenty-four. You're probably wondering about what I said just now, about him meeting Mr. Right? Well, we might as well get it out in the open, as the actress said to the bishop, you're going to have to know sooner or later. He won't be meeting any girl tonight. He's what you might call—cheerful. I can't bear that other word. He's been like it since—well—since he was born, I s'ppose. I didn't want him to turn out that way, of course, but I think I always knew, somehow. It's not as though he was ever a wimp or anything, any scrape, any adventure, even a punch-up, he was first in, last out, football was always his favorite game, and he's never liked pink as a color. So I think we both accepted the fact as a natural part of his life, and got on with living. Some of you'll be going tut-tut-tut, I s'ppose, but I don't really see why. He's a good, honest lad, with a heart as big as Western Australia, and he's as much a friend as a son. Mind you, he can be a nightmare to live with. Drives me up the wall sometimes.

Jeff comes back wearing jeans and taking a new shirt out of a wrapper, a pink one, arguing, "There's pink and pink. This is more like—warm white." Jeff goes to put the finishing touches on his array, and Dad explains to the audience that he himself is a ladies' man (in youth his nickname was Rabbit). He was faithful to his wife, though—she was killed by a drunken driver when Jeff was 10: "He's never talked about it, the way she died, but he won't drive when he's been drinking."

> *Jeff returns dressed to kill.*
JEFF: You reckon these jeans are all right, or should I wear the dark ones?
DAD: How many pairs of my socks did you borrow? I can almost see your religion.
> *Jeff, now in a fine humor, glances down at his crotch.*
JEFF: If you've got it, show it, I always say.
DAD: You haven't got that much to skite about.
JEFF: Yeah, well, size isn't everything, it's what you do with it that counts.
> *He goes into the kitchen. Dad glances uneasily at the audience.*
DAD: His mother always used to say that to me.

Jeff returns with a dish towel wrapped around his neck to protect his new shirt. The person he's meeting tonight isn't anybody special—yet. Dad is reading a book at the dinner table. It's about the explorer Sir Richard Burton, whom Dad much admires for his search for the source of the Nile. Jeff scoffs, "I don't want to go chasing all over Africa looking for somewhere to have a swim." He's not adventurous—not even, his father points out, in "love, the greatest adventure of all. Your Gran said it once, I've never forgotten it, 'The greatest explorers of all,' she said, 'are the explorers of the human heart.'"

"Is that why she became a dike?", Jeff counters, flustering his father, who objects principally to the word "dike."

DAD: I admit her relationship with Mary was—intimate—but she was not a dike. *(Pause.)* Lesbian, perhaps.
JEFF: Lezzo, dike, what's the diff?
DAD: What's the diff, what's the diff, there's a hell of a lot of flamin' diff! What's in a word, Shakespeare said, well, there's a whole bloody lot. Words give life to things and meaning and beauty. Like your grandma was a very beautiful woman, and just because she found a bit of happiness after your graddad died, just because in her grief she turned to Mary and they found a bit of comfort in each other's arms, that doesn't give you the right to call her names. How would you feel if I went round calling you a fairy, or a pansy, or a poofter?
JEFF: You do, half the time.

DAD: Only when you upset me. Eat your veggies.

Dad goes back to his reading, while Jeff shares his memories of his grandmother with the audience. He enjoyed visiting her very much. Her friend Mary was very religious, even to the point of forbidding the game Monopoly, but Gran had one hidden and played it with Jeff when Mary was out of the house. One morning when he saw Gran and Mary asleep in each other's arms, "It seemed—natural, somehow. I dunno. Like the most natural thing I'd ever seen. Like love." In the fervor of one of the Sunday meetings, Jeff, at 12, flung himself on the Mercy Seat as though his soul were being saved, just to please everybody—except his father, who was angry when he heard about it later. After an elaborate Sunday lunch, Gran and Mary would disappear upstairs, "Probably just slept, be too tired for anything else," Jeff surmises.

JEFF *(to the audience):* . . . . . The nicest thing about going to bed with someone on a regular basis is when they just let you go to sleep. That's the bit I like, snuggled up all safe and sound in their arms. Not that I'm an expert on relationships, mind you, but it happened to me once, and it worked real nice. For a while.
   He doesn't want to remember that.
I mean, you meet some blokes that treat sex like they're going twenty-seven rounds with Bruce Lee, but that wears me out. I don't see what it proves. Maybe that's why I've never had much luck in the romantic stakes. Maybe I haven't got a high enough sex drive. Maybe I'm a bit—ordinary.
   He glances at his father.
Or maybe it's him, there's such a thing as being too well adjusted. There's been a couple of times blokes have stayed here, stayed the night, y'know, and then in the morning he comes in, they're fast asleep in me arms, he comes in, taps 'em on the shoulder and says, "Do you take sugar in your tea?" It can be a bit unnerving, I s'ppose. So it could be him. More likely it's me. Maybe I am just a bit—dull.

Turning to his father, Jeff ascertains that the coast in this room will be clear tonight in case he brings his friend back. Dad will be watching a movie on TV in the other room. To Dad's satisfaction, Jeff, when offered a bit of cake for dessert, declines as expected.
Jeff goes to brush his teeth, while Dad remembers that, yes, his mother was prostrated with grief for two years after his father was killed at sea, and she began to come back to life only after she met Mary, a singer, at Salvation Army meetings, took her in as a lodger and found solace at last in her arms. When Dad realized what was happening, it made him furious: "I thought it was an insult to my dad's memory." His own conservative married life might have been to some extent a reaction. "Maybe I was trying to hang on to some sense of order."
Jeff comes back, on his way to meet someone at the Prinny, his favorite bar, someone "different . . . . . something else . . . . . he's, well, he's sincere, know what

Neil Maffin as Greg and Tony Goldwyn
as Jeff in David Stevens's *The Sum of Us*

I mean, genuine." He departs, and Dad reflects that his son lacks confidence. In the beginning Jeff was promiscuous, but he fell happily in love and was heartbroken when his lover left him after a short time. Like Jeff, Dad has never forgotten his first love, "Still, you can't live your life on memories, can you?"

Suiting his action to his words, Dad takes a note from his wallet and dials a number on the phone. He identifies himself as Harry Mitchell and asks for Joyce Johnson, referred to him by Desiree's Introduction Agency. In their phone conversation, Dad and Joyce quickly assert this is the first time they've done anything like this, that they are both looking for companionship. They make a date for the Footscray Social Club (to which Dad belongs) on the following Sunday. Hanging up the phone, Dad reflects, "I don't know about this one, at all. 'I'm not looking for a physical relationship in the first instance, you know.' Well, I am." The first one the agency introduced him to was "a bit of a disaster," but perhaps this one will turn out to be "a right little humdinger." Waltzing around the room in anticipation of adventure to come, he glances at himself in the mirror and comments, "Oh, there's life in the old dog yet."

Scene 2

Later that evening, Jeff, *"bright-eyed and eager,"* ushers in his friend Greg, who comments that this place looks very much like his own home. Greg is nervous, aware of Jeff's father's presence in the house, but Jeff reassures him, "It's all right . . . . . He knows all about me, what I do, and who I do it with. I bring back blokes all the time," and then wishes he hadn't expressed himself in quite that way, it makes him sound promiscuous. He fetches a couple of beers, and he and Greg sit on the sofa, at first in silence.

JEFF: Real glad you turned up tonight. Wasn't sure you would.

GREG: I said I would.

JEFF: Yeah, but some blokes don't keep their word.

GREG: I know. Been stood up a few times myself.

JEFF: Cripes, any bloke that stood you up must need his head read. I really liked you, first time I saw you, down at the pub. Took me yonks to pluck up courage to say g'day.

GREG: I thought you weren't interested. I'd seen you there before. And in the park, too. I work in the park, sometimes, and I've seen you there, jogging, in footy gear. Those shorts look really sexy on you.

> *Jeff can hardly believe his ears. Someone thinks he's sexy?*

JEFF: Ah. Just training. For the club.

GREG: You play footy?

JEFF: Just the local club. Amateur stuff. But it's a laugh.

GREG *(giggles):* More'n a laugh, what I've heard. What goes on in those locker rooms.

JEFF: That's just talk. Everybody's trying to out-butch everybody else, in there. It's all spit on the floor and how many sheilas did you root last night.

GREG: But haven't you ever—y'know—with any of 'em?

JEFF: Nah, not really. Oh, they know about me all right. Crack a few jokes sometimes. They call me Baxter—

GREG *(laughs):* Backs ter the wall, boys—

JEFF and GREG: —here comes Jeff!

> *They laugh together.*

JEFF: You play any sport?

GREG: Swimming. I do a lot of swimming. It keeps me away from home a bit, I s'ppose that's why. All by yourself, in the water, no one to hassle you, no one to give you a hard time. Won a few medals too, at school.

JEFF: Don't you get on at home?

GREG: Mum's all right, but Dad's a bit tricky, always picking on me, finding fault with everything I do. He went through the roof when I got my job.

JEFF: Gardening, what's wrong with that? That's butch enough.

GREG: He reckoned it wasn't good enough for me, there wasn't any future in it, but I'm bringing home nearly as much money as him already.

Greg's mother wanted him to take ballroom dancing classes, to meet people, but his father wouldn't hear of it. As the two sip their beers and talk, the sexual tension grows until Jeff puts his arm around Greg. As they kiss, Jeff's father comes in dressed in pajamas and dressing gown, greets the boys nonchalantly and goes to the kitchen for a beer. Greg jumps up, alarmed, but Jeff assures him that his father is accustomed to taking this sort of thing in stride (again embarrassing himself because this implies to Greg that he does this sort of thing all the time).

Dad comes back into the room to be introduced to Greg and join the lads in a chat whose overt friendliness, excessively outgiving with in-jokes about homosexuality, makes Greg a bit uncomfortable.

DAD: Don't you get on with your family? Greg.

JEFF: Greg's mum and dad don't know about him yet, Dad.

DAD: Oh, I see. That's a pity, don't you think, Greg? I mean, you're their son.

GREG: It's just—there's never been the chance.

DAD: I expect you could make the opportunity, if you really wanted to.

JEFF: Leave it, Dad—

DAD: I've always been very grateful that Jeff's been so honest with me. Not that I had a lot of choice, really, walking into the back shed when you were—what?—fourteen, and finding you up Willy Jones's bum.

JEFF: I wasn't up his bum!

DAD: As near as dammit.

GREG: You're very broad-minded, Mr.—um—

DAD: I try to be, lad. After all, this is Jeff's home, if he can't be himself here, where can he be? And you think of this place as a second home, Greg. You're welcome here any time you like. We don't have secrets from each other here.

GREG (touched): Thanks very much, Mr. Mitchell.

DAD: Oh, none of that. Either "Harry" or "Dad." But I suppose that depends on how long you plan to go on seeing my Jeffrey, doesn't it?

  Greg gives a half-smile of agreement.

JEFF: Nothing on telly, Dad?

DAD: Nothing worth watching. This is much more fun . . . . .

  Jeff throws his eyes to heaven.

They decide to switch to whiskey. Jeff goes to get the drinks. Dad tells Greg he wanted to know all about Jeff's lifestyle, so he went the rounds of the pubs with him. Dress and behavior seemed weird, but he soon realized "It was all a bit of a game."

Jeff comes back and pours the drinks. Greg is now much more relaxed, responding in kind to Dad's jokes, even telling Dad about his secret ambition.

GREG: I'd like to plant a forest.
DAD *(thunderstuck):* That is—magnificent.
GREG: Isn't it a beauty? You see, I met this bloke once, he was a violin maker, well, apprenticed to it, and he told me there's these famous violins made, oh, centuries ago, by some Stradivarius bloke, he used wood that was anything up to four or five hundred years old, and one of the reasons no one can make a violin as good as his is because they can't get wood that's old enough. All the forests being chopped down, the new trees aren't given time to grow any more. That's when I got the idea. To plant a whole forest, and watch it grow, and stand in the middle of all the great trees and say, I planted this, I made this.
DAD: Do it! That's wonderful, eh, Jeffrey?
Jeff thinks that Greg could walk on water if he wanted to.
JEFF: My oath. Make a fair old swag of violins too.
DAD: "A fair old swag of violins?" Haven't you got any respect for the English language?
JEFF: What's wrong with the way I talk?
GREG: I like it. It turns me on.
Jeff's chest swells about two inches.
Sorry, Mr. M—Harry—bit bold.
DAD: Please, pretend I'm not here.

Dad sends Jeff off to get Greg another drink, and after Jeff has gone to the kitchen, his father gives Greg three gay porn magazines he had stashed with the books. He bought them (he tells Greg) because he wanted to see what his son was doing, and he noticed an article on "Safe Sex," about AIDS, and this had him worried until Jeff told him he was always careful. Greg assures Dad that he practices safe sex too; so, when Jeff comes back, Dad goes to bed contented, leaving the field for the young men. He returns immediately to ask Greg how he likes his morning coffee, then finally goes.

Jeff tries to re-establish the mood, but now Greg pleads a headache: "Look—do you mind—I think I'll give it a miss." Jeff offers him medicine for the headache, and Greg admits, "Seeing you and your dad, I think it's terrific, it's how I'd like to be, bringing your boyfriend home and not having to lie or pretend." But it makes Greg feel guilty instead of sexy, and the domesticity of it all reminds him too much of his own home and his own father's hostile attitudes. "I'd like to see you again, I really would," Greg tells Jeff as he goes to the door. Jeff begs him to stay: "I like you, mate, true dinx. I don't mean just sex, we don't have to do that if you'd rather not. But—I like you, as a person, y'know. . . . . Even when we didn't talk, when we were just sitting together, I felt—comfy with you. Don't go, mate. Please. We could just talk, get to know each other a bit." But Greg apologizes and goes.

Jeff's chagrin reminds him of a time when he went to Sydney hoping for the best, but even with all the people there, he didn't make out any better than he does at home. His father believes it's because he's too shy. In the bar of the train to Sydney, he noticed a woman, alone, heavily made up and bejeweled, "mutton dressed as lamb, drinking gin and tonic." Finally she became extremely drunk and, repeating "Oh, the agonizing pain of it all," stumbled off, trying desperately to maintain her dignity. Jeff remembers, "'Oh, the agonizing pain of it all.' That's what she said. I've often wondered what she meant. But I suppose I know. She just wanted someone to talk to, to have a good time with, to laugh and get drunk with, and cuddle up to. That's all. Doesn't seem a lot to ask, does it? How can you be too bloody domestic, for Pete's sake? What was he looking for, Superman with a ten-inch schlong?"

Dad comes into the room, takes in the situation and pours himself a drink. Dad tries to cheer Jeff up by planning an especially good dinner for the next day, even suggesting that Jeff try "one of those introduction agencies." Jeff declines, and Dad leaves him sitting sipping his drink and remarking, "She comes into my mind from time to time. That woman on the train." *Curtain.*

ACT II

Scene 3

At Christmas, Jeff is trimming the tree and complaining about the number of requests for money from charitable groups. He lights up a joint in celebration of the holiday and offers it to Dad, who takes a puff and finds it "rather smooth." The Christmas decorations remind them both of Jeff's mother, and they both miss her, each in his own way. Jeff cracks a joke about his grandmother's relationship with her lodger, and Dad remembers that their obvious happiness made him begin to wonder if there might be something rewarding in this kind of relationship for men, too. It never interested him personally, but "I made up my mind that no matter what, you were going to be your own man, and I knew I'd love you." He warms to this subject and challenges Jeff.

DAD: . . . . . Be the man you ought to be.
JEFF: I am—
DAD: Sitting round here every night feeling sorry for yourself, getting stoned, when you should be out making some contribution to life, seeing the world, sowing your oats, falling in love, something wonderful—
JEFF: I make a contribution. I look after people's drains. That's a very important thing. Life would be pretty shitty without plumbers, I can tell you.
    He laughs smugly at his own joke.
DAD: Not very romantic, is it? Not like planting a forest.
JEFF: Ah, fair go. I'm just me—
DAD: I know you are. I gave you that freedom. So go on, prove to me that the

way I've brought you up wasn't wrong. Prove to me that my mother wasn't wrong, that what she found was wonderful, worth everything, all for love.

JEFF: It's not that flaming easy, it doesn't just happen to order. The choice is a bit more limited, for one thing. Well, maybe some places, San Francisco, all the blokes wear their dicks on their sleeves there, they reckon—

DAD: Ever thought of going there for a holiday?

JEFF: I don't want to live like that, Dad. I don't want to live in a world that begins and ends with being gay. I like having all sorts of people around and every sort of person there is. I like it at work or the footy where the other blokes rag me about what I am. I like knowing I can cope with all that. And I don't want to live in a world without women. I like women. Me and the girls at the office get on great. I've even fancied some of them, done it with a couple of 'em, just to make sure I wasn't missing out on anything.

DAD *(deeply shocked)*: You've done it with girls? You never told me.

JEFF: Yeh, well, I didn't want to get your hopes up.

DAD: Did you like it?

JEFF: See what I mean?

Jeff liked it all right, "But they just don't turn me on like the blokes do." He appreciates what his father has done for him, and he wouldn't like to be limited in any way. And Dad admits, "I've been a very lucky man to have a son like you."

Dad urges Jeff to look up Greg again. He has done so, several times, casually, but with no attempt at a closer tie after the rebuff suffered that first evening. Dad's insistence—even offering his son the money to take Greg somewhere for a week-end—annoys Jeff enough to bring on an outburst: he wants to fall in love but at the same time is afraid of it because of what happened when he did. He knows his own limitations: "I'm not one of your big explorers, discovering new countries, I'm never going to win any cups or prizes or be rich and famous. I'm never even gonna win Lotto, with my luck. And I'm never even gonna give you grandchildren, which is the least that most blokes can do. But I'm trying to do the best I can."

All Dad wants is for Jeff to be happy, he assures his son. He prayed for his son's happiness outside a locked church the day he brought baby Jeff home. Dad believes in God, in his own way, because it helps him sometimes to think of his wife surrounded by angels and waiting for him to join her.

Jeff assures him, "I am happy. Sort of," and challenges Dad to do some court-ing of his own: "Must be a few old widows floating round." Dad has enjoyed enough puffs from Jeff's cigarette to loosen his tongue, and he admits that he has already made a move in that direction, through an introduction agency. "I'm a man who likes women," says Dad. He gets very lonely at times.

DAD: I was beginning to give up hope, they'd introduced me to a dog first up. Joyce doesn't know that, of course, she thinks it's first time lucky for both of us. She's a wonderful woman, Jeffrey. My side of forty, of course, and her hair's a bit

Tony Goldwyn and Richard Venture (as Dad) in *The Sum of Us*

violent, but she's still got her figure, and she's a lovely personality. And a very generous nature.

     Jeff gives a small, dirty chuckle.

JEFF: You—um—you know, done it then?

DAD: You dirty little bugger.

JEFF: I thought you must have got into her knickers.

DAD: Don't talk about Joyce that way if you don't mind. She's a very refined type of person.

JEFF: Well I'll be—you old dog.

DAD: She's quite a catch, actually. I was worried about it being disloyal to your mum, to her memory, to bring someone else into her bed. But I think she'd understand.

JEFF: Is it love, then, Dad?

DAD: No, Jeff, I can't honestly say it is. It might be the next best thing, though. Do you mind? I've been worried about you.

JEFF: Me? Why me? I'm right. I don't come into this.

     He thinks he understands.

Y'mean, you want me to move out or something? Course I would. Give you two a bit of space.

DAD: No, Jeff, this is your home. I wouldn't want that, nor would Joyce. She knows all about you.

JEFF: Oh yeh?

DAD: She knows who you are, and that you live here, and all.

JEFF: Yeh, but you haven't told her everything, have you?

DAD: No, not that, not yet, there didn't seem to be any need. Let her meet you and get to know you a bit first.

JEFF: Come on, Dad. It's going to be hard enough for her coping with you, without your poofter son hanging around.

DAD: Joyce is a warm, understanding woman, you'll love her, you'll see. And if it all works out, because it will, you'll stay here, in your home, till the day comes when you want to move out. On your own. With someone.

He hasn't actually asked Joyce to marry him yet, but he will, soon. Each thinking his own thoughts, they sit in silence, broken by Dad who asks, "Are we going to have another joint?"

Scene 4

At night, the front door opens, and Dad carries Joyce over the threshold. Joyce looks around the room and likes what she sees. Dad fixes them a drink—a mixture of Irish Cream and Cointreau. Joyce notices the wedding photo Dad forgot to put away for her visit and admires his late wife. Of Jeff's picture, she comments, "It's a wonder some girl hasn't snatched him up," but Dad refuses to take the bait at this point.

Joyce admits she didn't expect much when she applied to the introduction agency, but now things seem to be getting very serious. She has to be extra careful, because "There's more to consider when one marriage has failed on you." Her former husband left her for another woman, quite a nice person.

JOYCE: With her he was a silly boy all over again, a young ram sowing his oats, and he hadn't looked at me that way for a long time, I can tell you. Oh, we still— you know—did it, but it was habit as much as anything, like doing the dishes or feeding the cat. But I've got my needs too. Like you have.

DAD: Oh. Um.

JOYCE: You probably think I'm a bit bold coming right out and talking about it, but it's best we put our cards on the table. I may not be very imaginative in the bed department, Harry, I'm not keen on all the sexual gymnastics you read about in the magazines these days, but I never said no to him, not in all the years we were together.

Dad is intrigued, of course, but tries not to show it.

DAD: Not once?

JOYCE: Well, obviously, there were certain times, after my daughter was born, and when I wasn't well. But apart from that, he always got his onions, whenever he wanted them. (*Giggles.*) He could have had 'em a bit more if he'd played his cards right. I like to be wooed.

DAD: I'll remember that.

JOYCE: So long as you're not too demanding, you'll get what you want on that score.

Joyce asks for another drink, but Dad decides to seize the moment. Kneeling, he asks her to marry him. Tears come to Joyce's eyes at the thought that her years of loneliness may be coming to an end, but she tells Dad, "No . . . . . It's too soon! I don't want to make another mistake. Let's give it six months, see how we go, see how I get on with Jeff, and if we still feel the same way then, I'll say yes."

Dad begs to have the waiting period shortened to three months, and Joyce agrees. They kiss to bind the bargain, and Dad goes to the kitchen to fetch a bottle of champagne. Joyce looks around the room, studying it as a place which she might call home some day. She notices the magazines stored with the books, picks one up and then holds it behind her back as Dad returns with the glasses of wine. He sees there is something wrong, and then Joyce shows him the magazine. She has guessed that it has to do with Jeff.

JOYCE: . . . . . I've been wondering why you never talk very much about Jeff's personal life, why he hasn't got a girl, or anything. But then I thought you would have told me, so I must be wrong.
DAD: I should have told you. Tomorrow, I kept saying, I'll do it tomorrow.
JOYCE: Why didn't you tell me before. Why couldn't you have been honest?
She almost breaks, her disappointment is so intense.
Oh, why didn't you have the guts to tell me before? You're ashamed of him, aren't you?

Dad turns to the audience and asserts that of course he has never been ashamed of Jeff—disappointed in certain respects, certainly, but ashamed, never. He remembers how he and his wife shared each other's lives—"the struggles and the fun"—watched their baby grow and dreamed of his future. "I remember the first time he went to school, he didn't seem old enough, he didn't seem big enough to be setting out on such an adventure, but he was a cocky little shit, all set to take on the world. But the night before, I was tucking him into bed, and I kissed him, and he whispered to me, he said, 'Is it going to be all right, Dad, at school, am I going to manage?' It nearly broke my heart." He's disappointed that Jeff will never know the joys he and his wife had, but "I want him to have all the things he can have."

Dad turns to Joyce and assures her he's not disappointed in his son. Joyce is calmer, but still upset.

JOYCE: You should have told me, Harry. It's not just that you know about it. You accept it. You encourage it.
DAD: It doesn't change anything between us, Joyce.
JOYCE *(cries from her heart):* It does! You lied to me, and let me fall in love with the lies!
DAD: Please, Joyce, just meet Jeff. You'll love him, you'll see.
JOYCE: I can't, Harry. I've met a couple of the gay boys, nice enough, I'm sure

Jeff is too, but I can't imagine how they can do what they do. The thought of two men, touching, doing what they do—or two women—it makes me—and I know it's not fashionable, but that doesn't help, it's how I feel, and what I know doesn't help how I feel.

DAD: Then what are we gonna do?

JOYCE: You said he was going to move out. That he was talking about it, anyway.

DAD *(immediately on guard)*: Don't make me choose, Joyce, please.
> *Moment.*

JOYCE: No. Well, perhaps not.

But Joyce would prefer not to meet Jeff tonight—she wants to think everything over first. Despite Harry's plea for her to stay, she puts on her coat and departs, telling him she'll give him a call in a day or two. After a moment alone, Dad gets his champagne and toasts Joyce's departure, "Up your dress, Henrietta!"

Scene 5

In the Park, on a sunny day, Dad is in a wheelchair, and Jeff is reading to him. When Jeff asks his father if he needs anything, it appears that Dad has lost the power of speech and now communicates by means of a buzzer attached to his chair. Jeff is making conversation about taking Dad on a vacation trip to the sea, when he sees someone approaching.

> *He tries to make himself look inconspicuous. After a moment, Greg arrives, wearing shorts and boots, pushing a wheelbarrow with plants.*

GREG: G'day, Jeff. Thought it was you.

JEFF: Greg—g'day. Fancy meeting you here.

GREG: I'm working here today, planting. G'day, Mr. Mitchell, remember me? Greg. You not well?

> *Dad buzzes on the arm of his chair.*

JEFF: Dad's had a bit of a stroke

GREG: That's bad luck, isn't it? Sorry to hear that, Mr. Mitchell.

JEFF: He can't answer or nothing, but he remembers you.

GREG: How can you tell?

JEFF: Oh, well, you work it out. He buzzes on his chair, once for yes, twice for no, and three times for silly.

Jeff admires Greg's tan and assures him that it's O.K. to speak frankly in front of Dad—he hasn't changed his attitudes just because he's sick. Greg informs Jeff that *his* father knows about him now, having seen him in town with a couple of friends and asking questions when Greg came home. Greg told him all, and his father threw him out of the house. He now has his own studio apartment in town, but shares it with no one at present.

The two young men decide to go for a walk, leaving Dad secure in his wheelchair, after Greg promises Dad to drop in to see him at home some Saturday.

When Dad is alone, we hear him speak his thoughts as though he could talk. "The trouble with having a stroke is that people treat you like a fuckwit afterwards . . . . . Jeff treats me like an imbecile. . . . . Doesn't want to know what I really feel. Likes to put his own interpretation on it, I'm the poor invalid, and he's the suffering only son who's got to stay home and look after Dad."

Jeff and Greg aren't fooling him with their talk of going for a walk: "There's a public convenience in the middle of the Park, I know what goes on in some of those places." Jeff has told his father he doesn't go in for brief encounters any more; and certainly he's stopped bringing friends home, possibly because he's ashamed of his father's condition. What bothered Dad greatly about the onset of his illness was that he never had the chance to tell Jeff goodbye.

Dad remembers the time that his mother and her friend Mary became too old to take care of each other, so Dad's brother decided to take Gran in and send Mary to a home, "For their own good, how many times did we tell ourselves that." The morning they were separated they were "two human beings in pain," saying nothing but holding hands until it was time for Mary to leave. Their hands had to be forced apart. Three months later they heard that Mary had died, and Gran died soon after: "I don't think it was that she wanted to go, so much as she couldn't see a reason to stay . . . . . I've always wanted to know what they said to each other that last night, lying in that great old brass bed, knowing it was for the last time, knowing they'd never see each other again, knowing that they were being taken away to different places to die . . . . . How on earth did they say goodbye? I can't imagine what they might have said. So I don't know what I would have said to Jeffrey, if I'd known the stroke was going to happen, and I was going to be left like this . . . . . but I know I would have said something, and now I'll never find out what it was."

Maybe Jeff will find somebody after he's gone, Dad surmises, but by that time Jeff may have forgotten how to love another person—"I can't think of a worse thing to happen to a human being than that." There is no happy ending to this story in sight, Dad warns, Jeff will come back and take him home and cook up some lasagna or fish for supper because he thinks, mistakenly, that Dad likes it, and maybe they'll grow to hate each other because of the limitations each is forced to impose on the other's life. "Not a very nice thing to look forward to, is it? Sometimes I think it would be easier all round if I just—ended it. After all, what have I got to look forward to, except a few years of him cooking fish or lasagna and wiping my bum, which is not exactly the plan I had for my later years. Nor for his. But there's nothing I can do. I can't even turn on the gas by myself, and anyway, our house is all electric. Pathetic, isn't it? I can't even kill myself."

Jeff returns *looking like a cat that's just had a bowl of cream.* But all he and Greg did was talk, he tells his father, and when Jeff got up the nerve to ask Greg home for tea "one night," to his astonishment Greg suggested that tomorrow would be fine. He's going to bring a couple of poetry books to read to Dad (and his toothbrush, Greg said with a wink, and was probably just joking). Jeff's plan is to play it cool, be himself, and cook up something special.

JEFF: . . . . . Couple of T-bones, that's the go, and there's asparagus in the shops already. I saw some the other day. Sorry, Dad, I meant three T-bones, of course. Though I don't suppose you'd be too keen on 'em, would you? Could be a bit difficult for you to chew. Fish, I'll get you a piece of fish. We'll have T-bones, you can have a nice bit of flounder, that all right? What's up, Dad? What's the matter, mate? You're crying. Ah, come on, it can't be that bad, whatever it is. Here, come on, dry your eyes, it'll be all right.
He wipes his father's eyes with his own hanky.
Don't, Dad, please stop. Breaks me up to see you like this. Come on, here—
He takes his father into his arms and hugs him hard.
There's nothing to get yourself all upset about, I'm here. I'll always be here, I promise. Is it Greg, don't you want him to come to tea? I won't. I'll stop him if you want to me to, I've got his phone number.
But his father is buzzing urgently.
Is that what it is? Tell me, come on, one buzz for yes, two buzzes for no.
One buzz.
Yes, you want me to cancel it?
Two buzzes.
No, you don't want me to?
One buzz.
Yes, that's what I thought.
He hugs his father.
You all right? You sure? Silly old bastard, aren't you? Getting yourself worked up over things. There's nothing to worry about, Dad. I promise yer. *(He smiles at the sun.)* Not a worry in the world. *(And at his dad.)* Turned out real nice, after all, didn't it? I wonder if he'll show up?
Dad throws his eyes to heaven. They sit there, in the sunlight. The father and the son. Curtain.

SHADOWLANDS

A Play In Two Acts

BY WILLIAM NICHOLSON

Cast and credits appear on page 312

WILLIAM NICHOLSON was born in Tunbridge Wells January 12, 1948. His father was a doctor whose career led to specializing in leprosy and other such diseases while practicing in Nigeria, but Nicholson grew up mostly in England, educated at Downside School and Christ College, Cambridge, graduating in 1970. In childhood he knew he wanted to be a writer; in grade school, assigned to draw a picture, he drew one of himself writing. During the decade after college he wrote eight novels—but seven of them were rejected and only one, The 7th Level, *has ever been published.*

In the meantime, Nicholson had distinguished himself at Cambridge with a very good degree—a double first in English literature—and won a place as a trainee with BBC-TV. He wrote every morning and spent the rest of the day forging himself into a director and producer of TV documentaries. In 1981, Martin Luther's 500th anniversary, he was planning a drama to be called Martin Luther—Heretic *with Jonathan Pryce in the title role. His boss had read Nicholson's novel and suggested he do the TV script himself. The rest is history. This first effort of*

Nicholson's was very well received, and by 1987 he was able to resign from the BBC and devote his entire time to writing.

Nicholson's award-winning TV scripts have included The Race for the Double Helix, Sweet as You Are, The Vision, New World *and* Shadowlands, *which began life on the small screen. Expanded into a full-length play,* Shadowlands *was produced in the English hinterlands in September 1989, opened in London at the Queen's Theater October 23, 1989, ran for about a year and crossed the Atlantic to open on Broadway Nov. 11, 1990, Nicholson's first Best Play.*

In addition to his many citations for TV plays and the stage version of Shadowlands, *Nicholson received the Royal Television Society Writers' Award in 1988. He lives outside London with his wife and son.*

The following synopsis of Shadowlands *was prepared by Sally Dixon Wiener.*

Time: The 1950s

Place: Oxford

ACT I

SYNOPSIS: The stage is divided into two areas, one within the other. The inner area takes up most of the space and is concealed by a translucent screen. Both areas represent a variety of places, and the action flows freely within each act. The settings are minimally furnished, which gives not a feeling of emptiness, but rather of essence, to the play. There is an overall atmosphere of other-worldliness, as if the physical setting of life were incidental and relatively unimportant in comparison to the richly overcrowded life of the mind. The furnishings are naturalistic, with the exception of the immense wardrobe upstage, of the size it might appear to a small child. The screen, with its panes and the arched design along the top outlined narrowly in black, rises and descends periodically and upon occasion becomes transparent rather than opaque.

At rise, *"Lewis enters, holding a newspaper and standing before the screen, and addresses the audience as if they have come to hear one of his popular talks. An Oxford don in his 50s, known as 'Jack,'"* he wears rumpled brown corduroy trousers and a v-necked sweater and jacket with elbow patches over his shirt and tie. His baggy clothing and balding head give him a look of a prototypical academic. He is going to speak on love "in the presence of pain and suffering," he announces, claiming that as a bachelor in comfortable circumstances he must be an authority on the subject. He proposes to ask and answer why, if God loves people, would He allow them to suffer? In the newspaper he is carrying, there is a report of an accident—a bus driving into a group of young cadets marching along an unlit road, ten-year-olds, 23 of them killed. No one can be blamed, unless . . .

He points an accusing finger upwards.

LEWIS: Where was He? Why didn't He stop it? What possible point can there be to such a tragedy? Isn't God supposed to be good? Isn't He supposed to love us? That's the nub of the matter: love. What do we mean by "love?" I think I'm right in saying that by "love," most of us mean either kindness or being "in love." But when we say "God loves us" I don't think we mean that God is in love with us, not sitting by the telephone, not writing us letters: "I love you madly, God, XXX and hugs." At least, I don't think so. Perhaps we mean a kind God. Kindness is the desire to see others happy. Not happy in this way or that, but just happy. Not so much a Father in heaven as a Grandfather in heaven. "I do like to see the young people enjoying themselves." Something like that? "What does it matter as long as it makes them happy?"

What I'm going to say next may come as a bit of a shock. I think that God doesn't necessarily want us to be happy. I think he wants us to be lovable. Worthy of Him. Able to be loved by Him. We don't start off by being very lovable, if we're honest. What makes someone hard to love? Isn't it what is called selfishness? Selfish people are hard to love because so little love comes out of them . . . . . God creates us free to be selfish, but he adds a mechanism which will penetrate our selfishness and wake us up to the presence of others in the world, and that mechanism is called "suffering." To put it another way, pain is God's megaphone to rouse a deaf world. Why must it be pain? Why can't He wake us more gently, with violins or laughter? Because the dream from which we must be woken is the dream that all is well. The most dangerous illusion of them all is the illusion that all is well. Self-sufficiency is the enemy of salvation. If you are self-sufficient, you have no need of God. If you have no need of God, you will not seek Him. If you do not seek Him, you will not find Him. God loves us, so He makes us the gift of suffering. Through suffering, we release our hold on the toys of this world and know that our true good lies in another world. We're like blocks of stone, out of which the sculptor carves the forms of men. The blows of his chisel, which hurt us so much, are what make us perfect. The suffering in the world is not the failure of God's love for us; it is that love in action. For believe me, this world that seems to us so substantial, is no more than the shadowlands. Real life has not begun yet.

The screen rises, revealing the traditional "high table" of an Oxford dining hall. Seated there are Christopher Riley, a pompous don; "Harry" Harrington, an Oxford chaplain; Maurice Oakley, a physician; Alan Gregg, considerably younger than the rest; and Lewis's bachelor brother, Warnie, a retired major. They represent the all-male milieu of which Lewis is a part. As Lewis enters, dons his robe and seats himself, Riley is going on about a dinner conversation he'd had some time previously with the lady at his left. The conversation was about "the moral superiority of herbivores to carnivores." At the end of it, Riley had suggested to the woman that she execute her cats. She'd wondered why he would attempt to upset her when he didn't even know her, Riley crows. Gregg, to whom Riley's remarks had been apparently directed, asks what that is supposed to prove.

LEWIS: I think Christopher means us to conclude that women are different.

RILEY: Thank you, Jack. Women are different.

GREGG: The poor woman was clearly terrified.

LEWIS: I like her saying, "Why are you upsetting me? You don't even know me." She's right, of course. One does only seek to distress one's friends.

GREGG: Different in what way, exactly?

RILEY: The point is this, Alan. She was unable to distinguish between an intellectual attack and an emotional attack.

HARRINGTON: Even so, Christopher, some women are very clever, you know.

OAKLEY: Jack, you don't hold with this, do you? You're a great respecter of women.

RILEY: Hah! It's all that depth of personal experience.

LEWIS: Christopher believes only practicing fornicators can teach him sexual morality. Or do you believe each man must fornicate for himself? I've never been quite clear.

RILEY: In a sense, perhaps I do. Morality presupposes choices. To fornicate or not to fornicate. The man who has never fornicated, or wanted to fornicate, or imagined fornicating, has no real moral choice in the matter.

LEWIS: Ah, Christopher. Beware solipsism. Soon you'll be believing if it hasn't happened to you, it doesn't exist.

RILEY: I'm sure you're right, Jack. Already I believe if it hasn't happened to me, it doesn't matter.

Both Harrington and Riley look to Lewis to speak up for women, Riley sarcastically, but Lewis defends himself by announcing he'd just recently spoken at a women's conference. He gets letters from women, and furthermore he answers them.

The group breaks up. Lewis, aware that his brother has had too much to drink, "is discreetly protective of him" as they walk home. As they stroll, Warnie remarks that Riley lives like a monk and always talks about women, whereas Harrington, a married man, never mentions his wife. Lewis wonders if they should conclude that women are more interesting in theory than in practice, but Warnie finds never concluding anything to be the safer course.

Alone in the study at the Kilns, Lewis's and Warnie's home, at the back of which is the giant wardrobe, Lewis dons a dressing gown over his jacket and sits at his desk to write letters.

A lighting change indicates it is now morning. What is obviously the domestic ritual begins with Warnie coming on with the breakfast tray, newspaper and mail. Lewis takes the mail, Warnie pours the coffee and takes up the newspaper. Their talk, the habit of years of living together, is not dialogue, "it is two intersecting *monologues."* Warnie talks about a dream he's had, and Lewis talks about another letter he's just opened from a Mrs. Gresham, "The Jewish Communist Christian American," he reminds Warnie. Warnie complains of the usual lack of news in the newspaper, and Lewis quotes from the letter. "I can't decide whether you'd rather be the child caught in the magic spell, or the magician casting it." Mrs. Gresham, whose first name is Joy, intrigues him, writing to him as if she knows him. Lewis assumes it's because she's read his books. Warnie chalks it up to Americans not understanding about inhibitions.

> *Lewis comes upon a surprising section in the letter. He takes it and*
> *shows it to Warnie.*

LEWIS: Look at that, Warnie.

WARNIE: She's coming to England.

LEWIS: Yes.

WARNIE: "I'm told you share a house with your brother, Major Lewis." Who can have told her that?

LEWIS: You remember that American who came and wrote a sort of book about me? She knows him.

WARNIE: Ah. "I imagine you telling your brother about me, and him saying, 'Is she a nut?', and you weighing this letter in one hand as if to weigh my respectability, and saying 'I'm not sure.'"

> *He gives the letter back*

Is she a nut?

> *Lewis smiles and weighs the letter in his hand.*

LEWIS: I'm not sure.

WARNIE: She seems to want to meet you.

LEWIS: Us.

WARNIE: Politeness.

LEWIS: A good sign.

WARNIE: You are curious.

LEWIS: When you correspond with someone, you do begin to form an impression.

They imagine what she probably looks like: short, dumpy, with spectacles. But she has shown some delicacy in suggesting that they meet for tea at a hotel—safe, neutral ground—so Lewis will agree to meet her. "She might be mad," Warnie fears. Lewis confesses she does write poetry, but assures Warnie they will be "just a day excursion" for her. He insists, however, that Warnie accompany him. Warnie agrees.

In the hotel tea room Lewis and Warnie are awaiting Joy's arrival with her young son. When the boy, Douglas, 8, comes on carrying a book, he's followed by *"a sensible-looking woman . . . . . She looks neither mad, nor obviously American. In fact, she is rather attractive."* The usual introductions follow. Douglas doesn't

Nigel Hawthorne as C.S. Lewis and Jane Alexander as Joy
Davidman in a scene from William Nicholson's *Shadowlands*

think Lewis looks like he thought he would. And after Warnie rings the bell for
tea, Lewis senses Joy's reaction to meeting him was much the same as Douglas's.
She confesses that the meeting was not as she'd imagined but expresses her
appreciation at Lewis's coming to meet her. His letters to her have been "the most
important thing" in her life. She's wanted to come to England for a long time, it
seems, but in answer to Warnie's query as to how she's found it, she claims it's too
quiet. The English seem tired, "timid and lethargic." (She has a theory that the
English are nocturnal, that somewhere there's a big party that goes on all night and
that during the day the English are sleeping it off.) Lewis claims it's just that the
English don't have the energy New Yorkers have. Joy is rather disparaging about
New York, but the discussion does reveal that her husband Bill is a writer—"or
would be, if he ever wrote."

Joy is intrigued to find that Lewis is called Jack and decides he does look like
one. "Not at all spiritual," is her answer when Lewis asks what a Jack looks like.
He's afraid he's disappointed her, but she assures him he's just "becoming real."

Douglas wants Lewis to sign one of the Narnia books he's brought with him.
It's *The Magician's Nephew*. "It's not true, is it?" Douglas wants to know, referring
to the book. It depends on what Douglas means by true, Lewis hedges. "Digory

put on the magic ring, and it magicked him into this palace, where there was this beautiful queen, except she was really a witch, and he found a magic apple, and he brought it back for his mother, and she was very sick, and she got well again," Douglas rapidly summarizes. But he doesn't believe it's true. Lewis insists it's true in the story. Douglas then wants to know if Lewis is capable of doing magic. When he confesses he isn't, the boy asks to be excused and goes running off.

Douglas's saying, "It isn't true," means he wants it to be true, Joy explains. She was the same at his age. Had she "secretly wanted to believe in God?" Lewis wonders. "In something," she concedes, but hadn't realized it then. But it hadn't started as atheism, it began with materialism. She'd had it all doped out early on, but it was a front because "inside there was somebody else." The somebody who wrote poetry, Lewis conjectures.

WARNIE: Ah? You're a poet, Mrs. Gresham?

JOY: Major Lewis, I know what you're thinking. You're thinking, God save us, she's going to start reciting.

WARNIE: I hope I'm not so bad-mannered.

JOY: No poetry at tea time. I know my manners too. But just to redeem myself a little, I must tell you that I did once win a national poetry award which I shared with Robert Frost. You have heard of Robert Frost?

WARNIE: Yes. Absolutely.

JOY: But that's all in the past now.

LEWIS: Why is that?

JOY: Let's say, I've turned away from the mirror.

Lewis is intrigued.

LEWIS: The mirror? Do you mean the reflection of yourself, or the reflection of the world?

JOY: The one being vanity, which is bad, the other being art, which is good?

LEWIS: Possibly.

JOY: I don't make that distinction. See yourself in the mirror, you're separate from yourself. See the world in the mirror, you're separate from the world. I don't want that separation any more.

LEWIS: I think I would argue that art has quite the opposite effect. Great art breaks through that separateness, to let us touch the very heart of reality.

JOY: Breaks through? That sounds as if art does all the work. I'd say we have to do the breaking through ourselves. Art teaches us how to know it when we see it, but art isn't it.

LEWIS: Oh, I see. Art is some sort of instruction manual for life, is it?

JOY: Hey! That's one of your favorite tricks, isn't it? Redescribe your opponent's argument with a dismissive image, and you think you've dismissed the argument.

Lewis is taken aback by her vigorous riposte, but he bows to the truth in her criticism.

LEWIS: I stand corrected.

Douglas has returned. After a bit more talk, Joy rises, having noticed Lewis glancing at his watch. Warnie and Lewis also rise. Douglas is longing to ring the bell on the tea table, but Joy forbids him to.

Warnie rings for the waiter. It seems Joy will stay in England until the end of December and could be in Oxford again, in which event Lewis suggests to Warnie that they might be able to provide a pot of home-brewed tea. Joy thanks him for the invitation. Lewis has gone off to pay the bill, and Warnie and Joy continue conversing as they go off.

> *Lewis is about to follow, when he sees Douglas, who is still hanging around the bell.*
>
> LEWIS: Do you remember the bell in the book?
>
> DOUGLAS: Yes. And the queen was sitting in a stone chair, and she was very beautiful, and she didn't move or even breathe. But she wasn't dead.
>
> LEWIS: No. She was waiting.
>
> DOUGLAS: Waiting for someone to ring the bell.
>
> LEWIS: Do you remember the writing on the pillar beneath the bell? "Make your choice, adventurous stranger. Strike the bell, and bide the danger."
>
> *Music begins: the music of the magic world.*
>
> DOUGLAS: Can I?
>
> LEWIS: It'll break the spell. It'll wake the queen.
>
> DOUGLAS: I don't care.
>
> LEWIS: All right, then.
>
> *Douglas rings the bell. The lights change. The screen rises. The door of the giant wardrobe slowly opens, to reveal a magical infinite space beyond: a child's vision of paradise. Douglas walks towards the opening wardrobe door, as if hypnotized. Lewis watches. Douglas enters the magic world, and the great door closes behind him. The music fades. The brief glimpse of another world is over.*

Lewis and Warnie are hanging Christmas paper chains in the study as they await the arrival of Joy and Douglas for tea. Somewhat apologetically, Lewis comments to Warnie that "At least one can talk to her." "Listen to her," is the way Warnie puts it, and he bets Lewis she'll make him listen to a poem and then ask him what he thinks of it.

Joy and Douglas arrive. Joy, curious, looks about, and Douglas goes directly to a bookcase and takes out books. Joy hopes Lewis doesn't mind (he doesn't). Warnie excuses himself, saying he's leaving Jack to entertain her, slyly adding as he departs that his brother is hopeful she'll introduce him to her poetry. She wonders if Lewis is really interested. He claims he is. Joy is walking about the study and learns that the brothers have lived here for more than 20 years—his friends refer to it as the Midden, Lewis confesses. He goes off to bring back the tea tray, with orange squash for Douglas.

Joy notes some of the book titles, and Lewis explains he's working on 16th century English literature for OHEL—the Oxford History of English Literature. He brings the conversation back to her poems and insists on hearing one. To get it over with, she recites a brief one, written when she was 22, about snow in Madrid during the Spanish Civil War. When he makes no comment, Joy feels he's embarrassed. Actually he was touched, and Joy regards that as a satisfactory response. She confesses she was never in Madrid, however.

LEWIS: Personal experience isn't everything.

JOY: You don't think so?

LEWIS: I've never been to Madrid, but I know it's there.

JOY: How about Narnia? Ever been there?

LEWIS: Interesting question. I'm not sure. I suppose I've sent surrogates of myself there. Children.

JOY: Yourself as a child.

LEWIS: Something like that.

JOY: It is different when you feel something for yourself. And it's a lot different when it hurts.

LEWIS: Just because something hurts, it doesn't make it more true. Or even more significant.

JOY: No. I guess not . . . . .

LEWIS: I'm not saying pain is purposeless, or even neutral. Not at all. But to find meaning in pain, there has to be something else. Pain is a tool. If you like, pain is God's mega—

JOY: God's megaphone to rouse a deaf world.

Lewis, caught out by Joy's quoting him, is embarrassed. She claims she knew him quite well before they met from reading his work. Joy asks Lewis if she might call him Jack, and they agree to calling each other by their first names.

Joy digs back into their previous conversation by inquiring whether or not he's ever been badly hurt. He evades the question, and she changes the subject to Christmas, asking what he does on the holiday. "Roast turkey, Christmas pud, far too much to drink," and what will Joy and Douglas do? Probably a hotel, Joy thinks, and then, yes, home for the New Year.

They fall silent, and then Lewis opens the floodgates. Indeed he has been hurt. His mother died when he was 8; the end of his world; his father crying; the big house with empty corridors; voices; doors opening and closing. He'd had the toothache and wanted his mother to come to him. She'd died of cancer. Joy wonders if he'd believed in heaven and that he'd see her again. He hadn't—she'd just gone. And, yes, he'd gone somewhere secret, but not to cry.

There is silence again, but before Joy can continue questioning him, Lewis turns to ask Douglas if he'd like more orange squash, and Joy insists they must leave. Almost as if on impulse, Lewis suggests they stay with him over Christmas. Of course he'll speak with Warnie, but he'd welcome their company. Joy at first demurs, but as they are leaving he assures them they'd be doing him a kindness and that Warnie would be delighted.

Riley, Oakley and Harrington are with Warnie and Lewis in the study, and a pre-Christmas drinks party is under way. Riley, typically, is resentful of the seasonal "presumption of good will." He feels ill will towards his fellow men. Harrington admits to feeling that Christmas is something of a lost cause, but Lewis says it's all in the manner in which it is presented. Telling people "It's about peace in the world, and being kind to the poor and needy" won't make anyone listen. Riley suggests the arch communicator give them the sales pitch. Lewis offers "Virgin Has Sex with Omnipotent Alien. Gives Birth To God."

Riley's view of the incarnation leads him to believe the deity is limited in intelligence: why would anyone voluntarily choose to be human when there's the option of remaining divine? But Lewis sees it as magic, "the coming of new life in the heart of winter when all the land is dead."

Joy enters. She has no sooner been introduced before Riley attempts a rather puerile put-down of her, as an American, in a sly joke involving the name of one of Lewis's books. Lewis tells him to behave, and Riley apologizes, claiming that Lewis's success as an author has made him envious. Joy is curious as to whether Riley's read any of Lewis's books for children. It seems Lewis, as one of his tests of friendship, has read extracts to Riley. Lewis has been reading Sir Philip Sidney to Joy, and she finds Sidney "glorious," which delights Lewis. She specifically mentions Sidney's image of desire as a baby that will not stop crying.

JOY: Babies just yell until they get what they want. That's what I love about the image. It's precise. Nowadays, poets are so lazy.

LEWIS: You sound like me, Joy. She's supposed to be dragging me kicking into the twentieth century.

JOY: I've been force-feeding Jack T.S. Eliot, but even Eliot can be lazy. "When the evening is spread out against the sky, like a patient etherized upon a table." What kind of image is that? He could just as easily have written, "Like a cocktail sausage upon a tray."

Riley is beginning to feel excluded.

RILEY: Congratulations, Jack. You seem to have found a soul mate.

LEWIS: I thought you believed we didn't have souls, Christopher.

RILEY: Well now, you see, I regard the soul as an essentially feminine accessory. "Anima." Quite different from "animus," the male variant. This is how I explain the otherwise puzzling difference between the sexes. Where men have intellect, women have soul.

JOY: Professor Riley, as you know, I'm an American, and different cultures have different modes of discourse. I need a little guidance here. Are you being offensive, or merely stupid?

Lewis, Harrington, Oakley and Warnie laugh. Riley pulls a face at

Lewis, rather put out, but trying to laugh it off.

LEWIS: Serves you right, Christopher. Don't be such a bully.

RILEY: I feel like calling for police protection. Where on earth did you find her?

HARRINGTON: How do you find England, Mrs. Gresham?

JOY: Cold. Dull.

RILEY: How very perceptive. How original.

JOY: And I don't much care for the weather, either. Will you excuse me, Jack? Mr. Harrington, Dr. Oakley, Professor Riley, it's been my pleasure.

After Joy's departure, the party breaks up; but before leaving, Riley advises Lewis to get rid of her. "She's ghastly" and has "her hooks into you." Lewis assures him she's married, "a committed Christian" and not likely to be interested in an adulterous relationship with him. Riley isn't convinced. "Never send to know for whom the wedding bell tolls, Jack," he warns him.

Afterward, when Lewis is alone with Joy, he apologizes for Riley's behavior, then becomes aware that the letter she's reading has her full attention. She's troubled by it but finds it difficult to talk about it, despite his obvious empathy. If she were home, she'd write him, asking him what to do.

LEWIS: That's easy.
    He takes a chair and turns it so that its back is to Joy. Then he sits, where she can't see him.
Tell me like a letter. Off you go.
    Joy falls in with his suggestion, at first tentatively, then with increasing feeling and fluency.

JOY: Dear Mr. Lewis. My husband has just written to me to tell me that he's fallen in love with another woman. Her name is Renee. He wants me to give him a divorce, so that he can marry her. I don't know what to do.
    She takes up the letter and reads from it.
"Renee and I are in love, and have been since about the middle of August. If it had not been for our love I could not have come through this summer with as little anguish as I have, for things have been rough financially." Perhaps you wonder if I knew about Renee. The answer is no. But Renee is not the first.

LEWIS: Do you love your husband?

JOY: I don't know how to answer that one. Bill's very talented, he wants to do right by everyone, he's a good man at heart, and I guess I love him. Bill's an alcoholic, he's compulsively unfaithful, he's sometimes violent, and I guess I haven't loved him for years. Once he broke a bottle over Douglas's head. Two days later he said, "When have you ever known me to do an unkind thing?"
    She begins to weep.
He's worn me out. That's the truth of it. The only thing that's new is, he wants a divorce.

LEWIS: I had no idea.

JOY: How could you? People never know about other people's lives. You have to live it to know it. Sorry. You don't agree with that.

LEWIS: Contrary to popular opinion, I don't know everything.

Joy pulls herself together, admitting that some good things happened to her during the marriage, which had begun happily. There was their son. And something had happened that began to change things for her, to change her, something she wants Lewis to know about. When Douglas was a baby, Bill called from his office one day, saying he was not ever going to come home again. Alone with the baby, she began to go to pieces late that night, when suddenly she was sure someone else was there, for "maybe half a minute." She knew it was a person—"More real than real. So real that everything else became like shadows." When she told Bill about it later, he believed her and wished God would come to him.

She sees no recourse but to go home. As for the divorce, she believes they would still be married in God's eyes, and she couldn't marry another man. Lewis agrees but is unable to say what she'd like him to say. Joy presumes the other woman is living with Bill, but there's no place else she can go. Lewis wishes there was a way he could help. There is a way, she insists; he can be her friend. He already is, he assures her.

On a morning sometime thereafter, when Lewis and Warnie are back in their bachelor routine, Riley appears. Told that Joy has departed, he's relieved, because "people talk." Lewis doesn't understand why a man and a woman can't be friends, complaining that friendship is "almost as quaint and outdated a notion as chastity." He imagines friends will become like elves, just mythical beings from the past. Riley feels it will be worse, that friendship will become illegal: "The accused has been found guilty of gross public friendship. I hereby pass sentence of five years marriage, with no remission," he pronounces.

Lewis becomes reflective.

LEWIS: Tell me something, Christopher. How can I put this? Would you say that you were . . . content?

RILEY: I am as I am. The world is as it is. My contentment or otherwise has very little to do with it.

LEWIS: You don't ever feel a sense of waste?

RILEY: Of course. All life is waste. Remember, I don't have your faith in divine recycling.

LEWIS: I've always found this a trying time of the year. The leaves not yet out. Mud everywhere you go. The frosty mornings gone, and the sunny mornings not yet come. The air dank and unhealthy. Give me blizzards and frozen pipes, but not this nothing time. Not this waiting room of a world.

RILEY: May will come, Jack. And June. And July.

LEWIS: And I have two books to finish, and six talks to write, and letters, letters, letters.

He turns to his work, waiting on the desk. Riley rises from his chair and watches him with some sympathy, understanding him better than his friend realizes. Then he exits.

Lewis finally settles to his work and is concentrating as Joy comes on, standing and watching him, greeting him only when he becomes aware someone is there. She and Douglas live in Oxford now, she reveals. But Lewis mustn't worry about it—they won't be any trouble, they have a house. Lewis, stunned, wonders why she hadn't written. Why should she have? she retorts. To ask his permission? And, yes, she's divorced. She hopes he doesn't mind she's there. He doesn't.

They are walking to Joy's house, when Lewis reports he might be offered a chair at Cambridge, teaching medieval and renaissance literature, and he'll probably take it. Joy wonders if that means he'll leave Oxford. He won't. He'll just teach in Cambridge. Joy is relieved.

He looks at her with affection,

LEWIS: I really am very—very surprised to see you, you know.

JOY: I think you're overdoing the surprise a bit, Jack. I wasn't dead. I was only in America.

LEWIS: Yes, of course. But you see, I've been thinking about—

He hesitates to say it; then decides he will.

I've been thinking about you.

JOY: I am honored.

LEWIS: Yes. I was thinking about you. And, there you were.

JOY: Here I am. Present tense. Present, and tense.

LEWIS: I really am very glad to see you again, Joy.

JOY: Thank you, Jack.

He has gone a little further than he intended and changes the subject .....

Lewis calls moving "a sort of revolution" as they arrive at Joy's house, where she begins to empty packing cases full of books. He evidently regards the whole process as hair-raising. Joy wonders when he last moved. It was 25 years ago, Lewis recalls: "Thank God that's over." He offers to help put books onto the shelves, but merely takes one and starts reading it.

It seems Bill wasn't keen on Joy's coming to England, but it's cheaper to live in England, and Bill can't afford to give her much. Lewis is worried she won't be able to manage on what she's getting and offers to help her out if she needs more— that's what friends are for.

Joy hopes the move will work out for her son. She likes Oxford, being among educated people in the same place as Lewis. He's delighted to have her as a neighbor, he insists, wondering why she looks at him as if he's lying. He means what he's said. "But you don't say it all, do you?" she rejoins. Saying it all would take too long, he sidesteps.

She takes a different tack. She wants to stay friends with him and wants to know anything that could make that difficult for him. She wants the subject fully aired. He pussyfoots around it, talking about people coming to conclusions, and how it angers him that people are not allowed to be "just friends." He regards friendship as very important, but it ought not be "turned into a watered-down version of something it is not." He deplores that romantic love is the only option men and women are allowed to indulge in. Actually, he believes that friendship is (and Joy finishes his thought) "a kind of love." He appreciates that she understands. She lays it flat out that she realizes he's a bachelor, she's divorced, and that some people might think he might consider marrying her, and that he doesn't have any such idea and she mustn't have any such expectations. She realizes that he wants this clearly understood, because he doesn't want her hurt.

Lewis doesn't know what to say. But she's just said it, she points out. He's unaccustomed to this . . . "Whatever it is." "Naming names" is what it is, Joy simplifies it for him, and now he needn't be afraid of her anymore.

Lewis insists there must be some way he can be of more help to her. She's fearful of exhausting his good will, but he believes it grows if drawn on. If she asked him for something he couldn't give, he would say so, wouldn't he, and without running away? she asks. There is something she wants, he realizes, but he turns it into a joke. She wants him to make the tea, he suggests. "I'll get it," she offers, and they exit in opposite directions.

Warnie and Lewis have come downstage separately, each with a deckchair, and have settled down to read.

WARNIE: So she's settled over here for good, has she?
LEWIS: Who knows? For the foreseeable future.
WARNIE: Why Oxford?
LEWIS: Why not Oxford? Dreaming spires, and so forth.
WARNIE: You know how it looks, don't you, Jack?
LEWIS: I know.
> *Neither of them have taken their noses out of their books. There follows a short silence. Then:*
She's a good friend to me, Warnie. That's all.
> *Warnie nods.*
WARNIE: Is that how she sees it?
LEWIS: I wouldn't presume to raise the matter.
WARNIE: No. Of course not.
> *Another short silence.*
LEWIS: There is something you should know, Warnie.
WARNIE: What's that, Jack?
LEWIS: I've agreed to marry her.

WARNIE: You have?

LEWIS: Yes. Seemed like the right thing to do.

WARNIE: You astound me. No, I mean . . .

LEWIS: It's all right, Warnie. Nothing's going to change. I'm not really going to marry Joy.

WARNIE: You're not?

LEWIS: The rumors are unfounded.

WARNIE: They are?

LEWIS: What I have agreed to do is extend my British citizenship to her, so that she can go on living in England.

WARNIE: By marrying her.

LEWIS: Only technically.

WARNIE: You're marrying Joy technically?

LEWIS: A true marriage is a declaration before God, not before some government official. This will be a bureaucratic formality, nothing more. Joy will keep her own name. We will all go on living exactly as before. No one will even know the marriage has taken place, apart from you, Somerset House, and the Department of Immigration. It is nothing more than a bureaucratic formality.

At the Registry Office, where Joy and the woman registrar are joined by Warnie, Lewis hurries in late, disheveled and with a pile of books, apologizing. As the registrar proceeds, Lewis speaks *"in an unduly clear voice . . . . . Joy's responses are more muted."* Asked if there is a ring, both Lewis and Joy say no, and both add, "Sorry." *"The whole affair is very awkward and embarrassing."* As the three leave the Registry, it is raining. Joy invites them to come for a drink, but Lewis has to get back to work and hurries off. Warnie accepts Joy's offer, which she appreciates. Warnie apologizes for Lewis, but Joy is understanding and appreciative of what Lewis has done for her. They refer briefly to the fact that the marriage is to be kept a secret. "It will be as if it never happened," is what Warnie tells her Lewis had said to him. "Jack plays safe, you see. Always has," Warnie explains as they go off.

Lewis is at Joy's house talking with Douglas, who is in his pajamas. It seems Douglas doesn't like being in England very much, and his mother had told him they needn't stay if they don't like it. His mother seems to like it, however. He wants to stay with his mother though, as he loves her better than his father. When Douglas is sent off to bed, Lewis remarks on his obedience and adds that he likes the boy. Douglas likes Lewis, too, Joy claims, and she believes he'll get used to England. As for her, she feels happier than she's felt in a long time, "mostly because of you" she confesses to Lewis. He teasingly asks her if she's not getting tired of seeing him. She isn't, but wonders what the neighbors must think about them.

JOY: Don't you sometimes burst to share the joke?

LEWIS: What joke?

JOY: Well. Here's the neighbors thinking we're unmarried and up to all sorts of wickedness, while all along we're married and up to nothing.

> *She sees that her joke makes him uneasy.*

Only technically married, of course.

LEWIS: Do you think I come round too often?

JOY: Too often for what? We're friends. That's what we agreed. Good friends.

> *Lewis prepares to leave. She gets his coat and helps him on with it. Her hands rest on his shoulders. He moves away.*

We won't talk of it again. I know you don't like it. You get that twitchy look in your eyes, and you start feeling in your coat pockets, as if there's something there you have to find.

> *Lewis is doing just as she describes. He stops and removes his hands from his pockets.*

LEWIS: You know me too well.

JOY: Don't say that. Just say, I know you.

LEWIS: You know me.

DOUGLAS (*from off*): Mom! I'm ready!

JOY: Coming! Goodnight, Jack.

LEWIS: Goodnight.

> *As Lewis leaves, a sudden pain strikes her.*

JOY: Ah!

LEWIS: What is it?

JOY: I don't know. It's all right. It's gone again.

LEWIS: I'll say goodnight, then.

JOY: Goodnight, Jack.

> *He pats her on one arm and they exchange a peck on the cheek. Lewis exits. Joy stands looking after him. Then she turns to go to Douglas. Her body twists, and her mouth opens in a silent scream. Suddenly, she crumples to the floor. Curtain.*

ACT II

Lewis enters, as at the beginning of the play, to speak to the audience as if giving another of his talks; but as he continues, it seems as if he is trying to reaffirm his own belief as well as convince the audience. He has been talking about a friend of his, "a brave and Christian woman," who had seemed well until she had suddenly collapsed in agony. She is now in the hospital and probably dying of cancer. He asks why.

LEWIS: I find it hard to believe that God loves her. If you love someone, you don't want them to suffer. You can't bear it. You want to take their suffering onto yourself. If even I feel like that, why doesn't God? Not just once in history, on the cross, but again and again? Today. Now. It's at times like this that we have to remind ourselves of the very core of the Christian faith. There are other worlds than this. This world, that seems so real, is no more than the shadow of the life to come. If we suppose that all is well in this present life, if we can imagine nothing more satisfactory than this present life, then we are under a dangerous illusion. All is not well. Believe me, all is not well.

> *His present experience, Joy's suffering, breaks through the familiar pattern of his lecture.*

Suffering . . . by suffering . . . through suffering, we release our hold on the toys of this world, and know that our true good lies in another world. But after they have suffered, must they still suffer more? And more?

> *He has no answer to this question, which torments him. All he can do is repeat his familiar lines, wanting to believe them.*

We are blocks of stone . . . . .

Warnie comes on with Douglas, who sits in a chair reading *The Magician's Nephew* while Lewis and Warnie talk. The prognosis isn't good, Lewis reports. The world seems full of "cutting edges" to him: "They give her morphine . . . . . No morphine for me." Lewis needs sleep, but he can't sleep, and it's too soon for her to die because he hasn't had the time to talk with her. It doesn't take much time, and he should get on with it, Warnie counsels.

When the nurse comes to take Douglas in to see his mother, Lewis tries to reassure the boy, and Warnie promises to take him afterward for a bun tea. As Lewis and Warnie wait, Lewis recalls the boy in the book who brings the magic apple to his dying mother to make her well again: "I'm a fraud, Warnie." The doctor comes on, acknowledging that Joy has been told the cancer had "eaten through her left femur" and that she has a malignant tumor in one breast. Of course she knows it's serious—the hip bone "snapped like a frozen twig." Lewis can't understand how that could happen without warning, but the doctor regards it as not that unusual. He won't say she's going to die but admits the cancer is very advanced.

Lewis is alone in the hospital room with Joy. She admits the pain is "kind of pushy." The hip operation is the next day, he informs her. She doesn't expect him to worry about her. She's his wife, Lewis points out. "Technically," she reminds him. Then he'll worry about her "technically."

LEWIS: Give me your hand.
> *Joy turns and looks at him. Slowly she raises her hand. But before she gives it to him, she pauses.*
JOY: Just how much is there to worry about, Jack? They won't tell me.
LEWIS: That's because they're not sure themselves.
JOY: Tell me, Jack.
LEWIS: I don't know any more than they do, Joy.
JOY: Please.

After a pause.
LEWIS: They expect you to die.
JOY: Thank you.
Having got what she wanted, she pauses to regain strength. Then:
What do you say, Jack? I'm a Jew. Divorced. Broke. And I'm dying of cancer.
Do I get a discount?
LEWIS: Oh, Joy.
JOY: You know something? You seem different. You look at me properly now.
LEWIS: Didn't I before?
JOY: Not properly.
LEWIS: I don't want to lose you, Joy.
JOY: I don't want to be lost.
LEWIS: Please.
He holds out his hand again. This time she gives him her hand. He holds it and strokes it.

Joy tells Jack she loves him. He almost responds to her declaration but can't quite manage to. Then a spasm of pain ends the visit.

Harrington and Riley are talking about Lewis's situation. When Lewis appears they are embarrassed to bring up the topic, but Lewis launches into it, assuring them Joy's being well taken care of. He's worried that her affairs are not in order, however, and about what will become of Douglas, as Joy doesn't want him to be with his father. Harrington assumes there are relatives. He realizes that Joy is Lewis's friend, but "She's not . . . well, family."

LEWIS: Not my wife?
Harrington gives a nervous laugh at such a prospect.
HARRINGTON: No. Of course not.
LEWIS: Of course not. Impossible. Unthinkable.
HARRINGTON: I only meant—
LEWIS: How could Joy be my wife? I'd have to love her, wouldn't I? I'd have to care more for her than for anyone else in this world. I'd have to be suffering the torments of the damned at the prospect of losing her.
Harrington is awed by Lewis's passionate outburst.
HARRINGTON: I'm sorry, Jack. I didn't know.
LEWIS: Nor did I, Harry.
Suddenly his manner changes. He becomes calm, almost businesslike.
I'm going to marry Joy. I've made up my mind. I want you to marry us properly, Harry, before God.
Harrington is now embarrassed professionally as well as personally.
HARRINGTON: I think it would be best if we talked about this later, Jack.
LEWIS: We haven't got a later.
HARRINGTON: Still. It's not entirely plain sailing, is it?
He looks to Riley for support.

RILEY: I think Harry's trying to say it's against the rules.

HARRINGTON: She's a divorced woman, Jack. The bishop would never let me . . . . . I don't make the rules.

RILEY: Jack. I can't pretend to understand what's happening to you, but if this is what you want, I wish you both happy.

HARRINGTON: I'm really sorry, Jack.

LEWIS: That's all right, Harry. I understand.

Lewis returns to Joy's room. She's been given more medication, but her mind is clear, he determines, and he announces he intends to marry her "before God and the world." "Make an honest woman of me," Joy comments. Lewis claims he's the one who has not been honest, that it took this situation to make him see sense. She reminds him there's a custom called proposing and wonders if she missed it. When he does propose, asking her, "marry this foolish, frightened old man, who needs you more than he can bear to say, and loves you even though he hardly knows how," she accepts.

Douglas comes on and stands watching. Then Warnie comes on with a young priest carrying a missal. The priest goes to Joy's bedside, Lewis takes Joy's hand, and the service begins. As it proceeds, the lights come up upstage on the Other World space, and the door of the big wardrobe opens. Only Douglas sees this happening, and he moves quietly from the group and goes into the Other World, reaches up and picks a magic apple from a tree and brings it back into the hospital room.

The service is now ended, and Joy is asleep. Warnie and the priest go off. Lewis goes downstage. Douglas puts the apple under Joy's pillow, kisses her. As he goes off, the Other World lights fade out.

Some time later, Lewis and the doctor are talking. "Cautiously optimistic" is the doctor's phrase. It confuses Lewis—he could understand "getting better" or "getting worse." The doctor says the rate of the spread of the cancer is slowing. Returning strength would be a good sign, he tells Lewis, who has pointed out that people have recovered from cancer. The doctor won't commit himself but does allow that remissions can happen.

Lewis arrives at the hospital to find Joy sitting up in bed cheerfully chattering away about the nurse's love life. The nurse has been going out with someone for two years and hopes he'll marry her. Lewis, pleased at Joy's improvement, asks what advice she gave the nurse. Joy told her, "Give him enough to make him want the rest, then nothing till he pays up."

And Lewis doesn't need to feel sorry for Joy anymore. "Nor for myself," he adds. All he wants is some time with her. *She glances upward, at God, who mustn't hear.* Which reminds her, she's been wondering how Lewis has squared it with God for marrying her. It seems he's rationalized it quite simply. Her husband had been married before, and if marriage is indissoluble he can't have married Joy, because he was still married; and therefore she was never married in the first place.

When Joy is able to walk again after the operation, the doctor tells Lewis and Warnie there is no need for her to stay at the hospital as long as the remission continues. That could be months or weeks, but not years as Lewis hopes—that would be unusual in a case as advanced as Joy's. They will go home, to Lewis's house, and Lewis and Warnie will take care of her, Lewis assures Joy. Joy wonders whether Lewis has consulted Warnie about this. He hadn't, and he does so. Warnie'd been prepared to find a new place, but Warnie now agrees to stay on.

As Lewis and Joy leave the hospital, he insists he doesn't want to hear anything about miracles, they frighten him, and he's frightened he will love God so much for giving Joy back to him that he could hate God afterward. It's her miracle, Joy warns him, and he should leave it alone. It isn't so big anyhow, Lewis believes, because she was alive before. He wasn't; he only began to live when he started to love her.

When they arrive at the Kilns he welcomes her home.

She hobbles into the room. Lewis pulls on his dressing gown.

JOY: Jack, I have a question I've never dared ask before. But now that we're married . . .

LEWIS: Anything, Joy.

JOY: Do you ever turn the heat on in here?

LEWIS: I'm afraid it's broken.

JOY: When did it stop working?

LEWIS: Good heavens, I can't remember. Ten years ago? Put your coat on, I always do.

JOY: This world is not a perfect place, Jack. And your house is less perfect than most of it. Will you let me purge it a little?

LEWIS: It's your home now, Joy. Purge away.

She hits chair with cane. Dust rises.

Look at that.

She turns to him and strokes his shoulder.

And how about you. I'm not caressing you lovingly, I'm removing the dust. Actually, I am caressing you lovingly.

They look into each other's eyes. They embrace and kiss. Lewis then helps her into her chair, brings a footstool for her legs and covers her with an afghan. He then brings her a crossword puzzle and a pen.

The scene is comfortably domestic, with Douglas and Warnie playing chess, until Lewis has something to say about a move Douglas has just made. Joy wants Douglas to work it out himself, provoking Lewis to suggest Douglas should be sent to "the University of Hard Knocks." Joy accuses Lewis of being an intellectual snob. He takes umbrage, but she claims she isn't insulting him, merely criticizing him—and the country's educational system. At Douglas's school the boys speak of going to a university in the same way as going to the moon. Lewis insists he'd like "as many boys to go to university as possible." "Like" isn't strong enough to suit Joy (and what about the girls?). The argument continues until Warnie interrupts.

WARNIE: Honeymoon.

JOY: What?

LEWIS: What was that, Warnie?

WARNIE: Marriage. Honeymoon. That's the way of it. You should have a honeymoon.

LEWIS: Joy's not up to travelling.

JOY: I suppose this is our honeymoon, Warnie.

LEWIS: I suppose it is.

JOY: So how come we're carrying on as if we've been married for years?

LEWIS: Is that what we're doing?

JOY: You are an intellectual bully, you know.

LEWIS: That makes two of us. I think I'm too old to change now. Do you mind?

JOY: You being too old or you being a bully?

LEWIS: Either.

JOY: No. I don't mind. Do you mind?

LEWIS: No. I don't want to be young any more. When you're young you're

Nigel Hawthorne and Jane Alexander in *Shadowlands*

always looking ahead, always waiting for something better to come round the next bend in the road. I'm not looking ahead any more. I'm with you, here, now, and that's enough.

JOY: People go on journeys for the honeymoon, Jack.

LEWIS: What, you mean abroad?

JOY: No need to sound so alarmed.

LEWIS: My mother took Warnie and me to Berneval, near Dieppe, the summer before she died. My one and only holiday abroad.

WARNIE: Nineteen hundred and seven.

LEWIS: Where do you want to go?

JOY: I've always wanted to go to Greece. To see the Parthenon. And the Temple of Apollo at Delphi. And the lion gates of Mycenae.

LEWIS: Where would we stay?

JOY: Some little Greek hotel.

LEWIS: Are you up to it?

JOY: Me? If you are.

LEWIS: I truly believe that if I had to go into an hotel with a woman and sign the register, I'd blush.

WARNIE: That's settled, then.

At the hotel in Greece, Lewis is ill-at-ease, but Joy loves hotels—and room service. Lewis admits he used to think room service was "saying prayers in bed." He's shocked when Joy wants him to order gin and tonic, shortly after breakfast, and is near panic when trying to deal with the waiter and oblivious as the waiter returns with the drinks and hopefully awaits a tip. Even the brightness of the sun upsets him. She encourages him to turn toward it and feel it on his face—he just doesn't know how to act in the sun. And the suggestion that he might take his jacket off is even more off-putting to him.

But they are happy, Joy never more so, Lewis as happy as the day he was elected a Fellow of Magdalen. The happiness won't last though, Joy warns him, wanting him to face it, wanting to know what he'll do when she dies. She wants to be "with him" then, and can be only if she talks about it now. Pain is part of the happiness they're enjoying now. "That's the deal," she insists.

LEWIS: We'll have no clocks. No calendars. No clocks.

JOY: I know your footsteps. I can tell it's you, long before you reach the house. I know it's you coming up the road.

LEWIS: I never thought I could be so happy, so late in life. Every day when I come home, there you are.

JOY: The first words you speak, I know what kind of a mood you're in. Just from the sound of your voice. I watch you when you're working at your desk. I study you. I learn you.

LEWIS: Every day. Every day when I come home, there you are. I can't get used to that. Every day it surprises me. There you are. It's the sheer availability of the happiness that takes my breath away. I reach out, and there you are. I hold you in my arms. I kiss you. All I have to do is reach out, and there you are. You've made the world kind to me, and I'm so grateful. Grateful for all the ordinary domestic pleasures.

Back home again, Joy is in pain, but trying not to show it. At least it keeps her quiet, she quips. Lewis can't bear to see her in pain: "When it gets close, you find out whether you believe or not." Joy reminds him of his own words—"Only shadows . . . . . Real life hasn't begun yet." He'd "better be right," she adds before falling asleep.

Douglas comes in, not knowing how to speak to his mother, and Lewis takes him aside and tells him she's very sick. Douglas asks if she's going to die. Lewis doesn't know what to say. Nor does he know why Joy is sick, he tells him. When Douglas asks if Lewis is able to do anything about it, he confesses he can't. Douglas utters a stoic "Okay" and goes off.

It is night, and Lewis, exhausted and half-asleep, is sitting in a chair next to Joy's bed when she awakens. Joy asks if it's been worth it, and his rhetorical answer is "Three years of happiness?" She worries about whether or not he will be all right. He claims he will be but wonders if she's afraid of dying. She's tired and wants to rest, she claims. She doesn't want to leave him, but there's "too much pain." There are other worlds, she reminds him, and she loves his other worlds— they were what made her begin to love him before they met.

Joy tells him he'll have to let her go but asks him to take care of her son. Douglas "pretends not to mind," she comments. Lewis is aware of that. He urges her not to try to talk anymore. As he continues to sit with her he calls her the "truest person" he's ever known, and pleads, "Sweet Jesus, be with my beloved wife, Joy." He begs forgiveness if he's loved her too much. When Joy finally convinces him he must go to bed, he kisses her and goes off.

At the college high table Riley, Harrington, Gregg and Warnie are conversing over their port. Riley accuses Harrington of telling a whopper when, at the service for Joy, he'd said something to the effect that "All who knew her loved her." Harrington didn't love her and Riley didn't either, he puts it baldly, and he isn't going to start to love her now that she's dead either. Harrington could hardly speak the truth with Jack nearby. But he wonders if Warnie liked Joy. "Not at first. But oh, yes," Warnie states.

Lewis joins them, appearing to be quite calm. Harrington asks Lewis about his address at the service, and Lewis admits to not having any idea of what Harrington said. Riley wonders if Lewis is all right. He isn't, Lewis confesses.

HARRINGTON: Thank God for your faith, Jack. Where would you be without that?
LEWIS: I'd be here, drinking my port.
HARRINGTON: What I mean to say, Jack, is that it's only faith that makes any sense of times like this.
    Lewis puts down his glass.

LEWIS: I'm sorry, Harry, but it won't do. This is a mess, and that's all there is to it.

HARRINGTON: A mess?

LEWIS: What sense do you make of it? You tell me.

HARRINGTON: But, Jack—we have to have faith that God knows—

LEWIS: God knows. Yes, God knows. I don't doubt that. "Are not five sparrows sold for two farthings, and not one of them is forgotten before God? Even the very hairs on your head are numbered." God knows. But does God care? Did He care about Joy?

HARRINGTON: Why are you talking like this, Jack? We can't see what's best for us. You know that. We're not the Creator.

LEWIS: No. We're the creatures. We're the rats in the cosmic laboratory. I've no doubt the great experiment is for our own good eventually, but that still makes God the vivisectionist.

HARRINGTON: This is your grief talking.

LEWIS: What was talking before? My complacency?

HARRINGTON: Please, Jack. Please.

LEWIS: I'm sorry, Harry. You're a good man. I don't mean to distress you. But the fact is, I've come up against a bit of experience recently. Experience is a brutal teacher, but you learn fast. I'm sorry. I shouldn't have come this evening. I'm not fit company.

Lewis rises, excuses himself and leaves. Warnie follows him, assuring Lewis, who apologizes to him, that his friends understand. Lewis is distressed that he cannot remember Joy's face. Warnie assumes it is shock. And Lewis is frightened of not ever seeing Joy again, and of thinking suffering is just suffering, that there isn't any cause, purpose, pattern or sense—"Just pain, in a world of pain."

Warnie is sympathetic but insists that Lewis must talk with Douglas, who has come on. Lewis's grief is Lewis's business, but Douglas is a child, Warnie lectures Lewis before going off.

> *Lewis walks slowly across to Douglas. He speaks to the boy in a matter-of-fact way; as if they are equals.*

LEWIS: When I was your age, my mother died. That was cancer too. I thought that if I prayed for her to get better, and if I really believed she'd get better, then she wouldn't die. But she did.

DOUGLAS: It doesn't work.

LEWIS: No. It doesn't work.

DOUGLAS: I don't care.

LEWIS: I do. When I'm alone, I start crying. Do you cry?

DOUGLAS: No.

LEWIS: I didn't when I was your age.

> *A brief pause.*

I loved your mother very much.

DOUGLAS: That's okay.

LEWIS: I loved her too much. She knew that. She said to me, "Is it worth it?" She knew how it would be later.

Suddenly the pain and anger explodes out of him.

Oh, it's not fair! If you want the love, you have to have the pain.

DOUGLAS: I don't see why she had to get sick.

LEWIS: Nor me.

Another pause.

You can't hold on to things. You have to let them go.

DOUGLAS: Jack?

LEWIS: Yes.

DOUGLAS: Do you believe in heaven?

LEWIS: Yes.

DOUGLAS: I don't believe in heaven.

LEWIS: That's okay.

DOUGLAS: I sure would like to see her again.

LEWIS: Me too.

Douglas cannot contain his grief any longer. In his anguish he throws himself against Lewis's body. Taken aback, Lewis puts his hands high up into the air where they remain, unused, until at last Lewis's grief bursts out as well, and his arms finally descend to go around Douglas in an embrace. When their tears subside, Douglas comes out of the embrace and goes off.

> *Lewis turns to face the audience and begins to speak quietly. His words are a version of the talk he has given earlier, now transformed by his own suffering.*

LEWIS: We are blocks of stone, out of which the sculptor carves the forms of men. The blows of his chisel, which hurt us so much, are what make us perfect. No shadows here. Only darkness, and silence, and the pain that cries like a child. It ends, like all affairs of the heart, with exhaustion. Only so much pain is possible. Then, rest. So it comes about that, when I am quiet, when I am quiet, she returns to me. There she is, in my mind, in my memory, coming towards me, and I love her again as I did before, even though I know I will lose her again and be hurt again. So you can say if you like that Jack Lewis has no answer to the question after all, except this: I have been given the choice twice in my life. The boy chose safety. The man chooses suffering.

He now speaks to her, in his memory.

I went to my wardrobe this afternoon. I was looking for my old brown jacket, the one I used to wear before—I'd forgotten that you'd carried out one of your purges there. Just before we went to Greece, I think it was. I want to hold you, but I have to let you go. That much I do understand. I find I can live with the pain, after all. The pain, now, is part of the happiness, then. That's the deal. Only shadows, Joy.

Curtain.

THE AMERICAN PLAN

A Play in Two Acts

BY RICHARD GREENBERG

Cast and credits appear on pages 350-351

RICHARD GREENBERG was born in 1958 in East Meadow, Long Island, the son of an executive of a film theater chain. He was educated in local schools and went to college at all of the Big Three: Princeton (B.A. 1980), Harvard (in a Ph.D. course in English literature, abandoned after less than a year) and Yale (M.F.A. from the Drama School in 1985, where he won the Molly Kazan Playwriting Award). He began writing fiction at Princeton, including a novel for his thesis; but it was his first play, started after the Harvard experience and later submitted to Yale, that won him a place in the latter's playwriting program under Oscar Brownstein.

Greenberg's first New York production took place while he was at Yale: The Bloodletters *off off Broadway November 17, 1984 at Ensemble Studio Theater. It won him the 1985 Oppenheimer Award for best new playwright. His one-acter* Life Under Water *was produced by the same OOB group later that season and was published in the* Best Short Plays *volume of its year. Ensemble also mounted his one-acters* Vanishing Act *(1986) and* The Author's Voice *(1987, also a* Best Short Plays *selection). Also in 1987, his adaptation of a Martha Clarke performance work based on Kafka writings,* The Hunger Artist, *appeared OOB as a Music*

Theater Group/Lenox Arts Center showcase.

Greenberg's first full off-Broadway production was The Maderati *at Playwrights Horizons February 19, 1987 for 12 performances. His first Best Play,* Eastern Standard, *opened October 27, 1988 at Manhattan Theater Club (after a run the previous season at Seattle Repertory Theater), played 46 off-Broadway performances, transferred to Broadway January 5, 1989 for 92 additional performances and was twice cited among the Outer Critics Circle nominees for the bests of the season. Greenberg's second Best Play, this season's* The American Plan, *was produced at Manhattan Theater Club December 16, 1990 for 37 performances.*

Greenberg is also the author of Neptune's Hips *(1988, Ensemble Studio Theater OOB) and the TV scripts* Trying Times *and the adaptation of his own* Life Under Water. *He is a member of the Dramatists Guild and Ensemble Studio Theater, lives in New York City and almost always starts a new play while in rehearsal for the previous one (his next,* The Extra Man, *was commissioned by Jujamcyn).*

Time and Place: The Catskills in the summer of 1960 and the Adlers' Central Park West apartment ten years later.

ACT I

Scene 1

SYNOPSIS: Lili Adler is lying in a hammock, reading a book, at her mother's summer place in the Catskills, with a resort hotel across the lake. Nick Lockridge enters dressed in bathing trunks and toweling himself after a swim. They introduce themselves to each other—strangers, sizing each other up with small talk and questions like Lili's "What brings you to the Catskills?" (Nick has come with friends to the hotel on the vacation) and "What do you do at present?" (Nick tells her he writes for the "weekly cultural epiphany," *Time*, while dreaming of becoming an architect); and Nick's "And what do you do?" (Lili is "pre-occupational," out of Sarah Lawrence). Lili invites him to make himself at home.

LILI: It's relaxing, don't you find?
NICK: Oh, yes. Especially after, you know . . . over there.
LILI: Are you getting tired of things?
NICK: Well, The American Plan—*what* Americans live like this? What Americans *eat* like this? The breakfasts and the lunches and the dinners and the coffees and the teas and the snacks and the hardly-any-exercise in between . . .
LILI: Are you getting at all tired of Mindy?
    Beat.

Wendy Makkena as Lili Adler and D.W. Moffett as
Nick Lockridge in a scene from *The American Plan*

NICK: I beg your . . . umm . . . Excuse me?

To Nick's surprise, Lili knows all about Nick and Mindy Kahkstein being
together most of the time at the hotel. Lili's mother encourages her to go over to

the hotel and mingle with the guests, and she has observed Nick with Mindy. In fact, Lili can see Mindy right now, in the distance—"the one with the turbulent thighs and exotic swim suit." Lili can see her mother over there, too—"that looming, late-Ibsenesque figure with the Mah Jong tiles"—together with her black companion, Olivia Shaw—"cooks a little, listens to my mother's tirades."

NICK: Your mother's the one they call "the Duchess," isn't she?

LILI: I wouldn't be the least bit surprised. She's really a dreadful woman.

NICK: I'm sure not.

LILI: Why—what do you know?

NICK: Well, if she were so dreadful, it's unlikely she'd have reared such a . . . charming . . . and mercurial daughter.

     Beat.

LILI: Protestant!

NICK: Guilty as charged. *(Looks across lake.)* Oh my God, they're playing more Simon Says. What a nightmare.

LILI: Simon Says: A witless unseen despot who derives his authority from God-knows-where instructs you to deform yourself in truly revolting ways; and if you dare, even accidentally, to act without his permission, you're exterminated. My mother thinks it's a great game for Jews.

NICK: I'm sorry—but I don't find that funny.

LILI: But my mother *is* a Jew.

NICK: All the same.

On the subject of Mindy, Lili seems to know quite a lot about her. She's an education major at N.Y.U. and "extremely rich" (when Nick suggests that he might be, too, Lili suggests he then ought to quit his job, which he hates, but he believes otherwise). They agree that Mindy is also a nymphomaniac. Lili wonders if that's fun for him, and Nick is noncommittal.

In New York, Nick lives in the Village and Lili in a Central Park West apartment which she describes as "a horrible place, and sort of disgraces us" because her father, an inventor, couldn't afford Park Avenue. In her fanciful way, Lili tells Nick that her mother murdered her father "with small doses of cyanide administered in his farina" but has avoided punishment by bribing the law and is now holding Lili captive because she's disappointed in Lili's not being an attractive daughter. Nick is protesting when they hear Eva Adler, Lili's mother, calling offstage. At the same time, Nick learns that this place is indeed private Adler property and appears to be embarrassed that he has unwittingly trespassed on it.

Olivia enters looking for Lili. Lili takes Nick's face in her hands and kisses him before they part.

Scene 2

The three women—Lili, her mother and Olivia—are breakfasting outdoors while Eva describes the festivities at the hotel, including a comedian "with vast jowls and this idiotic, juvenile voice, and, of course, his language was quite improper," and a huge meal. Eva hopes Lili will visit the hotel with her next time, but Lili makes it clear that she has no interest in so doing.

EVA: But . . . you must . . . Lili, you must come *out* a bit—
LILI: Why?
EVA: For your health.
LILI: My health is fine.
EVA: For your *well-being. (Beat.)* It is something all the doctors have agreed upon. All we are here for—all we want—Olivia and I—is for our girl to be happy again.
LILI: I am.
EVA: Yes?
LILI *(sullen):* Drunk with it.
    Beat.
EVA: Well, at any rate, I am pleased that you have not entirely confined your circle of acquaintances to us two old ladies—
LILI: What do you mean?
EVA: Nothing, nothing—
LILI: What do you mean?
EVA: . . . Merely that Olivia informs me she has seen you—on more than one occasion, I believe—in the company of a most attractive young man from across the lake.
LILI: Olivia should be shot between the eyes.
EVA: Lili!
    Olivia starts laughing.
What a thing to say! All I meant was I am terribly *pleased.*
LILI: And then her corpse should be thrown to the sharks—
EVA: My darling, no!
OLIVIA: She doesn't mean it.
LILI: Every word.
    Pause. Lili stares balefully at Olivia; Olivia looks back; her good humor gives way.

After Eva exits to bathe in salted water, Olivia grudgingly permits Lili to make up to her. Lili was "no picnic" as a child, Olivia remarks, and Eva had a hard time as a woman alone bringing her up and giving her all the advantages including good schools. Lili was born "a difficult girl" who doesn't treat her mother as she should (Olivia remarks). Lili remembers that her mother used to sing to her in her crib a song that went, "The Nazis haven't found us, but darling they're around us," as though this explained her behavior. Olivia cautions Lili not to make remarks without thinking but Lili continues to amuse herself by asking Olivia extravagant questions like "Are you a virgin?" Olivia maintains her cool.

OLIVIA: I'm going into town later to buy food. Is there anything special you want for dinner?

LILI: What did my father die of?

(Beat.)

OLIVIA: Pneumonia.

LILI: I thought it was malaria.

OLIVIA: Well, maybe it was.

LILI: Was he in Panama or something? Who dies of malaria on Central Park West?

OLIVIA: You ask and ask and ask. What are you planning to do with all these answers if you get them?

LILI: Make them into belts.

OLIVIA: Difficult. A difficult girl.

Olivia looks out and sees Nick and Mindy. Lili imagines that Nick is an eastern prince who "charges the fields of Greenwich and Darien. His life is a round of jousts and tourneys and tennis matches." She pretends that Nick has adventured into the Catskills in search of a fair lady to whom he can dedicate his victories— but when Eva is heard humming a lullaby offstage, Lili acts *as though physically stricken.* Abruptly, she informs Olivia that Nick has asked her to marry him, and she hurries off.

Scene 3

Lili is lying in her hammock listening to Bobby Darin on the radio. Nick hasn't been around in some time, but he's here now, accusing Lili: "You told Mindy I had the clap." Lili denies it, but Nick is getting strange looks from people at the hotel. He explains that he has been busy with a shuffleboard tournament, which he won, and with paying attention to the people he came with. Lili offers to go across the lake and apologize to Mindy for her capricious joke, but it's too late. Mindy's father heard the rumor and has taken the whole family away after hearing Mindy confess that she has slept with Nick often. Mr. Kahkstein was furious, but Mindy cooled him off with "Daddy, don't be ridiculous. He didn't take my virtue. I've slept with hundreds of men. I'm afraid *I* gave it to *him*." Nick figures the whole incident will soon blow over. His engagement to Mindy—a new development which comes as a surprise to Lili—will continue.

LILI (softly): You never told me

NICK: I know.

LILI: We walked together . . . Well then, why are you here?

NICK: I want to know why you did it.

LILI: . . . I missed you.

NICK: And this is the simplest way you could think of to deal with that problem?

LILI: My mind doesn't run to simple ways. How is it that you've been here so long, anyway? Don't you have a job to do? *Time* magazine must be incredibly liberal with its vacations. They ought to call it *Free Time*.

NICK: Lili—

LILI: Mindy has gone; why aren't you going too?

NICK: The room still belongs to me, and—

LILI: That's not a reason.

NICK: I want to see you.

LILI: Why?

NICK: . . . I don't know anyone like you.

LILI: Mindy's like me. Mindy's exactly like me. Except stupid and a cow.

NICK: She isn't anything like you—

LILI: —and a raving, famous nymphomaniac.

NICK: Granted.

LILI: I'll be a raving, famous nymphomaniac, maybe, some day—

NICK: That's not an ambition.

LILI: Did my mother give you money to stop seeing me?
        (Beat.)

NICK: You shouldn't have said that . . .

LILI: I'm sorry, I'm sorry—but it's something she'd try—

Lili informs Nick that she is rich in her own right, or will be next year when she takes possession of the money her father left her. Nick denies any interest at all in her money. He confesses that though he thinks her beautiful (which she can hardly believe) he stopped coming over because Mindy asked him to. He suggests a swim as a change of pace, but it turns out Lili can't swim. As Nick is offering to teach her, Olivia joins them and announces tea at a table set for four; Mrs. Adler is looking forward to meeting Nick. Lili hangs back, fearing to let Nick meet her mother, as the others exit.

Scene 4

Eva and Nick are seated, with Olivia managing the tea things. Lili *"idles, paces"* nearby. Eva is explaining that she prefers the mountains to the sea because the views are finite: "It is for this reason that we come here year after year. Though it means we must suffer proximity to some of the country's most comical misfits. But even *that* is a good thing—it is good to stay in touch with the lower life forms." Her name for her house is Nicht Ahin, Nicht Ahier.

Lili has told Eva of Nick's ambition to become an architect (she pretends that her mother had an affair with Mies Van der Rohe). Nick explains that his ambition is to design "a whole city," but family problems have prevented him from starting to study for a career. His father died in an accident with a gun the year after his mother died, and these events "sidetracked" him. Eva comments, "It is the people to whom random things happen, and who are then able to survive, flourish . . . it is these people who will see Damascus. My husband and I were in Germany until the last possible moment. We were to discover that the boat we took was the last boat out. What would have happened if we had missed that boat . . ."

Lili starts skipping rope like a little girl and accompanies it with a rhythmic chant about "Nicky and Lili."

LILI: First comes love/then comes marriage—
NICK: Lili!
EVA: Have you discussed this scenario, or is Lili improvising?
LILI: Then comes Nicky with the baby carriage—
NICK: That's very embarrassing.
EVA: My daughter is this way because her father indulged her; he found her irresistible—
NICK: What was it Mr. Adler did?
LILI: My father invented teflon—
EVA: Mr. Adler invented—
LILI: He invented Bakelite—
EVA: He had the patent on—
LILI: He blazed the trail for macaroni-and-cheese—
EVA: Mr. Adler's work was in—
LILI: He invented the reversible condom—
EVA (gently): Lili . . .
        Beat.
LILI (softly, chastened): Something in lamps. He invented something that's in lamps . . . something that's in lamps; excuse me, please . . .
        She exits quickly.
NICK: Lili—
        But she's gone.

Olivia goes to keep an eye on Lili while she's in this state. Eva explains to Nick that "Inside her head is a sort of masked ball; you never know with whom you are dancing." Lili isn't just another neurotic, it's more serious than that. She's been hospitalized.

Eva mentions that Lili often tells people that she murdered her husband. "I think she half believes it," Eva says. "I loved my husband for subtle reasons, and he was annihilated for a crude one." Eva doesn't explain further, because she feels this is not the right subject for this time and place, but adds that apparently they cannot relieve Lili of the sadness she acquired as a child. She is brought here every summer and inevitably makes contact with "some sweet boy from across the lake," but the experience never has a happy ending.

Eva inquires whether Nick's job and other responsibilities will cause him to depart soon. Apparently not; he seems to have no pressing engagements. When

Eva then suggests that maybe Nick is the solution to Lili's condition they've been hoping for, Nick remarks, "She thinks you want to keep me away from her." Eva asks Nick to tell Lili that the opposite is true, and to be good to Lili whatever happens. "We can't expect miracles," Eva comments as the scene ends.

Scene 5

Alone with Nick, Lili hears about his conversation with Eva. It was her mother who made her go to the hospital when really she felt perfectly all right, Lili tells Nick, and now Eva will be up to her old tricks and frighten Nick off somehow, without seeming to.

LILI: Why don't you just go away now? Why don't you just leave me alone?

NICK: Why are you going on like this?

LILY: Because I love you. *(Beat; simply.)* I know that sounds crazy, but I'm not crazy—I know my own name—I don't see things—and I love you . . . I know I can't ever have you, I know I lie . . . I do awful things . . . I don't know why . . . I can't explain it . . . I feel as if everything I've ever done was something that happened *to* me . . . That sounds crazy, too . . . Oh God, this isn't making you think any better of me . . . I'm sorry . . . I haven't meant anything . . . Just go . . .

   Beat.

NICK: Nothing you said sounds crazy—No, *listen* . . . Nothing you said sounds crazy. And I don't believe you've ever done anything so terrible. You have this way of seeing yourself—I think it just comes from living in dark rooms with bad air—Listen—all this stuff about what you've done—even if you *have* done it—Pasts are . . . they're nothing . . . Things can be so much simpler . . .

LILI: Look—she'll probably be here soon—It would be better if you just—

NICK: Forget her! . . . The hell with her . . . There are some people we have to pretend don't exist . . . We just have to forget about—no matter how it hurts . . . Some people we just have to get away from.

LILI: I can't do that.

NICK: I know you can.

LILI: She's what I have.

Nick confesses that he had lied to her, he really came to this resort to meet Lili, and he's never wanted anything so much as to be with her. He kisses her as a promise to be on her side, no matter what.

Scene 6

Eva, walking with a cane, calls Nick a wonder for making Lili so happy these past weeks, including teaching her to swim. Eva has found out a lot about Nick in the meantime, and she proceeds to tell him so. He doesn't work for *Time*, he was fired some months ago, and he has no money. He comes from a good but crumbling Social Register family. His father didn't die in a gun accident, he shot himself. Nick kind of lost his way after his father's suicide, and "Finally you arrived here and met my daughter and proceeded to tell not a single true thing about yourself . . . . . Is there anything you'd like to say?"

Indeed there is, and Nick explains at some length. His father gradually disintegrated after his mother's death, and all Nick's attempts to help him failed. He gradually lost touch with reality and finally had (Nick repeats) the "accident" with his gun. He didn't tell Lili because it would have been unpleasant, and "I wish you would let me tell Lili instead of you." But Eva does not mean to tell Lili. She has an entirely different program in mind.

EVA: After you marry, I will pay for your graduate school in architecture, then give you a start in business.

NICK: . . . What?

EVA: There—you made me give it away—that was meant to be my surprise.

NICK: I can take care of all that myself.

EVA: You mean with Lili's money. No, you see, this is where you are wrong. Has Lili told you she comes into her money on her twenty-first birthday? Yes; this is a thing she says. In truth, she does come into money. On her thirty-fifth birthday. Until then, it is only what she earns or what I give her. Now, tell me, what are your plans for getting through school and life? Go moment by moment. *(Beat.)* Yes, I will pay for you, gladly, for we will be related.

NICK: . . . That isn't right, somehow . . .

EVA: You have a conscience, excellent! I'll write that down. Oh, look! To deny happiness because it looks like something it is not . . . You have told me everything about yourself—now I understand and pity you. You love my daughter—you are in a condition I can remedy—what stupidity—what *cruelty*—not to let me.

   Beat.

NICK: Then I'll tell her about all this.

EVA: That I cannot allow.

NICK: . . . What?

EVA: If you will tell her, she will tell me; if she will tell me, I will renege.

NICK: Why?

EVA: Do you know how this would look to her? This lie and that lie. A few swimming lessons do not make one psychologically whole. I'm sorry if you thought that was the case. We don't want to risk your losing her affection, do we?

NICK: But—

EVA: Figure nothing out; look no further; all is well.

NICK: I don't understand. Why don't you just tell her everything and be rid of me?

EVA: Because there isn't very much we can hope for Lili, but at least we can hope for the best.

NICK: And what is the best, do you think?

EVA: An intricately unhappy life, I'm afraid, lived out in compensatory splendor.

NICK: I don't believe that!

   Beat.

EVA: And why not?

NICK *(pulling back a little):* I cause happiness; that's what I do.
> *Beat.*

EVA: How nice for you! Well—I believe I must go in—everything aches.

NICK: Eva—!

EVA: What?

NICK: I really do love her, you know.

EVA: That is no longer either here or there.
> *Fade out. Curtain.*

ACT II

Scene I

Olivia has made a cake as a special treat for tea, but Eva thinks longingly of the elaborate pastries of her European youth, and of demitasses stirred with tiny spoons. She confides in Olivia that she sometimes hears her husband walking up and down the hallway, as he once did, in despair because his partners had cheated him out of the credit, if not the money, for his invention, Eva insinuating that he was pushed into the background because he was a Jew.

Olivia remarks that she likes Nick. As Eva is protesting that she has done nothing—yet—to discourage the affair, Gil Harbison, a refugee from the activities and people at the hotel, enters in search of a little peace and quiet. The women introduce themselves and finally make Gil understand that this is private property and he is trespassing. He apologizes—he is in the publishing business and came here for a two-day rest but has found none until now. Eva invites him to stay to tea, and he readily accepts. "Two of you in one summer . . . " she remarks.

Nick and Lili enter, and Gil introduces himself to them. Gil thinks he may have met Nick previously, possibly at an annual event called the Gold and Silver Ball. Gil comments on the present state of his chosen field, book publishing. Lili states proudly that Nick is to become a great architect.

EVA: This is a policy of mine: Never doubt the young. Now, I must tell you all what the special treats are about. Nicky: This morning I called my accountant, and he is going to set up that special fund for your education, plus another to start you off professionally, as we have discussed. He says there will be no problem at all.

NICK: Eva—

LILI: *What?*
> *Beat. Nick stares at Eva, horrified.*

EVA: Oh, have I said something inopportune? Haven't you told her, Nicky? . . . Was I supposed to keep that to myself? I am old and often muddled these days.
> *No one speaks. Lili looks at Nick, who does nothing.*

GIL: So, I think that's great that you're helping out, just great.

EVA: Well, you know Nick is part of the mishpucha, now.

GIL: Part of the *what*? That doesn't sound like German.

EVA: It's the only kind of German I speak these days.

> *Lili has picked up the teapot and turned it over; tea trickles slowly onto the ground.*

OLIVIA: Lili!

NICK: Lili, I—

GIL *(overlapping)*: Is something going on?

> *Lili, for the rest of the scene, is trying to beat back an overwhelming emotion—panic and confusion and hysteria. When she speaks, it's tense, clenched, her breathing shallow.*

LILI: I don't care—

EVA: My darling, what have you done?

LILI: I don't care if it's the money—it doesn't make any difference to me . . .

NICK: Lili, please—

LILI: I still want—I still want to be with you—I'll pay! I'll pay for everything!

NICK: That isn't what this is—

LILI: But did you—did you make a *deal* with her?

NICK: Listen to me—

LILI: Are you—are you on her side?

NICK: No, listen—

LILI: I'll pay for anything, but please—please—be on my side—

EVA: My darling—

NICK: Lili, come with me.

LILI: STOP! I can't breathe! I can't breathe!.

> *She clutches herself tightly, and her mouth opens as if she's about to scream, but only a strangulated sob comes out.*

NICK: Lili—

> *She collapses. Blackout.*

Scene 2

Nick is lying in the hammock, telling Gil how much he loves Lili; but he has been banished from the Adler place as a "dangerous influence" on her.

GIL *(moves to behind the hammock)*: It's so quiet . . . so dark . . . a real country darkness.

NICK: The hotel's still blazing.

GIL: But behind us it's pitch black. *(Beat.)* No one around. *(Beat.)* No one anywhere.

> *Long pause. Then Gil leans over the hammock and kisses Nick on the mouth. Nick allows it, then pulls back.*

NICK: No.

GIL: What do you mean, "No"?

NICK: It's time to put away childish things.

GIL: . . . Well, I'm sorry, it's a nice quote and all, but that never felt like a childish thing, to me, that never—

NICK *(moving away):* How did you find me here anyway? . . . . . Mindy.

GIL: Mindy, yes! My research was pretty extensive.

NICK: Nothing's going to happen; why did you bother?

GIL: Don't you know yet, Nick? I'm here to save you.

NICK *(bursts out laughing):* I'm deeply touched.

GIL: I have spent months looking for you—I've come to these mountains to get you—who else would climb a mountain for you?

NICK: Lili would.

GIL: Yes—but when she got there would it matter?

Wendy Makkena, Joan Copeland (as Eva Adler)
and D.W. Moffett in Richard Greenberg's play

NICK: I'm marrying her.

Gil understands; he himself is marrying a girl Nick knows named Cinny in October and wants Nick for best man. She's beautiful, rich and wants a child, and Gil is happy to oblige. What's more, she likes Nick. It's Gil's plan that they both marry, have families and remain best friends for life; no one will ever guess their real relationship.

Nick is startled by a light being put out in the direction opposite from the hotel, but Gil dismisses it: "It was nothing," Nick is getting paranoid.

Nick protests that his affair with Gil was just a phase that has passed: "I'm not marrying Lili the way you're marrying Cinny." Gil challenges Nick that if his relationship with Lili is so perfect a union, why hasn't he told her about Gil? "I will, you know, if that's what you want," Gil warns. Nick turns to go, but Gil stops him with "You say it was what, a phase, but I was there too, buddy, and that's not how I remember it." Nick warns Gil to lower his voice and admits that he went through a confused, disintegrating time but is coming out of it now.

Nick pleads with Gil to go away, but Gil suggests they both go some place where "we don't have to lie . . . and . . . nobody cares . . . and people give us money for things we do." Alternatively (Gil continues) they could follow the course he first suggested, marry and remain the best of friends with no one the wiser.

NICK (quietly): I think there are some things you don't understand.

GIL: I think there's nothing I don't understand. And nothing I'm willing to give up. I think that's the situation.

Nick has been staring toward the house.

Why do you keep looking over there?

NICK: I'm trying to see Lili.

GIL: Why?

NICK: . . . Did you hear her before? It didn't matter what Eva said—she didn't care . . . She's staggering.

GIL: Nick—

NICK: She's under arrest; there is a moat around her—

GIL: Nick, come on—

NICK: You don't exist.

Beat.

GIL: Goddamn you.

NICK: You don't exist. Nothing's ever happened in my life. I'm a man who crosses moats.

Fade Out.

Scene 3

At night, Nick is joined by Lili, her first venture outside in some time. Eva has been keeping Nick away, but she is asleep and off guard now. Lili is sleepy from having taken pills, but Nick wants to tell her that he means to take her away from here and can explain about everything. Lili wants no more explanations, she doesn't care what Nick has done: "We don't ever have to talk about it. Just as long as you're mine now." Lili asks Nick to hold her in his arms and sing a lullaby, which he does.

Scene 4

Gil is saying his goodbyes to Eva, Lili and Olivia. Lili departs to go swimming, with Olivia following to keep an eye on her, giving Eva and Gil the opportunity to discuss Nick in private. Lili's swimming, Eva comments, is "another of your friend's dubious legacies to us," and Gil denies that Nick could be called his friend. Eva never trusted Nick (she claims) and wonders why he is still hanging around when he knows he can't see Lili. Nick is "a nice boy" with a conscience, Gil remarks, and at any rate Lili seems to be looking better than when he first met her and she made that nightmarish scene.

EVA: Finally she calmed down and fell asleep, but I couldn't sleep. After a while, I went outdoors to get some air. I stared out in space to try to calm myself— and do you know what I saw? Down by the lake where nobody but us ever goes?
GIL: . . . What?
EVA: Lovers kissing.
     Pause.
GIL: Huh!
EVA: Can you imagine that?
GIL: Well . . .
EVA: At first, I found it curiously . . . revolting. But after a while, you know . . . What haven't I seen?
GIL: . . . I'd guess . . . not too much. *(Beat.)* Well—
EVA: Gil—
GIL: Yes?
EVA: I was wondering if perhaps you had seen these lovers also.
GIL: . . . I think I may have; I think I may have passed them while I took a walk.
EVA: . . . Did they seem to you deeply in love? Did it seem to you a thing that would endure?
GIL: . . . No. I'd have to say it looked to me like the end of something.
EVA: Really?
GIL: A pretty bitter one, too.
EVA: Well, then it must have been true love!
GIL: Who knows?
EVA: And true love can always be rekindled, can't it, if necessary?
     Pause. Gil just looks at her, amazed by her audacity, then considering.
GIL: . . . Possibly.

Eva wonders if Gil could be persuaded to stay on. Gil hints that he might, if it were worth his while, and Eva hints that it will be. The mention of Lili leads them to the subject of life's disappointments. "You revise and revise the thing you want . . . and what are you left with?" asks Eva. "Other things you want. The trick is wanting a lot of things," Gil answers, smiling.

Scene 5

Nick isn't feeling well, and Gil massages his neck. Nick is departing that evening, and he admits that the relations between them aren't as they should be because Nick cheated Gil out of the chance to say goodbye properly.

GIL: Could be.
NICK: . . . What if . . . we did?
GIL: Did what?
NICK: Said goodbye . . . what if we said goodbye . . . would you . . . would you go away then, would you leave me alone then?
    Beat.
GIL: So how do we do that, say goodbye? How do we arrange it, when?
    Beat.
NICK: Now.
    Pause.
GIL: Where else does it hurt? *(Slips his hand inside Nick's shirt.)* Here?
    Fade out.

Scene 6

"Lili sits, staring out," as Eva enters and informs her that Nick won't be coming to see her tonight . . . "The spell is broken" . . . and it's time to pack up and go home. Lili wants to leave, but not to go home, especially home with Eva. "But you are my home, *mein kind,*" Eva tells her.

Scene 7

Ten years later, in the den of the Adlers' Central Park West apartment, Nick is explaining to Olivia that he decided to pay a visit to New York after he heard the news that Lili and Olivia are by themselves now—"Two old maids playing Jewish card games," as Olivia puts it. Olivia leaves Nick staring out the window at some sort of demonstration and goes to get the tea, as Lili enters, *"much more grandly dressed than we've ever seen her before—but somehow more severely, as well. She seems older and more studied, harder and more appraising than she used to be."*

Nick tells Lili, "I was sorry to hear about your mother," and she replies, "Yes . . . We're both orphans now." Catching up with each other, they sit, and Lili hears that Nick is living outside Cincinnati, teaching math at a school. He never built a whole city, or anything else.

Nick looks around the room and sees that it is just as Lili once described it to him, "Heavy with dark damask," surprising Lili because she redecorated the place last year. As Lili is wondering what is keeping Olivia so long over the tea, Nick comes to the point.

NICK: I'm sorry.
> *Beat.*

LILI: For what?

NICK: For what I did to you.

LILI: But what an egomaniac you are! Do you really think something you did ten years ago could possibly be of the least consequence?

NICK: ... It's been ... of consequence to me.
> *Lili rises, goes to window.*

I didn't just run out. It wasn't something I did lightly. I meant to talk to you ... I always intended to tell you why.

LILI: Then why didn't you?

NICK: Too much time passed, and I didn't know what to say. I wasn't lying to you when I told you I loved you.

LILI: This really couldn't matter in the least—

NICK: ... Somebody I'd been in love with came back to me ... There are some people you can't get rid of. This was one.

LILI *(quietly)*: And did you end up together?

NICK: Only for a little while.

LILI: Why?

NICK *(quietly)*: Things didn't work out the way we'd planned.

Lili asks Nick to tell him who her rival was. Nick hesitates but then says it was Cinny, a girl he knew back home. Olivia enters with the tea tray but departs to get her knitting. Lili looks out the window at the demonstration, then turns on Nick, *"as vulnerable and passionate as she used to be."*

LILY: *Cinny!* My God!

NICK: ... What?

LILI: Do you really think I didn't know? My mother found out—I didn't care! I wanted you anyway—I would have gone with you anyway—Anything to get out of this place! Anything to get out of this *place*! I would have let you have your life—I would have let you have your story, too. You could have built a whole city, and I would have lived in it!

NICK: Lili ...
> *Lili turns sharply away. A moment. She composes herself, draws her-*
> *self up. The ten years have returned. She's almost regal, perfectly*
> *philosophical.*

LILI: But that is *nicht ahin, nicht ahier* ... I haven't poured you any tea. How rude!

NICK: . . . I'll go.

LILI: You have to stay. You have to stay for tea. Do you take sugar? Oh no, I remember, now. No sugar.

>   *She pours.*

How is it teaching math? Do you enjoy it?

NICK: It's . . . all right.

LILI: I'm glad; it's such a relief to find your place in life, don't you think? *(He's just looking at her.)* You look tired.

NICK: I am, I guess.

LILI: Maybe I'll sing you a lullaby. You sang me one, once . . . remember? I thought it was hilarious!

NICK *(remembering):* Then you sang one back to me . . .

LILI: No. Did I?

NICK: Yes. It was something your mother used to sing to you . . . some German song . . . *"Nicht ist . . . Nict ist . . ."*

LILI *(singing sweetly): Nicht ist das gluck fur mich/Es ist fur andren menchen . . ."*

NICK: You told me what the words meant . . . something like, "There is no such thing as happiness."

LILI: No, wrong again!

NICK: What, then?

>   *Lili drifts toward the window, finds herself looking out of it, almost against her will.*

LILI: Happiness exists . . .

NICK: Happiness exists . . .

LILI: . . . but it's for other people.

NICK: That's right . . . that's right.

>   *She stares out the window; he is looking in the other direction. Fade out. Curtain.*

LOST IN YONKERS

A Play in Two Acts

BY NEIL SIMON

Cast and credits appear on page 316

NEIL SIMON was born in the Bronx, N.Y. on July 4, 1927. After graduating from DeWitt Clinton High School he managed to find time for writing while serving as a corporal in the USAAF, 1945-46. Writing soon became his profession without the formalities of college (except for a few courses at New York University and the University of Denver). His first theater work consisted of sketches for camp shows at Tamiment, Pa., in collaboration with his brother Danny. He became a TV writer, supplying a good deal of material for Sid Caesar ("Caesar's Hour") and Phil Silvers ("Sergeant Bilko").

On Broadway, Simon contributed sketches to Catch A Star *(1955) and* New Faces of 1956. *His first Broadway play was* Come Blow Your Horn *(1961), followed by the book of the musical* Little Me *(1962). His next play, the comedy* Barefoot in the Park *(1963) was named a Best Play of its season, as was* The Odd Couple *(1965). Neither of these had closed when the musical* Sweet Charity, *for which Simon wrote the book, came along early in 1966; and none of the three had closed when Simon's* The Star-Spangled Girl *opened the following season in December 1966—so that Simon had the phenomenal total of four shows running simultaneously on Broadway during the season of 1966-67. When the last of the four closed that summer, they had played a total of 3,367 performances over four theater seasons.*

Simon immediately began stacking another pile of blue-chip shows. His Plaza Suite *(1968) was named a Best Play of its year.* His book of the musical Promises, Promises *(1968) was another smash, and his* Last of the Red Hot Lovers *(1969) became his third show in grand simultaneous display on Broadway (and fourth Best Play).* Plaza Suite *closed before* The Gingerbread Lady *(1970, also a Best Play) opened, so that Simon's second stack was "only" three plays and 3,084 performances high.*

There followed The Prisoner of Second Avenue *(1971, a Best Play),* The Sunshine Boys *(1972, a Best Play),* The Good Doctor *(1973, a Best Play) and* God's Favorite *(1974). There was no new Neil Simon play on Broadway the following year because he was moving himself and his family from New York to California, partly for personal reasons and partly to base himself closer to his screen activities. Movies or not, by April 1976 he had* California Suite *ready for production at Center Theater Group in Los Angeles en route to the Eugene O'Neill Theater—which for a time he owned—in June 1976 as his 15th Broadway script and ninth Best Play.*

To continue: Simon's tenth Best Play was Chapter Two, *also produced at Center Theater Group before coming to New York in December 1977. He wrote the book for* They're Playing Our Song, *the long-run 1979 musical with a Marvin Hamlisch score and Carole Bayer Sager lyrics. His 11th Best Play,* I Ought To Be in Pictures, *went the California-to-New York route in 1980. His shortest-run New York play,* Fools *(1981) survived for only 40 performances, and an attempt to revise and revive* Little Me *in 1982 also fell short of expectations, with only 36 performances. But Simon came roaring back in 1983 with the first of three semi-autobiographical works,* Brighton Beach Memoirs *(the Critics Award winner), with the character "Eugene Jerome" standing in for Simon as an adolescent growing up in Brooklyn. This popular hit was still running when its sequel, the Jerome-in-the-Army Best Play* Biloxi Blues *opened in March 1985, both taking the California-to-New York route. The third play in the series was* Broadway Bound, *about "Jerome's" efforts at gag writing for radio in collaboration with his brother, which came in from a Washington, D.C. tryout to New York on December 4, 1986 as—let's see—its author's 23rd Broadway script and 13th Best Play.*

Prior to this third in the Jerome series was a revised version of The Odd Couple—*sex-changed so that the two leading characters were women instead of men as in the original version—produced on Broadway in June 1985. After* Broadway Bound *came* Rumors *for 531 Broadway performances beginning in November 1988. It had tried out at the Old Globe Theater in San Diego, as did Simon's next play,* Jake's Women—*but he withdrew the latter after a week of tryout performances in March 1990 and it hasn't yet reached New York. But the beat went on with* Lost in Yonkers *which arrived on Broadway this season, on Feb. 21, after tryouts at the North Carolina School of the Arts in Winston-Salem and the National Theater in Washington, D.C.—Simon's 27th produced playscript, 14th*

Best Play, and first Pulitzer Prize-winner.

Simon wrote the screen plays for his own Barefoot in the Park *(in its time the longest-runner at Radio City Music Hall),* The Odd Couple *(which broke that record the following year),* Plaza Suite, The Prisoner of Second Avenue, The Sunshine Boys, California Suite, Chapter Two, I Ought To Be in Pictures, Brighton Beach Memoirs *and* Biloxi Blues, *plus* The Out-of-Towners, The Heartbreak Kid, Murder by Death, The Goodbye Girl, The Cheap Detective, Seems Like Old Times, Only When I Laugh, Max Dugan Returns *and* The Slugger's Wife.

Simon's many honors and accolades have included Tony Awards every ten years: the 1965 Tony as author of The Odd Couple, *a special 1975 Tony for his overall contribution to the theater and the 1985 best-play Tony for* Biloxi Blues, *plus the 1991 best-play Tony for* Lost in Yonkers. *He received the Sam S. Shubert Award in 1968, Writers Guild motion picture awards in 1968, 1970 and 1975 and numerous Tony, Emmy and Oscar nominations—and two years ago Broadway's Alvin Theater was renamed the Neil Simon in his honor. He is a member of the Dramatists Guild and the Writers Guild of America and divides his time between New York and Los Angeles. He has been thrice married, with two daughters by his first wife.*

Time: 1942

Place: A two-bedroom apartment over Kurnitz's Kandy Store, Yonkers, New York.

ACT I

Scene 1: 6:30 p.m. on a hot Sunday evening in August

SYNOPSIS: The Kurnitz living room is neat and somewhat austere, with a large sofabed in the center, an armchair at left and dark wooden furniture in the background. At right, a window looks onto the street; upstage the dining room is visible with a door leading into the kitchen; upstage left is the door leading to a stairway to the candy and ice cream parlor on the first floor; and at left are the doors leading to the two bedrooms and the bathroom.

Fidgeting in the living room are the two Kurnitz boys—Arthur, 13 going on 14, *"looking apprehensive"* and *"wearing an old woolen suit, his only one, with knickered pants, a shirt, tie, long socks and brown shoes"*; and Jay, not quite 16, *"in a suit as well, but with long pants, shirt, tie and shiny black shoes. He looks more sullen and angry than apprehensive."* They both hate being here, visiting their grandmother who owns this apartment and the candy store below. For one thing, it's very hot, and for another, as Jay remarks, "I'd hate coming here if I was cool. Pop doesn't even like to come, and it's his own mother . . . I was so afraid of her when I was a kid. She'd come out of that door with a limp and a cane and look like she was going to kill you."

Arty hates kissing his grandmother, describing it as "putting your lips on a wrinkled ice cube." Besides her limp, their grandmother has one deaf ear, and Jay notes that there seems to be something amiss with every member of their father's family. Their father's sister, Aunt Bella, who lives here with her mother, apparently suffers from some kind of mental defect, possibly (the boys conjecture) from being hit on the head by Grandma's cane. But they like her better than their grandmother because Bella is warm-hearted and makes wonderful ice cream sodas.

The boys' father, Eddie Kurnitz, 41, comes into the room from the downstage bedroom door at left. *"He wears a suit and tie and seems hot and nervous. He wipes his brow with a hanky."* He admonishes his sons not to lounge around and wrinkle their clothes, then exits back into the bedroom like a soldier returning to the front.

Meanwhile, the boys examine a picture of their father's other sister, Aunt Gert, whose problem is that she doesn't seem to be able to breathe properly. As Jay has noticed, "She says the first half of a sentence breathing out and the second half sucking in." And as for the fourth Kurnitz sibling, their father's brother Louie, he seems to be some kind of gangster, probably a bagman for the mob.

Looking out of the window, the boys see their Aunt Bella coming toward the house. They shout to her, which brings their father out of the bedroom telling them Grandma wants them to pipe down, and they must stay neat, and they must refuse an ice cream soda if Bella offers them one, and Grandma wants Bella to rub her sore back when she comes in—and then he exits back into the bedroom.

Jay answers a knock at the door to the stairs. It's his Aunt Bella, mid-30s, *"as warm and congenial as she is emotionally arrested,"* neatly dressed but with nothing matching properly.

BELLA *(smiles):* I forgot my key.

JAY: How'd you get in downstairs?

BELLA: I used my spare key. I'm glad you called me. I walked right by the house, didn't I? Sometimes I daydream so much. I think I should carry an alarm clock . . . Oh, God, I'm so happy to see you. Arty! Jay! My two favorite cousins.

JAY: Aren't we your nephews?

BELLA: Of course you are. My cousins, my nephews, my boys. Come here. Give your Aunt Bella a kiss.

> *She puts down her purse, pulls Jay and Arty into her arms and kisses them both.*

Let me look at you. You both got so much bigger. You're growing up so fast, it almost makes me cry . . . Where's your father? I haven't seen your father in so long . . . *(Calls out.)* Eddie! It's Bella . . . Is he here?

ARTY: He's in there, talking to Grandma.

BELLA *(suddenly nervous):* Oh, I'd better not disturb them . . . Did she ask for me?

JAY: Pop said her back was hurting. She wanted you to give her a back rub when you came in.

BELLA: Oh. Did you tell her I was here?

JAY: No. You just came in.

BELLA: Did you tell her where I went?

JAY: We didn't know where you went.

BELLA: Well, let's not tell her I'm here yet. Then we won't be able to visit.

Bella chats with them about her favorite pastime, which is going to the movies. She offers them something from the ice cream parlor downstairs and tries to persuade them when they refuse, but they obey their father's order. Bella knows that the boys' mother is dead—through she is a bit confused about this—and remembers, "She didn't get along too well with your grandmother. Nobody does. My sister, Gert, was once engaged to a man. She brought him over to meet Grandma. The next day he moved to Boston."

Bella's father died before she was born. The Kurnitzes were a big family—"Big families are important when you have trouble in your life," Bella observes—with two other siblings, Aaron and Rose, who died young and the four now living.

Once again, Bella offers the boys ice cream and overreacts with anger and hurt feelings when they refuse. She takes refuge in the bathroom and slams the door, bringing the boys' father, Eddie, out of the bedroom to find out what the noise is all about. He knocks on the bathroom door, summoning Bella to tend to Grandma's sore back, then exits to the bedroom, obviously stressed.

Bella comes out of the bathroom, her flare-up forgotten. She insists that the boys are to stay to Sunday dinner topped off with an ice cream treat (Arty is more than willing).

The boys' harried father comes out of the bedroom feeling faint and needing a glass of water. His eyes fill with tears, as, solemnly, he explains his present predicament to his sons in detail. It seems that when Eddie learned that his wife, the boys' mother, had cancer, he spared no expense for her treatment in a hospital room with an attractive view of a tree through the window, and with the very best doctors. Eddie put every cent they owned into her treatment, and then some, at first borrowing to the limit and then going beyond the limit to a "Shylock," a moneylender. "Understand something," Eddie tells his boys, "This man kept your mother alive . . . kept that tree outside her window . . . It was his painkillers that made her last days bearable . . . And for that I'm grateful."

Eddie owes the Shylock $9,000 which he doesn't have and never will under the present circumstances. But World War II has greatly increased the demand for scrap iron, the product which his company sells. If Eddie can go on the road to the Southern states as a buyer for his company, he can make the $9,000 in less than a year. To do this, he must find a place for the boys to live while he's gone.

The boys are appalled by the implication that they would have to live here with Grandma. But Eddie has no choice—yesterday he told the landlady he was giving up their apartment because he can't pay the raise in the rent. The boys plead that they are dangerous to have around, they break and dirty everything, but Eddie insists. And Grandma hasn't made up her mind yet: "It's up to us to convince her that you two won't be any trouble . . . That's why I want you both looking so neat. Do you see how important this is?" It will be a disaster if she says no, Eddie reminds them as he exits again into the bedroom.

Arty's first impulse is to break something so that Grandma will refuse to house them, but Jay realizes that would be "like putting a gun to Pop's head and pulling the trigger." Trying to control Arty, Jay accidentally rips his collar, then

The Kurnitz family of Neil Simon's *Lost in Yonkers: top row*, Kevin Spacey as Louie, Lauren Klein as Gert, Mark Blum as Eddie; *seated on sofa*, Mercedes Ruehl as Bella, Irene Worth as Grandma; *on floor*, Jamie Marsh as Jay, Danny Gerard as Arty

catches his hand painfully in a drawer while looking for a pin to fix it, bringing tears to his eyes. So Eddie finds them in disarray when he comes back in. He is fussing with them when Bella comes in and throws herself onto the sofa, sobbing because of something her mother said to her about her back rubs. Eddie comforts Bella by reminding her that she won't be lonely with the boys staying here—and they can have all the ice cream they want. Eddie goes to the bedroom to get his mother.

> *Grandma Kurnitz enters slowly from the bedroom. She is a big woman, or, hopefully, gives that appearance. Not fat, but buxom, with a strong, erect body, despite her 70-odd years. She has white hair pulled back in European style with buns in the back. She carries a cane and walks with a slight dragging of one foot. She wears rimless glasses and has a pasty white complexion. She wears a large-print dress of the period with a cameo brooch pinned on. Authority and discipline seem to be her overriding characteristics, and she would demand attention in a crowd. She speaks with few, but carefully chosen words, with a clear German accent. She walks to the armchair, not looking at anybody, least of all the boys. Then she sits and looks at Eddie.*

GRANDMA: So?
> *Eddie motions with his head to the boys.*

JAY *(on cue):* Hello, Grandma.
ARTY: Hello, Grandma.
> *Eddie looks at them again and gives them another head signal. Jay steps up and kisses her quickly on her cheek and steps back. Arty does the same and steps back. Grandma Kurnitz hardly reacts.*

EDDIE: I know you haven't seen the boys in a long time, Mom. They wanted to come but with their mother sick so long, they felt they should spend as much time as they could with her . . . I bet they've grown since you've seen them, haven't they?

GRANDMA *(looks at them, then points her cane at Arty):* Dis iss da little one?
EDDIE: Yes. Arthur. He's two years younger, right, Arty?
ARTY: Yes. I'm two years younger . . . than him.
GRANDMA *(looks at Jay, points cane at him):* Dis one I remember more . . . Dis one looks like his mother.
JAY: Yes. A lot of people tell me that.
GRANDMA: Vot's wrong vit your eyes?
JAY: My eyes? Oh. They're a little red. I got something in them and I scratched them too hard.
GRANDMA: You vere crying maybe?
JAY: Me? No. I never cry.
GRANDMA: Big boys shouldn't cry.
JAY: I know. I haven't cried in years. A couple of times when I was a baby.

Grandma continues her interrogation of Eddie and his nervous, eager-to-please sons. She doesn't like the nickname "Jay," preferring the whole name "Yakob," nor "Arty," preferring "Artur," (as she pronounces it) which is O.K. with the latter because he likes King Arthur. She wants to know which is the smart one. Both, says Eddie, but Arty claims he's better at sports, Jay is the smart one.

Grandma wants the boys to tell her why they want to live here. Haltingly, Jay refers to their emergency but adds that in these bad times "families should sort of stick together."

GRANDMA *(points cane at Arty):* And vot about dis King Artur? . . . Vy do you vant to live vit Grandma?

ARTY *(after looking at Grandma):* . . . because we have no place else to go.

EDDIE: *Arty*!! . . . I think what Arty is trying to say, Momma—

GRANDMA *(points cane at Eddie):* No! He knows vot he vonts to say . . . *(She looks at Arty.)* I tink maybe *dis* iss da smart one.

EDDIE: He's always been very honest. But he's just a boy, Momma—

GRANDMA: So! You haff no place else to go. Dot's vy you vant to live vit Grandma . . . Alright . . . Alright . . . So now Grandma vill tell you vy she doesn't tink you should live vit her . . . Dis house iss no place for boys. I'm an old woman. I don't like to talk. I don't like noise. I don't like people in my house. I had six children once, I don't need more again . . . . .

There are no games or diversions for children in this house, not even radio, because they listen only to the news here, Grandma continues. She and Bella lead an austerely quiet life, and she doesn't want any intrusion that would effect Bella's tendency occasionally to get too excited. Eddie tries to interrupt, but Grandma raises her cane and continues: she doesn't owe Eddie the kind of help he's asking for, because Eddie's wife turned him against her and made strangers out of her grandchildren.

GRANDMA: . . . . . And now he comes to me for help? . . . He cried in my bedroom. Not like a man, like a child he cried. He vas always dot way . . . I buried a husband and two children und I didn't cry. I didn't haff time. Bella was born vit scarlet fever und she didn't talk until she was five years old, und I didn't cry . . . Your father's sister, Gertrude, can't talk vitout choking und I didn't cry . . . Und maybe one day, they'll find Louie dead in da street und I von't cry . . . Dot's how I vas raised. To be strong. Ven dey beat us vit sticks in Germany ven ve vere children, I didn't cry . . . You don't survive in dis vorld vitout being like steel. Your father vants you to grow up, first let *him* grow up . . . Ven he learns to be a father, like I learned to be a mother, den he'll be a man. Den he von't need my help . . . You tink I'm cruel? You tink I'm a terrible person? Dot a grandmother should say tings like dis? I can see it in your faces vot you tink . . . Goot, it'll make you hard. It'll make you strong . . . Den you'll be able to take care of yourselves vitout *any-*

body's help . . . So dot's my decision. Maybe one day you'll tank me for it.
>   *She gets up.*

Give da boys an ice cream cone, Bella. Den come inside and finish my legs.
>   *She starts for the bedroom. They all stand, stunned. Bella, who has remained seated, seems impervious to this.*

Calmly, Eddie agrees with his mother that he is the weak one of the family. He insists, though, that his wife Evelyn turned her family *toward* her with her love, not *against* Grandma. He apologizes to his mother for imagining that she would help him, sorry for what being a child in the Berlin of her era made of her but knowing full well how she'd react to his plea. He summons the boys to leave, homeless and ice cream cone-less, but Bella has another idea. She orders the boys to go home and pack their things, and she pulls out the sofabed and begins to make it up. Grandma protests, but Bella adds that the boys should bring back a picture of their mother for the table next to their bed.

GRANDMA: Bella! Nicht sprecken! Enough! . . . Dey're going. Dot's da end of it.
BELLA (*quite calmly*): No, Momma. They're not going. They're staying. Because if you make them go, I'll go too . . . I know I've said that a thousand times, but this time I mean it . . . I could go to the Home. The Home would take me . . . You're always telling me that . . . And if I go, you'll be all alone . . . And you're afraid to be alone, Momma . . . Nobody else knows that but me . . . But you don't have to be, Momma. Because we'll all be together now . . . You and me and Jay and Arty . . . Won't that be fun, Momma?
>   *They stand there, all frozen, except Bella, who is beaming . . . The stage goes to black.*

Scene 2: 11 p.m., a week later.

After the sound of a train, a letter to the boys from their father is heard in Eddie's voice-over. He's doing all right but has developed an irregular heartbeat.

The boys are in bed, wondering how they could get their hands on some real money to help their father—maybe cut off Grandma's braids and sell them, they wildly conjecture. Bella enters, hoping to tell the boys about her evening. But Grandma intrudes, having heard the sound of Bella's entry, immediately reproving her daughter for wasting her time on movies and coming home dangerously late. She humiliates Bella in front of the boys by confiscating a movie magazine Bella has brought home. Bella rushes into her bedroom and Grandma warns the boys not to touch her braids (she has overheard) and exits as the scene ends.

Scene 3: 4 p.m., Sunday afternoon, a month later.

Eddie's voice-over informs the boys that he suffered from exhaustion in Houston and had to take a week off to rest.

Artie is gleeful that both Grandma and Bella are out and they have the house to themselves, but Jay warns him that Grandma could come back at any minute. Two men in a black Studebaker have been inquiring for their Uncle Louie; from the window, they can see the car circling in the neighborhood.

Bella comes in with news she is dying to tell the boys, after solemnly swearing them to secrecy. She's going to get married and "have lots and lots of children" and set up her own home. The man's name is Johnny, he's an usher at the Orpheum Theater, and since Bella met him ten days ago she's been to that movie four times just to admire him in his uniform. They went out for coffee, and walks in the park, "And then today, just like in the movies, at exactly two o'clock . . . or two-fifteen . . . or two-thirty . . . he asked me to marry him . . . And I said I would have to think it over, but the answer was yes."

Johnny is 30 or 40 years old—Bella's not quite sure, and she's never bothered to ask him what his last name is. He's never been married before. He has a reading handicap and went to a special school. He dreams of opening a restaurant, and Bella could help him with the cooking and especially with the paper work. They need $5,000 to get it started, and maybe Grandma would give it to Bella (she tells the boys) out of the $10 or $15 thousand she has stashed away in cash somewhere on these premises, changing the hiding place yearly. She asks Jay and Arty to think the situation over for her, reminding them to keep all this a secret, then exiting into her bedroom.

It immediately crosses Jay's mind that they could "borrow" some of Grandma's cash to help their father, with possibly a whole year to replace it—if they could find it. (Blackout.)

Scene 4: Midnight, a week later

Eddie's voice-over "letter" to his sons tells of his difficulties in understanding the variety of Southern accents.

The room is moonlit. Jay comes back from the ice cream parlor, carrying a flashlight—he's been looking for Grandma's cache under the boysenberry ice cream, which, unlike other flavors, is a slow mover.

After the boys have gone to bed and turned out the light, a man enters slowly and carefully through the door to the stairs. Jay challenges him, but the man quickly identifies himself as the boys' Uncle Louie and turns on the lamp after the boys identify themselves.

> *Louie Kurnitz is about 36 years old. He wears a double-breasted suit, with a hanky in the breast pocket, black pointy shoes, a dark blue shirt and a loud tie. He also wears a fedora hat and carries a small black satchel, not unlike a doctor's bag.*

LOUIE: Whaddya know? Look at you! Couple a big guys now, ain't you?. . . You don't come around here for a while and you grow up on me . . . Come here. Come on. I want a hug. You heard me. Move it.

The boys look at each other, not thinking Louie was the hugging type. They quickly climb out of bed and go to him. He puts his arms around both their shoulders and pulls them in to him. He looks at Jay.

Picture of your mother. Pretty woman, your mother . . . *(To Arty.)* And you. You look like a little bull terrier. Is that what you are, a bull terrier?

He musses Arty's hair.

ARTY: Yeah, I guess so.

LOUIE *(fakes a punch at Jay's mid-section):* Hey, watch it! What are you, a middleweight or what? Who's been beefin' you up?

JAY: Aunt Bella. She's a good cook.

LOUIE *(taking off his hat):* And a couple a midnight trips down to the ice cream freezer, heh? Diggin' into the boysenberry with your flashlight? . . . That's breakin' and enterin', kid. Two to five years.

JAY: You saw me?

LOUIE *(crosses to Grandma's door and listens):* I been down there since Ma closed the store.

JAY: Sitting in the dark?

LOUIE: Yeah. Waitin' for her to go to sleep. I wasn't in no mood for long conversations.

JAY *(looks at Arty, then at Louie):* I just took a finger-full, that's all. I love boysenberry.

LOUIE: Big mistake, kid. Mom reads fingerprints. She'll nail you in the morning.

JAY: Are you serious?

LOUIE: Get outa here. What are you? A couple a pushovers? Like your old man . . . . .

Louie remembers how he and Eddie would never touch anything during the day but would make nightly raids on the store. He loved the danger, but Eddie couldn't stand up under his mother's interrogations. She knew what was going on—"She could tell if there was salt missin' from a pretzel." Her questions would reduce Eddie to tears, but not Louie—Louie actually loved the clash of wills.

Louie tells the boys he has to stay here for a week or so—a surprise visit—pretending that it's because his apartment is suddenly being painted. The boys are impressed with the pistol and holster revealed when Louie starts to undress—"I'm holdin' it for a friend," a policeman, he explains. He whips it out of the holster, mimicking a stickup, and offers to lend the boys a couple of bucks after they tell him they have no money at all.

LOUIE: . . . . . Doesn't your pop send you some loose change once in a while?

JAY: Oh, yeah. Whenever he can.

LOUIE: Like never, right? You think I don't know what's goin' on? The sharks are puttin' the bite on him, right? He shoulda come to me. There's lotsa ways of borrowing money. Your Pop don't unnerstand that. Sometimes bein' on the up and up just gets you down and down, know what I mean, Jay?

JAY: Yeah . . . I never knew a policeman could lend his gun to someone.

LOUIE *(looks at him, then at Arty):* You got a smart brother there, Arty, you know that? You're right, Jay. It's my gun. I'm a bodyguard for a very prominent and distinguished political figure. It's sort of like an FBI man, only they call it something else.

ARTY: You mean a henchman?

LOUIE *(glares at him):* Who's been telling you stories like that? Jay?

ARTY: No, I swear.

LOUIE: Don't ever repeat that word around to anyone again, you unnerstand?

He means it, but he is soon off on another tack, doing magic tricks to amuse the boys and offering to hire them for $5 a week. What he wants them to do is say nothing and tell no one anything if anyone should come around asking questions. The boys inform Louie that two men have already been here looking for him. From their description, Louie recognizes one of them as someone he knows, Hollywood Harry. Anyhow, they are to say nothing to anyone from now on. Jay wouldn't want to be doing anything wrong, but Louie reassures him, "You're my brother's kids, you think I'm gonna get you involved with somethin' stupid?" He pretends it's merely woman trouble, "a minor neighborhood problem," adds, "We'll bunk up together tonight, O.K.?", picks up his satchel and exits into the bathroom.

"He's incredible. It's like having a James Cagney movie in your own house," Arty declares. Jay knows what is really going on: "He's a bag man and he's got a bag and a gun," and their father wouldn't approve of their taking the money or having anything to do with Uncle Louie's problems.

Bella comes in, asks if the boys have thought of how she should break the news to Grandma of her forthcoming marriage. She offers them a dollar apiece if they can come up with something, then exits back into her bedroom. Jay remarks, "You know, we could make a great living from this family."

Louie comes out of the bathroom carrying his black bag, puts it where he can see it and gets into bed. He warns the boys not to get up during the night, it might disturb him and make him grouchy. Eddie's voice-over is heard: "Dear boys, the one thing that keeps me going is knowing you're with my family. Thank God you're in good hands. Love, Pop." *Curtain.*

ACT II

Scene 1: 3 p.m., a few days later.

"Train" music is heard, and in the dark a letter from Eddie in voice-over reveals that he was hospitalized for exhaustion but is all right now.

When the lights come up, Jay is bringing soup that Grandma made to Arty, who is in bed. Jay took a phone call this morning leaving a message for Louie (who is napping in Bella's room) that the "Goodbye Louie" dance is over on Friday night. The boys figure this may signify a double-cross and a rub-out.

Grandma comes in from the door to the stairs, wondering why this errand is taking Jay so long—he is needed for sweeping and keeping an eye on the young customers to see that they don't swipe anything. She pulls the covers from Arty and orders him out of bed to walk off the fever he claims he has. While he is in this house Arty is going to do what she tells him, including finishing the soup right now, getting dressed and coming downstairs to help clean up the soda fountain.

GRANDMA: . . . . . Put da soup in your mouth right now or I do it for you.
> *He looks at her. She obviously means business. He quickly puts the soup in his mouth. He keeps it there.*
ARTY: . . . I can't swallow it.
> *Grandma crosses to him, pulls his head back and the soup goes down.*
You could drown me like that . . . Why are you so mean to me? I'm your own grandson.
GRANDMA: Dot's right. And vot am I?
ARTY: What do you mean?
GRANDMA: *Vot am I?* . . . Am I a nobody?
ARTY: No. You're my grandmother.
GRANDMA: Den vere's da respect? Da respect I never got from you or your family since da day you vere born?
ARTY: You're just mad at my mother and you're taking it out on me. You don't care about your rotten soup or making me get better. You just want me to be miserable because somebody made you miserable in Germany. Even Pop said it . . . Well, that's not my fault. Take it out on Hitler, not me.
GRANDMA: Und if you vere a boy growing up in Germany, you vould be dead by now.
ARTY: That's right. Maybe I would. And if I ate this soup, I would be just as dead. Would that make you happy then? You want to be happy, Grandma? Watch!
> *And he quickly eats six or seven spoonfuls of the soup.*
Okay? Now you can stand there and watch me die.
GRANDMA: No. You von't die. You'll be better dis afternoon. It's not so important dot you hate me, Arthur . . . It's only important dot you live.
> *She crosses to the door and opens it.*
Dot's something dot I could never teach your father. *(She exits.)*

Louie comes out of Bella's room, tells Arty that he always hated that soup, too, but he used to eat it and ask for more to defy his mother. Arty delivers the phone message about the Friday night dance. Louie just smiles and remarks, "A couple a Bronx boys like to talk tough."

Louie sees that Arty is depressed about Grandma and explains to the boy that she hates her life here in Yonkers, is as hard on herself as on anyone else and has never been able to make friends: "I didn't like her, but I respected her. Hell of a teacher, Ma was." Her foot was crushed by a policeman's horse at a political rally in Germany when she was 12 years old, but she ignores the constant pain. She used to punish her own children by locking them in the closet, even for trivial offenses. Louie ran away from home so often that finally she wouldn't let him come back, "Told the policeman she didn't know me." Eddie was deathly afraid of his mother, but Bella thought being locked in the closet was fun, sort of. "Now, Gert—Gert was more scared than your old man. Gert used to talk in her sleep, and Mom heard her one night sayin' things she didn't like. So Gert didn't get supper that week. Until she learned to sleep holdin' her breath. I tried once to get her on that Believe It or Not show, but it was hard gettin' her to fall asleep on the radio."

"I don't blame you for hating her," Arty decides. "I didn't say 'hate,'" Louis replies, "I didn't *like* her. That's different."

Arty is feeling better now—apparently the awful soup is effective. Louie exits to the bathroom to get cleaned up before leaving (he admits to being in a spot of trouble, as always, and "No point waitin' till the dance is over").

Jay comes up from the store, furious that Grandma has charged him six cents for three pretzels some kids stole. He wants Louie to take him along with him and "teach me a few things"—if Jay goes, Arty wants to go too. Jay promises to send for Arty when he gets established.

Bella comes in looking for Jay at Grandma's request. She tells the boys that her sister Gertrude is coming to visit them tonight, and she confides that tonight's the night she's going to tell her mother about her coming marriage, with so many members of the family present to back her up. She has been so nervous all day, she ate three pretzels—and Grandma knows where the three went, Bella tells Jay before exiting, infuriating him.

Louie comes in and hears that Grandma has been up to her old tricks—she once charged Louie for a bag of pistachios she herself had taken. Jay announces to Louie his intention of leaving here and asks his advice. "It's cold out there. It's lonely out there . . . and it's dangerous out there," is Louie's advice. But Jay wants to risk it in order to get rich, for his father's sake.

Since Jay doesn't plan to rob anybody, Louie wonders how Jay plans to do it. "I got nothin' to teach you and nothin' I *wanna* teach you . . . Is that what you think I do? Rob banks? Rob liquor stores? Grocery stores? Little old ladies in the park?" No, Louie tells Jay, he's a business man, independent, a "free-lance money manager," and he's relocating out of town, so that there's no place in his business for Jay, who still asks to be taken along.

LOUIE: . . . . . What do I need you for? What can you do for me? Heh? *(He exits into the bathroom.)*

JAY: . . . . . I could carry your little black satchel.
        Louie comes in, wearing his shoulder holster. He has fire in his eyes. Louie moves toward Jay.

LOUIE: . . . You interested in my little black satchel?

JAY: No . . . I just thought—

LOUIE: No? But you want to carry it . . . Why? Does it look heavy to you? . . . You think I got a broken arm, I can't carry a little bag like that?

JAY: No.

LOUIE: So maybe you have some other interest in it . . . You been foolin' around with this bag?

JAY: I swear. No.

LOUIE: So what are you curious about? How much it weighs or something? . . . You want to pick it up, go ahead, pick it up.

JAY: I don't want to pick it up.

Despite Louie's insistence, Jay refuses to pick up the bag. Louie turns to Arty and orders him to pick it up. Arty is on the point of crying, but he holds back his tears and picks up the bag, finding it of medium weight.

LOUIE: . . . . . So what do you think is in the bag? . . . Money? . . . fives and tens and twenties and hundreds all stuck together with rubber bands? . . . WHAT??? . . . I said *WHAT!!!*

ARTY: I don't know.

LOUIE: You don't know . . . Well, then, maybe you'd better look in the bag and see . . . Why don't you do that, Arty? . . . Open the bag . . . Okay?

ARTY: Please, Uncle Louie—

LOUIE: *(takes a step closer)*: I'm only gonna ask you one more time, Arty . . . because I'm runnin' out of patience . . . Open—the bag!

    Arty looks at him helpless, terrified . . . and then suddenly . . .

JAY: Don't do it, Arty . . . Leave him alone, Uncle Louie. You want the bag open, do it yourself.

    He takes the bag from Arty and tosses it at Louie's feet.

Maybe you don't rob banks or grocery stores or little old women. You're worse than that. You're a bully. You pick on a couple of kids. Your own nephews. You make fun of my father because he cried and was afraid of Grandma. Well, everyone in *Yonkers* is afraid of Grandma . . . And let me tell you something about my father. At least he's doing something in this war. He's sick and he's tired but he's out there selling iron to make ships and tanks and cannons. And I'm proud of him. What are *you* doing? Hiding in your mother's apartment and scaring little kids and acting like Humphrey Bogart. Well, you're no Humphrey Bogart . . . And I'll tell you something else—No. That's all.

    Louie has hardly blinked an eye. He shifts his body and takes one
    small step towards Jay.

LOUIE *(smiles)*: That was thrilling. That was beautiful. I had tears in my eyes, I swear to God . . . You got bigger balls than I thought, Jay. You got a couple of steel basketballs there. You know what you got, Jay? You got Moxie.

Louie advises Jay not to go with him but to stay here and take care of Arty and the women—and maybe Jay will even have some reason to be proud of Uncle Louie some day. There's only dirty laundry in the satchel, Louie tells the boys.

Grandma enters, orders Jay to help Bella close the store and wants to talk to Jay later about some missing pistachio nuts. Jay and Louie exchange looks as Jay exits.

Grandma informs Louie that he is not leaving now, he is staying for dinner at Bella's request. She also returns $100 Louie had left for her as a birthday present; she refuses to take any of his "filthy money"—he's a survivor, yes, as she taught him, but at other people's expense. Louie smiles at her: "You can't get me down, Ma. I'm too tough. You taught me good. And whatever I've accomplished in this life, just remember—you're my partner." He blows her a *"ferocious kiss"* as the scene blacks out.

Scene 2: *After dinner, that same day*

Eddie's voice-over letter is addressed to Grandma, sending her $25 for expenses and expressing his amazement that, as Jay wrote him, pretzels and pistachios are still disappearing as they did thirty years ago.

Except for Eddie, the whole family is present: Bella and Jay clearing the table of dishes which Arty, unseen, is helping to wash in the kitchen; Grandma in her chair; Louie fidgeting, anxious to leave; and *"Aunt Gert, in her mid to late 30s, sits on the sofa. She holds a purse and her handkerchief, which she uses now and then to wipe her mouth."*

Bella sends Jay to the kitchen to get more coffee for Gert and places the dining room chairs in a circle in the living room. Louie starts to say his goodbyes, but Bella insists he stay—she has something to tell the whole family, and she calls Jay and Arty from the kitchen. And now as Aunt Gert speaks, *"Her affliction becomes apparent. She speaks normally for the first half of the sentence, and then somewhere past the middle she talks by sucking in her breath, so the words go to a higher pitch and it sounds very difficult for her:* Louie, can't you just sit for a few minutes until Bella tells us what it is—*(She sucks in now.)*—she wants to talk to us all about." Grudgingly, Louie finally takes a chair after his mother orders him to do so.

Bella doesn't know how to begin. Jay helps her by asking, "Have you been going to the movies lately, Aunt Bella?" This gets her started, and under further questioning she tells them how she met the head usher, Johnny, at the movies and got to know him. He wants to open a restaurant with Bella, who will be the book-keeper because Johnny has a reading handicap. All they need is $5,000 to start it.

LOUIE *(laughs)*: Five thousand dollars? Why not five million. And who's got the five grand. Him?
BELLA: I don't think so . . . He doesn't have any money.
LOUIE: Oh. Too bad . . . Well then, who does that leave?
BELLA: Don't yell at me, Louie.

LOUIE: I'm not yelling at you, Bella. I'm just asking you a question. Who does that leave to put up the five thousand dollars?

GERT: This is too terrible. Momma, please tell them— *(Sucks in.)* —to stop this awful thing.

LOUIE: Who does that leave, Bella?

BELLA: I'll get the money somewhere.

LOUIE: Where is somewhere, Bella? . . . There is no somewhere. You want Momma to sell the store? Is that what this guy asked you to do?

BELLA: He didn't ask me anything.

LOUIE: And he's either very smart or very dangerous. Well, he doesn't sound too smart to me. So that just leaves dangerous.

Bella denies that Johnny is dangerous. "They don't take you at the Home if you're dangerous," she argues, eliciting an explosive "Oh, my Gott!!" from her mother. Bella complains that Jay and Arty don't seem to be helping her as they should. Again, Louie suggests that Johnny is mainly after money.

BELLA: He wants *more* than that.

LOUIE: What could possibly be more than that, Bella?

BELLA: Me! He wants me! He wants to marry me! *(She starts to cry.)* I want to marry him . . . I want to have his children . . . I want my own babies.

LOUIE *(sits back):* Jesus Christ!

GRANDMA *(shocked at this):* Dot's enough! . . . I don't vant to hear dis any more!

BELLA: You think I can't have healthy babies, Momma? Well, I can . . . I'm as strong as an ox. I've worked in that store and taken care of you by myself since I'm twelve years old, that's how strong I am . . . Like *steel,* Momma. Isn't that how we're supposed to be? . . . But my babies won't die because I'll love them and take care of them . . . And they won't get sick like me or Gert or be weak like Eddie and Louie . . . My babies will be happier than we were because I'll teach them to be happy . . . Not to grow up and run away or never visit when they're older and not be able to breathe because they're so frightened . . . and never, *ever* to make them spend their lives rubbing my back and my legs because you never had anyone around who loved you enough to want to touch you because you made it so clear you never wanted to be touched with love . . . Do you know what it's like to touch steel, Momma? It's hard and it's cold and I want to be warm and soft with my children . . . Let me have my babies, Momma. Because I have to love somebody. I have to love someone who'll love me back before I die . . . Give me that, Momma, and I promise you, you'll never worry about being alone . . . Because you'll have us . . . Me and my husband and my babies . . . Louie, tell her how wonderful that would be . . . Gert, wouldn't that make her happy? . . . Momma? . . . Please say yes . . . I need you to say yes . . . Please?

> *It is deathly silent. No one has moved. Finally, Grandma gets up slowly, walks to her room, goes in and quietly closes the door. Bella*

Mercedes Ruehl and Irene Worth in *Lost in Yonkers*

> *looks at the others.*
> Hold me . . . Somebody please hold me.
> *Gert gets up and puts her arm around Bella and rocks her gently.*
> *Blackout.*

Scene 3: Noon, Sunday, three days later

This time the voice-over communication is Arty's, telling his father of his general misery.

Bella has been missing for two nights. Jay is worried, he tells his brother, but Gert comes out of Grandma's room and lets the boys know that Bella is at her house but doesn't want her mother to know where she is. And she reveals to Jay and Arty in passing that she doesn't have that much trouble with her voice impediment except when she visits here. She departs, leaving the boys her Westchester phone number in case they need her.

Grandma comes in, allowing as how she doesn't need to be kept company, the boys should be out playing (but she is nervously hoping Bella will phone). She orders the boys out, but at this moment Bella enters carrying her purse, a small suitcase and a cake box. Only the boys greet Bella—Grandma doesn't react but orders the boys out again, and they go. Bella has brought her mother a coffee cake and proceeds to get tea.

BELLA: . . . . . I know you must be very angry with me.

GRANDMA *(looks away from Bella):* You're home for goot or iss dis a visit?

BELLA: I don't know . . . I thought I'd come back and talk to you about it.

GRANDMA: Like you talked to me da night you left? . . . Vitout a word?

BELLA: You're the one who didn't talk, Momma. You never gave me a chance to say anything.

GRANDMA: I heard vot you had to say. I didn't haff to hear no more.

BELLA *(nods):* Look, Momma, I'm not crying . . . I know you're very angry with me, but I'm not crying. And it's not because I'm afraid to cry. It's because I have no tears left in me. I feel sort of empty inside. Like *you* feel all the time.

GRANDMA: How vould you know how I feel?

BELLA: You don't think I know anything, do you? You think I'm stupid, don't you, Momma?

GRANDMA: No. You're not stupid.

BELLA: Then what? Am I crazy? Do you think I'm crazy, Momma?

GRANDMA: Don't use dot word to me.

BELLA: Why not? Are you afraid of it? If that's what I am, Momma, then don't be afraid to say it. Because if I'm crazy, I should be in the Home, shouldn't I? But then you'd be alone and you wouldn't like that. Is that why you don't use that word, Momma?

GRANDMA: You vant to know vot you are, Bella? . . . You're a child. Dot's vot da doctors told me. Not crazy. Not stupid . . . a child! . . . And dot's how I treat you. Because dot's all you understand . . . . .

Grandma adds that Bella ought to be happy to live in peace as a child and be taken care of, the times being what they are. But it is not in a childish way that Bella now confronts her mother. She feels like a woman and wants to be no one's responsibility, particularly not Grandma's. She knows what she's talking about, although she's always been afraid to tell her mother—she let boys in school touch her and has met men downstairs in the store at night when her mother was asleep: "I needed somebody to touch me, Momma. Somebody to hold me. To tell me I was pretty . . . You never told me that."

Some of the men even told her they loved her, but Bella never believed them—she knew what they wanted, but John is different: "He *did* love me." He understood Bella, and she felt safe with him. She ran away from home because she felt that this was her only chance for real happiness, and she took $5,000 with her to give to John to open the restaurant.

GRANDMA *(looks at her disdainfully):* Is dis someting else you dreamed up? Vere vould you get five tousand dollars?
>   *Bella opens her purse and takes out a stack of bills tied in rubber bands. She puts it on the table.*

BELLA: Does this look like a dream, Momma?

GRANDMA *(picks up the bills and looks at them):* Vere did you get dis? *(She turns quickly, looks toward her room.)* Did you steal from me? You know vere I keep my money. Nobody else knows but you.
>   *She throws her cup of tea in Bella's face.*

You tief!! You steal from your own mother? Tief!!

BELLA *(screams at her):* Go on, hit me, Momma! Crack my head open, make me stupid and crazy, because that's what you really think anyway, isn't it?

GRANDMA: Get out of my house. Go live with your tief friend. You vant da rest of da money, go take it . . . It vont last you long . . . You'll both haff to steal again to keep alive, believe me.

BELLA: I don't want the rest of your money . . . You can have this too . . . Louie gave it to me. I stayed in Gertrude's house, the last two nights . . . Louie came to say goodbye and he gave me this out of his little black satchel and God knows how much more he had . . . I didn't ask him. Maybe he's a thief too, Momma, but he's my brother and he loved me enough to want to help me . . . Thieves and sick little girls, that's what you have, Momma . . . Only God didn't make them that way. You did. We're alive, Momma, but that's all we are . . . Aaron and Rose are the lucky ones.

Grandma begs Bella to stop and pleads that she hardened her heart after those two children of hers died because she couldn't bear to be hurt anymore. She is now resigned to Bella's leaving to start the restaurant, come what may, but Bella confesses, "There is no restaurant, Momma." John now doesn't want to get married and is afraid to take on more responsibility than he has as a movie usher; and he is content to keep on living with his parents because they love him. But Bella is resolved never to settle for the life she was living: "Maybe I'm still a child but now there's just enough woman in me to make me miserable." Bella picks up her things and exits to her room, while *"Grandma sits, stoically . . . and then her hand goes to her mouth, stifling whatever feelings are beginning to overcome her. Blackout."*

Scene 4: Late morning, eight months later.

This time the voice-over communication is a cheerful postcard from Bella to Eddie assuring him that his boys are fine. But the fact is, Eddie is back from his trip, visiting with his mother in her room, while the boys are dressed as they were in the first scene, with their suitcase packed and ready to go. "Ten months here and we're still alive," Jay comments to Arty. "We got through Grandma and we're all right." They miss Uncle Louie, though, who is now with the U.S. armed forces in the South Pacific.

Bella comes in with goodbye presents for the boys—a football and a basketball, which they much appreciate. Eddie enters, followed by Grandma, who comes in just as Arty throws the football to Jay. Grimly, she warns them that if they break anything they'll pay dearly for it. And she doesn't want protracted goodbyes.

EDDIE *(with some sincerity):* Well, Momma . . . I just wanted to say thank you. You did a lot for me and the boys. I don't know how to repay you for that.
GRANDMA: I'll tell you how. Don't do it again.
EDDIE: I pray to God I won't have to.
GRANDMA: And if you happen to, I'll say no again. And dis time I'll mean it . . . when Louie left for da Army, I thought about sending you the money. Even Bella asked me to. But den I said no . . . Eddie has to do things for himself. And you did it. Dot's goot.
EDDIE: Yes, Momma. I'm glad you finally approve of me.
GRANDMA: I didn't say dot. All I said was "Goot."
EDDIE: I'll accept that.

Promising that from now on the boys will no longer be strangers to Grandma, but grandchildren, Eddie exits *"before the tears come."* Grandma and Jay agree that this hasn't been easy for either of them, and Jay admits he learned a lot.

GRANDMA *(looks up to him):* You're not afraid to say da trut. Dot's goot . . . You vant to hear vot my trut is? . . . Everyting hurts. Votever it is you get goot in life, you also lose something.
JAY: I guess I'm too young to understand that.
GRANDMA: And I'm too old to forget it . . . Go on. Go home. Take care of your father. He's a goot boy but he always needs a little help.
Jay nods and crosses to the door, waiting for Arty.
ARTY: Well, you sure gave me and Yakob a lot of help, Grandma. Danker schein . . . That means "Thank you."
GRANDMA: He's sneaky, dis one. Tries to get around me . . . Don't try to change me. Sometimes old people aren't altogether wrong.
ARTY: You're absolutely right . . . Can King Artur give you a kiss goodbye?
He kisses her and crosses to the door.
GRANDMA: Vot vere you two looking for dot night under da boysenberry? My money maybe?

ARTY: No! I swear!

GRANDMA: You should have looked behind da malted machine.

The boys leave. Bella looks at her mother.

BELLA: Well, I'll get dinner started . . . Do you mind eating early, because I'm going out tonight. With a friend.

Grandma looks at her.

It's a girl, Momma. I have a new girl friend. She likes me and I like her . . . And she also has a brother I like . . . He works in the library . . . He can read everything . . . I'd like to have them both over for dinner one night . . . Can we do that, Momma?

Grandma looks away, not knowing how to deal with this.

It's all right . . . It's no rush. You don't have to make up your mind right now.

She turns on the radio.

. . . I thought Thursday would be a good night.

The music, "Be Careful, It's My Heart" sung by Bing Crosby, comes up. Bella hums along happily.

It's called music, Momma.

She disappears into the kitchen. Grandma watches Bella, then nods her head as if to say, "So it's come to this . . ." Curtain

THE SUBSTANCE OF FIRE

A Play in Two Acts

BY JON ROBIN BAITZ

Cast and credits appear on pages 342, 344

JON ROBIN BAITZ was born in Los Angeles in November 1961. His father was an executive in the international division of Carnation Milk, and at the time his son was 7 years old the family went on the move to Brazil for three years and then to South Africa for seven, not returning to California until young Baitz was 17 and ready to attend high school for one year, receiving his diploma in 1978. This was the extent of his formal education, but the experience of living abroad had inspired him to self-education, reading voluminously and beginning to write, in his early teens, with short stories ("A writer is a reader moved to emulation" is a Saul Bellow quote that Baitz likes to remember).

Listening to foreign languages, Baitz developed an ear for local dialects and expressions and returned to his native land with a special sensitivity to "the language under the surface of language" (he found the Watergate tapes particularly fascinating). In the early 1980s he apprenticed himself to the Padua Hills playwrights workshop in California, run by Sam Shepard and Murray Mednick. In 1985 his first formal production took place at L.A. Theater Works—Mizlansky/Zilinsky in repertory with a John Steppling play. His next, The Film Society, was produced January 22, 1987 at Los Angeles Theater Center and brought him national acclaim. The American Theater Critics Association cited it in The Best Plays of 1986-87 *as one of the outstanding scripts of the cross-country season.*

Baitz then moved to New York, where The Film Society *was produced OOB at Second Stage July 7, 1988, winning the Oppenheimer-Newsday Award, and where he became playwright-in-residence for the OOB group Stage and Film Company. The Mark Taper Forum back in Los Angeles commissioned Baitz's* Dutch Landscape *and produced it in January 1989. That year he started work on* The Substance of Fire, *workshopping the first act at his own OOB group, Naked Angels, and the whole play the following year in New Haven in the Long Wharf Theater's workshop series. Playwrights Horizons produced it off Broadway this season on March 17 in Baitz's New York professional theater debut, in which he received his first Best Play citation.*

Moving right along, Baitz is looking forward to the production of his The End of the Day *at Playwrights Horizons next season (it was staged at Seattle Repertory in April 1990). He is a recipient of Rockefeller and Revson fellowships and lives in Manhattan.*

The following synopsis of The Substance of Fire *was prepared by Sally Dixon Wiener.*

Time: *Spring, 1987, then three and a half years later.*

Place: *A conference room, Kreeger/Geldhart Publishers, then an apartment on Gramercy Park.*

ACT I

SYNOPSIS: The setting is a book-lined conference room at Kreeger/Geldhart Publishers, located in the area of Broadway and 23d Street. There is the conventional conference table, with five chairs. Three tall windows occupy the upstage area, and at stage left there is a rank of filing cabinets. Several manuscripts are on the table, and Sarah Geldhart, an attractive if slightly fey-looking young blonde in her middle 20s, is sitting and looking at one of them. She is smiling and nodding to herself as her older brother, Martin Geldhart, in his late 20s, comes on. He wears glasses, is bearded, and is as dark as she is fair. There is a certain aura of vulnerability about him, a quality she seems to share, but not to the same degree or in quite the same way. Martin is smiling as they greet each other and Sarah asks her brother what he thinks of all this, the world of publishing.

MARTIN (*thinks for a second, simple*): It's a bore. You know? What're you reading?

SARAH: Oh, something Dad's thinking of publishing. It was sitting here. God knows what he—what he's thinking. "Hobson-Jobson. A Glossary of Colloquial Anglo-Indian Words & Phrases." I mean, tell me, Martin, am I out of touch here or will, like, two people buy this?

MARTIN: Well, I mean, please. No wonder, is it, we're going bankrupt?

SARAH: No, but still, I do feel funny being dragged into it, don't you?

MARTIN (cheerful): Well, you are a stockholder.

SARAH: Right. I was kind of hoping that by the time I flew in, they'd have it all sorted out. You know? When you're actually happy they've delayed the flight? Anyway, I read the manuscript they're fighting about on the plane and, I mean—

MARTIN: It was bound to come to a head, wasn't it? Look—just take a look at these shelves. You can't do it . . . . . look at this: a two-volume tome on the destruction of the Sephardim during the Spanish Inquisition? Reprints of Traven and Pirandello. Firbank? That's big. How many Kreeger/Geldhart books do you see in the stores?

SARAH: Oh, please, we don't have bookstores on the Coast, Martin. Let me tell you, I went into a Crown or Dalton or something. You walk in. It's like a Burger King. There're "blips" from the video games . . . it's like, "Buy a Coke, getta Book." I said to the clerk, "I'm looking for E. E. Cummings." He said, "Self help, second aisle on the left." And I said, "Are you people still in the book business, or what?"

Martin wants to know what Sarah thought of the manuscript she'd read on the plane, the manuscript that's the bone of contention between their father and their brother Aaron. She admits to having just skimmed it—Martin understands she hates to read—but she'd thought "the dirty part, the thing with the two guys" was funny. Neither Sarah nor Martin are happy at being here, but to refuse the summons from their father was not a viable option, despite their father's ongoing condescension to them. The last time she was home, Sarah, who's involved in children's television on the Coast, was asked by her father how she remembers her lines, because he believes actresses are not bright. Their father refers to Martin, who teaches landscape architecture at Vassar, as a "gardener's apprentice" and asked him at Passover how "the tree-pruning business" was.

They're being kept waiting while their father and brother are conferring with the author of the manuscript under discussion, a novelist named Val Chenard. Sarah's show is going well, she reports. Martin has seen one of the programs. She was playing a cave man's wife, he recalls. Sarah wonders if Martin's having any kind of life. Martin thinks no one does—"People sit alone at diner counters eating meat loaf and thinking of Mom." But actually Martin enjoys his orchard, his bonsai. She hopes they can have dinner together when this is over, but Martin can't. He'll get home too late and has to be up at dawn. He confesses to still seeming to get tired.

They recall how, as children, they waited in this same room while something

The Geldharts: Martin (Patrick Breen), Aaron (Jon Tenney), Isaac (Ron Rifkin) and Sarah (Sarah Jessica Parker) in a scene from *The Substance of Fire* by Jon Robin Baitz

was going on down the hall, and their parents were screaming at each other. Sarah wonders if bankruptcy really means that their book-publishing firm will end.

Isaac, their father, comes in. He is wearing an impeccably cut suit and has a slight European accent. He is handsome, elegant and domineering, not without obvious charm. Isaac has overheard Sarah's question, and assures her the firm's situation isn't that bad, that Aaron is exaggerating.

It's some time before Isaac bothers to speak to Martin. He seems surprised that Martin's come and wants to know if he received the Edmund Wilson memoirs he'd sent but Martin hadn't acknowledged.

Aaron comes in—he's younger than Martin and looks more like an advertising executive than a publisher. He immediately addresses his father, as if they were continuing the discussion they'd had elsewhere, implying that Isaac had been rude to Val. Isaac thinks not but is annoyed that the author, Val, had denigrated one of their manuscripts. Aaron claims Val was right and that Val is likely to go off to Knopf, who will publish Val's book immediately and earn a lot of money in so doing.

ISAAC: So what do you think of your brother's little agenda to take over the company?
MARTIN: Oh come on, Isaac, you're not serious.

ISAAC: I've seen it fermenting in him! What do you think, I'm a village idiot?

AARON: Please.

ISAAC: Please! A blood lust for profit making. You knew the kind of work we publish—and you have this arrogant idea that you could—God knows the lingo you people use—

AARON: You people? *You people*? What is that supposed to mean?

ISAAC: You know exactly what I mean. You wanna accuse me of bigotry toward M.B.A.'s, fine, go ahead. You're not working at Gulf and Western.

AARON: Just this morning, he actually asked me if I wouldn't be happier as a sales rep.

SARAH: Oh dear.

There is a silence.

ISAAC: The reason the stock of this company has been kept in the family is because I wished to avoid precisely the kind of confrontation we are having now. If Aaron cannot make peace with the mandate by which *my* company is to be run, he should not be vice president. No company would settle for less. It is unfortunate, sure, I wanted at least one of you here, but perhaps—

AARON *(quiet)*: That's very clear, yeah. Thanks. But the reason I'm here, you know, is that I actually value the stock I hold in this house. Do you need to be reminded? I own twenty percent of this place, Martin, *a quarter*, and Sarah fifteen. And if you continue the course you're on, we will be flattened.

Isaac calls the Val Chenard book "crapola." Martin disagrees. He thinks it's powerful. He doesn't know why, but he cried when he read it. When Isaac reminds Martin that his is the literary judgement of a mere gardener, Martin smiles, remarking how much they've looked forward to seeing Isaac, how he makes everyone so welcome. Sarah reminds Isaac that Martin was a Rhodes scholar and announces that what she read of the book she also rather liked. Aaron is pleased they both liked it. Isaac is not. He has made up his mind to publish a six-volume work on the Nazi medical experiments and regrets letting Aaron even a decision on such a matter as the trash by "a slickohipster." Aaron wonders what he's doing there. Is it just to balance the books?

Isaac goes on about how Abraham Kreeger, "your mother's father," set about to publish serious work of importance to the world at large, a mandate he confesses they've sometimes ignored and made money, but that it's time now to get back to what's been lost. And again he reviles the Chenard book. Martin claims Isaac's misreading the book but Isaac insists he knows the lay of the land and has no doubt about his judgement.

AARON: Then tell me—why have we been losing so much money?

ISAAC *(softens, shakes his head)*: Something has happened. The way in which people read. Perceive. There used to be some silence to life. There is now none. Just static, white noise, fireworks, and boredom all around you. We lose money because we do something that is no longer held to be vital, we're a side-thought to life. And now here you come, Aaron, wanting to save us from destruction, running around here with your manuscript . . . . . *This ain't literature. It's a dress.* You don't read this book. You get a nice little, strung-out, anorexic model who doesn't need a lot of covering, and you put it on her to wear to a gallery opening.

    Beat.

So listen, Aaron, what I'm saying to you is—it's simple—you've never burdened anyone with your editorial ambitions until now. You're doing fine. You've learned a lot. But these are very tricky waters out there. Forget about this. Go back to your ledgers and you'll be fine. Leave the heavy stuff to me, okay?

Martin reports that Aaron has told him if Isaac publishes the Nazi medical experiment books they will be unable to do anything else for the spring list except a couple of reprints. Isaac claims he can't hold off producing the work the man has been writing for 34 years. It's not been a big house, now perhaps it will be smaller for a while. But it isn't bankruptcy—it is scale, Isaac insists, and he'll take a cut in his earnings.

Aaron reminds him disparagingly about his Visa bills and Isaac is livid, warning him never to dare to tell him how to spend, that nobody ever has, not Aaron's mother, not the banks, and not his son. And why won't the Nazi medical experiment work be read? he asks. Martin concedes that Isaac might not be wrong, but he doesn't see the harm in letting Aaron run with the other book at the same time. "A lot . . . . . it can all slip away, everything," his father believes.

Martin takes the bit in his teeth, speaking up for the three of them, pointing out that they all find Isaac is getting harder and harder to reach, as if he's on some self-destructive course. Isaac worries them, they're uncertain about what they should do. From the look of what he's been publishing, it seems as if it's time he took another tack. When Isaac reads aloud a sex scene from the novel Martin wants to publish, indicating his distaste for it, Sarah suggests he publishes political books because there's no sex in them.

Martin wants his father to understand clearly that he promised Aaron he'll stand behind him if he liked the book, and Martin had liked it. He reminds Isaac that he's made Aaron his partner. Isaac can be fair, upon occasion, Martin admits, and he doesn't see publishing the book as a big deal and urges Isaac to do so. Isaac suddenly feels threatened and demands to know what's going on. Aaron can't understand his father's obsession with the Nazis, citing some works that have been published in the last year that have taken the bread out of their mouths.

SARAH: Hey. It's just books. You know? I see what's happening here. You'll all use these issues as leverage, whatever the cost. Hey, I know what I'm talking about. Listen, I talk to other actors, and it's so fucking dull. It's just this crushing bore—they're all dying from their dogmas. What they will or will not do, and it's a total snooze. Who cares? It doesn't matter. It just doesn't make a difference.

ISAAC: Oh, sure it does. It matters to them. Otherwise, you end up? What? Heinrich Mann doing little drawings at his desk at Warner's. Kazan in a cold sweat, saying yes to anything. All the little failures of spirit—they add up, and they add up badly. But, of course, that's the American seduction, isn't it? Not a thing matters here, it's all disposable. Forget your history, forget what you believed in, forget your fire. Forget your fire.

Pause.

Leave your fire at the door. You see, Sarah, it matters very much what I choose to fight for.

Commercial considerations aside (Isaac challenges Aaron), what good literary reason is there for publishing this book? Aaron knows himself and his father well enough not to allow himself to be drawn into this type of discussion, however. If Aaron thinks the book deals with certain themes, his father would claim he's wrong, that it deals with other themes, and he would suggest that Aaron find "a nice German novel" set in 1934 that does deal with these themes and have it translated. But Aaron wonders if Isaac's literary opinions will get them to a point where his children have to stop him. Could it be that, since their mother died six years ago, Isaac's become suicidal? Insulted, Isaac claims he would not let his high standards get mixed up with the death of his wife.

Aaron backs down briefly, then counters with the claim that Isaac has lost his sense of humor. Martin backs Aaron up, terming Isaac a "Cotton Mather type" now. Sarah agrees that her father is increasingly intractable. He seldom sees anyone anymore or goes out, content with the company of his collection of first editions, letters, post cards. He does attend certain auctions and recently bought a postcard with a drawing by Adolf Hitler.

ISAAC: He painted, you know that, as a boy. I mean, once he was a boy. He sent a postcard on which he had painted a church. He painted mostly churches. Landmarks in old Vienna. It had a fascination for me. Done in 1916. It wasn't cheap, but it triggered something. I don't know. A view of a world. I am out of step with myself lately, here in New York. I am out of step with myself.

MARTIN: I understand all that, but I don't understand why that precludes publishing Aaron's book. It's a comic novel. A little book. You just can't give everything equal weight, equal moral weight—

ISAAC: Maybe you can. Maybe you should. Maybe that's exactly the problem.

MARTIN: No. I don't think so. For you, rejecting this book becomes this—affirmation—of how you're supposed to live your life, saying "no" to everything. Let me ask you this: You've become a pretty good publisher of books about horror. It's all death camps and napalm and atrocities with you.

ISAAC: Martin—

MARTIN: The question is—just because you've started to deal in historical hardware, do you imagine that makes you above some sort of reproach? It's "Oh, we can't criticize Isaac Geldhart, we've gotta take him dead serious. After all, he published *Hazlitt on Cannibalism*." Well, to my mind, all that makes you is a very cautious academic pornographer, a sensationalist with Sulka ties. "See the bodies pile up, watch the dead, see how bad everything is. Why bother engaging?"

ISAAC: This is rich coming from you who has deliberately shut himself away from all interaction up there in Poughkeepsie. You, with your seed-hybrids. Humorless? No, I don't think so. I am just so afraid of this trash piling up around us. I am afraid of the young. *You.* Let me tell you—I am. "Publish this book 'cause you're not funny any more." My God, I prefer at least your arguments about fiscal doom, but spare me that playing-to-the-balcony crap about missing your mom. I am destroying this company because life is not worth living without your mother? Let me tell you, that wasn't the greatest marriage in the world. I don't think about her a lot these days. So phooey to that approach—stick to the numbers, Aaron.

Sarah is angry at Isaac's references to her mother, and at the way he's treating Aaron, bullying him when he's trying to be helpful. Isaac admits he treats Aaron badly but claims that asking him to change the way the company's going would drive him mad. He wouldn't know how, anyway. He asks their forbearance for a while—not having a sense of humor isn't an excuse for their taking over.

Martin reminds his father about the last time they had dinner together, Isaac sending back the salmon three times. "It wasn't right" Isaac says of the salmon and shrugging. He'd thought they'd had a pleasant time.

Aaron points out to his father that the last time they had a best-seller was seven years ago, and that it kept them alive. The new book could do that, he pleads, urging Isaac to trust him this one time. Isaac refuses, and Martin announces he's signing over his shares to Aaron, making Aaron the majority stockholder. He doesn't like doing that to Isaac, but their mother left the shares to them to do with as they pleased.

Sarah is incredulous and warns them that families don't get over disputes like this and they might never speak to each other again. She insists they work out some sort of compromise. When Aaron assures his father he can't win, Sarah claims she doesn't want this; if Martin turns his stock over to Aaron, she will turn hers over to her father. Isaac pronounces it a stalemate.

Aaron remembers that the author, Val, is still in the library and might not wait. Isaac insists he will ask Val to wait, and before leaving the room tells them they should talk things over without him. But he won't compromise, he tells them, nor be manipulated.

Sarah argues that her father needs a negotiable way to get out of this, suggesting that Aaron give a little and then Isaac will. It's beyond that, Aaron believes. With Sarah's stock, Isaac will have 55 percent. If she gives it to him she will be killing Isaac, Aaron insists. Sarah's convinced that Aaron taking the control away from Isaac would do the same thing. Aaron is acting out of rage, she is sure. He's noncommittal about that but thinks it's equally bad if she gives in to Isaac out of "some need to be loved."

Martin leaves to get a drink, and Sarah and Aaron continue the conversation, with Aaron expressing concern for his own future. Sarah is sorry, but is just trying to do "the most right thing." Aaron denies this. What they've both been trying to do is get their father's approval. In all the time that he's been there, Aaron confesses, his father has never solicited his opinion, nor asked him what he was reading. Sarah empathizes with him, admitting that while on the plane she'd gone through magazines to find conversational gambits to dazzle her father with. Last month, it seems, her father sent her some Perelman first editions, with no note, and she's been trying to understand what he meant by that—"Be funnier?" Aaron confesses that when someone recently had asked Isaac about Sarah, he'd said she was "a clown for hire for children's birthday parties." And at the ABA, Aaron adds, Isaac had introduced him as his bookkeeper. Aaron hopes they'll be able to have a meal together, but Sarah has to take a plane, she's scheduled to act out the letter "K" on her children's program.

The last time Aaron and Sarah had seen each other, Sarah had been involved with her producer, an older man, and Aaron asks if she's still involved with him. He's been married for 15 years, Sarah reveals, and now it's boiled down to her waiting for days without him calling; probably a symptom of her father fixation.

What Aaron will have to do now is back off and get them through bankruptcy, he explains, but Sarah shouldn't worry. He confesses that he'd gone out with Val Chenard in college—but the book is good, he assures her. "I knew that you were . . . but I mean, I just didn't know," she sympathizes. In those days, "Everybody had a little 'thing,'" Aaron admits. His wife Judy doesn't know, nor anyone else. He and Chenard have dinner. Because Aaron's in publishing, they have "this link," he explains, assuring her that he's now "almost totally domesticated." Aaron describes himself as a seven-year-old in thinking that this book would be his chance to prove himself. Sarah claims he's ahead of her, at least. She's only a toddler.

Martin returns with a drink to report that Isaac is in the library with Val, giving his "Decline of the West, Part Three speech" and that Val is laughing. Sarah suggests all of them pulling back and starting over, to reason it out. But Martin won't. As far as he's concerned, it's in Aaron's control now, and Martin doesn't care what he publishes.

ISAAC (entering): So, it's getting late. We all have places to go, and I'm tired. How do you want to handle this?

MARTIN: Publish *Hustler* or publish Proust. I don't want to have anything to do with it any more. Your books. God. I am so tired of these books. And your endless posturing, position-taking, ranting, judging. The only thing I miss is Mom. She wouldn't have put up with any of this crap for a second. She'd know what to do. Damn it. I just—coming down here is too much. It's done me in. I miss

Mom.

ISAAC: The only part I believe is the last. Such poison. Why such poison, Martin? Always?

MARTIN: Poison! You want to talk about poison? Look at what you've done. You've created a family of literary zombies. You know that people are afraid of you. It's why you've gotten so far. Yes. "Isaac Geldhart knows something, he came from some awful childhood in Europe that nobody knows about." He has a "seer-like standing in the book world." Blah-Blah-Blah—phooey. Let me tell you, we're fucked up by it. I grew up running around this building. When I was eight, you gave me the *Iliad* in Greek so that some day I could read it. Monster! Peoples' lives are ruined by books, and they're all you know how to relate to, Dad. You, too, Aaron, for all your talk. You, too, Sarah, pretending you hate to read. Sometimes I want to take a pruning shears and do an Oedipus on myself. I counted my books last week. Do you know how many I have? Want to take a guess?

> *No one says anything.*

Fourteen thousand, three hundred and eighty-six. The sixty crates of books that Mom left me. Well, I finally had them carted up the Hudson, but I had to have shelves built. The whole house. Every room. And instead of just guessing—I was, I mean—speechless. A wreck of a life. It just flashed before my eyes. No sex, no people, just books 'til I die. Dickens. In *French*. The bastard didn't write in French. What the fuck am I doing with *Dombey and Son* in French? The twelve-volume *Conquest of Mexico*. Two hundred cookbooks. The *Oxford World Classics*, the little ones with the blue bindings, you know?

ISAAC: You got that?

MARTIN: They're all just words. And this is life, and besides, I hear the book chains are now selling pre-emptive strike video games, so why bother anyway? I'm out.

Martin refuses to waste his life being pulled into a confrontation that his father very much wants, by his standards "a dead waste." Martin spent almost a year, at age 16, in Sloan-Kettering having chemotherapy, time he won't get back, but which haunts him to this day. He is very concerned about how he spends his life. He wants it clear that he's not a gardener, despite his father's goading, and that his sister's not a children's birthday party clown, and his brother is not an accountant. And his father's fixation on Nazi books is frightening to Martin.

ISAAC: I spent a couple of days, a little boy, wandering around after the liberation. I saw a particular kind of man—a wraith-like figure—who could only have been in the camps. But with a brown pin-stripe suit, a fleur-de-lis on his tie and manicured nails, trying to pick up where he left off, as if you could. I never say anything about this. Why talk? Why bother? I wasn't in the camps. I was in a basement. You know? They're busy throwing the Farbers and the Hirsches into the ovens, and I'm happily eating smoked eels in the basement, with my Stendhal and Dumas. What did I know? I was protected, sheltered by my cousins. And then I got out of the basement and into the wrecked world. I came to this country. You reinvent yourself. Make it as a bon vivant in Manhattan. Meet this woman—this extraordinary woman. Marry. Have these kids. Go to so many cocktail parties, host so many more . . . and they . . . haunt.

    Beat.

I have kept my eyes closed to the world outside the basement for so long. The wrecked world all around us. But I can no longer close my eyes.

    He turns to Aaron.

My son. You are fired. I will give you a week to clear your desk, and I will give you letters of recommendation. But I will not speak to you, I will not communicate with you, I will not . . . (*Pause.*) . . . *give at all*. Kiddo. To the victor go the spoils.

Sarah calls Isaac down on this, claiming he is taking advantage of her offering her shares to him to hurt Aaron. She is enraged that Isaac would think she would permit that because she feels sorry for him. She is going to give her shares to Aaron instead, thereby giving Aaron control of the company.

Isaac's done this to himself, Aaron tells him. Despite Aaron's warnings, Isaac asked to be "usurped," and if Isaac wants to hate him he can do so. Aaron has had a Japanese offer. They'll be backed by people in Tokyo that won't care what they publish as long as it makes money. Aaron assures Isaac, however, that he'll be taken care of. He won't run the company, but he'll be on the board.

ISAAC: You've been talking to money people.

AARON: Yes. And I will publish Val's book, Dad.

ISAAC: You understand, Aaron, sweetheart. You will just be part of the big pile, the big carcinogenic pile of trash, building up all around you, as life itself no longer seems real.

AARON: Yeah, well, you know, that's not my problem. That's *your* problem, Dad. It's not my fault that life does seem real to me, and I can make peace with that. I don't have a holocaust to pin on my chest. I have my family. My city. Some continuity. The way I think. My friends. I don't want to set life back to its beginnings, and I'm not burdened by thinking I'm one of the world's great thinkers, either. All I can do with the "carcinogenic pile of trash" is sift through it. That's all anyone can do. But my life does seem totally real to me. I do not need to suffer in order to feel alive, Pop. I'm sorry. I'm going to have dinner with my author.

ISAAC: Aaron. I hope it works out for you.

    Aaron exits. Isaac crosses to the window, looks out.

This city. When I got off the boat, I said, "It's going to be so good now, this life, it's all going to be so full." It was snowing.

Sarah suggests that her father and she and Martin go out for dinner, and Martin

reinforces the offer. But for Isaac, turning to the window, it isn't possible.
Curtain.

ACT II

Three and a half years have passed. There is a snowstorm raging outside over
Gramercy Park, which the old Geldhart family apartment overlooks, and Isaac is
looking out the window. *"The apartment is not so much a home as it is an archive.*
Floor-to-ceiling—the room is dominated by books. Though there are also gaping
holes, gaps on the shelves where volumes are missing." Downstage center there is
a couch with a blanket. In front of the couch there is a coffee table, and there are
other chairs, one near the window upstage. Isaac is in his shirtsleeves with a shawl
around his shoulders and *"has a frayed, fogged-in air about him."* Time has taken
its toll of Isaac and the apartment as well.

When Isaac hears the door buzzer, he doesn't answer it but begins to pull himself together. Martin enters from the hallway at left, wearing heavy winter clothing. He puts his things in the hallway and mentions that he'd had to struggle with
his keys in the ice, then stops in mid-sentence to ask his father how he is. Isaac
shrugs. He's surprised Martin's there at all, but it seems Martin came to town last
night and stayed with a friend. Isaac barely listens, he's discouraged and in a rage
about his difficulties with housekeeping. He expects the woman who comes in
once a week to show up today, which he thinks is Tuesday; but actually, Martin
persuades him gently, today is Thursday. Isaac expects a Sotheby lady on
Thursday; but no, Martin reminds him, today is the day the psychiatric social worker is to call on Isaac.

ISAAC: Without Miss Barzakian, how'm I supposed to know my appointments?
Idiotic. To have even consented to this.

MARTIN: It would help if you could remember the days of the week.

ISAAC: What for? Just a slab of days, this. What do you do? You go back to
Aaron? With reports?

MARTIN: Yes. He asks.

ISAAC: He asks? And you tell him, "He's doddering, he's slobbering, he's mor-
tifying, the kitchen is a horror? He can't tie his shoes." That sort of thing?
Because frankly, if that's the case, I'm better off—

MARTIN: *(suddenly suspicious):* What do you mean the "Sotheby lady"—what
were you talking about before?

ISAAC: I didn't say anything, I didn't say—

MARTIN: What did you do? Have you been trying to get rid of more stuff?

ISAAC: Musselblat the attorney tells me if I can raise enough, I should be able to
make a reasonable offer to get back the company, so—

MARTIN *(disgusted and exhausted)*: Oh Jesus, Dad . . . . . What's the matter with you?

ISAAC: I've gotta try, don't I?

MARTIN: We're in Chapter 11. What do you think you can do? It would take a superhuman effort, and you're not in any shape . . .

ISAAC: What do you know about business? What have you ever known about business? Please. Please.

Martin changes the subject by asking Isaac if he's taken a walk in the park. Isaac doesn't respond, and in fact feels that talking to Martin is like talking to a stranger. He doesn't need him to make these trips in from the country. The unpleasantries continue. Martin is annoyed at the pile of unpaid bills. When Isaac notices Martin looking at the gaps in the shelves, he says he's had to sell some things, his disability checks will be ending soon. When Isaac asks Martin about his sister, Martin reports he's heard that Isaac still hangs up on her. A buzz indicates that the social worker is downstairs. Before she appears, Martin advises his father, now in his jacket and with his tie straightened, not to show off for her, to simply answer yes or no. Resenting the advice, Isaac goes off briefly.

Marge Hackett, an attractive, business-like but womanly woman, probably in her 50s, come on. Martin tells her he's concerned that it could not be a good time for her to see his father. Not to be put off, she reminds him that her department is busy, that his brother had been insistent, and to have someone come to the house is difficult. Eccentricity doesn't worry her. Martin wants her to understand that he thinks the whole thing is a bad mistake. "Noted," is her only comment as she goes off to the kitchen to check in with her office by telephone.

Martin plans to leave them alone and goes off before Marge returns to report the phone is not working ("It doesn't ring," Isaac tells her, as he re-enters and introduces himself). Isaac regards that as a relief. "The silence is welcome," Marge agrees.

Isaac again indicates he thinks it's Tuesday, and, when corrected by Marge, he states it's Thursday and that he's attempting to be competent, obviously aware that his competency or the lack thereof is the subject of her visit. She assures him that it's a process, that no one individual makes the decision. Isaac, embarrassed at the disarray of the apartment, then becomes angry that they would send a woman to his home to see if he's "whacko"—and then nothing is to be determined here. He demands she tell him what he has to do.

Martin, at the doorway, intervenes, but Marge insists they be left alone. She is here, Marge points out, because of Aaron's protectiveness and persuasiveness. Aaron had seen her organization's offices and hadn't wanted a nightmarish excursion there for his father. Isaac sarcastically comments on his gratefulness. He hasn't set eyes on Aaron for three and a half years ("And every day I don't see him is a victory"). Martin he sees only a couple of times a year. He dismisses the subject of his children with an obscenity.

Maria Tucci (as Marge) and Ron Rifkin in *The Substance of Fire*

ISAAC: So, how are things at Sotheby's?

MARGE: Sotheby?

ISAAC: What do you think of the collection?

MARGE: Pardon me? What are you talking about?

ISAAC *(pointing to some framed letters on the wall):* The illustrated letters, those. Believe me, I've seen you eyeing 'em. You'll see, just like I said on the phone, the collection—I have one piece that's exquisitely ironic.

MARGE: I'm not from Sotheby. I'm from Social Services.

ISAAC *(letting that one go):* I have here something that's not up on the walls . . . There was a filing system when—I used to have Miss Barzakian rummaging around in here doing alphabetical orders and such. The perfect job for a person who was never married. She had an Eastern European's passion for chaos.

    Isaac takes a moment.

Of course, what she is now is dead, of course. You know? And we had a link, let me tell you.

MARGE: What was that?

    Beat.

Mr. Geldhart?

ISAAC: We were both refugees. New York, for some of us, for many, who got out of "that kind of Europe"—how do you explain such a link? We didn't come as husks. We came with some decent socks and some handmade shoes. Our Europe.

    He stops, looks at her.

But you are not interested in this, forgive me.

MARGE: No, it's interesting.

ISAAC (*overriding her with a small, sad smile*): No, of course you're not. You came to look at the collection. Forgive me. My mind wanders, so they tell me.

Marge seems unsure of what tack to take with him. Isaac suspects he's making her nervous, and Marge admits it. She brings the discussion back to Aaron's request for competency proceedings since Isaac's shown a lack of ability in managing his affairs. Isaac sputters, finally stops and announces he cannot take all this seriously. His son Martin doesn't either, Marge admits; nevertheless, her agency was called upon, and Isaac had agreed to an evaluation. She wants to get on with the questions. He acquiesces but then refuses to answer what country, state and city they are in. As for what the month is, he acidly reports, "July, can't you tell?"

ISAAC: Okay. This is what it is. There is a book company. It has my name on it. And some forty percent of it still belongs to me. Some Japanese own the rest, along with Aaron, who has helped them grind it down into a kind of bankrupt pornographic dust. (*Beat.*) So, you see, I've been trying to put together a package. I still know a little money in this town and at the same time, my son, also wouldn't mind eighty-sixing the nips, and he thought if he could get me out of the picture, maybe he could use my forty as leverage. This is what we've got here.

MARGE: You're saying your son is doing all this just to get your stock?

ISAAC: Yes, so. You are a dupe, sweetie. Now, I've got coffee cake, linzer torte and sacher torte. You want a little?

Nobody says anything for a moment.

MARGE: Aaron tells me you spent $43,000 on hand-cut suits. What made you think you needed them?

ISAAC: I thought it was going to be a busy year.

MARGE: He says you hardly ever leave this apartment. Is that true?

ISAAC: It was *not* a busy year.

MARGE: And that you've cast off all your friends, you've disengaged.

ISAAC: This is Girl Scouts? I have to have friends?

MARGE: And the credit card bills?

ISAAC: Staggering! Guilty.

MARGE: You're living on—I mean—I don't understand. What did you think would happen to you when it was all gone?

ISAAC (*with exaggerated good cheer*): Who cares?

MARGE: You were diagnosed last year as chronically depressed. You've been on Elavil three times a day.

ISAAC: I stopped. I stopped. I didn't want to take it. I could not read. *That* I will not accept! No! No! No! . . . . .

Isaac changes the subject; he is enthusiastic about showing her his collection. Marge had said on the phone that she was a fan of Herzen, and he produces a 1921

English edition of a Herzen book, then a number of other volumes of value by different authors before he sits beside her on the sofa with the illustrated letters file on the coffee table in front of them. He has sold a couple of the letters because the Visa people were getting shrill. Marge makes a remark about his love for books, and he finds her tone, which he describes as anti-intellectual, amusing.

With almost an air of religious fervor Isaac opens the file and begins to show her the letters, recalling a time when there was reveling in words, in stories, when people used to write letters to each other and included a drawing with the letters—"a gesture of love." He shows her letters from Thackeray, Beerbohm, Grosz, Beckmann, Mandlestam, Babel and Orwell, insisting that she must take the whole collection, and that it must be sold in its entirety. He could not bear the idea of it being divided up. Marge concedes that she likes the collection; then, apologetically, she says she will have someone from her office call him. She's not the person to handle this situation. "Sometimes this job makes me sick," she admits. Isaac seems confused—has he said something? He wants her to see the rest of the collection, but she reminds him she's not from Sotheby's. She starts to leave but stops when Isaac reveals he has a letter from Hitler—the postcard on which Hitler has done a watercolor of a church. Hitler had bought art supplies from a Jew, who considered Hitler had talent and gave him materials. "I think about that," Isaac muses, "and what came after . . . It's the most crucial part of my collection." He shows Marge the card, hoping she'll see, as Isaac can, that Hitler had "a certain basic, rudimentary talent." The card has never been appraised, and that's why he'd called Sotheby's.

Marge asks if he truly believe she's from the auction houses. Isaac, after a pause, admits he has problems. Marge agrees. Isaac had thought the fog was from the pills, but when he stopped the pills, the fog still hadn't lifted, and he's aware he frequently gets things wrong. But he can't accept being helpless. He confesses he finds his dreams more interesting than his real life.

Isaac notes how dark it's getting, even though it's still early, and wonders if Marge has ever been in the park outside. She has, it seems, when her husband was alive. They'd had friends who took them into the park, but she hadn't liked the idea of the key. Isaac says he's always hated the park. Besides needing a key, there's no one ever there.

Marge, who had been about to leave, confesses to Isaac she's been here in this apartment before, at some meeting, a reading, during the fiscal crisis in 1974, and that she recognized his name from the case-load. "This room is the same . . . not what it was, but the same," she comments. Isaac felt that he had recognized her but couldn't place her. It was a fund-raiser for the library, Isaac figures out. Isaac remembers that the writer who was reading was someone he disliked, but Isaac's wife had insisted he publish the writer's books. Marge remembers standing in the kitchen talking to Isaac, who was annoyed at his wife, while Marge's husband was in the other room concentrating on the food, which was his main reason for attending such gatherings.

MARGE: My husband was Adrian Harrold.

ISAAC *(nods, getting it):* Oh, I see. Jesus Christ. And now you work for social services, shlepping around town with a little briefcase? I remember your husband. The Manhattan borough president. And in the end, made off with a couple of million, didn't he?

MARGE: The last editorial in the *Times* said, "Drinking from the public trough like a maddened pig . . ."

ISAAC: Please, I really, this is not. I did not . . .

MARGE: No. This is not professional. I know that. No. Do you know how they found him? My husband? On the road to Montauk. Actually, at the end of the road. God knows what he was doing. In February out there, by the lighthouse. He had a Biedermeier table in the back of his Lincoln. His wrists and ankles slashed and a bottle of pills on the floor. And then, for weeks afterwards, the funny part, these women would show up with outrageous claims.

> *Beat.*

Good for a laugh, at least.

ISAAC: I'm sorry. I am.

MARGE: My husband lied from morning 'til night, and they knew everything. The mayor. All of them. The only one, really, who knew nothing was, in fact, me.

ISAAC: So, your husband, he left you, what? Nothing?

MARGE: No. He left nothing. I mean, he had his hands in the till. And to me, this is funny—he never shared. It was all for him.

> *She looks at him.*

I expected to find a drooler. I thought I'd come over here and find a drooler who had had it easy in the old days.

ISAAC: No, unfortunately, I'm not a drooler. So, you came not for an "evaluation," you came 'cause you were curious.

MARGE: Yes.

ISAAC: You came to gloat. You came to see a "drooler."

MARGE *(ashamed, perhaps):* Maybe.

ISAAC: But this is pathetic. It's like nostalgia for a car wreck. So, terrific, you're just another hustler with an agenda.

MARGE: You could say that.

Isaac refers to her as a "self-righteous, social-worker-tootsie" and wonders whether she'll mention in her report she'd come there for vodka and flirting all those years ago. He tells her to go home and type up in her report that he has "delusions of persecution." Marge admits she's made a bad mistake. She's come for revenge, he claims. He knows revenge, he confesses. She thinks it's what keeps him alive, but she doesn't go around thinking of revenge—"It just wells up," she says.

Marge finds it odd that Isaac suddenly asks her to have dinner with him. Besides, it wouldn't be professional of her—she would be fired, or, even worse, there'd be a letter put in her file. Isaac becomes charmingly persuasive. He still has his Diners Club card, and the food nearby is good. She insists she can't. "Late in the game for romance?" he ventures. That's something she wouldn't consider. Isaac sympathizes, surmising she might have had "all the human traffic" she could bear. Marge agrees that's possible, and she doesn't think things look so good for him either.

Isaac wonders what chance she thinks she has in the world. What is she going to do? Is she waiting for a better deal or what? She is not waiting for anything, she declares. In the past five years she's put herself through school and now has a job, not exactly as she imagined it would be, but even so. And what has Isaac done of late? she wants to know. She also has a child—"a son who knows his father ripped off everything in this city that wasn't nailed down!" And now Isaac is asking her what chance does she have because she refuses to have dinner with him! She's furious, because years before he wouldn't have looked at her. Much as she loathes having dinner alone, she'd rather do that than have dinner with him. Isaac suggests she might be afraid she will see herself in him.

MARGE: We are nothing alike. Whatever has happened to you, you've done to yourself. You had everything and you threw it away. Is this how you imagined your life would go?

ISAAC: You can't even imagine. You have no idea. This is not how I saw my life turn out. But surprised I am not, Miss Hackett. I did this to myself? You don't see any other survivors in your files, do you? You don't see any brothers and sisters? Betrayal? I never even smelt it coming until the fucking *maid* turned us in. The *maid*. She was like my mother, and let me tell you—I don't have self-pity! You don't see a tattoo on my wrist, do you? But they got my grandparents, they got my mother and father, and they got . . . I came here to make a family and they trashed it, they got it.

MARGE: I am sorry. But really, I am going to leave.

ISAAC: Listen to me. You came here with an agenda, but now at least listen to what was taken away from me. *(Pause.)* I loved my children. I sure don't love them now. You walk into this house . . .

He points to a table.

Aaron cut his head on the tip of that table and I carried him to N.Y.U. Hospital when he was two. *(Beat.)* Sarah got laid for the first time in this house, and I thought I was quite literally going to die. *(Beat.)* My wife found this sofa in Kingston, and we had it carted down, and we sat on it, and it was the most perfect . . . my wife . . . my wife . . . my wife. *(Beat.)* My Martin. He comes in here from lacrosse when he was sixteen, sneezing, and the next thing, he was, just like that— no blood count at all. *(Beat.)* This house. I sleep now in the living room, because the bedrooms are too much to bear, literally. *(Beat.)* I am so stupid, Miss Hackett, I thought that if I published Hazlett and Svevo, I'd be spared. The silence, Miss Hackett. The silence. Pointless.

MARGE *(thinks before speaking):* I could never bear to play on my husband's connections. There were people who actually liked him, held a degree of sympathy for him. Because, mainly, he kept quiet. He had a thief's honor. I am owed favors. Specifically. I suppose, I am actually owed *one* favor. The way these things work. Because there are people in this town who actually think my husband *told* me things. Which is rich. *(Beat.)* But. I can make a call. I can call a judge. And they'll just drop it. Like that. And believe me, there'd be nothing your son can do.

ISAAC: Wouldn't that make you just like your husband?

MARGE: No—that's too damn tough, that's just too hard. We're just flesh and blood here. That's all we are. *(Beat.)* Hey, I'm offering you a good hand. What are you gonna do? Wait for a "better deal"? There are so few breaks.

ISAAC *(after a moment):* There are, that's true. *(Beat.)* Perhaps you're right. *(Tired.)* I *would* like a break.

MARGE: Then it'll be over.

ISAAC: Over? That would be lovely, if it were over . . . . .

Isaac has picked up the Hitler postcard and is musing over it again, wondering what sort of day it was when it was painted, and about "all the things to come." Marge calls it "just a lousy postcard." Her husband had put post-it notes up all over, but she did not save those. Isaac looks at her affectionately, still disappointed she won't have dinner with him. He assures her he is amusing, particularly if he takes the prescribed pills. "You do not have to eat alone," Marge admonishes as she turns to leave. Isaac thanks her and suggests that perhaps they could have dinner some other time, "Maybe when the weather turns kinder." It would be nice, she concedes, using his given name for the first time. She bids him good night and exits.

Isaac sets the postcard alight and puts it in an ashtray. He looks at it as it burns. The snow is still coming down heavily as Martin comes in, noting that Marge has gone and wondering what his father is doing. "Nothing," he tells Martin; and as for how the session went, he assures Martin he will not yet have to write his checks, hear his complaints about the cook or make sure his underwear's changed. But he wouldn't mind doing that, Martin tells his father.

ISAAC: You would. Yes, you would. Why wouldn't you mind, Martin? I don't understand . . . why you wouldn't mind after this . . . ?

MARTIN: Because I am not, unfortunately as strong as you.

ISAAC: What does that mean? Martin? Please? What?

MARTIN: I don't know. I don't have it in me to do this. To resolve, the way you have, to write people off, to write it all off. I don't. Believe me, I've tried.

ISAAC: And now what're you—you're going back upstate?

MARTIN: There's a train in forty minutes, yeah.

Silence. Isaac looks out the window.

ISAAC: Maybe I'll walk outside with you a bit. It's so lovely with the snow. Do you want to walk through the park?

MARTIN: Sure.

ISAAC: I need to find the key to the park. Let me find the key.

MARTIN: Wait. I've still got mine.

> Martin puts on his coat, hands Isaac his. They walk out to the hall.
> Martin turns off the light. Curtain.

MISS SAIGON

A Musical in Two Acts

BY ALAIN BOUBLIL AND CLAUDE-MICHEL SCHÖNBERG

MUSIC BY CLAUDE-MICHEL SCHÖNBERG

LYRICS BY RICHARD MALTBY JR. AND ALAIN BOUBLIL, ADAPTED FROM ORIGINAL FRENCH LYRICS BY ALAIN BOUBLIL

ADDITIONAL MATERIAL BY RICHARD MALTBY JR.

Cast and credits appear on pages 318-320

ALAIN BOUBLIL (co-author of libretto, lyrics and original French lyrics), with his composer-collaborator Claude-Michel Schönberg, has brought a French presence to the modern English-speaking musical stage with spectacular success. Their first French musical, La Révolution Française, established their musical-writing reputa-

tion in their native land in 1973 with the first French rock musical, with 350,000 double-albums sold. Boublil conceived the idea for a musical version of Victor Hugo's Les Misérables *in 1978, and with Schönberg and Jean-Marc Natel joining him as collaborators, he prepared the project over a two-year period as a record album. It had already sold more than 260,000 copies by the time the French stage version opened in Paris at the Palais des Sports in September 1980.*

Boublil made his entrance onto the British musical stage in 1983 with Abbacadabra *at the Lyric Theater, Hammersmith. He and his collaborators then proceeded to develop the English-language version of* Les Misérables *which was produced by Cameron Mackintosh and the Royal Shakespeare Company under the direction of Trevor Nunn and John Caird at the Barbican on October 8, 1985, then moving to London's Palace Theater December 4, 1985. Its American production under the same direction opened in Washington, D.C. at the Kennedy Center Opera House on December 20, 1986 and moved to Broadway on March 12, 1987 where it won a Best Play citation and the Critics and Tony Awards as the best musical of the season, with Boublil sharing the best-book and best-score Tonys. As of the Broadway opening date this season of* Miss Saigon, Les Misérables *was still running strong and pointing toward its 1,700th performance.*

Boublil has continued to interest himself in many aspects of Les Misérables *including the London and Broadway cast albums, a bilingual production in Montreal and a forthcoming new French production (for which latter two versions he has rewritten the lyrics in French). But since 1985 his principal concentration has been on the* Miss Saigon *collaboration, working with Schönberg on the book and with Richard Maltby Jr. on writing English lyrics. This show, a Vietnam variation on Puccini's* Madama Butterfly *dramatic theme, was produced by Mackintosh in London at the Theater Royal on September 20, 1989 and on Broadway April 11, 1991, winning Boublil his second Best Play citation.*

CLAUDE-MICHEL SCHÖNBERG (music and co-author of libretto) is a performer as well as a composer and recording artist and producer. He played King Louis XIV in the hit production of his first collaboration with Alain Boublil, La Révolution Française, in 1973, and in the show's double gold album which he co-produced. In 1974 Schönberg sang his own compositions and lyrics for another album, one of whose numbers, "Le Premier Pas," rose to the top of the popularity scale. His 1981 album of Les Misérables *received two gold discs, and he has continued to pay close attention to every aspect of its stage metamorphosis; the London and Broadway productions and cast albums, Japanese and Australian companies and a newly-released symphonic recording. His accolades for the score and book (with Boublil) of* Les Misérables *have so far included its 1987 Best Plays citation, the Critics and Tony Awards for best musical and, with Boublil, the Tonys for best book and score.*

In 1983 Schönberg produced an opera album in Paris with Julia Migenes-Johnson and the Monte Carlo Philharmonic Orchestra. Like his longtime collabo-

rator, he has been busy on the creation of Miss Saigon since 1985 and co-produced its London cast album in 1989. Now that it has arrived on Broadway, his honors continue with another Best Plays citation.

RICHARD MALTBY JR. (additional material and co-author of lyrics), son of a well-known orchestra leader, was born in Ripon, Wis. on Oct. 4, 1937. Early ambition to become a scene designer led him toward theater activity at Yale, where he found that the undergraduate organization (the Dramat) wasn't putting on the kind of shows he wanted to design—so he decided to try providing his own material. With a classmate, the composer David Shire, he wrote two shows for the Dramat, graduated B.A. in 1959 and spent a semester at the Yale Drama School before making the New York scene with the Maltby-Shire collaboration which has contributed so much to the modern musical stage.

The off-Broadway situation was beginning to develop and expand when the team put on their first New York show of record: The Sap of Life (book and lyrics by Maltby, music by Shire) October 2, 1961, for 49 performances at One Sheridan Square. There have followed several numbers in the long-run off-Broadway revue Graham Crackers January 23, 1963; the finale for Leonard Sillman's New Faces of 1968 on Broadway May 2 of that year; the revue Starting Here, Starting Now March 7, 1977 for 120 off-Broadway performances; Baby on Broadway December 4, 1983 for 241 performances, a Tony nominee for book and score; Urban Blight June 19, 1988 at Manhattan Theater Club, an organization with which Maltby has been associated for 15 years as a director and in other capacities; and the off-Broadway revue Closer Than Ever November 6, 1989 for 288 performances. Maltby's contributions to Miss Saigon receive his first Best Play citation but aren't his first association with one of those spectacular musicals from overseas. He wrote the American adaptation (with Don Black) and additional lyrics to the Andrew Lloyd Webber Song & Dance, produced on Broadway September 18, 1985 for 474 performances.

Maltby's other credits include, in addition to numerous directing stints, contributions to Daarlin' Juno, a 1976 Long Wharf Theater musical version of Juno and the Paycock; the concept with Geraldine Fitzgerald of her one-woman show Street Songs in 1979; the concept with Gretchen Cryer and Nancy Ford of the Manhattan Theater Club revue Hang On to the Good Times in 1985; and most particularly the concept and direction of the Fats Waller revue Ain't Misbehavin' on Broadway May 9, 1978 for 1,604 performances and revived for another 176 performances ten years later, winner of the Critics, Tony, Outer Critics and Drama Desk Awards for the best musical of its season, plus the best-musical-direction Tony.

Maltby's other honors have included the London Drama Critics and Evening Standard Awards for the British production of Closer Than Ever and a Grammy nomination for the original cast album of Starting Here, Starting Now. He is a member of the Dramatists Guild, ASCAP and the Society of Stage Directors and Choreographers, is married, with three sons and a daughter, and lives in Manhattan.

Our method of synopsizing Miss Saigon *in these pages differs from that of other Best Plays. In order to illustrate the distinctively theatrical "look" of its characters, setting, and choreography, the musical is represented here in photographs, with a few excerpts from its almost all-sung text to portray its verbal style and flavor. These Michael LePoer Trench/Joan Marcus photos of* Miss Saigon *depict scenes as produced on Broadway April 11, 1991 by Cameron Mackintosh and as directed by Nicholas Hytner, with scenery by John Napier, costumes by Andreane Neofitou and Suzy Benzinger and lighting by David Hersey.*

Our special thanks are tendered to the producer and his press representatives, the Fred Nathan Company and Marc Thibodeau, for making available these excellent photos of the show.

ACT I

SAIGON—APRIL 1975

1. "The Engineer," (Jonathan Pryce, *right),* a pimp, is squeezing the last drops of profit before the U.S. troops leave by presenting his girls in a "Miss Saigon" contest *(above).*

ENGINEER:
  They say Saigon has weeks, I
                think more like days
GIRLS:
  Tonight I will be Miss Saigon
ENGINEER:
  Each night these little buns of
                theirs are worth less and less
  I need a visa fast—that means
                there's cash to raise
  Look who I got out here
  I can still engineer

2. G.I.'s watch bar girls *(below)* compete for the "Miss Saigon" title, and Gigi (Marina Chapa, *right*) wins. She sings about "the movie in my mind," the universal Saigon dream of getting away to the U.S. with an American soldier.

An inexperienced new girl, Kim (Lea Salonga, *bottom of page* and *opposite page*), also has a movie in her mind: "I will not cry, I will not think/ I'll do my dance, I'll make them drink/When I make love, it won't be me/And if they hurt me, I'll just close my eyes/And see ... the movie in my mind."

3. Chris, a driver at the Embassy (Willy Falk, *below opposite page*) gets a night Kim as a present from a bu Kim is attracted to the ye Marine, and their night of lo more than casual. It leaves (wondering why, now that about to leave Saigon, he has denly had a wonderful experie

4. Chris leaves money on the table and goes but soon returns and hands Kim the money as she wakes. She refuses it, telling Chris she's never done this before. She had no choice but to run away after her village was burned and her parents (who'd promised her to a man she didn't love) were slaughtered. Now Kim has been blessed, along with Chris, singing, "You are my sunlight and I, moon/Joined here/Bright'ning the sky/With the flame of love." Rather than let Kim go back to working at the club, Chris asks her to live with him.

The Embassy is in chaos, preparing to evacuate. Chris gets his buddy John to cover for him while he goes to join Kim. The Engineer reneges on the deal for Kim's continuing services: he wants a visa instead of money. At gunpoint, Chris holds him to the deal as made.

Chris sets Kim up in new quarters, and friends join in a ceremony including a Vietnamese wedding chant. Thuy, Kim's village fiance, now a Vietcong soldier, forces his way into the party, intending to take Kim away with him. She refuses, as Thuy and Chris confront each other with pistols. Thuy curses her and flees.

Chris takes Kim in his arms and sings, "On the other side of the earth/There's a place where life still has worth/I will take you." "I'll go with you," Kim replies, and they cling to each other and dance as though this were "The last night in the world."

HO CHI MINH CITY—APRIL 1978

5. Three years later, Saigon has been renamed in the victor's honor. A massive celebration is in progress (*above* and *below*). The Engineer returns from a labor camp which has supposedly "re-educated" him. Not so: "Wherever I go, I speak Uncle Ho/And think Uncle Sam." Thuy (Barry K. Bernal, *opposite page*), now a uniformed commissar, orders the Engineer to find Kim, who has disappeared into the slums of the city.

Meanwhile, in America, Chris is now married but haunted by secret dreams which his loving wife Ellen wishes he'd share with her. In Vietnam, Kim still has faith that love cannot die and Chris will return.

6. The Engineer finds Kim for Thuy, who urges her to forget the past and come to him, as promised by their parents. Kim refuses, declaring, "I have a husband that I love/Real as the sun in the sky."

To demonstrate his power, Thuy directs his soldiers to commit an act of violence, but Kim still rejects him. After the Engineer is permitted to leave, Kim reveals to Thuy, "There is a secret/That you don't know/There is a force here/I never show/You say it's treason/To keep my vow . . . . . /If you want the reason/I will show you now."

Kim calls "Tam!" A two-year-old boy (Brian R. Baldomero, *below*) enters and runs into her arms. "Look Thuy," she sings, "This is my son/He has kept me alive/Now you see why/I must tell you No."

7. "That bastard fouls our name," Thuy exclaims, "When you're my wife/Keeping this child of his/Brands us for life/No alternative/This child cannot live." He pulls a knife, menacing the boy. Kim shouts "Run!", letting Tam hide behind the bed curtains as she points a pistol at Thuy.

> KIM:
> Don't touch my little boy
> And do not test my will
> For him I'll kill . . . . .
> THUY:
> You don't know how to kill
> KIM:
> I have no other choice
> What I must do I will

Thuy comes on, and Kim fires. Thuy falls dead in her arms.

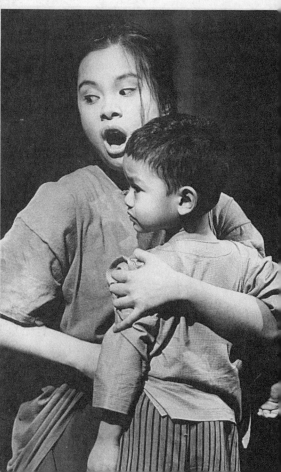

8. The Engineer retrieves a hoard of watches he stashed in better times. He prepares to flee: "Give me francs or dollars or yen/I'll set up a game/I know how it works." Kim finds him, and he suddenly realizes her Marine's child may be a passport to the U.S.A. He goes to make arrangements, while Kim comforts her son *(right):* "You will be who you want to be—you/Can choose whatever heaven grants/As long as you can have your chance/I swear I'll give my life for you."

The Engineer returns, and they exit with a group of boat people. *Curtain.*

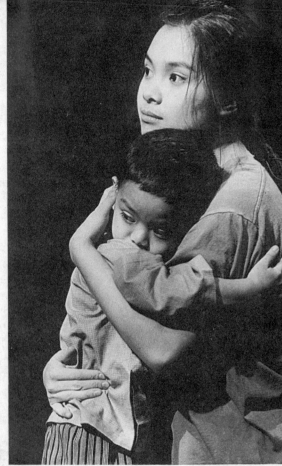

ACT II

U.S.A.—SEPTEMBER 1978

9. Chris's onetime Vietnam buddy, John (Hinton Battle, *left*), addresses a conference on the "bui-doi," the "dust of life," as the Vietnamese babies left behind by G.I.s are called. John tells his audience, "They are the living reminders/Of all the good we failed to do."

John has a staff working on this problem in Bangkok, and they have found Kim (John tells Chris after the lecture). And "She has a child/You have a son." Chris is bowled over: "I have a whole new life/I have a wife I love. She can't just disappear." John advises, "You must both go to Bangkok." Chris is telling his wife Ellen about Kim as the scene fades.

BANGKOK—OCTOBER 1978

10. In Bangkok, the Engineer is up to his old tricks *(right)*, working the tourists as a shill for a bevy of bar girls, one of whom is Kim.

John *(below)* finds Kim, who has applied for U.S. citizenship, and the Engineer, who is posing as her brother. John reveals that Chris is in Bangkok. Kim is so delighted, John can't tell her the rest ("They don't say in the files/There's a woman in love here"). He goes to find Chris and bring him to Kim.

The Engineer decides he doesn't trust either John or Chris. He resolves to send Kim to meet Chris and goes to get Chris's address. In his absence, Kim is haunted by a nightmare in which the ghost of Thuy taunts her: "You may think your Marine's not like other men/He betrayed you once and will again."

11. Kim's dream flashes back to Saigon, with Chris assuring her, "I'm getting you out!" From the Embassy, he obtains papers for her to board a carrier, declaring that he will marry her when they reach the U.S. After spending the night with Kim, Chris goes to work as usual (but leaves his gun with her) and tells her to pack her belongings. "We'll get plenty of word when the V.C. attack," he says, and leaves for the Embassy.

OFFICER *(immediately, at the Embassy):*
    Sorry, Sergeant, we must accelerate
    State Department says we evacuate
    The word is, we must be out by dawn
CHRIS: I have to get my girl!
ANOTHER OFFICER:
    Sorry, Sergeant, it's straight from Washington
    No one leaves the grounds now, not anyone
    As fast as we load the planes we're gone
CHRIS: But my girl is out there!
        A huge crowd of Vietnamese is at the Embassy gates (below).
MARINE CAPTAIN *(to the crowd):*
    Okay! Keep quiet! Don't shout!
    The Ambassador won't leave till everyone's out
(continued on the opposite page)

MARINE CAPTAIN *(continued):*
    The choppers on their way have room for all
ANOTHER MARINE:
    They're climbing over the wall!
MORE MARINES: Get back!
    Get back! I tell you, don't shout!
    The Ambassador won't leave till everyone's out!
MARINE *(entering):*
    The Ambassador just sent an order to freeze
MARINE CAPTAIN:
    That's it! No more Vietnamese! Get in!
CHRIS: But my girl is out there!

Kim is in the street, trying to get to the Embassy, and Chris is trying to get out to find her, but neither can go through the barriers. Both cry, "Please, get me through—I don't care how/Don't take my love away, not now!" A chopper lands on the Embassy roof *(above)*, while Marines hold the frantic Vietnamese (many of whom, like Kim, have the right papers to get away) at bay. Chris cries, "Why in the world should I be saved instead of her?" and John comments, "She's not the only one we'll have betrayed." Chris is forced to board the last helicopter out of Saigon, which rises with a roar and escapes before Kim and the others left behind can burst the barrier and swarm into the Embassy yard.

BANGKOK—OCTOBER 1978

12. The Engineer sends Kim to Chris's hotel room, where she is surprised to find Ellen (Liz Callaway, *above right*), Chris's wife. "Please tell me you're not married/You don't know, you can't know what I've done to be here," Kim begs, and Ellen replies, "You don't know how he needed/A new start." Ellen promises Kim she and Chris will take care of Kim and her child, but not take Tam to the U.S. where they hope to have children of their own. They must take Tam to America, Kim pleads, it's his only hope for a future. If not, Chris must tell her so, face to face. She exits.

ELLEN *(to herself):*
Now that I've seen her
There's no way to hide
She is not some fling
From long ago
Now that I've seen her
I know why he lied

And I think it was better
when I didn't know . . . . .
Now that I've seen her
She's more than a name
I don't hate this girl even so
Now that I've seen her
I can't stay the same . . . . .

Returning to the hotel with John, Chris reflects on how Kim seemed the only reality in a mad world and he wanted to protect her, but "All I made was a mess, just like everyone else/In a place full of mystery/That I never once understood." Then he began again with Ellen, and she is all he wants now. Chris won't abandon Tam but can't take Kim to America—she obviously still loves him—and won't separate mother and child. Chris makes the decision: "There's no choice/I think the answer's clear/They have to stay in Bangkok/We'll support them there."

13. The Engineer, self-described as the son of a Haiphong tattoo artist and a prostitute—"My job was bringing red-faced monsieurs to our huts"—believes he's on his way to the U.S., thanks to Kim and Tam. "I'll sell blondes there," he dreams *(below)*, "that they can charge on a card."

ENGINEER:
What's that I smell in the air
  The American Dream
Sweet as a suite in Bel-Air
  The American Dream
Girls can buy tits by the pair
  The American Dream
Bald people think they'll grow hair
  The American Dream

Call girls are lining Times Square
  The American Dream
Bums there have money to spare
  The American Dream

Cars that have bars take you there
  The American Dream
Onstage each night, Fred Astaire
  The American Dream

Come everyone, come and share
  The American Dream
Name what you want, and it's there
  The American Dream . . . . .
What other place can compare
  The American Dream
Come and get more than your share
  The American Dream

14. Backstage at the bar, Kim dresses Tam in his best clothes and holds him lovingly *(left)*.

KIM:
> Little god of my heart
> You must do what I say
> Soon, Tam
> Soon your father will come
> Look Tam
> See how happy I am
>
> He will come,
> Take you home
> All I want for you
> He'll do
> You're still mine
> But I can't go along
> Please don't ever be sad
> Though I seem far away
> I'll be watching you too . . . . .

15. Kim continues to Tam: "Look at me one last time/Don't forget what you see/Press your little hands to my face/And bless my journey." When she hears Chris, Ellen and the Engineer coming, she kisses the child one more time and then goes behind the bed curtain.

"A gunshot. Chris runs into the little room followed by the others. Kim's body falls out from behind the curtain."

Chris takes Kim in his arms *(right)* and hears her say, "The gods have guided you to your son," before she becomes lifeless. *Curtain.*

OUR COUNTRY'S GOOD

A Play in Two Acts

BY TIMBERLAKE WERTENBAKER

BASED ON THE NOVEL *The Playmaker*
BY THOMAS KENEALLY

Cast and credits appear on page 323

TIMBERLAKE WERTENBAKER, daughter of distinguished American journalists, was born and received early schooling in the U.S. but grew up in the south of France. Her professional activities have been concentrated in England, so that her Best Play and Critics Award-winning Our Country's Good *is classified as a foreign play. Prior to its arrival on these shores in a Mark Taper Forum production Sept. 13, 1989 and in a Hartford Stage Company production Oct. 5, 1990 brought to New York under the auspices of the Broadway Alliance April 29, 1991, this play in a London production had won the 1988 Evening Standard Most Promising Playwright Award and the Olivier Play of the Year Award.*

Now in her mid-40s, Wertenbaker has a long list of British playwriting accomplishments to her credit, including a stint as the Royal Court Theater's resident writer in 1984-85. Among her productions in various media have been the plays The Third *(All-London Playwrights Award);* Case to Answer; New Anatomies *(her second American offering, produced OOB at Home for Contemporary Theater Feb. 14, 1990 and cited by Mel Gussow in the 1989-90 Best Plays volume among the OOB season's best work);* Abel's Sister *(produced OOB by Echo Stage in 1985);* The Grace of Mary Traverse *(Plays & Players' Most Promising Playwright Award, 1985);* The Love of the Nightingale *(Eileen Anderson Central TV Drama Award, 1989); translations of Marivaux's* False Admissions, Successful Strategies *and* La Dispute, *Anouilh's* Leocadia, *Maeterlinck's* Pelleas and Melisaunde, *Lorca's* The House of Bernarda Alba *and Mnouchkine's* Mephisto; *and the screen plays* The Children *(based on Edith Wharton) and* Do Not Disturb.

In 1989 Wertenbaker was the recipient of a Mrs. Giles Whiting Award for her body of work. At present she is working on a translation of Sophocles's Theban Plays for the Royal Shakespeare Company.

In the following synopsis of Our Country's Good, *the scene divisions and their descriptions are reprinted from a published version of this play; they were not included in the Broadway Playbill.*

Time: 1788-89

Place: Sydney, Australia

ACT I

Scene 1: The voyage out

SYNOPSIS: Upstage left, a framework of timbers suggesting the skeleton of a ship remains in the background throughout the play, with a number of hangman's nooses suspended above the stage. In the opening scene at sea, the passengers, a group of convicts overseen by a military detachment, are huddled below while one of their number is being severely punished on deck above with fifty lashes being counted off *"in a barely audible, slow and monotonous voice"* by Marine 2d Lt. Ralph Clark. The punishment finished, the victim is dumped with the other convicts.

Scene 2: A lone aboriginal Australian describes the arrival of the First Convict Fleet in Botany Bay on Jan. 20, 1788

THE ABORIGINE: A giant canoe drifts onto the sea, clouds billowing from upright oars. This is a dream which has lost its way. Best to leave it alone.

Scene 3: Punishment

The governor of this New South Wales colony, Navy Capt. Arthur Phillip, is shooting birds with Marine Capt. Judge David Collins (the Advocate General),

Marine Capt. Watkin Tench and Midshipman Harry Brewer. They are discussing whether hanging—imposed under British law, which rules the colony—is a suitable or effective form of punishment for stealing and other crimes which are bound to take place among this population of convicted criminals. Gov. Phillip speaks for a more humane form of correction, but Capt. Tench argues, "Justice and humaneness have never gone hand in hand. The law is not a sentimental comedy."

PHILLIP: Have these men lost all fear of being flogged?

COLLINS: John Arscott has already been sentenced to 150 lashes for assault.

TENCH: The shoulder blades are exposed at about 100 lashes, and I would say that somewhere between 250 and 500 lashes you are probably condemning a man to death anyway.

COLLINS: With the disadvantage that the death is slow, unobserved and cannot serve as a sharp example.

PHILLIP: Harry?

HARRY: The convicts laugh at hangings, Sir. They watch them all the time.

TENCH: It's their favorite form of entertainment, I should say.

PHILLIP: Perhaps because they've never been offered anything else.

TENCH: Perhaps we should build an opera house for the convicts.

PHILLIP: We learned to love such things because they were offered to us when we were children and young men. Surely no one is born naturally cultured? I'll have the gun now.

COLLINS: We don't even have any books here, apart from the odd play and a few Bibles. And most of the convicts can't read, so let us return to the matter at hand, which is the punishment of the convicts, not their education.

Three soon to be hanged are an Irishman transported for assault, a marine who stole food and a 17-year old, Thomas Barrett, transported for stealing one sheep. Gov. Phillip would prefer to have the convicts see "real plays: fine language, sentiment" instead of watching hangings for their diversion, but he reluctantly assigns Harry to oversee the executions and persuade someone to fill the office of hangman. A fourth condemned, an 82-year-old woman sentenced for stealing a biscuit, will escape punishment—she hanged herself this very morning.

Scene 4: The loneliness of men

Lt. Ralph Clark speaks aloud that he is writing to his wife Alicia in his diary: "Dreamt, my beloved Alicia, that I was walking with you and that you was in your riding-habit." He watched a corporal flogging one of the women—Elizabeth Morden—for impertinence: "She has long been fishing for it." And he notes that some of the convicts have run away.

Midshipman Harry Brewer comes in and confesses that he could well be one of the prisoners instead of one of the guards—at one time he was an embezzler. Harry had a vision, or a nightmare, of one of the three men he hanged a month ago,

Peter Frechette as 2d Lt. Ralph Clark and Tracey Ellis as Mary
Brenham in *Our Country's Good* by Timberlake Wertenbaker

Handy Baker, who was a rival of Harry's for the affections of Harry's convict
mistress. Harry tells Ralph, "Duckling," as the mistress is called, "says she never
feels anything. How do I know she didn't feel something when she was with him?
She thinks I hanged him to get rid of him, but I didn't, Ralph." *(Pause.)* "Do you
know I saved her life? She was sentenced to be hanged at Newgate for stealing
two silver candlesticks, but I got her name put on the transport lists. But when I
reminded her of that, she says she wouldn't have cared. Eighteen years old, and
she didn't care if she was turned off."

Harry informs Ralph of the senior officers' conversation while out shooting,
about the possibility of putting on a play with the convicts as actors. Ralph wants
to be assigned to this task if the plan goes through. He asks Harry to put in a good
word for him and promises to put Harry's Duckling in the play if he gets the job.

Scene 5: An audition

The play project has been launched under Ralph's direction, and he is at work
casting *The Recruiting Officer*. Meg Long, *"very old and very smelly,"* hovers
over him. Having heard that Ralph was looking for women (he needs four for parts
in the play), Meg is only too willing to oblige: "You want women: you ask Meg . . . . . We
thought you was a madge cull. Ha! Ha! . . . . . You know, a fluter, a mollie.
(Impatiently.) A prissy cove, a girl. You having no she-lag on the ship. Nor here,

neither." Meg is glad to hear he now wants a lot of women all at once and is ready to supply them.

As Meg exits, Robert Sideway comes on with a theatrical flourish. A onetime pickpocket in the theater district, he begs Ralph for a part. As he exits, Dabby Bryant brings in Mary Brenham, whom Ralph has especially requested to see. Mary stands there, silent; but Dabby isn't shy about looking for a part: "In all these plays, there's always a friend. That's because a girl has to talk to someone, and she talks to her friend. So I'll be Mary's friend."

But it's Mary who interests Ralph. He wants Mary for the part of Sylvia. He auditions her (Mary can read), and she is fine. Dabby can't read but assures Ralph that Mary will read her lines aloud, and she'll memorize them.

While Ralph is explaining that the plot of *The Recruiting Officer* involves mistaken sexual identity, Liz Morden enters.

RALPH: Ah, here's your cousin.
> *There is a silence. Mary shrinks away. Dabby and Liz stare at each other, each holding her ground, each ready to pounce.*
Melinda. Sylvia's cousin.
DABBY: You can't have her in the play, Lieutenant.
RALPH: Why not?
DABBY: You don't have to be able to read the future to know that Liz Morden is going to be hanged.
> *Liz looks briefly at Dabby, as if to strike, then changes her mind.*
LIZ: I understand you want me in your play, Lieutenant. Is that it?
> *She grabs the book from Ralph and strides off.*
I'll look at it and let you know.

Scene 6: *The authorities discuss the merits of the theater*

Gov. Phillip, Marine Maj. Robbie Ross, Judge Collins, Capt. Tench, Marine Capt. Jemmy Campbell, Rev. Johnson, Marine Lt. George Johnston, Marine Lt. Will Dawes, Ralph Clark and Marine 2d Lt. William Faddy are discussing the play project. It is late at night, and tempers are on the rise. Rev. Johnson is concerned with morality implications; Capt. Tench with the criminality of the performers ("Many criminals seem to have been born that way"); Gov. Phillip with Rousseau's view of man's unhappy state and the possibility of redemption; Ralph with the possibility that putting the play on "could change the nature of our little society." He outlines the plot: "It's about this recruiting officer and his friend, and they are in love with these two young ladies from Shrewsbury, and after some difficulties, they marry them."

Gov. Phillip points out that some time in the future these convicts will either be reassimilated into the English population or found a colony of their own out here, and in either case they need to be encouraged "to think in a free and responsible manner." Capt. Tench doesn't believe a comedy will be that much help.

PHILLIP: The theater is an expression of civilization. We belong to a great country which has spawned great playwrights: Shakespeare, Marlowe, Johnson, and even in our own time, Sheridan. The convicts will be speaking a refined, literate language and expressing sentiments of a delicacy they are not used to. It will remind them that there is more to life than crime, punishment. And we, this colony of a few hundred, will be watching this together, for a few hours we will no longer be despised prisoners and hated gaolers. We will laugh, we may be moved, we may even think a little. Can you suggest something else that will provide such an evening, Watkin?

DAWES: Mapping the stars gives me more enjoyment, personally.

TENCH: I'm not sure it's a good idea having the convicts laugh at officers, Arthur.

CAMPBELL: No. Pheeoh, insubordination, heh, ehh, no discipline.

ROSS: You want this vice-ridden vermin to enjoy themselves?

COLLINS: They would only laugh at Sergeant Kite.

RALPH: Captain Plume is a most attractive, noble fellow.

REV. JOHNSON: He's not loose, is he Ralph? I hear many of these plays are about rakes and encourage loose morals in women. They do get married? Before, that is, before. And for the right reasons.

RALPH: They marry for love and to secure wealth.

REV. JOHNSON: That's all right.

TENCH: I would simply say that if you want to build a civilization there are more important things than a play. If you want to teach the convicts something, teach them to farm, build houses, teach them a sense of respect for property, teach them thrift so they don't eat a week's rations in one night, but above all, teach them how to work, not how to sit around laughing at a comedy.

PHILLIP: The Greeks believed that it was a citizen's duty to watch a play. It was a kind of work, in that it required attention, judgement, patience, all the social virtues.

TENCH: And the Greeks were conquered by the more practical Romans, Arthur.

COLLINS: Indeed, the Romans built their bridges, but they also spent many centuries wishing they were Greeks. And they, after all, were conquered by the barbarians, or by their own corrupt and small spirits.

TENCH: Are you saying Rome would not have fallen if the theater had been better?

RALPH (very loud): Why not? (Everyone looks at him, and he continues, fast and nervously.) In my own small way, in just a few hours, I have seen something change. I asked some of the convict women to read me some lines, these women who behave often no better than animals. And it seemed to me, as one or two— I'm not saying all of them, not at all—but one or two, saying those well-balanced lines of Mr. Farquhar, they seemed to acquire a dignity, they seemed—they seemed to lose some of their corruption. There was one, Mary Brenham, she read so well, perhaps this play will keep her from selling herself to the first Marine who offers her bread—

FADDY *(under his breath):* She'll sell herself to him, instead.

ROSS: So that's the way the wind blows—

CAMPBELL: Hooh. A tempest. Hooh.

RALPH *(over them):* I speak about her, but in a small way this could affect all the convicts and even ourselves, we could forget our worries about the supplies, the hangings and the floggings, and think of ourselves at the theater, in London, with our wives and children, that is, we could, euh—

PHILLIP: Transcend—

RALPH: Transcend the darker, euh—

REV. JOHNSON: Brutal—

RALPH: The brutality—remember our better nature and remember—

COLLINS: England.

RALPH: England.

Capt. Tench feels that a play will simply cause them to lose the convicts' labor for the two hours they are watching it. Judge Collins samples the views of the assembled company and finds that most are in favor of letting Ralph put the play on (Maj. Ross dissents strongly and exits with the intention of complaining to the Admiralty in writing). Gov. Phillip orders that the play project continue.

Scene 7: *Harry and Duckling go rowing*

Midshipman Harry Brewer takes Duckling Smith for a ride in a rowboat, trying to remind her of an outing on the Thames, but she remains morose and sulky. Harry has taken her out of the women's camp, where the other soldiers seek women, so as to have her to himself. But he remains jealous and suspicious: "You've found someone already, haven't you? Where do you go, on the beach? In my tent?" Duckling is willing to "open my legs wide" to him, but she yearns for freedom, without Harry following her around.

Harry offers to get Duckling a part in the play, and she accepts. In no way does Ralph represent a rival for Duckling's attentions, and Harry can come to watch the rehearsals.

Scene 8: *The women learn their lines.*

Dabby Bryant is sitting dreaming of Devon and its soft rain, "as soft as Lieutenant Clark's dimpled cheeks," she remarks to Mary Brenham. She assures Mary that the Lieutenant is ripe for Mary's plucking.

MARY: Don't start. I listened to you once before.

DABBY: What would you have done without that lanky sailor drooling over you?

MARY: I would have been less of a whore.

DABBY: Listen, my darling, you're only a virgin once. You can't go to a man and say, I'm a virgin except for this one lover I had. After that, it doesn't matter how many men go through you.

MARY: I'll never wash the sin away.

DABBY: If God didn't want women to be whores he shouldn't have created men who pay for their bodies. While you were with your little sailor, there were women in that stinking pit of a hold who had three men on them at once, men with the pox, men with the flux, men biting like dogs.

MARY: But if you don't agree to it, then you're not a whore, you're a martyr.

DABBY: You have to be a virgin to be a martyr, Mary, and you didn't come on that ship a virgin.

They discuss their roles. Mary is to play Sylvia, "brave and strong," and she fears she may not be able to become such a person: "I have to be her . . . . . that's acting." But for Dabby, acting is merely pretending, and she'll pretend to be Rose, not minding that Rose is an idiot.

Mary is trying out lines, when Liz Morden comes in and insists that Mary join her in reading aloud the first scene between Sylvia and Melinda (Liz's role).

    Liz looks at the book.

MARY: You start: "Welcome to town, Cousin Sylvia—"

LIZ: "Welcome to town, Cousin Sylvia—"

MARY: Go on: "I envied you—"

LIZ: "I envied you." You read it first.

MARY: Why?

LIZ: I want to hear how you do it.

MARY: Why?

LIZ: 'Cause then I can do it different.

MARY: "I envied you your retreat in the country; for Shrewsbury, methinks, and all your heads of shires—"

LIZ: You're saying it too fast.

MARY: Well, you can say it slower.

LIZ: No. You do it slower, then I'll do it fast.

DABBY: Why don't you read it? You can't read!

LIZ: What?

    She lunges at Dabby.

MARY: Liz, I'll teach you the lines.

DABBY: Are you her friend now, is that it? Mary the holy innocent and thieving bitch—

    Liz and Dabby seize each other. Ketch Freeman appears.

KETCH *(with nervous affability):* Good morning ladies. And why aren't you at work instead of at each other's throats?

    Liz and Dabby turn on him.

LIZ: I wouldn't talk of throats if I was you, Mr. Hangman Ketch Freeman.

DABBY: Crap merchant.

LIZ: Crapping a cull. Switcher.

MARY: Roper.

KETCH: I was only asking what you were doing, you know, friendly like.

LIZ: Stick to your ropes, my little galler, don't bother the actresses.

KETCH: Actresses? *(Pause.)* You're doing a play.

LIZ: Better than dancing the Paddington Frisk in your arms—noser!

KETCH: I'll nose you, Liz, if you're not careful.

LIZ: I'd take a leap in the dark sooner than turn off my own kind. Now take your whirligigs out of our sight, we have lines to learn.

> *Ketch slinks away as Liz and Dabby spit him off.*

DABBY *(after him):* Don't hang too many people, Ketch, we need an audience!

MARY: "Welcome to town, cousin Sylvia." It says you salute.

LIZ *(giving a military salute):* "Welcome to town, cousin—Sylvia."

Scene 9: *Ralph Clark tries to kiss his dear wife's picture.*

Ralph is talking to his "darling tender wife" in his imagination, reading aloud comforting passages from the Bible and telling her of brutalities here in the camp. This being Sunday, he takes out her picture to kiss it, *"goes down on his knees and brings the picture to himself,"* when Ketch Freeman enters. Ralph jumps to his feet to ask "What do you want?"; but Ketch, believing he has interrupted Ralph's prayers, launches into a detailed account of his own strong religious beliefs. In sum, Ketch blames his guardian angel for not taking better care of him and allowing him to get into a situation where, after a dockside murder he didn't commit, he was threatened with being hanged unless he gave out the names of the killers.

"It's because I'm so friendly, see," Ketch goes on, "so I go along, and then I'm the one who gets caught . . . . . I was just there, keeping a lookout, just to help some friends, you know. But when they say to you, hang or be hanged, what do you do? Someone has to do it. I try to do it well. God had mercy on the whore, the thief, the lame, surely he'll forgive the hang—it's the women—they're without mercy . . . . ." Finally Ketch arrives at the point of his visit: he wants a part in the play.

Scene 10: *John Wisehammer and Mary Brenham exchange words*

John Wisehammer pauses in piling bricks and observes Mary copying from *The Recruiting Officer* and reading some of the lines aloud, one of which includes the word "country." Wisehammer muses, "'Country' can mean opposite things. It renews you with trees and grass, you go rest in the country, or it crushes you with power: you die for your country, your country doesn't want you, you're thrown out of your country."

As a child, Wisehammer had access to a dictionary and grew to love words. He compliments Mary on her handwriting, adding that he too can write. Mary suggests he speak to Ralph about helping with the copying.

WISEHAMMER: No . . . no . . . I'm—
MARY: Afraid?
WISEHAMMER: Diffident.
MARY: I'll tell him. Well, I won't. My friend Dabby will. She's—
WISEHAMMER: Bold. *(Pause.)* Shy is not a bad word, it's soft.
MARY: But shame is a hard one.
WISEHAMMER: Words with two L's are the worst. Lonely, loveless.
MARY: Love is a good word.
WISEHAMMER: That's because it only has one L. I like words with one L. Luck. Latitudinarian.
    Mary laughs.
Laughter.

Scene 11: The first rehearsal

Sideway, Wisehammer, Mary, Liz, Dabby, Duckling and Ketch are assembled and welcomed by Ralph. Sideway brings up traditions observed by theater folk on the first day of rehearsal: the director, to begin with, must punctiliously introduce the members of the cast to each other. Ralph does so, announcing their roles and ignoring the flashes of hostility which break out from time to time among the convicts. Two cast members, Henry Kable and John Arscott, haven't shown up, so Ralph reads the Captain Plume part in a scene with Sideway, who overacts a simple entrance with every overblown mannerism he can remember having seen onstage. Ralph cautions him to try to perform more naturally.

Black Caesar comes in, determined to play a part—"There is always a black servant in a play"—and attaches himself to Sideway, though there is no servant written for Sideway's role of Worthy. Caesar argues that being from Madagascar, he'll speak in French, and having a French servant will make Worthy seem more of a gentleman.

"I'll think about it," Ralph allows tolerantly and proceeds to rehearse the Melinda and Sylvia parts. Liz speaks Melinda's lines very rapidly, demonstrating that she has learned them. Gently, Ralph informs her that she might like to act them as well as speak them. He instructs her to act like a rich lady while she talks.

RALPH: Have you ever seen a lady in her own house?
LIZ: I used to climb into the big houses when I was a girl, and just stand there, looking. I didn't take anything. I just stood. Like this.
RALPH: But if it was your own house, you would think it was normal to live like that.
WISEHAMMER: It's not normal. It's not normal when others have nothing.
RALPH: When acting, you have to imagine things. You have to imagine you're

someone different. So, now, think of a rich lady and imagine you're her.
>   *Liz begins to masticate.*
What are you doing?

LIZ: If I was rich I'd eat myself sick.

DABBY: Me too, potatoes . . . . .

LIZ: Eels, oysters—

RALPH: Could we get on with the scene, please? Brenham, it's your turn to speak.

MARY: "Oh, madam, I have heard the town commended for its air."

LIZ: "But you don't consider, Sylvia, how long I have lived in't!"

RALPH *(to Liz):* I believe you would look at her.

LIZ: She didn't look at me.

RALPH: Didn't she? She will now.

LIZ: "For I can assure you that to a lady the least nice in her constitution, no air can be good above half a year . . . . ."

MARY: "But prithee, my dear Melinda, don't put on such an air to me."

RALPH: Excellent, Brenham. You could be a little more sharp on the "don't."

MARY: "Don't." *(Mary now tries a few gestures.)* "Your education and mine were just the same, and I remember the time when we never troubled our heads about air, but when the sharp air from the Welsh mountains made our noses drip in a cold morning at the boarding school."

RALPH: Good! Good! Morden?

LIZ: "Our education, cousin, was the same, but our temperaments had nothing alike." .

RALPH: That's a little better, Morden, but you needn't be quite so angry with her. Now go on, Brenham.

LIZ: I haven't finished my speech!

RALPH: You're right, Morden, please excuse me . . . . .

LIZ: "You have the constitution of a horse."

RALPH: Much better, Morden. But you must always remember you're a lady . . . . .

The rehearsal continues. Duckling is reluctant to fetch a piece of wood (representing a fan) for Liz, but she complies when she understands that it is her role to do so; she is playing Liz's servant, Lucy. The rehearsal moves forward under Ralph's tutelage, until the convicts are suddenly cowed by the entrance of Maj. Ross and Capt. Campbell.

ROSS: Where are the prisoners Kable and Arscott, Lieutenant?

CAMPBELL: Eh?

RALPH: They seem to be late.

ROSS: While you were rehearsing, Arscott and Kable slipped into the woods with three others, so five men have run away, and it's all because of your damned play and your so-called thespists. And not only have your thespists run away, they've stolen food from the stores for their renegade escape, that's what your play has done.

RALPH: I don't see what the play—

ROSS: I said it from the beginning. The play will bring down calamity on this colony.

RALPH: I don't see—

ROSS: The devil, Lieutenant, always comes through the mind, here, worms its way, idleness and words.

RALPH: Major Ross, I can't agree—

ROSS: Listen to me, my lad, you're a second lieutenant and you don't agree or disagree with Major Ross.

CAMPBELL: No discipline, tchhha.

ROSS (looks over the convicts): Caesar! He started going with them and came back.

RALPH: That's all right, he's not in the play.

CAESAR: Yes I am, please Lieutenant, I am a servant.

ROSS: John Wisehammer!

WISEHAMMER: I had nothing to do with it!

ROSS: You're Jewish, aren't you? You're guilty. Kable was last seen near Wisehammer's hut. Liz Morden! She was observed next to the colony's stores late last night in the company of Kable, who was supposed to be repairing the door. (To Liz.) Liz Morden, you will be tried for stealing from the stores. You know the punishment? Death by hanging. And now you may continue to rehearse, Lieutenant.

Ross goes. Campbell lingers, looking at the book.

CAMPBELL: Ouusstta. The Recruiting Officer. Good title. Arara. But a play, tss, a play.

He goes. Ralph and the convicts are left in the shambles of their rehearsal. A silence. Curtain.

ACT II

Scene 1: Visiting Hours

Liz, Wisehammer, Arscott and Caesar are huddled in chairs. Liz is describing how bad luck has undermined her life from the beginning. She and her five brothers were abandoned by her mother, and then her father had her stripped and beaten in the street for stealing a lady's handkerchief, which in fact he himself had stolen. She fled her father's home and went to her older brother.

LIZ: . . . . . Liz, he says, why trine for a make, when you can wap for a winne? I'm no dimber mort, I says. Don't ask you to be a swell mollisher, sister, men want

Miss Laycock, don't look at your mug. So I begin to sell my mother of saints. I thinks I'm in luck when I meet the swell cove. He's a bobcull. He says to me, it's not enough to sell your mossie face, Lizzie, it don't bring no shiners no more. Shows me how to spice the swells. So. Swell has me up the wall, flashes a pocket watch, I lifts it. But one time I stir my stumps too slow, the swell squeaks beef, the snoozie hears, I'm nibbed. It's up the ladder to rest, I thinks when I go up before the fortune teller, but no, the judge's a bobcull, I nap the King's pardon and it's seven years across the herring pond. Jesus Christ, the hunger on the ship, sailors won't touch me: no rantum scantum, no food, but here, the Governor says, new life. You could nob it here, Lizzie, I thinks, bobcull Gov, this niffynaffy play, not too much work, good crew of rufflers, Kable, Arscott, but no, Ross don't like my mug, I'm nibbed again and now it's up the ladder to rest for good. Well, Lizzie Morden's life. And you, Wisehammer, how did you get here.

WISEHAMMER: Betrayal. Barbarous falsehood. Intimidation: injustice.

LIZ: Speak in English, Wisehammer.

WISEHAMMER: I am innocent. I didn't do it, and I'll keep saying I didn't.

LIZ: It doesn't matter what you say. If they say you're a thief, you're a thief.

WISEHAMMER: I am not a thief. I'll go back to England to the snuff shop of Rickett and Loads and say see, I'm back, I'm innocent.

LIZ: They won't listen.

WISEHAMMER: You can't live if you think that way.

Caesar longs to get back to his native Madagascar, hoping that next time he tries to escape his ancestors will help him. Arscott, in despair, cries that there is no escape from Australia, he had hoped to walk north to China, but his compass didn't work and he walked in circles. He shows Wisehammer his "compass"—a piece of paper with "north" written on it, acquired from a sailor who deceived Arscott into believing it would point the way for him.

Sideway, Mary and Duckling enter.

SIDEWAY: Madam, gentlemen, fellow players, we have come to visit, to commiserate, to offer our humble services.

LIZ: Get out!

MARY: Liz, we've come to rehearse the play.

WISEHAMMER: Rehearse the play?

DUCKLING: The Lieutenant has gone to talk to the Governor. Harry said we could come see you.

MARY: The Lieutenant has asked me to stand in his place so we don't lose time. We'll start with the first scene between Melinda and Brazen.

WISEHAMMER: How can I play Captain Brazen in chains?

MARY: This is the theater. We will believe you.

ARSCOTT: Where does Kite come in?

SIDEWAY *(bowing to Liz):* Madam, I have brought you your fan.

Scene 2: His Excellency exhorts Ralph

Gov. Phillip is inquiring why Ralph seeks to discontinue the play. "Half my cast is in chains, Sir," Ralph points out, to which the Governor replies, "That is a difficulty, but it can be overcome." There is so much opposition to the project, Ralph continues, that he fears to offend his superiors. "Would you have a world without Socrates?" Gov. Phillip counters and cites the Meno's argument that "A slave boy can learn the principles of geometry as well as a gentleman . . . . . It is a matter of reminding the slave of what he knows, of his own intelligence. And by intelligence you may read goodness, talent, the innate qualities of human beings."

But even the Reverend has given up trying to search out the goodness and redeem Liz Morden, who is probably doomed to be hanged, Ralph notes. Gov. Phillip asked Ralph to put her in the play just because she is the most difficult woman in the colony. Even she might be redeemed by kindness, Gov. Phillip believes, and he certainly doesn't want any woman under his authority to be hanged. He had retired from military service when they assigned him to run this colony—he doesn't know why—but he means to accept the responsibility under any circumstances. "What is a statesman's responsibility?" Gov. Phillip asks himself. "To ensure the rule of law. But the citizens must be taught to obey that law of their own free will. I want to rule over responsible human beings, not tyrannize over a group of animals. I want there to be a contract between us, not a whip on my side, terror and hatred on theirs."

The Governor looks for Ralph's help, the play being a sort of diagram in the sand to remind the slave of his intelligence. And there may be great difficulties ahead. Opponents are trying to convince the Admiralty that the Governor is out of his mind. They might also hinder Ralph's expected promotion in rank. And, more seriously, supplies are running so low that Gov. Phillip may have to cut the rations again, and they'll run out entirely if a ship doesn't arrive within three months.

Ralph promises to do his best, adding, "It's a wonderful play, Sir. I wasn't sure at first, as you know . . . . ."

Scene 3: Harry Brewer sees the dead

Harry is in an alcoholic daze, talking to the ghosts of hanged men, including the youth Thomas Barrett and Handy Baker, his predecessor in Duckling's affections. Duckling comes in to find out what is causing the screams she has heard, and she agrees to let him make out with her in order to calm him down—but he still suspects that she's been down on the beach with a rival, possibly even the ghost of her dead lover.

Scene 4: The Aborigine muses on the nature of dreams

THE ABORIGINE: Some dreams lose their way and wander over the earth, lost.

But this is a dream no one wants. It has stayed. How can we befriend this crowded, hungry and disturbed dream?

Scene 5: The second rehearsal

Ralph, Mary and Sideway await the arrival of other cast members. Maj. Ross and Capt. Campbell bring in prisoners—Caesar, Wisehammer and Liz—in chains, then release the two former but refuse to take the chains off the latter and risk her trying to escape. She is to be tried the next day. Arscott is absent because he's been sentenced to a whipping at which he fainted with 53 lashes still to go.

Ross wants to stay and watch the rehearsal, but Ralph asks him to respect the natural modesty of performers in the process of developing their roles. Ross scoffs at the word "modesty" and demonstrates his intimate knowledge of Sideway's lacerated back after two whippings on the ship coming over, of Dabby's willingness to demean herself by imitating a dog in order to beg for food, and of the intimate location of Mary's tattoo. Liz and Sideway take the bull by the horns and rehearse in spite of Ross's presence. But Ross sends Campbell to order the continuation of Arscott's punishment, and the victim's offstage cries disturb the actors and bring the rehearsal process to a standstill.

Scene 6: The science of hanging

Liz has been tried and sentenced to be hanged, and Harry Brewer has directed the colony hangman—Ketch Freeman—to prepare for the execution. Ketch is apologetic to Liz for examining and lifting her, but he needs details of weight and measurement to make sure of doing the job cleanly. When he executed young Thomas Barrett he made a mess of it, and he doesn't want to repeat his mistake with Liz, his first woman victim. "I don't want to do this," Ketch tells Liz, "I know, you're thinking in my place you wouldn't, but somebody will do it if I don't, and I'll be gentle."

In the midst of these grisly details, Harry is again possessed by the ghosts of his former victims but is lucid enough to remark, "There's no food in the colony and she steals it and gives it to Kable to run away." Ketch agrees that this was a major offense, but he promises not to shame her at the execution. Liz finally breaks her silence during these proceedings, asking Ketch, "Tell Lieutenant Clark I didn't steal the food. Tell him—afterwards. I want him to know." Harry, now totally possessed by his demons, screams and falls.

Scene 7: The meaning of plays

Dabby, Wisehammer and Arscott watch Mary and Ralph rehearse. So does the Aborigine, who comments, "Ghosts in a multitude have spilled from the dream. Who are they? A swarm of ancestors comes through the unmended cracks in the sky. But why? What do they need? If we can satisfy them, they will go back. How can we satisfy them?"

There is a mention of a will and testament in the play, which causes the actors to break off to discuss its meaning: an act of faith, a contract between lovers who are to be married.

Wisehammer tells Ralph, "I've written something. The prologue of this play won't make any sense to the convicts: 'In ancient times, when Helen's fatal charms,' and so on—I've written another one." He gives it to Ralph, who glances at it, finds it interesting and promises to look at it carefully later. They argue about a piece of business that isn't in the script but that Wisehammer wants to add to his character of Brazen. As the rehearsal continues, Ralph asks Wisehammer to play another role, Bullock, in addition to Brazen.

WISEHAMMER: What? Play two parts?

RALPH: Major Ross won't let any more prisoners off work. Some of you will have to play several parts.

WISEHAMMER: It'll confuse the audience. They'll think Brazen is Bullock and Bullock Brazen.

RALPH: Nonsense, if the audience is paying attention, they'll know that Bullock is a country boy and Brazen a captain.

WISEHAMMER: What if they aren't paying attention?

RALPH: People who can't pay attention should not go to the theater.

MARY: If you act well, they will have to pay attention.

WISEHAMMER: It will ruin my entrance as Captain Brazen.

RALPH: We have no choice, and we must turn this necessity into an advantage. You will play two very different characters and display the full range of your abilities.

WISEHAMMER: Our audience won't be that discerning.

RALPH: Their imagination will be challenged and trained. Let's start the scene . . . . .

DABBY: I think *The Recruiting Officer* is a silly play. I want to be in a play that has more interesting people in it.

MARY: I like playing Sylvia, She's bold, she breaks rules, and out of love for her captain she's not ashamed.

DABBY: She hasn't been born poor, she hasn't had to survive, and her father's a Justice of the Peace. I want to play myself.

ARSCOTT: I don't want to play myself. When I say Kite's lines I forget everything else. I forget the judge said I'm going to have to spend the rest of my natural life in this place getting beaten and working like a slave. I can forget that out there it's trees and burnt grass, spiders that kill you in four hours, and snakes. I don't have to think about what happened to Kable, I don't have to remember the things I've done, when I speak Kite's lines I don't hate any more. I'm Kite, I'm in Shrewsbury. Can we get on with the scene, Lieutenant, and stop talking?

DABBY: I want to see a play that shows life as we know it.

WISEHAMMER: A play should make you understand something new. If it tells you what you already know, you leave as ignorant as when you went in.

DABBY: Why can't we do a play about now?

WISEHAMMER: It doesn't matter when a play is set. It's better if it's set in the past, it's clearer. It's easier to understand Plume and Brazen than some of the officers we know here.

Ralph puts another scene into rehearsal, playing Plume in Kable's absence, but finds they can't go through it without Sideway, who's so upset about Liz that he hasn't showed up. Arscott is asked to try one of his major scenes. Dabby, watching him, feels that his fictional character is very much like her real one, and she doesn't see why she can't be allowed to play Kite—she feels she could easily portray a man. She leaves in a huff, as Ketch Freemen comes in. Ralph decides to rehearse one of his scenes with Mary, angering Arscott, who walks out on the rehearsal. Mary tries to rehearse the scene; but working with Ketch while remembering what he's going to do to Liz is too much for her, and, overcome with emotion, she runs off, followed by Wisehammer.

"We're not making much progress today," comments Ralph (they have been rehearsing for five months), and he goes, leaving Ketch alone and bewildered.

Scene 8: Duckling makes vows

Harry Brewer is ill, with Duckling nursing him and swearing that if he lives she will no longer give him the silent treatment but treat him tenderly. But Harry dies, leaving Duckling genuinely grieving.

Scene 9: A love scene

At night on the beach, Ralph comes upon Mary rehearsing her lines. Ralph picks up the Captain Plume role in the scene, kissing "Sylvia" (who in the play is disguised as a man) and reaching the lines, "'Will you lodge at my quarters in the meantime? You shall have part of my bed,'" adding "Sylvia. Mary," extending the play's invitation into reality.

RALPH: Will you?
    Pause.
MARY: Yes.
    They kiss.
RALPH: Don't lower your head. Sylvia wouldn't.
    She begins to undress, from the top.
I've never looked at the body of a woman before.
MARY: Your wife?
RALPH: It wasn't right to look at her. Let me see you.
MARY: Yes. Let me see you.
RALPH: Yes.
    He begins to undress himself.

Scene 10: The question of Liz

Ralph, Maj. Ross, Gov. Phillip and Judge Collins are discussing Liz's situation.

COLLINS: She refused to defend herself at the trial. She didn't say a word. This was taken as an admission of guilt, and she was condemned to be hanged. The evidence against her, however, is flimsy.

ROSS: She was seen with Kable next to the food stores. That is a fingering fact.

COLLINS: She was seen by a drunken soldier in the dark. He admitted he was drunk and that he saw her at a distance. He knew Kable was supposed to be repairing the door, and she's known to be friends with Kable and Arscott. She won't speak, she won't say where she was. That is our difficulty.

ROSS: She won't speak because she's guilty.

PHILLIP: Silence has many causes, Robbie.

RALPH: She won't speak, Your Excellency, because of the convict code of honor. She doesn't want to beg for her life.

They know that Liz spoke about this to Harry Brewer (Ketch Freeman reported to Ralph what she told him), but Liz won't confirm it and Harry, who was present when Liz spoke to Ketch, died before he could testify. Ralph is in favor of getting at the truth, and so is Gov. Phillip, but Maj. Ross argues that truth is an insignificant problem compared with the hellish situation they all find themselves in here, isolated, short on supplies, in the midst of "800 thieves, perjurers, forgers, murderers, liars, escapers, rapists, whores, coiners, in this scrub-ridden, dust-driven, thunder-bolted, savage-run, cretinous colony."

Judge Collins calls for Capt. Campbell to bring in the prisoner. Collins explains to Liz that if she doesn't speak they'll have to hang her, but if she defends herself the verdict might be overruled. Still she remains silent. Gov. Phillip urges her to have the courage to tell the truth and if necessary suffer the contempt of her fellow-convicts. Maj. Ross resents the implication that the soldiers who testified against Liz might be lying, just as he resents the portrayal of officers in the play as liars and cheats. Finally Gov. Phillip reminds Liz of the play: "Don't you want to be in it, Liz?" He urges her to speak, for the good of the play.

> *A long silence.*

LIZ: I didn't steal the food.

COLLINS: Were you there when Kable stole it?

LIZ: No. I was there before.

ROSS: And you knew he was going to steal it?

LIZ: Yes.

ROSS: Guilty. She didn't report it.

COLLINS: Failure to inform is not a hangable offense.

ROSS: Conspiracy.

COLLINS: We may need a retrial.

PHILLIP: Why wouldn't you say any of this before?

ROSS: Because she didn't have time to invent a lie.

COLLINS: Major, you are demeaning the process of the law.

PHILLIP: Why, Liz?

LIZ: Because it wouldn't have mattered.

PHILLIP: Speaking the truth?

LIZ: Speaking.

ROSS: You are taking the word of a convict against the word of a soldier—

COLLINS: A soldier who was drunk and uncertain of what he saw.

ROSS: A soldier is a soldier and has a right to respect. You will have a revolt on your hands, Governor.

PHILLIP: I'm sure I will, but let us see the play first. Liz, I hope you are good in your part.

RALPH: She will be, Your Excellency, I promise that.

LIZ: Your Excellency, I will endeavor to speak Mr. Farquhar's lines with the elegance and clarity their own worth commands.

J. Smith-Cameron as Dabby Bryant made up for her role in *Our Country's Good*'s play-within-the-play

Scene 11: Backstage

On the night of the performance, the actors are making up and putting on their costumes, as the Aborigine comments, "Look: oozing pustules on my skin, heat on my forehead. Perhaps we have been wrong all this time and this is not a dream at all." Australian natives near the camp are suffering from smallpox caught from the settlers.

Liz reassures Duckling that if Duckling forgets a line, Liz will prompt her. Sideway insists that they rehearse their bow, showing them how David Garrick used to do it. When Dabby tells them all how much she misses Devon, Wisehammer remarks, "I don't want to go back to England now. It's too small, and they don't like Jews. Here, no one has more of a right than anyone else to call you a foreigner. I want to become the first famous writer."

Sideway means to start a theater company, and Liz offers to join it. Ralph comes in, gives them a few last-minute instructions, then goes to Duckling to console her about Harry's death. "I loved him," she admits, "but now he'll never know that. I thought if he knew he would become cruel." She means to go on in the play, despite her feelings, because she remembers that Harry liked to hear her rehearse her lines.

After telling Mary how beautiful she looks, Ralph hears that Mary has dreamed of having three children. If they have a boy, Ralph informs her, they'll call him Harry and a girl Betsey Alicia.

Arscott brings in Caesar, whom he found on the beach, drunk. Caesar thinks his ancestors will be angry at him if he takes part in the play. It takes the threat of hanging for treason from Ralph and Ketch to make Caesar agree to go through with his role.

Sideway has brought each of them a pinch of salt, for luck. Wisehammer reminds Ralph of his proposed new prologue, and Ralph asks to hear it again.

WISEHAMMER:
From distant climes o'er wide-spread seas we come,
Though not with much eclat or beat of drum,
True patriots all; for be it understood,
We left our country for our country's good;
No private views disgraced our generous zeal,
What urg'd our travels was our country's weal,
And none will doubt but that our emigration
Has prov'd most useful to the British nation.
Silence.
RALPH: When Major Ross hears that, he'll have an apoplectic fit.
MARY: I think it's very good.
DABBY: So do I. And true.
SIDEWAY: But not theatrical.

RALPH: It is very good, Wisehammer, it's very well written, but it's too—too political. It will be considered provocative.

WISEHAMMER: You don't want me to say it.

RALPH: Not tonight. We have many people against us.

WISEHAMMER: I could tone it down. I could omit "We left our country for our country's good."

DABBY: That's the best line.

RALPH: It would be wrong to cut it.

WISEHAMMER: I worked so hard on it.

LIZ: It rhymes.

SIDEWAY: We'll use it in the Sideway Theater.

RALPH: You will get much praise as Brazen, Wisehammer.

WISEHAMMER: It isn't the same as writing.

RALPH: The theater is like a small republic, it requires private sacrifices for the good of the whole. That is something you should agree with, Wisehammer. *(Pause.)* And now, my actors, I want to say what a pleasure it has been to work with you. You are on your own tonight, and you must do your utmost to provide the large audience out there with a pleasurable, intelligible and memorable evening.

LIZ: We will do our best, Mr. Clark.

MARY: I love this!

RALPH: Arscott.

ARSCOTT *(to Caesar):* You walk three steps ahead of me. If you stumble once, you know what will happen to you later? Move.

RALPH: You're on.

ARSCOTT *(about to go on, then remembers):* Halberd! Halberd!

> *He is handed his halberd and goes on, preceded by Caesar beating the drum.*

"If any gentleman soldiers, or others, have a mind to serve Her Majesty, and pull down the French King; if any prentices have severe masters, any children have undutiful parents; if any servants have too little wages or any husband too much wife; let them repair to the noble Sergeant Kite at the Sign of the Raven, in this good town of Shrewsbury, and they shall receive present relief and entertainment..."

> *And to the triumphant music of Beethoven's Fifth Symphony and the sound of applause and laughter from the First Fleet audience, the first Australian performance of "The Recruiting Officer" begins. Curtain.*

THE GOOD TIMES
ARE KILLING ME

A Play in Two Acts

BY LYNDA BARRY

Cast and credits appear on pages 362-363

LYNDA BARRY was born in Richland Center, Wis. in 1956. Her father, a butcher, moved the family to Seattle, so that she was educated in Seattle schools and at Evergreen State College in Olympia, Wash., graduating in 1978 with a B.A. An artist as well as a writer, Barry is the creator of the comic strip Ernie Pook's Comeek, *which now runs in 55 newspapers. She has been a frequent contributor of cartoons to* Esquire *and even more frequently of articles of all kinds to that magazine and others, as well as to newspapers, and of commentary to National Public Radio's program* Morning Edition.

Barry's The Good Times Are Killing Me *won the Washington State Governor's Writer's Award and was selected as editor's choice on the American Library Association's book list when it appeared as its author's first novel. She adapted it into the play of the same title, first workshopped at the City Lit Theater Company in Chicago in 1989 and there honored with six Joseph Jefferson Awards. Further adapted by Barry, it was presented off off Broadway by Second Stage Theater on April 18, and after 37 performances and enthusiastic reception by both critics and public moved up to off-Broadway status May 21, becoming Barry's New York professional theater debut and first Best Play.*

Barry is now at work on a second novel, My Perfect Life, *scheduled for publication in the spring of 1992. She is single and lives in Chicago.*

Time: The mid-1960s

Place: A working class neighborhood

ACT I

Scene 1: What is music?

SYNOPSIS: We are instantly introduced to Edna Arkins, a white girl in her early teens. She addresses the audience from her front porch.

EDNA: Do you ever wonder what is music? Who invented it and what for and all that? And why just hearing a certain song can make a whole entire time of your life suddenly rise up and stick in your brain?

Scene 2: My street

Edna continues to address us, joined now by her younger sister Lucy. While waiting for their mother to return from work, Edna tells us the recent history of her street. It started off "mostly white." Edna can remember when the houses went "White, White, White, Japanese, White, White." Then one black family moved in. And a white one moved away. Then more blacks came in, more whites left. And now the street is "White, Negro, Negro, White, Negro, White." The neighborhood in general has gone that way.

Their exhausted Mom enters, late and carrying groceries. She is upset to learn from her daughters that Dad hasn't come home yet. Lucy follows Mom into the house.

Scene 3: On the street

Edna remains outside and continues to confide in us. She tells us her favorite time was "at night after dinner in the summer when all the radios were on, and the lit-up front doors were open, and you hear all the people on their front porches." As she speaks, we indeed hear music from radios, and people in their houses join in with them. Some of it is black pop music of the 1960s.

EDNA: I remember laying in the grass feeling the perfect temperature of the air and just listening. It was like the whole entire world just fell off a cliff, except for

Angela Goethals as Edna Arkins and Chandra Wilson as Bonna
Willis in *The Good Times Are Killing Me* by Lynda Barry

the sound of the voices and the beautiful sky of telephone wires and stars and the
lights of airplanes flying over.

Edna's mother and the parents of other neighborhood kids call their children
home.

Scene 4: Edna Meets Bonna

Edna now tells us she remembers the first time she saw her young black
neighbor Bonna Willis. Bonna turns to us and chimes in that she remembers the
occasion, too. It was during this after-dinner time. Bonna and her younger brother
Elvin were being called into the house by Mrs. Willis, their mother. Bonna and
Edna remember some things differently.

EDNA: She was wearing a pink dress.
BONNA: It was blue.
EDNA: And I wondered if she was my same age because there weren't any girls
my age in our neighborhood.
BONNA: I wondered about you too.
EDNA: I stood up and shouted "Excuse me, girl!" but she didn't answer me, so I
figured either she was hard of hearing or boy was she ever stuck up.

BONNA: I heard you.

MRS. WILLIS: Bonna Willis! You better get your brother back over here! If he gets hit by a car, whose fault will that be? Don't let me have to tell you twice!

Bonna and Elvin disappear into the house. At the Arkins's, Mom asks Lucy to call the store to find out why Dad is so late coming home.

Scene 5: "The Sound of Music"

To the accompaniment of the title song of *The Sound of Music*, Edna tells us of her powerful attachment to the song and how much she wanted to be Julie Andrews in the movie so she could talk back to Nazis, cheer up sad kids and make their father forget their dead mother and fall in love with her. "Me," says Edna. "Beautiful me with the British accent who can sing so beautifully that everybody knows I am God's first pick, no contest." She'd think of the song sometimes when she was trying to get to sleep, staring "at the silver spot coming through our bedroom curtains. My little sister Lucy told me one time that she used to think that street light was in reality God. I don't see how she can even stand to admit that. She's a lot different than me, and it's not just because I'm older. I could always tell the difference between God and a street light."

Scene 6: Dad's home

Finally Dad returns. Very late. He tries to charm Mom out of her unhappiness by singing romantically to her and telling her about his getting carried away and working all this time on a friend's Buick. Mom tells him she was worried. He hugs her. "Oh Sweetheart. Nothing's going to happen to me." And with more sweet words he walks her into the house.

Scene 7: "I Could Write a Book"

Now it's morning. Bonna's mother, Mrs. Willis, comes outside with laundry, happily singing "I Could Write a Book" along with the radio. As we see the dynamic of Mrs. Willis with Bonna and her young mischievous son Elvin, Edna tells us that Mrs. Willis used to sing professionally. When she married, Mr. Willis told her to quit "because it caused attraction." We also learn that Bonna misses their old home. A phone call—probably from Mr. Willis—summons the Willis family indoors. As she goes in, Bonna sees Edna looking at her. Bonna looks away abruptly and goes in.

Scene 8: Borrowing things

The focus switches to the Arkins's house and a visit from Uncle Jim, Aunt Margaret and their teenage daughter Ellen and son Steve. Aunt Margaret is on crutches from a sprained ankle and playing nobility in the face of suffering for all it's worth. The agony of her ankle won't keep her from bravely going away with her family on vacation as promised. There is friction between the families. Edna explains: "Uncle Jim is my dad's older brother. And they haven't liked each other much since we were kids, because me dad constantly wrecked things of Uncle Jim's. And took away Uncle Jim's girl friends . . . . . Aunt Margaret hated us for us owing so much money. Like it was our fault they lent it to us."

Now, over dinner, Dad wants to borrow something else: Jim's tape recorder. Jim hesitates but agrees. Suddenly Aunt Margaret has a headache. She'll wait in the car until Jim is ready to drive home. She starts to leave without the crutches, a fact which escapes nobody's attention. She returns and retrieves the crutches. Now, off to the side, Margaret and Jim quarrel. Margaret didn't want him to lend the tape recorder, but Jim didn't know how to say no. Edna is in her room eavesdropping on this when cousin Steve marches in.

STEVE (dead pan): If your dad breaks that tape recorder. That's it. I'm killing you.

EDNA: And then he said what he always says to me every time we are ever alone together.

STEVE: And if your dad and mom die, and if my dad and mom die, remember. You owe all that money to me.

Scene 9: Hey girl

Back out on the street, we see a little bit of the flirtation between Earl Stelley and Bonita, two young black teenagers, Earl calling her "Bonita banana" because of the yellow go go boots she's wearing, Bonita waving him away. Bonna, Elvin and Edna have all been watching this exchange. When Earl and Bonita leave, Edna sees Bonna and tries to strike up a conversation. "Hey girl," she says. "You live in the Mitchell's old house." Bonna suppresses an initial desire to talk with Edna, instead snapping back, "Don't call me girl. And it's not their house any more." Elvin approaches Edna, imitating Earl, but Bonna drags him away.

Scene 10: Tape recorder

Dad enters with the tape recorder he's borrowed from Uncle Jim. Mom starts chastising him for borrowing other things, but, instead of listening to what she says, Dad records it. He then encourages each member of the family to "do something into the microphone to save for the people of the future." Dad tells a bad joke. Mom recites a poem. Edna reads a report she did on a book about rodents. Lucy grabs the microphone and sings a TV commercial. Edna is disgusted. She can't imagine that the people of the future will be interested in this. But it turns out they won't get the chance. Later Uncle Jim uses that tape to record Eddie Arnold singing, erasing everything they recorded that day.

Scene 11: The console

The chief source of music in the Arkins's house is a console they keep in the kitchen. Edna remembers that Mom and Dad danced there a lot. They bought it second hand from Uncle Jim after he got promoted. Aunt Margaret chimes in, "We wanted to get rid of everything old we ever had because none of it was going to match everything new we were going to buy!"

EDNA: The console was a big tall thing. Too tall for me and Lucy to reach into without standing on a chair. And the lid had a way of suddenly falling WHAM! right onto our fingers to remind us.

MOM: You have no business playing with it in the first place.

EDNA: But it was hard not to give our plastic barnyard animals rides on the turntable sometimes.

LUCY: We all did our best to take care of the record player, but after the knobs were missing and we had to start turning it on with pliers Mom started calling it . . .

MOM: The piece of junk.

EDNA: For me the best part of the record player was the gold upholstery cloth stretched tight over the speaker which I could not resist poking a pencil into even though I know it ruined it.

   Music: Blue Hawaii hits.

The way the pencil would punch through the fabric and the sound it would make gave me such a strange perfect feeling in my pants. And listening to music with this feeling was all I ever wanted to do for the rest of my life. I remember this one time I was listening to Elvis Presley's beautiful voice singing about Hawaii. About him and me going swimming in the moonlight of Hawaii, and I was listening, listening, listening, just staring at the dust floating in the air, feeling so hypnotized, just punching the pencil in and out and in and out over and over until I suddenly noticed my mother's legs about five inches from my face.

MOM: Why do you insist on doing this? Is it to torment me? Do you do it just to torment me?

Scene 12: Elvin and Earl

Back outside now. Earl Stelley calls to Bonna to get Elvin away from him. Little Elvin's getting on his nerves, imitating everything Earl says and does. Earl leaves as Bonna takes charge of Elvin, who keeps bouncing around as kid brothers do. Edna, who has been watching, exchanges a hello with Bonna. Bonna doesn't object.

Mr. Willis returns home from work now, and we see something of his loving if overprotective relationship with Mrs. Willis. And we see a little of his friction with his wife's aunt Martha, who thinks Mrs. Willis could have married better. Mr. and Mrs. Willis, Elvin and Aunt Martha go into the Willis house, leaving Edna and Bonna alone together.

EDNA: That was the first time I had ever seen Bonna Willis close up before. The main thing I noticed was that for earrings she had little pieces of broom straws with the ends burnt stuck through her ears. I asked her way later what was the first thing she noticed about me . . .

BONNA: How much you looked like that what-me-worry guy on Mad Magazine. I'm not saying it to be cold. You can't control the first thing you notice about somebody.

Bonna is summoned for a chore by her mother. *"Lucy joins Edna on the porch. Edna puts her arms about her absentmindedly."* Lucy asks Edna, "Do you like me?" "No," says Edna in a dreamy way. "Sorry."

Scene 13: My record player

Dad comes home with a record player for Lucy and Edna to share. He tells Mom that it's something a friend was going to throw away. Edna tells us, "It turned out it used to belong to the kids of a girl friend we didn't know about yet. The one he would eventually marry." Dad has also brought along a lot of old 45 r.p.m. records. He and Mom and Lucy begin to goof and sing "Volare" together. Edna watches, then as the song "Chances Are" begins to play, she turns to us again.

EDNA: Before he gave it to us, he got the idea to spray it with a heavy coat of red enamel paint, and he painted every part including the needle and the masking tape holding the tone arm together. And he must have tried to pick it up when it was still wet because one day, a long time after he was gone, I found it sitting in the basement, and I noticed for the first time the print of part of his hand on the side. It made me think of fossils, a million years old.

Scene 14: My father

> Lucy and Dad begin to dance. Mom picks up the record player and records, exits. Edna watches.

EDNA: If you try to talk to Lucy about my father now she'll say she doesn't remember anything. But I think she is just being stubborn. I remember everything. Sometimes I remember so much that I about hate him for it. Everything was sad when he left. I think even the dogs in the street were sad. When he had days off sometimes we would play a game with him called . . .

DAD: Get lost!

EDNA: He would take us on long rides . . .

DAD: All over. In any direction!

EDNA: He bet us our allowance that we couldn't get him lost. He would turn wherever we said. . .

LUCY: Are you lost yet?

DAD: Nope!

EDNA: I have a song that automatically reminds me of him, and sometimes when I hear it by accident I imagine that he is secretly thinking of me and the song is the sign of it. Do you think it is possible that a song could be a message from someone? And I don't know why that song would remind me of him. It was just a song, a dumb song that we played all the time when things were still normal and I never even noticed that they were.

Scene 15: Ass beater

Elvin comes running onstage, Earl on his heels. Calling for Bonna, Elvin dashes into the Willis house. Bonna comes out, looking to deal with Earl for messing with her younger brother. Earl tries to laugh her off, but, even though she is smaller than he is, Bonna's fierceness gives him pause. He retreats. Edna tells us that Bonna had a reputation for threatening to beat the asses off anybody who got in her face. "That was the main topic of her conversation. Ass beating."

Bonita now arrives and asks Earl how he fared with Bonna. He insists he faced her down with a laugh. He asks Edna to confirm this. Edna doesn't contradict him at first. She walks to a "safe" place, then turns and shouts out that Bonna could beat Earl's ass any day. Earl, embarrassed in front of Bonita, blusters at Edna. Bonita mocks him and leaves. Earl trails after. Bonna has overheard this.

Scene 16: Record Player Nightclub

Lucy watches smugly as Mom tells Edna that she doesn't want her "getting mixed up with those people." Mom leaves. Lucy chimes in. Edna tells Lucy to shut up. Lucy runs to tell Mom on her. Edna grumpily retreats to the basement. Upstairs, Dad emerges carrying a bowling bag, claiming that he has to go to "an emergency game." Mom is upset that he won't stay for dinner. His explanations regarding the game don't sound quite right. He takes off, almost forgetting his bowling bag.

Lucy enters the basement, trying to carry the record player. Edna rushes to help her. They tell us of the Record Player Nightclub they created together, each claiming credit for key aspects. They hung the 152 records on separate nails hammered into the wall and put the record player in the center of the room. They were very impressed with the coolness of what they had created.

Scene 17: My genius

Edna tells us of a great idea to improve the club. In the middle of the night she sneaks down and puts a red darkroom bulb into the socket. "Boy, is Lucy ever going to be surprised. Being in the pitch dark Record Player Nightclub with only the red light on would put us in the perfect mood to listen to records, because music always sounds completely different in the dark."

Scene 18: She came over

Edna and Lucy come up with a dance using flashlights in which they "move around like we were sad lonely ghosts who loved all music." In the middle of their dance, Elvin and Bonna show up unannounced. Bonna's heard about their record player, wants to play it. The arrival of the Willis kids puts Edna into a quandary because they still had a rule of "No Negro Kids Can Come In Our House." Then Edna decides that it is O.K. because the basement wasn't inside the "real" part of their house.

The records Bonna and Elvin have brought over introduce Edna to a different sound: James Brown. One of the lyrics ("Say it loud. I'm black and I'm proud.") confuses Edna. "I had never heard of being proud about being a Negro before, so I wondered, is this a joke song or what? She also told me that Black Panthers were coming to beat Whitey's ass, and I didn't know what she was talking about." Edna tries not to betray her ignorance, though. Bonna offers to teach Edna the Tighten Up. Edna claims she already knows it. Bonna knows she doesn't and tells Elvin to demonstrate. Little Elvin dances sensationally and Edna nearly dies with envy.

Mrs. Willis's voice summons Bonna and Elvin away. Mom calls for Lucy and Edna. Edna tells Lucy not to tell Mom about Bonna and Elvin's visit. She sends Lucy up to deal with Mom.

Scene 19: My imagination

Edna turns to us and tells us that that night she imagined what it would be like to be best friends with Bonna. She imagined renaming the nightclub after the two of them, and how everybody in the neighborhood would treat her with respect or have their asses beaten off by Bonna. And she imagined being able to dance the Tighten Up so well as to do it in school with Bonna as part of the President's Council on Fitness. Mom interrupts, calling Edna upstairs.

Scene 20: Why bother?

As Edna watches unseen, Mom confronts Dad on the front porch when he returns. Dad apologizes for coming home so late. He has excuses. Work. "I thought Frosty was never going to let us leave the store." Mom replies, "I don't even know why you bother."

Scene 21: Teenagers

> We hear Steve playing "The Lonely Bull" (a popular tune of the time) offstage. Sharon and Ellen rush on. Lucy follows and Edna joins them. Sharon and Ellen listen to him for a split second and decide to tease him by singing the chorus.

ELLEN and SHARON (singing): Ahhh- ahhh- ahhh- ahhh.

STEVE (deadpan and offstage): Shut up.

EDNA: For awhile before I was old enough to babysit Lucy by myself, we'd have to walk up to my Aunt Margaret's. We hated that because she wanted us to . . .

MARGARET: Stay in the basement!

EDNA: To keep us from messing up the plastic she had . . .

MARGARET (lovingly): On her new furniture!!

EDNA: There wasn't anything to do there except sit around on their old couch in the part she called . . .

MARGARET: My future rec room!!

> Steve plays "The Saber Dance" offstage.

EDNA: We had to listen to my cousin Steve practice the trumpet. (To Steve.) Can't you learn no other songs?

STEVE *(off)*: Shut up.

> *Aunt Margaret reappears.*

MARGARET: Steven! The trash needs disposing!

STEVE: Make Ellen.

ELLEN: As if!

MARGARET: Steve Alfonse Arkins! Be my little gentleman please.

LUCY: We complained about it a lot.

> *They all cross to Edna's front porch.*

EDNA: Finally Mom fixed it so that Ellen came over and baby sat us for twenty-five cents.

ELLEN: Which was a gyp because my mom just takes the money from me to put toward my college education.

EDNA: That's when Ellen was the queen of being stuck up. A lot of times her best friend Sharon would come with her, and they would sit around our kitchen acting big and smoking the cigarettes they stole from Sharon's mom who must have had a pile of them not to notice.

SHARON: You think I would look better with your hair?

ELLEN: Oh God. You'd look wicked.

> *Ellen leans over Sharon so that her hair falls over Sharon's head. Sharon looks into a compact.*

SHARON: God. I want your hair.

EDNA: Ellen. Can I try your hair?

ELLEN and SHARON: As if!

EDNA: Ellen hated us. But I loved her.

SHARON: And Sharon.

ELLEN and SHARON: Because they were both so beautiful and developed.

EDNA: And I didn't care when they invented the game of ignoring me and Lucy. Hey, you guys.

ELLEN: Did you hear something?

SHARON: No, I didn't hear anything.

ELLEN: It must have been . . .

ELLEN and SHARON: The wind!

LUCY: Shut your lip, potato chip.

> *Ellen and Sharon crack up.*

EDNA: In a way it was better because if we didn't exist, they couldn't tell me to bug off when I sat there watching them and listening and imagining how great it would be to have their lives.

SHARON: Hey, you want to call up Brian Bano and tell him he's a spaz?

ELLEN: Yeah!

Scene 22: Pimpwalking

On the street, Edna is pleased when Bonna and Elvin say hi. They run to see what Earl is up to. He demonstrates a crazy new dance step. Bonna makes fun of it. Earl tells her to watch her mouth.

Edna and Lucy explain to us that, since none of the teens on the block had licenses to drive, after dinner they would hit the street and chase around with each other. "Some nights the older boys did a kind a dance parade where they would get in a line and start singing these things, these poems."

And now there is an extended sequence of the mostly black neighborhood boys and girls strutting around like pimps, dancing and trading rude rhymes in rhythm about the sexual habits of a mythical girl named April Arnold. (We get the idea half the kids don't know what's being talked about.) The sequence builds to a verbal duel between Bonna and Earl, Bonna making Earl retreat pretty swiftly. The boys run off, and the girls congratulate Bonna on her victory. Edna stands to the side. Bonna waves that she should join them. They're about to run off together when Mrs. Arkins and Mrs. Willis call their children to come home. Bonna and Elvin exit into the Willis house. Lucy and Edna join their mother on the porch.

Scene 23: Calling Dad

Lucy volunteers to call Dad at the store, to see if he's there. "No!" Mom explodes. Then, getting control, she says quietly, "No, honey. That's O.K." She and Lucy disappear into the house.

Scene 24: At the lake

A phone call at the Willis house. Mrs. Willis answers and cries out, "No!" and runs off. Edna is on her way to Bonna's house when she runs into Earl, who tells her that Elvin has drowned at the lake. Overwhelmed by the news, Edna hugs her mother, who tries to comfort her. Mom goes inside while Edna sits on the front porch, waiting for Bonna and her family to come home. Finally, Mom tells Edna she should come inside and go to bed. Now Mrs. Arkins looks for a sign of her husband coming home. Nothing. "Damn him," she says. She goes inside.

Scene 25: The street light

EDNA: That night I lay in bed just staring at the street light. Wondering if Bonna was doing the same thing. Staring at the same street light. Staring at it until it turned off and was finally morning.

Scene 26: "It's Not for Me to Say"

Edna awakens to learn the Dad didn't return the night before. Whatever is going on is serious, because Mom has arranged for Aunt Margaret to come and take them to stay at her place awhile. Mom leaves, and the girls wait, afraid even to turn on the TV in case that might jinx things between Mom and Dad. Finally, Aunt Margaret arrives.

MARGARET: Come on, you two. Let's go.

LUCY: Is our dad coming home?

MARGARET: Oh, now don't you worry, Lucy, everything is going to be fine. Isn't it, Edna? Tell your sister. *(Aunt Margaret winks at her. We hear "It's Not for Me to Say.")*

EDNA: I knew right then that whatever happened was really bad, because she looked at me with a look I have never seen on her face in my life. She looked . . . I don't know how else to say it . . . Friendly.

Lucy begins to cry.

MARGARET: Oh now Lucy, you'll just make it worse for your mom if you cry. Fish some Kleenex out of my purse, will you Edna honey? And there's a stick of Juicy Fruit in there, but you'll have to split it.

EDNA: The radio was on, and that was the first time I heard that song, the one I hate. Whenever I hear it, all I can think of is that very day riding in the front seat with Lucy leaning against me and the smell of Juicy Fruit making me want to throw up. How can a song do that? Be like a day whose guts you hate? You hear it, and all of a sudden everything comes hanging back in front of you, all tangled up in that music.

Ellen appears.

ELLEN: God, I feel so sorry for you guys.

MARGARET: Ellen, get the hell back inside. *(To Lucy.)* Come on honey.

Margaret and Lucy exit. Ellen remains looking at Edna, then exits.

EDNA: Ellen wasn't supposed to tell us, but it was from her I found out that the name of Dad's girl friend was Pat. And I guess he was going to be living with her now. Ellen let me sleep in her bed for the whole week we had to stay there. Sometimes it doesn't matter when your dream finally comes true, does it? She slept with her radio playing, and during the night when I couldn't sleep I would lay there and wonder if I had heard every song in the world yet.

Scene 27: Walk me

Back in the neighborhood, Bonita and Earl are practicing a dance step, when Bonna emerges from her house. Everyone on the street turns to look at her. "What are you looking at," Bonna demands. And Edna invites Bonna to join her, crossing to take her by the hand and walking her back to the Arkins's front porch. Referring to Elvin's drowning, Bonna says, "It wasn't my fault."

EDNA: Shoot. I know that. Who doesn't know that? Heck, everybody in the world knows that.

Earl and Bonita keep staring at Bonna.

BONNA: I gotta go.

EDNA: O.K.

Bonna starts to leave.

Bonna! Wait for a sec. I'll walk you.

Bonna turns. Edna steps towards Bonna as lights black out. Curtain.

ACT II

Scene 1: Best friends

One evening some time later, Edna and Bonna have become close friends. They sit on Edna's front porch singing together with the radio. We see, too, that Earl and Bonita have become closer. Together, they walk past where Edna and Bonna sit, Bonita resplendent in a dreadful wig. Hearing the girls sing, Earl howls softly.

EARL: Sound like Lassie. Don't it sound like Lassie? *(He howls again, and Bonita laughs.)*
BONNA: Nobody's talking to you.
EARL: Oooooooh, look like Lassie too. And smell.
BONNA: Shut up, fool.
BONITA: Who you calling fool? Me or my man.
BONNA: Nobody.
EARL: I know that's right.
BONITA *(to Earl):* Was somebody talking to you? *(To Bonna.)* Girl, you better watch that tacky mouth of yours.
　　　Earl and Bonita start walking away, and Bonna stands up.
BONNA: Her "man." She must mean "her boy." And see how she's trying to get stylish, too. Wearing her grandma's tired old wig. Nasty as her hair is, she need it. And you know why. Girl has hot combed herself bald headed.
EDNA *(to audience):* By the end of summer things seemed pretty much back to normal. If you can call it normal without Elvin. Or if you can call it normal over at my house. It wasn't my first pick of normal.

We see, too, that in becoming best friends with Bonna, Edna has picked up some of Ellen's behavior with Sharon. Ellen and Sharon pretended Edna wasn't there. Now Edna and Bonna pull the same "It must have been the wind" routine on Lucy.

Neither has yet stayed over at the other's house. Bonna doesn't think it would be a problem with her mom if Edna stayed over. Edna says she thinks Bonna could stay over, too, but Bonna suspects otherwise. She doesn't think Mrs. Arkins likes her, and she has a pretty good idea why.

The summer days have settled into a pattern. Whoever gets up first goes to the other's house, and they do "it didn't matter what." And at night, one would walk the other home. Then they'd turn around and walk back to the other's house. And then turn around again. Back and forth until one of their mothers lost patience and they'd have to go to their separate homes. "And I thought it was going to be like that forever," Edna tell us. "I thought we would grow up, get married to twins, and live next door to each other for the rest of our lives."

Scene 2: My disappointment

Lucy complains to Mom about how Edna treats her. Mom is otherwise occupied, getting dressed to go out. Ellen comes over to baby-sit Edna and Lucy while Mom goes to a movie with Mr. Gunderson, a man Mom knows from work. Edna doesn't understand why Mom is spending time with him. Don't they see enough of each other at work?

Sharon comes by to join Ellen. The two teen-agers start watching an episode of *Bonanza* and ignore their charges. Lucy claims the right to show the two older girls the Record Player Nightclub. Edna insists it's *her* right, shoving Lucy to make the point. Edna instantly apologizes, but it's not good enough. Lucy, very upset, shouts that she wishes everybody in the world would "just shut up!" Edna moves to the Record Player Nightclub.

EDNA: Ever since we made the Record Player Nightclub, all I could think about was wait until Ellen and Sharon see it. I knew that it would make them realize how great I was, how incredibly mod I was, and they'd automatically start begging me to be their friend and spend the night with them and hang around them and do everything with them for the rest of their lives . . . . . I imagined how when they saw it, they'd say "Oh Edna, please be our best friend forever." And I practiced how at first I'd say "Nope. No way. Serves you right for ignoring me all those times." Then after they begged me and begged me I'd finally say "Well, O.K.," and they would be so happy that we would wear matching clothes and have matching hair, and they would put make up on me like they did that one time before they became such snobs. *(Calling.)* Ellen! Sharon! Come down here! I got something to show you!

Initially Sharon and Ellen ignore her, but Edna continues to beg them. They relent and come down to the basement. At first, Sharon and Ellen pretend to admire the place, cooing over the modness of the decor and the records. Edna picks up on their sarcasm.

EDNA: That was the day I learned that it's not good enough to have a record player and a bunch of records.
SHARON: You have to have a bunch of the right records.
EDNA: And it doesn't matter if you like the records you have because there are only certain songs that are good to listen to.
SHARON: All the rest are corny.
ELLEN: Turns out all the ones you have are corny.
SHARON: So Ed, when are you going to have your Shindig Party down here?
ELLEN: We wouldn't want to miss that!
SHARON: You've got to invite us. O.K.? Promise?
SHARON and EDNA: Promise?!!!
EDNA: Oh just go shut up and flake off and get out and drop dead!

Sharon and Ellen laugh and exit singing "Volare." Lucy walks in the room and goes to the record player and puts on "Put Your Head on My Shoulder" and closes her eyes and sways by the table while listening to it.

Scene 3: Church

Mrs. Willis invites Edna and Lucy to join her husband and Bonna going to church. Going to church has become a big part of Mrs. Willis's life since Elvin's death. And she doesn't sing around the house the way she used to, and she's pulled the flowers off her hat.

Overcoming her misgivings, Mom lets Edna and Lucy go. It is a Baptist church and an eye-opening experience for the girls. The singing! The exaltation! The leaping up from the chairs! At one point, Lucy wants to leap up, too, but Edna yanks her back down. Later, Lucy eludes Edna and accepts the invitation to sway with the others in the choir.

The whole experience puzzles Edna. The congregation here are all "laughing, touching each other and giving kisses." Doing this kind of thing in Edna's church

Angela Goethals (Edna), Lauren Gaffney (Lucy), Kim Staunton (Mrs. Willis), Ellia English (Aunt Martha), Chandra Wilson (Bonna), Wendell Pierce (Mr. Willis) and John Lathan (Preacher) in the church scene of *The Good Times Are Killing Me*

would earn you a ticket to hell. But here it seems to be O.K.

Scene 4: The solution

Edna has sampled some of the black world. Now Bonna is going to have a chance to taste some of the white. The self-appointed guide is Aunt Margaret who, all fired up about racism from a TV documentary, decides to make Bonna the beneficiary of her project by inviting her along on a family camping trip. It's partially motivated out of self-interest. Aunt Margaret is afraid that if white people don't do their part and reach out, then Negroes are going to get mad, join the Black Panthers and burn down the white world. Uncle Jim would just as soon send them all to Africa. Wouldn't they be happier there? Aunt Margaret is appalled by this. She extends the invitation to the Willises.

Scene 5: Camping

Margaret has a few uncomfortable minutes with Mr. Willis. She's a little miffed that Mr. Willis insisted on meeting her before allowing his daughter to go. But this isn't said. Mr. Willis and Margaret are painfully polite with each other. Alone with Bonna, Mr. Willis asks Bonna if she really wants to go. Bonna says she does. Mr. Willis tells her to call him if she has "any trouble with that crazy woman." He kisses her goodbye, and Bonna joins Edna, Lucy, Sharon, cousins Ellen and Steve and Aunt Margaret and Uncle Jim in the station wagon. Aunt Margaret leads a family singalong of something called "The Beaver Song." After a long drive, they arrive at an acceptable campsite.

Aunt Margaret has intended this excursion to be something of a demonstration of a model of a happy white family. The white kids don't cooperate. There is constant bickering. Bonna and Edna are glad to get away together on an errand to fetch water.

BONNA: Why does your aunt keep saying do I like everything? Do I like the mountains? Do I like the fresh air? Do I like eating off a paper plate? Don't she think I never been outside before?

EDNA: My aunt is a dirty son of a bitch.

BONNA: Edna!

EDNA: I don't know how I said that. I had never said anything like that before in my life.

BONNA: Aw, your aunt isn't so bad.

Returning to the campsite, Margaret has come up with a fun family activity. She's brought along a song book, and she commands them all to run through the repertoire, which includes Stephen Foster songs like "Old Black Joe" and "Massa's in de Cold Cold Ground." Margaret reads from the book how influenced Foster was by "the music of the colored people." She asks Bonna how she's enjoying her first camping trip. Bonna tells her that it isn't her first camping trip. "I've been camping with my cousins in South Carolina about a million times." Aunt Margaret tries to contain her disappointment.

Scene 6: My singing

Despite her desires and fantasies, Edna is not much of a singer and knows it. "I've been tested," she says. This means that in school she can't be in the choir but instead is assigned to take music appreciation from a Mrs. Hosey, which in turn means singing "Go Tell Aunt Rhody" with other ungifted singers and having to suffer through assemblies when the choir gets to show off. "And after Mrs. Hosey, you get only one more chance at music," says Edna.

Scene 7: Girl Scouts

We hear a group of girls singing "Kumbiya." Edna and Bonna have joined the Girl Scouts. Though she gets pretty sick of "Kumbiya," Edna is thrilled to be one. Beyond the usual kick of the uniform and the privilege of accosting strangers to buy cookies, there's the opportunity to hang around with Joycie Mercer, the most popular girl in the troop. Joycie lives in a big house and sleeps in a canopy bed. "She was my dream," says Edna.

The troop Enda and Bonna are in is run by Mrs. Doucette, who smokes and comes up with implausible reasons why the badges the girls have given her money to order haven't arrived yet. She also has the girls get their mothers to buy meat for the camp-outs, but somehow the meat never appears during the camp-outs. Bonna and Edna are onto Mrs. Doucette's game. They don't care much for Mrs. Doucette's daughter, Theresa, either.

THERESA: Edna, Joycie Mercer wants to talk to you.

EDNA: She does?!

BONNA: Don't she got legs? Can't she come over here and tell us her own self?

THERESA: Excuse me, but I'm afraid I was talking to Edna.

EDNA: Bonna, I'll be back in one sec . . . okay? *(Bonna looks at Edna.)* Tell Joycie I'll be there in a minute.

THERESA: It's about her party.

BONNA: What party?

THERESA: It's gonna be a blast.

EDNA: Theresa! Just go tell her I'll be there in a sec.

THERESA: Okay then. *(Theresa exits with a salute.)*

BONNA: Ask your mama where that badge money at. *(To Edna.)* What party?

EDNA: Don't ask me. I don't know. *(Edna watches in the direction of Joycie Mercer.)*

BONNA: If you want to talk to Joycie Mercer so bad then just go.

EDNA: Bonna.

BONNA: I'm quitting Girl Scouts. I am.

EDNA: No, you're not.

BONNA: I am. I hate. I always hated it. I'm sick of that old Mrs. Doucette with her greasy two-colored hair. That "Kumbiya"-singing heifer. Making me wear ugly uniforms and sell nasty cookies.

EDNA: If you hate it so much, then why did you even join?

BONNA *(looks at her):* You asked me to, remember? *(Exits.)*

EDNA: Bonna! *(Edna crosses to her porch.)* Well she didn't quit Girl Scouts. Not right then, anyway. She just paid me back by acting like she hated me for around two days. Then things turned pretty much back to normal.

Scene 8: The Projects

Edna and Bonna visit Edna's cousins and return to find that Bonna's mother has been frantic with worry about her absence. Bonna's father tells Bonna of Mrs. Willis's agitation. "Look," he says firmly. "You have one responsibility. One. To help me take care of your mother. You know exactly what I'm talking about." Looking for Bonna, Mrs. Willis has searched as far as Aunt Martha's apartment in Dunbar Vista Projects. Mr. Willis tells Bonna to stay put while he phones Aunt Martha's to tell his wife that Bonna has turned up and that they will drive by to pick her up. As Mr. Willis goes inside to make the call, Bonna asks Edna to come with her. "She won't yell at me if you're there." Edna is reluctant. She doubts her mother would like her visiting that neighborhood. Bonna prevails. Mr. Willis returns, and he and the girls drive toward the projects, Edna ducking as they pass her house so her mother won't see her.

At the projects, Aunt Martha gives Bonna a bad tongue-lashing. Angrily, Bonna takes off. Edna follows. A black boy named Marcus they pass yells out at Bonna, calling her an Uncle Tom and an Oreo. Bonna is determined to beat Marcus's ass. Edna reluctantly follows her into Marcus's house. It seems Bonna and Marcus have tangled before. Marcus taunts Bonna for hanging around with a white girl. Edna feels very uncomfortable.

EDNA: I stare at the linoleum and notice that it is exactly like the linoleums at my cousin Ellen's and that makes me feel better. There are pictures of people taped everywhere on the walls, also, the most pictures of Jesus I have ever seen in one place. I want to ask him, "Does your mother collect Jesus?" but I figure he would slap me silly. To some people, "Your mother" is a swear word. I imagine what my mother would do if a voice suddenly started talking to her from out of nowhere like in a laundry commercial to tell her what I was doing.

VOICE: "Mrs. Arkins, right at this very second while you are trying to untangle that garden hose, your daughter is standing with some Negroes over inside a Negro project."

EDNA: Bonna, come on. Let's go back.

MARCUS: Ummmmm, hmmmmm and I see she tells you what to do now, too.

BONNA: Better shut your mouth, Marcus Davis, before I shut it up for you.
MARCUS: Ummm. Hmmmm.
EDNA: Bonna, let's go back. *(Bonna look at Edna to shut her up.)*

Bonna asks to have one of Marcus's cigarettes. They offer one to Edna, too, who accepts the challenge. She takes a puff and quotes a line from a TV commercial. Bonna and Marcus laugh. Edna runs. Bonna runs after her.

EDNA: Thanks a lot.
BONNA: For what?
EDNA: You know for what.
BONNA: Oh Edna, we were just playing with you.
EDNA: Oh sure. Right.

Returning to Aunt Martha's, they find that the Willis car is gone. Aunt Martha tells them that Bonna's folks got upset all over again. They'd better walk back home. The two take off. It is a tense walk for Edna. "Boys honked their horns and yelled words at us from cars."

Finally, when they get back to their neighborhood, Edna says goodbye. Bonna notes that Edna isn't walking her home, as per their usual goodbye ritual. Edna says she'll do it if Bonna wants. Bonna says she doesn't want. The two part.

When Edna returns to her home, a worried Mom wants to know where she's been. "No place," says Edna.

Scene 9: The invitation

Some time later, Theresa Doucette stops by Edna's with the party prize Edna left behind at Joycie Mercer's house. Bonna overhears this, realizes that Edna went to Joycie's party without her. Hurt, Bonna retreats to her house. After Theresa leaves, Edna tries to figure things out. Even though there was supposed to be "no such thing as the color of your skin in Girl Scouting," it did not pass unnoticed that only white girls ended up being invited to the Mercers' for Joycie's party. Mrs. Mercer insists that the choice of the guest list was her daughter's.

Edna has divided feelings. On the one hand, she's thrilled that Joycie Mercer has decided to bestow upon her the treasured gift of her acquaintance, which gift includes access to the Mercers' fancy house. On the other, Bonna continues to be angry all summer that Edna went to a party where she (Bonna) was unwelcome. "I knew she wanted to talk to me as bad as I wanted to talk to her. But whenever I saw her I got this feeling in my stomach of two magnets pointing the wrong way, and I couldn't get them to point back right."

Scene 10: Seventh Grade

Now they've moved out of grade school into junior high school, and Edna notices a change. "From the second we walked through those school doors we all automatically split into groups of who was alike. Everyone knew exactly what to do. Like someone was whispering instructions to our hands and eyes and feet and hair." Black and white kids who had been friends till now no longer talk and walk together.

EDNA: We had to constantly read books and poems about equality in English, and I wondered sometimes if Bonna thought of me in the way I thought of her when I read them. *To Kill a Mockingbird. A Raisin in the Sun.*

BONNA: "What happens to a dream deferred?" Yeah. I thought of you.

EDNA: If she didn't that's O.K. It wouldn't hurt my feelings. We had to write our own stories and poems and discuss them, and it would put us in a mood so real and true to us because we could each write the answer, and the answer was always the same.

BONNA: Love each other, love each other, love each other.

EDNA: And we really thought that things could change until the bell would ring, and we would go back into the hallway and know there is no way some puny little poem or story could change anything.

Confrontations between the kids are common. One day, Kimmy, one of Bonna's friends, slams into Edna. Edna appeals to Bonna to get Kimmy to stop harassing her. Bonna does nothing. Edna, agitated, yells at Bonna, calling her stupid. Bonna's friends tell Bonna she can't let a white girl get away with talking like that. Other kids gather around, egging the two of them on, chanting "Fight! Fight!"

Edna can't believe Bonna would hit her. Despite everything, she's sure they're still friends "inside." The crowd continues to chant. Edna pleads with Bonna, "Remember? Don't you even remember? I know your mother and father! I knew Elvin! I know your house and everything in your house! I know the color of the walls in your room." Bonna slaps Edna anyway.

BONNA: The next thing I knew we were snatched by the arms and dragged down to the office just like I had seen girls being dragged every day since I got there.

EDNA: We sat in chairs in front of the secretary waiting for the vice principal to come. I tried looking at Bonna but she kept staring straight ahead. I could see the streaks on her face.

BONNA: I heard Edna crying but I couldn't look at her.

   Bell rings.

EDNA: In the vice principal's office, we acted like we had never met. Like all it was was any black girl slapping any white girl that mouthed off to her. Something that happened every single day and would just keep on happening world without end. When he called my mother to tell her, she never knew that the girl they were talking about was Bonna. Just like Bonna's father never knew that the other girl was me.

The cast sings the song "Unclouded Day," as the lights fade. *Curtain.*

Special Citation for Verse

○○○
○○○
○○○
○○○
○○○
○○○ LA BÊTE

A Comedy of Manners in Two Acts

BY DAVID HIRSON

Cast and credits appear on pages 315-316

DAVID HIRSON was born in New York City in 1958. His father, Roger Hirson, was a writer who was soon to have Broadway and off-Broadway productions to his credit, so it didn't take his son long to begin writing plays. At Yale, from which he graduated in 1980, young Hirson was commissioned to adapt Alessandro Scarlatti's 1690 comic opera Gli Equivoci nel Sembiante *which was put on at Yale and later broadcast on public radio. He went on to get his D.Phil. degree at Magdalen College, Oxford. La Bête, produced on Broadway by Stuart Ostrow and Andrew Lloyd Webber, was Hirson's professional theater debut; it opened on Feb. 10 for 25 performances and received the John Gassner Award from the Outer Critics Circle, the Oppenheimer Award, five Tony nominations and six Drama Desk nominations, including Best Play. He is the author of essays and criticism for numerous publications and lives in Manhattan.*

Time: 1654

Place: Prince Conti's estate, Pezenas, France (Languedoc)

Specially cited for its imaginative and functional use of rhymed couplets in the modern Broadway theater, *La Bête* begins with the leader of a theatrical troupe, Elomire (an anagram of Molière), and his assistant, Bejart, intensely troubled. They have just stormed out of the dining room into its ante-chamber (where the play takes place), furious because their princely patron has demanded that their troupe take on an actor-writer, Valere, whom the Prince finds amusing, and stage his comic verse. *"This play is meant to be performed in an absurdly high comic style, at lightning speed and with rhymes and iambs stressed . . . . . The pace is frantic,"* reads a stage direction. Elomire is certainly frantic, willing to add another player at the Prince's command but adamant against it being Valere, while Bejart feels they have no choice under the circumstances. They fall on their knees and thank God for the blessing of the Prince's favor but beg His mercy in this new predicament.

At this moment, Valere—extravagantly and indefatigably mannered—enters from the dining room. His opening monologue, comprising virtually half of Act I, appears here in its entirety as in *La Bête's* playscript.

VALERE:
    Well Heaven Bless Us! *NOW* I see:
    It was a sudden burst of piety
    That took you from the table, am I right?
        Bejart opens his mouth to speak.
    I'm *so* relieved! I thought, perhaps, your flight
    Was caused by something *I* had said or done . . .
        Elomire opens his mouth to speak.
    No, don't explain. GOD BLESS US, EVERY ONE!
    I, too, am *very* pious, *most* devout:
    I cross myself . . . twelve times (or thereabout)
    Before I take my morning tea each day!
    At lunch I'm up to forty; and I'd say
    By nightfall it's . . . a staggering amount;
    But what a foolish waste of time to count!
        Sniffs and extends handkerchief.
    DEVOTION COMES TO NOTHING IF WE COME
    TO SUMMARIZE DEVOTION IN A SUM.

A slight cough, eyelids flutter, and a self-loving bow.
A tiny play on words . . . doth please you not?
I swear I made it up right on the spot!
I don't know *how* I do it, I just . . . do.
These epigrams, they . . . come to me as dew
Collects upon a budding daffodil . . .
A curse? A blessing? Call it what you will,
It's mine to bear this "genius of the word"—
DID I SAY "GENIUS?": I think it's absurd
When people call you that, don't you agree?
To us it comes like breath: so naturally.
It seems like sorcery to those below!
I cite that telling phrase from Cicero:
"DE BONUM EST" . . . "DIS BONUM EST" . . . O, shit . . .
Well, anyway, you get the gist of it.
I *do* love Latin. Does it show? It's *true!*
I'm something of a scholar in it, too.
I've read them all (yes, even *I'm* impressed)
From Cicero to . . .
        Nervous gulp.
. . . you know . . . all the rest . . .
Whom I could quote in full without abatement:
But I digress . . .

ELOMIRE *(under his breath):*
    O, what an understatement.

VALERE:
    That meal! You must have gone to great expense!
    How cruel of me to keep you in suspense!
    DID I enjoy it? *WAS* the meal a hit?
        A long pause.
    He turns them slowly, slowly on the spit.
        Thinking he has tortured them, he expounds jubilantly.
    Be at your ease, my friends! I thought the meal
    Was excellent . . . if not . . . you know . . . "ideal."
    The vinaigrette: a touch acidic, no?
    And I prefer less runny *haricots;*
        Singing this line.
    More butter in the velouté next time;
    And who, for heaven's sake, told you that lime
    Could substitute for lemon in soufflé . . .?
    These tiny points aside, please let me pay
    My compliments to all your company,
    So generous in breaking bread with me
    (Albeit bread that was a wee bit stale);

But I don't want to nit-pick. Did I fail
To mention what a charming group they *are*?
Marquise-Therese! *She's* going to be a *star*!
No, no . . . I'm *sure* of it! I *know* these things!
So . . .

> *Cupping his hands over imaginary breasts.*

. . . "gifted," and I'm told she even sings!
As for the others, well they tend to be
A little too . . .

> *With a theatrical flourish.*

. . . "theatrical" for me . . .
But, *darling*, otherwise, words can't *describe*
My deep affection for your little tribe
With whom, I do amuse myself to think,
I shall be privileged to eat and drink
(As we have done this evening) every night!
This is, of course, assuming it's all right.
Am I mistaken? Stop me if I am . . .
But it seemed obvious to this old ham
That we had an immediate rapport!
Well-educated people I adore!
It's such a joy to know there's no confusion
When I, whose speech is peppered with allusion,
Refer to facts which few but scholars know:
Arcane, pedantic things like . . .

> *Nervous gulp.*

. . . Cicero . . .
And . . . other larnèd oddments of that kind

> *Indicating himself.*

(Which, to the truly cultivated mind,
Are common knowledge more than erudition . . .)
But I digress! . . .

> *Slapping his own wrist.*

. . . O, Damn me to perdition!

> *To himself:*

"SHUT UP! SHUT UP! GIVE SOMEONE *ELSE* A CHANCE!"

> *He covers his mouth with his hands for a beat; then, unable to contain
> himself for more than a second, he plows on.*

I've had that said to me all over France . . .
All over Europe, if the truth be told:
To babble on completely uncontrolled
Is such a dreadful, *dreadful, DREADFUL* vice!
Me, I keep my sentences concise
And to the point . . . (well, nine times out of ten):

Yes, humanly, I falter now and then
And when I do, näive enthusiasm
Incites a sort of logorrheic spasm:
A flood! I mean I don't come up for air!
And even though such episodes are rare
I babble on . . . you can't *imagine* how . . .
(My God! I'm almost doing it right now!)
NO, NO! I'M ONLY JOKING! NOT TO FEAR!
In fact, I'm far *more* guilty, so I hear,
Of smugly showing that "My lips are sealed . . ."
When *I'm* the leading expert in the field!
Of haughtily refusing to debate
When I could easily pontificate!
Instead, I turn away with icy mien
And look . . . intimidatingly serene:
As if—you know—the wisdom of the ages
Were silently inscribed upon the pages
Of some majestic tablet in my mind.
But I lay claim to nothing of the kind!
It's others who surround me with this lore;
Myself, I know I'm just a troubadour
With very few accomplishments to boast . . .
But, then, I'm more self-critical than most.
You think me *too* self-critical?! Alack,
Ten thousand *more* have launched the same attack!
        Weighing the gem.
That's awfully good: ". . . have launched the same attack!"
"Ten thousand *more* have launched the same attack!"
        With an oratorical flourish.
"YOU THINK ME TOO SELF-CRITICAL?! ALACK,
TEN THOUSAND *MORE* HAVE LAUNCHED THE SAME ATTACK!"
        The gem is priceless! Thunderstruck.
That's VERY close to genius, don't you think?
If only . . .
        Searching the room with his eyes.
. . . YES! You *HAVE* a quill and ink!
        Rushes to them.
I *would* be very grateful . . . may I please?
No time to lose when lightning strikes the trees!
What did I say again? How did it go?
        As he thinks, a rolling hand gesture to Elomire and Bejart.
(Keep talking . . . I'm still listening, you know:
This won't take me a second.) Yes, that's right!
        Scribbling it down.

"Ten thousand more . . . " O, what a pure delight!
One must act quickly on one's inspirations
That they're preserved for future generations;
Behaving otherwise, it seems to me,
Ignores the grave responsibility
Imposed on us (for it's not ours to choose)
By . . . what? . . .

    Forms inverted commas with fingers.
. . . "the lyric gift" . . . "the tragic muse" . . .
I translate rudely from the words in Greek;
But any tongue sounds coarse when used to speak
Of something so ineffable and high.
Believe me, greater scriveners than I . . .
(All right, not "greater," "different": is that fair?)
Have wracked their brains and torn out all their hair
In vain pursuit of some linguistic sign
By which mankind might utter the divine.
But what?—"afflatus"? "talent"?—they're too crude,
And I'm a stickler for exactitude
Who chafes at clumsy, earth-bound turns of phrase.
True eloquence rings out like godly praise:
There's no mistaking it, it just takes wing.
And, frankly, my own phrase, "THE WONDROUS *THING*,"
Seems loftiest . . . more lofty than the Greek!
O! HOW DISGRACEFUL! SLAP ME ON THE CHEEK!
WHAT HUBRIS! WHAT VULGARITY! WHAT NERVE!
NO, SLAP ME! SLAP ME! THAT'S WHAT I DESERVE!
What gall that *I*, the commonest of sods,
Presume to speak more finely than the gods!
Of *course* it may be true, that's not the *point*!
What's ugly is my choosing to anoint
Myself instead of giving you the chance.
No doubt you both must look at me askance
For such a gross, conceited indiscretion:
I pray it won't affect your good impression.
I'm so relieved to get *that* off my chest!
Now that we've put that nagging point to rest
I shall return to my initial theme,
Which is, in short, in fact, to wit, I deem
By way of introduction, SILENCE ALL:

    A pause. Then, with fatuous self-ridicule.
I HAVEN'T GOT A CLUE! BLANK AS A WALL!
NO, *REALLY*, I'M QUITE SENILE! IT'S NO JOKE!
MY HEAD IS LIKE AN EGG WITHOUT A YOKE!

AND DON'T THINK THIS IS JUST A WAY OF STALLING . . .
MY MIND HAS *BUCKLED*—ISN'T THAT *APPALLING?*
THERE'S NOTHING BUT A SPACE BETWEEN MY EARS!
    Change of tone.
One time I had amnesia in Algiers,

Tom McGowan as Valere in David Hirson's *La Bête*

Where everyone is *black* who isn't *white*!
(But that's another tale . . .
    With a wink.
. . . some other night)
Suffice to say I lost a whole December . . .
Or was it August? . . . Whoops, I don't remember!
You see how absent-minded I can get!?
    Acting both parts.
"WHEN DID YOU HAVE AMNESIA?" "I FORGET!"
    He laughs, thrilled.
Is that not comic genius? I must use it!
I'd better write it down before I lose it!
What did I say . . . again . . . about forgetting . . . ?
O CHRIST! I've just FORGOTTEN! How UPSETTING!
    Shaking his fist at the sky.
COME BACK! COME BACK! YOU TANTALIZING GEM!
YOU TEASE! YOU BITCH! YOU FICKLE APOTHEGM!
I GAVE YOU LIFE, AND NOW YOU FLY FROM ME!!
    Apologetically.
This happens with annoying frequency.
It leads me to exclaim and caterwaul!
Well! Now you've *really* seen me, *warts and all* . . .
    Suddenly remembering.
ALGERIAN AMNESIA! . . .
    Disappointed.
. . . no, that's wrong;
Oh, never mind. More gems will come along;
They always do. Now *where* was I? . . . Ah, yes:
You've seen me in a state of stark undress,
My warts exposed, my manner slightly odd:
Well, what would you prefer? Some cheap facade
Of blemish-less perfection? Not from ME!
    With a dismissive flick of the wrist.
GO ELSEWHERE, YE WHO SEEK DISHONESTY;
MY LIFE IS TRUTH, AND TRUTH MY GREATEST PASSION!
    Dawning, a revelation.
Good heavens, both of you are looking . . . ashen!
I've been *too* honest, haven't I? But *when*?
WHY CAN'T I LEARN RESTRAINT LIKE OTHER MEN
INSTEAD OF SPILLING EVERYTHING AT ONCE?
    Realizing.
THE VINAIGRETTE! OF COURSE! I'M SUCH A DUNCE!
HOW COULD I? Please accept my deep regret!
    Putting on his best face.

Look, I . . . *enjoy* . . . acidic . . . vinaigrette . . .
It really makes me . . .
>   *Exploding.*

. . . GAG!!! . . . O!!! THERE, YOU SEE!
I CANNOT LIE! *DAMN* MY INTEGRITY!
I *want* to spare your feelings, yes I do;
But that means saying things that aren't true,
And of my meagre talents, that's not one.
You see, I find that dwelling in the sun
Of honest criticism brings more joy
Than rotting in the darkness of some coy
And sycophantic coterie of slaves.
God! Eloquence comes over me in waves!
Did you hear *that* one? We *all* raised our brows . . .
Permit me . . . just the . . . tiniest of bows.
>   *He bows.*

I thank you very much, you're far too kind;
As Cicero has famously opined,
"To hear one's peers applaud," . . . no! that's not it!
You know the one . . . the *famous* one . . .
>   *Exasperated*

. . . O, shit!
THE . . . ONE ABOUT . . . THE NOBLEMEN . . . COMPETING . . .
>   *After a desperate pause.*

Well it's so famous it's not worth repeating.
The point is, when a man whom I revere
As highly as the famous Elomire
>   *Bows to him.*

Should greet my stabs at wit with such approval,
I faint . . .
>   *He slumps into a chair.*

. . . go fetch a cart for my removal!
It's true. No, absolutely, I'm not acting:
The lights grow dim, my pupils are contracting,
My knees go wobbly and my knuckles white,
I'm fading out. Goodnight, sweet world, goodnight . . .
>   *Pause.*

I'm totally unconscious now, I swear.
CAN ANYBODY HEAR ME? ARE YOU THERE?
Perhaps you think I'm being too dramatic;
But, really, I just droop when I'm ecstatic.
>   *Snaps wide awake.*

What *causes* that? Do either of you know?
A mystic in Gibraltar said I'm low

In some peculiar energy which lies
(For Leos, Capricorns, and Geminis)
Astride the cusp of Saturn's largest moon.
Well, *fine.* But does that tell me *why* I swoon?
Of course it doesn't! What a lot of bunk!
Believe in that stuff and you're really sunk!
Thank God our age has banished superstitions!
(Except for things like sprites and premonitions
Which I think almost certainly are true;
And voodoo dolls and fetishism, too,
Seem eminently credible to me—
And tarot cards and numerology
And cabalistic rituals and such . . .)
But that *astrology!* Now there's a *crutch*
That's used by *fools* with *half* a brain, or *none* . . .
    Slaps his forehead, and is struck by a vision.
WELL, SPEAK OF VISIONS! SOFT! I'M HAVING ONE!
    He describes the vision, eyes half closed.
We're standing in a public square in Ghent
(I think it's Ghent. It looks like Ghent . . . . . It's *Ghent.*)
A scarlet banner reads: "A Great Event:
AUGUSTE VALERE and ELOMIRE Present
Their Brilliant Spectacle Hailed All Through France . . ."
(And then the title:) "ROMAN . . .", no, "ROMANCE
OF . . ."
    Trying to make it out.
". . . SOMETHING . . . SOMETHING. . ." Then: "The Town of Ghent."
    Impatiently triumphant.
(I . . . *told* you it was Ghent). Then there's a tent
Around which throngs the very cream of Flanders!
    Pauses to savor it.
A rousing vision (though it almost panders—
By promising *such* glory—to my dream
That like two cloths sewn neatly at the seam
Our talents might, someday, this world enfold.)
A fancy, merely? Or a truth foretold?
Won't someone say which of the two he thinks it?
No, no. Don't answer: that would only jinx it,
And fate's a cranky governess gone gray
(I coined that phrase in Zurich, by the way,
When I was EIGHT YEARS OLD! YES, ONLY *EIGHT!*
Precocious? *Try* PHENOMENAL! *Try* GREAT!
The envy I provoked just knew no ends . . .
    Rubbing his hands together.

Imagine how despised I was by friends!
My tutor fell in love with me of course;
He thought my every word a *tour-de-force!*
I pitied him for doting on me so,
But, then, I *was* a . . . *strapping* lad, you know. . .
Don't look at me as if I led him on!
> *With increasing vehemence, obviously reliving some past tribunal.*
You'd blame a *child* before you'd blame a *don*!!??
I ONLY DID WHAT I WAS TOLD TO DO!!
> *Full abreaction.*
LIES! I NEVER JUMPED HIM! THAT'S NOT TRUE!
> *Quickly regaining himself.*
Good Heavens! Suddenly it all came back!
So sorry . . . seems I wandered off the track . . .)
Um . . . FATE! . . . that's right . . . a governess gone gray:
She guides our every movement, and I'd say
Her stewardship goes well beyond the grave;
But if all things are fated, why be brave . . . ?
Or noble? Or industrious? Or fair?
> *Schoolmasterish pause, "Do I see hands?"*
Is that all you can do? Just blankly stare?
Don't tell me this has *never* crossed your mind!
If not, you've waltzed through life completely blind!
Such questions are essential, don't you see?
A solid grounding in philosophy
Is vital to a proper education!
It never entered my imagination
That you could lack this bare necessity . . .
(The things I just *assume!* Well, foolish me!)
At risk of sounding pompous or uncouth,
I'd like to list some volumes from my youth
Which might flesh out the . . .
> *Expressing this as if it were the perfect metaphor, unconscious of the contradiciton.*
. . . bald spots in your learning.
They've made *my* brain more subtle and discerning,
Those great Moroccan-bound and gold-tooled classics,
Which we—the prefects—in our flowing cassocks
Had tucked beneath our arms . . .
> *Bringing fingers to nose.*
. . . I smell them, still!
Indulge me for a moment, if you will.
I recommend you read . . . no, I insist . . .
An author whom, *remarkably*, you've missed

Since he's the cornerstone of ancient thought
(And—if he's not already—*should* be taught
To every child in every French lycée:)
His name, of course, is . . . wait, it *starts* with "A" . . .
A *very* famous name, don't help me out;
I *know* it's "A"; it's "A" without a doubt.
It starts with "A." It's "A" . . .
> *Slight pause.*
. . . Or *maybe* "D."
> *Banishing the ambiguity.*
No, "A." It's "A." I'm sure it's "A" . . .
> *Another ambiguity.*
. . . Or "P."
It *could* be "P" . . .
> *Slight pause.*
. . . Or "M" . . .
> *Now he's got it!*
. . . IT'S "M!" IT'S "*M!!!*"
> *Crestfallen.*
O, never mind. It could be all of them.
Well, this is terrible; I'm just appalled.
My God! He wrote the famous . . . WHAT'S-IT-CALLED,
COME ON! Don't leave me hanging on a limb!
You're acting like you've never heard of him,
And *everybody* has. He's world renowned!
His writings turned philosophy around
By altering the then-prevailing view—
That what is real is really falsely true—
To what is true is really falsely real . . .
> *A perplexed squint; then, resuming.*
Well, *either* way, it's BRILLIANT! Don't you feel?
And I'm not saying I don't see the *holes*;
Still, it's a stunning glimpse into our souls
No matter *how* you slice it, Q.E.D.
(He won a prize for it . . . deservedly.)
But who remembers prizes? It's the *FAME!*
The names of brilliant men like . . . what's his name. . .
Can never be forgotten: *that*'s the PRIZE!
Such men live on when everybody dies!
They *laugh* at famine, pestilence and drought:
And isn't that what life is all about?
> *Deep breath, as a signal of summation.*
In any case, we've really talked a streak!
Aren't you exhauted? Me? I'm feeling WEAK!!

We've hardly met, and yet you're like my brother
     Playfully sparring.
The way we banter and play off each other.
We've chatted, chortled, changed our points of view,
We've laughed a little, cried a little, too,
We've had some hills, some valleys and plateaus,
We've traded secrets, quipped in cryptic prose,
We've dropped our guards, we've learned to give a damn!
We've proudly cried, "Yes! This is who I am!"
We've said it all, and then: . . . found more to say;
In short, we've, quote, "just talked the night away."
And surely that's a sign, at least to me,
That this—our partnership—was *meant* to be!
For though we're strangers (in a narrow sense),
In several ways more striking and intense—
Our gift for words, our love of the sublime—
We've known each other since the dawn of time!
     Weighing the gem.
O, *very* pretty: ". . . since the dawn of time!"
     With an oratorical flourish.
"WE'VE KNOWN EACH OTHER SINCE THE DAWN OF TIME!"
     Concluding, slapping hands together.
Well, good! That's all I really planned to *say,*
Except to thank you for a fine soirée
     Treading on egg-shells, as if he's saying it for the first time.
Spoiled only by acidic vinaigrette,
     Hearing a bell.
But then I've said that . . . more than once, I'll bet!
My head is in the clouds: pay no attention!
It's off in some etherial dimension
Where worldly thoughts not instantly deleted
Are roundly and mechanically repeated
As if to pacify the earth below.
How galling it must be for you to know
That even as we speak, within my mind
I might be off in some place more refined—
That even though I'm present by convention,
You may not really have my full attention . . .
I don't mean *you specifically,* dear friend!
Good Heavens! Would I dare to condescend
To someone as illustrious as you!?
I mean, of course, the *common* people who
Would stoop to kiss my hem they so adore me:
Forgive them, Lord! They know not how they bore me

With idle chatter of their simple ways!
I'm sorry, but my eyes begin to glaze
And it's a chore to keep myself awake
When someone's telling me about a rake
Or if his soil will yield a healthy grape.
I smile and nod, but silently escape
To knowledgable regions in my dome
More crowded than a Roman Hippodrome!
I have, for instance (and it's not a fluke)
Verbatim recall of the Pentateuch!
Incredible? It's *true!* Just watch and see:
From Genesis to Deuteronomy
I now recite the Scriptures, LEARNED BY HEART!!:
"*IN THE BEGINNING*" . . .
> *Squinting, trying to remember more.*
. . . yes, well that's the start;
> *Moving right along.*
It goes on just like that till Moses dies.
A superhuman task to memorize?
Not really. It's so *good*, it rather *stuck* . . .
> *To himself.*
But I digress! SHUT UP YOU STUPID CLUCK,
AND LET *THESE* GENTLE PEOPLE TALK A MITE!
> *Dramatically extending handkerchief.*
Look, gag me with this handkerchief, all right?
I know that sounds extreme, and I'm a stranger,
But trust me: you are in the gravest danger!
For my digressions (left unchecked) can reach
The vast proportions of a major speech;
And you have no *idea* how close I am
To just that sort of frantic dithyramb!
So why not spare yourselves a living hell
And gag me! . . .
> *Valere touches the handkerchief to his mouth, snapping it away long*
> *enough to finish the line; he continues to do so, the handkerchief*
> *hovering.*
. . . GAG ME! TIE ME UP, AS WELL!
RESTRAIN ME! DISCIPLINE ME! HOLD ME BACK!
HUMILIATE ME! GIVE THE WHIP A CRACK!
DISGRACE ME: MAKE ME BARK AND WEAR A DRESS
AND LICK THE FILTHY FLOOR WHEN I DIGRESS!
But in the meantime, gagged I *should* remain:
It's better that way, no? It's such a sane
And healthy way to curb my domination.

I find it a *complete* abomination
(No matter how distinguished one might be)
When every word is "ME ME ME ME ME."
ME, I'm far too interested in others;
And frankly, friends, were I to have my "druthers"
I'd utter not a peep for weeks untold,
Preferring to . . . absorb the manifold
Of human speech: the "babel" of the masses.
Just stop and *listen* to the lower classes!
You'll have an education when you're done
That rivals twenty years at the Sorbonne!
For in their mindless grunts, the bourgeoisie
Express what I call "wise stupidity."
But no one listens anymore, I fear,
And when I die, so too will disappear
That subtle art, whose practice now grows faint.
And I'm not saying I'm some stained-glass saint
Who *always* listens. Always? No, indeed!
My God! I'm human! Cut me and I bleed!
It's simply that, as far as mortals go,
I'm sensitive (and some say too much so)
To any nuance in a conversation
Which *might, PERHAPS*, suggest my domination.
Thus, in mid-sentence often I just cease . . .
(Despite the countless times I've held my peace
When, in the end, I might as well have chattered
Since only *I* said anything that mattered!
I know that sounds repulsive, but it's true.)
The point is, this is something that I do
Against all logic; so don't be distraught
If, in the middle of a brilliant thought,
I stop like this . . .

     Freeze; continues.

. . . depriving you of more;
Or if, commanding reverence from the floor
For awesome skills debating pro *or* con,
I simply stop like this . . .

     Freeze; continues.

. . . and don't go on!
A trifle strange, *n'est-ce pas?* But, if you please,
Ask any of my many devotees:
They'll tell you that this quirk (at first appearing)
In time becomes . . .

     Freeze; continues.

... incredibly endearing!
> *Guffaw of self-delight.*

To *me* it seems *obnoxious*, heaven knows;
But most say it's a charming trait that grows
More sweet with each encounter! TELL ME WHY!
I just don't see it . . . but: then who am I?
At any rate, THE GAG! OF COURSE! Let me:
Observe with what profound simplicity
It does the job. I think you'll be surprised.
VOILA! . . .
> *He stuffs the gag into his mouth, then continues, half-audibly.*

. . . Now isn't this more civilized!
I'm silenced and I think we're *all* relieved!
We've nipped me in the bud, and thus retrieved
The limelight for our precious Elomire.
Speak on, my friend! This player longs to hear
If in posterity you'll deign to share
Your splendid name with one AUGUSTE VALERE!
Please answer lest I talk you both to death:
> *Removes the gag.*

I wait on your reply with bated breath.
> *He stuffs the gag back into his mouth, assumes a theatrical pose and: blackout.*

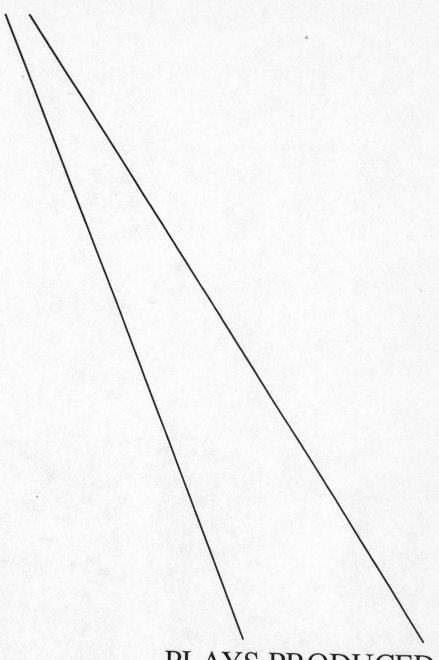

PLAYS PRODUCED
IN NEW YORK

PLAYS PRODUCED ON BROADWAY

Figures in parentheses following a play's title give number of performances. These figures are acquired directly from the production offices and do not include previews or extra non-profit performances. In the case of a transfer, the off-Broadway run is noted but not added to the figure in parentheses.

Plays marked with an asterisk (*) were still in a projected run June 1, 1991. Their number of performances is figured through May 31, 1991.

In a listing of a show's numbers—dances, sketches, musical scenes, etc.—the titles of songs are identified wherever possible by their appearance in quotation marks (").

HOLDOVERS FROM PREVIOUS SEASONS

Plays which were running on June 1, 1991 are listed below. More detailed information about them appears in previous *Best Plays* volumes of appropriate years. Important cast changes since opening night are recorded in the Cast Replacements section of this volume.

*Cats (3,610). Musical based on *Old Possum's Book of Practical Cats* by T.S. Eliot; music by Andrew Lloyd Webber; additional lyrics by Trevor Nunn and Richard Stilgoe. Opened October 7, 1982.

*Les Misérables (1,696). Musical based on the novel by Victor Hugo; book by Alain Boublil and Claude-Michel Schönberg; music by Claude-Michel Schönberg; lyrics by Herbert Kretzmer; original French text by Alain Boublil and Jean-Marc Natel; additional material by James Fenton. Opened March 12, 1987.

*The Phantom of the Opera (1,398). Musical adapted from the novel by Gaston Leroux; book by Richard Stilgoe and Andrew Lloyd Webber; music by Andrew Lloyd Webber; lyrics by Charles Hart; additional lyrics by Richard Stilgoe. Opened January 26, 1988.

Black and Blue (824). Musical revue with musical numbers by various authors. Opened January 26, 1989. (Closed January 20, 1991)

Jerome Robbins' Broadway (634). Musical dance revue conceived, choreographed and directed by Jerome Robbins; music and lyrics by various authors. Opened February 26, 1989. (Closed September 1, 1990)

The Heidi Chronicles (621). Transfer from off Broadway of the play by Wendy Wasserstein. Opened December 11, 1988 off Broadway where it played 81 performances through February 19, 1989; transferred to Broadway March 9, 1989. (Closed September 1, 1990)

Meet Me in St. Louis (253). Musical based on *The Kensington Stories* by Sally Benson and the M-G-M motion picture *Meet Me in St. Louis*; book by Hugh Wheeler; songs by Hugh Martin and Ralph Blane. Opened November 2, 1989. (Closed June 10, 1990)

*Grand Hotel (647). Musical (subtitled *The Musical*) based on Vicki Baum's *Grand Hotel*; book by Luther Davis; songs by Robert Wright and George Forrest; additional music and lyrics by Maury Yeston. Opened November 12, 1989.

A Few Good Men (497). By Aaron Sorkin. Opened November 15, 1989. (Closed January 26, 1991)

*Gypsy (477). Revival of the musical suggested by the memoirs of Gypsy Rose Lee; book by Arthur Laurents; music by Jule Styne; lyrics by Stephen Sondheim; original production directed and choreographed by Jerome Robbins. Opened November 16, 1989. (Closed January 6, 1991) Reopened in a return engagement April 28, 1991; see its entry in the Plays Produced on Broadway section of this volume.

*City of Angels (611). Musical with book by Larry Gelbart; music by Cy Coleman; lyrics by David Zippel. Opened December 11, 1989.

Tru (295). By Jay Presson Allen; adapted from the works of Truman Capote. Opened December 14, 1989. (Closed September 1, 1990)

Cat on a Hot Tin Roof (149). Revival of the play by Tennessee Williams. Opened March 21, 1990. (Closed August 1, 1990)

The Grapes of Wrath (188). Adapted by Frank Galati from the novel by John Steinbeck. Opened March 22, 1990. (Closed September 2, 1990)

Lettice & Lovage (284). By Peter Shaffer. Opened March 25, 1990. (Closed December 23, 1990)

Aspects of Love (377). Musical with book by Andrew Lloyd Webber, adapted from the novel by David Garnett; music by Andrew Lloyd Webber; lyrics by Don Black and Charles Hart. Opened April 8, 1990. (Closed March 2, 1991)

The Piano Lesson (329). By August Wilson. Opened April 16, 1990. (Closed January 27, 1991)

Accomplice (52). By Rupert Holmes. Opened April 26, 1990. (Closed June 10, 1990)

Prelude to a Kiss (440). By Craig Lucas. Opened off Broadway March 14, 1990 where it played 33 performances. (Closed April 19, 1990) Transferred to Broadway May 1, 1990. (Closed May 19, 1991)

Some Americans Abroad (62). By Richard Nelson. Opened May 2, 1990. (Closed June 17, 1990)

Zoya's Apartment (45). By Mikhail Bulgakov; translated by Nicholas Saunders and Frank Dwyer. Opened May 10, 1990. (Closed June 17, 1990)

The Cemetery Club (56). By Ivan Menchell. Opened May 15, 1990. (Closed July 1, 1990)

PLAYS PRODUCED JUNE 1, 1990-MAY 31, 1991

Stand-Up Tragedy (13). By Bill Cain. Produced by Charles B. Moss Jr., Brent Peek and Donald Taffner in the Center Theater Group/Mark Taper Forum, Gordon Davidson artistic director, and Hartford Stage Company, Mark Lamos artistic director, production at the Criterion Center Stage Right. Opened October 4, 1990. (Closed October 16, 1990)

Marco Ruiz	Anthony Barrile	Freddy	Robert Barry Fleming
Lee Cortez	Marcus Chong	Burke Kendall	Dan Gerrity
Father Ed Larkin	Charles Cioffi	Carlos Cruz	Darrin DeWitt Henson
Tom Griffin	Jack Coleman	Henry Rodriguez	Ray Oriel
Mitchell James	John C. Cooke		

Standbys: Messrs. Cioffi, Coleman, Cooke, Gerrity—Christopher Cass; Messrs. Chong, Barrile—Robert Barry Fleming; Mr. Oriel—Darrin DeWitt Henson; Messrs. Henson, Fleming—Marc Joseph.

Directed by Ron Link; scenery, Yael Pardess; costumes, Carol Brolaski; lighting, Michael Gilliam; sound, Jon Gottlieb; original music, Craig Sibley; rap choreography, Charles Randolph-Wright; production stage manager, Franklin Keysar; stage manager, Ruth E. Sternberg; press, Bill Evans & Associates, Jim Randolph.

Time: 1980s. Place: A small Catholic school for Hispanic boys on New York's Lower East Side. Act I: First semester. Act II: Second semester.

Dedicated teacher tries to rescue a gifted student from the consequences of urban poverty and prejudices. Previously produced in regional theater in Los Angeles, Hartford and the Marines Theater in San Francisco.

Circle in the Square Theater. 39th anniversary schedule of three programs. **The Miser** (93). Revival of the play by Molière; translation by John Wood. Opened October 11, 1990. (Closed December 30, 1990) **Taking Steps** (78). By Alan Aykbourn. Opened February 20, 1991. (Closed April 28, 1991) And *Getting Married*, revival of the play by George Bernard Shaw, scheduled to open 6/27/91. Produced by Circle in the Square Theater, Theodore Mann artistic director, Paul Libin producing director, at Circle in the Square Theater.

THE MISER

Dame Claude	Jennifer Roblin	Frosine	Carole Shelley
Valere	Christian Baskous	Maitre Jacques	John Christopher Jones
Elise	Mia Dillon	Brindavoine	Willis Sparks
Cleante	Thomas Gibson	La Merluche	Joseph Jamrog
Harpagon	Philip Bosco	Marianne	Tracy Sallows
La Fleche	Adam Redfield	Police Officer	Tom Brennan
Maitre Simon;		Anselme	John MacKay
Officer's Assistant	Bill Buell		

Understudies: Mr. Bosco—John MacKay; Misses Dillon, Sallows—Jennifer Roblin; Messrs. Baskous, Gibson—Willis Sparks; Mr. Redfield—Bill Buell; Messrs. MacKay, Brennan—Joseph Jamrog; Messrs. Sparks, Jamrog, Buell—John Tyrell; Misses Shelley, Roblin—Lucy Martin.

Directed by Stephen Porter; scenery, James Morgan; costumes, Gail Brassard; lighting, Mary Jo Dondlinger; production stage manager, William Hare; press, Merle Debuskey, Susan Chicoine.

Time: 1668. Place: Harpagon's house in Paris. The play was presented in two parts.

The last major New York revival of *The Miser* was a Broadway production by Repertory Theater of Lincoln Center 5/8/69 for 27 performances.

TAKING STEPS

Elizabeth	Jane Summerhays	Roland	Christopher Benjamin
Mark	Jonathan Hogan	Leslie Bainbridge	Bill Buell
Tristram	Spike McClure	Kitty	Pippa Pearthree

Directed by Alan Strachan; scenery, James Morgan; costumes, Gail Brassard; lighting, Mary Jo Dondlinger; production stage manager, William Hare.

The play was presented in two parts.

Elaborate farcical structure of family relationships and attitudes, set in a home which happens to be a former brothel and is haunted. A foreign play previously produced in England in 1979, in Scarborough and elsewhere.

*Jackie Mason: Brand New (195). One-man show created, written and performed by Jackie Mason. Produced by Old Friends Group, Jyll Rosenfeld executive producer, at the Neil Simon Theater. Opened October 17, 1990.

Design and lighting, Neil Peter Jampolis; sound, Bruce Cameron; production stage manager, Don Myers; press, Zarem, Inc., Robert M. Zarem, Jason Weinberg.

Standup comedy treatment of various subjects as per Jackie Mason's recent previous Broadway appearances 12/22/86 for 367 performances and 5/2/88 for 203 performances.

*Once on This Island (258). Transfer from off Broadway of the musical based on the novel *My Love, My Love* by Rosa Guy; book and lyrics by Lynn Ahrens; music by Stephen Flaherty. Produced by The Shubert Organization, Capital Cities/ABC Inc., Suntory International Corp. and James Walsh in association with Playwrights Horizons at the Booth Theater. Opened October 18, 1990.

Daniel	Jerry Dixon	Armand	Gerry McIntyre
Erzulie	Andrea Frierson	Agwe	Milton Craig Nealy
Mama Euralie	Sheila Gibbs	Andrea	Nikki Rene
Ti Moune	La Chanze	Papa Ge	Eric Riley
Asaka	Kecia Lewis-Evans	Tonton Julian	Ellis E. Williams
Little Ti Moune	Afi McClendon		

Understudies: Misses Gibbs, Lewis-Evans, Frierson—Fuschia Walker; Misses La Chanze, Rene—PaSean Wilson; Miss McClendon—Desiree Scott; Messrs. Dixon, McIntyre, Williams, Nealy—Keith Tyrone; Mr. Riley—Gerry McIntyre.

Musicians: Steve Marzullo conductor, keyboards, piano; Garth Roberts assistant conductor, keyboards; Tony Conniff bass; Norbert Goldberg percussion; Richard Prior woodwinds.

Directed and choreographed by Graciela Daniele; musical direction, Steve Marzullo; scenery, Loy Arcenas; costumes, Judy Dearing; lighting, Allen Lee Hughes; sound, Scott Lehrer; orchestrations, Michael Starobin; associate choreographer, Willie Rosario; production stage manager, Leslie Loeb; stage manager, Fred Tyson; press, Philip Rinaldi, Tim Ray.

Time: Night, in a storm. Place: An island in the French Antilles. The play was performed without intermission.

Group of people on a Caribbean island pass the time during a storm by telling (and acting out) a fairy tale about gods, "grands hommes" and ordinary folk involved in the adventures of a peasant waif who falls in love with an aristocrat. Previously produced by Playwrights Horizons off Broadway 5/6/90 for 24 performances and named a Best Play of 1989-90.

The list of musical numbers in *Once on This Island* appears on page 415 of *The Best Plays of 1989-90*.

Lillias White replaced Kecia Lewis-Evans 1/8/91.

Oh, Kay! (77). Revival of the musical with book by Guy Bolton and P.G. Wodehouse; music by George Gershwin; lyrics by Ira Gershwin; adapted by James Racheff; concept by Dan Siretta. Produced by David Merrick at the Richard Rodgers Theater. Opened November 1, 1990. (Closed January 5, 1991; see note)

Billy Lyles . . . . Gregg Burge
Dolly Greene . . . . Kyme
Duke. . . . . Stanley Wayne Mathis
Nick; Sam . . . . David Preston Sharp
Joe . . . . Fracaswell Hyman
Waiter; Jake . . . . Frantz Hall
Larry Potter . . . . Kevin Ramsey
Shorty . . . . Helmar Augustus Cooper
B.J. . . . . Keith Robert Bennett
Floyd . . . . Frederick J. Boothe

Zeke. . . . . Ken Roberson
Jimmy Winter . . . . Brian Mitchell
Constance DuGrasse. . . . . Tamara Tunie
Bouquett
Chauffeur . . . . Byron Easley
Kay Jones . . . . Angela Teek
Janson . . . . Mark Kenneth Smaltz
Rev. Alphonse
DuGrasse . . . . Alexander Barton

Ensemble: Keith Robert Bennett, Jacquelyn Bird, Frederick J. Boothe, Cheryl Burr, Byron Easley, Robert H. Fowler, Karen E. Fraction, Frantz Hall, Garry Q. Lewis, Greta Martin, Sharon Moore, Elise Neal, Ken Roberson, David Preston Sharp, Allyson Tucker, Mona Wyatt.

Duo Pianists: Donald Johnston, Robert Colston.

Orchestra: Suzanne Ornstein concert mistress, violin 1; Peter Dimitriades, Andy Stein, Martin Agee violin; Maxine Roach, Crystal Garner viola; Garfield Moore, Rachel Steuermann cello; Anthony Cecere, Virginia Benz horn; Wilmer Wise, Jeff Kievit, Danny Cahn trumpet; Morty Bullman trombone; Les Scott, John Moses, Ric Heckman, Gene Scholtens reeds; Linc Milliman bass; Tony Tedesco drums; Rick Loewus guitar, banjo; Marty Grupp percussion.

Understudies: Miss Teek—Tamara Tunie Bouquett; Miss Kyme—Sharon Moore; Miss Bouquett—Karen E. Fraction; Messrs. Cooper, Barton, Smaltz—Fracaswell Hyman; Swings—Melissa Haizlip, Ken Leigh Rogers.

Directed and choreographed by Dan Siretta; musical direction and vocal and additional dance arrangements, Tom Fay; scenery, Kenneth Foy; costumes, Theoni V. Aldredge; lighting, Craig Miller; orchestrations, Arnold Goland; dance arrangements, Donald Johnston; sound, Jan Nebozenko; assistant choreographer, Ken Leigh Rogers; executive producer, Natalie Lloyd; associate producer, Leo K. Cohen; production stage manager, Harold Goldfaden; stage manager, Tracy Crum; press, the Joshua Ellis Office, Susanne Tighe, John Barlow.

Time: 1926. Place: Harlem.

The 1926 Gershwin musical revised to take place in modern Harlem. *Oh, Kay!* was first produced on Broadway 11/8/26 for 256 performances. Its producers brought it back in a return engagement 1/2/28 for 16 performances, and it was revived off Broadway in the 1959-60 season for 89 performances. This revival is credited with being "inspired by" recent productions at the Goodspeed Opera House, East Haddam, Conn. and the Birmingham, Mich. Theater.

Note: This production of *Oh, Kay!* reopened in previews 4/2/91 at the Lunt-Fontanne Theater with Rae Dawn Chong, Ron Richardson and Natalie Oliver replacing Angela Teek, Brian Mitchell and Tamara Tunie Bouquett, respectively, in the leading roles. It closed in previews 4/14/91.

ACT I

Scene 1: Onstage at the Paradise Club
"Slap That Bass" . . . . Billy, Dolly, Ensemble
Scene 2: Backstage at the Paradise Club
Scene 3: Jimmy Winter's townhouse, late that night
"When Our Ship Comes Sailing In" . . . . Duke, Shorty, Male Ensemble
"Dear Little Girl" . . . . Jimmy, Shorty
"Maybe" . . . . Jimmy, Kay
Scene 4: Jimmy Winter's townhouse, the next morning
"You've Got What Gets Me" . . . . Billy, Dolly
"Do, Do, Do" . . . . Jimmy, Kay
"Clap Yo' Hands" . . . . Potter, Ensemble

ACT II

Scene 1: Jimmy's terrace, that afternoon
"Oh, Kay!" . . . . Billy, Kay, Ensemble
(lyrics by Ira Gershwin and Howard Dietz)
"Ask Me Again" . . . . Jimmy
"Fidgety Feet" . . . . Duke, Ensemble

"Ask Me Again" (Reprise).. Jimmy
"Someone to Watch Over Me" .... Kay
Scene 2: Onstage at the Paradise Club
"Heaven on Earth" .... Potter, Duke, Billy
    (lyrics by Ira Gershwin and Howard Dietz)
Scene 3: Backstage at the Paradise Club
Scene 4: Onstage at the Paradise Club
"Show Me the Town/Sleepless Nights"......... Kay, Billy, Dolly, Potter, Duke, Ensemble
"Someone to Watch Over Me" (Reprise)...................... Jimmy, Kay

Buddy: The Buddy Holly Story (225). Musical written by Alan Janes; songs by Buddy Holly and others. Produced by Paul Elliott, Laurie Mansfield and Greg Smith (for International Artistes) and David Mirvish at the Sam S. Shubert Theater. Opened November 4, 1990. (Closed May 19, 1991)

ACT I

Hipockets Duncan .... Fred Sanders
Engineer (KDAV);
    DJ (WWOL) .... Philip Anthony
Buddy Holly .... Paul Hipp
Joe B. Maulin .... Bobby Prochaska
Jerry Allison .... Russ Jolly
Decca Producer; DJ (WCLS)... David Mucci
Decca Engineer .... Paul McQuillan
Decca Engineer; DJ (KPST);
    DJ at Apollo .... Don Stitt
Norman Petty .... Kurt Ziskie
Vi Petty .... Jo Lynn Burks
4th Cricket.............. Ken Triwush
DJ (WDAS); Man at Apollo ... Demo Cates
Candy .... Melanie Doane
Performer at Apollo...... Jerome Smith Jr.

Jingle Singers: Jo Lynn Burks, Caren Cole, Liliane Stilwell.

The Hayriders: Melanie Doane, Kevin Fox, Tom Nash, Steve Steiner, Don Stitt.

Boppers, Autograph Hunters: Jill Hennessey, Paul McQuillan, Ken Triwush.

Decca Session Musicians: Kevin Fox, Tom Nash, Ken Triwush, Steve Steiner.

Couples in Woods: Jo Lynn Burks, Caren Cole, Kevin Fox, Jill Hennessey, Liliane Stilwell, Ken Triwush.

Apollo Singers: Sandra Caldwell, Denese Matthews, Lorraine Scott.

Musicians at Apollo: Demo Cates, Alvin Crawford, Jerome Smith Jr., James H. Wiggins Jr.

BUDDY: THE BUDDY HOLLY STORY—Paul Hipp in the title role of the Alan Janes musical about the rock star's life and career

ACT II

Maria Elena . . . . Jill Hennessey
Murray Deutch; Jack Daw . . . . . Steve Steiner
Shirley; Mary Lou Sokoloff . . . . . Caren Cole
Maria Elena's Aunt . . . . Liliane Stilwell
English DJ; Dion . . . . Paul McQuillan
Peggy Sue . . . . Melanie Doane
DJ (KRWP). . . . . Kurt Ziskie
Clearlake MC. . . . . Don Stitt
The Big Bopper. . . . . David Mucci

The Belmonts . . . . Russ Jolly, Tom Nash
Ritchie Valens . . . . Philip Anthony
Tommy . . . . Ken Triwush
  Jingle Singers, WWOL: Sandra Caldwell,
Denese Matthews, Lorraine Scott. Photo-
graphers, Band and Backup Singers at Clearlake:
Members of the Company. The Snowbirds: Jo
Lynn Burks, Caren Cole, Melanie Doane, Jill
Hennessey, Liliane Stilwell.

Understudies: Buddy Holly Alternate—Ken Triwush; Messrs. Prochaska, Triwush—Kevin Fox; Messrs. Jolly, McQuillan—Tom Nash; Messrs. Mucci, Sanders, Stitt—Steve Steiner; Messrs. Anthony, Ziskie, Steiner—Paul McQuillan; Misses Burks, Doane, Stilwell—Caren Cole; Messrs. Cates, Smith—Alvin Crawford; Misses Hennessey, Jingle Singers, Cole—Melanie Doane; General Understudy—Louis Tucci.

Directed by Rob Bettinson; musical direction, Paul Jury; scenery, Andy Walmsley; costumes, Bill Butler, Carolyn Smith; lighting, Graham McLusky; sound, Rick Price; jingles composed by Paul Jury; musical consultant, Bruce Welch; executive producer, Brian Sewell; associate producer, Contracts International Ltd.; production stage manager, Peter B. Mumford; stage managers, Shirley Third, Gary M. Zabinski; press, Adrian Bryan-Brown.

The life and performing career of the rock star Buddy Holly, from an original idea by Laurie Mansfield.

MUSICAL NUMBERS, ACT I: "Texas Rose," "Flower of My Heart," "Ready Teddy," "That's All Right," "That'll Be the Day," "Blue Days, Black Nights," "Changing All These Changes," "Peggy Sue," "Looking for Someone to Love," "Mailman Bring Me No More Blues," "Maybe Baby," "Everyday," "Sweet Love," "You Send Me," "Not Fade Away," "Words of Love," "Oh Boy."

ACT II: "Listen to Me," "Well All Right," "It's So Easy to Fall in Love," "Think It Over," "True Love Ways," "Why Do Fools Fall in Love," "Chantilly Lace," "Maybe Baby," "Peggy Sue Got Married," "Heartbeat," "La Bamba," "Raining in My Heart," "It Doesn't Matter Anymore," "Rave On," "Johnny B. Goode."

Those Were the Days (130). Musical revue in English and Yiddish; concept and continuity by Zalmen Mlotek and Moishe Rosenfeld; songs by various authors (see listing below). Produced by Moe Septee and Emanuel Azenberg in association with Victor H. Potamkin, Zalmen Mlotek and Moishe Rosenfeld at the Edison Theater. Opened November 7, 1990. (Closed February 24, 1991)

Bruce Adler
Robert Abelson
Mina Bern

Eleanor Reissa
Lori Wilner

The Golden Land Klezmer Orchestra: Zalmen Mlotek conductor, piano; Howard Leshaw woodwinds; Alkiviades Steriopoulos keyboards; Allen Herman, John Redsecker drums; Edward Conte bass.

Understudies: Mr. Adler—Stuart Zagnit; Mr. Abelson—Norman Atkins; Miss Bern—Shifra Lerer; Misses Reissa, Wilner—Sandra Ben Dor.

Directed and choreographed by Eleanor Reissa; musical direction, Zalmen Mlotek; costumes, Gail Cooper-Hecht; lighting, Tom Sturge; sound, John Badrak, Alan Gregorie; production stage manager, Charles Blackwell; stage manager, Greta Minsky; press, Max Eisen, Madelon Rosen Solomon.

Additional material by E. Cecuona, J. Offenbach, M. Makeba, F. Loesser, M. Hadjidakis, B. Towne, B. Adler, R. Abelson, M. Bern, E. Reissa.

Jewish musical theater selections from the shtetl to Second Avenue to Broadway, where this was its first appearance in 20 years.

ACT I—THE SHTETL

Overture . . . . Golden Land Orchestra
Prologue—Nigunim (Melodies)
   "Lomir Loybn" (Let Us Praise), "Sha Shtil" (The Rabbi's Coming)—folk songs . . . Company
"Oyfn Pripetshik" (At the Fireplace) . . . . Bruce Adler
   (words and music, M. Warshavsky)

"On a Moonlit Night" . . . . Eleanor Reissa, Lori Wilner
    (based on a story by I. L. Peretz)
"Ver Der Ershter Vet Lakhn" (Who Will Laugh First?). . . . . Reissa, Wilner
    (words and music, M. Gebirtig)
"Motele". . . . . Robert Abelson, Reissa
    (words and music, M. Gebirtig)
"Hudl Mitn Shtrudl" (Hudl With the Shtrudl) . . . . Adler
    (words and music, A. Lebedeff)
Kasrilevke Restoran (A Restaurant in Kasrilevke). . . . . Adler, Abelson, Mina Bern
    (based on a story by Sholom Aleichem)
"Di Dinst" (The Maid)—folk song . . . . Reissa
Shalakh-Mones (Gifts for Purim). . . . . Reissa, Wilner
    (based on a story by Sholom Aleichem)
"Yosl Ber" . . . . Adler with Wilner and Reissa
    (words, Itsik Manger; music, folk melody)
"Shabes, Shabes, Shabes" (Welcoming the Sabbath) . . . . Bern
    (words, Ben Bonus; music, Ben Yomen)
"Chelm" . . . . Company
"Litvak/Galitsyaner" . . . . Adler, Reissa
    (words and music, Hymie Jacobson)
"Halevay Volt Ikh Singl Geven" (I Wish I Were Single Again) . . . . Abelson, Bern
    (American folk song adapted by M. Younin)
"Shloymele-Malkele". . . . . Wilner, Adler
    (music, J. Rumshinsky)
"Mamenyu Tayere" (Dear Mama) . . . . Wilner, Bern
    (words, Mani Leib; music, folk melody; from the repertory of Menashe Oppenheim)
"Nokhumke, Mayn Zun" (Nochum, My Son)—folk song . . . . Abelson, Adler
"Saposhkelekh" (The Boots). . . . . Reissa
    (folk song from the research of Michael Alpert)
"The Wedding" . . . . Company
    "Khosn-Kale Mazl Tov" (Congratulations to the Bride and Groom), folk song; "Di Rod" (The
    Circle), words and music, M. Warshavsky; "Der Ayznban" (The Train), folk song; "Yoshke
    Fort Avek" (Yoshke's Going Away), folk song; "Mayn Alte Heym" from the "forbidden
    songs" of Soviet Jews, as recorded by David Eshet

ACT II—THE MUSIC HALL

Entr'acte . . . . Golden Land Orchestra
"Those Were the Days" . . . . Reissa, Abelson
    (words and music, Gene Raskin)
"Shpil Gitar" (Play Guitar) . . . . Wilner
"The Palace of the Czar" . . . . Adler
    (words and music, Mel Tolkin)
"Di Mame" (The Mother)—Monologue . . . . Bern
"Yiddish International Radio Hour". . . . . Company
    (Yiddish lyrics, Chana Mlotek)
"Figaro's Aria" (from The Barber of Seville). . . . . Abelson
    (music, Gioacchino Rossini; Yiddish, R. Abelson, M. Rosenfeld)
"My Yiddishe Mame" . . . . Reissa
    (words, Jack Yellen; music, Lew Pollack)
"Hootsatsa". . . . . Adler
    (based on a song by Fishl Kanapoff)
"Bei Mir Bist Du Schoen" (To Me, You're Beautiful) . . . . Reissa, Wilner, Adler
    (words, Jacob Jacobs; music, Sholom Secunda; English, Sammy Cahn, Saul Chaplin)
"In an Orem Shtibele" (In a Poor Little House)—folk song. . . . . Bern
"A Khazndl Oyf Shabes" (A Cantor for the Sabbath)—folk song . . . . Abelson
"Papirosn" (Cigarettes) . . . . Wilner
    (words and music, Bella Meisel, Herman Yablokoff)
"Yosl, Yosl". . . . . Reissa
    (words, Nellie Casman; music, Samuel Steinberg)

"Rumania, Rumania" . . . . Adler
    (words and music, A. Lebedeff, Sholom Secunda)
"Those Were the Days" . . . . Company

*Lincoln Center Theater. Schedule of two programs (see note). ***Six Degrees of Separation** (234). Transfer from off Broadway of the play by John Guare. Opened November 8, 1990. **Mule Bone** (67). By Langston Hughes and Zora Neale Hurston; prologue and epilogue by George Houston Bass; music by Taj Mahal. Opened February 14, 1991. (Closed April 14, 1991 matinee) Produced by Lincoln Center Theater, Gregory Mosher director, Bernard Gersten executive producer, at the Vivian Beaumont Theater (*Mule Bone* at the Ethel Barrymore Theater).

SIX DEGREES OF SEPARATION

Ouisa	Stockard Channing	Woody	Gus Rogerson
Flan	John Cunningham	Ben	Anthony Rapp
Geoffrey	Sam Stoneburner	Dr. Fine	Stephen Pearlman
Paul	Courtney B. Vance	Doug	Evan Handler
Hustler	David Eigenberg	Policeman; Eddie	Philip LeStrange
Kitty	Kelly Bishop	Trent	John Cameron Mitchell
Larkin	Peter Maloney	Rick	Robert Duncan McNeil
Detective	Brian Evers	Elizabeth	Mari Nelson
Tess	Robin Morse		

Understudies: Misses Channing, Bishop—Patricia Hodges; Mr. Cunningham—Brian Evers; Mr. Maloney—Brian Evers, Philip LeStrange; Messrs. Stoneburner, Pearlman—David Little; Messrs. Eigenberg, Rapp, Mitchell—Ray Cochran; Misses Morse, Nelson—Catherine Curtain; Messrs. Rogerson, Handler—Anthony Rapp.

Directed by Jerry Zaks; scenery, Tony Walton; costumes, William Ivey Long; lighting, Paul Gallo; sound, Aural Fixation; poster art, James McMullan; production stage manager, Steve Beckler; stage manager, Sarah Manley; press, Merle Debuskey, Susan Chicoine.

Time: Today. Place: New York City. The play was presented without an intermission.

Black impostor intrudes on a white family by pretending to be a college chum of their son's. Produced off Broadway 6/14/90 for 155 performances in this production; see its entry in the Plays Produced Off Broadway section of this volume.

A Best Play; see page 89.

MULE BONE

Zora; Teets	Joy Lee	Mattie Clark	Myra Taylor
Dave Carter	Eric Ware	Luther	Bron Wright
Jim	Kenny Neal	Matilda	Shareen Powlett
Daisy	Akosua Busia	Willie Lewis	Robert Earl Jones
Deacon Hambo	Sonny Jim Gaines	Tony Taylor	Mansoor Najeeullah
Old Man Brazzle	Clebert Ford	Sister Taylor	Marilyn Coleman
Lum Boger	Paul S. Eckstein	Rev. Simms	Leonard Jackson
Lige Mosely	Reggie Montgomery	Jesse; Julius	T.J. Jones
Robena	Pauline Meyer	Katie Pitts	Theresa Merritt
Joe Lindsay	Allie Woods Jr.	Sister Lewis	Frances Foster
Walter Thomas	Donald Griffin	Sister Thomas	Fanni Green
Mayor Joe Clark	Samuel E.Wright	Sister Hambo	Edwina Lewis
Sister Blunt	Ebony Jo-Ann	Sister Lindsay	Peggy Pettitt
Senator	Pee Wee Love	Rev. Singletary	Arthur French
Bootsie	Vanessa Williams		

Musicians: Kester Smith conductor, drums; Calvin "Fuzzy" Samuel acoustic and electric bass; Kim D. Jordan keyboards, synthesizer; Abdul Wali electric guitar, banjo.

Understudies: Misses Lee, Lewis, Pettitt—Myra Taylor; Miss Busia—Vanessa Williams; Messrs. Neal, Ware, Eckstein, Najeeullah—Guy Davis; Mr. Wright—Arthur French; Misses Jo-Ann, Foster—Peggy Pettitt; Mr. Love—T.J. Jones; Messrs. Ford, Griffin, Woods—Billy Ray Tyson; Misses Williams,

Taylor, Green—Oni Faida Lampley; Miss Powlett—Pauline Meyer; Miss Meyer, Mr. Jones (Julius)—Shareen Powlett; Miss Merritt—Ebony Jo-Ann, Edwina Lewis; Mr. Montgomery—Mansoor Najeeullah; Miss Coleman—Fanni Green; Mr. T.J. Jones (Jesse)—Bron Wright; Mr. Wright—Pee Wee Love; Messrs. French, Gaines, Jones, Jackson—George Lee Miles.

Directed by Michael Schultz; dance staging, Dianne McIntyre; musical supervisor, Taj Mahal; scenery, Edward Burbridge; costumes, Lewis Brown; lighting, Allen Lee Hughes; sound, Serge Ossorguine; fight staging, Ron Van Clief; poster art, James McMullan; production manager, Jeff Hamlin; production stage manager, Maureen F. Gibson; stage manager, Fredric H. Orner; press, Merle Debuskey, Susan Chicoine.

Time: Saturday, Nov. 8, sometime in the 1920s. Place: Eatonville, Fla. Prologue: Just outside of Eatonville. Act I: Joe Clark's General Store. Act II Prologue: A barn. Dave Carter's house, Saturday night. Scene 1: Macedonia Baptist Church, the following Monday. Scene 2: A high stretch of railroad tracks a mile out of town, the same day, late afternoon.

Comic treatment of an all-black town turned upside down over the rivalry between two young men over the town flirt, with further implications of Baptist vs. Methodist confrontation and embellished with several musical numbers. Written in 1930 by the late Langston Hughes and Zora Neale Hurston, it was never produced until this 1991 staging with embellishments.

Note: Lincoln Center Theater also presented 16 special performances of Spalding Gray's *Monster in a Box* at the Vivian Beaumont Theater; see its entry in the Plays Produced Off Broadway section of this volume.

Christmas Spectacular (181). Revised version and return engagement of the spectacle originally conceived by Robert F. Jani. Produced by Radio City Music Hall Productions, David J. Nash, executive producer, at Radio City Music Hall. Opened November 9, 1990. (Closed January 3, 1991)

CHRISTMAS SPECTACULAR

Scrooge; Narrator;
Santa . . . . Charles Edward Hall
Mrs. Santa . . . . Marty Simpson
Bob Cratchit . . . . David Elder
Scrooge's Nephew . . . . . Frank DiPasquale
1st Man . . . . Joe Bowerman
2d Man . . . . Robert Ashford
Marley's Ghost . . . . Scott Spahr
Ghost of Christmas
Past. . . . . Pascale Faye-Williams
(Parentheses indicate roles in which the actors alternated)

Ghost of Christmas Present . . . Tim Hamrick
Mrs. Cratchit . . . . Karen Longwell
Belinda Cratchit . . . . Suzanne Phillips
(Sarah Cratchit) . . . . Laura Bundy,
Christen Tassen
(Peter Cratchit) . . . Sean Dooley, Joey Rigol
(Tiny Tim). . . . . . . Joey Cee, Art Vernon
Poultry Man . . . . Todd Hunter

Skaters: Laurie Welch & Randy Coyne, Shelly Winters-Stein & Bruce Hurd.

The New Yorkers: Ellyn Arons, David Askler, Michael Berglund, Maria Calabrese, John Clonts, James Darrah, John Dietrich, Frank DiPasquale, Jane Labanz, Keith Locke, Karen Longwell, Michelle Mallardi, Wendy Piper, Marty Simpson, Jennifer Smith, Mary Jayne Waddell, Jim Weaver, David Wood.

Elves: Jiggle—Michael Lee Gogin; Squiggle—R. Lou Carry; Wiggle—John Edward Allen; Giggle—Michael J. Gilden; Bruce—Leslie Stump; Understudies—Elena Bertagnolli, Phil Fondacaro.

Dancers: Robert Ashford, Joe Bowerman, Tina DeLeone, David Elder, Pascale Faye-Williams, Christopher Gattelli, Steve Geary, Tim Hamrick, Todd Hunter, Terry Lacy, Bonnie Lynn, Marty McDonough, Joan Mirabella, Suzanne Phillips, Scott Spahr.

Rockettes: Pauline Achilles, Catherine Beatty, Linda Beausoleil, Dottie Bell, Kiki Bennett, Susan Boron, Katy Braff, Julie Branam, Janice Cavargna, Connie Cittadino, Eileen Collins, Lilian Colon, Marylee Dewitt, Susanne Doris, Colleen Dunn, Phyllis Frew, Prudence Gray, Susan Heart, Vicki Hickerson, Ginny Hounsell, Stephanie James, Jennifer Jones, Dee Dee Knapp, Judy Little, Sonya Livingston, Setsuko Maruhashi, Lori McMacken, Mary McNamara, Lori Mello, Laraine Memola, Lynn Newton, Rosemary Noviello, Kerri Pearsall, Joan Peer, Gerri Presky, Laureen Repp, Linda Riley, Mary Six Rupert, Jereme Sheehan, Terry Spano, Maureen Stevens, Lynn Sullivan, Susan Theobald, Scotti Tittle, Carol Toman, Jill Turnbull, Darlene Wendy, Beth Woods, Eileen Woods.

Orchestra: Don Pippin conductor; Bryan Louiselle assistant conductor; Louann Montesi concert mas-

CHRISTMAS SPECTACULAR—The Rockettes in the Music Hall's Christmas show

ter; Gilbert Bauer, Carmine Delco, Howard Kaye, Joseph Kowalewski, Julius J. Kunstler, Nannette Levi, Samuel Marder, Holly Ovenden violin; Barbara H. Vaccaro, Andrea Andros viola; Frank Levy, Sarah Carter cello; Dean Crandell bass; Kenneth Emery flute; Gerald S. Niewood, Richard Oatts, John M. Cippola, Joshua Siegel, Kenneth Arzberger reeds; George Bartlett, Nancy Freimanis, French horn; Richard Raffio, Zachary Shnek, Norman Beatty trumpet; John Schnupp, Thomas B. Olcott, Mary Johansen trombone; John Bartlett tuba; Thomas J. Oldakowski drums; Mario DeCiutiis, Maya Gunji percussion; Anthony Cesarano guitar; Susanna Nason, Henry Aronson piano; Jeanne Maier harp; George Wesner, Robert Maidhof, Frederick P. Davies, Paul Fleckenstein organ.

Directed by Scott Salmon; original direction, Robert F. Jani; original staging and choreography restaged by Violet Holmes and Linda Lemac; choreography for "Carol of the Balls" and "We Need a Little Christmas," Scott Salmon; choreography for "Christmas in New York," Marianne Selbert; musical direction and vocal arrangement, Don Pippin; scenery, Charles Lisanby; original costumes, Frank Spencer; additional costumes, Jose Lengson; costumes for "Carol of the Bells" and "We Need a Little Christmas," Pete Menefee; lighting, Ken Billington; dance music arrangements, Marvin Laird; orchestrations, Michael Gibson, Danny Troob, Jonathan Tunick, Jim Tyler, Bob Wheeler; Rockette director, Violet Holmes; Rockette captain, Joyce Dwyer; production stage manager, Howard Kolins; stage managers, Mimi Apfel, Travis DeCastro, Peter Muste; press, Sandra Manley, Kevin M. Brockman, Alyce Fisher.

Special music credit: "Silent Night" arrangement by Percy Faith. Original music: "They Can't Start Christmas Without Us" lyrics by Fred Tobias; "Christmas in New York" music by Stan Lebowsky, written by Billy But Galahad Music, Inc. Original orchestrations: Elman Anderson, Robert N. Ayars, Michael Gibson, Don Harper, Arthur Harris, Bob Krogstad, Phillip J. Lang.

The Music Hall's annual Christmas show starring the Rockettes, with its famous Nativity pageant last offered 11/10/89 for 188 performances, includes three new numbers: "We Need a Little Christmas," "Carol of the Bells" and *Charles Dickens' A Christmas Carol*, a play by Charles Lisanby.

SCENES AND MUSICAL NUMBERS: Greeting (Herald Trumpeters). Scene 1: "We Need a Little Christmas" (Rockettes, Company). Overture (Radio City Music Hall Orchestra). Scene 2: *The Nutcracker*, A Teddy Bear's Dream. Scene 3: *Charles Dickens' A Christmas Carol* by Charles Lisanby. Scene 4: "Christmas in New York" (The New Yorkers, Rockettes, Radio City Music Hall Orchestra, Company). Scene 5: Ice Skating in the Plaza. Scene 6: The Story of Santa

Claus. Scene 7: "They Can't Start Christmas Without Us" (Santa, Mrs. Claus, Elves). Scene 8: The Parade of the Wooden Soldiers (Rockettes). Scene 9: Beginning of Santa's Journey. Scene 10: "Carol of the Bells" (Rockettes, Company). Scene 11: The Living Nativity. Scene 12: Jubilant, "Joy to the World" (Radio City Music Hall Orchestra).

Shadowlands (169). By William Nicholson. Produced by Elliot Martin, James M. Nederlander, Brian Eastman, Terry Allen Kramer and Roger L. Stevens at the Brooks Atkinson Theater. Opened November 11, 1990. (Closed April 7, 1991)

C.S. Lewis . . . . Nigel Hawthorne	Alan Gregg; Doctor . . . . . Edmund C. Davys
Christopher Riley . . . . Paul Sparer	Maj. W.H. Lewis . . . . Michael Allinson
Rev. Harry Harrington . . . . Robin Chadwick	(Douglas) . . . Jonathan Gold, Lance Robinson
Dr. Oakley; Waiter; Clerk;	Joy Davidman . . . . Jane Alexander
Priest . . . . Hugh A. Rose	Registrar; Nurse . . . . Mary Layne

(Parentheses indicate role in which the performers alternated)

Standby: Mr. Hawthorne—Michael Allinson; Understudies: Miss Alexander—Mary Layne; Messrs. Allinson, Rose—Ian Sullivan; Mr. Sparer—Edmund C. Davys; Messrs. Davys, Chadwick—Hugh A. Rose; Miss Layne—Jennifer Sternberg.

Directed by Elijah Moshinsky; design, Mark Thompson; lighting, John Michael Deegan; production stage manager, Elliott Woodruff; stage manager, Wally Peterson; press, Jeffrey Richards Associates, David LeShay.

Time: The 1950s. Place: Oxford. The play was presented in two parts.

The love story of C.S. Lewis and Joy Davidman. A foreign play previously produced in a TV version on British and American television and onstage in London.

A Best Play; see page 140.

*Fiddler on the Roof (222). Revival of the musical based on Sholom Aleichem's stories; book by Joseph Stein; music by Jerry Bock; lyrics by Sheldon Harnick. Produced by Barry and Fran Weissler and Pace Theatrical Group at the Gershwin Theater, Opened November 18, 1990.

Tevye. . . . . Topol	Lazar Wolf . . . . Mark Zeller
Golde . . . . Marcia Lewis	Mordcha . . . . David Masters
Tzeitel. . . . . Sharon Lawrence	Nachum. . . . . Michael J. Farina
Hodel . . . . Tia Riebling	Yente . . . . Ruth Jaroslow
Chava . . . . Jennifer Prescott	Rabbi . . . . Jerry Matz
Shprintze;	Avram. . . . . Jerry Jarrett
Grandma Tzeitel . . . . . . Kathy St. George	Constable . . . . Mike O'Carroll
Bielke. . . . . Judy Dodd	Mendel . . . . David Pevsner
Motel . . . . Jack Kenny	Fiddler . . . . Stephen Wright
Perchik. . . . . Gary Schwartz	Fruma-Sarah . . . . Jeri Sager
Fyedka . . . . Ron Bohmer	Shandel . . . . Panchali Null

Bottle Dancers: Kenneth M. Daigle, David Enriquez, Craig Gahnz, Keith Keen.

Russian Dancers: Brian Arsenault, Michael Berresse, Brian Henry.

Villagers: Brian Arsenault, Michael Berresse, Joanne Borts, Stacey Lynn Brass, Lisa Cartmell, Kenneth M. Daigle, David Enriquez, Craig Gahnz, Brian Henry, Todd Heughens, Keith Keen, Panchali Null, Marty Ross, Jeri Sager, Beth Thompson, Lou Williford.

Standby: Topol—Mark Zeller. Understudies: Miss Lewis—Lou Williford; Miss Lawrence—Lisa Cartmell; Miss Riebling—Beth Thompson; Misses Prescott, St. George (Shprintze), Dodd—Stacey Lynn Brass; Mr. Kenny—David Pevsner; Mr. Zeller—Mike O'Carroll; Mr. Schwartz—Keith Keen; Mr. Bohmer—Brian Henry; Miss Jaroslow—Lou Williford; Mr. Matz—David Masters; Messrs. O'Carroll, Jarrett, Masters—Marty Ross; Mr. Pevsner—Todd Heughens; Mr. Wright—David Enriquez; Mr. Farina—Newton Cole; Miss St. George (Grandma Tzeitel)—Judy Dodd; Swing Dancers—Chris Jamison, Newton Cole.

Original production directed and choreographed by Jerome Robbins; direction reproduced by Ruth Mitchell; choreography reproduced by Sammy Dallas Bayes; musical direction and vocal arrangements, Milton Greene; scenery, Boris Aronson; costumes based on original designs by Patricia Zipprodt; lighting, Ken Billington; sound, Peter J. Fitzgerald; music coordinator, John Monaco; technical supervisor, Arthur Siccardi; associate producer, Alecia Parker; produced in association with C. Itoh & Co.,

Ltd./Tokyo Broadcasting System International, Inc. and A. Deshe (Pashanel); production stage manager, Martin Gold; stage manager, David John O'Brien; press, Shirley Herz Associates, Pete Sanders.

Time: 1905, on the eve of the Russian revolution. Place: Anatevka, a small village in Russia.

The last major New York revival of *Fiddler on the Roof* took place on Broadway 7/9/81 for 53 performances.

The list of musical numbers in *Fiddler on the Roof* appears on page 303 of *The Best Plays of 1964-65*.

ACT I—Prologue. Scene 1: Kitchen in Tevye's house. Scene 2: Exterior of Tevye's house. Scene 3: Interior of Tevye's house. Scene 4: The inn. Scene 5: Street outside the inn. Scene 6: On a bench outside Tevye's house. Scene 7: Tevye's bedroom. Scene 8: Village street and Motel's tailor shop. Scene 9: Section of Tevye's yard.

ACT II—Prologue. Scene 1: Exterior of Tevye's house. Scene 2: Village street. Scene 3: Exterior of railroad station. Scene 4: Village street. Scene 5: Motel's tailor shop. Scene 6: Somewhere on the outskirts of the village. Scene 7: The barn. Scene 8: Outside Tevye's house. Epilogue.

Shogun: The Musical (72). Musical based on the novel by James Clavell; book and lyrics by John Driver; music by Paul Chihara. Produced by James Clavell, Joseph Harris and Haruki Kadokawa at the Marquis Theater. Opened November 20, 1990. (Closed January 20, 1991)

John Blackthorne . . . . Philip Casnoff	2d Samurai Guard . . . . Marc Oka
Crew of the Erasmus:	3d Samurai Guard . . . . . . Owen Johnston
Roper. . . . . Ron Navarre	Lord Toranaga . . . . Francis Ruivivar
Pieterzoon . . . . Lee Lobenhofer	Sazuko. . . . . Jenny Woo
Sonk . . . . Terry Lehmkuhl	Osagi; Ishido's General; Acolyte . . Jason Ma
Father Alvito . . . . John Herrera	Lady Mariko . . . . June Angela
Lord Buntaro . . . . Joseph Foronda	Capt. Gen. Ferriera . . . . . Lee Lobenhofer
Omi . . . . Eric Chan	Lord Ishido. . . . . Alan Muraoka
Captured Samurai; Ishido's Head	Ninja . . . . Andrew Pacho
Samurai . . . . Tito Abeleda	Fujiko . . . . Leslie Ishii
Gyoko. . . . . Freda Foh Shen	Osaka Guards . . Kenji Nakao, Andrew Pacho
Kiku. . . . . JoAnn M. Hunter	Chimmoko . . . . Kiki Moritsugu
1st Samurai Guard; Courtier of	Red Guards of Osaka Castle . . . . Marc Oka,
Osaka . . . . Darren Lee	Alan Ariano

Catholic Daimyos: Cholsu Kim, Marc Oka, Kenji Nakao. Slatterns of the Hovel: Tina Horii, Linda Igarashi, Chi-en Telemaque. Ninja Attackers: Cheri Nakamura, Andrew Pacho, Darren Lee, Owen Johnston, Tito Abeleda, Jason Ma, Terry Lehmkuhl, Cholsu Kim, Ron Navarre. Taiko Drummers: Jason Ma, Marc Oka, Leslie Ishii, Lee Lobenhofer. Swings: Ted Hewlett, Herman Sebek, Victoria Lee, Lyd-Lyd Gaston.

Dancers, Act I—Storm Scene "Karma": JoAnn M. Hunter, Kiki Moritsugu, Kathy Wilhelm, Darren Lee, Cholsu Kim, Andrew Pacho. Toranaga's Entrance: 1st Guard—Darren Lee; 2d Guard—Marc Oka; 3d Guard—Owen Johnston; and Tito Abeleda, Cholsu Kim, Andrew Pacho. "An Island": Kuroko Falcon Handler—Lee Lobenhofer. "Karma": Tito Abeleda, Betsy Chang, Deborah Geneviere, Tina Horii, JoAnne M. Hunter, Linda Igarashi, Jason Ma, Kiki Moritsugu, Cheri Nakamura, Kenji Nakao, Chi-en Telemaque, Kathy Wilhelm, Jenny Woo.

Dancers, Act II—"Fireflies": JoAnn M. Hunter, Eric Chan, Betsy Chang, Deborah Geneviere, Linda Igarashi, Kiki Moritsugu, Kathy Wilhelm, Jenny Woo, Tito Abeleda, Owen Johnston, Darren Lee, Jason Ma, Marc Oka, Cholsu Kim. Kuroko/"Fireflies": Alan Ariano, Tina Horii, Andrew Pacho, Cheri Nakamura, Kenji Nakao, Ron Navarre. "Rum Below": Betsy Chang, Tina Horii, Linda Igarashi, Kiki Moritsugu, Kathy Wilhelm, Jenny Woo, Cholsu Kim, Owen Johnston, Darren Lee, Jason Ma, Marc Oka, Andrew Pacho. "One Candle": JoAnn M. Hunter, Kiki Moritsugu.

Directed and choreographed by Michael Smuin; musical direction, Edward G. Robinson; scenery, Loren Sherman; costumes, Patricia Zipprodt; lighting, Natasha Katz; orchestrations, David Cullen; additional orchestrations, Steven Margoshes; sound, Tony Meola; co-choreographer, Kirk Peterson; assistant director, J. Steven White; fight instructor, Mashiro Kunii; co-producers, Hiroshi Sugawara, Lloyd Phillips; production stage manager, S. Randolph Post; stage managers, Deborah Clelland, Michael Pule, Donna A. Drake; press, Shirley Herz Associates, Sam Rudy, Miller Wright.

Romance and violent strife in Japan in 1600, per the Clavell novel and TV miniseries. Previously produced at Kennedy Center, Washington, D.C.

SHOGUN—Francis Ruivivar (*center*) with members of the company

ACT I

"Karma". . . . . Orchestra
"Night of Screams" . . . . Sailors, Blackthorne, Ensemble
"This Is Samurai" . . . . Samurai
"How Nice to See You" . . . . Toranaga, Buntaro, Alvito, Mariko
"Impossible Eyes" . . . . Mariko, Blackthorne
"He Let Me Live" . . . . Mariko
"Honto" . . . . Blackthorne
"Assassination". . . . . Alvito, Ferriera
"Shogun" . . . . Hostages
"Royal Blood". . . . . Ishido, Toranaga
"An Island" . . . . Toranaga
"No Word for Love" . . . . Mariko
"Mad Rum Below/Escape" . . . . Blackthorne, Ensemble
"Karma". . . . . Toranaga, Ensemble
"Born to Be Together" . . . . Mariko, Blackthorne

ACT II

"Fireflies". . . . . Ensemble, Mariko, Blackthorne
"Sail Home". . . . . Blackthorne
"Rum Below". . . . . Blackthorne, Toranaga, Ensemble
"Pillowing" . . . . Gyoko, Kiku, Ladies
"Born to Be Together" (Reprise) . . . . Meriko, Blackthorne
"No Man" . . . . Blackthorne
"Cha-No-Yu" . . . . Mariko, Buntaro
"Absolution". . . . . Alvito, Acolyte, Ensemble, Mariko
"Poetry Competition" . . . . Ishido, Sazuko, Mariko
"Death Walk" . . . . Ensemble, Blackthorne
"One Candle" . . . . Mariko, Blackthorne
"Ninja Raid" . . . . Orchestra
"One Candle" (Reprise). . . . . Mariko, Blackthorne
"Winter Battle" . . . . Orchestra
"Resolutions" . . . . Toranaga, Ensemble
"Trio" . . . . Toranaga, Blackthorne, Mariko
Finale . . . . Ensemble

Peter Pan (45). Revival of the musical production of the play by James M. Barrie; music by Moose Charlap; lyrics by Carolyn Leigh; additional music by Jule Styne; additional lyrics by Betty Comden and Adolph Green; original production conceived, directed and choreographed by Jerome Robbins. Produced by James M. Nederlander and Arthur Rubin in the Thomas P. McCoy-Keith Stava production in association with P.P. Investments, Inc. and Jon B. Platt at the Lunt-Fontanne Theater. Opened December 13, 1990. (Closed January 20, 1991)

Wendy Darling; Jane	Cindy Robinson	1st Twin	Janet Kay Higgins
John Darling	Britt West	2d Twin	Courtney Wyn
Michael Darling	Chad Hutchison	Slightly	Christopher Ayers
Liza	Anne McVey	Tootles	Julian Brightman
Nana	Bill Bateman	Mr. Smee	Don Potter
Mrs. Darling;		Cecco	Calvin Smith
Wendy Grown Up	Lauren Thompson	Gentleman Starkey	Carl Packard
Mr. Darling; Capt. Hook	Stephen Hanan	Noodler; Crocodile	Barry Ramsey
Peter Pan	Cathy Rigby	Bill Jukes	Andy Ferrara
The Never Bear	Adam Ehrenworth	Tiger Lily	Holly Irwin
Curly	Alon Williams		

Pirates and Indians: Bill Bateman, Andy Ferrara, Anne McVey, Christian Monte, Carl Packard, Barry Ramsey, Joseph Savant, Calvin Smith, Timothy Talman, David Thome, John Wilkerson.

Musicians: Kevin Farrell conductor; Brian Tidwell assistant conductor, piano, synthesizer; Craig Barna keyboards, Tinkerbell; Steve Bartosik drums; Sally Foster harp; James Saporito percussion; Bruce Uchitel guitar; Diana Halprin (concertmaster); Maura Giannini, Cecelia Hobbs Gardner, Lisa Brooke violin; Roger Shell, Eliana Mendoza cello; Joe Bongiorno acoustic bass; Jaime Austria electric bass; Dan Gerhart flute, piccolo; David Weiss flute, baritone sax; Alva Hunt clarinet, tenor sax; John Winder clarinet, bass clarinet, bassoon; David Kossoff oboe, English horn; Chris Jaudes, John Frosk, Larry Lunetta trumpet; Dan Cloutier trombone; Ron Sell, French horn.

Understudies: Miss Rigby—Cindy Robinson; Mr. Hanan—Carl Packard; Miss Thompson—Anne McVey; Mr. Potter—Bill Bateman; Miss Robinson—Courtney Wyn; Mr. West—Christopher Ayers; Miss Irwin—Courtney Wyn; Misses Higgins, Wyn, Williams, Mr. Hutchison—Adam Ehrenworth; Messrs. Brightman, Ayers—Janet Kay Higgins; Ensemble Swing—Jim Alexander.

Directed by Fran Soeder; choreography, Marilyn Magness; musical supervision and direction, Kevin Farrell; flying by Foy; costumes, Mariann Verheyen; lighting, Natasha Katz; sound, Peter J. Fitzgerald; Neverland scenery, James Leonard Joy; additional arrangements, M. Michael Fauss, Kevin Farrell; production stage manager, John M. Galo; stage manager, Eric Insko; press, Shirley Herz Associates, Glenna Freedman.

The last major New York revival of *Peter Pan* took place on Broadway 9/6/79 for 551 performances. The list of scenes and musical numbers in *Peter Pan* appears on page 370 of *The Best Plays of 1954-55*.

La Bête (25). By David Hirson. Produced by Stuart Ostrow and Andrew Lloyd Webber at the Eugene O'Neill Theater. Opened February 10, 1991. (Closed March 2, 1991)

Elomire (anagram of Molière)	Michael Cumpsty	Madeleine Bejart	Patricia Kilgarriff
Bejart	James Greene	De Brie	John Michael Higgins
Valere	Tom McGowan	Catherine De Brie	Holly Felton
Dorine	Johann Carlo	Rene Du Parc	William Mesnik
Prince Conti	Dylan Baker	Marquise Therese Du Parc	Suzie Plakson

Servants: Cheryl Gaysunas, Ellen Kohrman, Michael McCormick, Eric Swanson.

Understudies: Mr. McGowan—John Michael Higgins; Mr. Cumpsty—Michael James Reed; Mr. Greene—William Mesnik; Misses Carlo, Plakson—Ellen Kohrman; Messrs. Baker, Higgins—Eric Swanson; Mr. Mesnik—Michael McCormick; Misses Felton, Kilgarriff—Cheryl Gaysunas.

Directed by Richard Jones; scenery and costumes, Richard Hudson; lighting, Jennifer Tipton; sound, Peter J. Fitzgerald; production stage manager, Bob Borod; stage manager, Glen Gardali; press, John Springer Associates, Gary Springer.

Time: 1654. Place: Prince Conti's estate, Pezenas, France (Languedoc). The play was presented in two parts.

Highly stylized comedy, in the Molière manner with the script in rhymed couplets, lightly concerning itself with artistic integrity when a prince forces an acting troupe to make room for one of his cronies.

A Best Plays special citation; see page 282.

*Lost in Yonkers (114). By Neil Simon. Produced by Emanuel Azenberg at the Richard Rodgers Theater. Opened February 21, 1991.

Jay . . . . Jamie Marsh	Grandma Kurnitz. . . . . Irene Worth
Arty . . . . Danny Gerard	Louie . . . . Kevin Spacey
Eddie . . . . Mark Blum	Gert . . . . Lauren Klein
Bella . . . . Mercedes Ruehl	

Standbys: Miss Worth—Pauline Flanagan; Misses Ruehl, Klein—Didi Conn; Messrs. Spacey, Blum—David Chandler; Mr. Gerard—Justin Strock; Mr. Marsh—David Neipris.

Directed by Gene Saks; scenery and costumes, Santo Loquasto; lighting, Tharon Musser; sound, Tom Morse; production supervisor, Peter Lawrence; stage manager, Jim Woolley; press, Bill Evans & Associates, Jim Randolph, Becky Flora.

Time: 1942. Place: A two-bedroom apartment over Kurnitz's Kandy Store, Yonkers, N.Y. Act 1, Scene 1: 6:30 p.m. on a hot Sunday evening in August. Scene 2: 11 p.m. a week later. Scene 3: 4 p.m. Sunday afternoon, a month later. Scene 4: Midnight a week later. Act II, Scene 1: 3 p.m. a few days later. Scene 2: After dinner that same day. Scene 3: Noon Sunday, three days later. Scene 4: Late morning eight months later.

Second generation German Americans and their children strive to rise above their individual shortcomings while coping with their tyrannical old-country matriarch.

A Best Play; see page 183.

The Speed of Darkness (36). By Steve Tesich. Produced by Robert Whitehead and Roger L. Stevens with Robert L. Sachter and the American National Theater and Academy at the Belasco Theater. Opened February 28, 1991. (Closed March 30, 1991)

Joe . . . . Len Cariou	Lou . . . . Stephen Lang
Anne . . . . Lisa Eichhorn	Eddie . . . . Robert Sean Leonard
Mary. . . . . Kathryn Erbe	

Understudies: Messrs. Cariou, Lang—William Wise; Miss Eichhorn—Lisa Sloan; Miss Erbe—Abigael Sanders; Mr. Leonard—Alan Mozes.

Directed by Robert Falls; scenery, Thomas Lynch; costumes, Merrily Murray-Walsh; lighting, Michael S. Philippi; music and sound, Rob Milburn; associate producers, Howard Platt, Sheila Hanaghan, Michael Cullen, Constance Towers; production stage manager, William Dodds; stage manager, Jay Adler; press, David Powers, David Roggensack.

Time: The recent past. Place: South Dakota. The play was presented in two parts.

Echoes of the Vietnam experience deeply disturb a family when a homeless Vietnam veteran comes to visit his onetime buddy. This was the first production of the new Broadway Alliance reduced-cost plan for both production and admission. Previously produced at the Goodman Theater, Chicago.

The Big Love (41). One-woman performance by Tracey Ullman; written by Brooke Allen and Jay Presson Allen; based on the book by Florence Aadland and Tedd Thomey. Produced by Lewis Allen Productions, Robert Fox Ltd., Witzend Productions and the Landmark Entertainment Group in association with Home Box Office, Inc. at the Plymouth Theater. Opened March 3, 1991. (Closed April 7, 1991)

Directed by Jay Presson Allen; scenery and projections, David Mitchell; costumes, Jane Greenwood; lighting, Ken Billington; sound, Otts Munderloh; original music, Stephen Lawrence; production stage manager, Dianne Trulock; stage manager, Jane Grey; press, the Fred Nathan Company, Merle Frimark.

Time: 1961. Place: Los Angeles. The play was presented in two parts.

Character study of Florence Aadland (co-author of the book about the real-life episodes on which this play is based), whose daughter had a much-publicized affair with Errol Flynn. The play was presented in two parts. Previously produced at the Coconut Grove Playhouse, Miami, Fla.

*Penn & Teller: The Refrigerator Tour (67). Magic show with Penn Jillette and Teller. Produced by Richard Frankel, Thomas Viertel and Steven Baruch at the Eugene O'Neill Theater. Opened April 3, 1991.

Special guest: Carol Perkins.

Original music: "Liftoff/Ripoff of Love" by Gary Stockdale, Penn Jillette and Teller; "Burnin' Luv" by Gary Stockdale. Ambient music: Yma Sumac.

Scenery, John Lee Beatty; lighting, Dennis Parichy; sound, T. Richard Fitzgerald and Craig Van Tassel; "director of covert activities," Robert P. Libbon; "director of internal affairs," Mike Wills; associate producer, Marc Routh; production stage manager, Cathy B. Blaser; stage manager, Marilyn Helinek; press, Chris Boneau, Jackie Green.

Mixture of magic and humor in the Penn & Teller style, as in previous appearances off Broadway 4/18/85 for 666 performances and on Broadway 12/1/87 for 130 performances.

ACT I: Amanao 'Damocles, A Card Trick, Liftoff to Love/Ripoff of Love, Two Modern Fakir Tricks, Quotation of the Day, Two Houdini Tricks.

ACT II: Mofo, the Psychic Gorilla, By Buddha This Duck Is Immortal!, Cuffed to a Creep, Burnin' Luv, Shadows, King of Animal Traps.

Penn & Teller: The Refrigerator Tour—Penn Jillette *(left)* and Teller in a scene from their comedy and magic show

Lucifer's Child (28). One-woman performance by Julie Harris in a play by William Luce; based on the writings of Isak Dinesen. Produced by Ronald S. Lee at the Music Box. Opened April 4, 1991. (Closed April 27, 1991)

Directed by Tony Abatemarco; incidental music, Charles Gross; scenery, Marjorie Bradley Kellogg; costumes, Noel Taylor; lighting, Pat Collins; sound, T. Richard Fitzgerald; production stage manager, Patrick Horrigan; stage manager, Jack Doulin; press, David Rothenberg Associates.

Place: Karen Blixen's study at Rungstedlund, Denmark. Time: Act I, New Year's Eve, 1958. Act II: April, 1959.

Julie Harris as the author "Isak Dinesen" (Baroness Karen Blixen), based on her autobiographical writings about Africa and her personal drama. Previously performed at Duke University (where it was developed), Washington, D.C. and Boston.

*I Hate Hamlet (62). by Paul Rudnick. Produced by Jujamcyn Theaters, James B. Freydberg, Robert G. Perkins and Margo Lion at the Walter Kerr Theater. Opened April 8, 1991.

Felicia Dantine	Caroline Aaron	Lillian Troy	Celeste Holm
Andrew Rally	Evan Handler	John Barrymore	Nicol Williamson
Deirdre McDavey	Jane Adams	Gary Peter Lefkowitz	Adam Arkin

Understudies: Mr. Williamson—Richard M. Davidson; Messrs. Handler, Arkin—Andrew Mutnik; Misses Holm, Aaron—Marilyn Pasekoff; Misses Aaron, Adams—Deanna Dunmyer.

Directed by Michael Engler; scenery, Tony Straiges; costumes, Jane Greenwood; lighting, Paul Gallo; sound, Scott Lehrer; music, Kim Sherman; fight direction, B.H. Barry; associate producers, 126 Second Avenue Corporation, William P. Wingate; production stage manager, Pat Sosnow; stage manager, Eric S. Osbun; press, Adrian Bryan-Brown, John Barlow, Cabrini Lepis.

Time: The present. Place: New York City. The play was presented in two parts.

John Barrymore's ghost appears to help a soap-opera actor play Hamlet in Central Park.

Andrew Mutnick replaced Evan Handler 5/2/91.

*Miss Saigon (58). Musical with book by Alain Boublil and Claude-Michel Schönberg; music by Claude-Michel Schönberg; lyrics by Richard Maltby Jr. and Alain Boublil; adapted from the original French lyrics by Alain Boublil; additional material by Richard Maltby Jr. Produced by Cameron Mackintosh at the Broadway Theater. Opened April 11, 1991.

ACT I

Saigon—1975

The Engineer	Jonathan Pryce
Kim	Lea Salonga
Kim (Wed. mat., Sat. eve.)	Kam Cheng
Gigi	Marina Chapa
Mimi	Sala Iwamatsu
Yvette	Imelda de los Reyes
Yvonne	JoAnn M. Hunter
Chris	Willy Falk
John	Hinton Battle
Thuy	Barry K. Bernal

Marines: Paul Dobie, Michael Gruber, Leonard Joseph, Paul Matsumoto, Sean McDermott, Thomas James O'Leary, Gordon Owens, Christopher Pecaro, Matthew Pedersen, Kris Phillips, W. Ellis Porter, Alton F. White, Bruce Winant.

Barmen: Zar Acayan, Alan Ariano, Jason Ma.

Vietnamese Customers: Tony C. Avanti, Eric Chan, Francis J. Cruz, Darren Lee, Ray Santos, Nephi Jay Wimmer.

Embassy Workers, Inhabitants of Saigon, Vendors: Company.

Ho Chi Minh City (formerly Saigon)—April 1978

Ellen	Liz Callaway
Tam	Brian R. Baldomero
Tam (Mon., Wed., Fri., Sat. eve.)	Philip Lyle Kong
Guards	Tony C. Avanti, Francis J. Cruz
Asst. Commissar	Eric Chan

Dragon Acrobats: Darren Lee, Michael Gruber, Nephi Jay Wimmer.

Soldiers: Zar Acayan, Alan Ariano, Jason Ma. Citizens of Ho Chi Minh City, Refugees: Company.

ACT II

USA—September 1978

Conference Delegates	Company

Bangkok—October 1978

Owner of Moulin Rouge	Francis J. Cruz

Hustlers: Zar Acayan, Jason Ma, Paul Matsumoto, Ray Santos, Nephi Jay Wimmer.

Inhabitants of Bangkok, Bar Girls, Vendors, Tourists: Company.

Saigon—April 1975
    Shultz . . . . Thomas James O'Leary
    Antoine . . . . Alton F. White
    Reeves . . . . Bruce Winant
    Gibbons. . . . . Paul Dobie
    Troy . . . . Leonard Joseph
    Nolen . . . . Gordon Owens

Huston . . . . Matthew Pedersen
Frye . . . . Sean McDermott
Marines, Vietnamese Civilians: Company.
Bangkok—October 1978.
    Inhabitants of Bangkok, Customers of the
Moulin Rouge: Company.

Orchestra: Robert Billig conductor; Jay Alger associate conductor, keyboards; Braden Toan assistant conductor, bassoon; Louann Montesi concertmaster; Mineko Yajima, Ming Yeh, Sandra Billingslea violin; Mitsue Takayama viola; David Bakamjian, Julie Green cello; Douglas Romoff bass; Timothy Malosh, David Weiss flute; Lino Gomez clarinet; Sal Spicola clarinet, saxophone; Blair Tindall oboe; Russell Rizner, Daniel Culpepper, French horn; Richard Henly, Anthony Gorruso trumpet; Jack Gale trombone; John Hahn bass trombone, tuba; Peter Calandra keyboards; Doug Quinn guitars; Michael Hinton, Howard Joines percussion.

Understudies: Mr. Pryce—Tony C. Avanti, Paul Matsumoto; Misses Salonga, Cheng—Annette Calud, Imelda de los Reyes, Melanie Mariko Toji; Mr. Falk—Sean McDermott, Christopher Pecaro; Mr. Battle—Leonard Joseph, Alton F. White; Miss Callaway—Jane Bodle; Mr. Bernal—Zar Acayan, Jason Ma; Swings: Sylvia Dohi, Henry Menedez, Marc Oka, Todd Zamarripa.

Directed by Nicholas Hytner; musical staging, Bob Avian; scenery, John Napier; costumes, Andreane Neofitou, Suzy Benzinger; lighting, David Hersey; sound, Andrew Bruce; orchestrations, William D. Brohn; musical supervision, David Caddick, Robert Billig; associate director, Mitchell Lemsky; executive producers, Mitchell Lemsky, Richard Jay-Alexander; associate producer, Martin McCallum; production stage manager, Fred Hanson; stage managers, Sherry Cohen, Tom Capps; press, the Fred Nathan Company, Marc Thibodeau.

Variations on the *Madama Butterfly* theme, as an American G.I. meets and loves a Vietnamese bar girl during the last stages of the U.S. withdrawal from Saigon, leaving her with a child. A foreign play previously produced in London, with some changes made for this New York production.

A Best Play; see page 225.

A Best Play; see page 225.

ACT I

Saigon—April 1975
    "The Heat Is on in Saigon" . . . . Engineer, Girls, Marines, Company
    "The Movie in My Mind" . . . . Gigi, Kim, Girls
    "The Transaction" . . . . John, Engineer, Chris, Company
    "Why God Why?" . . . . Chris
    "Sun and Moon" . . . . Kim, Chris
    "The Telephone" . . . . John, Chris, Engineer
    "The Ceremony" . . . . Kim, Chris, Girls
    "The Last Night of the World" . . . . Kim, Chris
Ho Chi Minh City—April 1978
    "The Morning of the Dragon" . . . . Company, Thuy, Engineer
    "I Still Believe" . . . . Kim, Ellen
    "Back in Town" . . . . Kim, Engineer, Thuy
    "You Will Not Touch Him" . . . . Kim, Thuy
    "If You Want to Die in Bed" . . . . Engineer
    "I'd Give My Life for You" . . . . Kim, Company

ACT II

USA—September 1978
    "Bui-Doi" . . . . John, Company
Bangkok—October 1978
    "What a Waste" . . . . Engineer, Company
    "Please" . . . . John, Kim
    "The Guilt Inside Your Head" (the fall of Saigon, April 1975) . . . . Thuy, Kim,
                                                                         Chris, John, Company
    "Sun and Moon" (Reprise) . . . . Kim
    "Room 317" . . . . Ellen, Kim
    "Now That I've Seen Her" . . . . Ellen
    "The Confrontation" . . . . Ellen, Chris, John

"The American Dream" . . . . Engineer, Company
"Little God of My Heart" . . . . Kim, Tam

*The Secret Garden (42). Musical based on the novel by Frances Hodgson Burnett; book and lyrics by Marsha Norman; music by Lucy Simon. Produced by Heidi Landesman, Rick Steiner, Frederic H. Mayerson, Elizabeth Williams, Jujamcyn Theaters/TV ASAHI and Dodger Productions at the St. James Theater. Opened April 25, 1991.

Lily . . . . Rebecca Luker
(Mary Lennox) . . . . Daisy Eagan,
Kimberly Mahon

In Colonial India, 1906:
Fakir. . . . . Peter Marinos
Ayah . . . . Patricia Phillips
Rose . . . . Kay Walbye
Capt. Albert Lennox . . . . Michael De Vries
Lt. Peter Wright. . . . . Drew Taylor
Lt. Ian Shaw . . . . Paul Jackel
Maj. Holmes . . . . Peter Samuel
Claire . . . . Rebecca Judd
Alice. . . . . Nancy Johnston

At Misselthwaite Manor, North Yorkshire, England, 1906:
Archibald Craven . . . . . . Mandy Patinkin
Dr. Neville Craven . . . . Robert Westenberg
Mrs. Medlock . . . . Barbara Rosenblat
Martha . . . . Alison Fraser
Dickon . . . . John Cameron Mitchell
Ben . . . . Tom Toner
Colin. . . . . John Babcock
Jane. . . . . Teresa De Zarn
William . . . . Frank DiPasquale
Betsy . . . . Betsy Friday
Timothy . . . . Alec Timerman
Mrs. Winthrop . . . . Nancy Johnston
Others . . . . Ensemble

(Parentheses indicate role in which the actors alternated)

Orchestra: Michael Kosarin conductor; Jeanine Levenson associate conductor, keyboard; Jeff Carney basses; Kevin Kuhn guitar; Steve Schneider hammered dulcimer; Susan Jolles harp; James Saporito percussion; Neil Balm trumpet; Matt Finders trombone; Kaitlin Mahoney, Katharine Dennis, Leise Anscheutz, French horn; Keith Underwood, Andrew Sterman, Vicki Bodner, Don McGeen woodwinds; Dale Stuckenbruck concert master; Cecelia Hobbs Gardner, Ann Labin, Rudy Perrault, Evan Johnson, Yong Tae Kim violin; Julien Barber viola; Mark Shuman, Maria Kitsopoulous cello.

Standby: Mr. Patinkin—Greg Zerkle. Understudies: Miss Luker—Teresa De Zarn, Nancy Johnston; Misses Eagan, Mahon—Melody Kay; Mr. Patinkin—Michael De Vries, Paul Jackel; Miss Rosenblat—Rebecca Judd, Jane Seaman; Miss Fraser—Betsy Friday, Jennifer Smith; Mr. Mitchell—Kevin Ligon, Alec Timerman; Mr. Toner—Bill Nolte, Drew Taylor; Mr. Babcock—Joel E. Chaikin; Miss Walbye—Teresa De Zarn, Betsy Friday; Mr. De Vries—Paul Jackel, Greg Zerkle; Mr. Marinos—Kevin Ligon, Alec Timerman; Miss Phillips—Rebecca Judd, Jennifer Smith; Mr. Taylor—Frank DiPasquale, Bill Nolte; Mr. Jackel—Kevin Ligon, Alec Timerman; Mr. Samuel—Frank DiPasquale, Bill Nolte; Miss Judd—Betsy Friday, Jane Seaman; Miss Johnston—Betsy Friday, Jennifer Smith; Miss Johnston—Rebecca Judd, Jennifer Smith; Swings—Kevin Ligon, Bill Nolte, Jane Seaman, Jennifer Smith.

Directed by Susan H. Schulman; choreography, Michael Lichtefeld; musical direction and vocal arrangements, Michael Kosarin; scenery, Heidi Landesman; costumes, Theoni V. Aldredge; lighting, Tharon Musser; sound, Otts Munderloh; orchestrations, William D. Brohn; dance arrangements, Jeanine Levenson; senior associate producer, Greg C. Mosher; associate producers, Rhoda Mayerson, Playhouse Square Center, Dorothy and Wendell Cherry, Margo Lion, and 126 Second Ave. Corp.; production stage manager, Perry Cline; stage managers, Francis Lombardi, Maximo Torres; press, Adrian Bryan-Brown.

Mysteries of life and death, as per the 1911 novel on which the show is based. Previously produced at Skidmore College and the Virginia Stage Company, Norfolk, Va.

ACT I

Opening
"Opening Dream" . . . . Lily, Fakir, Mary, Company
India
"There's a Girl" . . . . Company
The library at Misselthwaite Manor; A train platform in Yorkshire; The door to Misselthwaite Manor
"The House Upon the Hill" . . . . Company
Mary's room; The gallery
"I Heard Someone Crying". . . . . Mary, Archibald, Lily, Company
Scene 1: Mary's sitting room
"A Fine White Horse" . . . . Martha

THE SECRET GARDEN—Rebecca Luker and Mandy
Patinkin in the Marsha Norman–Lucy Simon musical

Scene 2: The ballroom
  "A Girl in the Valley" . . . . Lily, Archibald, Dancers
Scene 3: In the maze; The greenhouse; The edge of the moor
  "It's a Maze" . . . . Ben, Mary, Dickon
  "Winter's on the Wing" . . . . Dickon
  "Show Me the Key" . . . . Mary, Dickon
Scene 4: Archibald's library
  "A Bit of Earth" . . . . Archibald
Scene 5: The gallery
  "Storm I" . . . . Company
  "Lily's Eyes" . . . . Archibald, Neville
Scene 6: The hallway
  "Storm II" . . . . Mary, Company
Scene 7: Colin's room
  "Round-Shouldered Man" . . . . Colin
Scene 8: On the grounds; The door to the garden
  "Final Storm" . . . . Company

ACT II

Scene 1: The tea party dream; The other side of the door
"The Girl I Mean to Be" . . . . Mary, Company
Scene 2: Archibald's dressing room
"Quartet" . . . . Archibald, Neville, Rose, Lily
Scene 3: Colin's room
"Race You to the Top of the Morning" . . . . Archibald
Scene 4: The greenhouse
"Wick" . . . . Dickon, Mary
Scene 5: Colin's room
"Come to My Garden" . . . . Lily, Colin
Scene 6: In the maze; The garden
"Come Spirit, Come Charm" . . . . Mary, Martha, Dickon, Fakir, Ayah, Lily, Company
"A Bit of Earth" (Reprise) . . . . Lily, Rose, Albert
Scene 7: The library
"Disappear" . . . . Neville
Scene 8: Mary's room; Paris
"Hold On" . . . . Martha
"Letter Song" . . . . Mary, Martha
Scene 9: Archibald's rooms in Paris
"Where in the World" . . . . Archibald
"How Could I Ever Know" . . . . Lily, Archibald
Scene 10: The garden
Finale . . . . Company

*Gypsy (38). Return engagement of the revival of the musical suggested by the memoirs of Gypsy Rose Lee; book by Arthur Laurents; music by Jule Styne; lyrics by Stephen Sondheim; original production directed and choreographed by Jerome Robbins. Produced by Barry and Fran Weissler, Kathy Levin and Barry Brown at the Marquis Theater. Opened April 28, 1991.

Uncle Jocko; Kringelein	Stan Rubin	Tulsa	Robert Lambert
George;		Yonkers	Bruce Moore
Mr. Goldstone	Victor Raider-Wexler	L.A.	Craig Waletzko
Clarence.	Bobby John Carter	Kansas	Paul Geraci
Balloon Girl	Jeana Haege	Flagstaff.	Kevin Petitto
Baby Louise.	Kristen Mahon	St. Paul	Cory English
Baby June	Susan Cremin	Mrs. Cratchitt; Tessie Tura. . .	Barbara Erwin
Rose	Tyne Daly	Agnes	Lori Ann Mahl
Pop; Cigar.	Ronn Carroll	Pastey; Bougeron-Cochon	Jeff Brooks
Weber; Phil.	Richard Levine	Mazeppa.	Jana Robbins
Herbie	Jonathan Hadary	Electra.	Anna McNeely
Louise	Crista Moore	Maid	Ginger Prince
June	Tracy Venner		

Newsboys: Bobby John Carter, Thomas Fox, Danny Cistone, Tony Yazbeck. The Cow: Crista Moore, Barbara Folts, Robin Robinson, Cory English, Kevin Petitto. Hollywood Blondes: Teri Furr, Barbara Folts, Michele Pigliavento, Nancy Melius, Robin Robinson.

Swings: Laurie Crochet, George Smyros.

Standbys: Misses Robbins, Erwin, McNeely—Ginger Prince; Miss Moore—Michele Pigliavento; Mr. Hadary—Richard Levine; Miss Daly—Jana Robbins. Understudies: Messrs. Carroll, Brooks—Victor Raider-Wexler; Mr. Lambert—Craig Waletzko; Misses Mahl, Venner—Teri Furr; Misses Mahon, Cremin—Jeana Haege; Mr. Levine—Stan Rubin.

Directed by Arthur Laurents; Jerome Robbins's choreography reproduced by Bonnie Walker; musical direction, Michael Rafter; scenery, Kenneth Foy; costumes, Theoni V. Aldredge; lighting, Natasha Katz; sound, Peter J. Fitzgerald; automation and showdeck, Feller Precision; orchestrations, Sid Ramin, Robert Ginzler; dance music arrangements, John Kander; assistant director, Richard Sabellico; musical coordinator, John Monaco; produced in association with Tokyo Broadcasting International, Inc. and Pace Theatrical Group; production stage manager, Craig Jacobs; stage manager, James Bernandi; press, Shirley Herz Associates, Robert W. Larkin.

Time: A period from the 1920s to the 1930s. Place: various cities throughout the U.S.A. The play was presented in two parts.

This production of *Gypsy* was originally produced on Broadway 11/16/89-1/6/91 for 477 performances. The list of musical numbers in *Gypsy* appears on page 338 of *The Best Plays of 1958-59*.

*Our Country's Good (38). By Timberlake Wertenbaker; based on the novel *The Playmaker* by Thomas Keneally. Produced by Frank and Woji Gero, Karl Sydow, Raymond, L. Gaspard, Frederick Zollo and Diana Bliss in the Hartford Stage Company production, Mark Lamos artistic director, David Hawkanson managing director, at the Nederlander Theater. Opened April 29, 1991.

Capt. Arthur Phillip;	Rev. Johnson; Liz Morden . . . . . Cherry Jones
John Wisehammer . . . . Richard Poe	Lt. George Johnston;
Maj. Robbie Ross;	Mary Brenham . . . . Tracey Ellis
Ketch Freeman . . . . Adam LeFevre	Lt. Will Dawes; Duckling Smith;
Capt. David Collins;	Meg Long . . . . Amelia Campbell
Robert Sideway. . . . . . . Sam Tsoutsouvas	2d Lt. Ralph Clark . . . . Peter Frechette
Capt. Watkin Tench; Aboriginal	2d Lt. William Faddy;
Australian; Black Caesar. . . Gregory Wallace	Dabby Bryant. . . . . J. Smith-Cameron
Capt. Jemmy Campbell; Midshipman	Convicts . . . . . Neville Aurelius, John Hickok
Harry Brewer; John Arscott . . . Ron McLarty	

Understudies: Messrs. McLarty, Poe, Wallace—Neville Aurelius; Messrs. Frechette, LeFevre, Tsoutsouvas—John Hickok; Misses Campbell, Ellis, Jones, Smith-Cameron—Orlagh Cassidy.

Directed by Mark Lamos; scenery, Christopher Barreca; costumes, Candice Donnelly; lighting, Mimi Jordan Sherin; sound, David Budries; associate producer, Jeffrey A. Sine; production stage manager, Fredric H. Orner; stage manager, Barbara Reo; press, Chris Boneau & Associates, Adrian Bryan-Brown, Susanne Tighe.

Time: 1788-89. Place: Sydney, Australia. The play was presented in two parts.

British military officers attempt to bring a humanizing element into the lives of convicts deported to Australia for "our country's good" by helping them put on a play, George Farquhar's *The Recruiting Officer*. A foreign play previously produced at the Royal Court Theater in London in 1988 and the Hartford, Conn. Stage Company.

A Best Play; see page 241.

*The Will Rogers Follies (35). Musical with book by Peter Stone; music composed and arranged by Cy Coleman; lyrics by Betty Comden and Adolph Green. Produced by Pierre Cossette, Martin Richards, Sam Crothers, James M. Nederlander, Stewart F. Lane and Max Weitzenhoffer in association with Japan Satellite Broadcasting, Inc. at the Palace Theater. Opened May 1, 1991.

Ziegfeld's Favorite . . . . Cady Huffman	Betty Blake . . . . Dee Hoty
Indian of the Dawn . . . . Jerry Mitchell	Will Rogers Jr. . . . . Rick Faugno
Indian Sun Goddess . . . . . . Jillana Urbina	Mary Rogers . . . . Tammy Minoff
Will Rogers . . . . Keith Carradine	James Rogers . . . . Lance Robinson
Unicyclist; Roper . . . . Vince Bruce	Freddy Rogers . . . . . Gregory Scott Carter
Wiley Post . . . . Paul Ukena Jr.	Voice of Mr. Ziegfeld . . . . . . Gregory Peck
Clem Rogers. . . . . Dick Latessa	

Will's Sisters: Roxane Barlow, Maria Calabrese, Colleen Dunn, Dana Moore, Wendy Waring, Leigh Zimmerman. Betty's Sisters: Roxane Barlow, Maria Calabrese, Colleen Dunn, Dana Moore, Wendy Waring, Leigh Zimmerman. The Will Rogers Wranglers: John Ganun, Troy Britton Johnson, Jerry Mitchell, Jason Opsahl.

The Wild West Show: Bonnie Brackney, Tom Brackney with B.A., Cocoa, Gigi, Rusty, Trixie, Zee.

The New Ziegfeld Girls: Roxane Barlow, Maria Calabrese, Ganine Derleth, Rebecca Downing, Colleen Dunn, Sally Mae Dunn, Toni Georgiana, Eileen Grace, Luba Gregus, Tonia Lynn, Dana Moore, Amiee Turner, Jillana Urbina, Wendy Waring, Christina Youngman, Leigh Zimmerman.

Orchestra: Eric Stern conductor; Karl Jurman associate conductor, keyboards; Joe Passaro assistant conductor, percussion; Patrick Brady keyboards; Ray Marchica drums; Richard Sarpola bass; Scott Kuney, Larry Campbell guitar; Robert Paparozzi harmonica; John Frosk, Joe Mosello, Danny Cahn trumpet; Jim Pugh, Larry Farrell, Paul Faulise trombone; Anthony Cecere, French horn; Chuck Wilson,

Dale Kleps, Alva Hunt, Vincent DellaRocca, Frank Santagata reeds; Amy Hiraga Wyrick concert mistress; Heidi Carney, Rob Shaw violin; Crystal Garner viola; Joe Kimura cello.

Standbys: Mr. Latessa—Tom Flagg; Miss Minoff, Messrs. Robinson, Carter—Erica Dutko. Understudies: Mr. Carradine—Paul Ukena Jr.; Miss Huffman—Dana Moore; Mr. Faugno—Lance Robinson. Swings: Marylee Dewitt, Jack Doyle, Augie L. Schworer.

Directed and choreographed by Tommy Tune; musical direction, Eric Stern; scenery, Tony Walton; costumes, Willa Kim; lighting, Jules Fisher; sound, Peter J. Fitzgerald; projection design, Wendall K. Harrington; orchestrations, Bill Byers; wig design, Howard Leonard; associate director, Philip Oesterman; associate choreographer, Jeff Calhoun; production stage manager, Peter von Mayrhauser; stage manager, Patrick Ballard; press, the Jacksina Company, Judy Jacksina, Julianne Waldheim.

Time: The present. Place: The Palace Theater.

Subtitled "A Life in Revue," a musical comedy celebration of the career and character of Will Rogers.

ACT I

Prelude: "Let's Go Flying"
Scene 1: The *Follies*
 "Will-a-Mania"... Ziegfeld's Favorite, Company
 "Give a Man Enough Rope" .... Will, Will Rogers Wranglers
Scene 2: The ranch
 "It's a Boy!".. Clem, Will's Sisters
 "So Long Pa" .... Will
Scene 3: The moon
 "My Unknown Someone".. Betty
Scene 4: The *Follies*
Scene 5: The St. Louis Exposition
 "We're Heading for a Wedding".. Will, Betty
Scene 6: Vaudeville
 "The Big Time" .... Will, Betty, Children
 "My Big Mistake"... Betty
Scene 7: The *Follies*
 "The Powder Puff Ballet" ("My Big Mistake") .... New Ziegfeld Girls
 "Marry Me Now"/"I Got You".................................... Will, Betty
Act I Wedding Finale

ACT II

Entr'Acte
Scene 1: The *Follies*
 "Give a Man Enough Rope" (Reprise)................. Will, Will Rogers Wranglers
 "Look Around" .... Will
Scene 2: The convention
 "Favorite Son".. Will, Chorus
Scene 3: The Hollywood ranch
 "No Man Left for Me"... Betty
 "Presents for Mrs. Rogers"........... Will, Will Rogers Wranglers, New Ziegfeld Girls
Scene 4: The bare stage
 "Will-a-Mania" (Reprise).. Will, Clem
 "Without You" (Reprise of "I Got You"). .... Betty
Scene 5: The finale
 "Never Met a Man I Didn't Like"............................... Will, Company

PLAYS WHICH CLOSED
PRIOR TO BROADWAY OPENING

Productions which were organized by New York producers for Broadway presentation but which closed in 1990-91 during their production and tryout period are listed below.

Kiss of the Spider Woman. Musical based on the novel by Manuel Puig; book by Terrence McNally; music by John Kander; lyrics by Fred Ebb. Produced in tryout by New Musicals, Martin J. Bell producing director, in association with and at the Performing Arts Center of the State University of New York at Purchase. Opened May 1, 1990. (Closed June 24, 1990)

Valentin . . . . Kevin Gray	Marta . . . . Lauren Mufson
Marcus . . . . Philip Hernandez	Piano Player . . . . Carl Maultsby
Warden; Monster . . . . Harry Goz	Armando . . . . Donn Simione
Esteban . . . . John Norman Thomas	Drag Queen . . . . Aurelio Padron
Guard . . . . Adam Heller	Gabriel . . . . Greg Zerkle
Molina . . . . John Rubinstein	Jose . . . . Jonathan Brody
Aurora; Spider Woman . . . . Lauren Mitchell	Jorge . . . . Forest Dino Ray
Sra. Molina . . . . Barbara Andres	

Prisoners, Insurgents, Ensemble: Jonathan Brody, Bill Christopher-Myers, David Koch, Rick Manning, Casey Nicolaw, Aurelio Padron, Forest Dino Ray, Matt Zarley, Greg Zerkle. Nurses, Parrot Girls, Ensemble: Karen Giombetti, Ruth Gottschall, Dorie Herndon, Lauren Mufson, Lorraine Serabian, Wendy Waring.

Orchestra: Donald Chan conductor; James Sedlar trumpet I; Charles Affelt trumpet II; Joseph Petrizzo trombone I; James Miller trombone II; Kaitlin Mahoney, French horn I; Leise Anschautz,

KISS OF THE SPIDER WOMAN—John Rubinstein and Kevin Gray in the musical with book by Terrence McNally, music by John Kander, lyrics by Fred Ebb

French horn II; Mimi Dye viola, violin I; Dan Seidenberg viola, violin II; Brian Zenone viola III; Don Krishnaswami viola IV; Albert Block reed I; Charles Millard reed II; David Diggs reed III; Matthew Bennett reed IV; Jay Mattes drums; Ian Finkel percussion; Luther Rix, Latin percussion; Joe Leisa bass; Robby Kirshoff guitar; David Pogue assistant conductor, piano; Carl Maultsby synthesizer; David Berkjamian cello I; Marisol Espada cello II.

Directed by Harold Prince; choreography, Susan Stroman; musical direction, Donald Chan; scenery, Thomas Lynch; costumes, Florence Klotz; lighting, Peter A. Kaczorowski; sound, Alan Stieb; orchestrations, Michael Gibson; dance arrangements, David Krane; assistant to Harold Prince, Ruth Mitchell; musical coordinator, John Monaco; production stage manager, Beverly Randolph; stage manager, Michael Pule; press, Mary Bryant, Joshua Ellis, Susanne Tighe.

Time: The present. Place: A prison in Latin America and in the minds of some of the characters. Criminal distracts a rebel leader by entertaining him with the details of movie plots.

MUSICAL NUMBERS, ACT I: "Her Name is Aurora"—John Rubinstein, Lauren Mitchell, Company; "Over the Wall I"—Male Ensemble; "Dear One"—Barbara Andres, Lauren Mufson, Kevin Gray, Rubinstein; "Man Overboard"—Mitchell, Male Ensemble; "I Do Miracles"— Mitchell, Mufson; "Over the Wall II"—Male Ensemble; "Every Day"—Donn Simione; "I Don't Know"—Mitchell, Rubinstein; "Tango"—Female Ensemble; "You Could Never Shame Me"— Andres; "Letter From a Friend"—Aurelio Padron; "Letter From Gabriel"—Greg Zerkle; "The Day After That"—Gray; "She's a Woman"—Rubinstein; "Gimme Love"—Mitchell, Company.

ACT II: "Good Clean Fight"—Male Ensemble; "Cookies"—Rubinstein, Gray; "Never You"— Simione, Mitchell; "Mama, It's Me"—Rubinstein; "Over the Wall III—Male Ensemble; "Kiss of the Spider Women"—Mitchell; "The Day After That"—Gray, Simione, Company; "Over the Wall IV"—Male Ensemble; "Only in the Movies"—Rubinstein, Karen Giombetti, Ruth Gottschall, Dorie Herndon, Wendy Waring.

Grandma Moses—An American Primitive. By Stephen Pouliot.   Produced on tour by Palm Tree Productions, Dennis Babcock executive producer, and Bob Banner Associates' Paradigm Entertainment, with the Lamb's Theater. Opened at the Fargo, N.D. Theater April 25, 1990. (Closed at Ford's Theater, Washington, D.C. June 24, 1990)

CAST: Grandma Moses—Cloris Leachman; Others—Peter Thoemke.

Directed by Howard Dallin; scenery, Michael Beery; costumes, Stephanie Schoelzel; lighting, Duane Schuler; projections, John Boesche; press, Peter Cromarty.

Grandma Moses (Anna Mary Robertson), the distinguished painter, age 45 through age 100. Previously produced on a 14-city tour in 1989.

PLAYS PRODUCED OFF BROADWAY

Some distinctions between off-Broadway and Broadway productions at one end of the scale and off-off-Broadway productions at the other are blurred in the New York Theater of the 1990s. For the purposes of the *Best Plays* listing, the term "off Broadway" is used to distinguish a professional from a showcase (off-off-Broadway) production and signifies a show which opened for general audiences in a mid-Manhattan theater seating 499 or fewer and 1) employed an Equity cast, 2) planned a regular schedule of 8 performances a week in an open-ended run and 3) offered itself to public comment by critics at designated opening performances.

Occasional exceptions of inclusion (never of exclusion) are made to take in visiting troupes, borderline cases and nonqualifying productions which readers might expect to find in this list because they appear under an off-Broadway heading in other major sources of record.

Figures in parentheses following a play's title give number of performances. These figures do not include previews or extra non-profit performances.

Plays marked with an asterisk (*) were still in a projected run on June 1, 1991. Their number of performances is figured from opening night through May 31, 1991.

Certain programs of off-Broadway companies are exceptions to our rule of counting the number of performances from the date of the press coverage. When the official opening takes place late in the run of a play's regularly-priced public or subscription performances (after previews) we count the first performance of record, not the press date, as opening night—and in each such case in the listing we note the variance and give the press date.

In a listing of a show's numbers—dances, sketches, musical scenes, etc.—the titles of songs are identified wherever possible by their appearance in quotation marks (").

HOLDOVERS FROM PREVIOUS SEASONS

Plays which were running on June 1, 1990 are listed below. More detailed information about them appears in previous *Best Plays* volumes of appropriate date. Important cast changes since opening night are recorded in the Cast Replacements section of this volume.

*The Fantasticks (12,898; longest continuous run of record in the American theater). Musical suggested by the play *Les Romanesques* by Edmond Rostand; book and lyrics by Tom Jones; music by Harvey Schmidt. Opened May 30, 1960.

*Nunsense (2,261). Musical with book, music and lyrics by Dan Goggin. Opened December 12, 1985.

*Perfect Crime (1,677). by Warren Manzi. Opened October 16, 1987.

Tamara (1,036). By John Krizanc; conceived by Richard Rose and John Krizanc. Opened December 2, 1987. (Recessed January 18, 1988) Reopened February 2, 1988. (Closed July 15, 1990)

*Other People's Money (954). By Jerry Sterner. Opened February 16, 1989.

Closer Than Ever (288). Musical revue conceived by Steven Scott Smith; music by David Shire; lyrics by Richard Maltby Jr. Opened November 16, 1989. (Closed July 1, 1990)

Forbidden Broadway 1990-91 (576). New edition of the musical revue with concept and parody lyrics by Gerard Alessandrini. Opened January 23, 1990. (Closed June 9, 1991)

By and for Havel (256). Transfer from off off Broadway of the program of two one-act revivals: *Audience* by Vaclav Havel and *Catastrophe* by Samuel Beckett. Opened April 17, 1990. (Closed October 28, 1990)

The Rothschilds (379). Transfer from off off Broadway of the revival of the musical based on *The Rothschilds* by Frederic Morton; book by Sherman Yellen; music by Jerry Bock; lyrics by Sheldon Harnick. Opened April 27, 1990. (Closed March 24, 1991)

Spunk (165). Program of three one-act plays adapted by George C. Wolfe from tales by Zora Neale Hurston: *Sweat, Story in Harlem Slang* and *The Gilded Six-Bits*; music by Chic Street Man. Opened April 18, 1990. (Closed September 2, 1990)

Talking Things Over With Chekhov (62). By John Ford Noonan. Opened May 10, 1990. (Closed July 1, 1990)

Each Day Dies With Sleep (44). By Jose Rivera. Opened May 16, 1990. (Closed June 10, 1990)

Further Mo' (174). Musical conceived and written by Vernel Bagneris. Opened May 17, 1990. (Closed October 14, 1990)

The B. Beaver Animation (25). Revival of the play by Lee Breuer. Opened May 20, 1990. (Closed June 10, 1990)

*Forever Plaid (428). Musical by Stuart Ross. Opened May 20, 1990.

The Grand Guignol (94). Program of three one-act plays: *Experiment at the Asylum* by Annie C. Hogue and Mitch Hogue, *The Treatment of Dr. Love* by William Squier and *Orgy in the Air-Traffic Control Tower* by Sean Burke and Steve Nelson. Opened May 24, 1990. (Closed August 12, 1990)

PLAYS PRODUCED JUNE 1, 1990—MAY 31, 1991

Manhattan Theater Club. 1989-90 season concluded with **Prin** (35). By Andrew Davies. Produced by Manhattan Theater Club, Lynne Meadow artistic director, Barry Grove managing director, at City Center Stage I. Opened June 6, 1990. (Closed July 6, 1990)

Prin . . . . Eileen Atkins	Walker . . . . John Christopher Jones
Dibs . . . . Amy Wright	Kite . . . . Remak Ramsay
Boyle . . . . John Curless	Melanie . . . . Wendy Makkena

Directed by John Tillinger; scenery, John Lee Beatty; costumes, Jane Greenwood; lighting, Richard Nelson; sound, Bruce Ellman. Production stage manager, Travis DeCastro; press, Helene Davis, Clay Martin.

Study of a school principal who is overly zealous in her striving for perfection. A foreign play previously produced in London.

Elliot Loves (44). By Jules Feiffer. Produced by Roger Berlind at the Promenade Theater. Opened June 7, 1990. (Closed July 15, 1990)

Elliot . . . . Anthony Heald	Phil . . . . David Pierce
Joanna . . . . Christine Baranski	Larry . . . . Oliver Platt
Vera . . . . La Tanya Richardson	Bobby . . . . Bruce A. Young

Directed by Mike Nichols; scenery, Tony Walton; costumes, Ann Roth; lighting, Paul Gallo; sound, Tom Sorce; associate producer, Susan MacNair; stage manager, John Brigleb; press, Bill Evans & Associates.

Time: The mid-1980s. Place: Chicago. The play was presented in two parts.

Neurotic man subjects his lover to review by his neurotic friends as a sort of audition for marriage—with devastating results. Previously produced at the Goodman Theater, Chicago.

Roundabout Theater Company. 1989-90 season concluded with **Price of Fame** (31). By Charles Grodin. Opened June 13, 1990. (Closed July 8, 1990) And **Light Up the Sky** (40). Revival of the play by Moss Hart. Opened August 21, 1990. (Closed September 23, 1990) Produced by Roundabout Theater Company, Todd Haimes producing director, Gene Feist founding director, at the Christian C. Yegen Theater.

PRICE OF FAME

Roger . . . . Charles Grodin	Karen . . . . Lizbeth Mackay
Pete . . . . W.J. Paterson	Evelyn . . . . Jeannie Berlin
Matt . . . . Jace Alexander	Cappy . . . . Michael Ingram
Mario . . . . Joseph R. Sicari	Bob . . . . Sam Groom

Directed by Gloria Muzio; scenery, David Jenkins; costumes, Jess Goldstein; lighting, Tharon Musser; sound, Philip Campanella; production stage manager, Kathy J. Faul; press, Josh Ellis, Susanne Tighe.

Hollywood star confides his career and personal woes to a female reporter.

LIGHT UP THE SKY

Miss Lowell . . . . Elaine Bromka	Sven; Shriner; Plainclothes Cop . . Paul Nielsen
Carleton Fitzgerald . . . . Charles Keating	Irene Livingston . . . . Linda Carlson
Frances Black . . . . Betsy Joslyn	Tyler Rayburn . . . . John C. Vennema
Owen Turner . . . . . . Humbert Allen Astredo	Max . . . . Max Robinson
Stella Livingston . . . . Peggy Cass	Shriner . . . . Peter Robinson
Peter Sloan . . . . John Bolger	William H. Gallegher . . . . . Bill McCutcheon
Sidney Black . . . . Bruce Weitz	

Directed by Larry Carpenter; scenery, Andrew Jackness; costumes, Martin Pakledinaz; lighting, Dennis Parichy; sound, Philip Campanella; production stage manager, Roy W. Backes.

Light Up the Sky was originally produced on Broadway 11/18/48 for 216 performances. This is its first major New York revival. The play was presented in three parts.

Jason Alexander replaced Bruce Weitz 8/28/90.

Lincoln Center Theater. 1989-90 season concluded with **Six Degrees of Separation** (155). By John Guare. Produced by Lincoln Center, Gregory Mosher director, Bernard Gersten executive producer, at the Mitzi E. Newhouse Theater. Opened June 14, 1990. (Closed October 28, 1990 and transferred to Broadway status at the Vivian Beaumont Theater; see its entry in the Plays Produced on Broadway section of this volume)

Ouisa . . . . Stockard Channing	Woody . . . . Gus Rogerson
Flan . . . . John Cunningham	Ben . . . . Anthony Rapp
Geoffrey . . . . Sam Stoneburner	Dr. Fine . . . . Stephen Pearlman
Paul . . . . James McDaniel	Doug . . . . Evan Handler
Hustler . . . . David Eigenberg	Policeman; Doorman . . . . . . Philip LeStrange
Kitty . . . . Kelly Bishop	Trent . . . . John Cameron Mitchell
Larkin . . . . Peter Maloney	Rick . . . . Paul McCrane
Detective . . . . Brian Evers	Elizabeth. . . . . Mari Nelson
Tess . . . . Robin Morse	

THE TAMING OF THE SHREW—Morgan Freeman as Petruchio and Tracey Ullman as Katherina in the New York Shakespeare Festival production

Understudies: Misses Channing, Bishop—Sarba Jones; Mr. McDaniel—Gregory Simmons; Messrs. Cunningham, Maloney—Brian Evers; Messrs. Stoneburner, Pearlman—David Little; Messrs. McCrane, Mitchell—Evan Handler; Messrs. Rogerson, Handler—David Eigenberg; Misses Morse, Nelson—Laura Linney; Messrs. Rapp, Eigenberg—Ray Cochran.

Directed by Jerry Zaks; scenery, Tony Walton; costumes, William Ivey Long; lighting, Paul Gallo; sound, Aural Fixation; production stage manager, Steve Beckler; stage manager, Sarah Manley; press, Merle Debusky, Susan Chicoine.

Time: Today. Place: New York City. The play was presented without intermission.

Black impostor intrudes on a white family by pretending to be a college chum of their son's.

Swoosie Kurtz replaced Kelly Bishop 8/20/90.

New York Shakespeare Festival Shakespeare Marathon. Schedule of four revivals of plays by William Shakespeare (see note). **The Taming of the Shrew** (27). Opened June 22, 1990; see note. (Closed July 22, 1990) **Richard III** (27). Opened August 3, 1990; see note. (Closed September 2, 1990) Produced by New York Shakespeare Festival, Joseph Papp producer, in association with New York Telephone and with the cooperation of the City of New York, David N. Dinkins mayor, Mary Schmidt Campbell commissioner of cultural afffairs, Elizabeth F. Gotbaum commissioner of parks & recreation, at the Delacorte Theater in Central Park.

Also **Henry IV, Part 1** (23) and **Part 2** (23). Opened February 26, 1991 (Part 1) and February 27, 1991 (Part 2). (Closed April 7, 1991, Part 1 at matinee, Part 2 in evening). Produced by New York Shakespeare Festival, Joseph Papp producer, at the Public Theater (see note).

ALL PLAYS: Associate producer, Jason Steven Cohen; plays and musicals development director, Gail Merrifield; production manager, Andrew Mihok; press, Richard Kornberg, Barbara Carroll, Reva Cooper, Carol Fineman.

THE TAMING OF THE SHREW

Lucentio	Graham Winton	Curtis	Michael Gaston
Tranio	Robert Joy	Nathaniel	Joe Zaloom
Baptista Minola	George Guidall	Joe Bob	Wade Williams
Katherina	Tracey Ullman	Walter	Tim Perez
Bianca	Helen Hunt	Sugarsop	Timothy D. Stickney
Gremio	Mark Hammer	Beau	Peter Ryan
Hortensio	Tom Mardirosian	Travelling Actor	William Duff-Griffin
Biondello	Peter Appel	Tailor	Norris Shimabuku
Petruchio	Morgan Freeman	Vincentio	Thomas Barbour
Grumio	Jose Perez	Widow	Leah Maddrie
Bartender	Royal E. Miller		

Understudies: Mr. Winton, Ensemble—Royal E. Miller; Mr. Joy—Tim Perez; Messrs. Freeman, Guidall, Barbour—Michael Gaston; Miss Ullman—Leah Maddrie; Misses Hunt, Maddrie— Giovanna Sardelli; Messrs. Hammer, Shimabuku, Ensemble—Peter Ryan; Mr. Mardirosian, Ensemble—Wade Williams; Messrs. Appel, Gaston, Ensemble—Timothy D. Stickney; Mr. Perez— Joe Zaloom.

Directed by A.J. Antoon; scenery, John Lee Beatty; costumes, Lindsay W. Davis; lighting, Peter Kaczorowski; music, Claude White; fights, B.H. Barry; production stage manager, Ron Nash; stage manager, Lisa Buxbaum.

Shakespeare's comedy adapted as a tale of the 19th century American West, presented in two parts. The last major New York production of *The Taming of the Shrew* was by New York Shakespeare Festival at the Delacorte Theater 8/3/78 for 28 performances.

THE TRAGEDY OF KING RICHARD III

Richard, Duke of Gloucester	Denzel Washington	Hastings	Jeffrey Nordling
Duke of Clarence	Joseph Ziegler	Lady Anne	Sharon Washington
Robert Brakenbury; Bishop of Ely	John Newton	Tressel; Father John; Oxford	Royal E. Miller

Berkeley; Christopher Urswick;
  Messenger . . . . John Miskulin
Halberdier; Messenger . . . . . Justin Thompson
Guard; Messenger;
  Derby's Messenger . . . . . Michael McElroy
Queen Elizabeth . . . . Nancy Palk
Lord Rivers . . . . Philip Moon
Lord Grey . . . . Richard Holmes
Dorset . . . . David Aaron Baker
Buckingham . . . . Daniel Davis
Earl of Derby . . . . Ben Hammer
Queen Margaret . . . . Mary Alice
Catesby. . . . . Jake Weber
1st Murderer; Blunt . . . . Wade Williams
2d Murderer . . . . Tim Nelson
Edward IV . . . . Sam Tsoutsouvas
Ratcliffe. . . . . Jonathan Fried
Duchess of York. . . . . . . Virginia Downing

Edward Plantagenet . . . . . . Reese Madigan
Margaret Plantagenet . . . . Jenny Nichols
1st Citizen . . . . Tracey Copeland
2d Citizen . . . . Lisa Arrindell
3d Citizen; Archbishop
  of Canterbury . . . . Tom Hewitt
Archbishop of York; Lovell . . . . Curt Hostetter
Duke of York. . . . . Jesse Bernstein
Prince Edward. . . . . Seth Gilliam
Lord Mayor; Tyrrel . . . . Peter McRobbie
Jane Shore . . . . Erin J. O'Brien
Vaughan . . . . William Moses
Duke of Norfolk . . . . Bruce Katzman
Messenger; Sheriff of Wiltshire . . Brett Rickaby
Richmond . . . . Armand Schultz
Sir Walter Herbert . . . . Chris DeBari
Surrey . . . . Jean-Paul Moreau

Guards, Halberdiers, Gentlemen, Lords, Ladies, Citizens, Attendants, Soldiers, Monks: Lisa Arrindell, David Aaron Baker, Rafeal Clements, Tracey Copeland, Chris DeBari, Todd Eastland, Seth Gilliam, Steve Graham, Robert Harryman, Richard Holmes, Reese Madigan, Michael McElroy, Royal E. Miller, John Miskulin, Philip Moon, Jean-Paul Moreau, William Moses, Tim Nelson, Jenny Nichols, Erin J. O'Brien, Brett Rickaby, Richard Roy, Justin Thompson, Wade Williams.

Understudies: Mr. Washington—Jake Weber; Mr. Ziegler—Armand Schultz; Mr. Hewitt—Curt Hostetter; Mr. Nordling—Wade Williams; Misses Washington, Nichols, Mr. Bernstein—Erin J. O'Brien; Messrs. Miller, Moses, Rickaby—Chris DeBari; Mr. Miskulin—Justin Thompson; Misses Palk, Downing—Tracey Copeland; Messrs. Holmes, Katzman—Rafeal Clements; Mr. Baker—Jean-Paul Moreau; Mr. Davis—Tom Hewitt; Messrs. Hammer, Newton—Bruce Katzman; Miss Alice—Lisa Arrindell; Mr. Weber—William Moses; Messrs. Williams, McRobbie—Richard Holmes; Mr. Nelson—Steve Graham; Mr. Tsoutsouvas—Jonathan Fried; Messrs. Fried, McElroy—Brett Rickaby; Misses Copeland, Arrindell, Mr. Hewitt—Todd Eastland; Mr. Hostetter—Robert Harryman; Mr. Schultz—Michael McElroy.

Directed by Robin Phillips; scenery and costumes, Elis Y. Lam; lighting, Louis Guinand; music, Louis Appelbaum; fight staging, Martino N. Pistone; production stage manager, Susie Cordon; stage manager, Allison Sommers.

The last major New York revival of *Richard III* took place on Broadway 6/14/79 for 33 performances. The play was presented in three parts.

HENRY IV
PART 1

The Court:
  Henry IV . . . . Larry Bryggman
  Henry, Prince of Wales (Hal) . . Thomas Gibson
  John of Lancaster. . . . . Arnold Molina
  Thomas of Clarence. . . . . Roger Bart
  Humphrey of Gloucester. . . . Reese Madigan
  Westmoreland. . . . . Norris Shimabuku
  Lord Chief Justice . . . Richard Russell Ramos
  Blunt . . . . Kelly C. Morgan
The Rebels:
  Henry Percy
    of Northumberland. . . . . . Miguel Perez
  Henry Percy (Hotspur). . . . . . Jared Harris
  Lady Percy (Kate) . . . . . Lisa Gay Hamilton
  Thomas Percy of Worcester . . Daniel Oreskes
  Owen Glendower. . . . . Traber Burns
  Mortimer. . . . . Mark Deakins
  Lady Mortimer . . . . Moon Hi Hanson

  Douglas . . . . John Wojda
  Archbishop of York . . . Rodney Scott Hudson
  Brother Michael . . . . Richard Spore
  Morton. . . . . Tom Nelis
The Tavern: Eastcheap, London
  Sir John Falstaff. . . . . Louis Zorich
  Bardolph . . . . David Manis
  Peto . . . . David J. Steinberg
  Gadshill . . . . Tim Perez
  Poins. . . . . Rene Rivera
  Mistress Quickly . . . . Ruth Maleczech
  Francis . . . . Roger Bart
  Vintner. . . . . J. David Brimmer
Others:
  Carrier #1 . . . . Richard Spore
  Carrier #2 . . . . William Duell
  Chamberlain . . . . Susan Wands
  Guards . . . . . . Kent Gash, Rafeal Clements

PART 2

Rumor. . . . . Caris Corfman
The Court:
Henry IV . . . . Larry Bryggman
Henry, Prince of Wales (Hal) . Thomas Gibson
John of Lancaster. . . . . Arnold Molina
Thomas of Clarence. . . . . Roger Bart
Humphrey of Gloucester. . . . Reese Madigan
Westmoreland. . . . . Norris Shimabuku
Lord Chief Justice . . . Richard Russell Ramos
Harcourt . . . . Kelly C. Morgan
The Rebels:
Henry Percy of Northumberland . Miguel Perez
Lady Northumberland. . . . . Caris Corfman
Lady Percy (Kate) . . . . . Lisa Gay Hamilton
Archbishop of York . . . Rodney Scott Hudson
Brother Michael . . . . Richard Spore
Lord Bardolph . . . . Daniel Oreskes
Morton. . . . . Tom Nelis
Travers. . . . . Kent Gash
Hastings. . . . . Traber Burns
Mowbray. . . . . Mark Deakins
Coleville . . . . John Wojda

The Tavern: Eastcheap, London
Sir John Falstaff. . . . . Louis Zorich
Page. . . . . Jason S. Woliner
Bardolph . . . . David Manis
Peto . . . . David J. Steinberg
Pistol. . . . . Jared Harris
Poins. . . . . Rene Rivera
Mistress Quickly . . . . Ruth Maleczech
Doll Tearsheet . . . . Susan Wands
Fang . . . . Tim Perez
Snare. . . . . J. David Brimmer
Francis . . . . Roger Bart
The Country: Gloucestershire
Shallow . . . . William Duell
Silence. . . . . Richard Spore
Davy . . . . Peter Schmitz
Mouldy. . . . . Tim Perez
Shadow . . . . Tom Nelis
Wart. . . . . Arnold Molina
Feeble . . . . Jared Harris
Bullcalf . . . . Miguel Perez
Others:
Guards . . . . . . Kent Gash, Rafeal Clements

BOTH PLAYS: Messengers, Soldiers, Musicians, Street and Tavern People (in Part I); Same and Circus (Part II): Roger Bart, J. David Brimmer, Traber Burns, Rafeal Clements, Caris Corfman, Mark Deakins, William Duell, Kent Gash, Mel Duane Gionson, Lisa Gay Hamilton, Moon Hi Hanson, Rodney Scott Hudson, Reese Madigan, David Manis, Arnold Molina, Kelly C. Morgan, Tom Nelis, Daniel Oreskes, Miguel Perez, Tim Perez, Richard Russell Ramos, Rene Rivera, Peter Schmitz, Norris Shimabuku, Mia Sneden, Richard Spore, David J. Steinberg, Susan Wands, John Wojda, Jason S. Woliner.

Musicians: Alan Johnson keyboards; Jon Gibson clarinet, saxophone; William Trigg percussion.

Directed by JoAnne Akalaitis; scenery, George Tsypin; costumes, Gabriel Berry; lighting, Jennifer Tipton; original music, Philip Glass; musical direction, Alan Johnson; sound, John Gromada; projections, John Boesche; fight direction, David S. Leong; production stage manager, Lisa Buxbaum; stage manager, Buzz Cohen.

The last major New York production of *Henry IV, Part 1* was by New York Shakespeare Festival at the Delacorte Theater in Central Park 8/27/87 for 16 performances; of *Henry IV, Part 2* was in Classic Stage Company repertory 10/22/78.

Note: Press date for *The Taming of the Shrew* was 7/12/90, for *The Tragedy of King Richard III* was 8/16/90.

Note: In Joseph Papp's Public Theater there are many auditoria. *Henry IV* played the Estelle R. Newman Theater.

Note: New York Shakespeare Festival Shakespeare Marathon will continue through following seasons until all of Shakespeare's plays have been presented. *A Midsummer Night's Dream, Julius Caesar* and *Romeo and Juliet* were presented in the 1987-88 season; *Much Ado About Nothing, King John, Coriolanus, Love's Labor's Lost, The Winter's Tale* and *Cymbeline* were presented in the 1988-89 season; and *Twelfth Night, Titus Andronicus, Macbeth* and *Hamlet* were presented in the 1989-90 season (see their entries in *Best Plays* volumes of appropriate years).

Jekyll and Hyde (45; see note). Musical based on the book by Robert Louis Stevenson; book and lyrics by David Crane and Marta Kauffman; music by Michael Skloff. Produced by Theaterworks USA, Jay Harnick artistic director, Charles Hull managing director, in the 1990 Free Summer Theater Program, Mrs. George Bush honorary chairman, at the Promenade Theater. Opened June 25, 1990. (Closed July 22, 1990)

Henry. . . . . Christopher Scott
Stuart . . . . Eric Ruffin
Marissa; Mother . . . . Amanda Green
Chelsea . . . . Emily Bear
Vernicker; Father . . . . Frederick Einhorn

Directed by Jay Harnick; choreography, Helen Butleroff; musical direction, Wayne Abravanel; scenery, Vaughn Patterson; costumes, Ann-Marie Wright; lighting, Mathew J. Williams; musical arrangements, Steve Orich; sound consultants, Gary and Timmy Harris; production stage manager, Ronald A. Koenig; press, Judith Rabitcheff.

Rock 'n roll musical version of the Stevenson classic, designed for family audiences.

Note: *Jekyll and Hyde* played 45 performances during its regular run, plus 6 special performances 10/27/90, 10/28/90, 11/3/90 and 11/4/90.

Playwrights Horizons. 1989-90 season concluded with **Falsettoland** (215). Musical by William Finn and James Lapine; music and lyrics by William Finn. Produced by Playwrights Horizons, Andre Bishop artistic director, Paul S. Daniels executive director, at Playwrights Horizons. Opened June 28, 1990; see note. (Closed January 27, 1991)

Mendel	Chip Zien	Trina	Faith Prince
Marvin	Michael Rupert	Dr. Charlotte	Heather MacRae
Jason	Danny Gerard	Cordelia	Janet Metz
Whizzer	Stephen Bogardus		

Musicians: Michael Starobin piano, James Kowal synthesizer, Glenn Rhian drums, percussion.

Understudies: Miss Prince—Janet Metz; Messrs. Rupert, Zien, Bogardus—Tim Ewing; Misses MacRae, Metz—Ellen Zachos.

Directed by James Lapine; musical direction and arrangements, Michael Starobin; scenery, Douglas Stein; costumes, Franne Lee; lighting, Nancy Schertler; sound, Scott Lehrer; production stage manager, Kate Riddle; stage manager, Benjamin Gutkin; press, Philip Rinaldi.

An all-sung musical, third in the "Marvin Trilogy," the two previous ones being *In Trousers* and *March of the Falsettos.* AIDS intrudes into this mixture of sexual identities, in events which bring Marvin and his son closer together but leave him loverless. The play was presented without an intermission.

Note: *Falsettoland* recessed 8/12/90-9/13/90 after 54 performances and reopened at the Lucille Lortel Theater for an additional 161 performances, produced by Maurice Rosenfield, Lois F. Rosenfield and Steven Suskin with Playwrights Horizons in this production.

Lonny Price replaced Chip Zien 9/14/90.

A Best play; see page 106.

MUSICAL NUMBERS

Scene 1
"Falsettoland" . . . . Company
"About Time" . . . . Marvin
"Year of the Child" . . . . Dr. Charlotte, Cordelia,
Marvin, Trina, Mendel, Jason

Scene 2
"Miracle of Judaism" . . . . Jason

Scene 3
"The Baseball Game" . . . . Company

Scene 4
"A Day in Falsettoland"
Mendel at work . . . . Mendel
Trina and Mendel's house . . . . Trina, Mendel
Dr. Charlotte and Cordelia's house. . . . . Dr. Charlotte, Cordelia
Racquetball court . . . . Marvin, Whizzer

Scene 5
"Planning the Bar Mitzvah" . . . . Jason, Trina, Mendel, Marvin

Scene 6
"Everyone Hates His Parents" . . . . Mendel, Jason

Scene 7
"What More Can I Say?" . . . . Marvin

Scene 8
"Something Bad Is Happening" . . . . Dr. Charlotte, Cordelia

Scene 9
"More Racquetball" . . . . Marvin, Whizzer

Scene 10
    "Holding to the Ground" . . . . Trina
Scene 11
    "Days Like This" . . . . Marvin, Whizzer, Cordelia, Trina, Mendel, Jason, Dr. Charlotte
Scene 12
    "Canceling the Bar Mitzvah". . . . . Trina, Mendel, Jason
Scene 13
    "Unlikely Lovers". Marvin, Whizzer, Cordelia, Dr. Charlotte
Scene 14
    "Another Miracle of Judaism" . . . . Jason
Scene 15
    "You Gotta Die Sometime" . . . . Whizzer
Scene 16
    "Jason's Bar Mitzvah" . . . . Jason, Whizzer, Marvin, Trina, Mendel, Cordelia, Dr. Charlotte
Scene 17
    "What Would I Do?" . . . . Marvin, Whizzer

Broadway Jukebox (50). Musical revue conceived by Ed Linderman. Produced by Eric Krebs in association with Joanne Macan and Carol Wernli at the John Houseman Theater. Opened July 19, 1990. (Closed September 2, 1990)

Robert Michael Baker	Gerry McIntyre
Susan Flynn	Amelia Prentice
Beth Leavel	Sal Viviano

Musicians: Ed Linderman, Ken Lundie piano.
Standby: Ken Lundie.

Directed and choreographed by Bill Guske; production supervised by Ed Linderman; scenery, James Morgan; costumes, Barbara Forbes; lighting, Stuart Duke; sound, E.F. Morrill; production stage manager, Michael J. Chudinski; press, David Rothenberg Associates, Terence Womble.

Compendium of song numbers from relatively obscure Broadway musicals, some of them selected by audience voting on items in a list of 90 numbers, with 30 songs offered at each performance

*Smoke on the Mountain (332). Transfer from off off Broadway of the Gospel musical comedy conceived by Alan Bailey; written by Connie Ray; musical numbers by various authors (see credits below). Produced by the Lamb's Theater Company, Carolyn Rossi Copeland producing director, at the Lamb's Theater. Opened August 14, 1990.

Burl Sanders . . . . Reathel Bean	Dennis Sanders . . . . Robert Olsen
Mervin Oglethorpe . . . . . . Kevin Chamberlin	Denise Sanders . . . . Jane Potter
Vera Sanders . . . . Linda Kerns	June Sanders . . . . Connie Ray
Stanley . . . . Dan Manning	

Directed by Alan Bailey; musical direction, John Foley, Mike Craver; scenery, Peter Harrison; costumes, Pamela Scofield; lighting, Don Ehrman; musical arrangements, Mike Craver, Mark Hardwick; production stage manager, Tom Clewell; press, Cromarty & Co., Peter Cromarty, Patrick Paris.

Time: A Saturday night, June 1938. Place: Mount Pleasant Baptist Church, Mount Pleasant, N.C. The show was presented in two parts.

Depression-era family on tour in the South with cheerful religion-oriented song and instrumental numbers. Previously produced in this run as an OOB production opening 5/13/90 and raised to off-Broadway status.

MUSICAL NUMBERS: "Wonderful Time Up There" by Lee Roy Abernathy, "No Tears in Heaven" by Robert S. Arnold, "Christian Cowboy" by Cindy Walker, "The Filling Station" by April Ann Nye, "I'll Never Die (I'll Just Change My Address)" by J. Preston Martinez, "Jesus Is Mine" by Wally Fowler and Virginia Cook, "I'll Live a Million Years" by Lee Roy Abernathy, "I Wouldn't Take Nothing for My Journey Now" by Charles Goodman and Jimmy Davis, "I'm Using My Bible for a Roadmap" by Don Reno and Charles Schroeder, "I'm Taking a Flight" by Kathryn Boyington, "I'll Walk Every Step of the Way" by Mike Craver and Mark Hardwick, "Smoke on the Mountain" by Alan Bailey, "I'll Fly Away" by Albert E. Brumley.

Quiet on the Set (47). Transfer from off off Broadway of the play by Terrell Anthony. Produced by Coup de Grace Productions in association with the 126 Second Ave. Corp. in the Westbeth Theater Center production at the Orpheum Theater. Opened August 15, 1990. (Closed Sept. 23, 1990)

Judith Petri/Barbara Stewart . . . . Kate Collins
Taylor Lydell/
  John Whittington . . . . . . Robert Newman
Tamra Lydell/Bridget Stewart . . . . Beth Ehlers

Bruce Mitchell/
  Bart Whittington . . . . Trent Bushey
Director/Characters . . . . Matt Servitto

SMOKE ON THE MOUNTAIN—At top, John Foley, Mimi Bessette, Susan Mansur, Kevin Chamberlin and Reathel Bean, and *at bottom,* Connie Shulman and Robert Olsen, three members of the original cast (Chamberlin, Bean, Olsen) and subsequent replacements in the Gospel musical

Understudies: Misses Collins, Ehlers—Britt Helfer; Messrs. Newman, Bushey—Marc Kudish; Mr. Servitto—Michael Musick.

Directed by A.C. Weary; scenery, Rick Dennis; costumes, Colleen McFarlane; lighting, Nancy Collings; production stage manager, Susan Whelan; press, Cromarty & Co., Peter Cromarty, David Lotz.

Act I: Early evening on the sound stage of *Sunset*, a highly-rated television soap opera. Act II: Later the same evening.

The lives of a soap opera cast are entangled in events similar to those of their show. Previously presented OOB at Westbeth Theater Center in this production 6/18/90-7/1/90.

New York Shakespeare Festival Public Theater. Schedule of 11 programs. **Indecent Materials** (14). Limited engagement of a program of two one-act plays: *Indecent Materials* adapted for the stage by Edward Hunt and Jeff Storer from a text by Sen. Jesse Helms; and *Report From the Holocaust* adapted for the stage by Edward Hunt and Jeff Storer from a book by Larry Kramer; presented in the Manbites Dog Theater Company production. Opened August 27, 1990. (Closed September 9, 1990) **Through the Leaves** (33). Revival of the play by Franz Xaver Kroetz; translated by Roger Downey; presented in the Interart Theater, Margot Lewitin artistic director, and Mabou Mines 20th anniversary production. Opened September 16, 1990. (Closed October 14, 1990) **Machinal** (48). Revival of the play by Sophie Treadwell. Opened October 15, 1990. (Closed November 25, 1990) **Gonza the Lancer** (Yari no Gonza Kasane Katabira) (16). Revival of the play by Chikamatsu Monzaemon; translated by Donald Keene. Opened October 22, 1990. (Closed November 4, 1990) **The Fever** (12). Limited engagement of the one-man show by and with Wallace Shawn. Opened November 17, 1990. (Closed December 1, 1990)

Also **The Caucasian Chalk Circle** (24). Revival of the play by Bertolt Brecht; adapted by Thulani Davis from the translation by William B. Spiegelberger. Opened December 2, 1990. (Closed December 23, 1990) **The Big Funk** (8). By John Patrick Shanley. Opened December 10, 1990. (Closed December 16, 1990) **A Bright Room Called Day** (14). By Tony Kushner. Opened January 7, 1991. (Closed January 20, 1991) **Dead Mother, or Shirley Not All in Vain** (14). By David Greenspan. Opened January 31, 1991. (Closed February 10, 1991) **The Way of the World** (16). By William Congreve. Opened May 21, 1991. (Closed June 2, 1991) **Casanova** (8). By Constance Congdon. Opened May 28, 1991. (Closed June 2, 1991) Produced by New York Shakespeare Festival, Joseph Papp producer, at the Public Theater (see note).

ALL PLAYS: Associate producer, Jason Steven Cohen; plays and musical development director, Gail Merrifield; production manager, Andrew Mihok; press, Richard Kornberg, Reva Cooper, Carol Fineman.

INDECENT MATERIALS

and

REPORT FROM THE HOLOCAUST

CAST: Patricia Esperon, David Ring. Dancer: Rebecca Hutchins.

Indecent Materials: 1. I Have the Photographs Here at My Desk; 2. Pictures of Male Genitals Placed on a Table; 3. Unspeakable Portrayals; 4. Sickening Obscenity in My Home State; 5. Indecent Materials; 6. Bosh and Nausea; 7. Well, La-Di-Da; 8. Hate the Sin.

BOTH PLAYS: Directed by Jeff Storer; choreography, Barbara Dickinson; photographic design, Alan Dehmer; stage manager, Andrea Ball.

Indecent Materials features excerpts from Sen. Helms's speeches attacking the National Endowment for the Arts for its policies and programs. *Report From the Holocaust* is a cry for help and compassion in the AIDS crisis. Originally produced in Durham, N.C.

THROUGH THE LEAVES

Annette . . . . Ruth Maleczech
Victor . . . . Frederick Neumann

Directed by JoAnne Akalaitis; scenery, Douglas Stein; costumes, Teresa Snider-Stein; lighting, Frances Aronson; sound, L.B. Dallas; stage manager, Jack Doulin.

Time: The present. Place: Queens.

The human condition viewed as the strife and isolation of brutish lovers. A foreign (German) play written in 1976 and first produced here by Interart Theater in this production 3/16/84 for 53 performances, with these two actors receiving a best-performance Obie.

MACHINAL

CAST: Announcer, Bellboy, Waiter, Defense Attorney, Jailer—Timothy Britten Parker; Adding Clerk, Prosecuting Attorney, 1st Barber—Ralph Marrero; Filing Clerk, Neighbor, Boy at Speakeasy Table #3, Reporter—Omar Carter; Stenographer, Neighbor, Nurse, Final Speakeasy Woman, Reporter—Linda Marie Larson; Telephone Girl, Neighbor, Court Stenographer—Kristine Nielsen; Husband—John Seitz; Young Woman—Jodie Markell; Mother—Marge Redmond; Singer, Neighbor—Darby Rowe; Doctor, Salesman at Speakeasy Table #1, Neighbor, Reporter, 2d Barber—Christopher Fields; Lover—William Fichtner; Man at Speakeasy Table #3, Priest, Neighbor—Rocco Sisto; Woman at Speakeasy Table #2, Neighbor, Matron—Regina Taylor; Man at Speakeasy Table #2, Neighbor, Bailiff, Reporter, Guard—Gareth Williams; Judge, Final Speakeasy Man, Convict—Michael Mandell.

Directed by Michael Greif; scenery, David Gallo; costumes, Sharon Lynch; lighting, Kenneth Posner; original music and sound, John Gromada; production stage manager, Jess Lynn; stage manager, Allison Sommers.

This melodrama suggested by the Ruth Snyder-Judd Gray murder case was first produced on Broadway 9/7/28 and was named a Best Play of its season. It was revived off Broadway in the 1949-50 and 1959-60 seasons. This 1990 revival was presented without an intermission.

GONZA THE LANCER

CAST: Kawazura Bannojo, Kakusuke, Asaka Ichinoshin—Ron Bagden; Iwaki Chutabei, Okiku—Fanni Green; Sasano Gonza—Koji Okamura; Governess of Oyuki, Narrator B—Tim Perez; Oyuki, Torajiro, Min, Sugi, Namisuke, Osute, Servant, Boatman—Keenan Shimizu; Osai, Mother of Osai—Mary Shultz; Narrator A, Iwaki Jimbei—Ching Valdes/Aran.

Directed by David Greenspan; scenery, William Kennon; costumes, Elsa Ward; lighting, David Bergstein; fights, B.H. Barry; production stage manager, Diane Hartdagen; stage manager, Mark McMahon.

Prologue (by David Greenspan): The long flat plane (1982). Scene 1: The Japan seacoast, north of Matsue, summer. Scene 2: Asaka Ichinoshin's house. Scene 3: The journey of Gonza and Osai from Matsue to Fushimi. Scene 4: Iwaki Chutabei's house, some weeks later. Scene 5: The Capital Bridge at Fushimi. The play was presented in two parts.

18th century Japanese domestic tragedy (originally written for puppet theater but performed here by live actors) translated and re-set in the 20th century.

THE FEVER

105-minute monologue presented without intermission on a bare stage set with only a chair, with no Playbills, with author-performer Wallace Shawn deploring the economic inequality and unfairness of modern society, in which he characterizes himself as comfortable while others are starving. Presented for 12 performances prior to an English tour beginning 1/7/91 at the Royal Court Theater in London, then returning to New York City in various engagements including Second Stage 2/18/91, the Public Theater for 7 more performances 3/4/91-3/10/91 and the Mitzi E. Newhouse Theater at Lincoln Center for 18 performances 4/2/91-4/21/91. Previously performed more than 50 times in private sessions for invited audiences in residences and other locales.

THE CAUCASIAN CHALK CIRCLE

The Noble Child
Storyteller; Griot;
  Woman Cook . . . . Novella Nelson
Casbeque . . . . L. Peter Callender
Mme. Le Gouverneur . . . Sharon Washington
Doctor; Architect;
  Chambermaid . . . . Cynthia Martells
Doctor; Architect . . . . Luis A. Ramos
Aide-de-Camp . . . . M.W. Reid
Nurse . . . . Fanni Green
Messenger; Fire . . . . Patrick P. Mathieu

Simon Chachava . . . . Kevin Jackson
Grusha Vasne . . . . Charlayne Woodard
Man Cook . . . . . Raymond Anthony Thomas

The Flight to the Northern Mountains
Mon Oncle; House Servant . . Novella Nelson
Elderly Lady; Trader . . . . . . Luis A. Ramos
Younger Lady; Trader . . . . Cynthia Martells
Landlord; Shadow Puppeteer . . Kevin Jackson
Corporal . . . . L. Peter Callender
Blackshirts . . . . Patrick P. Mathieu,
    M.W. Reid, Raymond Anthony Thomas

Peasant Woman . . . . . . Sharon Washington
Trader . . . . Fanni Green

In the Northern Mountains
Laurent . . . . L. Peter Callender
Anique . . . . Sharon Washington
Mother-in-Law . . . . Fanni Green
Jussup . . . . M.W. Reid
Monk . . . . . . Raymond Anthony Thomas
Michel Abasville
    Puppeteer . . . . Patrick P. Mathieu

The Story of the Judge/The Chalk Circle
Azdak . . . . Reggie Montgomery

The Fugitive; Le Grand Blanc;
    Lame Man . . . . Kevin Jackson
Shauva . . . . Fanni Green
Blackshirt; Ludo; Lawyer. . . Cynthia Martells
Blackshirt; Invalid; Enrique the Bandit;
    Lawyer . . . . Luis A. Ramos
Casbeque's Nephew; Doctor;
    Old Woman . . . Raymond Anthony Thomas
Extortionist; Rich Peasants . . . . . M.W. Reid
Landlord; Old Couple . . . . L. Peter Callender
Hired Hand . . . . Patrick P. Mathieu

Musicians: Kweyao Agyapon percussion, mbira, flute; Kevin Burrell percussion; Tom Murray guitar.
Directed by George C. Wolfe; choreography, Hope Clarke; scenery, Loy Arcenas; costumes, Toni-Leslie James; lighting, Don Holder; music and vocal arrangements, Kweyao Agyapon; additional vocal arrangements, Carol Maillard; mask and puppet design, Barbara Pollitt, Stephen Kaplin; production stage manager, Jana Llynn; stage manager, Jenny Peek.

Time: The present. Place: L'Ile Antillais de Gonave. The play was presented in two parts with the intermission following *In the Northern Mountains*.

The first New York production of *The Caucasian Chalk Circle* was by Repertory Theater of Lincoln Center in an Eric Bentley English version 3/24/66 for 93 performances. In this, its first major New York revival, the play has been adapted to take place in a Caribbean setting and to include Afro-Caribbean music, dance, puppets, and masks.

THE BIG FUNK

Jill . . . . Jeanne Tripplehorn
Fifi . . . . Jayne Haynes
Omar . . . . Graham Beckel

Austin . . . . Jake Weber
Gregory . . . . Skip Sudduth

Directed by John Patrick Shanley; scenery, Nancy Winters; costumes, Lindsay W. Davis; lighting, Arden Fingerhut; sound, John Gromada; production stage manager, Pamela Singer; stage manager, John M. Atherlay.

Time: Now. Place: Here. The play was presented in two parts.

Subtitled "A casual play, or a talk around the polls" and described by its author as "Naked cursing actors, engaged in a topical conversation," as its characters seek self-fulfillment, sometimes with bodies unclothed.

A BRIGHT ROOM CALLED DAY

Zillah Katz . . . . Reno
Agnes Eggling . . . . Frances Conroy
Annabella Gotchling . . . . . . Joan MacIntosh
Paulinka Erdnuss . . . . . . Ellen McLaughlin
Vealtninc Husz . . . . Olek Krupa

Gregor Bazwald . . . . Henry Stram
Die Alte . . . . Marian Seldes
Roland; Emil Traum. . . . . . Kenneth L. Marks
Rosa Malek . . . . Angie Phillips
Gottfried Swetts . . . . Frank Raiter

Directed by Michael Greif; scenery, John Arnone; costumes, Walker Hicklin; lighting, Frances Aronson; sound, John Gromada; projections, Jan Hartley; production stage manager, Marjorie Horne; stage manager, Stephen Zorthian.

Time: 1990 and 1932-33. Place: An apartment in Berlin. The play was presented in two parts.

The failure of the Weimar Republic viewed as history we should avoid repeating.

DEAD MOTHER,
OR SHIRLEY NOT ALL IN VAIN

CAST: Character 1—David Greenspan; Character 2—Ben Bodé; Character 3—Terra Vandergaw; Character 4—Mary Shultz; Character 5—Ron Bagden; Character 6—Stephen Mellor.

Directed by David Greenspan; scenery, William Kennon; costumes, Elsa Ward; lighting, David Bergstein; production stage manager, Diane Hartdagen; stage manager, Mark McMahon.

Act I: Introduction; Sylvia Remembers; Daniel Reminds Harold; Arriving at the Hotel; Harold in the Bathroom; Melvin Arrives. Act II: Eris; Peleus and Thetis; Prometheus; Zeus; Paris. Act III: Lynn's Saga. Act IV: Back From the Play; The Ferry Tale. Act V: All That Sprawl; Shirley Talks Business to Saul; The Family Has a Discussion; Sylvia's Epilogue. The play was presented in two parts with the intermission following Act III.

Family clashes, particularly involving a dominant mother, alternating with episodes of classical mythology.

THE WAY OF THE WORLD

Fainall	Rene Rivera	Lady Wishfort	Ruth Maleczech
Mirabell	Andre Braugher	Mrs. Millamant	Jayne Atkinson
Witwoud	Joe Urla	Mrs. Marwood	Caris Corfman
Petulant	Burke Moses	Mrs. Fainall	Mary Shultz
Sir Wilfull Witwoud	Joseph Costa	Foible	Angie Phillips
Waitwell	James Lally	Mincing	Terra Vandergaw
Servant; Messenger; Coachman;		Betty; Peg; Mrs. Hodgson	Ami Brabson
Footman	John Elsen		

Directed by David Greenspan; scenery, William Kennon; costumes, Elsa Ward; lighting, David Bergstein; choreography, James Cunningham; production stage manager, Diane Hartdagen; stage manager, Mark McMahon.

Time: Equal to that of the presentation. Act I: A chocolate-house. Act II: St. James's Park. Acts III, IV and V: A room in Lady Wishfort's house. The play was presented in two parts with the intermission following Act III.

Congreve's comedy transposed to contemporary times and environment. The last major New York production of *The Way of the World* took place off Broadway at the Brooklyn Academy of Music 2/13/74 for 5 performances.

CASANOVA

ACT I

Rousseau's Girl	Erika Alexander	Lady	La Tanya Richardson
Therese	Margaret Gibson	Old Count	Jack Stehlin
In Paris:		Girl	Liana Pai
Sophie	Kaiulani Lee	Bellino	Martha Thompson
Bobo	Jeff Weiss	Salembini	Jack Stehlin
The Hague:		Monsignor	James Noah
Girl Sophie	Liana Pai	Bobo's Childhood (Paris):	
Giacomo Casanova	John Seitz	Boy Bobo	Martha Thompson
On the Road:		Countess	Marylouise Burke
Uta	Erika Alexander	French Fop	Jack Stehlin
Casanova's Childhood (Venice):		Home From the Seminary:	
Girl Therese	Martha Thompson	Old Servant	James Noah
Young Casanova	Ethan Hawke	Venetian Fop	Robert Stanton
Therese's Mother	Erika Alexander	Caterina	Liana Pai
Grandma; Sorceress	Marylouise Burke	At the Convent in Murano:	
Priest	Jack Stehlin	Laura	Marylouise Burke
Man at Festival	Robert Stanton	Idiot Woman	Martha Thompson
Zanetta	La Tanya Richardson	Marina	La Tanya Richardson
Grimani	James Noah	At the Riddoto, Venice:	
Dead Gaetano	Robert Stanton	Count DeBernis: Sbirri #1	Jack Stehlin
Woman Wearing Hoops	Liana Pai	Sbirri #2	Robert Stanton
At the Seminary:		Manuzzi	James Noah
Priest	Robert Stanton	Woman Passing By	Martha Thompson

ACT II

At Riombi Prison:		Ladies at Damiens'	
Jailer	James Noah	Execution	La Tanya Richardson, Martha Thompson
Inquisitor #1	La Tanya Richardson	Marcoline	La Tanya Richardson
Inquisitor #2	Jack Stehlin	At Versailles:	
Inquisitior #3	Robert Stanton	Paris-Duverny	Robert Stanton
On the Way to Paris:		Emaciated Woman	Martha Thompson
Traveler #1	Jack Stehlin	Court Lady	Liana Pai
Traveler #2	James Noah	In the Ballet Box:	
In Paris:		Lady	Liana Pai
Dancing Master	Robert Stanton		

THE WAY OF THE WORLD—Jayne Atkinson, Mary Shultz, Ruth Maleczech, Joseph Costa and Joe Urla in the New York Shakespeare Festival revival of William Congreve's comedy

Man . . . . James Noah	Jacomine . . . . Liana Pai
Mme. D'Urfé . . . . Marylouise Burke	In the Opera Box:
Charpillon's Rooms:	DaPonte . . . . James Noah
Charpillon's Mother. . . . . Marylouise Burke	In Sophie & Bobo's Rooms:
Charpillon . . . . Erika Alexander	Alain . . . . Robert Stanton
Mariucci's Home:	Julien. . . . . James Noah
Mariucci . . . . La Tanya Richardson	At the Ball:
Mariucci's Husband . . . . James Noah	Footman. . . . . Robert Stanton
Guillelmine . . . . Martha Thompson	Guests . . . . Company

Musicians: Jill Jaffe violin, viola, keyboards, percussion; John David Scott keyboards, percussion.

Directed by Michael Greif; scenery, John Arnone; costumes, Gabriel Berry; lighting, Frances Aronson; music and sound, John Gromada; musical direction, Jill Jaffe; choreography, James Cunningham; production stage manager, Jess Lynn; stage manager, Allison Sommers.

The life of Casanova as a feminist object lesson, as told by his daughter, her mother and a transvestite. The play was presented in two parts.

Note: In Joseph Papp's Public Theater there are many auditoria. *Indecent Materials, Gonza the Lancer, The Fever, Dead Mother* and *The Way of the World* played the Susan Stein Shiva Theater; *Through the Leaves* played the Estelle R. Newman Theater; *Machinal* and *A Bright Room Called Day* played LuEsther Hall; *The Caucasian Chalk Circle* and *Casanova* played Martinson Hall; *The Big Funk* played the Anspacher Theater.

Money Talks (5). By Edwin Schloss. Produced by Arthur Cantor at the Promenade Theater. Opened September 6, 1990. (Closed September 9, 1990)

Phyllis Stein	Dolores Gray	Morty Drexler	Arnie Kolodner
Vivian Newhouse	Helen Hanft	Allan Rothenberg	Ted Neustadt
Adrienne	Judith Cohen	Claudia Stein	Julie Halston
Irma Katzenbach	Janet Sarno	Carla Axelrod	Jill Wisoff
Lucille Blumenthal	Lucille Patton	Cesare Rotini	John Braden
Natalie Kilroy Axelrod	Helen Gallagher		

Directed by David Kaplan; continuity, Cindy Adams; scenery, James Noone; costumes, David Woolard; lighting, Dan Kotlowitz; sound, Aural Fixation; production stage manager, J.P. Elins; press, Arthur Cantor Associates.

Women members of an investment club and their eccentricities. The play was presented in two parts.

*Playwrights Horizons. 20th anniversary season schedule of five programs. **The 1990 Young Playwrights Festival** (20). Program of four one-act plays: *Mutterschaft* by Gregory Clayman, *Believing* by Allison Birch, *Psychoneurotic Phantasies* by Gilbert David Feke and *Hey Little Walter* by Carla D. Alleyne; presented in the Foundation of the Dramatists Guild production, Nancy Quinn producing director, Sheri M. Goldhirsch managing director. Opened September 18, 1990. (Closed October 6, 1990) **Subfertile** (39). By Tom Mardirosian. Opened November 7, 1990. (Closed December 9, 1990) **Assassins** (25). Musical with book by John Weidman; music and lyrics by Stephen Sondheim. Opened January 27, 1991. (Closed February 16, 1991) ***The Substance of Fire** (84). by Jon Robin Baitz. Opened March 17, 1991. **The Old Boy** (33). By A.R. Gurney. Opened May 5, 1991. (Closed June 2, 1991) Produced by Playwrights Horizons, Andre Bishop artistic director, Paul S. Daniels executive director, at Playwrights Horizons.

THE 1990 YOUNG PLAYWRIGHTS FESTIVAL

Mutterschaft

Mom	Leslie Lyles
Opal	Jane Adams
Evan	Harold Perrineau
Klaus	Victor Slezak

Directed by Michael Mayer; dramaturge, Morgan Jenness; stage manager, Cathy Diane Tomlin. Satirical reversal of the usual mother-daughter relationship.

Believing

Miss Agnes	Marjorie Johnson
Thelma	Cynthia Martells
Lawna	Tonya Pinkins
Martin	Kevin Jackson
Sharon	Sasha Mujica
David	Zakee Howze
Leater	Chandra Wilson
Frank	Michael Rogers
Boysie	Wendell Pierce

Directed by Clinton Turner Davis; fights, B.H. Barry; dramaturge, Karen Jones-Meadows; stage manager, Liz Small. Melodrama in a community of West Indians.

Psychoneurotic Phantasies

Elaine	Jane Adams
Joshua	Christopher Shaw
Freud	Walter Bobbie

The Psychocompany: Mia Korf, Leslie Lyles, Bruce MacVittie, Wendell Pierce, Angela Pietropinto, Tonya Pinkins, Kevin Rock, Victor Slezak, Jill Tasker, Lenny Venito.

Directed by Gloria Muzio; dramaturge, Victoria Abrash; stage manager, Liz Small. Lampoon of Freud and his successors.

Hey Little Walter

Walter	Harold Perrineau
Rakim	Seth Gilliam
Mama	Cynthia Martells
Albert	Merlin Santana
Latoya	Natalia Harris
Nicky	Lisa Carson
Treybag	Sean Nelson

Directed by Mark Brokaw; dramaturge, OyamO; stage manager, Cathy Diane Tomlin. A young city dweller resorts to drug trafficking, with dire consequences.

ALL PLAYS: Scenery, Alan Moyer; costumes, Claudia Stephens; lighting, Pat Dignan; sound, Janet Kalas; production stage manager, James FitzSimmons; press, Shirley Herz Associates, Sam Rudy.

These four plays by young authors (Gregory Clayman 17, Allison Birch 17, Gilbert David Feke 15, Carla D. Alleyne 16 at the time of submission) were selected from hundreds of entries in the Foundation of the Dramatists Guild's 9th annual playwriting contest for young people. The program was presented in two parts with the intermission following *Believing*.

SUBFERTILE

CAST: Tom Mardirosian, Richard Council, Kitty Crooks, Susan Knight, Frederica Meister.

Directed by John Ferraro; scenery, Rick Dennis; costumes, Abigail Murray; lighting, Brian MacDevitt; sound, Frederick Wessler; production stage manager, Karen Armstrong; press, Philip Rinaldi, Tim Ray.

Comedy, the efforts of a 40-ish couple to have a child. The play was presented without intermission.

ASSASSINS

Proprietor; James Garfield;		John Wilkes Booth	Victor Garber
Gerald Ford	William Parry	Balladeer	Patrick Cassidy
Leon Czolgosz	Terrence Mann	David Harold; Hangman	Marcus Olson
John Hinckley	Greg Germann	Bartender; James Blaine;	
Charles Guiteau	Jonathan Hadary	Warden	John Jellison
Giuseppe Zangara	Eddie Korbich	Emma Goldman	Lyn Greene
Samuel Byck	Lee Wilkof	Benjamin's Mother	Joy Franz
Lynette "Squeaky" Fromme	Annie Golden	Benjamin; Billy	Michael Shulman
Sara Jane Moore	Debra Monk	Lee Harvey Oswald	Jace Alexander

Bystanders: Joy Franz, Lyn Greene, John Jellison, Marcus Olson, William Parry. Fairgoers: Lyn Greene, John Jellison, Marcus Olson, William Parry.

Musicians: Paul Ford piano, Paul Gemignani percussion, Michael Starobin synthesizer.

Understudies: Messrs. Korbich, Jellison, Olson—Ted Brunetti; Messrs. Cassidy, Hadary—Davis Gaines; Misses Golden, Greene—Julia Kiley; Master Shulman—J.R. Nutt; Miss Monk—Joy Franz; Messrs. Garber, Parry—John Jellison; Messrs. Germann, Alexander—Marcus Olson; Messrs. Mann, Wilkof—William Parry.

Directed by Jerry Zaks; choreography, D.J. Giagni; musical direction, Paul Gemignani; scenery, Loren Sherman; costumes, William Ivey Long; lighting, Paul Gallo; sound, Scott Lehrer; production stage manager, Clifford Schwartz; stage manager, Karen Armstrong; press, Philip Rinaldi, Tim Ray.

Presented without intermission, *Assassins* portrays the killers and would-be killers of Presidents of the United States, ironically, as victims of the societies directed by the Presidents they have attacked, in a series of episodes.

MUSICAL NUMBERS

Scene 1: A booth at a carnival
"Everybody's Got the Right" . . . . Proprietor, Assassins
Scene 2: A tobacco barn, Virginia, April 1865
"The Ballad of Booth" . . . . Balladeer, Booth
Scene 3: A saloon
Scene 4: Bayfront Park, Miami, Fla., Feb. 15, 1933
"How I Saved Roosevelt" . . . . Bystanders, Zangara
Scene 5: A street in Chicago
Scene 6: A public park
Scene 7: "Gun Song" . . . . Czolgosz, Booth, Guiteau, Moore
Scene 8: The Pan American Exposition, Buffalo, N.Y., Sept. 6, 1901
"The Ballad of Czolgosz" . . . . Balladeer, Crowd
Scene 9: A city sidewalk
Scene 10: A basement rumpus room; then outside the Washington Hilton Hotel,
        Washington, D.C.,March 20, 1981
"Unworthy of Your Love" . . . . Hinckley, Fromme
Scene 11: A park; then the Baltimore and Potomac Railroad Station,
        Washington, D.C., July 2, 1881
Scene 12: A gallows
"The Ballad of Guiteau" . . . . Guiteau, Balladeer
Scene 13: Outside a hotel in California
Scene 14: A highway in Maryland, Feb. 22, 1974
Scene 15: "Another National Anthem" . . . . Assassins
Scene 16: A storeroom
Scene 17: "Everybody's Got the Right" . . . . Assassins

THE SUBSTANCE OF FIRE

Sarah Geldhart	Sarah Jessica Parker	Aaron Geldhart	Jon Tenney
Martin Geldhart	Patrick Breen	Marge Hackett	Maria Tucci
Isaac Geldhart	Ron Rifkin		

Directed by Daniel Sullivan; scenery, John Lee Beatty; costumes, Jess Goldstein; lighting, Arden Fingerhut; sound, Scott Lehrer; production stage manager, Roy Harris; stage manager, Jane Seiler; press, Philip Rinaldi, Tim Ray.

Act I: Spring, 1987. A conference room, Kreeger/Geldhart Publishers, New York City. Act II: Three and a half years later. An apartment on Gramercy Park.

Immigrant publisher struggles to defend the business he has built from being taken over and to cope with damaging emotions left over from the cruel Nazi-haunted past.

A Best Play; see page 205.

THE OLD BOY

Dexter	Richard Woods	Harriet	Nan Martin
Bud	Clark Gregg	Perry	Matt McGrath
Sam	Stephen Collins	Alison	Lizbeth Mackay

Directed by John Rubinstein; scenery, Nancy Winters; costumes, Jane Greenwood; lighting, Nancy Schertler; sound, Bruce Ellman; fight direction, B.H. Barry; production stage manager, Michael Pule; stage manager, Deborah Clelland.

Time: Graduation weekend in early June in the early 1990s. Place: A private boarding school in New England. The play was presented in two parts.

Eminent prep school graduate returns to make a fund-raising speech and finds himself face to face with his too-facile past and unfulfilled present self.

About Time (15) by Tom Cole, opened October 9, 1990 (closed November 11, 1990); and **Handy Dandy** (12) by William Gibson, opened October 22, 1990 (closed November 12, 1990); repertory of two programs. Produced by Eric Krebs at the John Houseman Theater.

PERFORMER	"ABOUT TIME"	"HANDY DANDY"
Audra Lindley	Old Woman	Molly Egan
James Whitmore	Old Man	Henry Pulaski

BOTH PLAYS: Directed by Tony Giordano; coordinating designer, Neil Peter Jampolis; sound supervisor, Tom Gould; executive producer, Roger Alan Gindi; production stage manager, Christine Michael; stage manager, Jonathan Shulman; press, David Rothenberg, Terence Womble.

ABOUT TIME: Scenery, Kent Dorsey; lighting, Kent Dorsey, Neil Peter Jampolis; costumes, Christine Dougherty.

A couple at various mealtimes, trying to straighten out their longstanding differences. The play was presented in two parts. Previously produced with this cast at George Street Playhouse, New Brunswick, N.J.

HANDY DANDY: Scenery and lighting, Neil Peter Jampolis; costumes, Barbara Forbes.

Conservative New England judge coping in court with an activist, a liberal minded nun. The play was presented in two parts. Previously produced at the Pasadena Playhouse and the George Street Playhouse, New Brunswick, N.J.

*The Sum of Us (259). By David Stevens. Produced by Dowling Entertainment, Duane Wilder, Gintare Sileika Everett in association with Chantepleure, Inc. at the Cherry Lane Theater. Opened October 16, 1990.

Jeff	Tony Goldwyn	Greg	Neil Maffin
Dad	Richard Venture	Joyce	Phyllis Somerville

Understudies: Mr. Goldwyn—Neil Maffin; Mr. Venture—Richard Thomsen; Mr. Maffin—Matthew Ryan. Standby: Miss Somerville—Monica Merryman.

Directed by Kevin Dowling; scenery, John Lee Beatty; costumes, Therese A. Bruck; lighting, Dennis Parichy; sound, Darron West; associate producers, Jay Hass, Donald R. Stoltz; stage manager, Larry Bussard; press, Bill Evans & Associates, Becky Flora.

Place: The sitting room of a house in Footscray—an industrial suburb of Melbourne, Australia—and later in the local park. The play was presented in two parts.

The close relationship of a father and his gay son. A foreign (Australian) play previously produced at

THE OLD BOY—Stephen Collins and Matt McGrath
in the play by A.R. Gurney at Playwrights Horizons

the Williamstown, Mass. Theater Festival and A Director's Theater, Los Angeles.

Neil Maffin replaced Tony Goldwyn and Matthew Ryan replaced Neil Maffin 1/29/91. Robert Lansing replaced Richard Venture 4/9/91. Matt Salinger replaced Neil Maffin 5/28/91.

A Best Play; see page 124.

*Roundabout Theater Company. 25th anniversary season schedule of four revivals. **King Lear** (80). By William Shakespeare. Opened October 9, 1990 (see note). (Closed December 16, 1990) **The Country Girl** (55). By Clifford Odets. Opened December 26, 1990 (see note). (Closed February 10, 1991) **Pygmalion** (64). By George Bernard Shaw. Opened March 6, 1991 (see note). (Closed April 28, 1991) ***The Subject Was Roses** (19). By Frank D. Gilroy. Opened May 15, 1991 (see note). Produced by Roundabout Theater Company, Todd Haimes producing director, Gene Feist founding director, at the Christian C. Yegen Theater.

KING LEAR

King Lear	Hal Holbrook	Lear's Fool	Christopher McCann
King Lear (weekday matinees)	Peter Aylward	Oswald	Gary Sloan
Goneril	Suzy Hunt	Knight	Kevin McCarty
Regan	Margery Murray	Curan	Peter Aylward
Cordelia	Gloria Biegler	Cornwall Servants	Darrell Starnick, Justin Thompson
Albany	John Buck Jr.		
Cornwall	Andrew Boyer	Messenger to Albany	David Ruckman
King of France	Simon Brooking	Messenger to Cordelia;	
Burgundy	Patrick Mulcahy	2d Messenger to Albany	Eric Vogt
Gloucester	Ron Randell	Herald	William Wilson
Edgar	Michael James-Reed	Captain	Andrew M. Segal
Edmund	John Hutton	Albany Officer	Eric Nolan
Kent	John Woodson		

Knights of Lear's Train, Servants, Soldiers, Attendants, Gentlemen: Simon Brooking, Richard Long, Patrick Mulcahy, Eric Nolan, Stephan Roselin, David Ruckman, Andrew M. Segal, Darrell Starnik, Justin Thompson, Eric Vogt, William Wilson.

Understudies: Mr. Holbrook—Peter Aylward; Mr. James-Reed—Simon Brooking; Mr. Woodson—Kevin McCarty; Mr. Hutton—Patrick Mulcahy; Mr. Boyer—Eric Nolan; Messrs. Randell, McCann—David Ruckman; Mr. McCarty—Andrew M. Segal; Messrs. Sloan, Aylward—Justin Thompson; Messrs. Brooking, Mulcahy—Eric Vogt; Mr. Buck—William Wilson.

Directed by Gerald Freedman; scenery, John Ezell; costumes, Robert Wojewodski; lighting, Thomas R. Skelton; music, John Morris; sound, Tom Mardikes; fight direction, Robert L. Behrens; production stage manager, Kathy J. Faul; press, the Joshua Ellis Office, Susanne Tighe, John Barlow.

Time: Ancient time. The play was presented in two parts.

The last major New York revival of *King Lear* was in the Georgian (Russian) language 4/2/90 for 5 performances. The Roundabout revival was originally produced in regional theater by Great Lakes Theater Festival, Gerald Freedman artistic director, Mary Bill managing director.

THE COUNTRY GIRL

Bernie Dodd	Paul McCrane	Nancy Stoddard	Geraldine Leer
Larry	Stephen Mendillo	Frank Elgin	David Rasche
Phil Cook	George Morfogen	Georgie Elgin	Karen Allen
Paul Unger	Jim Abele	Ralph	Henry LeBlanc

Understudies: Mr. Mendillo—Daniel Costigan; Messrs. McCrane, Morfogen—Henry LeBlanc; Miss Allen—Geraldine Leer; Mr. Rasche—Stephen Mendillo; Miss Leer—Mary Shaw; Messrs. Abele, LeBlanc—William Wilson.

Directed by Kenneth Frankel; scenery, Hugh Landwehr; costumes, David Murin; lighting, Stephen Strawbridge; sound, Philip Campanella; production stage manager, Roy Backes.

Act I, Scene 1: The stage of a New York theater. Scene 2: A furnished room, later the same day. Scene 3: The stage, ten days later. Scene 4: The furnished room, a week later. Scene 5: A dressing room in a Boston theater, a week later. Act II, Scene 1: The Boston dressing room, a few nights later. Scene 2: The same, the next day. Scene 3: Opening night, New York.

The last major New York revival of *The Country Girl* took place off Broadway 10/18/84 for 45 performances.

PYGMALION

Clara Eynsford-Hill	Pamala Tyson	Henry Higgins	Anthony Heald
Mrs. Eynsford-Hill	Annie Murray	Mrs. Pearce	Joyce Worsley
Bystander	Edwin J. McDonough	Alfred Doolittle	Charles Keating
Freddy Eynsford-Hill	Willis Sparks	Mrs. Higgins	Anne Pitoniak
Eliza Doolittle	Madeleine Potter	Parlormaid	Page Clements
Col. Pickering	Earle Hyman		

Bystanders: Lester Chit-Man Chan, Daniel Tedlie, Henry Traeger, Angela Schreiber, Michael Schwendemann.

Understudies: Miss Tyson—Page Clements; Messrs. Hyman, Keating—Edwin J. McDonough; Miss Worsley—Annie Murray; Miss Murray—Angela Schreiber; Mr. Heald—Willis Sparks; Messrs. Sparks, McDonough—Daniel Tedlie; Miss Potter—Pamala Tyson; Miss Pitoniak—Joyce Worsley.

Directed by Paul Weidner; scenery, John Conklin; costumes, Martin Pakledinaz; lighting, Natasha Katz; sound, Philip Campanella; production stage manager, Kathy J. Faul.

Act I, Scene 1: The portico of St. Paul's Church, Covent Garden, 11:15 p.m. Scene 2: Higgins's laboratory, Wimpole Street, the next morning. Scene 3: Mrs. Higgins's drawing room, Chelsea Embankment, two months later. Act II, Scene 1: Higgins's laboratory, four months later, midnight. Scene 2: Mrs. Higgins's drawing room, the following morning.

The last major New York revival of *Pygmalion* took place on Broadway 4/26/87 for 113 performances.

THE SUBJECT WAS ROSES

John Cleary	John Mahoney	Timmy Cleary	Patrick Dempsey
Nettie Cleary	Dana Ivey		

Directed by Jack Hofsiss; scenery, David Jenkins; costumes, Michael Krass; lighting, Beverly Emmons; sound, Philip Campanella; production stage manager, Kathy J. Faul.

Time: May 1946. Place: an apartment in the Bronx. Act I, Scene 1: Saturday morning. Scene 2: Saturday afternoon. Scene 3: 2 a.m. Sunday morning. Act II, Scene 1: Sunday morning. Scene 2: Sunday evening. Scene 3: 2 a.m. Monday morning. Scene 4: Monday morning.

The Subject Was Roses was first produced on Broadway 5/25/64 for 832 performances and was named a Best Play of 1964-65. This is its first major New York revival.

Note: Press date for *King Lear* was 11/15/90, for *The Country Girl* was 1/10/91, for *Pygmalion* was 3/24/91, for *The Subject Was Roses* was 6/5/91.

Circle Repertory Company. 22nd season schedule of five programs. **The Colorado Catechism** (25). By Vincent J. Cardinal. Opened October 21, 1990. (Closed November 11, 1990) **Love Diatribe** (32). By Harry Kondoleon. Opened December 18, 1990. (Closed January 13, 1991) **Road to Nirvana** (30). By Arthur Kopit. Opened March 7, 1991. (Closed March 31, 1991) **Walking the Dead** (25). By Keith Curran. Opened May 12, 1991. (Closed June 2, 1991) And *The Balcony Scene* by Wil Calhoun scheduled to open 6/30/91. Produced by Circle Repertory Company, Tanya Berezin artistic director, Terrence Dwyer managing director, at Circle Repertory.

THE COLORADO CATECHISM

Ty	Kevin James O'Connor
Donna	Becky Ann Baker

Directed by Mark Ramont; scenery, James Youmans; costumes, David C. Woolard; lighting, Pat Dignan; sound, Stewart Werner, Chuck London; production stage manager, Denise Yaney; press, Gary Murphy.

Rehabilitation memories and present romance of recovered alcoholics.

LOVE DIATRIBE

Frieda	Martha Gehman	Dennis	Edward Seamon
Orin	Barry Sherman	Mike	Michael Rispoli
Sandy	Amy Aquino	Gerry	Lynn Cohen
Mrs. Anderson	Jane Cronin		

Directed by Jorge Cacheiro; scenery, G.W. Mercier; costumes, Walter Hicklin; lighting, Dennis Parichy; sound, Scott Lehrer; production stage manager, Fred Reinglas.

Time: The present. Place: A suburb of a large city, the "family room." The play was presented without intermission.

Grownup children retreat from life to the shelter of their parents' home.

ROAD TO NIRVANA

Al	Jon Polito	Ramon	James Puig
Lou	Saundra Santiago	Nirvana	Amy Aquino
Jerry	Peter Riegert		

Directed by Jim Simpson; scenery, Andrew Jackness; costumes, Ann Roth; lighting, Scott Zielinski; sound, Stewart Werner, Chuck London; "Who Am I" words and music by Arthur Kopit and Frank Wildhorn; production stage manager, Fred Reinglas.

Act I: Al's place, day. Act II: Nirvana's place, that evening.

Hollywood movie producers and superstar will suffer and inflict any indignity and/or mutilation to achieve success. First produced as *Bone-the-Fish* at the Actors Theater of Louisville and subsequently at the Alley Theater, Houston and American Repertory Theater, Cambridge, Mass.

WALKING THE DEAD

Veronica Tass	Ashley Gardner	Bobby Brax	Cotter Smith
Dottie Tass	Scotty Bloch	Dr. Drum	Tyrone Wilson
Maya Deboats	Myra Taylor	Stan	Joe Mantello
Chess Wysynsky	Christopher Shaw		

Directed by Mark Ramont; scenery, Tom Kamm; costumes, Toni-Leslie James; lighting, Kenneth Posner; sound, Scott Lehrer; fight direction, Rick Sordelet; production stage manager, Denise Yaney.

Time: Right Now. Place: Here.

A murdered person's episode of transsexualism is recalled by her living friends.

Pretty Faces (49). Musical by Robert W. Cabell. Produced by Tommy DeMaio at the Actors Outlet Theater. Opened October 21, 1990. (Closed December 2, 1990)

Monique	Lynn Halverson	Patricia	Heather Anne Stokes
Jimmy	Ron Meier	Pleasure	Amy Ryder
Carter	Michael Winther	Paulette	Margaret Dyer
Bobby-Joy	Kathleen Rosamond Kelly	Deloris	Liz Leisek
Daphne	Amy Jo Phillips	Roger	Charles Mandracchia

Musicians: Jim Mironchik conductor, 1st keyboard; Mark Berman 2d keyboard; Don Perlman percussion.

Directed and choreographed by Gene Foote; musical direction, Jim Mironchik; scenery, Peter Rogness; costumes, George Bergeron; lighting, Clifton Taylor; musical supervisor/arranger, Arnie Gross; production stage manager, John Frederick Sullivan; press, Jeffrey Richards Associates, David LeShay.

Time: Now. Act I: Rehearsals for the Pageant. Act II: Onstage and backstage at the Pageant.

A beauty contest to select "Miss Global Glamour Girl."

ACT I

"Taking Chances"	Jimmy, Girls
"42-32-42" (Soliloquies #1)	Girls
"How Do You Like Your Men"	Deloris, Girls
"42-32-42" (Soliloquies #2)	Girls
"Furs, Fortune, Fame, Glamor"	Daphne
"Interviews"	Girls

ROAD TO NIRVANA—Saundra Santiago, Jon Polito and Peter Riegert in Arthur Kopit's play at Circle Rep

"Sleep Walkers Lament #1". . . . . Monique, Roger
"Too Plump for Prom Night" . . . . Patricia, Girls
"Heartbreaker" . . . . Monique, Carter
"What's Missing in My Life". . . . . Monique
"Sleep Walkers Lament #2" . . . . Jimmy, Girls
"Pretty Faces" . . . . Roger
"Daddy Doesn't Care". . . . . Pleasure
"Sleep Walkers Lament #3" . . . . Company
"Solo for the Telephone". . . . . Paulette
"Waiting for the Curtain" . . . . Carter, Jimmy, Company

ACT II

"Global Glamor Girls" . . . . Roger, Girls
"Woman That I Am" . . . . Monique
"Purple Hearted Soldiers" . . . . Daphne
"Song for Jesus" . . . . Bobby-Joy
"Are You the One" . . . . Carter, Bobby-Joy
"On With the Show" . . . . Monique, Pleasure
"Tears and Tears Ago" . . . . Pleasure
"What Is Missing in My Life" . . . . Monique, Roger
"This Moment Is Mine" . . . . Finalist
"42-32-42". . . . . Girls

Yiddle With a Fiddle (55). Musical in English based on the Yiddish movie *Yitl Midn Fidl* by Joseph Green; books and lyrics by Isaiah Sheffer; music by Abraham Ellstein. Produced by Raymond Ariel and Lawrence Toppall at Town Hall. Opened October 28, 1990. (Closed December 30, 1990)

Yiddle . . . . Emily Loesser
Aryeh . . . . Mitchell Greenberg
Wagon Driver; Tavern Keeper;
  Rabbi; Mr. Becker . . . . Steve Sterner
Kalamutke . . . . Michael Ingram
Froym . . . . Robert Michael Baker
Truck Driver; Zalmen Gold; Stationmaster;
  Prof. Zinger . . . . Danny Rutigliano

Waitress; Cook;
  Stage Manager . . . . Andrea Green
Chauffeur; Yossel . . . . Steven Fickinger
Cook's Helper;
  Musician's Assistant . . . . . . Rachel Black
Teibele . . . . Patricia Ben Peterson
Teibele's Mother; Channah . . . . Susan Flynn

Townspeople, Tavern Patrons, City Folk: Steve Sterner, Danny Rutigliano, Andrea Green, Steven Fickinger, Rachel Black, Susan Flynn.

Musicians: Lanny Meyers keyboards, Greg Venuta percussion, Juliene Purefoy woodwinds, Susan Shumway solo violinist.

Understudies: Misses Loesser, Flynn, Green, Black—Patti Mariano; Miss Peterson—Andrea Green, Rachel Black; Miss Green—Rachel Black; Mr. Greenberg—Steve Sterner; Mr. Ingram—Danny Rutigliano; Messrs. Rutigliano, Fickinger, Sterner—Gary John La Rosa; Messrs. Rutigliano, Baker—Steven Fickinger.

Directed by Ran Avni; choreography, Helen Butleroff; musical direction and orchestration, Lanny Meyers; scenery, Jeffrey Schneider; costumes, Karen Hummel; lighting, Robert Bessoir; sound, David Smith; production stage manager, D.C. Rosenberg; press, Shirley Herz Associates, Pete Sanders.

Time: Summer 1936. Place: Poland.

Adventures of a father and daughter (disguised as a boy) as travelling musicians, the show that once made a star of Molly Picon. Previously produced in West Orange, N.J.

ACT I

Scene 1: Village marketplace
  "Come Gather 'Round" . . . . Yiddle
  "If You Wanna Dance" . . . . Yiddle Villagers
Scene 2: Village street, outside Aryeh's home
  "Music, It's a Necessity". . . . . Aryeh
Scene 3: On the road
  "Yiddle With a Fiddle" . . . . Yiddle, Aryeh

Scene 4: Courtyard in the small town of Droghobyeh
"Come Gather 'Round" (Reprise). . . . . Yiddle
"New Rhythm". . . . . Kalamutke, Froym, Yiddle, Aryeh, Townspeople
"Help Is on the Way!" . . . . Kalamutke, Froym, Yiddle, Aryeh
Scene 5: On the road
"Yiddle With a Fiddle" (Reprise) . . . . Yiddle, Aryeh, Kalamutke, Froym
Scene 6: The barn
"I'll Sing" . . . . Froym
Scene 7: The tavern
"Hard as a Nail" . . . . Yiddle, Tavern Patrons
Scene 8: The barnyard
"Man to Man". . . . . Froym, Yiddle
"Oh Mama, Am I in Love" . . . . Yiddle
Scene 9: On the road
"Travelling First Class Style" . . . . Kalamutke, Aryeh, Yiddle, Froym, Chauffeur
Scene 10: The wedding
"Badchen's Verses" . . . . Rabbi
"Only for a Moment". . . . . Teibele
Wedding Bulgar: Dance . . . . Wedding Guests
"Help Is on the Way!" (Reprise) . . . . Kalamutke, Yiddle, Froym, Aryeh, Teibele

ACT II

Scene 1: Zamosc, a small-town railway station
"Come Gather 'Round" (Reprise) . . . . Teibele, Yiddle, Aryeh, Froym, Kalamutke
"Warsaw!" . . . . Kalamutke, Yiddle, Teibele, Froym, Aryeh
"How Can the Cat Cross the Water?". . . . . Yiddle
Scene 2: On the railroad
"Yiddle With a Fiddle" (Reprise) . . . . . . Yiddle, Aryeh, Teibele, Froym, Kalamutke, Passengers
Scene 3: Warsaw, Channah's home
"Stay Home Here With Me". Channah, Kalamutke
"Take It From the Top". . . . . Channah, Teibele, Yiddle
Scene 4: Warsaw, a busy street
"Come Gather 'Round" (Reprise). . . . . Teibele, Yiddle,
                                                                    Aryeh, Froym, Kalamutke
Scene 5: Channah's house
"Yiddle With a Fiddle" (Reprise). . . . . Yiddle, Aryeh, Froym, Kalamutke, Channah
Scene 6: The Variety Theater, backstage/dressing room
"Only for a Moment" (Reprise) . . . . Teibele, Yossel
Scene 7: The Variety Theater, onstage
"To Tell the Truth" . . . . Yiddle
"We'll Sing". . . . . Yiddle, Froym, Ensemble
"Help Is on the Way!" . . . . Finale

Manhattan Theater Club. Schedule of eight programs. **Abundance** (32). By Beth Henley. Opened October 30, 1990. (Closed November 25, 1990) **The Wash** (16). By Philip Kan Gotanda; produced in association with the Mark Taper Forum. Opened November 6, 1990. (Closed November 18, 1990) **The American Plan** (37). By Richard Greenberg. Opened December 16, 1990. (Closed January 18, 1991) **Absent Friends** (47). By Alan Ayckbourn. Opened February 12, 1991. (Closed March 24, 1991) **Life During Wartime** (16). By Keith Reddin. Opened March 5, 1991. (Closed March 17, 1991) **Black Eagles** (33). By Leslie Lee; produced in association with Crossroads Theater Company, Ricardo Khan artistic director. Opened April 21, 1991. (Closed May 19, 1991) **The Stick Wife** (14). By Darrah Cloud. Opened May 9, 1991. (Closed May 19, 1991) And *Lips Together, Teeth Apart* by Terrence McNally scheduled to open 6/25/91. Produced by Manhattan Theater Club, Lynne Meadow artistic director, Barry Grove managing director. *Abundance, The American Plan, Absent Friends* and *Black Eagles* at City Center Stage I, *The Wash, Life During Wartime* and *The Stick Wife* at City Center Stage II.

ALL PLAYS: Artistic associate, Michael Bush; press, Helene Davis, Linda Feinberg, Stephen Hancock.

ABUNDANCE

Bess Johnson . . . . Amanda Plummer	William Curtis . . . . Lanny Flaherty
Macon Hill. . . . . Tess Harper	Prof. Elmore Crome . . . . Keith Reddin
Jack Flan. . . . . Michael Rooker	

Understudies: Messrs. Rooker, Flaherty, Reddin—Murphy Guyer; Misses Plummer, Harper—Lindsey Margo Smith.

Directed by Ron Lagomarsino; scenery, Adrianne Lobel; costumes, Robert Wojewodski; lighting, Paulie Jenkins; music and sound, Michael Roth; fight director, J. Allen Suddeth; production stage manager, Ruth Kreshka; stage manager, Buzz Cohen.

Time: The play spans 25 years, starting in the late 1860s. Place: Wyoming Territory and later St. Louis. The play was presented in two parts.

The experiences of mail-order brides living often distressed lives in the American West of the 19th century.

THE WASH

Nobu Matsumoto. . . . . Sab Shimono	Kiyoko Hasegawa. . . . . Shizuko Hoshi
Masi Matsumoto. . . . . Nobu McCarthy	Blackie . . . . Marshall Factora
Marsha Matsumoto . . . . Diane Takei	Sadao Nakasato . . . . George Takei
Judy Adams . . . . Jodi Long	Chiyo Froelich . . . . Carol A. Honda

Directed by Sharon Ott; scenery, James Youmans; costumes, Lydia Tanji; lighting, Dan Kotlowitz; original music and sound, Stephen LeGrand; production stage manager, Renee Lutz.

Time: The present. Place: San Jose, Calif. The play was presented in two parts.

In a Japanese-American family, a wife leaves her husband but continues to visit and look after him. Previously produced at the Eureka Theater Company, San Francisco and the New Theater for Now Festival at the Mark Taper Forum, Los Angeles.

THE AMERICAN PLAN

Lili Adler. . . . . Wendy Makkena	Olivia Shaw . . . . Yvette Hawkins
Nick Lockridge. . . . . D.W. Moffett	Gil Harbison . . . . Jonathan Walker
Eva Adler . . . . Joan Copeland	

Directed by Evan Yionoulis; scenery, James Youmans; costumes, Jess Goldstein; lighting, Donald Holder; sound and original music, Thomas Cabaniss; production stage manager, Richard Hester; stage manager, Carol Dawes.

Time and place: The Catskills in the summer of 1960 and the Adlers' Central Park West apartment ten years later. The play was presented in two parts.

Square pegs in the round holes of mainstream America's lifestyle and mores, portraying an ill-fated romance.

A Best Play; see page 165.

ABSENT FRIENDS

Evelyn . . . . Gillian Anderson	Paul. . . . . David Purdham
Diana. . . . . Brenda Blethyn	John . . . . John Curless
Marge . . . . Ellen Parker	Colin . . . . Peter Frechette

Directed by Lynne Meadow; scenery, John Lee Beatty; costumes, Jane Greenwood; lighting, Ken Billington; production stage manager, Pamela Singer; stage manager, William Joseph Barnes.

Time: Saturday, around 3 p.m. Place: The living room of Paul and Diana's home. The play was presented in two parts.

Reunion of old friends, with two of the group conspicuously missing. A foreign play previously presented in London in 1975.

LIFE DURING WARTIME

CAST: Heinrich—W.H. Macy; Sally, Mrs. Fielding, Megan—Welker White; Tommy—Bruce Norris; John Calvin, Fielding, Lt. Waters, DeVries—James Rebhorn; Gale—Leslie Lyles; Howard, Waiter, Richie, Delivery Boy—Matt McGrath.

Directed by Les Waters; scenery, James Noone; costumes, David C. Woolard; lighting, Michael R. Moody; original music and sound, John Kilgore; production stage manager, Tom Aberger.

Salesman of home security systems unwittingly becomes involved in violence. The play was presented in two parts. Previously produced in regional theater at the La Jolla Playhouse and the Berkeley Repertory Theater.

BLACK EAGLES

Elder Clarkie	Lawrence James	Buddy	Reggie Montgomery
Elder Nolan	Robinson Frank Adu	Leon	David Rainey
Elder Leon	Graham Brown	Othel	Brian Evaret Chandler
Gen. Lucas	Michael Barry Greer	Pia	Illeana Douglas
Clarkie	Raymond Anthony Thomas	Dave Whitson	Larry Green
Roscoe	Damien Leake	Roy Truman	Milton Elliott
Nolan	Scott Whitehurst		

Conceived and directed by Ricardo Khan; scenery, Charles McClennahan; costumes, Beth A. Ribblett; lighting, Natasha Katz; choreography, Hope Clarke; sound, Rob Gorton; fight direction, Rick Sordelet; music coordination, Robert La Pierre; "Julius Theme" by Damien Leake; ventriloquy consulting, Robert Aberdeen; artistic associate, Michael Bush; production stage manager, Cassandra Scott; stage manager, Bonnie L. Becker.

Time and Place: 1989, Washington, D.C., reunion of the Tuskegee Airmen; 1944, Italy during World War II. The play was presented in two parts.

ABSENT FRIENDS—Peter Frechette, Brenda Blethyn and David Purdham (*top*) in Alan Ayckbourn's comedy at Manhattan Theater Club

Dramatic reminiscence of America's first black air-war unit, the Army Air Force's 99th Fighter Squadron, in the Second World War. Commissioned and previously produced by Crossroads Theater Company and further developed at Ford's Theater, Washington, D.C.

THE STICK WIFE

Jessie Bliss . . . . Lindsay Crouse   Big Albert Connor . . . . Lanny Flaherty
Ed Bliss . . . . Murphy Guyer   Betty Connor . . . . Margo Martindale
Marguerite Pullet . . . . Julie White   Tom Pullet . . . . Michael Countryman

Directed by David Warren; scenery, James Youmans; costumes, David C. Woolard; lighting, Donald Holder; sound, John Kilgore; fight direction, J. Allen Suddeth; production stage manager, Christine Michael.

Time: 1963. Place: The backyard of the Bliss home in Birmingham, Ala. The play was presented in two parts.

Wives of Ku Klux Klan members suffer some of the consequences of their husbands' actions and support each other. Previously produced off off Broadway at Ensemble Studio Theater and in regional theater at L.A. Theater Center, Berkeley Repertory Theater, Hartford Stage Company and Trinity Square, Providence, R.I.

Life on the Third Rail (30). By Mitchell Uscher. Produced by Michael Thompson and Florence Hohenstein at the Theater at St. Peter's Church. Opened November 1, 1990. (Closed November 25, 1990)

CAST: Jim Walton, Lee Meredith, Courtenay Collins, Kathleen McCall, Leon B. Flagg, Jim Boyd, Florence Hayle, Tim Loughrin, Jack Mahoney.

Directed by Patricia Carmichael; scenery, William John Aupperlee; costumes, Clifford Capone; lighting, Vivien Leone; press, Becky Flora.

Romantic comedy set in various locations in New York City.

American Place Theater. Schedule of three programs. **Mambo Mouth** (114). One-man performance by John Leguizamo; written by John Leguizamo. Opened November 8, 1990. (Closed April 28, 1991; scheduled to reopen June 4, 1991) **Struck Dumb** by Jean-Claude van Itallie and Joseph Chaikin and **The War in Heaven** by Sam Shepard and Joseph Chaikin (13). Opened in repertory with *Mambo Mouth* March 24, 1991. (Closed April 7, 1991) **States of Shock** (19). By Sam Shepard. Opened May 16, 1991. (Closed June 2, 1991) Produced by American Place Theater, Wynn Handman director, Dara Hershman general manager, at American Place Theater.

MAMBO MOUTH

Directed by Peter Askin; scenery, Philipp Jung; lighting, Graeme F. McDonnell; sound, Bruce Ellman; production stage manager, Michael Robin; press, David Rothenberg, Terence Womble.

Subtitled "A Savage Comedy," a portrayal by John Leguizamo of Latino street personalities named Agamemnon, Angel Garcia, Loco Louie, Pepe, Manny the Fanny, Inca God and Crossover King. The play was presented without intermission.

STRUCK DUMB *and*
THE WAR IN HEAVEN

Struck Dumb
Adnan . . . . Joseph Chaikin

The War in Heaven
Angel . . . . Joseph Chaikin

Directed by Nancy Gabor; scenery, Woods Mackintosh; costumes, Mary Brecht; lighting, Beverly Emmons; composer/musician, Edwina Lee Tyler; production stage manager, Lloyd Davis Jr.

Monologues, *Struck Dumb* concerning the life of a Lebanese in America and *The War in Heaven* (subtitled "Angel's Monologue") about a fallen angel.

STATES OF SHOCK

Colonel	John Malkovich	White Man	Steve Nelson
Glory Bee	Erica Gimpel	Stubbs	Michael Wincott
White Woman	Isa Thomas	Percussionists	Richard Dworkin, Joseph Sabella

Directed by Bill Hart; scenery, Bill Stabile; costumes, Gabriel Berry; lighting, Pat Dignan, Anne Militello; composer, J.A. Deane; production stage manager, Lloyd Davis Jr.

War and its aftermath bitterly considered in the contrasting environment of a family restaurant, representative of a well-meaning society at large. The play was presented without intermission.

Catch Me If I Fall (16). Musical with book, music and lyrics by Barbara Schottenfeld. Produced by The Never or Now Company at the Promenade Theater. Opened November 12, 1990. (Closed November 25, 1990)

Lonny Simon	James Judy	Godiva Harris	Ronnie Farer
Brian Simon	David Burdick	Domnica Gruia	Laura Dean
Laurie Simon	Jeanine Morick	Andrei Gruia	A.D. Cover
Peter Bennington	Sal Viviano		

Orchestra: Joseph Church conductor; Daryl Goldberg cello; Andrew Sturman woodwinds; Gary Hoss bass; Mark Belair percussion.

Directed by Susan Einhorn; additional staging, Stuart Ross; musical supervision and direction, Joseph Church; scenery and costumes, G.W. Mercier; lighting, Richard Nelson; sound, Gary and Timmy Harris; orchestrations, Joe Gianono; associate producers, Frederick Schultz, Terry A. Johnston; production stage manager, John C. McNamara; press, David Rothenberg, Terence Womble.

Time: The late fall of 1939. Place: New York City.

A sculptor with many career and family problems. Previously produced in regional theater at Norwood, Mass.

ACT I

Opening Number/"Catch Me If I Fall"	Lonny, Company
"Business Is an Art"	Lonny, Domnica
"Veterinarian"	Lonny, Godiva
"The Love That Came Before"	Lonny, Laurie
"Sometimes at Night"	Domnica
"The Beach House"	Domnica, Lonny, Peter
"I Want You To Be. . ."	Peter
"It's Not a Real Wedding"	Lonny, Peter, Domnica, Godiva, Brian
"I Know the Feeling/Home Never Leaves You"	Lonny, Domnica

ACT II

"When You Live in New York"	Domnica, Company
"Libertate"	Andrei
"Isn't It Strange"	Domnica
"Timing and Lighting"	Domnica, Lonny
"Chaperone"	Domnica, Laurie, Godiva
"Never or Now"	Lonny
"Isn't It Strange" (Reprise)	Lonny, Domnica

Chelsea Stage. Schedule of two programs. **The March on Russia** (24). By David Storey. Produced in association with the Cleveland Play House. Opened November 12, 1990. (Closed December 2, 1990) **The Voice of the Prairie** (2). By John Olive. Opened December 18, 1990. (Closed December 20, 1990) Produced by Chelsea Stage (see note), Geoffrey Sherman artistic director, Dara Hershman managing director, at the Hudson Guild Theater.

THE MARCH ON RUSSIA

Colin	Sean Griffin	Wendy	Carol Locatell
Mr. Pasmore	John Carpenter	Eileen	Susan Browning
Mrs. Pasmore	Bethel Leslie		

Directed by Josephine R. Abady; costumes, Linda Fisher; lighting, Marc B. Weiss; sound, Jeffrey Montgomerie; production stage manager, Robert Bennett; press, Jeffrey Richards Associates, David LeShay.

Time: The present, the Pasmores' 60th wedding anniversary. Place: The Pasmores' retirement bungalow in northern England near the Yorkshire coast. Act I, Scene 1: 3 a.m. Scene 2: Morning. Act II, Scene 1: Early evening. Scene 2: The following morning.

The attenuating life of a retired university professor and the relationships within his troubled family. A foreign play previously produced by the National Theater in London and in regional theater by the Cleveland Play House.

THE VOICE OF THE PRAIRIE

Actor 1 . . . . Kevin Geer   Actor 3 . . . . Wendy Barrie-Wilson
Actor 2 . . . . Jack Cirillo

Directed by John Daines; scenery, Randall Etheredge; lighting, Philip Monat; costumes, Kathryn Wagner; sound, Richard Rose; sound consultant, Stuart Bernstein; production stage manager, Randy Lawson.

A rural radio star in the 1920s, with the three members of the cast playing numerous roles. Previously produced in regional theater at the Hartford Stage Company.

Note: Chelsea Stage, which had taken over the quarters formerly occupied by the Hudson Guild Theater, discontinued operations and shut down the week that *The Voice of the Prairie* opened and ended the play's run prematurely.

Lincoln Center Theater. Schedule of three programs. **Monster in a Box** (59; see note). One-man performance by Spalding Gray; written by Spalding Gray. Opened November 14, 1990. (Closed January 20, 1991; see note) **Township Fever** (39). Musical with book, music and lyrics and conceived by Mbongeni Ngema. Produced in association with the Brooklyn Academy of Music, Harvey Lichtenstein president and executive producer, in the Committed Artists production, Voza Rivers executive director, Duma Ndlova trustee. Opened December 19, 1990. (Closed January 20, 1991) And *Mr. Gogol and Mr. Preen* by Elaine May scheduled to open 6/9/91. Produced by Lincoln Center Theater, Gregory Mosher director, Bernard Gersten executive producer, at the Mitzi E. Newhouse Theater (*Township Fever* at the Majestic Theater, Brooklyn).

MONSTER IN A BOX

Directed by Renee Shafranzky; production manager, Jeff Hamlin; press, Merle Debuskey, Susan Chicoine.

The "monster" referred to in the title is the manuscript of the author's autobiographical novel *Impossible Vacation*, and this monologue—Gray's 13th—concerns his difficulties in writing it. The performance was presented without intermission. Previously produced in regional theater at Woodstock, N.Y., the Goodman Theater in Chicago and Emerson College, Boston.

Note: After the end of its regular run, *Monster in a Box* was presented in a series of 11 special performances on Monday evenings at Lincoln Center's Vivian Beaumont Theater, plus 5 special performances on Sunday and Monday evenings.

TOWNSHIP FEVER

Jazz Mngadi . . . . Brian Mazibuko
Tonko Mnisi . . . . Sindiswa Dlathu
Mr. Sibisi . . . . Bhoyi Ngema
Bra Cobra . . . . Bheki Mqadi
Phillidelphia . . . . John Lata
Priest . . . . David Manqele
Mrs. Mngadi . . . . Mamthandi Zulu
American Molefe . . . . Themba Mbonani

Manyewu Mnisi . . . . Dieketseng Mnisi
Dzehwe, The Leg; Rockman . . . Mike Motsogi
Fireman . . . . Sduduzo Mthethwa
Master of Ceremony . . . . Sphamandla Ngcamu
Kiriman . . . . Siphiwe Nkosi
News Presenter; Pregnant Woman . Clara Reyes
Policeman . . . . Mabonga Khumalo

Hostel Workers: Faca Khulu, Mabonga Khumalo, Sbusiso Ngema.
Lead Singers: Sindiswa Dlathu, Faca Khulu, Nomasonto Khumalo, Thembi Kubheka, John Lata,

TOWNSHIP FEVER—Bhoyi Ngema *(standing, rear)*, Themba Mbonani *(standing, foreground)*, Bheki Mqadi *(seated, right foreground)* and other members of the cast in a scene from the South African musical by Mbongeni Ngema at Lincoln Center Theater

David Manqele, Futhi Mhlongo, Dieketseng Mnisi, Mthandeni Mvelase, Zamagema Nene, Khululiwe Sithole, Mamthandi Zulu.

Dancers: Sindiswa Dlathu, Mabusi Gumede, Thapi Khambule, Skhumbuzo Kubheka, John Lata, Brian Mazibuko, Themba Mbonani, Gugulethu Mkhize, Batho Mhlongo, Futhi Mhlongo, Sduduzo Mthethwa, Sphamandla Ngcamu.

Chorus: Mabusi Gumede, Thapi Khambule, Faca Khulu, Mabonga Khumalo, Skhumbuzo Kubheka, John Lata, David Manqele, Themba Mbonani, Batho Mhlongo, Gugulethu Mkhize, Dieketseng Mnisi, Mike Motsogi, Sduduzo Mthethwa, Mthandeni Mvelase, Cry Ncube, Sphamandla Ngcamu, Sbusiso Ngema, Siphiwe Nkosi, Clara Reyes, Mamthandi Zulu.

Musicians: Mthandeni Mvelase conductor; Barney Bophela, Eddie Mathibe keyboards; Christopher Dlathu bass guitar; Jerry Kunene alto and tenor saxophone; Mfiliseni Magubane rhythm guitar; Wake Mahlobo drums; Duke Makasi tenor and soprano saxophone; Baba Mokoena, Sandile Shange lead guitar; Nathi Msomi trumpet, trombone; Sinelili Tshawe percussion; Brian Thusi trumpet, trombone, flugel horn, harmonica; Mfaniseni Thusi trombone.

Directed and choreographed by Mbongeni Ngema; scenery and costumes, Sarah Roberts; lighting, Mannie Manim; sound, Rick Rowe; original sound design (South Africa), Mark Malherbe; musical arrangements and orchestrations, Mbongeni Ngema; horn arrangements, Brian Thusi, Eric Norgate; additional choreography, Clara Reyes; stage manager, Michelle Lowry.

Inspired by the 1987 South African transit strike, the story of a jazz musician caught up in those troubled events. A foreign (South African) play previously produced at the Market Theater, Johannesburg.

MUSICAL NUMBERS (by Mbongeni Ngema unless otherwise noted), ACT I: "Ngatheth 'Amacala," "Hear My Prayer," "Daveyton," "Mfoka Ngema," "Intombenjani" (traditional), "Meleko," "Township Fever," "Blazing Like Fire," "Amasendenduna" (chant), "Izintombi Zomjolo," "Umandel 'Uthayihlome" (freedom song), "Ekufikeni" (the prophet Isaiah Shembe adapted by Mbongeni Ngema), "Isidudla" (adapted by Mbongeni Ngema), "Beautiful Little Mama," "The Lord Is My Shepherd" (prayer adapted by Mbongeni Ngema), "Xolisinhlizyo."

ACT II: "Mngani Wamina," "Wasiqoqela Ndawonye" (adapted by Mbongeni Ngema), "Oliver Tambo" (freedom song), "Nduna Ngibolekinduku" (the Zulu warriors), "Ufil 'Ubotha" (chant), "Ngobammakhosi," "Corruption," "U Mandela Uthayihlome" (freedom song), "Hohihlahla Mandela" (adapted by Mbongeni Ngema), "Freedom Charter" (original charter by the A.N.C. adapted musically by Mbongeni Ngema).

Sex, Drugs, Rock & Roll (36). Return engagement of the one-man performance by Eric Bogosian; written by Eric Bogosian. Produced by Frederick Zollo and Robert Cole in association with 126 Second Avenue Corp. and Sine/D'Addario Ltd. at the Orpheum Theater. Opened November 16, 1990. (Closed January 6, 1991)

Directed by Jo Bonney; scenery, John Arnone; lighting, Jan Kroeze; sound, Jan Nebozenko; associate producers, Ethel Bayer, William Suter; production stage manager, Pat Sosnow; press, Philip Rinaldi, Tim Ray.

These Bogosian character monologues, presented with one intermission, were previously produced off Broadway 2/8/90 for 103 performances. The program was named a Best Play of 1989-90.

The Gifts of the Magi (32). Return engagement of the musical adapted from Christmas tales by O. Henry; book and lyrics by Mark St. Germain; music and lyrics by Randy Courts. Produced by the Lamb's Theater Company, Ltd., Carolyn Rossi Copeland producing director, at the Lamb's Theater. Opened December 4, 1990. (Closed December 30, 1990)

Willy	Richard Blake	Jim Dillingham	Paul Jackel
City Her	Sarah Knapp	Della Dillingham	Lyn Vaux
City Him	Gordon Stanley	Soapy Smith	Ron Lee Savin

The Band: Steven M. Alper piano, conductor; David Nyberg percussion.

Directed by Carolyn Rossi Copeland; choreography, Richard O'Conner; musical direction and original incidental music, Steven M. Alper; costumes, Hope Hanafin; costume associate, Kathryn Wagner; lighting, Heather Carson; orchestrations, Douglas Besterman; production stage manager, Robin Anne Joseph; press, Peter Cromarty.

Time: Dec. 23 through 25, 1905. Place: New York City. The play was presented without intermission.

The Lamb's Theater Company's annual show, usually presented on an off-off-Broadway schedule but offered this year as a full off-Broadway production with some performances presented as dinner theater.

MUSICAL NUMBERS

"Star of the Night"	City Him, City Her
"The Gifts of the Magi"	Willy, Company
"Jim and Della"	Willy, Jim, Della
"Christmas to Blame"	Willy, City Him, City Her
"How Much to Buy My Dream"	Jim
"The Restaurant"	Soapy, City Him, City Her
"Once More"	Jim, Della
"Bum Luck"	Soapy, Jim
"Greed"	Jim, Della, City Him, City Her
"Pockets"	Willy
"Bum Luck" (Reprise)	Soapy
"The Same Girl"	Della

"The Gift of Christmas" . . . . Willy, Company
"The Gifts of the Magi" (Reprise) . . . . Company

Lyndon (46). By James Prideaux; based on *Lyndon: An Oral Biography* by Merle Miller.
Produced by Eric Krebs in association with Don Buford at the John Houseman Theater.
Opened January 17, 1991. (Closed March 3, 1991)

Lyndon Johnson . . . . Laurence Luckinbill

   Directed by Richard Zavaglia; makeup designed by Kevin Haney; press, David Rothenberg.
   Time: 1968, immediately after the announcement by the 36th President that he would not run for
re-election.
   Portrayal of President Johnson reflecting on his past, including his early political years and his
entanglement with the Vietnam War.

The Wizard of Hip (31). One-man performance by Thomas W. Jones II; written by Thomas
W. Jones II. Produced by National Black Touring Circuit, Inc., Woodie King Jr. and Art
D'Lugoff at the Top of the Gate Cabaret Theater. Opened January 20, 1991. (Closed
February 24, 1991)

   Directed by Kenny Leon; scenery, Tony Loadholt; lighting, Jeff Guzik; original score, James
Pelton Jr.; presented by special arrangement with Jomandi Productions of Atlanta; production stage
manager, Lisa L. Watson; press, Max Eisen.
   Young black man named Afro Jo in search (according to a program note) of "self-identity and self-
discovery . . . being who you are without apology." Previously produced at Newark Symphony Hall
1990 Theater Festival in April 1990 and in the Jomandi, Atlanta, Ga., mainstage season in June 1990.

An Unfinished Song (25). Musical with book, music and lyrics by James J. Mellon.
Produced by Cheryl L. Fluehr and Starbuck Productions, Ltd. at the Provincetown
Playhouse. Opened February 10, 1991. (Closed March 3, 1991)

Worth . . . . Aloysius Gigl   Mort . . . . Ken Land
Debbie . . . . Joanna Glushak   Beth . . . . Beth Leavel
Brad . . . . Robert Lambert

   Musicians: Marc Irwin piano, keyboards; Brad Fleckinger percussion.
   Understudies: Messrs. Land, Gigl, Lambert—Kevin Bailey; Misses Leavel, Glushak—Brad
Fleckinger.
   Directed by Simon Levy; musical direction, Mark Mitchell; scenery, Scott Bradley; costumes, Jeffrey
Ullman; lighting, Robert M. Wierzel; sound, Raymond D. Schilke; musical supervision and arrange-
ments, Lawrence Yurman; production stage manager, Karen Moore; press, Chris Boneau, Joe
D'Ambrosia.
   Exploring the complexities of falling in love.

ACT I

"Things We've Collected" . . . . Worth, Beth, Brad, Debbie
"Balance the Plate" . . . . Company
"Crossing Boundaries" . . . . Mort
"The Frying Pan" . . . . Beth
"Being Left Out" . . . . Debbie, Brad, Ensemble
"As I Say Goodbye" . . . . Beth
"Hobby Horses/How Could I Let You Leave Me" . . . . Company

ACT II

"New Hampshire Nights" . . . . Beth
"Blonde Haired Babies" . . . . Debbie
"Is That Love" . . . . Brad, Worth, Mort
"Crossing Boundaries" (Reprise) . . . . Mort
"An Unfinished Song" . . . . Mort
"We Were Here" . . . . Worth, Beth, Brad, Debbie

A Room of One's Own (98). One-woman performance by Eileen Atkins; adapted by Patrick Garland from the book by Virginia Woolf. Produced by Arthur Cantor at the Lamb's Theater. Opened March 4, 1991. (Closed June 9, 1991)

Directed by Patrick Garland; scenery, Bruce Goodrich; lighting, Lloyd Sobel; associate producer, Alexander Racolin; production manager, Mitchell Erickson; press, Arthur Cantor Associates.

The noted writer portrayed by Miss Atkins, with emphasis on her 1929 views on the status of women.

The Little Tommy Parker Celebrated Colored Minstrel Show (25). By Carlyle Brown. Produced by The Negro Ensemble Company, Douglas Turner Ward artistic director, Susan Watson Turner general manager, at the Master Theater. Opened March 17, 1991. (Closed April 7, 1991)

Henry . . . . Douglas Turner Ward	Soloman . . . . Ed Wheeler
Doe . . . . Helmar Augustus Cooper	Archie . . . . Kevin Smith
Tambo . . . . O.L. Duke	Percy . . . . Charles Weldon

Directed by Douglas Turner Ward; scenery, Michael Green; costumes, Gregory Glenn; lighting, William H. Grant III; sound, Selina Dixon; production stage manager, Femi; stage manager, Lisa Watson; press, Howard Atlee.

Tribulations of turn-of-the-century minstrel-show performers in their struggles for survival, as they must parody themselves onstage. The play was presented in two parts.

*And the World Goes 'Round (85). Musical revue with music by John Kander; lyrics by Fred Ebb; conceived by Scott Ellis, Susan Stroman and David Thompson. Produced by R. Tyler Gatchell Jr., Peter Neufeld, Patrick J. Patek and Gene R. Korf in association with the McCarter Theater at the Westside Theater. Opened March 18, 1991.

Bob Cuccioli	Jim Walton
Karen Mason	Karen Ziemba
Brenda Pressley	

Directed by Scott Ellis; choreography, Susan Stroman; musical direction and vocal and dance arrangements, David Loud; scenery, Bill Hoffman; costumes, Lindsay W. Davis; lighting, Phil Monat; sound, Gary Stocker; orchestrations, David Krane; production stage manager, Michael A. Clarke; stage manager, Valerie Lau-Kee; press, Philip Rinaldi, Mary Bryant, Tim Ray.

Standbys: George Dvorsky, Andrea Green.

Orchestra: David Loud musical director, piano; Stephen Milbank assistant musical director, synthesizer; Dennis Anderson woodwinds; David Brown trumpet; Bruce Doctor drums, percussion; Ronald Raffio bass, tuba.

Subtitled "The Songs of Kander & Ebb," a collection of their popular Broadway, movie and other songs. The show was presented in two parts. Previously produced at the Whole Theater, Montclair, N.J.

MUSICAL NUMBERS. ACT I: "And the World Goes 'Round" from *New York, New York*—Brenda Pressley; "Yes" from *70, Girls, 70*—Company; "Coffee in a Cardboard Cup" from *70, Girls, 70*—Company; "The Happy Time" from *The Happy Time*—Bob Cuccioli; "Colored Lights" from *The Rink*—Karen Mason; "Sara Lee"—Jim Walton, Ladies; "Arthur in the Afternoon" from *The Act*—Karen Ziemba, Cuccioli; "My Coloring Book"—Pressley; "I Don't Remember You" from *The Happy Time*—Cuccioli; "Sometimes a Day Goes By" from *Woman of the Year*—Walton; "All That Jazz" from *Chicago*—Ziemba, Walton; "Class" from *Chicago*—Pressley, Mason; "Mr. Cellophane" from *Chicago*—Walton; "Me and My Baby" from *Chicago*—Company; "There Goes the Ball Game" from *New York, New York*—Ladies; "How Lucky Can You Get" from *Funny Lady*—Mason, Men; "The Rink" from *The Rink*—Company.

ACT II: "Ring Them Bells"—Mason, Company; "Kiss of the Spider Woman" from *Kiss of the Spider Woman*—Cuccioli; "Only Love" from *Zorba*—Pressley; "Marry Me" from *The Rink*—Walton; "Quiet Thing" from *Flora, the Red Menace*—Ziemba; "When It All Comes True"—Walton, Ziemba; "Pain"—Company; "The Grass Is Always Greener" from *Woman of the Year*—Pressley, Mason; "We Can Make It" from *The Rink*—Cuccioli; "Maybe This Time" from the movie *Cabaret*—Pressley; "Isn't This Better?" from *Funny Lady*—Mason; "Money, Money" from the movie *Cabaret*—Company; "Cabaret" from *Cabaret*—Company.

Pvt. Wars (22). By James McLure. Produced by East-West Theater Productions at Actor's Playhouse. Opened March 21, 1991. (Closed April 7, 1991)

Woodruff Gately . . . . Jason Werner   Natwick . . . . Adrian Basil
Silvio . . . . Richard Werner

Understudies: Jason Werner—Gregory Gallagher; Richard Werner—Joseph Bronzi; Mr. Basil—Daniel Pearce.

Directed by Sylvia Caminer; scenery, Michael Lalicki; costumes, Joseph Petrollese; lighting, Eric Thoben; production stage manager, Lori Mudge; press, David Rothenberg Associates, Terence Womble.

Time: The 1970s. Place: On an outdoor terrace of an army veterans' hospital. The play was presented in two parts.

Echoes of war among hospitalized veterans.

The Kingfish (41). One-man performance by John McConnell as Huey P. Long in a play written by Larry L. King and Ben Z. Grant. Produced by Claudet & Christen Productions, Inc. (Michel Claudet and Darryl L. Christen) at the John Houseman Theater. Opened March 24, 1991. (Closed April 28, 1991)

Directed by Perry Martin; scenery, R.S.E. Limited; lighting, F. Mitchell Dana; sound, Tom Gould; production stage manager, Susan Whelan; press, Peter Cromarty, David Lotz.

The life, times and character of the colorful Louisiana Governor who was assassinated at age 42 in 1935. The play was presented in two parts. Previously produced at various Louisiana theaters.

Advice From a Caterpillar (54). By Douglas Carter Beane. Produced by John Nassivera and Don Schneider by special arrangement with Lucille Lortel at the Lucille Lortel Theater. Opened April 3, 1991. (Closed May 19, 1991)

Missy . . . . Ally Sheedy   Voice of Linda Lee. . . . . . . Gretchen Krich
Suit . . . . Harley Venton   Brat . . . . David Lansbury
Spaz . . . . Dennis Christopher

Understudies: Miss Sheedy—Gretchen Krich; Messrs. Venton, Christopher, Lansbury—Eric Swanson.

Directed by Edgar Lansbury; scenery, Rick Dennis; costumes, Jonathan Bixby; lighting, Brian Nason; original music, David Abir; production stage manager, Robert Bennett; stage manager, Gretchen Krich; press, Keith Sherman, Chris Day, Jim Byk.

Time: The present. Place: Act I, several locations in New York City's East Village and Soho; Act II, a country house in Old Chatham, N.Y.

Modern artist's bisexual lifestyle. Previously produced at the Dorset, Vt. Theater Festival.

Remembrance (40). Transfer from off off Broadway of the play by Graham Reid. Produced by the Irish Arts Center, Jim Sheridan artistic director, Georganne Heller and Nye Heron at the Irish Arts Center. Opened April 16, 1991. (Closed May 19, 1991)

Bert Andrews. . . . . Henry J. Quinn   Joan Donaghy. . . . . Ann Dowd
Victor Andrews . . . . Mickey Kelly   Deirdre Donaghy . . . . Terry Donnely
Theresa Donaghy . . . . Aideen O'Kelly   Jenny . . . . Ellen Tobie

Directed by Terence Lamude; scenery, Duke Durfee; costumes, C. Jane Epperson; lighting, John McLain; sound, Tom Gould; additional costumes, Richard Hieronymus; associate producer, Daniel P. Quinn; production stage manager, Kurt Wagemann; press, Francine L. Trevens.

Time: The present. Place: Belfast. The play was presented in two parts.

Catholic widow and Protestant widower meet at the graves of their children and form a loving attachment resented by their surviving children. Previously produced in Stamford, Conn. and in this run for 153 performances as an OOB production 10/7/90, later to off-Broadway status.

Mickey Kelly replaced John Finn and Henry J. Quinn replaced Malachy McCourt in the OOB cast prior to the off-Broadway opening.

*The Haunted Host and **Pouf Positive** (49). Program of two plays by Robert Patrick. Produced by Lawrence Lane at Actors' Playhouse. Opened April 19, 1991.

The Haunted Host

Jay Astor . . . . Harvey Fierstein
Frank . . . . Jason Workman

Time: 1964. Place: Jay's apartment on Christopher Street, Greenwich Village, New York City.
Scene 1: 8:30 p.m. Scene 2: 6:30 a.m. Scene 3: 7:30 p.m. The play was presented without intermission.

A Greenwich Village writer is haunted by the ghost of his protege when the dead man's look-alike
turns up. Previously produced off off Broadway at the Caffe Cino in the 1960s and 3/1/91 at La Mama
E.T.C.

Pouf Positive

Harvey Fierstein as a Greenwich Village playwright in the final hour of his life, a 25-minute monologue set in the present.

BOTH PLAYS: Directed by Eric Concklin; production design, David Adams; associate producers,
Steven J. Korwitch, Wayne Hamilton; production stage manager, Joe McGuire; press, Shirley Herz
Associates, Sam Rudy.

Ivy Rowe (40). One-woman performance by Barbara Bates Smith in a play by Mark Hunter
and Barbara Bates Smith; adapted from the novel *Fair and Tender Ladies* by Lee Smith.
Produced by The Ivy Company at the Provincetown Playhouse. Opened April 21, 1991.
(Closed May 25, 1991)

Directed by Mark Hunter; scenery, James Morgan; costumes, Vicki S. Holden; lighting, Ken
Kaczynski; production stage manager, Suzanne V. Beerman; press, Cromarty & Co., David Katz.

Time: Between 1912 and 1974. Place: Various locations in Southwest Virginia, including Ivy's
mountain home at Sugar Fork, the village of Majestic and the mining town of Diamond. The play was
presented in two parts.

Miss Smith as "Ivy Rowe," an Appalachian mountain woman remembering various episodes in her life.

*Pageant (34). Musical conceived by Robert Longbottom; book and lyrics by Bill Russell
and Frank Kelly; music by Albert Evans. Produced by Jonathan Scharer at the Blue Angel.
Opened May 2, 1991.

Miss Bible Belt . . . . Randl Ash
Miss Deep South . . . . David Drake
Miss Texas . . . . Russell Garrett
Miss Industrial Northeast . . . . Joe Joyce

Miss West Coast;
  Miss Glamouresse 1990 . . . . . John Salvatore
Miss Great Plains . . . . Dick Scanlan
Frankie Cavalier . . . . J.T. Cromwell

Directed and choreographed by Robert Longbottom; scenery, Daniel Ettinger; costumes, Gregg
Barnes; lighting, Timothy Hunter; co-choreographer, Tony Parise; musical direction, orchestrations and
arrangements, James Raitt; associate producer, Chip Quigley; production stage manager, Debora
Porazzi; press, Shirley Herz Associates, Glenna Freedman.

Standbys: Contestants (Miss U.S. Territories and Possessions)—Tony Parise; Mr. Cromwell—Larry
Hansen.

Musicians: James Raitt conductor, piano; Martin Erskine synthesizer programmer; Jeff Potter drummer.

Beauty contest with the contestants played by male performers, with the audience helping to select
"Miss Glamouresse 1991." The play was presented without intermission.

MUSICAL NUMBERS: The Miss Glamouresse Pageant—"Natural Born Females," "Something
Extra"; The Talent Competition—"It's Gotta Be Venus," "Girl Power," "Good Bye," "Miss Glamouresse."

*Breaking Legs (13). By Tom Dulack. Produced by Elliot Martin, Bud Yorkin and James
and Maureen O'Sullivan Cushing at the Promenade Theater. Opened May 19, 1991.

Lou Graziano . . . . Vincent Gardenia
Angie . . . . Sue Giosa
Terence O'Keefe . . . . Nicolas Surovy

Mike Francisco . . . . Philip Bosco
Tino De Felice . . . . Victor Argo
Frankie Salvucci . . . . Larry Storch

Standbys: Messrs. Gardenia, Bosco—Vince Viverito; Mr. Surovy—Virgil Roberson; Miss Giosa—
Kelleigh McKenzie. Understudy: Messrs. Argo, Storch—Brian Dykstra.

SONG OF SINGAPORE—Michael Garin, Robert Hipkens and Donna Murphy in the musical written by Allan Katz, Erik Frandsen, Michael Garin, Robert Hipkens and Paula Lockheart

Directed by John Tillinger; scenery, James Noone; costumes, David C. Woolard; lighting, Ken Billington; production stage manager, Elliott Woodruff; stage manager, Brian Dykstra; press, Jeffrey Richards.

Time: The present. Place: A restaurant in a New England university town. The play was presented in two parts.

College professor seeks backing for his play from gangsters. Previously produced in regional theater at the Old Globe Theater, San Diego.

*The Good Times Are Killing Me (12). Transfer from off off Broadway of the play by Lynda Barry. Produced by Second Stage Theater, Robyn Goodman and Carole Rothman artistic directors, at Second Stage Theater. Opened May 21, 1991; see note.

Edna Arkins. . . . . Angela Goethals	Cousin Ellen; Mrs. Hosey;
Lucy Arkins . . . . Lauren Gaffney	Mrs. Mercer. . . . . Jennie Moreau
Mom; Mrs. Doucette . . . . Holly Felton	Sharon; Theresa Doucette . . Kathleen Dennehy
Aunt Martha; Bonita . . . . Ellia English	Uncle Jim . . . . Ray DeMattis
Mr. Willis. . . . . Wendell Pierce	Dad; Cousin Steve . . . . Peter Appel
Mrs. Willis. . . . . Kim Staunton	Bonna Willis. . . . . Chandra Wilson
Aunt Margaret . . . . Ruth Williamson	Elvin Willis. . . . . Brandon Mayo
Earl Stelly; Preacher; Marcus . . . . John Lathan	

Neighborhood Kids, Teachers, 7th Graders: Company.

Directed by Mark Brokaw; scenery, Rusty Smith; costumes, Ellen McCartney; lighting, Don Holder; sound, Janet Kalas; musical direction, Steve Sandberg; choreography, Don Philpott; production stage manager, James Fitzsimmons; stage manager, Lori Lundquist; press, Richard Kornberg.

Time: Mid 1960s. Place: A working class neighborhood. The play was presented in two parts.

Affection and friction between two early teen-aged girls, one white and one black, growing up in a racially mixed neighborhood, with considerable emphasis on music, both recorded and sung, adapted by the playwright from her own novel of the same title. Previously produced in a different version by the City Lit Theater Company, Chicago.

Note: This production of *The Good Times Are Killing Me* opened at Second Stage as an off-off-Broadway production 4/18/91 and played 37 performances before transferring to off-Broadway status.

A Best Play: see page 262

*Song of Singapore (10). Musical with book by Allan Katz, Erik Frandsen, Michael Garin, Robert Hipkens and Paula Lockheart; music and lyrics by Erik Frandsen, Michael Garin, Robert Hipkens and Paula Lockheart. Produced by Steven Baruch, Richard Frankel and Thomas Viertel in association with Allen Spivak and Larry Magid at Song of Singapore Theater (17 Irving Place). Opened May 23, 1991.

Spike Spauldeen	Inpector Marvin Kurland;
(uke, guitar, vocals). . . . . . . Erik Frandsen	Others (vocals) . . . . Francis Kane
Freddy S. Lyme (piano, vocals). . Michael Garin	Kenya Ratamacue (drums) . . Oliver Jackson Jr.
Hans van der Last (trumpet,	Taqfim Arco (bass) . . . . Earl C. May
dobro, guitar, vocals) . . . . Robert Hipkens	Zoot DeFumee (saxophone,
Rose (vocals). . . . . Donna Murphy	clarinet). . . . . Jon Gordon
Chah Li (vocals). . . . . Cathy Foy	T-Bone Kahanamoku (trombone) . . . Art Baron

Directed by A.J. Antoon; scenery, John Lee Beatty; costumes, Frank Krenz; lighting, Peter Kaczorowski; sound, Stuart J. Allyn; musical supervision, Art Baron; orchestrations, John Carlini; vocal arrangements, Yaren Gershovsky; jazzaturg, Paula Lockheart; associate producer, Marc Routh; additional music staging, Lynne Taylor-Corbett; production stage manager, Ron Nash; stage manager, Mary E. Lawson; press, Chris Boneau & Associates, Jackie Green.

Time: Early December 1941. Place: Freddy's Song of Singapore Cafe, a nightclub on the Singapore waterfront.

Zany musical melodrama in a night club environment, with performer-musicians acting out an episode of jewel robbery and providing their own music and underscoring.

ACT I

"Song of Singapore"	Band
"Inexpensive Tango"	Spike
"I Miss My Home in Haarlem"	Hans
"You Gotta Do What You Gotta Do"	Rose
"The Rose of Rangoon"	Spike
"Necrology"	Band
"Sunrise"	Rose
"Never Pay Musicians What They're Worth"	Freddy
"Harbour of Love"	Kurland
"I Can't Remember"	Rose
"I Want to Get Offa This Island"/"Harbour of Love"	Band/Kurland

ACT II

"Foolish Geese"	Chah Li
"Serve It Up"	Rose
"Fly Away Rose" . . . . Hans, Freddy, Spike
"I Remember" . . . . Rose, Band
"Shake, Shake, Shake" . . . . Freddy, Band
"We're Rich"	Band
"Sunrise"/"Song of Singapore"	Band

Mump and Smoot in "Caged". . . With Wog (12). Written and created by Michael Kennard and John Turner. Produced by Arthur Cantor and Hollywood Canada Productions, Inc. at the Astor Place Theater. Opened May 29, 1991. (Closed June 9, 1991)

Mump . . . . Michael Kennard	Wog . . . . Debbie Tidy
Smoot . . . . John Turner	

Directed by Karen Hines; lighting, Michel Charbonneau; art direction, John Dawson; music and sound, Davis Hines; production stage manager, Louise Hines; press, Arthur Cantor Associates, Bob Grogan.

Clowns as the subjects and perpetrators of a horror show, created by Canadian performers. The play was presented without intermission.

CAST REPLACEMENTS AND
TOURING COMPANIES

The following is a list of the major cast replacements of record in productions which opened in previous years, but were still playing in New York during a substantial part of the 1990-91 season; or were still on a first-class tour in 1990-91 (replacements in first-class touring companies of previous seasons which were no longer playing in 1990-91 appear in previous *Best Plays* volumes of appropriate years).

The name of each major role is listed in *italics* beneath the title of the play in the first column. In the second column directly opposite appears the name of the actor who created the role in the original New York production (whose opening date appears in *italics* at the top of the column). Indented immediately beneath the original actor's name are the names of subsequent New York replacements, together with the date of replacement when available.

The third column gives information about first-class touring companies produced under the auspices of their original New York managements. When there is more than one roadshow company, #1, #2, etc., appear before the name of the performer who created the role in each company (and the city and date of each company's first performance appears in *italics* at the top of the column). Their subsequent replacements are also listed beneath their names, with dates when available.

ASPECTS OF LOVE

New York 4/8/90

George Dillingham

Kevin Colson
   Walter Charles
   John Cullum 10/22/90
   Barrie Ingram 1/7/91

Rose Vibert

Ann Crumb
   Elinore O'Connell 9/90
   Sarah Brightman 12/14/90

BLACK AND BLUE

New York 1/26/89

Singer

Ruth Brown
   LaVern Baker

CATS

New York 10/7/82

Bustapher Jones; Asparagus;
  Growltiger

Stephen Hanan
   Timothy Jerome
   Gregg Edelman
   Bill Carmichael

Stephen Hanan
Paul Harman
Dale Hensley
John Dewar

Cassandra

Rene Ceballos
Christina Kumi Kimball
Nora Brennan
Charlotte d'Amboise
Jessica Northrup
Roberta Stiehm
Julietta Marcelli
Leigh Webster
Darlene Wilson

Coricopat; Mungojerrie

Rene Clemente
Guillermo Gonzalez
Joe Antony Cavise
Johnny Anzalone
Ray Roderick·
Johnny Anzalone

Loni Ackerman *(right)* as Grizabella with members of the cast of *Cats*

Demeter	Wendy Edmead
	Marlene Danielle
	Jane Bodle
	Patricia Ruck
	Beth Swearingen
	Brenda Braxton
Grizabella	Betty Buckley
	Laurie Beechman
	Loni Ackerman
Jennyanydots	Anna McNeely
	Marcy DeGonge
	Cindy Benson
Mistoffelees	Timothy Scott
	Herman W. Sebek
	Jamie Torcellini
	Michael Scott Gregory
	Barry K. Bernal
	Don Johanson
	Kevin Poe
	Michael Barriskill
	Michael Arnold
	Gen Horiuchi
Munkustrap	Harry Groener
	Claude R. Tessier
	Mark Fotopoulos
	Rob Marshall
	Robert Amirante
	Greg Minahan
Old Deuteronomy	Ken Page
	Kevin Marcum
	Clent Bowers
	Larry Small
	Ken Prymus
Plato; Macavity; Rumpus Cat	Kenneth Ard
	Scott Wise
	Brian Andrews
	Jamie Patterson
	Randy Wojcik
Rum Tum Tugger	Terrence Mann
	Jamie Rocco
	Rick Sparks
	Steve Yudson
	Frank Mastrocola
Rumpleteazer	Christine Langner
	Paige Dana
	Kristi Lynes
Skimbleshanks	Reed Jones
	Michael Scott Gregory
	Robert Burnett
	Reed Jones
	Richard Stafford
	Eric Scott Kincaid
	Michael Scott Gregory

THE FANTASTICKS

New York 5/3/60

El Gallo	Jerry Orbach
	    David Brummel 12/25/90
	    Michael Licata 1/8/91
	    Kenneth Kantor 2/12/91
	    Scott Willis 3/26/91

Luisa	Rita Gardner Marilyn Whitehead 1/23/89

Matt	Kenneth Nelson
	    Matthew Eaton Bennett 5/30/89
	    Rex Nockengust 7/31/90
	    Kevin R. Wright 11/6/90
	    Rex Nockengust 5/7/91

Note: Only this season's or the most recent cast replacements are listed above under the names of the original cast members. For previous replacements, see previous volumes of *Best Plays*.

A FEW GOOD MEN

New York 11/25/89

Lt. j.g. Daniel A. Kaffee	Tom Hulce Timothy Busfield 5/14/90

Lt. Cmdr. Joan Galloway	Megan Gallagher
	    Pamela Blair 6/25/90
	    Kathleen McNenny 1/7/91

Lt. Col. Nathan Jessep	Stephen Lang
	    Ron Perlman
	    Perry King 12/3/90

FOREVER PLAID

	New York 5/20/90	*#1 Washington, D.C. 3/12/91* *#2 St. Louis 5/12/91*
Sparky	Jason Graae Dale Sandish 4/15/91	#1 Michael Winther #2 Dan Brunson
Smudge	David Engel	#1 Greg Jbara #2 Tom Cianfichi
Jinx	Stan Chandler	#1 Paul Binotto #2 Buck Dietz
Francis	Guy Stroman Drew Geraci 4/30/91	#1 Neil Nash #2 Alan Souza

GRAND HOTEL

	New York 11/12/89	*Tampa 11/27/91*
Otto Kringeline	Michael Jeter Chip Zien 9/12/90	Mark Baker

Baron Felix Von Gaigern	David Carroll
	    Brent Barrett 5/8/90
	    Rex Smith 5/29/90
	    David Carroll 12/2/90
	    John Schneider 3/4/91
		Brent Barrett

Elizaveta Grushinskaya	Liliane Montevecchi	Liliane Montevecchi
	Rene Ceballos 11/12/90	
Flaemmchen	Jane Krakowski	DeLee Lively

GYPSY

New York 11/16/89

Rose

Tyne Daly
  Jana Robbins 2/20/90
  Tyne Daly 2/25/90
  Linda Lavin 7/30/90

Herbie

Jonathan Hadary
  Jamie Ross 10/30/90

THE HEIDI CHRONICLES

N.Y. Off B'way 12/11/88
N.Y. B'way 3/9/89   *Los Angeles 10/2/90*

Heidi Holland

Joan Allen   Amy Irving
  Christine Lahti 9/5/89   Stephanie Dunnam 1/8/91
  Brooke Adams 1/2/90
  Mary McDonnell 7/2/90

Peter Patrone

Boyd Gaines   Robert Curtis-Brown
  David Pierce 9/5/89
  David Lansbury 3/6/90

Scoop Rosenbaum

Peter Friedman   Mark Harelik
  Tony Shalhoub 9/5/89
  Kario Salam 7/2/90

LES MISERABLES

#1 Boston 12/5/87
#2 Los Angeles 5/21/88
New York 3/12/87   *#3 Tampa 11/28/88*

Jean Valjean

Colm Wilkinson   #1 William Solo
  Gary Morris 11/30/87   Craig Schulman 4/88
  Timothy Shew 5/30/88   J. Mark McVey
  William Solo 7/3/89   Gary Morris
  Craig Schulman 1/13/90   Mark McKerracher
  J. Mark McVey 1/22/91   #2 William Solo
                                          Jordan Bennett
                                          Rich Hebert
                                          Kevin McGuire
                                          Richard Poole
                                       #3 Gary Barker
                                          Richard Poole
                                          Brian Lynch

Javert

Terrence Mann   #1 Herndon Lackey
  Anthony Crivello 11/30/87   Charles Pistone
  Norman Large 1/18/88   Robert DuSold
  Anthony Crivello 3/14/88   Richard Kinsey
  Norman Large 7/19/88   #2 Jeff McCarthy
  Herndon Lackey 1/17/89   Richard Kinsey

J. Mark McVey (Jean Valjean) and Robert DuSold (Javert) in *Les Misérables*

Peter Samuel 1/15/90
Robert Westenberg
Robert DuSold

Tim Bowman
#3 Peter Samuel
Paul Schoeffler
David Jordan

Fantine

Randy Graff
Maureen Moore 7/19/88
Susan Dawn Carson 1/17/89
Laurie Beechman 1/15/90
Christy Baron

#1 Diane Fratantoni
Ann Crumb
Hollis Resnik
Kathy Taylor
Susan Dawn Carson
Laurie Beechman 1/89
Susan Gilmour
Anne Runolfsson
#2 Elinore O'Connell
Kelly Ground
#3 Hollis Resnik
Christy Baron
Lisa Vroman

Enjolras

Michael Maguire
Joseph Kolinski
Joe Locarro 1/15/90
Joseph Kolinski

#1 John Herrera
Joe Locarro
Pete Herber
Christopher Yates
#2 Greg Blanchard
Raymond Sarr
Craig Oldfather

		#3 Greg Zerkle Jerry Christakos Aloysius Gigl
Marius	David Bryant Ray Walker Hugh Panaro Matthew Porretta	#1 Hugh Panaro John Ruess Peter Gunther #2 Reece Holland Peter Gantenbein Matthew Porretta John Ruess #3 Matthew Porretta Gilles Chiasson
Cosette	Judy Kuhn Tracy Shayne Jacqueline Piro	#1 Tamara Jenkins Melissa Errico Kimberly Behlman #2 Karen Fineman Jacqueline Piro Ellen Rockne #3 Jacqueline Piro Tamra Hayden Lisa Vroman Marian Murphy
Eponine	Frances Ruffelle Kelli James 9/15/87 Natalie Toro 7/88	#1 Renee Veneziale Jennifer Naimo Susan Tilson #2 Michelle Nicastro Michele Maika Candese Marchese Misty Cotton #3 Michele Maika Dana Lynn Caruso Candese Marchese
Thenardier	Leo Burmester Ed Dixon	#1 Tom Robbins Neal Ben-Ari 12/5/88 Drew Eshelman #2 Gary Beach #3 Paul Ainsley J.P. Dougherty
Mme. Thenardier	Jennifer Butt Evalyn Baron 1/15/90	#1 Victoria Clark Rosalyn Rahn #2 Kay Cole Gina Ferrall #3 Linda Kerns Diana Rogers

LOVE LETTERS

	N.Y. Off B'way 8/22/89 *N.Y. B'way 10/31/89*	*Seattle 1/15/91*
Melissa Gardner	Stockard Channing Dana Ivey 8/29/89 Swoosie Kurtz 9/5/89 Elaine Stritch 9/12/89	Stephanie Powers

Jane Curtin 9/19/89
Colleen Dewhurst 9/26/89
Kate Nelligan 10/3/89
Joanna Gleason 10/10//89

Colleen Dewhurst
Stockard Channing 11/7/89
Swoosie Kurtz 11/14/89
Elizabeth Montgomery 11/21/89
Jane Curtin 11/28/89
Nancy Marchand 12/5/89
Kate Nelligan 12/12/89
Elizabeth McGovern 12/19/89
Lynn Redgrave 12/26/89
Polly Bergen 1/2/90
Kate Nelligan 1/9/90
Elaine Stritch 1/16/90

Andrew Makepeace Ladd III	John Rubinstein George Segal 8/29/89 Richard Thomas 9/5/89 Jason Robards 9/12/89 Edward Herrmann 9/19/89 Josef Sommer 9/26/89 Treat Williams 10/3/89 John Rubinstein 10/10/89	Robert Wagner

Jason Robards 10/31/89
John Rubinstein 11/7/89
Richard Thomas 11/14/89
Robert Foxworth 11/21/89
Edward Herrmann 11/28/89
Fritz Weaver 12/5/89
David Dukes 12/12/89
Timothy Hutton 12/19/89
John Clark 12/26/89
Robert Vaughn 1/2/90
Treat Williams 1/9/90
Cliff Robertson 1/16/90

M. BUTTERFLY

	New York 3/20/88	*Boston 9/26/90*
Rene Gallimard	John Lithgow David Dukes 8/22/88 John Rubinstein 2/20/89 Tony Randall 8/21/89	Philip Anglim
Song Liling	B.D. Wong A. Mapa 9/25/89	A. Mapa

ONCE ON THIS ISLAND

	N.Y. Off B'way 5/6/90 *N.Y. B'way 10/18/90*	
Ti Moune	La Chanze	
Daniel	Jerry Dixon	
Asaka	Kecia Lewis-Evans Lillias White 1/8/91	

OTHER PEOPLE'S MONEY

	New York 2/26/89	*Baltimore 3/20/90*
Lawrence Garfinkel	Kevin Conway Jon Polito 1/21/90 Kevin Conway 4/24/90 Steven Keats 7/3/90 Dan Lauria 4/16/91	Tony Lo Bianco
Kate Sullivan	Mercedes Ruehl Janet Zarich 4/18/89 Mercedes Ruehl 10/24/89 Priscilla Lopez 1/21/90	Julie Boyd

THE PHANTOM OF THE OPERA

	New York 1/26/88	*#1 Los Angeles 5/31/90* *#2 Chicago 5/24/90*
The Phantom	Michael Crawford Timothy Nolen 10/10/88 Cris Groenendaal 3/20/89 Steve Barton 3/19/90 Kevin Gray Mark Jacoby 2/21/91	#1 Michael Crawford Robert Guillaume 5/1/90 Michael Crawford Davis Gaines #2 Mark Jacoby Kevin Gray
Christine Daaé	Sarah Brightman Patti Cohenour 6/7/88 Dale Kristien (alt.) 7/88* Rebecca Luker (alt.) 3/89* Rebecca Luker 6/5/89 Katherine Buffaloe (alt.)* Karen Culliver	#1 Dale Kristien Mary Darcy (alt.)* #2 Karen Culliver Teri Bibb (alt.)* Sara Pfisterer (alt.)*
Raoul	Steve Barton Kevin Gray 9/18/90 Davis Gaines 3/12/90 Hugh Panaro	#1 Reece Holland Michael Piontek #2 Keith Buterbaugh

*Alternates play the role of Christine Daaé Monday and Wednesday evenings.

THE PIANO LESSON

	New York 4/16/90
Boy Willie	Charles S. Dutton
Lymon	Rocky Carroll
Berniece	S. Epatha Merkerson
Wining Boy	Lou Myers Ernie Scott 7/15/90

PRELUDE TO A KISS

	N.Y. Off B'way 3/14/90 *N.Y. B'way 5/1/90*
Peter	Alec Baldwin

	Timothy Hutton
	    John Dossett 10/16/90
	    Steve Guttenberg 3/16/91

Rita	Mary-Louise Parker Ashley Crow 10/26/90
Old Man	Barnard Hughes John Randolph 1/18/91

THE ROTHSCHILDS

	New York 4/27/90
Nathan Rothschild	Bob Cuccioli John Loprieno 12/19/90
Mayer Rothschild	Mike Burstyn

TRU

	New York 12/14/89	*Buffalo 10/2/90*
Truman Capote	Robert Morse	Robert Morse

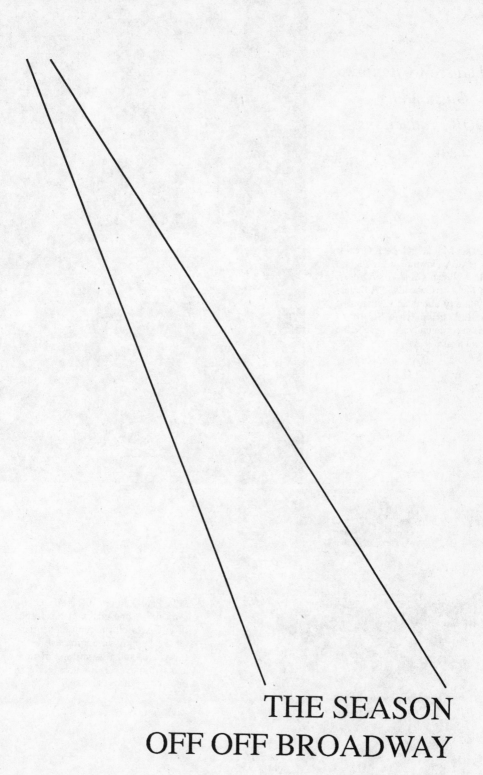

THE SEASON
OFF OFF BROADWAY

Mel Gussow Citations:
Outstanding
OOB Productions

Right, Dan Moran and Zach Grenier in the BACA Downtown production of Mac Wellman's *Sincerity Forever*, which Mel Gussow calls, "A fantastical comedy about an invasion of 'furballed' aliens in a Southern American community..... an acerbic attack on racism."

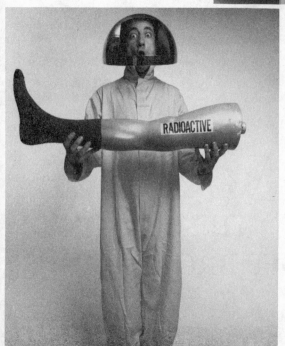

Left, Paul Zaloom in his *My Civilization:* "A one-man tabletop frolic. ..... As a clown-cum-puppetmaster, he has grown enormously over the years, and this collage of new and semi-new performance pieces is one of his wittiest to date."

OFF OFF BROADWAY

By Mel Gussow

IN COMMON with the rest of the theater (and, of course, the arts in general), off off Broadway was feeling the effects of cutbacks in funding this season. Economically, OOB has always been a marginal arena where no profits are made and less has to speak for more. A small grant from a federal, state or city agency can mean the difference between survival and failure. During the 1990-91 season, several OOB companies went out of business, including the New Theater of Brooklyn, Chelsea Stage (the shortlived successor to the Hudson Guild Theater) and BACA Downtown (in Brooklyn). Other companies, feeling extreme financial pressure, reduced the number and the size of productions and went, hat in hand, looking for substitute support. Certainly any theater can be revived, but, as the season ended, prospects were dim.

The most substantial loss is BACA Downtown, an outpost of experimental theater (and art, in an adjacent gallery). Under the artistic direction of Bonnie Metzgar, the company focused on challenging new voices in the theater, this past season with Mac Wellman's *Sincerity Forever*, cited as an outstanding 1990-91 OOB production.* This was a fantastical comedy about an invasion of "furballed" aliens in a southern American community. In this acerbic attack on racism, coneheaded Ku Klux Klansmen received their comic comeuppance. Brightening the cast under Jim Simpson's nimble direction were Stephen Mellor, Jan Leslie Harding, Amy Brenneman and Leslie Nipkow. BACA also presented *The Death of the Last Black Man in the Whole Entire World*, a slashing new play by Suzan-Lori Parks, and *The Almond Seller*, Oana-Maria Hock's provacative attempt to come to terms with the revolution in Romania.

Political commentary preoccupied Paul Zaloom in his one-man tabletop frolic

---

* *Editor's Note:* Sincerity Forever *was also cited by the American Theater Critics Association as one of the season's outstanding offerings in cross-country theater. Porter Anderson of the Dallas* Times Herald *introduces an excerpt from the script in The Season Around the United States section of this volume and provides the following footnote:* "Sincerity Forever *is one of the country's most scathing and yet artistically viable responses to the censorship/funding issues that threaten to overwhelm the National Endowment for the Arts. When Rep. Dana Rohrbacher called its conclusion 'a four-letter version of the Sermon on the Mount' and the play itself 'yet another NEA outrage,' the NEA wrote to Wellman to remove credit to the Endowment for assistance in the creation of the play, despite the $15,000 playwriting fellowship Wellman had been granted by the NEA for the spring 1990 period of the script's inception.*

"*As ready to respond to the NEA as he had been to the rightist conservatives who inspired the play— Wellman dedicated the show 'to Jesse and the Wildman,' referring to Sen. Jesse Helms and the Rev. Donald Wildmon of the American Family Association—the playwright added a note to his script: 'The author would like to amend the error of his ways. I was wrong.* Sincerity Forever *was not made possible by the generous assistance of the NEA. I don't know what I was thinking.'"*

entitled *My Civilization* (cited as an outstanding OOB production) at Dance Theater Workshop. As a clown-cum-puppetmaster, he has grown enormously over the years, and this collage of new and semi-new performance pieces is one of his wittiest to date. In it, he recycles the detritus of our civilization (including boxes, bottles, tools and other objects and ephemera) into a rudely comic environment that might have been co-designed by Gary Trudeau, Andy Warhol and the Monty Pythons. Zaloom trashes such icons of conservatism as Sen. Jesse Helms along with aspects of a compulsively consumerist society.

Karen Finley, whose own battle with the National Endowment for the Arts was featured prominently in Zaloom's comedy, brought her controversial one-woman show *We Keep Our Victims Ready* to New York and revealed herself as an intuitive and outspoken commentator for feminism and freedom.

Ellen Stewart's La Mama continued to be a thriving showplace for experimental theater, welcoming Ping Chong with his cyberpunk fantasy, *Elephant Memories*, and Richard Foreman with *Eddie Goes to Poetry City: Part 2*, another elliptical portrait by this symbolist director. Jean-Claude van Itallie also returned to La Mama with *Ancient Boys*, a disappointing look at the death of an artist from AIDS. While wandering through the chaotic legalistic landscape of George F. Walker's *Love and Anger*, the forward-looking New York Theater Workshop also presented Caryl Churchill's informative English history lesson, *Light Shining in Buckinghamshire*. In *Blue Heat* at INTAR, John Jesurun continued his investigation of methods of non-communication. On other stages, Allan Havis intriguingly restudied the legend of *Lilith* in his new play by that title, and John Kelly took a playfully idiosyncratic look at growing up in *Maybe It's Cold Outside*.

Battling the recession and the trend, the Soho Rep reopened in a new space in Tribeca—with Eric Overmyer's *Native Speech*, a high-intensity comedy about an inner city talk radio host named Hungry Mother (a prodigious performance by Kario Salem). Theater for the New City, refurbishing its facilities into a Lower East Side cultural center, opened a partly renovated theater late in the season with *Fata Morgana*, a ship-of-fools mystery journey directed by Paul Zimet. Everett Quinton stayed on track in his post-Charles Ludlam comeback phase at the Ridiculous Theatrical Company. *When Lightning Strikes Twice*, a doubleheader of loopy H.M. Koutoukas yarns, was followed by a bellringing camp quasi-musical derived from *The Hunchback of Notre Dame*, starring Quinton as a lecherous keeper of the cathedral (and the hunchback).

Anne Hamburger's En Garde Arts continued to pride itself on being homeless— and site-specific—setting up shows in the strangest of places, including the meatpacking district for *Father Was a Peculiar Man*, an environmental play that borrowed freely (but not wisely) from *The Brothers Karamazov* and other sources. Following up the En Garde's early residency in the reclaimed Victory Theater in Times Square, Theater for a New Audience presented a youthful production of *Romeo and Juliet* in that historic space.

The prolific Romulus Linney had a rewarding season, with the first New York production of *Unchanging Love*, an evocative adaptation of Chekhov's *In the Ravine*, offered by the Triangle Theater. At season's end, he became the first subject of the innovative Signature Theater, which is devoting an entire year to a single playwright, beginning with Linney's doubleheader, *The Love Suicide at Schofield Barracks*, in a new and improved one-act version, and a revival of his *F.M.*, a mirthful satire about a class in creative fiction.

While the WPA was still immersed in its so-called "silly phase," with *Grotesque Love Songs* and *Red Scare on Sunset* (a Charles Busch sendup of the blacklist), the CSC branched out with Molière's *The Learned Ladies*, starring Jean Stapleton, and a rare revival of *The Resistible Rise of Arturo Ui*, starring John Turturro in the Hitler-like title role. The Women's Project followed some dubious one-acts with *Night Sky*, Susan Yankowitz's deeply personalized study of aphasia, starring Joan MacIntosh and staged by Joseph Chaikin.

Tisa Chang's Pan Asian Repertory Theater opened the season with an oddity, *Lucky Come Hawaii*, a raucous comedy about the Japanese bombing of Pearl Harbor, and closed it with *Letters to a Student Revolutionary*, Elizabeth Wong's tender tale of a friendship by mail that ended with the uprising in Tiananmen Square. OyamO's *Let Me Live* was a fervid play about black labor unionism, and Richard Dresser's *Better Days* humorously contemplated post-recession America. Among the seasonal fizzles was Cornerstone's *The Video Store Owner's Significant Other*, a leaden attempt to reinterpret Lorca's *The Shoemaker's Prodigious Wife*. Elizabeth McGovern added necessary elevation to the Atlantic Theater's otherwise amateurish performance of David Mamet's adaptation of *Three Sisters*.

OOB continued to be a fertile ground for one-act plays, with festivals at the Ensemble Studio Theater, Manhattan Punch Line and the Working Theater. The Ensemble Studio's annual Marathon was a crosspatch of name authors (including Arthur Miller) and newcomers, with the most noteworthy play coming from Frank D. Gilroy, the very amusing *A Way with Words*, which could serve as a one-act model for aspiring writers.

One of the most sheerly entertaining shows was *Le Cirque de Soleil*, a French Canadian circus that set up its show in a tent in Battery Park City. Animal-less, fun-filled, it featured the antics of the clown, David Shiner.

Many other seasonal high points were of an international nature, in the fall with BAM Next Wave's *Ninagawa Macbeth*, a ritualized Japanese experiment with Shakespeare, and in June with the second New York International Festival of the Arts. The Festival brought a cornucopia of distinguished foreign companies to off-off venues as well as more central locations. Poland's Cricot 2 company returned to La Mama after the death of its director Tadeusz Kantor, presenting a revival of *The Dead Class* and Mr. Kantor's final play, *Today Is My Birthday*. The Suzuki Company of Japan offered a different *Dionysus*, and the Reduced Shakespeare Company put the collected works of Shakespeare on the head of a pin—all the plays excerpted in less than two hours. The outstanding event was the arrival after June 1 of Ingmar Bergman with a trio of plays from the Royal Dramatic Theater of Sweden. His innovative Swedish-language versions of *Miss Julie*, *Long Day's Journey Into Night* and *A Doll's House* (at the Brooklyn Academy of Music's Majestic Theater) gave distinction to the festival and to the season. Details of their casts and credits will appear in *The Best Plays of 1991-92*.

PLAYS PRODUCED
OFF OFF BROADWAY

AND ADDITIONAL PRODUCTIONS

Here is a comprehensive sampling of off-off-Broadway and other experimental or peripheral 1990-91 productions in New York, compiled by Camille Croce. There is no definitive "off-off-Broadway" area or qualification. To try to define or regiment it would be untrue to its fluid, exploratory purpose. The listing below of hundreds of works produced by more than 100 OOB groups and others is as inclusive as reliable sources will allow, however, and takes in all leading Manhattan-based, new-play producing, English-language organizations.

The more active and established producing groups are identified in **bold face type**, in alphabetical order, with artistic policies and the names of the managing directors given whenever these are a matter of record. Each group's 1990-91 schedule is listed with play titles in CAPITAL LETTERS. Often these are works-in-progress with changing scripts, casts and directors, sometimes without an engagement of record (but an opening or early performance date is included when available).

Many of these off-off-Broadway groups have long since outgrown a merely experimental status and are offering programs which are the equal in professionalism and quality (and in some cases the superior) of anything in the New York theater, with special contractual arrangements like the showcase code, letters of agreement (allowing for longer runs and higher admission prices than usual) and, closer to the edge of the commercial theater, a so-called "mini-contract." In the list below, all available data on opening dates, performance numbers and major production and acting credits (almost all of them Equity members) is included in the entries of these special-arrangement offerings.

A large selection of lesser-known groups and other shows that made appearances off-off-Broadway during the season appears under the "Miscellaneous" heading at the end of this listing.

Amas Musical Theater. Dedicated to bringing all people, regardless of race, creed, color or economic background, together through the creation and development of new American musicals. Rosetta LeNoire founder and artistic director.

JUBA (32). Book and lyrics by Wendy Lamb; music by Russel Walden. February 8, 1991. Director, Sheldon Epps; choreography, Mercedes Ellington; scenery, James Leonard Joy; lighting, Susan White; costumes, Daniel Lawson; musical director, Ted Kociolek. With Kevin Ramsey, James Brennan, Katherine Buffaloe, Lawrence Clayton, Ken Prymus, Terri White, Mark Hardy, Steve Boles.

Workshop Productions:

JUBA. September 19, 1990. With Lawrence Clayton, Evan Matthews, Jane Bodle, Michael McCormick, Ken Prymus, Brenda Pressley, Paul Kassel, Edwin Louis Battle.

WASN'T IT YOU? Book and lyrics by Bryan D. Leys, based on Richard Boleslavsky's *Acting, the First Six Lessons;* music by James Campodonico. May 30, 1991. Directed by Mark S. Herko; with Kip Niven, Monica Pege.

American Place Theater. In addition to the regular off-Broadway season, other special projects are presented. Wynn Handman director, Dara Hershman general manager.

CALVIN TRILLIN'S WORDS, NO MUSIC (13). Written and performed by Calvin Trillin. October 11, 1990. Director, Wynn Handman; scenery, Bill Stabile; lighting, Andrew James Meyer.

MIDNIGHT CARNIVAL (12). Conceived and created by Robert Faust, Faustwork Mask Theater and Wynn Handman. December 13, 1990. With Robert Faust, Cecil MacKinnon, Michael Preston, Paola Styron.

AMERICAN PLACE THEATER—A scene from *Midnight Carnival,* a dance and performance work by Faustwork Mask Theater

American Theater of Actors. Dedicated to providing a creative atmosphere for new American playwrights, actors and directors. James Jennings artistic director.

TOWN MEETING. By Gene Ruffini. June 20, 1990. Director, Mark Corum. With Donna Avery, Courtney Everette, Lou Lagalante, Mat Sarter.

WOLVES. By Marc Garcia. June 27, 1990. Director, James Jennings. With Kerry Mortell, Pati Sands, Victoria Kelly.

STORIES WOMEN TELL. By Janet Overmyer. August 15, 1990. Director, James Jennings. With Carrie James Hall, Tracy Lundell, Janice Bremec, Pati Sands.

THE ROCK. By David Lessoff. September 12, 1990. Director, Shep Pamplin. With Don Draxler, Duggins King, Brad Larimore.

NIGHT OF THREE MOONS. Written and directed by James Crafford. September 19, 1990. With Bob Crafford, Gene Gerrity, James Crafford.

MORTAL ENEMY. Written and directed by James Jennings. October 3, 1990. With Judy Ramakers, John Koprowsky, Lonnie Jones.

SECOND HAND KID. By Craig Sodaro. October 17, 1990. Director, Gayther Myers. With Irving Gale, Alan Gordon, Jennifer Capriano.

PROMISES. Written and directed by James Jennings. October 24, 1990. With Gregory Pekar, Kirsten Stammer, Ed Jupp Jr.

SCREAMING FOR TRAINS. Written and directed by Mitch Ganem. November 1, 1990. With Melania Levitsky.

TEXACO STAR. By Margo Haas. November 7, 1990. Director, James Jennings. With Jacqueline Wolff, Kelly Moore, Gary Williams.

LAND OF FIRE. By Glenn Allen Smith. November 28, 1990. Director, Mark Corum. With Pamela Dean Kenny, Mat Sarter.

THE FILE. By Stuart Edelson. December 12, 1990. Director, James Jennings. With Judy Ramakers, Tom Bruce, Tom Bolster.

WOLVES. By Marc Garcia. January 16, 1991. Director, James Jennings. With Tracy Lundell, Michael Bleasdale, Jennifer Townsend.

BREAD AND BUTTER. By Peter Chelnik. January 30, 1991. Director, James Jennings. With Seamus McNally, Charles Quinn.

THEN CAME JACK. By Stuart Edelson. February 13, 1991. Director, James Jennings. With Marc Holzman, Peg O'Donoghue, Sara Watchman, Tom Bruce.

EYE TO EYE. By Matthew Davis. February 13, 1991. Director, Donald L. Brooks. With Edie Falco, Daniel Pardo, Doug Von Nessen.

FRIENDLY FIRE. Written and directed by James Jennings. February 27, 1991. With Eric Lutes, Melanie Johnson, James Shanley.

GO. By Joseph P. McDonald. February 27, 1991. Director, James Jennings. With James Lorinz, Ed Marcowitz, Victoria Miner.

DANNY ROCHA. By Kevin Kelly. March 13, 1991. Director, Robin Haywood. With Michael Karon, Vincent Curatola, Lou Lagalante, Jerome Weinstein.

THE MIND IS A STRANGER. By Lori Peters. March 27, 1991. Director, Craig Moncho. With Paul Gubbay, Kim Manning, Powell Leonard.

THE MAGI. Written and directed by Tom LaBar. April 17, 1991. With Tom Brangle, Frank Deriso, John Flick.

SHADOW OF AN OUTCAST. By Richard Davidson. May 1, 1991. Director, Allan Michael Grosman. With Byron Allen, Helen Cazey, Tom Bruce, Joel Filderman.

A LEARNED EMOTION. By Robert L. Ford. May 8, 1991. Director, Lou Sapone. With Jeff Constan, Beta Levin, Raissa Radell.

AFTER THE PARTY. By Ellen Besserman. May 8, 1991. Director, John Plansse. With Eileen Dulen, Ken Kamlet.

HARRY'S MIRACLE CURE. By John Voulgaris. May 15, 1991. Director, Donald L. Brooks. With Tom Bruce, Sarah Himsel, Bill Maloney.

HOMETOWN APPLAUSE. By Michael Jones and Linda Renye. May 22, 1991. Director, Martin Flowers.

WAREHOUSE MOON. By Adam Kraar. May 29, 1991. Director, Gregg Brevoort. With Ken Kamlet, Dina Pearlman, Kelly Dacus, Helen Palladino.

Circle Repertory Projects-in-Progress. Developmental programs for new plays. Tanya Berezin artistic director, Terrence Dwyer managing director.

ROAD TO NIRVANA. By Arthur Kopit. October 22, 1990. Director, Jim Simpson.

GIGGLE AND SCREAM. By David Steven Rappoport. November 5, 1990. Director, Jorge Cachiero.

SERVY-N-BERNICE 4 EVER. By Seth Zvi Rosenfeld. March 11, 1991. Director, June Stein.

Extended Readings:

APPOINTMENT WITH A HIGHWIRE LADY. By Russell Davis. October 15, 1990. Director, Abigail Adams.
ONE FAMILY. By Jim Leonard Jr. December 17, 1990. Director, Mark Ramont.
TRUST. Written and directed by Steven Dietz. January 14, 1991.
LESSER LIGHT OF HEAVEN. By Tom Cumella. February 25, 1991. Director, Tee Scatuorchio.
AUTUMN AND WINTER. By Lars Noren. April 1, 1991. Director, Syd Sidner.
17 BLACK. By William S. Leavengood. May 13, 1991. Director, John Bishop.
MORTAL ACTS. By Tom Huey. May 20, 1991. Director, Russell Treyz.

CSC Repertory, Ltd. (Classic Stage Company). Aims to produce classics with a bold, contemporary sensibility. Carey Perloff artistic director.

HAPPY DAYS (42). By Samuel Beckett. October 10, 1990. Director, Carey Perloff; scenery, Donald Eastman; lighting, Frances Aronson; costumes, Julie Weiss. With Charlotte Rae, Bill Moor.

THE LEARNED LADIES (40). By Molière, translated and adapted by Freyda Thomas; additional adaptive material by Richard Seyd and Freyda Thomas. March 6, 1991. Director, Richard Seyd; scenery, Richard Hoover; lighting, Mary Louise Geiger; costumes, Beaver Bauer; music, Gina Leishman. With Jean Stapleton, Georgine Hall, Julia Gibson, Nestor Serrano, Peter Francis James, Frank Raiter, Merwin Goldsmith, Alice Haining, Martin B. Nathan, Michael Reilly, Amy Brenneman, Michael R. Wilson, Peter Bartlett.

THE RESISTIBLE RISE OF ARTURO UI (30). By Bertolt Brecht, translated by Ralph Manheim. May 8, 1991. Director, Carey Perloff; scenery, Douglas Stein; lighting, Stephen Strawbridge; costumes, Donna Zakowska; music, David Lang. With Larry Joshua, Michael McCormick, Miguel Perez, Keith R. Smith, Richard Ziman, Ron Faber, Sam Gray, Ted Ragg, Nicholas Turturro, Michael Reilly, John Turturro, Olek Krupa, Katherine Borowitz, Zach Grenier, Michael R. Wilson, David Patrick Kelly, Tom Delling.

En Garde Arts. Dedicated to developing the concept of "site-specific theater" in the streets, parks and buildings of the city. Anne Hamburger founder and producer.

FATHER WAS A PECULIAR MAN (16). By Reza Abdoh and Mira-Lani Oglesby. June 30, 1990. Director, Reza Abdoh; scenery, Kyle Chepulis; lighting, Brian Aldous; costumes, Claudia Brown; music, Eric Liljestrand. With a cast of 60 including Banipal Babilla Ebrahim, Leyla Ebtehadj, Tom Fitzpatrick, Jan Leslie Harding, Meg Kruszewska, Irma Paule, Ken Roht, Davidson Thomson.

OCCASIONAL GRACE (16). By Michael Ahn, Neena Beber, Migdalia Cruz, Talvin Wilks. March 2, 1991. Director, Bill Rauch; lighting, Brian Aldous; costumes, Claudia Brown; music, Amina Claudine Myers. With Christopher Adams, Kana Aoki, J. Ed Araiza, Sonnie Brown, Reg E. Cathey, Engle Cheung, John Cheung, Adam Dyer, Sara E. Erde, Robert James Gardner, Ruthanna Graves, Helen Greenberg, Sea Glassman, Barry Gunn, Brian Herrera, Andy Inkavat, Greg Jackson, Marie La Ferrara, Joel Leffert, Lori Leshner, Jory Levine, Carol Jean Lewis, Hollis Lewis, Bill Lin, Phillip Lin, Cathey Markoff, Johnny Martinez, Adelaide Mestre, Joy Pak, Mary Lou Snyder, Tami Tyree, Cherisa Villafana, Nela Wagman, Wei Wang Stevens, Peter Yoshida.

Ensemble Studio Theater. Membership organization of playwrights, actors, directors and designers dedicated to supporting individual theater artists and developing new works for the stage. Over 250 projects each season, ranging from readings to fully-mounted productions. Curt Dempster artistic director, Christopher A. Smith associate artistic director, Dominick Balletta managing director.

CHINESE COFFEE. By Ira Lewis. July 26, 1990. Director, Jack Gelber. With Al Pacino, Dominic Chianese.

OCTOBERFEST. Festival of 68 new plays by members. October 11-30, 1990.

GO TO GROUND. By Stuart Spencer. December 7, 1990. Director, Matthew Penn. With Baxter Harris, Mary Kane, Salty Loeb, James G. Macdonald, Richard Joseph Paul, Emma Walton.

KICKIN' THE SCIENCE. By Melvin Van Peebles. January 24, 1991. Director, Curt Dempster. With Melvin Van Peebles.

GRANG. By Frank D. Gilroy. March 14, 1991. Director, Christopher A. Smith. With Richard Council, Steve Jacobs, Anna Levine Thompson.

PROJECT 20: IN PURSUIT OF AMERICA. Festival of 28 new plays by members. March 26-April 10, 1991.

APPOINTMENT WITH A HIGHWIRE LADY. By Russell Davis. April 18, 1991. Director, Michael Mantell. With Jayne Atkinson, Victor Slezak, Suzanne Shepherd.

NEW VOICES (staged readings): AS SURE AS YOU LIVE by Roger Hedden; THE BRIDE OF OLNEYVILLE SQUARE by Edward Allan Baker; RON'S GARDEN by Julie McKee; MAGIC VALLEY by Jack Gelber; THE NEWS FROM PUERTO RICO by Jack Agueros; THE GIRL NEXT DOOR by Laurence Klavan. January 16-March 2, 1991.

MARATHON 1991 (festival of one-act plays). NAOMI IN THE LIVING ROOM written and directed by Christopher Durang; WHERE WERE YOU WHEN IT WENT DOWN? by David Mamet, directed by Billy Hopkins; INTIMACY written and directed by Harris Yulin; YOU CAN'T TRUST THE MALE by Randy Noojin, directed by Melodie Somers; A WAY WITH WORDS by Frank D. Gilroy, directed by Christopher A. Smith; PRACTICE by Leslie Ayvazian, directed by Elinor Renfield; FACE DIVIDED by Edward Allan Baker, directed by Risa Bramon Garcia; OVER TEXAS by Michael John LaChiusa, directed by Kirsten Sanderson; RAPID EYE MOVEMENT by Susan Kim, directed by Margaret Mancinelli; CAN CAN by Romulus Linney, directed by David Shookhoff; THE WORLD AT ABSOLUTE ZERO by Sherry Kramer, directed by Jason McConnell Buzas; SALAAM, HUEY NEWTON, SALAAM by Ed Bullins, directed by Woodie King Jr.; THE LAST YANKEE by Arthur Miller, directed by Gordon Edelstein; BIG AL by Bryan Goluboff, directed by Peter Maloney. May 15-June 23, 1991.

INTAR. Mission is to identify, develop and present the talents of gifted Hispanic American theater artists and multicultural visual artists. Max Ferra artistic director, Eva Brune managing director.

INTAR—Xonia Benguria, Olga Merediz and Alina Troyano in *The Lady from Havana* by Luis Santierio

THE LADY FROM HAVANA (39). By Luis Santiero. October 17, 1990. Director, Max Ferra; scenery and costumes, Campbell Baird; lighting, Debra Dumas. With Olga Merediz, Xonia Benguria, Alina Troyano.

BLUE HEAT (25). Written, designed and directed by John Jesurun. February 23, 1991. Lighting, Jeffrey Nash. With Oscare de la Fe Colon, Divina Cook, Larry Tighe, Michael Tighe, Sanghi Wagner, Eileen Vega.

THE HAVE-LITTLE (40). by Migdalia Cruz. June 9, 1991. Director, Nila Cruz; scenery, Donald Eastman; lighting, Ken Posner; costumes, Gabriel Berry. With Divina Cook, Gabriella Diaz-Farrar, Marisol Massey, David Roya.

INTAR II

NEWSTAGES (festival of multimedia performances). Schedule included: NECROPOLIS (opera/music theater work) by Jorge Cachiero; THE OPIUM WAR by Ana Maria Simo, music by Zeena Parkins; appearances by Reno, Penny Arcade. March 29-May 5, 1991.

Interart Theater. Committed to producing innovative work by women theater artists and to introducing New York audiences to a bold range of theater that is non-traditional in form or theme. Margot Lewitin artistic director.

Schedule included:

THROUGH THE LEAVES. (Co-produced by Mabou Mines. See Mabou Mines entry.)

Irish Arts Center. Provides a range of contemporary Irish drama, classics and new works by Irish American playwrights. Nye Heron artistic director.

REMEMBRANCE (200). By Graham Reid. October 7, 1990. Director, Terence Lamude; scenery, Duke Durfee; lighting, John McLain; costumes, C. Jane Epperson. With Malachy McCourt, John Finn, Aideen O'Kelly, Ann Dowd, Terry Donnely, Ellen Tobie. (Produced in association with Stamford Theater Works; also see its entry in the Plays Produced Off Broadway section of this volume.)

La Mama (a.k.a. LaMama) Experimental Theater Club (ETC). A busy workshop for experimental theater of all kinds. Ellen Stewart founder and artistic director.

Schedule Included:

HELLO, BOB. Written and directed by Robert Patrick. October 11, 1990. With Carol Nelson, Edmond Ramage, Jeffrey J. Albright, Stephen Engle.

ELEPHANT MEMORIES. Conceived and directed by Ping Chong in collaboration with the company. November 1, 1990. Choreography and text, Ping Chong, John Fleming, Brian Hallas, Jeannie Hutchins, Larry Malvern, Johanna Melamed, Ric Oquita, Louise Smith; song, Meredith Monk. With Ping Chong and company.

COSECHA and FRESH RUINS (performance art) by and with Federico Restrepo and company. November 7, 1990.

A LIGHT FROM THE EAST. Conceived, translated and directed by Virlana Tkacz; poems, Taras Shevchenko, Pavlo Tychyna, translated by Virlana Tkacz, Wanda Phipps. November 23, 1990. Scenery and lighting, Watoku Oeno; costumes, Carol Ann Pelletier. With Jason Bauer, Sean Eden, Amy Grappell, Timothy Greer, Peter McCabe, Rebecca Moore, Shona Tucker. (Yara Arts Group).

NEW MONOLOGUES (performance art) by and with David Cale and Frank Maya. November 29, 1990.

TROCKADERO GLOXINIA BALLET. December 1, 1990. With Ekathrina Sobechanskaya.

THE JAZZ PASSENGERS IN EGYPT (jazz opera-in-progress) libretto, Ray Dobbins; music, Roy Nathanson. December 13, 1990. Director, Sara Driver.

THE PATH OF ASHES (multimedia performance piece). Conceived and directed by Nicole Dreiske; music, Michael Zerang. December 13, 1990. Lighting, Roma Flowers. With the Dreiske Performance Company.

EROS. By Maureen Fleming and Yoshito Ohno; music, Mickey Hart. January 3, 1991.

WHITE STONES. By Bill Boesky. January 5, 1991. Director, Toni Kotite.

AMERICAN GRIOT (A JAZZ AUTOBIOGRAPHY). By Ed Bullins, and Idris Ackamoor. February 4, 1991.

SAINT TOUS. Conceived and directed by Andre De Shields. February 3, 1991.

BELLE REPRIEVE. Devised and performed by Lois Weaver, Peggy Shaw (Split Britches), Bette Bourne, Precious Pearl (Bloolips), inspired by Tennessee Williams's *A Streetcar Named Desire;* music, Laka Daisical, Phil Booth. February 14, 1991. Director, Lois Weaver; scenery, Nancy Bardawil, Matthew Owens; lighting, Howard Thies; costumes, Susan Young.

ANCIENT BOYS. By Jean-Claude van Itallie; music, Tony Scheitinger. February 16, 1991. Director, Gregory Keller; choreography, John Goodwin; design concept, Jun Maeda; lighting, Michael Smith; costumes, Mary Brecht. With Tom Bozell, Preston Dyar, Wayne Maugans, Michael Ornstein, Rosemary Quinn.

THE HAUNTED HOST. By Robert Patrick. February 28, 1991. Director, Eric Concklin; scenery, lighting, costumes, David Adams. With Harvey Fierstein, Jason Workman.

SPIRITFLESH. By Poppo and the Go-Go Boys. March 14, 1991.

THE FEVER (one-man show). By and with Wallace Shawn. March 21, 1991.

EDDIE GOES TO POETRY CITY: PART 2. Written, directed and designed by Richard Foreman. April 3, 1991. Lighting, Heather Carson; costumes, Donna Zakowska. With Kyle de Camp, Brian Delate, Rebecca Ellens, Colin Hodgson, Henry Stram. (Co-produced by Ontological-Hysteric Theater.)

WALKING THE BLONDE. By Leigh Curran. April 4, 1991. Director, Leonard Foglia; scenery, H.G. Arrott; lighting, Eileen Dougherty; costumes, Nina Canter. With Lee Brock, Marcia DeBonis, Keely Eastley, Tom Riis Farrell, Martha French, Isiah Whitlock Jr., Missy Yager.

WHEN THE BOUGH BREAKS. Conceived and directed by Lawrence Sacharow; text, Darrah Cloud; music, Carman Moore. April 26, 1991. Scenery, John Brown; lighting, Howard Thies. With Arlene Chadnow, Judy DiMenna, Peter Fontes, Roseann Lattarulo, Lurline Martineau, Florence Rader, Elizabeth Waslin, Anita Weinstein. (Produced in association with Daytop Family Association, Etan Merrick and River Arts.)

BANG ON A CAN FESTIVAL (new music). May 10, 1991.

ENCIRCLING TIDES. Written and directed by Beth Skinner, Ed Herbst. May 16, 1991. Scenery, lighting, costumes, Jun Maeda. With Thunder Bay Ensemble.

EAST; AN ELEGY FOR THE EAST END. By Steven Berkoff. May 17, 1991. Director, Paul Hellyer; scenery and lighting, Jeff Rowlings. With Paul Finnocchiaro, Stephanie Hunt, Delia MacDougall, Dennis Matthews, Joel Mullennix.

Mabou Mines. Theater collaborative whose work is a synthesis of motivational acting, narrative acting and mixed-media performance. Collective artistic leadership.

THROUGH THE LEAVES. By Franz Xaver Kroetz, translated by Roger Downey. September 14, 1990. Directed by JoAnne Akalaitis. With Ruth Maleczech, Frederick Neumann. (Co-produced by Interart Theater.)

C.E.O. By Stig Larsson, translated by Joe Martin. November 27, 1990. Director, Frederick Neumann; scenery, Kevin J. Roach from a concept by Frederick Neumann; lighting, Mahlon Kruse; costumes, Anna Gorman. With Brenda Daly, Dylan Price, Larry Pine, Marc Romeo, Claude Wampler.

THE BRIBE (work-in-progress). By Terry O'Reilly; music, John Zorn. May 9, 1991. Director, Ruth Maleczech. With Black-Eyed Susan, Terry O'Reilly and the voices of Jim Neu, Bob Holman, Kaja Gam, Bill Raymond.

Manhattan Punch Line. New York's only theater company devoted to comedy. Steve Kaplan artistic director.

Schedule included:

THE MENSCH. By Steven Kronovet. October 1, 1990. Director, Joel Bassin; scenery, Vaughn

Patterson; lighting, Danianne Mizzi; costumes, Kitty Leech. With Rick Zieff, Ed Setrakian, Virginia Dillon, Claudia Silver.

FESTIVAL OF ONE-ACT COMEDIES. Schedule included VARIATIONS ON THE DEATH OF TROTSKY by David Ives, directed by Jason McConnell Buzas; GORGO'S MOTHER by Laurence Klavan, directed by Steve Kaplan; GANGSTER APPAREL by Richard Vetere, directed by Matthew Penn; STAY CARL STAY by Peter Tolan, directed by Charles Karchmer. February 9-March 10, 1991. With Michael Aschner, Ronnie Farer, David Goldman, Daniel Hagen, Cheryl Hulteen, Chris Lutkin, Nora Mae Lyng, Michael Raynor, Elaine Rinehart, Steven Rodriguez, Kathrin King Segal, Ben Siegler, Joseph Siravo, Christine Toy.

Musical Theater Works. Developmental workshop where writers of musical theater learn by doing. Anthony J. Stimac artistic director.

WHATNOT (34). Conceived and written by Mark Waldrop and Howard Crabtree; music and lyrics by Dick Gallagher. September 5, 1990. Director, Mark Waldrop; scenery, James Noone; lighting, Kendall Smith; special effects, Howard Crabtree; musical director, Dick Gallagher. With Howard Crabtree, John Treacy Egan, Mark Lazore, Jennifer Smith.

LOVE IN TWO COUNTRIES: THAT PIG OF A MOLETTE, based on Guy DeMaupassant's *Ce Cochon de Morin;* and A QUESTION OF FAITH, based on Nickolai Semyenovich Leskov's *A Slight Error;* librettos by Sheldon Harnick, music by Thomas Z. Shepard (one-act operas) (26). March 20, 1991. Director, Michael Montel; choreography, Karen Azenberg; scenery, Marie Anne Chiment; lighting, Betsy Adams; costumes, Amanda J. Klein; musical director, Albert Ahronheim. With Scott Robertson, Bill Carmichael, Elizabeth Walsh, Suellen Estey, Lannyl Stephens, Michael Brian, Tim Ewing, Caryn Kaplan.

COLETTE COLLAGE (26). Book and lyrics by Tom Jones, music by Harvey Schmidt. April 24, 1991. Directors, Tom Jones, Harvey Schmidt; choreography, Janet Watson, Scott Harris; scenery and costumes, Ed Wittstein; lighting, Mary Jo Dondlinger; musical director, Norman Weiss. With Betsy Joslyn, Joanne Beretta, Paul Blankenship, John Bransdorf, Jaime Zee Eisner, Ralston Hill, Hilary James, Kenneth Kantor, James J. Mellon, Mary Setrakian, Craig Wells.

Music-Theater Group. Pioneering in the development of new music-theater. Lyn Austin producing director, Diane Wondisford associate producing director.

ENDANGERED SPECIES (14). Conceived and directed by Martha Clarke, created with the company; text adapted by Robert Coe from Walt Whitman's *Leaves of Grass.* October 7, 1990. Scenery and costumes, Robert Israel; lighting, Paul Gallo; sound, Richard Peaslee, Stanley Walden. With Michael J. Anderson, Felix Blaska, Alistair Butler, Courtney Earl, Lisa Dalton, David Grausman, Paul Guilfoyle, Valarie Eileen Henry, Judy Kuhn, Peter McRobbie, Frank Raiter. (Co-produced by Brooklyn Academy of Music as part of the Next Wave Festival, in association with Circus Flora. See also Brooklyn Academy of Music Miscellaneous entry.)

New Dramatists. An organization devoted to playwrights; member writers may use the facilities for anything from private cold readings of their material to public script-in-hand readings. Joel Ruark managing director.

Rehearsed Readings

THE GLOBAL GENERATION. By Antoine O'Flaherty. September 11, 1990. Director, Paul Walker. With Sophie Maletsky, Anne O'Sullivan, Calista Flockhart, Patrick Fitzgerald, Cuivan Kelly, Michael Mantell.

BIG DEAL. By Stuart Duckworth. November 29, 1990. Director, Casey Childs. With Karen Shallo, Steve Keyes, Ralph Marrero, Judson Camp, Alba Olms, Kara Greene, Gina Gionfriddo.

STATIC. By Ben Siegler. December 3, 1990. With Danny Hilfer, Ben Siegler, Susan Knight, Peter

Guttmacher, Bill Wise, Zach Grenier, Jonathan Hogan, Angela Pietropinto.

BEYOND THE RUINS. By Marco Micone, translated by Jill MacDougall. January 21, 1991. Director, Liz Diamond. With Antonia Rey, George McGrath, Rocco Sisto, Becky Borczon, Danny Zorn.

FLIPPING THE BIRD. By Wendy MacLeod. March 4, 1991. Director, Lisa Peterson. With Yusef Bulos, Angela Pietropinto, Susan Knight, Ben Siegler, Matt McGrath, Amelia Campbell.

THE OPIUM WAR. By Ana Maria Simo. March 12, 1991. Director, Linda Chapman. With Elizabeth Clemens, Jose Febus, J. Ed Ariaza, Peter Jay Fernandez, Anita Lobel.

BETTY AND THE KOOL KAT CLUB. Book and lyrics, Phil Bosakowski; music, Catherine Stone. April 6, 1991. Director, Roger Ames. With Lisa Beth Miller, Gary Richardson, Steve Coats, Patti Onorato, Frankie Sepulveda, Warren Bradley, Darryl Williams, Gordon Pettiford.

THERESA. By Dan Therriault. April 10, 1991. With William Wise, Tom Kopache, George McGrath, Erica Honda, Margery Shaw, Sharon Brady.

FABIOLA. By Eduardo Machado. May 1, 1991. Director, Anne Bogart. With Christopher McCann, Rafael Baez, Becca Lish, Pamela Stewart, Suzanne Costallos, George Bartenieff, Lynn Cohen, Jennifer Rohn, Elzbieta Czyzewska.

New Federal Theater. Dedicated to presenting new playwrights and plays dealing with the minority and Third World experience. Woodie King Jr. producer.

THE WIZARD OF HIP (OR WHEN IN DOUBT SLAM DUNK) (34). Written and performed by Thomas W. Jones II. October 17, 1990. Director, Kenny Leon. Scenery, Tony Loadholt; lighting, Jeff Guzik; music, James Pelton Jr.

JELLY BELLY (30). By Charles Smith. November 7, 1990. Director, Dennis Zacek; scenery and lighting, Richard Harmon; costumes, Judy Dearing. With Gina Torres, Weyman Thompson, Donald Douglass, Ramon Melindez Moses, Tony Smith.

THE BALM YARD (34). By Don Kinch. March 13, 1991. Director, Shauneille Perry; choreography, Thomas Pinnock; scenery, Robert Joel Schwartz; lighting, Sandra Ross; costumes, Judy Dearing; musical director, Julius Williams. With Ras Tesfa, Nichole Thompson, Nick Smith, Roxie Roker, Gary Dourdan, Kim Weston Moran, Donna Manno, Trevor Thomas, Carla Williams, Irene Datcher, Mac Arthur, Larry McDonald.

New York Shakespeare Festival Public Theater. Schedule of special projects, in addition to its regular off-Broadway productions. Joseph Papp, producer.

FESTIVAL LATINO IN NEW YORK. Schedule included: CRONICA DE UNA MUERTE ANUNCIADA (CHRONICLE OF A DEATH FORETOLD) written and directed by Salvador Tavora, based on a text by Gabriel Garcia Marquez, translated by Melia Bensussen, with Manuel Vera, Concha Tavora, Leonor Alvarez-Ossorio, Angel Monteseirin, Margot Linares, Yolanda Lorenzo, Juan Romero, Jose Luis Fernandez, Evaristo Romero, Isabel Vasquez; LA MISMA SANGRE (THE SAME BLOOD) by Carlos Velis, with texts by Jose Roberto Cea, Roque Dalton, translated by Melia Bensussen, directed by Emilio Carballido, with Mauricio Gonzalez, Aida Mancia de Tobias, Aida Parraga, Boris Barraza, Edwardo Fuentes, Juan Salomon Paredes, German Jaime Paz; DE DONDE? by Mary Gallagher, directed by Sam Blackwell, with Enrique Munoz, Bill Cwikowski, Socorro Santiago, Betty Miller, Mary Gallagher, Ted Minos, Steve Mones, Rene Moreno, John Ortiz, Robert Reilly, Phil Soltanoff, Marta Vidal; THE GAMMA RAYS IN NEW YORK book and lyrics by Silverio Perez, directed and performed by Jacobo Morales, Johanna Ferran, Horacio Olivo, Erick Perez, Silverio Perez, Georgina Borri; SIN TESTIGOS (WITHOUT WITNESSES) by Sofiya Prokofyeva, translated by Nina Miller, directed by Inda Ledesma, with Susu Pecoraro, Miguel Angel Sola; EL PALOMAR (THE PIGEON HOUSE) by Carlos Catania, translated by Melia Bensussen, directed by Alfredo Catania, with Eugenia Chavarri, Carlos Ovares,

NEW YORK THEATER WORKSHOP—Cherry Jones and Philip Goodwin in
the American premiere of Caryl Churchill's *Light Shining in Buckinghamshire*

Ruben David Pagura, Grettel Cedeno, Jacqueline Stellar, Juan Carlos Calderon, Rodolfo Araya,
Luis Fernando Gomez; VOCES DE ACERO (VOICES OF STEEL) by Pregones Theater Group,
directed by Alvan Colon Lespier, with Sandra Berrios, Jose Joaquin Garcia, Jorge B. Merced,
Judith Rivera, Rosalba Rolon; ANDAR POR LA GENTE (WALKING AMONG THE PEOPLE)
directed and performed by Inda Ledesma, translated by Nina Miller; O DOENTE IMAGINARIO
(THE IMAGINARY INVALID) by Molière, translated by Marcia Abujamra, directed by Caca
Rosset, with Caca Rosset, Maria Alice Verguiero, Christiane Tricerri, Ary Franca; MATATAN-
GOS by Marco Antonio de la Parra, directed by Abel Lopez, Hugo Medrano, with Mario Marcel,
Hugo Medrano, Yayo Grassi; MONDO MAMBO (musical revue) conceived and directed by Adal
Alberto Maldonado, written by Pedro Pietri, music by Tito Puente, with Edwin de Asis, Tito
Puente; LA SECRETA OBSCENIDAD DE CADA DIA (SECRET OBSCENITIES) by Marco
Antonio de la Parra, directed by Hugo Medrano, Sonia Castel, with Hugo Medrano, Mario Marcel;
ROMEO AND JULIET by William Shakespeare, adapted and directed by Maria Alicia Martinez,
Hugo Medrano, translated by Martin Perez Dzul, Carlos Yocupicio, with Octavio Cervantes, Lesvi
Vazquez, Luz Emilia Vazquez, Gavino Campos, Juan Francisco Tun, Victor Bacasehua, Eusebio
Penuelas. August 1-September 17, 1990.

Studio A Series (staged readings)
ROUNDHEADS AND PEAKHEADS. By Bertolt Brecht, translated by N. Goold-Verschoyle.
November 15, 1990. Director, Melia Bensussen. With Leon Addison Brown, Rene Moreno, Steve
Zahn, Anne O'Sullivan, Robert Jimenez, Victoria G. Platt.

A DREAM OF WEALTH. By Arthur Giron; music, Kim Sherman. December 13, 1990. Director,
Melia Bensussen. With Jesse Corti, John Hutton, Brett Rickaby, Socorro Santiago, Randy Vasquez,
Kathleen McNenny.

THE SUPPLIANT WOMEN. By Euripides, translated by Frank William Jones, adapted and directed by Melia Bensussen. February 7, 1991. With Randy Danson, Sam Tsoutsouvas, Jesse Corti, Angie Phillips, Mark Hammer, Sharon Washington.

STY FARM and GHOST TRAIN. By Franz Xaver Kroetz, translated and adapted by Regina Taylor and Mario Ernes. March 7, 1991. Director, Melia Bensussen. With Mary Alice, Paul Butler, Kenya Scott, Paul Benjamin. (Repeated April 18, 1991.)

New York Theater Workshop. Dedicated to the production of plays of intelligence and conscience and the development of new plays and emerging stage directors. James C. Nicola artistic director, Nancy Kassak Diekmann managing director.

LOVE AND ANGER (36). By George F. Walker. December 4, 1990. Directors, James C. Nicola, Christopher Grabowski; scenery, James Schuette; lighting, Christopher Akerlind; costumes, Gabriel Berry. With Saul Rubinek, Tonia Rowe, Kristine Nielsen, Arthur Hanket, Steve Ryan, Deirdre O'Connell.

LIGHT SHINING IN BUCKINGHAMSHIRE (39). By Caryl Churchill. February 12, 1991. Director, Lisa Peterson; scenery, Bill Clark; lighting, Brian MacDevitt; costumes, Michael Krass; music and sound, Mark Bennett. With Bill Camp, Philip Goodwin, Steve Hofvendahl, Cherry Jones, Shona Tucker, Gregory Wallace.

JEFFREY ESSMANN'S ARTIFICIAL REALITY (37). Written and performed by Jeffrey Essmann. April 3, 1991. Director, David Warren; scenery, George Xenos; lighting, Pat Dignan; costumes, David C. Woolard; music, Michael John LaChiusa.

EVE'S DIARY and THE STORY OF THE TIGER (one-act plays) (18). By Dario Fo, translated by Ron Jenkins. April 9, 1991. Director, Christopher Ashley; scenery, George Xenos; lighting, Pat Dignan; costumes, David C. Woolard. With Jane Kaczmarek, Rocco Sisto.

The Open Eye: New Stagings. Goal is to gather a community of outstanding theater artists to collaborate on works for the stage for audiences of all ages and cultural backgrounds. Jean Erdman founding director, Amie Brockway artistic director.

A PLACE BEYOND THE CLOUDS (one-act plays) (4). By Sandra Biano. November 4, 1990. Director, Sharone Stacey; choreography, Susan Jacobson; scenery, lighting, costumes, Adrienne J. Brockway. With Catherine Gale, Cynthia Kaplan, Valerie Williams, Joey A. Chavez, John DiLeo, Doug Jewell.

A WOMAN CALLED TRUTH (10). By Sandra Fenichel Asher. January 19, 1991. Director, Ernest Johns; choreography, Jamale Graves; scenery, lighting, costumes, Adrienne J. Brockway; musical director, Charles Brown. With Patricia R. Floyd, Kim Bey, Jen Wolfe, Garrett Walters, Ricky Genaro, Doug Jewell.

EAGLE OR SUN (AGUILA O SOL) (4). By Sabina Berman, translated by Isabel Saez, edited, adapted and directed by Amie Brockway. April 7, 1991. Choreography, Leslie Dillingham; scenery, lighting, costumes, Adrienne J. Brockway. With Joey A. Chavez, John DiLeo, Ricky Genaro, Martha Gilpin, Doug Jewell, Tara Mallen.

THE OPEN EYE: NEW STAGINGS LAB/CHICAGO NEW PLAYS (staged readings): THE IDEA OF CHAOS (SEX, DEATH, LIFE AND ORDER) AT KEY WEST by Nicholas A. Patricca, directed by Amie Brockway; CHILDREN LAST by Anne McGravie, directed by Alyce Mott; HOUSTON'S BLOOD by Ron Mark and Connie Rodgers, directed by Kim Sharp. April 13-14, 1991.

EYE ON DIRECTORS FESTIVAL (one-act works): THE JET OF BLOOD by Antonin Artaud, directed by Ernie Barbarash; NOBODY WAS SUPPOSED TO SURVIVE: THE MOVE MASSACRE by Alice Walker, directed by Patricia R. Floyd; SUCH SWEET THUNDER (excerpts from William Shakespeare's works) directed by James Furlong; PHAEDRA (excerpt) by Jean Racine, translated by Margaret Rawlings, directed by Lisa Brailoff; A DREAM DEFERRED by Celeste A. Frazier, directed by Joan Kane; HERE WE ARE by Dorothy Parker, directed by Susan Jacobson; THE INCREDIBLE SHRINKING FAMILY by Alice Elliot, directed by Kim T. Sharp; NAIM by A.B. Yehoshua, adapted by Nola Chilton, directed by Marc Weiner; DON SURREALISM by Elena Penga, directed by Sherry Teitelbaum; LEONCE AND LENA by Georg Buchner, translated by Hedwig Rappolt, directed by Brian Leahy Doyle. May 5-12, 1991.

Pan Asian Repertory Theater. Strives to provide opportunities for Asian American artists to perform under the highest professional standards and to create and promote plays by and about Asians and Asian Americans. Tisa Chang artistic/producing director.

LUCKY COME HAWAII (38). By Jon Shirota. October 24, 1990. Director, Ron Nakahara; scenery, Robert Klingelhoefer; lighting, Victor En Yu Tan; costumes, Maggie Raywood. With Tom Matsusaka, Mel Duane Gionson, Norris Shimabuku, Kati Kuroda, Les J.N. Mau, Ann M. Tsuji, James Jenner, Stan Egi, Joe Fiske.

LETTERS TO A STUDENT REVOLUTIONARY (17). By Elizabeth Wong. May 15, 1991. Director, Ernest Abuba; scenery, Kyung Won Chang; lighting, Anne Somogye; costumes, Maggie Raywood. With Caryn Ann Chow, Karen Tsen Lee, Andrew Ingkavet, Keenan Shimizu, Christen Villamor, Mary Lum.

Playwrights Horizons New Theater Wing. Full productions of new works, in addition to the regular off-Broadway productions. Andre Bishop artistic director, Paul S. Daniels executive director.

MIRIAM'S FLOWERS (14). By Migdalia Cruz. June 13, 1990. Director, Roberta Levitow; scenery, Tom Kamm; lighting, Kenneth Posner; costumes, Mary Myers. With Alex Caicedo, Monique Cintron, Divina Cook, Peter Jay Fernandez, Ralph Marrero.

Puerto Rican Traveling Theater. Professional company presenting bilingual productions primarily of Puerto Rican and Hispanic playwrights, emphasizing subjects of relevance today. Miriam Colon Valle founder and producer.

42 performances each
THE ENGLISH ONLY RESTAURANT. By Silvio Martinez Palau; music, lyrics and musical direction, Sergio Garcia-Marruz, Saul Spangenberg. June 18, 1990. Director, Susana Tubert; choreography, Ron Brown; scenery and costumes, Michael Sharp; lighting, Rachel Budin. With Alberto Guzman, Al D. Rodriguez, Miguel Sierra, Jose Rey, Emma Mio, Hal Blankenship, Sheila Kay, Adriano Gonzalez, David J. Seatter, Jeanette Toro.

IN MIAMI AS IT IS IN HEAVEN. By Raul de Cardenas, translated by Asa Zatz. January 16, 1991. Director, Alba Oms; scenery, Michael Sharp; lighting, Rachel Budin; costumes, Mary Marsicano. With Emilio del Pozo, Suzanne Costallos, Cari Gorostiza, Eileen Galindo, Orlando George.

SABINA AND LUCRECIA. By Alberto Adellach, translated by Jack Agueros. March 13, 1991. Director, Alba Oms; scenery, Edward T. Gianfrancesco; lighting, Rick Butler; costumes, Mary Marsicano. With Cordelia Gonzalez, Nancy Walsh.

CHARGE IT, PLEASE. Book, music and lyrics by Carlos Gorbea, translated by Walter Krochmal. May 15, 1991. Director, William Martin; choreography, Dennis Dennehy; scenery and lighting, Rick Butler; costumes, Mary Marsicano; musical director, David Wolfson. With Fred Barrows, Mel Gorham, Alberto Guzman, Joan Jaffe, Iraida Polanco, Jeanette Toro.

Quaigh Theater. Primarily a playwrights' theater, devoted to the new playwright, the established contemporary playwright and the modern (post-1920) playwright. Will Lieberson artistic director.

SUBLIME LIVES (20). By Paul Firestone. June 28, 1990. Director, Jay E. Raphael; scenery, Josh Rothenberg; lighting, Deborah Matlack; costumes, Jan Finnell. With Matthew Loney, Eugene J. Anthony, Nick Plakias, Woody Dahlia, Sharon Cornell, Steven Dennis, Maggie Wood.

THE MAN WHO FELL IN LOVE WITH HIS WIFE (20). By Ted Whitehead. August 9, 1990. Directors, Will Lieberson, Kevin Conway; scenery, Jeff Read Freund; lighting, Graeme F. McDonnell; costumes, V. Jane Suttell. With Kevin Conway, Mila Burnett, Julia Gibson, Holly Barron.

THE CRITIC: THE FUN I'VE HAD (10). By Ward Morehouse III. November 2, 1990. Director, Will Lieberson. With Sean O'Sullivan.

MR. DOOM (20). By Ward Morehouse III. March 5, 1991. Directors, Will Lieberson, Gerard J. Gentleman; lighting, John Wooding; costumes, Renee Davenport; music, Bill Zeffiro. With Steve Shoup, Tom Lytel, Peter Gregory Thomson, Jennifer Ann Kelly, Martha Whitehead, Lynne Wilson, Paul Campana.

QUAIGH THEATER—Mila Burnett, Kevin Conway and Holly Barron in *The Man Who Fell in Love With His Wife* by Ted Whitehead

Lunchtime Series. 10 performances each

UP THE CREEK. By Will Lieberson. October 1, 1990. Director, Dennis Rickabee. With Bernard Roundtree, Lester Fiedler, Ruth Wolf.

IAGO 1991. By Guillamo Amourfils. October 15, 1990. Director, Keith Brown. With Edith Kandell, Alex Boyar, Roland Felicie, Todd Hirch.

BOXER: OLD By Wolf Henryl. October 29, 1990. Director, Albert Brower. With Tom Kilpatrick.

THE WORLD'S UNFAIR. By Jennie DiDato. November 12, 1990. Director, Dennis Lieberson. With Beverly Ramey, John Fountain, Randy Kirk, Donna Lewis.

THE DEAD DON'T SLEEP. By Kevin Stewart. November 26, 1990. Director, Joyce Ring. With Victor Glass, Harry Cousins, Francine Sullivan, Helen Stewart.

THE ETERNAL PLEDGE (OR A LOOK AT CHANNEL 13). By Kenneth Ducore. December 10, 1990. Director, Midge Warren. With Tom Bradbury, Vincent Ryan, Didi Hopkins, Karen Kimberly.

THE FIRST APOLOGY. By Edward Mintzer. January 7, 1991. Director, John Powers. With Barbara Lee, Alison Tremont, Eleanor Siranko.

YUK YUK. Written and directed by Will Lieberson. January 21, 1991. With Joyce Bell, Will Lieberson.

ON WHO DID THE BERLIN WALL FALL. By Sasha Litvak. February 4, 1991. Director, Marilyn Norman. With Fred Lynch, Sarah Hopkins, Derek Henderson, Frank MacQue, Marge Loft.

INDIAN NUTS. By Rhoda Levine. February 18, 1991. Director, Freida Washington. With Candice O'Brien, Jack Freuberg.

THE KISS OFF. By Jason O'Toole. March 4, 1991. Director, Warren Johns. With Daphne Keel, Amanda Miller, Woody Johnson, Ernest Carter.

THE ARTIFICAL MINK. By Bobo Diago. March 18, 1991. Director, Susan Drury. With Mollie Stott, Scruffie Lee, Alan Johns, Dusty Humes, Carol Olson.

Reading Series

THE BUG. By Richard Strand. October 7, 1990.
YUK YUK. By Will Lieberson. November 11, 1990.
YOLANDA SAY GO. By Adam Kraar. December 9, 1990.
TRUTH IN ADVERTISING. By Alan Glass. January 20, 1991.
MY SON THE DOCTOR. By Mark Bielski. February 10, 1991.
PERFECT STRANGERS. By R.E. Durain. February 17, 1991.
DYING TO SEE YOU. By Alan Glass. March 10, 1991.
THE NERD. By Larry Shue. April 13, 1991.
STANDING ROOM ONLY. By Bill Henry. March 5, 1991.

The Ridiculous Theatrical Company. The late Charles Ludlam's comedic troupe devoted to productions of his original scripts and new adaptations of the classics. Everett Quinton artistic director, Steve Asher managing director.

CAMILLE (149). By Charles Ludlam. August 14, 1990. Director, Everett Quinton; scenery, Mark Beard; lighting, Terry Alan Smith; costumes, Elizabeth Michal Fried. With H.M. Koutoukas, Stephen Pell, Everett Quinton, Kevin Scullin, Carl Clayborn, Cheryl Reeves, Bobby Reed, Eureka, Jim Lamb, Georg Osterman, Jean-Claude Vasseux, James Eckerle.

WHEN LIGHTNING STRIKES TWICE (one-act plays): AWFUL PEOPLE ARE COMING OVER SO WE MUST BE PRETENDING TO BE HARD AT WORK AND HOPE THEY WILL GO AWAY and ONLY A COUNTESS MAY DANCE WHEN SHE'S CRAZY (24). By H.M.

Koutoukas. January 8, 1991. Scenery, Tom Moore; lighting, Richard Currie; costumes, Daniel Boike. With Everett Quinton, Eureka.

THE HUNCHBACK OF NOTRE DAME (45+). Written and directed by Everett Quinton, freely adapted from Victor Hugo's novel; music, Mark Bennett; lyrics, Everett Quinton and Mark Bennett. May 16, 1991. Scenery, Tom Moore; lighting, Richard Currie; costumes, Everett Quinton. With Hapi Phace, Everett Quinton, Stephen Pell, Cheryl Reeves, Gary Mink, Sophie Maletsky, Bobby Reed, Eureka.

Second Stage Theater. Committed to producing plays believed to deserve another look, as well as new works. Robyn Goodman, Carole Rothman artistic directors.

JERSEY CITY (17). By Wendy Hammond. July 10, 1990. Director, Risa Bramon; scenery, James Youmans; lighting, Anne Militello; costumes, Sharon Sprague. With Alison Bartlett, Eddie Castrodad, Jude Ciccolella, Adina Porter.

LAKE NO BOTTOM (24). By Michael Weller. November 29, 1990. Director, Carole Rothman; scenery, Adrianne Lobel; lighting, Kevin Rigdon; costumes, Jess Goldstein. With Marsha Mason, Robert Knepper, Daniel Davis.

EARTH AND SKY (22). By Douglas Post. February 4, 1991. Director, Andre Emotte; scenery, William Barclay; lighting, Phil Monat; costumes, Deborah Shaw. With Jennifer Van Dyck, Ted Marcoux, Ron Nakahara, Justin Deas, Lisa Arrindell, Michael Genet, Evan Thompson, Lisa Beth Miller, Paul Kandel.

THE GOOD TIMES ARE KILLING ME (27). By Lynda Barry. April 18, 1991. Director, Mark Brokaw; choreography, Don Philpott; scenery, Rusty Smith; lighting, Don Holder; costumes, Ellen McCartney; musical director, Steve Sandberg. With Angela Goethals, Lauren Gaffney, Holly Felton, Ellia English, Wendell Pierce, Kim Staunton, Ruth Williamson, John Lathan, Jennie Moreau, Kathleen Dennehy, Ray DeMattis, Peter Appel, Chandra Wilson, Brandon Mayo. (Also see its entry in the Plays Produced Off Broadway section of this volume.)

Soho Rep. Dedicated to new, non-naturalistic plays. Marlene Swartz, Julian Webber artistic directors.

HANGING THE PRESIDENT (17). By Michele Celeste. July 6, 1990. Director, Julian Webber; scenery, Stephan Olson; lighting, Donald Holder; costumes, Patricia Samataro. With Dan Moran, Peter Drew Marshall, Peter Crombie, Themba Ntinga.

NATIVE SPEECH (19). By Eric Overmyer. April 4, 1991. Director, John Pynchon Holms; scenery, Kyle Chepulis; lighting, Steve Shelley, costumes, Steve Sarnataro. With Kario Salem, SaMi Chester, James Encinas, Fracaswell Hyman, Deborah Mansy, Iona Morris, J. Reuben Silverbird, Sixto Ramos, Jennifer Parsons, Allan Tung.

YOKOHAMA DUTY (20). By Quincy Long. May 17, 1991. Director, Julian Webber; scenery, Stephan Olson; lighting, Donald Holder; costumes, Patricia Sarnataro. With Nesbitt Blaisdell, Michael Cullen, Susanna Frazer, Bruce Katzman, Cheri Nakamura, Brett Rickaby, Preston Keith Smith, Peter Yoshida.

Theater for the New City. Developmental theater and new American experimental works. George Bartenieff, Crystal Field artistic directors.

Schedule included:

THE CENSUS TAKER (13). Music, Christopher Cherney; lyrics and direction, Crystal Field. August 4, 1990. Scenery, Anthony Angel; costumes, Marc Borders, Allan Charlet, Renee Kraus, Margaret Lalwani, Katie O'Keefe, Nancy Karp. With Beth Boone, Jacque Lynn Colton, Joseph C. Davies, Crystal Field, Michael-David Gordon, Jerry Jaffe, Lillian Jenkins, Daniel Wilkes Kelley, T. Scott Lilly, Margaret Miller, Mira Rivera.

BITCH, DYKE, FAGHAG, WHORE. By Penny Arcade. October 13, 1990.

BIZARRE BAZAAR: Festival including new work by David Finkelstein, Alvin Only, Rachel Hennely, 9th Street Theater, Sarah Hauser, The Holy Cows, Allan Charlet, Shaun Ader, Richie Rish, Mark Marcante, steve ben israel, George Belleci, Judy Gorman, Bronx Magic, The Harris Sisters, Jungle Jim's Revenge, Phoebe Legere, Red & Black Masque, Penny Arcade. October 31, 1990.

ALAN ROY'S SPIRAL PRESENTS: 12 PERFORMANCES BY 12 ARTISTS: Sylvain Sylvain, Phoebe Legere, Walter Lure, Maria Excommunikata, Cheeta Chrome, Eddie Van Bach, Annie Golden, Frank Carillo, The Holy Cows, Penny Arcade, James Saleeby, Natasha, The Psycho-Billies. November 15, 1990.

HARVEST MOON CABARET. November 24, 1990. With Hot Peaches.

FLO 'N RIC and THE BIG COUNTDOWN (one-act plays). By Jack Brown. November 30, 1990.

KINGS MUST DANCE. Adapted by Paul Ratliff from Mohammad Ben Abdallah's *The Witch of Mopti*. December 1, 1990. Director, Daisy Von Scherler Mayer. With Francis Blackchild, Robin Corrett, Majora Carter, Dwight Donaldson, Kara Flannery, Yvette Grant, Arthur Halpern, Tony Maxwell, Jean Villefranche.

RAP 'N STEIN. Book, music, lyrics and directed by Exavier Mohammed. December 7, 1990.

THE WITCH WAY? TRAVEL AGENCY, OR OUR ADVENTURES ON THE DIS-ORIENT EXPRESS. December 8, 1990. With The Wycherly Sisters.

AMY COLEMAN WITH A LITTLE HELP FROM HER FRIENDS. By Amy Coleman. January 12, 1991.

FIRE (EMPTY YOUR CLOSETS IF YOU WANT NO FIRE). Written and directed by Bina Sharif. January 21, 1991.

THE BUNNY AND DORIS SHOW. By Sebastian Stuart. February 22, 1991.

FELICIA. By Patricia Cobey. March 2, 1991.

A FESTIVAL FOR PEACE (one-day marathon of over 200 performances, readings) including works by Barbara Barrie, Vinie Burrows, Vira and Hortensia Colorado, Roger Durling, steve ben israel, Zohra Lampert, The Living Theater, Eduardo Machado, Karen Malpede, Bob Morris, Lola Pashalinski, Bina Sharif, Spiderwoman Theater, Sebastian Stuart, The Talking Band, Jeff Weiss, Alien Comic, Robbie McCauley, Reno, Carmelita Tropicana, Paul Zaloom, Allen Ginsberg, Bob Heide. March 9, 1991.

WISE GUISE. Music, dance and sketches by T. Scott Lilly, Craig Meade, Juan Villegas, Daniel Wilkes Kelley. Director, Craig Meade. March 22, 1991.

CHARLOTTE IN WONDERLAND. By Steve Lott. April 11, 1991. Director, Sebastian Stuart.

FATA MORGANA. By and with The Talking Band. April 18, 1991. Director, Paul Zimet.

HUIPIL. By Vira and Hortensia Colorado. May 9, 1991.

Ubu Repertory Theater. Committed to acquainting American audiences with new works by contemporary French-speaking playwrights from around the world. Francoise Kourilsky artistic director.

THE CHAIRS. By Eugene Ionesco, translated by Donald Watson. October 2, 1990. Director, Francoise Kourilsky. With Clement Fowler, Elizabeth Perry, Waguih Takla.

GRAND FINALE (23). By Copi, translated by Michael Feingold. April 15, 1991. Director, Andre Ernotte; scenery, William Barclay; lighting Phil Monat; costumes, Carol Ann Pelletier. With Keith McDermott, Margo Skinner, David Pursley, Jack Koenig, Delphi Harrington, Robertson Carricart.

WPA THEATER—Kyra Sedgwick, Laila Robins and Elizabeth
McGovern in *Maids of Honor* by Joan Casademont

The Vineyard Theater. Multi-art chamber theater dedicated to the development of new
plays and musicals, music-theater collaborations and innovative revivals. Douglas Aibel
artistic director, Barbara Zinn Krieger executive director, Jon Nakagawa managing director.

NIGHTINGALE (15). By Elizabeth Diggs. December 2, 1990. Director, John Rubinstein; scenery,
William Barclay; lighting, Phil Monat; costumes, James Scott; music, Robert Waldman. With
Kathryn Pogson, Robertson Carricart, John Curless, Jane Lanier, Edmund Lewis, Elizabeth Logun,
Jodie Lynn McClintock, Emily Arnold McCully, Patrick O'Connell, Pippa Pearthree, Greg Porretta,
Sloane Shelton, James A. Stephens, Diana Van Fossen.

BODONI COUNTY (13). Book and lyrics by Frank Gagliano; music by Claibe Richardson. March
15, 1991. Director, Andre Ernotte; scenery, William Barclay; lighting, Robert A. Jared; costumes,
Muriel Stockdale. With Sally Mayes, Veanne Cox, Lyn Greene, Mary Beth Piel, Tom Wood,
Stephen Geoffreys, John Kildahl.

THE DON JUAN AND THE NON DON JUAN (13). Book and lyrics, James Milton, David
Goldstein, based on Marvin Cohen's writings; music, Neil Radisch. April 16, 1991. Director, Evan
Yionoulis; scenery, William Barclay; lighting, Robert A. Jared; costumes, Teresa Snider-Stein;
musical director, Jan Rosenberg. With Joseph Adams, Lyn Greene, Ann Harada, Deirdre Lovejoy,
Sharon Scruggs.

FOOD AND SHELTER (19). By Jane Anderson. May 30, 1991. Director, Andre Ernotte; scenery,
Ann Sheffield; lighting, Donald Holder; costumes, Muriel Stockdale. With Kelly Coffield, Philip
Seymour Hoffman, John Speredakos, T-F Walker, Isiah Whitlock Jr., Virginia Wing.

The Women's Project and Productions. Nurtures, develops and produces plays written
and, for the most part, directed by women. Julia Miles founder and artistic director.

28 performances each

DAYTRIPS. By Jo Carson. October 30, 1990. Director, Billie Allen; scenery, James Noone; lighting, Anne Militello; costumes, Barbara Beccio. With Linda Atkinson, Barbara Barrie, Beth Dixon, Helen Stenborg.

THE ENCANTO FILE by Rosa Lowinger, directed by Melia Bensussen; THAT MIDNIGHT RODEO by Mary Sue Price, directed by Melanie Joseph; BUT THERE ARE FIRES by Caridad Svich, directed by Susana Tubert; RELATIVITY by Marlane Meyer, directed by Melanie Joseph; PAGAN DAY by Sally Nemeth, directed by Melanie Joseph. March 19, 1991. Scenery, Mark Fitzgibbons; lighting, Franklin Meissner Jr.; costumes, Barbara Beccio. With Dana Bate, Divina Cook, Dorrie Joiner, Thomas Kopache, Wendy Lawless, Patrick McNellis, Faye M. Price, Cliff Weissman.

NIGHT SKY. By Susan Yankowitz. May 22, 1991. Director, Joseph Chaikin; scenery, Watoku Ueno; lighting, Beverly Emmons; costumes, Mary Brecht. With Joan MacIntosh, Edward Baran, Tom Caylor, Aleta Mitchell, Paul Zimet, Lizbeth Zindel.

WPA Theater. Produces new American plays and neglected classics in the realistic idiom. Kyle Renick artistic director, Edward T. Gianfrancesco resident designer, Donna Lieberman managing director.

MAIDS OF HONOR (31). By Joan Casademont. June 8, 1990. Director, Max Mayer; scenery, Edward T. Gianfrancesco; lighting, Craig Evans; costumes, Mimi Maxmen. With Elizabeth McGovern, Kyra Sedgwick, Laila Robins, Kristine Nielsen, John Michael Higgins, Jake Weber, Joe Urla.

GROTESQUE LOVE SONGS (35). By Don Nigro. October 30, 1990. Director, Kenneth Elliott; scenery, Edward T. Gianfrancesco; lighting, Craig Evans; costumes, Debra Tennenbaum. With Felicity Huffman, Ted Marcoux, Suzanne Collins, Stephen Mendillo, Chad Lowe.

THE MY HOUSE PLAY (22). By Wendy MacLeod. January 17, 1991. Director, Rob Greenberg; scenery, James Schuette; lighting, Craig Evans; costumes, Candice Donnelly. With Leslie Lyles, Kathryn Erbe, Jayce Bartok, Lewis J. Stadlen, Welker White, David Eigenberg.

RED SCARE ON SUNSET (49). By Charles Busch. March 19, 1991. Director, Kenneth Elliott; scenery, B.T. Whitehill; lighting, Vivien Leone; costumes, Debra Tennenbaum. With Charles Busch, Andy Halliday, Julie Halston, Arnie Kolodner, Ralph Buckley, Roy Cockrum, Mark Hamilton, Judith Hansen.

York Theater Company. Specializing in producing new works, as well as in reviving great musicals. Janet Hayes Walker producing director.

EAST TEXAS (22). By Jan Buttram. September 28, 1991. Director, Alex Dmitriev; scenery, James Morgan; lighting, May Jo Dondlinger; costumes, Holly Hynes. With Venida Evans, Peter Brouwer, Susanne Marley, Dorothy Lancaster, Page Johnson.

THE LUNATIC, THE LOVER, THE POET (one-man show) (17). Shakespeare anthology by and with Brian Bedford. November 28, 1990.

PHILEMON. Book and lyrics by Tom Jones, music by Harvey Schmidt. January 11, 1991. Director, Fran Soeder. With Michael Tucci, Kenneth Kantor, Tony Floyd, Joel Malina, Jean Tafler, Kim Crosby, Kathryn McAteer.

A FUNNY THING HAPPENED ON THE WAY TO THE FORUM. Book by Burt Shevelove and Larry Gelbart, music and lyrics by Stephen Sondheim. March 22, 1991. Director, Pamela Hunt. With Jack Cirillo, John Remme, Chris Callen, Jeffrey Herbst, Jason Graae, Jim Harder, Ken Parks, Tony Aylward, Hope Harris, Denise Ledonne, Isabel Rose, Valerie Macklin, Sloan Wilding, Deborah Graham, John Dietrich, Mark DiNoia, Barry Finkel.

Miscellaneous

In the additional listing of 1990-91 off-off-Broadway productions below, the names of the producing groups or theaters appear in CAPITAL LETTERS and the titles of the works in *italics*. This list consists largely of new or reconstituted works and excludes most revivals, especially of classics. It includes a few productions staged by groups which rented space from the more established organizations listed previously.

ACTOR'S OUTLET. *Pretty Faces* (musical) by Robert W. Cabell. October 21, 1990. Directed by Gene Foote. *The Jack the Ripper Revue* (musical revue) book and lyrics by Peter Mattaliano; music by Stephen Jankowski. February 14, 1991.

ACTORS' PLAYHOUSE. *It's Still My Turn* (one-man show) by and with Terry Sweeney. August 9, 1990. Directed by Bill Lovejoy. *Hosanna* by Michel Tremblay. September 5, 1990. Directed by Charlie Hensley. *Guilty Innocence* written and directed by Matthew Lombardo. January 14, 1991. *The Haunted Host* by Robert Patrick. April 19, 1991. Directed by Eric Concklin; with Harvey Fierstein, Jason Workman.

ALGONQUIN. *Jeff Harnar Sings the 1959 Broadway Songbook* (cabaret). February 5, 1991.

AMERICAN JEWISH THEATER. *I Ought To Be in Pictures* by Neil Simon. November 11, 1990. Directed by Stanley Brechner; with Jenn Thompson, Betsy Friday, David Bailey. *Grown Ups* by Jules Feiffer. January 20, 1991. Directed by Lonny Price; with Rosemary Prinz, Len Stanger, Barbara Niles, Barry Craig Friedman, Lisa Emery, Lauren Gaffney. *I Can Get It for You Wholesale*, book by Jerome Weidman, based on his novel; music and lyrics by Harold Rome. March 15, 1991. Directed by Richard Sabellico; with Evan Pappas, Patti Karr, Carolee Carmello, Vicki Lewis, Jim Bracchitta, Deborah Carlson, Alix Korey, Richard Levine, Sam Brent Riegel, Joel Rooks. *Fayebird* by Diane Amsterdam. May 19, 1991. Directed by Stanley Brechner; with Elinor Basescu, Janet Sarno.

APPLE CORPS THEATER. *A Silent Thunder* by Eduardo Ivan Lopez. July 5, 1990. Directed by John Cappelletti; with Nestor Carbonell, Suzen Murakoshi.

ATLANTIC THEATER COMPANY. *Three Sisters* by Anton Chekhov, adapted by David Mamet from Vlada Chernomordik's translation. April 17, 1991. Directed by W.H. Macy; with Melissa Bruder, Mary McCann, Elizabeth McGovern, Herbert DuVal, Todd Weeks, Jordan Lage. *The Virgin Molly* by Quincy Long. May 28, 1991. Directed by Sarah Eckhardt; with Robert Bella, Neil Pepe, Jordan Lage, Todd Weeks, Christopher McCann, Raymond Anthony Thomas.

BACA DOWNTOWN. *The Death of the Last Black Man in the Whole Entire World* by Suzan-Lori Parks. September 13, 1990. Directed by Beth A. Schachter; with Pamala Tyson, Leon Addison Brown, Jasper McGruder, Fanni Green, Ann Harada, James Himelsbach, Michael Jayce, Patrice Johnson, John Steber, Ching Valdes/Aran. *The Egg Eating Contest, or How Much Is That Nigger in the Window* written and directed by William Pope O. October 18, 1990. *Sincerity Forever* by Mac Wellman. November 29, 1990. Directed by Jim Simpson; with Stephen Mellor, Jan Leslie Harding, Amy Brenneman, Leslie Nipkow. *The Almond Seller* by Oana-Maria Hock. February 14, 1991. Directed by Tina Landau; with Paul Zimet, Maria Porter, Nina Mankin, Theresa McCarthy, Nancy Hume, Thomas Nahrwold, Kirk Johnson. *The Saint Plays* (14 one-act plays), text by Eric Ehn. March 21, 1991. Directed by Fritz Ertl, Thalia Field, Jennifer McDowall, Brian Mertes, Bonnie Metzgar, Randolyn Zinn.

BANDWAGON. *The Day Before Spring*, book and lyrics by Alan Jay Lerner; music by Frederick Loewe. June 28, 1990. Directed by Dania Krupska, Jerry Bell; with Rebecca Hoodwin, Gerald Sell, Michael Harrington.

BATTERY MARITIME BUILDING. *Love of a Poet* (performance art) based on Robert Schumann's "Dichterliebe," by and with John Kelly. October, 1990.

BATTERY PARK CITY. *Le Cirque du Soleil* (circus). April 13, 1991. With Brian Dewhurst, Vladimir Kekhaial, France La Bonte, Anne Lepage, David Shiner.

BILLIE HOLIDAY THEATER. *Camp Logan* by Celeste Bedford-Walker. February 8, 1991. Directed by A. YuJuan Carriere-Anderson; with Chaz McCormack, Kelly Lamarr, Darrell Hughes, LeVerne Summers, Kevin Richardson, Alvin Walker, Zaria Griffin.

BROOKLYN ACADEMY OF MUSIC NEXT WAVE FESTIVAL. Works included *Endangered Species* (see Music-Theater Group entry); *Ninagawa Macbeth* by William Shakespeare, translated by Yushi Odashima. October 19, 1990. Directed by Yukio Ninagawa; with Masane Tsukayama, Komaki Kurihara, Norihiro Inoue, Haruhiko Joh, Kazuhisa Seshimo. *Polygraph* by Marie Brassard and Robert Lepage, translated by Gyllian Raby. October 23, 1990. Directed by Robert Lepage; with Pierre Auger, Marc Beland, Marie Brassard. *Hydrogen Jukebox* (song cycle in two parts) poetry by Allen Ginsberg; music by Philip Glass. May 7, 1991. Directed by Ann Carlson; with James Butler, Richard Fracker, Suzan Hanson, Mary Ann Hart, Daryl Henriksen, Lynnen Yakes.

CHELSEA STAGE (HUDSON GUILD THEATER). *Theme and Variations* by Samuil Alyoshin, translated by Michael Glenny. October 3, 1990. Directed by Geoffrey Sherman; with Ethan Phillips, Kathleen McCall, William Wise. (Also see Chelsea Stage's entry in the Plays Produced Off Broadway section of this volume.)

CORNER LOFT THEATER *My Married Friends* written and directed by Steven Salinaro. October 19, 1990. With Michael Azzolina, Tom Riis Farrell, Martha French.

CORNERSTONE THEATER COMPANY. *The Video Store Owner's Significant Other* adapted by Cornerstone Theater Company, with Dyann Simile, from Federico Garcia Lorca's *The Shoemaker's Prodigious Wife,* translated by James Graham Lujan, Richard L. O'Connell. September 14, 1990. Directed by Bill Rauch; with Amy Brenneman, Christopher Moore, Ashby Semple, Peter Howard, Alison Carey, Jeff Branion.

COURTYARD PLAYHOUSE. *Men of Manhattan* (one-acts) by John Glines. June 14, 1990. Directed by Charles Catanese; with T.L. Reilly, Cy Orfield, Steve Liebhauser, Richard Skipper, David Baird, Leslie Roberts. *The Histories of Gladys* by and with Jane Young, Thomas Keith. November 28, 1990. Directed by Edward Cornell.

CUCARACHA THEATER. *Famine Plays* (13) written and directed by Richard Caliban; music by John Hoge. October 28, 1990. With Lauren Hamilton, Mollie O'Mara, Vivian Lanko, Glen M. Santiago, Lia Chang, Steven Bland. *Amerikamachine* written and directed by Peter Mattei. May 17, 1991. With Glen M. Santiago, Damian Young, Elizabeth Woodruff, Lauren Hamilton, Garrick Ambrose, Les Baum, Joey L. Golden, Damon Grant, Kirk Jackson, Christie MacFadyen, Freja Mitchell, Brennan Murphy, David Simonds.

DANCE THEATER WORKSHOP. *My Civilization* by and with Paul Zaloom. January 8, 1991; *Winter Man* by Andy Teirstein. February, 1991 (music/theater works). Directed by Victoria Bussert; with J. Reuben Silverbird, Eric Hanson, Simon Brooking, Marin Mazzie, Neal Ben-Ari, Michelle St. John, Richard Ortiz, Robert Zolli, Machiste, James Apaumut Fall, Steve Ortiz, Maria Antoinette Rogers, Jody Kruskal.

DIRECTORS COMPANY. *Of Blessed Memory* by George Rattner. April 4, 1991. Directed by David McKenna; with T. Ryder Smith, Nicolette Vatjay, Richard Allen Petrocelli, Jose Zuniga, Scott Sowers.

DOUBLE IMAGE THEATER. *Daugherty and Field Off Broadway,* special material written and composed by Robin Field. November 9, 1990. With Bill Daugherty, Robin Field.

FASHION INSTITUTE OF TECHNOLOGY. *Narnia,* book by Jules Tasca, based on C.S. Lewis's *The Lion, the Witch and the Wardrobe;* music by Thomas Tierney; lyrics by Ted Drachman. January 7, 1991. Directed by Shela Xoregos; with New York State Theater Institute members.

FESTIVAL '91 (black theater festival). Schedule included *General Hag's Skeezag* by Amiri Baraka; *The Hill* by Zakes Mda; *To Gleam It Around to Show My Shine* by Lee Rattner, based on Zora Neale Hurston's works. January 27-February 4, 1991.

FLORENCE GOULD HALL. *Fifty Million Frenchmen,* book by Herbert Fields; music and lyrics by Cole Porter. May 9, 1991. Directed by Larry Carpenter; with Peggy Cass, Kim Criswell, Jason Graae, James Harder, Kay McClelland, Howard McGillin, Susan Powell, Scott Waara, Karen Ziemba.

FREDERICK DOUGLASS CREATIVE ARTS CENTER. *Telltale Hearts* by Joe Barnes. November,

1990. Directed by Dean Irby; with Iona Morris, Tony Evans, Count Stovall, Petronia Paley, Elain Graham, Kim Sykes, Jack Landros, Fred Anderson.

THE GLINES. *High Strung Quartet* by Evan Bridenstine. April 17, 1991. Directed by Leslie Irons; with John Carhart III, Suzanne Cryer, Dane Hall, Mark Leydorf.

HOME FOR CONTEMPORARY THEATER AND ART. *Lilith* by Allan Havis. September 12, 1990. Directed by Robert Bailey; with Zach Grenier, Allison Janney, Joel Rooks, Lindsey Margo Smith, Carl Purcell.

IRISH REPERTORY THEATER COMPANY. *Philadelphia, Here I Come!* by Brian Friel. June 12, 1990. Directed by Paul Weidner; with Pauline Flanagan, Patrick Fitzgerald, Ciaran O'Reilly, W.B. Brydon, Madeleine Potter, Chris Carrick, Frank McCourt, Paddy Croft, Bernard Frawley, John William Short, Colin Lane, Brian F. O'Byrne, Denis O'Neill, Dermot McNamara. *Making History* by Brian Friel. April 10, 1991. Directed by Charlotte Moore; with Ray Fitzgerald, Robert Murch, Ciaran O'Reilly, W.B. Brydon, Miriam Foley, Angela Cooper Scowen.

JEAN COCTEAU REPERTORY. *The Infernal Machine* by Jean Cocteau, translated by Albert Bermel. October, 1990. Directed by Robert Hupp; with Mark Waterman, Elise Stone, Harris Berlinsky, Pascale Roger, Keith Hamilton Cobb. *When We Dead Awaken* by Henrik Ibsen, translated by Rolf Fjelde. January 10, 1991. Directed by Eve Adamson; with Craig Smith, Elise Stone, Mark Waterman, Joseph Menino, Angela Vitale, Grant Neale. *Leonce and Lena* and *Woyzeck* by Georg Buchner, translated by Eric Bentley. February 8, 1991. Directed by Robert Hupp; with Harris Berlinsky, Craig Smith, Elise Stone, Joseph Menino, Mark Waterman. *The Emigrants* by Slawomir Mrozek. May 24, 1991.

JEWISH REPERTORY THEATER. *What's Wrong With This Picture* by Donald Margulies. June 21, 1990. Directed by Larry Arrick; with Stephen Mailer, Michael Lombard, Dolores Sutton, Salem Ludwig, Barbara Spiegel, Lauren Klein. *Spinoza* by Dimitri Frenkel Frank, translated by Martin Cleaver. October 20, 1990. Directed by Robert Kalfin; with Diego Matamoros, W.B. Brydon, Salem Ludwig, Pamela Burrell, Karen McLaughlin, Jeffrey Logan, William Duff-Griffin, Funda Duyal. *Taking Stock* by Richard Schotter. January 10, 1991. Directed by Marilyn Chris; with Lee Wallace, George Guidall, Stephen Singer. *A Fierce Attachment* adapted from Vivian Gornick's book *Fierce Attachments* and directed by Edward M. Cohen. March 3, 1991. With Tovah Feldshuh. *Modigliani* by Dennis McIntyre. April 25, 1991. Directed by Bryna Wortman; with David Beach, Ronald Guttman, Daniel James, Dane Knell, Martin Rudy, Will Scheffer, Karen Sillas.

JOYCE THEATER. *We Keep Our Victims Ready* (performance art) with Karen Finley. September 18, 1990.

KAUFMAN THEATER. *Carnal Knowledge* by Jules Feiffer. November 19, 1990. Directed by Martin Charnin; with Jon Cryer, Judd Nelson, Justine Bateman, Karen Byers, Mimi Quillin, Laura Rogers, Arminae Azarian.

NEW YORK STREET THEATER CARAVAN. *Blues in Rags* written and directed by Marketa Kimbrell. April 9, 1991.

LIGHT OPERA OF MANHATTAN. *Babes in Toyland*, book by William Mount-Burke and Alice Hammerstein Mathias; music by Victor Herbert; lyrics by Alice Hammerstein Mathias. December 19, 1990.

LINCOLN CENTER. *Serious Fun!* Schedule included *You Could Be Home Now* by and with Ann Magnuson, directed by David Schweizer; *The Manson Family: Helter Five-O* (multimedia music drama) by John Moran, directed by Bob McGrath, with the Ridge Theater; *The Men's Room: Wipe the Dirt Off Your Legs and Stroke the Mystery* by and with Christian Swenson; *A Short History of Romance* by Tom Cayler, Kay Cummings, Clarice Marshall, with Tom Cayler, Clarice Marshall; songs by Harry Shearer; *Big Time!* works by Pat Oleszko, Leo Bassi, The Shrimps, David Ives; *We Keep Our Victims Ready* by and with Karen Finley. July 13-August 2, 1990. *Lincoln Center Out-Of-Doors* schedule included performances by Puerto Rican Traveling Theater; Commedia Dell'Arte; Cooperativa del Teatro Laboratorio of Verona; *The Great Illusion* (magic and juggling) with Jim Moore, Doug Skinner, Vince Bruce, Mark Nizer, Jack Adams, Clown Theater Day; Bread and Puppet Theater. August 1-28, 1990.

LIVING THEATER. *Humanity* by Walter Hasenclever. May 29, 1991. Directed by Elena Jandova,

Martin Reckhaus; with Alan Arenius, Philip Brehse, Joanie Fritz, Laura Kolb, Chris Maresca, Pat Russell.

MANHATTAN CLASS COMPANY.   One-acts: *A Snake in the Vein* by Alan Bowne, directed by Jimmy Bohr; *Forgetting Frankie* by Annie Evans, directed by Melia Bensussen; *Lonely on the Bayou*, book and lyrics by Lynn Ginsburg, music by Catherine Stone, directed by Robert LuPone; *Research and Development* written and choreographed by Fay Simpson.   November 3-17, 1990.   With Kent Adams, Gil Bellows, Charles Cragin, Margaret Eginton, Tony Gilbert, Sarah Knapp, Joseph Knight, John Kozeluh, Ilana Levine, Micah Lewis, Laura Linney, Ken Marks, Beth McGee-Russell, Edward Miller, Ross Mondschain, Patti Onorato, Connie Ray, Philip J. Reilly, Gregory Wolfe, Sam Zuckerman.

MAZUR THEATER. *Thoughts of a Confused Blackman* by and with Kwaku Sintim-Misa.   April 27, 1991.   Directed by Anthony Andresakis.

MICHAEL'S PUB.   Rupert Holmes (cabaret).   July 31, 1990.   *Follies*, book by James Goldman; music and lyrics by Stephen Sondheim.   April, 1991.   With Jo Sullivan, Emily Loesser, Virginia Sandifur, David Cryer, Don Stephenson.

NAT HORNE THEATER.   *Midsummer* by Paul Parente.   September 11, 1990.   Directed by Rick Lombardo.

OHIO THEATER—Jerry Kernion in *The History of Pornography,* a multimedia performance work

NEW YORK PUBLIC LIBRARY FOR THE PERFORMING ARTS. *Reading Room Readings.* Schedule included *The Tyranny of Blood* by Larry Kramer, directed by Marshall W. Mason. February 25, 1991. With Brad Davis. *Success* by Arthur Kopit; *Heatstroke* by James Purdy; *Teeth* by Tina Howe; *The Last Yankee* by Arthur Miller. May 13, 1991. With William Hurt, Nathan Lane, Marian Seldes, Mike Nussbaum, Patricia Hodges, Paul Calderon.

NEW YORK STREET THEATER CARAVAN. *Blues in Rags* (music-theater piece) written and directed by Marketa Kimbrell; with Ariel Joseph, Marcia Donalds, Jennifer Johnson.

NORTHERN LIGHTS THEATER *Five Women in a Chapel* by Arto Seppala, translated by Philip Binham, adapted by Kevin Kane. May 28, 1991. Directed by Oeyvind Froeyland; with Betty Aberlin, Shami Chaikin, Diane Kagan, Geraldine Singer, Reenie Upchurch.

OHIO THEATER. TWEED (Theater Works: Emerging/Experimental Directions) New Works Festival. Schedule included: *The History of Pornography* (multimedia performance work) written and directed by Kevin Malony; music by Carol Lipnik. January 12, 1991. With Jerry Kernion.

ONE DREAM THEATER. *The True Story of a Woman Born in Iran and Raised to Heaven in Manhattan* written and directed by Assurbanipal Babilla. April 27, 1991. With Leyla Ebtehadj, Donna Linderman, Jessie Marquez, Tom Pearl, Assurbanipal Babilla.

PEARL THEATER COMPANY. *The Fine Art of Finesse* by Pierre de Marivaux, translated by Alex Szogyi. December 15, 1990. Directed by Richard Morse; with Robin Leslie Brown, Christopher L. Cook, Frank Geraci, Stuart Lerch, Matthew Loney, Laura Rathgeb, Ahvi Spindell, Hank Wagner, Donnah Welby. *Dance of Death* by August Strindberg, translated by Harry G. Carlson. January 20, 1991. Directed by Shepard Sobel; with Richard Fancy, Joanne Camp, Janet Kingsley, Paul O'Brian. *The Farewell Supper* and *Countess Mitzi* by Arthur Schnitzler. February 23, 1991. Directed by Frank Geraci, Tom Bloom; with Stuart Lerch, Arnie Burton, Robin Leslie Brown, Hank Wagner, Richard Seff, Joanne Camp, Frank Geraci, Richard Bourg.

PERFORMANCE SPACE 122. *Das Vedanya Mama* written and directed by Ethyl Eichelberger. July 19, 1990. With Gerard Little, Joan Marie Moossy, Helen Shumaker, Black-Eyed Susan, Ethyl Eichelberger. *World Without End* by and with Holly Hughes. October 4, 1990. Directed by Kate Stafford. *Vid* (monologue) by and with John O'Keefe. November 8, 1990. *Sixth Annual Veselka Festival.* Schedule included *For Crying Out Loud* by Rocky Bornstein; performances by Michael Kaniecki, Mabou Mines. May 10-13, 1991.

PERRY STREET THEATER. *Big, Fat and Ugly With a Moustache* by Christopher Widney. September 19, 1990. Directed by Stone Widney; with Alison Martin, David Beach, Brian Howe, Evan O'Meara, Jane Gabbert, Gordon Stanley. *The Goat* by Ben Morse. May 29, 1991. Directed by Beatrice Winde.

PLAYWRIGHTS PREVIEW PRODUCTIONS. *Pokey: Confessions of an Inconsequential Man* written and directed by Paul Darvis. May 9, 1991. With Michael Santero, Amy Stiller, Kathleen Gati, Tara Dolan, Sandy Moore, Diane Cossa, Julie Alesander, Karen Marek.

PRIMARY STAGES COMPANY. *Swim Visit* by Wesley Moore. June 10, 1990. Directed by William Partlan; with Caroline Lagerfelt, Alice Haining, Pirie MacDonald, Mark Metcalf. *Lusting After Pipino's Wife* by Sam Henry Kass. September 9, 1990. Directed by Casey Childs; with Joseph Siravo, Wayne Maugans, Alexandra Gersten, Debra Riessen. *Better Days* by Richard Dresser. January 27, 1991. Directed by John Pynchon Holms; with Daniel Ahearn, Kevin McClarnon, Susan Greenhill, James Gleason, Ann Talman, Larry Pine.

RAPP ARTS CENTER. *Moe Green Gets It in the Eye* by Anthony DiMurro. May 9, 1991. Directed by R. Jeffrey Cohen; with John Bakos, Vinnie Edghill, Darian Sartain, Howard Wesson, Anthony DiMurro.

THE RED MOON ENSEMBLE. *Junglebird* by Martha Horstman. December 3, 1990. Directed by Seth Gordon; with The Red Moon Ensemble.

REGENESIS. *Stealing Souls (Bring Your Camera)* by Mira-Lani Oglesby; original music by Marc Ryan. March 17, 1991. Directed by Thomas Calabro.

RIVERSIDE SHAKESPEARE COMPANY. *Fridays* by Andrew Johns. May 16, 1991. Directed by Gus Kaikkonen; with Kent Adams, Henderson Forsythe, David Edward Jones, Stephanie Madden, John Peakes, Alice White.

SIGNATURE THEATER. *F.M.* and *The Love Suicide at Schofield Barracks* (one-act plays) written and directed by Romulus Linney. May 15, 1991. With Elizabeth Lewis Corley, Ann Sheehy, Scott Sowers, Adrienne Thompson, Kernan Bell, Constance Boardman, Fred Burrell, S.J. Floyd, Gordon G. Jones, Garrison Phillips, James Seymour, Mary Jane Wells, John Woodson.

SOUTH STREET THEATER. *My Father, My Son* by Ken Wolf and Henry E. Wolf. September 6, 1990. Directed by Frank Trezza; with Steve Parris, Ken Wolf.

SPUYTEN DUYVIL THEATER COMPANY. *Them* by Tom Coffey. November 1, 1990. Directed by Dennis Delaney; with Casey McDonald, Robert Poletick, Joan Penn, Clarke Gordon, Janelle Sperow, Rusty Owen.

SQUAT THEATER. *Full-Moon Killer* written and directed by Stephan Balint. January, 1991. With Eszter Balint, Michael Thomas, Augustin Rodriguez, Kelvin Garvanne, Michael Strumm, David Lee, Nelson Nazario, Delroy Simpson, Masashi Ohtsu, Richard Jones.

STEVE MCGRAW'S (cabaret). *An Evening of Loesser and Sondheim.* January 4, 1991. Directed by Mark Waldrop; with Meg Bussert.

THEATER ARIELLE. *Guilt Without Sex* (one-woman show) by and with Marilyn Sokol. January 22, 1991. *Don't Get Me Started* (one-woman show) by and with Tina Smith. April 11, 1991. Directed by Kathy Najimy.

THEATER FOR A NEW AUDIENCE. *The Mud Angel* by Darrah Cloud. November 8, 1990. Directed by Kevin Kuhlke; with Seane Corn, Alyssa Breshnahan, Andrew Weems, David Neipris, Sofia Landon. *Romeo and Juliet* by William Shakespeare. January 27, 1991. Directed by Bill Alexander; with Mark Niebuhr, Miriam Healy-Louie.

THEATER LABRADOR. *Ever After What? Women Repossess Fairy Tales* compiled by Susan Bernfield, Nela Wagman from women's poetry. January 30, 1991. Directed by Maureen Clarke; with Susan Bernfield, Nela Wagman.

THEATER ROW THEATER (formerly South Street Theater). *Pals* by Stephen Mantin. April 10, 1991. Directed by Martin Shakar; with Anthony Spina, Ivan Kronenfeld, Sam Coppola, Victor Arnold.

TRIANGLE THEATER COMPANY. *Two by Two,* book by Peter Stone; music by Richard Rodgers; lyrics by Martin Charnin. October 7, 1990. Directed by Michael Ramach; with Kip Niven. *Unchanging Love* by Romulus Linney, from *In the Ravine* by Anton Chekhov. February 3, 1991. Directed by John Dillon; with Jennifer Parsons, Jacqueline Knapp, T. Cat Ford, Tom McDermott, Scott Sowers, Elizabeth Lewis Corley.

TRIPLEX. *The Mermaid Wakes* text by Lora Berg, music and directed by Elizabeth Swados; additional music by Barrington Antonio Burke-Green and Leopoldo Fleming; choreography, Thuli Dumakude. February 14, 1991. With Judy Bennett, Barrington Antonio Burke-Green, Leslie Arlette Boyce, Natalie Carter, Jerriese Daniel Johnson, Jesse Moore, Percy Pitzu, Silindile Sokutu, Felicia Wilson. *A Teacher of Russian* by Aleksandr Buravsky, translated by Alexander Gelman. March, 1991. Directed by Yevgeny Kamenkovich; with Vladimir Mashkov, Irina Petrova, Aleksandr Marin, Mariya Miranova.

29TH STREET PLAYHOUSE. *The Catalyst* by Ronald Duncan. April 11, 1991. Directed by Stephen Jones; with William Charlton, Lyndawn Couch, Ilva Dulack.

VILLAGE GATE. *Yesterdays* by Reenie Upchurch. October 5, 1990. Directed by Woodie King Jr.; with Reenie Upchurch, Herb Lovelle, Weldon Irvine. *Love Lemmings* (revue) by Joe DiPietro; music by Eric Thoroman; lyrics by Joe DiPietro, Eric Thoroman. April 18, 1991. Directed by Melia Bensussen; with Steve Ahern, Becky Borczon, John Daggett, Helen Greenberg.

VILLAGE LIGHT OPERA GROUP. *Carousel,* book and lyrics by Oscar Hammerstein II; music by Richard Rodgers. May 1, 1991. Directed by Margaret Rose; with Rodne Brown, Teresa Lane Hoover, James Lightstone, Kim Stengel, Mira Stunkel.

VORTEX THEATER COMPANY. *The Sacrificial Murders of Maine Virgins for the Sake of Art* written and directed by David Steinhart. August 31, 1990.

WESTBETH THEATER CENTER. *Undying Love (L'Amour, Toujours, La Morte)* by Charles Horine. January 18, 1991. Directed by George Elmer; with George Wolf Reily, Nicola Sheara. *Custody*, book and lyrics by Sandra Hochman based on her book, *Walking Papers*; music by Marsha Singer. April, 1991. Directed by Mina Yakim; with Martin Austin, Robin Boudreau, Lenny Mandel, Barbara J. Mills, Tara Sands.

WESTSIDE ARTS THEATER. *Only the Truth Is Funny* (one-man comedy) written, directed, performed by Rick Reynolds. April 16, 1991.

WILLIAM REDFIELD THEATER. *Ball* by John Jiler. November 4, 1990. Directed by Steve Stout; with Margaret Hunt.

WINGS THEATER. *We've Got Today!*, book by Sidney Morris, music and lyrics by Michael Hansen. December 20, 1990. Directed by John Wall; with Ron Golding, Chris Fields.

WORKING THEATER. *Let Me Live* by OyamO; music by Olu Dara. January 9, 1991. Directed by Bill Mitchelson; with Monte Russell, Randy Frazier, Leland Gantt, Earl Hagan, Rande Harris, Lawrence James, Robert Jason, Mitchell Marchand, Jasper McGruder, Eugene Nesmith.

ZENA GROUP THEATER. *Momentary Lapses* (one-act plays): *Valentine's Day* by Kathleen Chopin, directed by Kate Cummings; *What She Found There* by John Glore, directed by Libba Harmon; *Out the Window* by Neal Bell, directed by Tracy Brigden; *Mixed Emotions* by Bob Krakower, directed by Rod McLachlan; *Really Bizarre Rituals* by Reid Davis, directed by Jameel Khaja; *After You* by Steve Dietz, directed by Alex Aron; *The Problem Solver* by Michael Bigelow Dixon and Valerie Smith, directed by Kate Cummings; *The Last Supper* by Reid Davis, directed by Libba Harmon. May 23, 1991. With Diane Casey, Kara Flannery, Jeremy Gold, Arthur Halpern, Margaret Howard, Marta Johnson, Matt Kozlowski, Josh Liveright, Belinda Morgan, Bruce Marshall Romans, Kate Splaine.

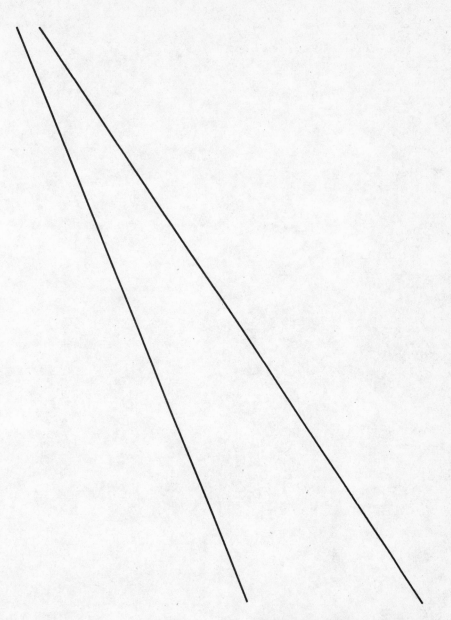

THE SEASON
AROUND
THE UNITED STATES

OUTSTANDING NEW PLAYS CITED BY AMERICAN THEATER CRITICS ASSOCIATION

and

A DIRECTORY OF NEW-PLAY PRODUCTIONS

THE American Theater Critics Association (ATCA) is the organization of 250 leading drama critics in all media in all sections of the United States. One of this group's stated purposes is "To increase public awareness of the theater as a *national* resource" (italics ours). To this end, ATCA has cited three outstanding new plays produced this season around the country, to be represented in our coverage of The Season Around the United States by excerpts from each of their scripts demonstrating literary style and quality. And one of these—*Two Trains Running* by August Wilson—was designated the first-place play and received the fifth annual ATCA New Play Award of $1,000.

The process of selection of these outstanding plays is as follows: any ATCA member critic may nominate a play if it has been given a production in a professional house. It must be a finished play given a full production (not a reading or an airing as a play-in-progress). Nominated scripts were studied and discussed by an ATCA play-reading committee chaired by T.H. McCulloh of the Los Angeles *Times* and comprising Porter Anderson of the Dallas *Times Herald*, Jeffrey Borak of the *Berkshire Eagle*, Richard Christiansen of the Chicago *Tribune*, Damien Jaques of the Milwaukee *Journal*, Dan Sullivan of the Los Angeles *Times* and

Gerald Weales. The committee members made their choices on the basis of script rather than production, thus placing very much the same emphasis as the editors of this volume in making the New York Best Play selections. There were no eligibility requirements except that a nominee be the first full professional production of a new work outside New York City within this volume's time frame of June 1, 1990 to May 31, 1991. If the timing of nominations and opening prevent some works from being considered in any given year, they will be eligible for consideration the following year if they haven't since moved on to New York production. We offer our sincerest thanks and admiration to the ATCA members and their committee for the valuable insight into the 1990-91 theater season around the United States which their selections provide for this *Best Plays* record, in the form of the following excerpts from outstanding scripts illustrating their style and the nature of their content, with brief introductions provided by T.H. McCulloh (*The Ohio State Murders*), Porter Anderson (*Sincerity Forever*) and Richard Christiansen (*Two Trains Running*).

Cited by American Theater Critics
as Outstanding New Plays
of 1990-91

TWO TRAINS RUNNING

A Play in Two Acts

BY AUGUST WILSÒN

Cast and credits appear on page 526 of *The Best Plays of 1989-90*

TWO TRAINS RUNNING: This is the fifth work in August Wilson's planned cycle of plays dealing with the African-American experience in the United States in each decade of the 20th century; and it is the third Wilson drama in that cycle, following *Fences* and *The Piano Lesson,* to be cited as an outstanding new work of its season by members of the American Theater Critics Association.

The play is set in Pittsburgh, Wilson's home town, in 1969, one year after the assassination of the Rev. Dr. Martin Luther King Jr. and the turbulent racial confrontations that followed his death. The scene is a four-stool, three-booth restaurant, specializing in cheap down-home cooking. It is owned by Memphis, a former Southern farmer who, like many of Wilson's characters, has moved North to face the changes and inequalities of a complex urban world.

Across the street from Memphis's place are two businesses that also play a key part in the drama: Lutz's meat market, site of a small but significant indignity done more than nine years ago to a simple-minded black man named Hambone; and West's Funeral Home, jammed at this time by hundreds of faithful followers who have come to pay last respects to their late, legendary and very wealthy leader, the Prophet Samuel.

As in all of Wilson's plays, the themes of disenfranchisment and disorientation are very much in evidence in *Two Trains Running*, and, again, these themes are expressed in the rich, vibrant, poetic argot of Wilson's people.

Here is an excerpt from Act I, Scene 2 of *Two Trains Running*. In addition to Memphis, the characters include Wolf, the local numbers runner; Holloway, a regular customer; and Risa, the cook-waitress.

> *The lights come up on the restaurant. Wolf is looking out the window of the door. Memphis is at the end of the counter. Risa is at the back.*

WOLF: Here he comes now. Lutz coming down the street. Hambone standing there.

> *Memphis comes around the corner of the counter and walks to the door. Looks out.*

MEMPHIS: What's Holloway doing?

WOLF: He watching him. He just standing there. We wanna hear what they say. Look at him . . . look at him. Look at Hambone.

> *Risa enters from the back.*

RISA: What you all looking at?

WOLF: We watching Hambone. We want to see what he say to Lutz. Holloway went over there to stand on the corner. Hambone talking to Lutz now.

MEMPHIS: That's the damnest thing I ever seen. (*He walks around the counter.*) Risa, you been here for half an hour and ain't got the coffee on. What you doing back there? Get them grits cooked up. I told you put the bread in the refrigerator . . . keep it fresh.

WOLF: Lutz going in his store. He turned his back to him and opening up his store. Holloway still standing there. (*Turning from the window.*) Lutz ought to go on and give him a ham.

MEMPHIS: Lutz ain't gonna give him no ham . . . cause he don't feel he owe him. I wouldn't give him one either.

WOLF: After all this time it don't make no difference. He ought to go on and give him a ham. What difference do it make? It ain't like he ain't got none. Got a whole store full of hams.

MEMPHIS: What you do with that flour? Ain't even got the oven turned on. How you gonna cook biscuits without turning on the oven? Where the flour? I brought ten pound of flour in here yesterday.

RISA: It's in the back.

MEMPHIS: Here's the sifter. Sift the baking soda and flour together. You ain't used this sifter in a month. And get on up to the bakery and get West his pie before he get over here.

WOLF: I hear tell somebody tried to break in West's last night to steal Prophet Samuel's money and jewels. Set off the burglar alarm . . . woke West up. He said he gonna hire Mason to sit in there tonight with his shotgun.

> *Holloway enters.*

Hey Holloway, we was watching you. What Hambone say? We seen Lutz when he came down the street. What he say?

HOLLOWAY: He told him he wanted his ham, that all. Said, "I want my ham." Lutz told him take a chicken, then he went on in his store. That was it. He ain't

Ella Joyce as Risa in the Yale Repertory Theater
production of August Wilson's *Two Trains Running*

said nothing back to him. The only words exchanged was, "I want my ham" and "Take a chicken."

MEMPHIS: I would just like to know . . . after nine and a half years . . . am I right, Holloway? . . . after nine and a half years . . . every day . . . I wish my arithmetic was right to tell you how many days that is . . . nine and a half years . . . every day . . . how . . . in his right mind . . . do you think Lutz is gonna give him his ham? You answer me that. That's all I want to know.

WOLF: Anybody can see he ain't in his right mind.

HOLLOWAY: I don't know. He might be more in his right mind than you are. He might have more sense than any of us.

WOLF: Would you stand there every morning for nine and a half years?

HOLLOWAY: I ain't saying that. Naw . . . hell no . . . I wouldn't stand over there for nine and a half years. But maybe I ain't got as much sense as he got.

MEMPHIS: You tell me how that makes sense. You tell me what sense that make?

HOLLOWAY: All right. I'll tell you. Now you take me or you. We ain't gonna do that. We gonna go ahead and forget about it. We might take a chicken. Then we gonna go home and cook that chicken. But how it gonna taste? It can't taste good to us. We gonna be eating just to be eating. How we gonna feel good about ourselves? Every time we even look at a chicken we gonna have a bad taste in our mouth. That chicken's gonna call up that taste. It's gonna make you feel ashamed. Even if it be walking around flapping it's wings it's gonna remind us of that bad taste. We ain't gonna tell nobody about it. We don't want nobody to know. But you can't erase it. You got to carry it around with you. This fellow here . . . he say he don't want to carry it around with him. But he ain't willing to forget about it. He trying to put the shame on the other foot. He trying to shame Lutz into giving him his ham. And if Lutz ever break down and give it to him . . . he gonna have a big thing. He gonna have something he be proud to tell everybody. He gonna tell his grandkids if he have any. That's why I say he might have more sense than me and you. Cause he ain't willing to accept whatever the white man throw at him. It be easier. But he say he don't mind getting out of the bed in the morning to go at what's right. I don't believe you and me got that much sense.

MEMPHIS: That's the old backyard Southern mentality. When I come up here they had to teach these niggers they didn't have to tip their hat to a white man. They walking around here tipping their hat, jumping off the sidewalk, talking about, "Yessir Captain, how do Major."

WOLF: How long you been up here, Memphis?

MEMPHIS: I been up here since thirty-six. They run me out of Jackson in thirty-one. I hung around Natchez for three or four years, then I come up here. I was born in Jackson. I used to farm down there. They ran me out in thirty-one. Killed my mule and everything. One of these days I'm going back and get my land. I still got the deed.

HOLLOWAY: I got an uncle and a bunch of cousins down in Jackson.

MEMPHIS: When I left out of Natchez I said I was gonna buy me a V-8 Ford and drive by Mr. Henry Ford's house and honk the horn. If anybody come to the window I was gonna wave. Then I was going out and buy me a thirty-oh-six and drive up to Mr. Stovall's house and honk the horn. Only this time I wasn't waving. Only thing was, it took me thirteen years to get the Ford. Six years later I traded that in on a Cadillac. There wasn't no way in the way in the world I was going back to Natchez then. Do you know what they do to a nigger they see driving a Cadillac in Natchez? But I'm going back one of these days. I ain't even got to know the way. All I got to do is find my way down to the train depot. They got two trains running every day. I used to know the schedule. They might have changed it . . . but if they did, they got it posted up on the board.

RISA: The oven's on. I'm going to get the pie.

Risa exits as Memphis watches after her.

The first production of record of Two Trains Running *took place at Yale Repertory Theater March 27, 1990 under the direction of Lloyd Richards. There have been subsequent productions at the Huntington Theater, Boston, October 26, 1990, at Seattle Repertory January 2, 1991 and at the Old Globe Theater, San Diego, March 14, 1991.*

THE OHIO STATE MURDERS

A Full-Length Play in One Act

BY ADRIENNE KENNEDY

Cast and credits appear on page 430

THE OHIO STATE MURDERS: Suzanne Alexander is a "well-known black writer" who attended Ohio State from 1949 to 1950. She has been asked to return to give a talk to students and faculty on the violent imagery in her work: "bloodied heads, severed limbs, dead father, dead Nazis, dying Jesus." They are, of course, interested in her brief years at the school but are more concerned with the violent imagery of her writing.

Playwright Adrienne Kennedy and her protagonist have a surprise in store for the complacent school, beginning with the de facto segregation of black students during Suzanne's stay on campus, and the fact that entry into the exclusively white ranks of English majors was denied her. Only one white man saw her potential, English Professor Robert Hampshire. In 1949, after reading her first paper, on *Tess of the d'Urbervilles*, he summons her to his office.

Suzanne narrates in the present from her prepared lecture:

SUZANNE: Before Christmas of my Freshman Quarter, Professor Hampshire wrote on my paper, "Make appointment to see me."
     Scene: English office, Suzanne and Hampshire, 1949.
His office in the English Department was along a path beyond the Oval. I seldom walked there, and once I left the Oval I got lost on the streets on that side of the campus and was almost late for my 4:00 appointment. It was dark. He was sitting in

a greyish office with several empty desks.

> *Suzanne, 1949, in saddle oxfords, skirt, matching sweater, cloth woolen coat . . . . . She wears powder blue, a popular color in 1949.*

I was quite nervous. It was the first time a professor at Ohio State had asked to see me.

> *She sits opposite Hampshire.*

He was crouched over his desk, writing, and seemed smaller than in class, very pale, glasses, the same greyish woolen suit. (*In 1949, to the Professor.*) Professor Hampshire, you wrote on my paper you wanted to see me.

HAMPSHIRE: Oh yes, Suzanne, sit down, please. Did you bring your paper?

SUZANNE: Yes.

HAMPSHIRE: Let me see it.

SUZANNE (*in the present*): For a moment he seemed to forget me and read the brief paper in its entirety. For a moment watching him, I realized he was a man of about thirty. I later was to discover he was a lecturer and this was his first year at Ohio State.

> *In 1949, Hampshire looks up and speaks quickly.*

HAMPSHIRE: What is your major?

SUZANNE: I am undeclared. But if I do well this quarter I want to apply to take another course in the spring, but I know I have to have special permission for any further English courses. (*In the present.*) He didn't seem to hear me.

HAMPSHIRE: Did you write this paper yourself?

SUZANNE: Yes, Professor Hampshire.

HAMPSHIRE: What reference books did you use?

SUZANNE: I used no reference books. I wrote the paper late one night in the dorm, the night before it was due. (*In the present.*) He returned the paper to me, staring at the desk top. Suddenly he looked up.

HAMPSHIRE: Have you read Hardy before? (*He does not smile.*)

SUZANNE (*in the present*): He didn't seem to want to continue speaking. I tried to tell him that I wanted to study more English courses, how much I loved literature. But he stood up, interrupting me. He didn't speak, but gathered his books together. And stared at me, then nodded. I saw the conference was over.

> *In 1949, Suzanne stands, moves away, staring back at Hampshire, as the scene ends . . . . .*
>
> *Immediately after Suzanne sees Hampshire, she is walking in darkness across the campus.*

SUZANNE: I got lost again between two buildings behind University Hall. Walking back in the darkness I remembered passages of my paper. And I remembered the comments Professor Hampshire had written on the margins. (*In 1949.*) "Paper conveys a profound feeling for the material". . . "Paper has unusual empathy for Tess" . . . "The language of the paper seems an extension of Hardy's own language."

> *She hears Hampshire's voice.*

HAMPSHIRE: It's brilliant. It's brilliant.

> *Suzanne's face shines.*

The following Christmas, 1950, Suzanne became pregnant. She told no one the father of her twins, Cathi and Carol, was the white Professor Hampshire.

Scene: path near Quonset hut.

SUZANNE: I had not seen him after the spring quarter ended. In fact, I did not see him until next fall (1950). I had applied to be an English major but had been denied. They let me take a trial course on Shaw, Wilde . . . . . I had seen Professor Hampshire on his way to the Quonset hut. (*In 1950.*) I am taking a trial course.

HAMPSHIRE: It's a shame.

SUZANNE (*in the present*): The previous quarter I had taken his course on *Beowulf.* Again he had liked my papers.

HAMPSHIRE: It's not necessary for you to take a trial course. It's a shame.

SUZANNE: He hurried on.

End of scene.

Bellary Darden (*top*) as Suzanne in the past and Hazel J. Medina as Suzanne in the present, in the Great Lakes Theater Festival production of *The Ohio State Murders* by Adrienne Kennedy

On that same path in one year we would meet. It was February, 1951 when I told him I was pregnant. He was on the same walkway that led to the hut. Within the Quonset I could see students gathering. I had not seen him since December, when I had gone to his house above the ravine.

       Scene: near Quonset hut.

On that cold morning I stopped him as he came toward me. I had been waiting for him as he came up the steps of University Hall and onto the Oval. The immense circle of buildings was majestic amid dark trees and snow. I told him I was pregnant. (*1951; hardly audible.*) I am pregnant. (*In the present.*) He stopped an instant.

HAMPSHIRE: That's not possible. We were only together twice. You surely must have other relationships. It's not possible.

SUZANNE: He walked past me.

Later, still reading from her lecture, Suzanne states: "Then it happened. Near the beginning of March, Robert Hampshire kidnapped and murdered our daughter. She was the one called Cathi. He drowned her in the ravine. For a year detectives questioned me. Did I have enemies? Had I ever observed anyone following me? At that time they didn't ask me about Cathi's father."

Suzanne slowly and carefully drops incidents before her lecture audience, stories of rebuilding her life after her dismissal from Ohio State, after the murder of one of her twins. She is relentless in the coolness of her retelling.

Finally her landlady, Mrs. Tyler, tells her she is expecting a college researcher studying negroes in the Columbus area. One evening when she returned from the law library at 10:05, "the Ohio State murders had occurred."

SUZANNE: Robert Hampshire, posing as a researcher, had killed Carol—our twin—and himself. It seems that once inside Mrs. Tyler's living room he had told her he was the father of the twins, that he had never been able to forget their existence. They ruined his life. He said he knew that one day I would reveal this, that he would be investigated, there would be tests and his whole career would fail. He admitted he had waited for me outside the doctor's office and had taken Cathi. He told her he tried to follow the advice of his father who lived near London, who told him to just ignore me, but he had been unable to do that. He was quite mad, she said, and had pushed her into the hallway and down the cellar stairs. When her son returned at 8:55 he had found her crying and injured on the dark stairwell. Upstairs in the small sewing room where Carol and I slept, Robert had killed himself and Carol with a knife he had taken from the kitchen sink.

Suzanne Alexander's lecture is almost over. Her story is told. Her point is made: "And that is the main source of the violent imagery in my work. Thank you."

The Ohio State Murders was commissioned in the Ohio Arts Council's new works program and premiered in workshop under the direction of Gerald Freedman June 16, 1990 at Great Lakes Theater Festival, Case Western Reserve University, Cleveland.

SINCERITY FOREVER

A Full-Length Play in One Act

BY MAC WELLMAN

Cast and credits appear on page 454

SINCERITY FOREVER: The generally acknowledged leader of the "language poet playwrights," an unofficial genus that includes Suzan-Lori Parks, Eric Overmyer, Len Jenkin, Jeffrey Jones, Constance Congdon and others, Mac Wellman at this writing remains largely untried by the established regional houses of the country, which the playwright vehemently derides for their conservative dependency on what he calls "touching little neo-realistic melodramas about family life." *Sincerity Forever*, described by Wellman as "a nasty little parable," is a 70-minute one-act of eight scenes set in a rural American burg named Hillsbottom. The action takes place in and around a parked convertible. With the exception of Christ and two Furballs—the deity arrives to condemn Hillsbottom, the demons to corrupt it—each character in Hillsbottom, male or female, wears full Ku Klux Klan regalia.

Under a summer moon, these adamant rednecks discuss how "an Intelligent Being out there" is responsible for the fact that they are "forever ignorant of the true nature of things, ignorant forever in absolute sincerity."

And in the final scene, the character of Christ (played in a later off-off-Broadway production by a black actress) "speaks to the company," as Wellman's stage directions indicate, "assembled at his feet, including the Furballs," as follows.

CHRIST:

Do you think I come here to reconcile you,
brother to sister, father to son, mother
to mother-in-law, second cousin twice-removed
to step-aunt from out of state, Cincinnati
maybe? Furball to Furball? Shitass no!
I came here to raise badass, obstreperous,
antisocial, pestiferous, brutalitarian, loud-
mouthed and chaotic bloody hell. The roaring kind!
You swinish, mealy-mouthed bunch of hypocrites
wouldn't know the Lord God of Hosts if he swope
down and bit you on the ass. All you care about
is what you look like, what you look like in a
mirror, a mirror some monster Furball dreamt up
for you to look at to make you blind. America,
you got your eyes open so wide you can't see a
fucking thing. America, you're crazy if you
think your limpdick, milksop, harebrained
Christianity has anything whatsoever to do with
Jesus H. Christ, because that's who's standing
here before you in the dusty ruination of the open
road, because the whole point of what I am
about is to shake up belief, to shake up belief
and make people stop being so goshdarned pleased
with theyselves, and take a good look at what a
sorry place this world is, what with all the jive
ass bullslinging, and endless justifying. And
mudslinging. And monumental cheapness of heart,
and moral stinginess. Furthermore, whosoever
puts words in my mouth concerning they fears
of the so-called cabal of international faggotry,
the scourge of the children of Ham, and the Hebrew
contagion—different folks who ought to be viewed
with a skeptical eye as total washouts at maintaining correck social decorum and avoidance of the
misnormal—all those who puts words in my mouth
concerning these things I have no use for. What
the fuck do I care who fucks with who? They
fucking is they own concern; and may they use it
wisely, and well. Furthermore, whosoever puts
words in my mouth, he too fucks with me in the
abstrack sense; therefore, I do not like him,
because . . . Because, you go figure: If'n I,
Jesus H. Christ, had any desire to speak your

language, the debased patois of late capitalism,
I woulda done so roundabout here likemost, right
from the start; but I didn't, so I don't; I
won't give you the satisfaction. Because I
got nothing to say to you, America. America,
I have nothing to say. I prefer the language
of Furballs, although they are a wicked awful
bunch, and spirits of negation, and the mere
sight of 'em like to make my skin crawl. I prefer
their language because you so much despise it . . .
No, all I wanted, pure and simple, was to create a
context for something powerfully human, great
and beautiful; it being the state of nature to
leave off with telling who to do what, X in the
name of Y, for no other reason than general cussidness.
The door opens on your side, I always say—
I can't open it! I mean, the handle's on your
side and if you don't want to see that, tough
shit, it's your problem and none of mine. Face it,
you a sleazy, lying conniving bunch of dickheads.
If you fuck up, it's your fault, not mine. And if
I had to do it all over again, I'd give the whole
matter serious thought. Because of doubts I now
possess about the entire enterprise. Because you
know what I got in this bag, do you?
        Pause.
I mean, do you know what this load is
which I have chosen to lug with me
all down through the ages, through the
peaks and canyons of oblivion, up to now,
do you?
GEORGE: Nope.
JUDY: No, we don't sir.
CHRIST:
    OF COURSE YOU DON'T, DICKHEADS. Because
you lack imagination, wit, manners
and any sense of humor.
        Pause.
Because anything simple and decent
escapes you . . .
        Pause.
Because you get lost in insane manias that
devolve into nightmares of control, slaughter,
rapine, and nontemporal unaccountability.

You get caught in dumbass things like sincerity
and infinite regress . . . Sincerity!?
I'll tell you about sincerity! It's not
about all the hooting and hollering. It's
about the stillness after all the hooting

Jason Duchin, Ntare Mwine and Tom Hildreth in a scene from the Berkshire Theater
Festival, Stockbridge, Mass. production of *Sincerity Forever* by Mac Wellman

and hollering has stopped.
        Pause.
WHAT THE FUCK DO I CARE ABOUT YOUR
FUCKING SINCERITY?! You can go shove
your fucking sincerity up your tailpipe.
        Pause.
In here is the quietest poem ever written.
And it is heavy. It is really, really heavy.
You *(To George.)*, you meathead, yes you, you
want to try to pick it up?
        Pause.
Go on. Just try. Pick it up.
        George can't do it.
I am Jesus H. Christ AND
I am John Q. Fedup.
        Pause.
When your time comes you too, each
one, will cry out . . . and be gone.
You're looking for the wrong event, that's
what you're looking for.
        Picks up the suitcase.
Wake up to the hollow time that is, because
that's where your parlous asses are,
each and every one.
        He goes—long pause.
MOLLY: The Lord giveth and the Lord taketh away.
TOM: Who was that African-American gentleman?

Sincerity Forever *was commissioned by the Roger Nathan Hirshl Playwriting Award for the Unicorn Company of the Berkshire Theater Festival at Stockbridge, Mass. and was presented there on July 25, 1990. It is doubly cited in this volume, since its off-off-Broadway production in the Fringe Series at BACA Downtown on November 29, 1990 was selected by Mel Gussow as one of the outstanding events of the OOB season (see report in the Plays Produced Off Off Broadway section of this volume).*

A DIRECTORY OF NEW-PLAY PRODUCTIONS

Compiled by Sheridan Sellers

Professional 1990-91 productions of new plays by leading companies around the United States that supplied information on casts and credits at Sheridan Sellers's request, plus a few reported by other reliable sources, are listed below in alphabetical order of the locations of the 75-plus producing organizations. Date given is opening date, included whenever a record was obtainable from the producing management. All League of Resident Theaters (LORT) and other Equity groups were queried for this comprehensive Directory. Those not listed here either did not produce new or newly-revised scripts in 1990-91 or had not responded by press time. Most of the productions listed—but not all—are American or world premieres. Some are new revisions, second looks or scripts produced previously but not previously reported in Best Plays.

Albany: The New York State Theater Institute

(Literary manager, James Farrell)

VASILISA THE FAIR. Book by Sofiya Prokofyeva and Irina Tokmakova; music by Alla Lander; translated by Sabina Modzhalevskaya and Harlow Robinson; edited by Harlow Robinson; adapted by Adrian Mitchell. May 11, 1991. Directors, Patricia Di Benedetto Snyder, Adrienne Posner; scenery, Richard Finkelstein; lighting, John McLain; costumes, Brent Griffin; sound, Matt Elie.

Tsar of Russia . . . . John Romeo
Ivan-Tsarevich . . . . Richard Barrows
Foma-Tsarevich. . . . . David Bunce
Danila-Tsarevich. . . . . . Michael P. Fitzgerald
Akulina . . . . Betsy Riley-Normile
Pava . . . . Etta Caren Fink
Vasilisa the Fair. . . . . Marlene Goudreau
Kashchey the
    Deathless . . . . . . John Thomas McGuire III
Misha-Medved. . . . . Joel Aroeste
Baba Yaga . . . . Joseph Larrabee-Quandt
Stroganov-Sabaka. . . . . David Bunce
Golubtsy-Koshka . . . . Etta Caren Fink

Sasha-Shpionka. . . . . Jeneane Schmidt
Zamok . . . . John Robert McEnerney
Sea Tsar . . . . John Romeo
Baba Yaga's Hut. . . . . . Raymond C. Harris
Ensemble Musician . . . . George Fortune
Iva. . . . . Ewa Lewinska
    Fences: Bonnie Jeanne Howland, Gary D. Marshall, Tara Raucci, Michael John Ziccardi. Spirits: Gary D. Marshall, Christina Patrick, Tara Raucci, Jennifer Williams. Guards: Raymond C. Harris, Gary D. Marshall, John Robert McEnerney, Michael John Ziccardi. Ensemble: David Bunce, Etta Caren Fink, Michael P. Fitzgerald, Raymond C. Harris, Bonnie Jeanne Howland, Ewa Lewinska, Gary D. Marshall, John Robert McEnerney, Christina Patrick, Tara Raucci, Jeneane Schmidt, Jennifer Williams, Michael John Ziccardi.

New Play Reading Series:
A STRAY DOG. By William S. Yellow Robe Jr. February 7, 1991. Director, Mark Dalton.

Allentown, Pa.: Pennsylvania Stage Company

(Producing director, Peter Wrenn-Meleck)

KURU. By Josh Manheimer. February 6, 1991. Director, Peter Wrenn-Meleck; scenery and lighting, Bennet Averyt; costumes, David Brooks.
Dr. Arthur Roman . . . . Brad Bellamy
Mary Lou Anderson . . . . Sue Brady

Mokina . . . . Kathi Kennedy
    Time and Place: A lecture hall of an American University, late 1970s; Dr. Roman's jungle hut deep in the highlands of New Guinea, 1959; and Stockholm, 1979. One intermission.

Atlanta: Academy Theater

(Artistic director, Frank Wittow; managing director, Lorenne Fey)

TRAINS. By Barbara Lebow. Director, Barbara Lebow; scenery, Michael Halpern; lighting, R. Scott Preston; costumes, Anita Beaty.

Businessman; Gabriel; Dennis . . . Thomas Byrd
Backpacker; John; Harvey . . . . Haynes Brooke

Three Plays in May:

HOUSEBREAKING. By Dennis Camilleri. May, 1991. Director, Frank Wittow; scenery, Elliott Berman; lighting, Adam Dowis.

William . . . . Gregg Wallace
Becca . . . . Nancy Lewis
Connie . . . . Mira Hirsch
Man . . . . Al Choy
Mike . . . . Charles Reed
  Time: The present. Place: The suburbs. One intermission.

WALKIN' TA HEAVEN. By Stephen Peace. May, 1991. Director, Frank Wittow; scenery, Elliott Berman; lighting, Adam Dowis.

Angel . . . . Kelly Lawrence
Don. . . . . John Rice
Junior . . . . Tom Pollock
Stevie . . . . Evan Pinto
  Time: The present. Place: Southeast Atlanta.

KAFKAPHONY. By Frank Wittow. May, 1991. Director, Frank Wittow; scenery, Elliott Berman; lighting, Adam Dowis.

Joseph . . . . Stephen Coulter
Grete; Berthe; Mother #1 . . . . . Nancy Lewis
Father . . . . Al Choy
Mother #2 . . . . Susan Thompson
  Time: 1924. Place: Prague, Czechoslovakia. One intermission.

PENNSYLVANIA STAGE COMPANY, ALLENTOWN—Sue Brady and Kathi Kennedy in the world premiere of Josh Manheimer's *Kuru*

Baltimore: Center Stage

(Artistic director, Stan Wojewodski Jr.)

THE HELIOTROPE BOUQUET BY SCOTT JOPLIN AND LOUIS CHAUVIN. By Eric Overmyer. February 16, 1991. Director, Stan Wojewodski Jr.; scenery, Christopher Barreca; lighting, Richard Pilbrow; costumes, Catherine Zuber; sound, Janet Kalas.

Spice . . . . Ellen Bethea
Keeler . . . . L. Peter Callender
Hannah . . . . Linda Cavell
Felicity . . . . Denise Diggs
Trick John; Disappearing Sam . . . Dion Graham
Stark . . . . Wil Love
Chauvin . . . . Victor Mack
Spanish Mary; Lottie; Belle. . . . . . Essene R
Joplin . . . . Monti Sharp
Turpin . . . . Jeffery V. Thompson
Joy . . . . Gina Torres

Berkeley, Calif.: Berkeley Repertory Theater

(Artistic director, Sharon Ott; managing director, Susan Medak)

FISH HEAD SOUP. By Philip Kan Gotanda. Director, Oskar Eustis; scenery, lighting, Kent Dorsey; costumes, Lydia Tanji; sound, James LeBrecht.

Papa. . . . . Alberto Isaac
Victor . . . . Kelvin Han Yee
Dorothy . . . . Dian Kobayashi
Mat. . . . . Stan Egi

Boston: Huntington Theater Company

(Producing director, Peter Altman)

TWO TRAINS RUNNING. By August Wilson, in the Yale Repertory Theater production. October 26, 1990. Director, Lloyd Richards; scenery, Tony Fanning; lighting, Geoff Korf; costumes, Chrisi Karvonides.

Memphis . . . . Al White
Wolf . . . . Anthony Chisholm
Risa . . . . Ella Joyce
Holloway . . . . Ed Hall
Hambone . . . . Sullivan Walker
Sterling . . . . Jonathan Earl Peck
West. . . . . Chuck Patterson
Time: 1969. Place: Lee's Restaurant in the Hill District of Pittsburgh. One intermission. (An ATCA selection; see introduction to this section).

Bristol, Pa.: Bristol Riverside Theater

(Artistic Director, Susan D. Atkinson)

MALICE AFORETHOUGHT. By Erik Jendresen. November 1, 1990. Director, Frederick Rolf; scenery, Bart Healy; lighting, Dean Seabrook; costumes, Bradford Wood, Gregory A. Poplyk.
Paul. . . . . Chad Restum
Nicole . . . . Elaine Princi
Graham. . . . . Randell Haynes
Kramer. . . . . Morton Banks
Feinsod. . . . . Frank Collins
Fitzhugh. . . . . John Wool
One intermission.

Cambridge, Mass.: American Repertory Theater

(Artistic director, Robert Brustein)

POWER FAILURE. By Larry Gelbart. Director, Michael Engler; scenery, Philipp Jung; lighting, Natasha Katz; costumes, Candice Donnelly.
Will; Snow; Graves . . . . . Christopher Lloyd
Coyne; Keene . . . . Christine Estabrook
Billings; Armor . . . . David Margulies
Worth. . . . . Jeremy Geidt
Myra . . . . Candy Buckley
Little . . . . Thomas Derrah
Time and Place: Several cities in America, over a period of several months.

THE WRITING GAME. By David Lodge. March 16, 1991. Director, Michael Bloom; scenery, Bill Clarke; lighting, Richard Riddell; costumes, Ellen McCartney; sound, Maribeth Back.

Jeremy Deane . . . . Jerry Pavlon
Leo Rafkin . . . . David Margulies
Maude Lockett. . . . . . . Christine Estabrook
Voice of Henry Lockett . . . . . Jeremy Geidt
Penny Sewell . . . . Yanna McIntosh
Simon St. Clair . . . . Steven Skybell

STEEL. Book and lyrics by Derek Walcott, music by Galt MacDermot. April 14, 1991. Director, Derek Walcott; choreography and musical staging, Mary Barnett; musical direction, Galt MacDermot; scenery, Richard Montgomery;

lighting, Richard Riddell; costumes, Catherine Zuber; sound, Maribeth Back; produced in association with American Music Theater Festival.

With Norman Matlock, Leon Morenzie, Debra Byrd, Mansur, Jahneen, Lisa Vidal, Edwin Louis Battle, Ron Bobb-Semple, Michael Starr, Patric Lacroix, Larry Marshall, P.J. Adamson, Ras Iginga, Joseph Siravo, Candy Buckley, Roderick Dudley, Celeste Ciulla, Brigette Dunn, Margarita Taylor.

One intermission.

Chicago: Goodman Theater

(Artistic director, Robert Falls; producing director, Roche Schulfer)

DEEP IN A DREAM OF YOU. By David Cale. February 4, 1991. Director, David Petrarca; music, Roy Nathanson; scenery, Linda Buchanan; sound, Rob Milburn.
Performer . . . . David Cale

Tenor, Alto and
  Soprano Saxophones . . . . . . Roy Nathanson
Bass . . . . Bradley Jones
Cello . . . . Laura Blanchet, Sara Wollan
Percussion. . . . . E.J. Rodriguez

Chicago: Northlight Theater

(Artistic director, Russell Vandenbroucke; managing director, Jeffrey Woodward)

ELEANOR: IN HER OWN WORDS. Adapted from the writings of Eleanor Roosevelt by Russell Vandenbroucke. October 3, 1990. Director, Russell Vandenbroucke; scenery, James Maronek; lighting, Rita Pietraszek; costumes, Gayland Spaulding; sound, Joseph F. Cerqua.
Eleanor Roosevelt . . . . Lois Markle
  Voices: Bradley Armacost, Saralynne Crittenden, Ellen Jane Smith, Kraig Swartz.
  One intermission.

UNCOMMON GROUND. By Jeremy Lawrence. January 9, 1991. Director, Gwen Arner; scenery, Michael Philippi; lighting, Linda Essig; costumes, Jessica Hahn; sound, Joseph F. Cerqua.
Alexsander Karpowicz . . . . . Donald Moffat
Marat; Josef . . . . Christopher Pieczynski
Nathan Freund; The Man;
  Minister of the Interior. . . . . . David Downs
Eric Morgenstern; Stainslaw
  Czabanski . . . . Ned Schmidtke

Lillian Morgenstern . . . . Lauren Charles
Rita Stricker; Babcia . . . . Lorna Raver
Jenny Simpson . . . . Anna Kathryn Gunn
Guards; Secret Police . . . . . . Michael Rohd,
                             Michael McNeal
Time and Place: New York City and Poland during the years 1967-68 and 1976. The play also takes place in Alexsander's memories of the years 1936 through 1952. One intermission.

WOODY GUTHRIE'S AMERICAN SONG. Musical revue by Peter Glazer, adapted from the songs and writings of Woody Guthrie. April 10, 1991. Director, Peter Glazer; choreography, Jennifer Martin; musical direction, Malcolm Ruhl; scenery, Philipp Jung; lighting, David Noling; costumes, Baker S. Smith; sound, Rick Netter.

Wtih Brian Gunter, Ora Jones, Susan Moniz, John Reeger, Christopher Walz.

Chicago: Organic Theater Company

(Artistic director, Richard Fire; executive director, Richard Friedman)

THE MURDERER. By Jack Clark and Bob Meyer. October 24, 1990. Director, Bob Meyer; scenery and lighting, Randy Buescher. With Consuelo Allen, Vito Bitondo, Amelia Buescher, Randy Buescher, Suellen Burton, Thomas Carroll, Michael Cates, Charles Clement, Paul Connel, Caroline Cygan, Peter DeFaria, Ben Harrison, Elyssia Jackson Hatch, Joy Jones, Katy Jones, Bob Kohut, Nicole Luzietti, Noel Olken,

Jim Ortlieb, Robin Rauch, Janet Roderick, Wendy Goldman Rohm, John Clayton Schafer, Rose Spinelli, Martin Stewart.

AMERICAN ENTERPRISE. By Jeffrey Sweet. February 14, 1991. Director, Wesley Savick; scenery, Richard and Jacqueline Penrod; lighting, Kevin Snow; costumes, Yslan Hicks.
George Pullman . . . . Gary Houston

J. Patrick Hopkins . . . . Larry Russo
George Jr.;
   Rev. E.C. Oggel . . . . . Michael A. Krawic
Eugene V. Debs . . . . Juan Ramirez
Governor John P. Altgeld; Mary
   Carter Harrison; Supervisor . . . . Phillip East
Stephens; Harahan; Wright . . . . . L.D. Barrett
Thomas Wickes;
   Commissioner Worthington. . . . Peter Garino

Jackson; Beman . . . . Edmund Wyson
Richard T. Ely. . . . . Colin K. Jones
Heathcote . . . . Chris Farrell
Clayton . . . . McKinley Johnson
Jennie Curtis . . . . Tonray Ho
Florence Pullman . . . . Paula Harrigan
Mrs. Kelsey; Soloist . . . . Jamie O'Reilly

Chicago: Second City

(Artistic director, Joyce Sloane)

WINNER TAKES OIL. Musical comedy revue (the group's 74th) written by the cast. April 24, 1991. Director, Tom Gianas; choreography, Jim Corti; musical direction, Ruby Streak; scenery and lighting, Craig Taylor; additional set design, Aaron Rhodes; sound, Mike Konopka.
   With Cynthia Caponera, Tim O'Malley, Steven Carell, John Rubano, Michael McCarthy, Jill Talley, Ron West.
   One intermission.

Chicago: Steppenwolf Theater Company

(Artistic director, Randall Arney; managing director, Stephen B. Eich)

WRONG TURN AT LUNGFISH. By Garry Marshall and Lowell Ganz. June 17, 1990. Director, Garry Marshall; scenery, Michael Merritt; lighting, Kevin Rigdon; costumes, Erin Quigley; sound, Richard Woodbury.
Peter Ravenswaal . . . . John Mahoney

Nurse . . . . Mariann Mayberry
Anita Merendino . . . . Laurie Metcalf
Dominic De Caesar . . . . Tim Hopper
   Time: The present. Place: A hospital room somewhere in New York City. One intermission.

Chicago: Wisdom Bridge Theater

(Producing director, Jeffrey Ortmann)

SOFT REMEMBRANCE. By Sol Saks. July 11, 1990. Director, Arnie Saks; scenery and lighting, Michael S. Philippi; costumes, Lynn Sandberg; sound, Robert Neuhaus.
Mike Banlon . . . . Malachy McCourt
Sam Green. . . . . Byrne Piven
Mrs. Banlon . . . . Linda Stephens
Mrs. Green. . . . . Etel Billig
Morty; Silent Cop . . . . Fredric Stone
Priest . . . . Gerry Becker
Dorothy. . . . . Rengin Altay
Caroline. . . . . Erin Creighton
   One intermission.

THE GREAT GATSBY. By John Carlile, adapted from the F. Scott Fitzgerald novel. April 19, 1991. Director, John Carlile; scenery, John Murbach; lighting, Peter Gottlieb; costumes, Claudia Boddy; incidental music, Evan Chen.
Nick Carraway . . . . Alan Ruck
Jay Gatsby . . . . Harry J. Lennix
Daisy Buchanan. . . . . Kate Goehring
Tom Buchanan . . . . Si Osborne
   One intermission.

Cincinnati: Cincinnati Playhouse in the Park

(Artistic director, Worth Gardner)

LOST ELECTRA. By Bruce E. Rodgers. May 16, 1991. Director, Margaret Booker; scenery, Joseph P. Tilford; lighting, Kirk Bookman; costumes, Scott Chambliss; sound, David Smith.

With Frank Muller, Brian David Price, Jacqueline Knapp, Kathleen Marsh, Paul Hebron.
   One intermission.

GOODMAN THEATER, CHICAGO—The entire cast of the world premiere production of *Deep in a Dream of You* by David Cale *(center).*

Cleveland: The Cleveland Play House

(Artistic director, Josephine R. Abady)

HEART'S DESIRE. Book by Stuart Dybek, Beverly Lowry, Armistead Maupin and Treva Silverman; music and lyrics by Glen Roben. October 9, 1990. Director, Jack Hofsiss; musical direction, Henry Aronson; choreography, Jerry Mitchell; scenery, Kevin Rigdon; lighting, Beverly Emmons; costumes, Michael Krass; sound, Jeffrey Montgomerie.

With Mary Gordon Murray, James Clow, Evan Pappas, Bradford Minkoff, Dana Moore, Jack Noseworthy, Lannyl Stephens, Cass Morgan, Marji Dodrill, Elaine Wright, Larry K. Collis, Roxane Barlow, David Davalos, Angelo H. Fraboni, Sara Beth Lane, Stephanie Pierce, Eric Porter, Kristie Tice, Sergio Trujillo, Rocker Verastique.

One intermission.

BRAVO, CARUSO! By William Luce. January 8, 1991. Director, Peter Mark Schifter; scenery, David Potts; lighting, Ann G. Wrightson; costumes, C.L. Hundley; sound, Jeffrey Montgomerie.

Mario Fantini . . . . Joseph R. Sicari
Enrico Caruso . . . . Joseph Mascolo
  One intermission

In repertory February 10, 1991:

BY THE POOL. By Stewart Conn. Director, Josephine R. Abady; scenery, David Potts; lighting, Richard Winkler; costumes, C.L. Hundley. With Angela Thornton, Robert Murch, Tonia Rowe, Tyrone Wilson, Laura Gardner, Bill Cwikowski, Walter Hudson.

One intermission.

SAY ZEBRA. By Sherry Conan. Director, Michael Breault; scenery, David Potts; lighting, Richard Winkler; costumes, C.L. Hundley. With Toni Ann Johnson, Walter Hudson, Tyrone Wilson, Tonia Rowe, Laura Gardner, Bill Cwikowski, Nikita Glover, Ebani Edwards, Leilani Barrett, Tusiimee Jackson, Akanna Thomas, Camille Harvey, Karena Farris, Gloria Ross, LeChone Salter, John Jacobs.

One intermission.

Cleveland: Cleveland Public Theater

(Artistic director, James A. Levin)

TALKING POLITICS. By Geralyn Horton; director, Christine Sell, and MAKE WAY FOR DYKLINGS by Aubrey Wertheim, director, Amanda Shaffer. February 7, 1991. Scenery, R. C. Naso; lighting, Michael Murray; costumes, Elizabeth Gardner; sound, Christopher Shimp.
Talking Politics

Peggy . . . . Linda Mason
Mitsuko . . . . Toni Dell
Clorinda . . . . Nancy Burkinshaw
Critic . . . . Vincent Taylor-Hart
Make Way for Dyklings
Loretta . . . . Kim Kohler
Sandra . . . . Carolyn Kmiek
Spender . . . . Christopher Shimp
Carter; 1st Male Bowler. . . . . . Sean Powers
T.X.; 2d Male Bowler . . . . . Allen Branstein
1st Woman Bowler; Janice. . . . . . Toni Dell
2d Woman Bowler; Robbie . Nancy Burkinshaw
Video Woman . . . . Linda Mason
Pool Player. . . . . Andrew Kaletta

STREET SENSE (opera based on the five senses: *The Sighting, Manuel's Tongue, The Touch of an Angel, Yet Another Girl Named Maria, The Man Who Stole a Smell).* Libretto by Migdalia Cruz; music by Linda Eisenstein. May 2, 1991. Director, Stephen Pickover; musical direction, Scott Myers; scenery, David Ellison, John Rivera-Resto; lighting, Dennis Dugan; costumes, Terri Gelzer, Vanne J. Furlan; sound, Christopher Shimp.

With Kirk Anderson, Angeles Martinez-Casado, Eileen Marie Moore, Tafee Patterson, Darnell Suttles, Troy Tinker. Musicians: Karen E. Bull, Gerald E. Evans, Jeramy Bleich, Linda Thomas-Jones.

9th Festival of New Plays: January 11-27, 1991
WHO COOKS FOR YOU ALL? By Michael Geither. Director, Paul Moser.
KITCHEN TABLE U. Constructed by Yvetta and K.J. Warren; contributions by Andika, Yvetta, Linda Thomas-Jones, Kenyette Adrine-Robinson.
DON THE WORKING MAN. By Richard A. Gaeta. Director, Jane Latman.
ATAHUALPA DOES TIME. By Masha Mildon. Director, James Slowiak.
RESUSCITATION OF A TRINITY. By Shanna Beth McGee. Director, Beverly Wykoff.
PABLO AND CLEOPATRA. By Rosanna Yamagiwa Alfaro. Director, Jane Armitage.
MAXIMUM TUMESCENCE: A TRIPTYCH OF THE GEOMETRY OF LOVE. By Ed SantaVicca. Director, Alan Trethewey.
THE MISSION ROMANCE and FAREWELL TO HOLLYWOOD. By Guillermo Reyes. Director, Paul Floriano.
4:15. By Peter Manos. Director, Harriett Logan.
THE BEAN PICKER. By Peter Manos. Director, Alec Rubin.
DOOMSDAY. By Craig Strasshofer. Director, Michael Salinger.
MOTOWN AT THE MOON PALACE. By Christine Child. Director, Amanda Shaffer.
THE DISMAY OF OUR LIVES. By Bob Vance. Director, Susan Speers.
LETTERS HOME. By Bob Vance. Director, Bill Modic.

Festival director, Linda Eisenstein; dramaturg, James A. Levin; lighting, Leslie Moynihan.

Cleveland: Great Lakes Theater Festival

(Artistic Director, Gerald Freedman; managing director, Mary Bill)

THE OHIO STATE MURDERS. By Adrienne Kennedy. June 16, 1990. Director, Gerald Freedman; scenery and projections, Kurt Sharp; lighting, Cynthia Stillings; costumes, Susan Bakula; sound, Stan Kozak.
Suzanne Alexander (present) . . Hazel J. Medina
Suzanne (1949, 1950, 1951) . . . Bellary Darden
David Alexander; Suzanne's
  Father; Val . . . . Marcus Naylor
Robert Hampshire . . . . Allan Byrne
Iris Ann . . . . Leslie Holland
Miss D; Aunt Louise;
  Mrs. Tyler . . . . Edythe Davis
  Time: The present, night, winter. Place: The

stacks on O Level beneath the library at Ohio State. No intermission. (An ATCA selection; see introduction to this section.)

DIVIDING THE ESTATE. By Horton Foote. October 13, 1990. Director, Gerald Freedman; scenery, John Ezell; lighting, Mary Jo Dondlinger; costumes, Al Kohout; sound, Stan Kozak. With Elizabeth Atkeson, Erma Campbell, Bellary Darden, Jack Davidson, Elizabeth Franz, Jennifer Harmon, Annalee Jeffries, Brian Keeler, Nan Martin, Logan Ramsey, Christine Segal, W. Benson Terry, Lucinda Underwood.
  One intermission.

Costa Mesa, Calif.: South Coast Repertory

(Producing artistic director, David Emmes; artistic director, Martin Benson)

ALEKHINE'S DEFENSE. By Robert Daseler. November 9, 1990. Director, Eli Simon; scenery, Cliff Faulkner; lighting, Peter Maradudin; costumes, Sylvia Vega-Vasquez.

Alan	Robert Sicular
June	Julie Fulton
Hal	Don Took

Time: The present. Place: The patio of a single-story Southern California home. One intermission.

PIRATES. By Mark W. Lee. January 11, 1991. Director, Martin Benson; scenery, Marjorie Bradley Kellogg; lighting, Tom Ruzika; costumes, Walker Hicklin; music and sound, Michael Roth; fight director, Kristina Lankford.

Jack Rackham; Nathan Taylor	Robert Sicular
Anne Bonney	Katherin Cortez
Helen Raymond	Joan McMurtrey
Stewart Crawley; Isaac Fletcher; Porterfield	Richard Doyle
Michael Dobbs; Captain; Soldier; Parson	Larry Paulsen
Cafeteria Worker; Rebecca Skolnik; Mary Read	Katherine Hiler

Time and Place: The Caribbean during the early 18th century and at a contemporary American university. One intermission.

EL DORADO. By Milcha Sanchez-Scott. April 19, 1991. Director, Peter C. Brosius; scenery, Loy Arcenas; lighting, Peter Maradudin; costumes, Lydia Tanji; music and sound, Michael Roth.

Sonsita	Christine Avila
Nestor	Michael Cerveris

Indians; Soldiers; Orderlies; Construction Workers; Rebels	Anthony Hernandez, Bernardo Rosa Jr.
Inez	Joan Stuart-Morris
Julio	George Ede
President	Julian Gamble
Michael	David Hayward
Sister Ann	Karen Landry

Place: A mythical South American country. One intermission.

Staged Readings:

A DREAM OF WEALTH by Arthur Giron.
FLOORSHOW: DONNA SOL AND HER TRAINED DOG by Edwin Sanchez.
PROSPECT by Octavio Solis.
THE NEWS FROM PUERTO RICO by Jack Agueros.
SCARLET MACAW by Bernardo Solano.
GLEANING/REBUSCA by Caridad Svich.

Staged Readings from New Scripts Series:

THINGS BEING WHAT THEY ARE by Wendy MacLeod.
EL DORADO by Milcha Sanchez-Scott.
BOUNDARY WATERS by Barbara Field.
THE EXTRA MAN by Richard Greenberg.
CUSTER'S LAST BAND by Abe Polsky.

Staged Readings from California Play Festival:

NOAH JOHNSON HAD A WHORE by Jon Bastian.
LA ILLUMINATA by Octavio Solis.
SHOW AND TELL by Anthony Clarvoe.

Dallas: Dallas Theater Center

(Artistic director, Ken Bryant; managing director, Jeff West)

HIS UNCONQUERABLE ENEMY. By W.C. Morrow. December 4, 1990. Adapted and directed by Bill Bolender; scenery, Tristan Wilson; lighting, Russell H. Champa; costumes, Donna M. Kress.

Doctor; Narrator	Sean Hennigan
The Rajah	Kurt Rhoads
Neranya	Michael A. Massari
Musician	Buddy Mohmed
The Man	Price Carson
The Woman	Erin Hawley

Time and place: India, 1910.

Denver: The Changing Scene

(Founders, Maxine Munt and Alfred Brooks)

HYAENA. By Ross MacLean. January 10, 1991. Director, Tricia Stevens; scenery, Rennick Stevenson; lighting, Sue Griffiths; costumes, Tricia Stevens.

Hyaena	Curt Pesicka
Patient	Tony Catanese
Wife	Toni Brady
Friend	Andrew Pollet
Nurse	Kendra White

One intermission.

THE CHERRY ORCHARD, PART II. By William M. Hoffman and Anthony Holland. April 18, 1991. Director, Steven St. James; scenery, Rennick Stevenson; lighting, Steven Eagleburger; costumes, Tricia Stevens; sound, Chuck Rhodes.

Firs Nikolayevich . . . . Otto Rieth
Irina Sergeyevna Prozorova . . Diane Buglewicz

Countess Vera Semyonova
  Danchencko . . . . Tere Edelen
Lev Davidovich Zibershtayn . . . Michael Roark
Yermolai Alexeyevich
  Lopakhin. . . . . Mark Lawrence
Mishka. . . . . Kevin Smith
Vilis Vilisovich Rittmanis . . . . . Dan Wiley
Agafia. . . . . Elizabeth Rose
One intermission.

Denver: Denver Center Theater Company

(Artistic director, Donovan Marley)

NEW BUSINESS. By Tom Williams. May 15, 1991. Director, Steven Dietz; scenery, Richard Hay; lighting, Charles MacLeod; costumes, Janet S. Morris.

Jerry Stewart . . . . Jeffrey Combs
Maxwell Greene . . . . James J. Lawless
Lisa Kane . . . . Leslie Hendrix
Rose . . . . Kathleen Brady-Garvin
Larry "Wooly" Pulaski. . James Michael Connor
Stevie McGlynn . . . . . Jacqueline Antaramian
Sid Holloway . . . . Jim Baker
Charles Hartman . . . . Stephen Lee Anderson
GRZBD . . . . Michael X. Martin
KNSTR . . . . Dee Maaske

BACK TO THE BLANKET. By Gary Leon Hill. May 17, 1991. Director, Roberta Levitow; scenery, lighting, and costumes, Pavel Dobrusky; sound, Scott R. Bradford.

James Moody. . . . . Jamie Horton
Major . . . . Ron Headlee
Major's Daughter . . . . Suzanne Fountain
Dr. Charles Western . . . . . Randolph Mantooth
Agent Roper . . . . Robert Eustace
Winona Marsh . . . . Kamella Tate

Sweet Lumps. . . . . Laura Vega
Buffalo Soldier. . . . . Harvy Blanks
  Ensemble: Robert Standley, Scott McKinstry, Vincent C. Robinson

JUNK BONDS. By Thomas Babe. May 28, 1991. Director, Anthony Powell; scenery and costumes, Andrew V. Yelusich; lighting, Daniel L. Murray; sound, Scott R. Bradford.

Joe . . . . Michael Ian Schwartz
Bobbie . . . . Matthew Vipond
Sylvia . . . . Chelsea Altman
Mrs. Elizabeth Rostenkowski . . . . Suzy Hunt
Mr. George
  Rostenkowiski . . . . . William M. Whitehead
A Cop. . . . . Jeffery Paul Reid

OKIBOJI. By Conrad Bishop and Elizabeth Fuller. May 30, 1991. Director, Frank Georgianna; scenery, Richard Hay; lighting, Charles MacLeod; costumes, Laura K. Love; sound, Daniel R. McLaughlin.

Mag . . . . Dee Maaske
Rae . . . . Kay Doubleday

Detroit: Detroit Repertory Theater

(Artistic/managing director, Bruce E. Millan)

LOVER'S COVE: A CONSPIRACY OF SILENCE. By Frederick St. John. May 16, 1991. Director, William Boswell; scenery, Robert Katkowski; lighting, Kenneth R. Hewitt Jr.; costumes, B.J. Essen; sound, Burr Huntington.

Beth . . . . Dee Andrus
Jessica . . . . Annie Cross
Doc; Jim . . . . Andrew Dunn

Stritch. . . . . Tom Emmott
Randy . . . . David L. Glover
Marcy . . . . Stacey Herring
Jud . . . . Rob Rucker
Fred. . . . . John W. Pulchalski
  Time: Present and then some. Place: A grove on top of a hill not far from town. One intermission.

Dorset, Vt.: Dorset Theater Festival

(Artistic director, Jill Charles; producing director, John Nassivera)

ADVICE FROM A CATERPILLAR. By Douglas Carter Beane. August 23, 1990. Director, Edgar Lansbury; scenery, William John

Aupperlee; lighting and sound, Jeffrey Bernstein; costumes, Eric Hansen.

Missie . . . . Jennie Moreau
Suit . . . . Harley Vinton
Spaz . . . . Eric Swanson

Brat . . . . Michael Liani
One intermission.

Hartford, Conn.: Hartford Stage

(Artistic director, Mark Lamos; managing director, David Hawkanson)

THE MASTER BUILDER. By Henrik Ibsen. New translation by Gerry Bamman and Irene B. Berman. December 29, 1990. Director, Mark Lamos; scenery, Marjorie Bradley Kellogg; lighting, Pat Collins; costumes, Jess Goldstein; sound, David Budries.

Knut Brovik . . . . Jack Bittner
Kaja Fosli . . . . Tracey Ellis
Ragnar Brovik . . . . Mark Nelson
Halvard Solness . . . . Sam Waterston
Aline Solness . . . . Veronica Cartwright
Dr. Herdal . . . . Frederick Neumann
Hilde Wangel . . . . Cynthia Nixon
  Townspeople: Denise Joughin Casey, Claire Cousineau, Peggy Johnson, Pauline Bruce Thompson.
  One intermission.

THE SNOW BALL. By A.R. Gurney. February

9, 1991. Director, Jack O'Brien; scenery, Douglas W. Schmidt; lighting, David F. Segal; costumes, Steven Rubin; sound, Jeff Ladman.

Cooper Jones . . . . James R. Winker
Lucy Dunbar . . . . Kandis Chappel
Liz Jones . . . . Katherine McGrath
Van Dam; Baldwin Hall . . . . Tom Lacy
Young Jack . . . . Christopher Wells
Young Kitty . . . . Susan J. Coon
Saul Radner . . . . Robert Phalen
Joan Daley . . . . Deborah Taylor
Jack Daley . . . . Donald Wayne
Kitty Price. . . . . Rita Gardner
  Various Members of the Community as Children and Adults: Mary R. Barnett, Terrence Caza, Brian John Driscoll, Cynthia D. Hanson, Robert Phalen, Mimi Quillin, Deborah Taylor, John Thomas Waite.
  One intermission.

HARTFORD STAGE—Susan J. Coon and Christopher Wells in the rhumba scene of A.R. Gurney's *The Snow Ball*

Houston: AD Players

(Artistic director, Jeannette Clift George)

ROWENA. By Jeannette Clift George. November 29, 1990. Director, Jeannette Clift George, Sissy Pulley; scenery, Don Hollenbeck Jr.; lighting, Sissy Pulley; costumes, Patty Tuel Bailey.

Rowena . . . . Debra Paget
Eloise . . . . Deborah Eckols
Drake. . . . . , ... Larry Balfe
Acting Ensemble . . . . . Sherry Joy Rathbun,
Marion Arthur Kirby
Time: A span of 20 years. One intermission.

THE CELEBRANT. Adapted from the Charles Turner novel by Lisa Armstrong. February 14, 1991. Director, Larry Balfe; scenery, Robert Howery; lighting, Dan Flahive; sound, Christopher Dunn.
Louis Schuyler. . . . . Don Hollenbeck Jr.
Helen Schuyler;
Miss Alberson. . . . . . . Susan Guthrie Dunn
Monty Schuyler;
Dr. William Dalzell . . . . . Christopher Dunn
Winifred Pell; Sister Constance;
Sister Frances . . . . Sherry Joy Rathbun
Father Benson; Dr. Tschiffeley;
Nurse . . . . Ric Hodgin

Mrs. Moffat; Sister Ruth . . . . . Sharla Boyce
Father Sword; Dr. Smith. . . . . . Dan Flahive
Mother Harriet. . . . . Barbara Jenkins
Sister Catherine; Fern . . . . Angela Turley
Mrs. Potts; Sister Hughetta;
Madame Annie;
Cook . . . . Elizabeth Pentak Averill
Dr. Houghton;
Dean George Harris . . . Marion Arthur Kirby
Bishop Charles Quintard . . . . Eric Moore
Father James Wheatley;
Dr. Bob. . . . . John Picciuto
Dr. Montgomery Schuyler;
Mr. Alberson . . . . Jerry Averill
Conductor; Baptist Doctor . . . . Robb Brunson
Young Lady on Train;
Sister Thecla; Cora . . . . Connie Embesi
Red-Headed Woman; Sister
Clare; Miss Randolph . . . . Carol Dougherty
Mrs. Bulloch. . . . . Barbara Jenkins
Jack . . . . Eric Moore
Time: Two weeks in the summer of 1978. Place: The play reflects, through dreams, memories and reality, the times, people and events in Louis Schuyler's journey. One intermission.

Houston: Alley Theater

(Artistic director, Gregory Boyd)

JEKYLL & HYDE. Book and lyrics by Leslie Bricusse; music by Frank Wildhorn; adapted from Robert Louis Stevenson. June 1990. Director, Gregory Boyd; choreography, Jerry Mitchell; scenery, Peter David Gould; lighting, Robert Jared; costumes, V. Jane Suttell; sound, Karl Richardson.
Sir Danvers Carew. . . . . . . Edmund Lyndeck
Henry Jekyll . . . . Chuck Wagner
Poole . . . . Eddie Korbich
Prince Michael. . . . . . . Martin van Treuren
Simon Stride . . . . Bill Nolte
Utterson . . . . Philip Hoffman
Lisa . . . . Rebecca Spencer
Gen. Glossop. . . . . Bob Wrenn
Bishop of Basingstoke . . . . . Dave Clemmons
Sir Archibald Proops . . . . Bob Zolli
Lady Beaconsfield . . . . Lee Merrill
Lord Savage . . . . Tug Wilson
Nellie . . . . Nita Moore
Lucy. . . . . Linda Eder
One intermission.

THE CZAR OF ROCK & ROLL. Book by Rand Foerster; music and lyrics by Rusty Magee. December 1990. Director, Rand Foerster;

scenery, Jay Michael Jagim; lighting, Christina Giannelli; costumes, Deborah Rosenberg; sound, Kevin Dunayer.
Martin . . . . Jeffrey Bean
Zeena . . . . Mary Hooper
Eugene . . . . Brian Sutherland
Mel; Ollie North; The Elk . . . . Charles Sanders
Dasha. . . . . Karen Trott
Bulba . . . . Anderson Matthews
Lupe; Wardrobe Mistress. . . . Laurie Galluccio
Eva . . . . Deborah Graham

SVENGALI. Book by Gregory Boyd; lyrics by John Bettis, Gregory Boyd and Frank Wildhorn; music by Frank Wildhorn. April 3, 1991. Director, Gregory Boyd; scenery, Jerome Sirlin; lighting, Howell Binkley; costumes, V. Jane Suttell; sound, Karl Richardson.
Svengali. . . . . Chuck Wagner
Gecko . . . . Philip Hoffman
Mme. Poussin . . . . Marty Simpson
Mme. Desmoulins;
Mme. Durian; Mme. Vinard . . . Sarah Knapp
Talbot Wynne . . . . Gerald Hiken
Alexander McAllister . . . . . Noble Shropshire
Model. . . . . Gage Tarrant

Trilby . . . . Linda Eder
Billie . . . . Dave Clemmons
Zou Zou . . . . Bjorn Johnson
Fabre; Impresario. . . . . John Feltch
Gaspardi; Impresario . . . . Jeffrey Bean
Herr Meinigen . . . . Tug Wilson
Dodor . . . . Peter Webster
Waiter; Philippe . . . . Jonathan Allore
Two Poets. . . . . Laurence Ruffo, Jon Hawkins
Two Policemen. . . . Peter Webster, John Feltch
Functionary. . . . . Tug Wilson

Two House Detectives . . . . . Peter Webster,
                                    John Feltch
Doctor . . . . Peter Webster
Four Ladies: Laurie Galluccio, Gage Tarrant,
Monique Maley, Marty Simpson. Four Grisettes:
Gage Tarrant, Monique Maley, Marty Simpson,
Laurie Galluccio.
Time and place: Act I: Paris, and then a small
provincial theater, 1894. Act II: Five years later.

Houston: Stages Repertory Theater

(Artistic director, Peter Bennett)

TALKING PICTURES. By Horton Foote. May
3, 1991. Director, Peter Masterson; scenery, Jay
Michael Jagim; lighting, Jerry Ford; costumes,
Nanette Griffin; sound, Darryl Akin.
Gerard Anderson . . . . . . Big Skinny Brown
Ashenback. . . . . Rutherford Cravens
Katie Bell . . . . Nicole Feenstra
Gladys . . . . Annalee Jefferies

Vesta . . . . Martha Mazeika
Pete . . . . Nick Merritt
Mr. Jackson . . . . Patrick Mitchell
Willis . . . . James Hansen Price
Myra . . . . Barbara Sims
Mrs. Jackson . . . . Ellen Swenson
Estaquio . . . . John Valasquez
One intermission.

Indianapolis: Indiana Repertory Theater

(Associate artistic director, Janet Allen; managing director, Victoria Nolan)

TALES FROM OLYMPUS. By Tom Evans.
March 26, 1991. Director, Linda Atkinson;
scenery and costumes, Jennifer Q. Smith; lighting
and sound, Martha Mountain.
   Horace; Zeus—Bob Berry. Latona; Servant #1;
Hera; Glamour—Connie Oates. Hera; Clymene—

Lynne Perkins. Rustic; Polichus; Computer;
Mercury; Vertumnus—Rick Walters. Rustic
Horse; Io; Pomona—Constance Macy. Rustic;
Phaethon; Argus; Cycle—Tif Luckenbill. Apollo;
Zeus—David Alan Anderson

Jackson City, Tenn.: The Road Company

(Artistic director, Robert H. Leonard; general manager, Linda Kesler)

A PREACHER WITH A HORSE TO RIDE. By
Jo Carson. December 13, 1990. Director, David
Johnson; scenery, Randy Ingram; lighting, Lee-
Zen M. Chen; costumes, Cheri Vasek.
George Black. . . . . Lawrence Adams
Hearing Monologue. . . . . . . Sharon Adams
Cecil Powers . . . . William V. Blevins
Marie . . . . Aimee M. Bruneau
John Dos Passos . . . . Pete Burris
George Sweet. . . . . Bill Cave
H.J. Blair . . . . Doug Chancey
Militia Man . . . . Bill Counts
Girl Who Sings #1. . . . . Sharon Marie Denson
Jeff Caldwell. . . . . Barry Ellenberger
Callaway Hobbs . . . . Ted Farmer
Jimmy Caldwell; Elizabeth Wilson . Peg Gannon
Theodore Dreiser. . . . . Bill Ogilvie
Hershel Lilly . . . . Frank Taylor
Molly Jackson . . . . . . Elizabeth McCommon
Hoit Bessman . . . . . . William W. Richardson

Jeff Caldwell. . . . . Barry Ellenberger
New Secreatary . . . . Suzen Haller
Helen . . . . Sioux Madden
Woman Who Will Not
   Say Her Name . . . . Lynn Marie
Girl Who Sings #2 . . . . Melissa Munson
Reporter . . . . Cary Nothnagel
Preacher . . . . W. Scott Self
Adam Karp. . . . . Howard Simpson
Paul Foot . . . . Todd Whitson
One intermission.

DESCENT TO THE GODDESS. By Amy
Appleyard, Emily Green, Sheila A. Malone, Ellen
Norris Spencer and Ginger West. March 5, 1991.
Director, Emily Green; scenery, Linda
Benemann; lighting, Amy Appleyard, Sheila A.
Malone.
   With Amy Appleyard, Sheila A. Malone, Ellen
Norris Spencer, Ginger West.

INDIANA REPERTORY THEATER, INDIANAPOLIS—Tif Luckenbill as Phaethon and David Alan Anderson in a scene from *Tales From Olympus* by Tom Evans

Kansas City: Missouri Repertory Theater

(Artistic director, George Keathley)

LIVING IN EXILE. By Jon Lipsky, music by Stephen Cummings. January 31, 1991. Director, Mary G. Guaraldi; scenery, Gary S. Mosby; lighting, Rob Murphy; costumes, Rebecca S. Larson; co-produced by Unicorn Theater (Cynthia Lewis, artistic director).

Patroklos	Phil Fiorini
Achilles	Larry Greer
Agammemnon	Robert Elliott
Briseis	Cynthia Hyer

One intermission.

La Jolla, Calif.: La Jolla Playhouse

(Artistic director, Des McAnuff; managing director, Alan Levey)

LIFE DURING WARTIME. By Keith Reddin. June 19, 1990. Director, Les Waters; scenery, Loy Arcenas; lighting, Stephen Strawbridge; costumes, David C. Woolard; sound, John Kilgore.

Heinrich	Stephen Markle
Sally	Colette Kilroy
Tommy	Josh Hamilton
John Calvin	Tony Amendola
Gale	Leslie Lyles
Howard; Delivery Boy	Talbert Morton
Walter; Richie	Jefferson Mays
Fielding; Lt. Waters; DeVries	Tony Amendola
Mrs. Fielding	Colette Kilroy
Megan	Kari McGee

One intermission.

DON QUIXOTE DE LA JOLLA. By Eric Overmyer. August 7, 1990. Director, Stan Wojewodski Jr.; scenery, Neil Patel; lighting, Stephen Strawbridge; costumes, Christine Dougherty; sound, James LeBrecht.

Don Quixote	Geoff Hoyle
The Band	Bina Leishman
Sancho Panza	Robert Dorfman
Dulcinea	Ellen McElduff
A Boy	Jonah Hoyle

Los Angeles: East West Players

(Literary manager, Dick Dotterer)

SONGS OF HARMONY. By Karen Huie. October 17, 1990. Director, Heidi Helen Davis; scenery and lighting, Rae Creevey; costumes, Dori Quan.

Mr. Song	Rodney Kageyama
Mrs. Song	Cici Lau
Elaine Song	Lauren Tom
Emily Song	Kimiko Gelman
Susanne Song Anderson	Nancy Long
Wellington Yes	Francois Chau

DOUGHBALL. By Perry Miyake. Director, Patricia S. Yasutake; scenery and lighting, Rae Creevey; costumes, Diane J. Winesburg.

George	Henry Hayashi
Tammy	Jill Ito
Yuki	Alice Kushida
Andrea	Lissa Ling Lee
Vicky	Marlo Miyashiro
Wayne	Craig Ng
Eric	Yuji Okumoto
David	Steve Park
Mits	Michael Shibata
Frank	Ken Takemoto
Melinda	Patricia Ayame Thomson

Time: Christmas, 1990 and the summer of 1970. Place: Venice, California. One intermission.

CANTON JAZZ CLUB. Book by Dom Magwili; lyrics by Tim Dang, music by Nathan Wang and Joel Iwataki. Director, Tim Dang; scenery, Gronk; lighting, Jose Lopez; costumes, Terence Tam Soon.

Joe E. Lee	Alvin Ing
Jack Kan	Robert Ito
Roxy Gow	Emily Kuroda
Jimmy	Ken Takemoto
Tony Dunn	Edmund Eng
Philip Wing	Robert Almodovar
Joy Yuen	Ren Hanami
Mimi Dunn	Sekiya Billman
Carmen Fund	Karen Lew
Johnny Kwan	Jusak Bernhard
Susan Koh	Theresa Lam
Ah Yee	Takayo Fischer
Sid MacNally	Tom Donaldson

Quartet: Mary Ann Hu, Susan Haruye Ioka, Paul Wong, Warren Sata.

Time: July, 1943. Place: Los Angeles. One intermission.

Mid winter Playreading Series:

UNCLE TADAO. By R.A. Shiomi.
CHINA MAMA. By C.Y. Lee.
MAIDEN VOYAGE. By Karen Huie.
EYE OF THE COCONUT. By Jeannie Barroga.
INTERRACIAL RELATIONS. By Perry Miyake.

Spring Playreading Series:

ATOMIC NANCY. By Marilyn Tokuda.
CHRISTMAS CAKE. By Velina Hasu Houston.
WIDESCREEN VERSION OF THE WORLD. By Han Ong.
NOT A THROUGH STREET. By Wakako Yamauchi.

Los Angeles: Los Angeles Theater Center

(Artistic director, Bill Bushnell; producing director, Diane White)

VIVA DETROIT. By Derek Walcott. Director, Claude Purdy; scenery, John Dexter; lighting, Douglas D. Smith; costumes, Ann Bruice; sound, Mark Friedman.

Barman	Moses Gunn
Pat	Gates McFadden
Sonny	Robert Gossett
Gretchen	Cheryl Gates

Time and place: Three weeks on the island of St. Lucia in the winter season. One intermission.

STRONG MAN'S WEAK CHILD. By Israel Horovitz. Director, Israel Horovitz; scenery and lighting, D. Martyn Bookwalter; costumes, Ann Bruice; sound, Jon Gottlieb.

Evvie	Meg Foster
Dede	Sheridan Gayr, Sally Levi
Auggie	Peter Iacangelo
Franny	Nick Mancuso
Fast Eddie	Don Yesso

Time: A succession of early mornings, the present. Place: Francis Farina's garage, Gloucester, Massachusetts.

THE JONI MITCHELL PROJECT. By Henry Edwards and David Schweizer; songs by Joni Mitchell. November 1, 1990. Director, David Schweizer; musical direction, Richard Bronskill; scenery and lighting, Timian Alsaker; costumes, Donna Barrier; sound, Mark Friedman.

With Hinton Battle, Noreen Hennessy, Philip Littell, Lisa Harlow Stark, Ren Woods.

One intermission.

AUGUST 29. By Violeta Calles. Director, Jose
Luis Valenzuela; scenery, Gronk and Douglas D.
Smith; lighting, Douglas D. Smith; costumes,
Gronk; sound, Mark Friedman.

Ruben . . . . E.J. Castillo
Lucero. . . . . Evelina Fernandez
Frank. . . . . Abel Franco
Rudy . . . . Mike Gomez
Benny . . . . Sal Lopez
Williams . . . . Tony Maggio
Lucy . . . . Vanessa Marquez
Molly. . . . . Angela Moya
Trini . . . . Lupe Ontiveros
Dancer. . . . . Olga M. Perez
   Time: 1970, 1990. Place: East Los Angeles/
Montebello. One intermission.

THE HIP-HOP WALTZ OF EURYDICE. By
Reza Abdoh. Director, Reza Abdoh; scenery and
costumes, Timian Alsaker; lighting, Rand Ryan;
sound, Erik Blank, Raul Vincent Enriquez.
A Hound . . . . . Borracha, Joselito Amen Santo
Eurydice (Dora Lee);
   Travel Agent. . . . . Tom Fitzpatrick
Captain. . . . . Alan Mandell
Orpheus (Tommy) . . . . Julia Mengers
   Time and Place: A multi-media performance
event set in an almost-future world.

VEINS AND THUMBTACKS. By Jonathan
Marc Sherman. February 7, 1991. Director,
David Saint; scenery, David Gallo; lighting,
Kenneth Posner; costumes, Marianna Elliott;
sound, Jon Gottlieb.

Annie . . . . Elizabeth Berridge
Arturo Constantini . . . . . . Bruce MacVittie
Grandmother . . . . Beatrice Manley
Chapel Owner; Divorce Guy;
   Caller. . . . . William Marquez
Wendy Bonaparte . . . . . . Mercedes McNab
Nurse; Tralice . . . . Noelle Parker
Jimmy Bonaparte . . . . Fisher Stevens
   Time: 1978 to 1989. Place: New Jersey.

ABSOLOM'S SONG. By Selaelo Maredi. Direc-
tor, Ann Bowen; scenery and costumes, Timian
Alsaker; lighting, Douglas D. Smith; sound,
Jon Gottlieb.
Absalom Makgato . . . . Sam Motaoana Phillips
Lynette Bloomfield . . . . Maggie Soboil
   Time and Place: A suburban area of Johannes-
burg known as Lower Houghton, on the brink of
change. One intermission.

DAY OF HOPE. By Birgir Sigurdsson, adapted
by Patrick Tovatt from the British translation by
Jill Brooke. March 7, 1991. Director, Bill
Bushnell; scenery and costumes, Timian Alsaker;
lighting, Douglas D. Smith; sound, Jon Gottlieb.
Gunnar . . . . Gregory Wagrowski
Alda. . . . . Ann Hearn
Lara . . . . Salome Jens
Gudny . . . . Julianna McCarthy
Hordur . . . . Richard Ortega
Reynir. . . . . Kyle Secor
   Time: 1955. Place: A port city in the Northern
Hemisphere. One intermission.

Los Angeles: Mark Taper Forum

(Artistic director/producer, Gordon Davidson; managing director, Stephen J. Albert)

HOPE OF THE HEART. Adapted by Adrian
Hall from the writings of Robert Penn Warren.
September 16, 1990. Director, Adrian Hall;
scenery, Eugene Lee; lighting Natasha Katz,
Eugene Lee; costumes, Dona Granata.
   With Vaughn Armstrong, Casey Biggs,
Sherritta Duran Burns, Russell Curry, Clifford
David, Doug Hutchison, Jeff Jeffcoat, Jeffrey
King, Richard Kneeland, Charles McCaughan,
Patrick McCollum, John Morrison, James Ellis
Reynolds, Margo Skinner, Emilie Talbot, Rose
Weaver, Nance Williamson.
   One intermission

JELLY'S LAST JAM. Book by George C.
Wolfe, music by Jelly Roll Morton. February 24,
1991. Director, George C. Wolfe; scenery,
George Tsypin; lighting, James F. Ingalls;
costumes, Toni-Leslie James; sound, Jon
Gottlieb.

Jelly Roll Morton . . . . Obba Babtunde
Chimney Man . . . . Keith David
Maman. . . . . Karole Foreman
Gran Mimi. . . . . Freda Payne
Anita. . . . . Tonya Pinkins
Mabel. . . . . Leilani Jones
Young Jelly . . . . Robert Barry Fleming
Eulalie . . . . Peggy Blow
Viola . . . . Phylliss Bailey
Amede. . . . . Patty Holley
Buddy Bolden . . . . . Ruben Santiago-Hudson
Blues Singer . . . . Mary Bond Davis
Three Finger Jake;
   Hick Man . . . . Gill Pritchett III
Too Tight Nora . . . . Deborah L. Sharpe
Jack the Bear . . . . Stanley Wayne Mathis
Hick Woman . . . . Regina Le Vert
Grieving Widow. . . . . Patty Holley
Dead Man . . . . Jerry M. Hawkins
Pool Player . . . . Patrick McCollum

Melrose Brothers; Agents;

Gangsters. . Jerry M. Hawkins, Timothy Smith
Loose Lil . . . . Linda Twine
L'il Moe. . . . . Garnett Brown
Hot Daddy . . . . Richard Grant
Too Sharp . . . . Jeffery Clayton
Left Foot . . . . Quentin Dennard
Joe. . . . . Karl Vincent
The Hunnies: Phylliss Bailey, Patty Holley, Regina Le Vert. The Ancestors: Timothy Smith, Mary Bond Davis, Patrick McCollum, Peggy Blow, Gil Pritchett III. The Crowd: Peggy Blow, Mary Bond Davis, Robert Barry Fleming, Karole Foreman, Jerry M. Hawkins, Stanley Wayne Mathis, Patrick McCollum, Freda Payne, Tonya

Pinkins, Gil Pritchett III, Ruben Santiago-Hudson, Deborah L. Sharpe, Timothy Smith.

Time: The eve of Jelly Roll Morton's death. Place: The Jungle Inn, a lowdown club somewhere between heaven and hell. One intermission.

FREEDOM SONG. By Peter Mattei. Director, Peter C. Brosius; scenery, Victoria Petrovich; lighting, Tom Dennison; costumes Lydia Tanji.
Ocie . . . . Jorge Galvan
Aunt D. . . . . Joyce Guy
Pimo . . . . Ivan G'Vera
Imogene . . . . Karen Maruyama
Uncle Snoo . . . . Patrick Roman Miller
The Mayor . . . . Rick Perkins

Louisville: Actors Theater of Louisville

(Producing director, Jon Jory)

15th Annual Humana Festival of New American Plays March 5-April 14, 1991.

A PASSENGER TRAIN OF SIXTY-ONE COACHES. By Paul Walker. Director, Paul Walker; scenery, Paul Owen; lighting, Mary Louise Geiger; costumes, Marcia Dixcy; sound Darron West.

Anthony Comstock—Robert Machray.

Comstock's Sister; Mrs. Motts; Young Woman on the Train; Victoria Woodhull; Mrs. Heywood; Madame Restell's Servant Girl; Lady Customer; Deputy Marshall; Actress Playing Evvie; George Bernard Shaw; Second Prostitute—Pamela Stewart. Comstock's Mother; Woman; 2d Lady;

ACTORS THEATER OF LOUISVILLE—Sally Parrish, Cynthia Carle and Peggity Price in *Cementville* by Jane Martin

Teacher of the Colored People; Mother from Chinatown; Madame Restell's Maid; Stage Manager; Brothel Madam—Ching Valdes/Aran. Comstock's Father; Drunk Soldier; Maggie; Mr. DeRobigne; M. Bennett; Dr. Morrison; Producer; 1st Member of the Society for the Suppression of Vice —V. Craig Heidenreich. Boy With Wine; Young Soldier; Adele; Tennessee Claflin; Widow's Children; 2d Anti-Vice Woman; Husband in Audience; 2d Member of the Society for the Suppression of Vice—Matthew Aibel. Comstock's Baby Brother Chet; Old Soldier; 1st Lady Teacher of the Colored People; Comstock's 1st Maid Servant; Young Lady Playing Croquet; Mrs. Prosch; Widows; Madame Restell; Actress Playing Mrs. Warren; George Bernard Shaw; Comstock's 2d Maid Servant; 1st Prostitute—Lynn Cohen. Soldier With Fiddle; Mrs. Mott's Butler; Boy on the Street; Young Gentleman Playing Croquet; Mr. Prosch; Ezra Heywood; 1st Anti-Vice Woman; Wife in Audience; Boy in Brothel—Scott Facher. Little Girl With the Message at Mrs. Motts's; Little Girl on the Train; Lillie; Little Girl Backstage—Leah Jones.

Time: 1844-1915. Place: America. One intermission.

DOWN THE ROAD. By Lee Blessing. Director, Jeanne Blake; scenery, Paul Owen; lighting, Mary Louise Geiger; costumes, Hollis Jenkins-Evans; sound, Darron West.

Dan Henniman . . . . Mark Shannon
Iris Henniman . . . . Bernadette Sullivan
William Reach . . . . Markus Flanagan
Time: The present. Place: A maximum security prison and a motel.

NIGHT-SIDE. By Shem Bitterman. Director, Frazier W. Marsch; scenery, Paul Owen; lighting, Mary Louise Geiger; costumes, Hollis Jenkins-Evans; sound, Darron West.

S . . . . Pamela Gien
Place: Boston and environs, both real and imagined.

CEMENTVILLE. By Jane Martin. Director, Jon Jory; scenery, Paul Owen; lighting, Mary Louise Geiger; costumes, Marcia Dixcy; sound, Darron West.

Dwayne Pardee . . . . Jim Petersmith
Tiger . . . . Suzanna Hay
Nola. . . . . Corliss Preston
Dani . . . . Annette Helde
Netty . . . . Adale O'Brien
Lessa. . . . . Kimberley LaMarque
Bigman . . . . Fred Major
Mother Crocker . . . . Sally Parrish
Dottie . . . . Peggity Price
Dolly . . . . Cynthia Carle
Miss Harmon. . . . . Jessica Jory
One-Eye Deneauve. . . . . Bob Burrus
Kid. . . . . Lex Monson
Eddie. . . . . Tom Stechschulte

Time: The present. Place: The locker room of a boxing arena in Cementville, Tennessee. One intermission.

A PIECE OF MY HEART. By Shirley Lauro. Director, Allen R. Belknap; scenery, Paul Owen; lighting, Karl Haas; costumes, Michael Krass; sound, Darron West.

Martha. . . . . Annette Helde
Mary Jo . . . . Cynthia Carle
Sissy . . . . Corliss Preston
Whitney . . . . Sharon Schlarth
Leeann . . . . Kim Miyori
Steele. . . . . Novella Nelson
All the American Men. . . . . Tom Stechschulte
Time: The very recent past. One intermission

THE DEATH OF ZUKASKY. By Richard Strand. Director, Nagle Jackson; scenery, Paul Owen; lighting, Karl Haas; costumes, Michael Krass; sound, Darron West.

Theodore Zukasky. . . . . Tom Lenoci
Barry Mills . . . . Rod McLachlan
Anne Desmond . . . . Monica Merryman
A.C. Tattums. . . . . William McNulty
Henry Marlino . . . . Ray Fry
Place: On the 22nd floor of a Chicago corporate headquarters.

IN THE EYE OF THE HURRICANE. By Eduardo Machado. Director, Anne Bogart; scenery, Paul Owen; lighting, Karl Haas; costumes, Michael Krass; sound, Darron West.

Manuela . . . . Diane D'Aquila
Maria Josepha . . . . Lynn Cohen
Mario. . . . . Christopher McCann
Oscar . . . . Bob Burrus
Sonia . . . . Pamela Stewart
Hugo . . . . Rafael Baez
Rosa . . . . Suzanne Costallos
Antonio . . . . Robert Machray
Fulgencio. . . . . V. Craig Heidenreich
Milciano . . . . . Michael Weis, Arthur Aulisi
Time: 1960. Place: Guanabacoa, Cuba. One intermission.

OUT THE WINDOW. By Neal Bell. Director, Bob Krakower; scenery, Paul Owen; lighting, Karl Haas; costumes, Hollis Jenkins-Evans; sound, Darron West.

Jake . . . . Tom Stechschulte
Andy . . . . Suzanna Hay
Time: The present. Place: New York.

WHAT SHE FOUND THERE. By John Glore. Director, Jon Jory; scenery, Paul Owen; lighting, Karl Haas; costumes, Hollis Jenkins-Evans; sound, Darron West.

Lou. . . . . V. Craig Heidenreich
Celia . . . . Jennifer Hubbard
Time: The present. place: A motel room.

Malvern, Pa.: *The People's Light and Theater Company*

(Producing director, Danny Fruchter)

SISTER CARRIE. By Louis Lippa, adapted from Theodore Dreiser. March 27, 1991. Director, Ken Marini; scenery, James F. Pyne Jr.; lighting, James L. Leitner; costumes, Lindsay W. Davis.

Caroline Meeber	Elizabeth Meeker
George W. Hurstwood	Tom Teti
Charles H. Drouet	Stephen Novelli
Ray Trafford; Shaughnessy	Pearce Bunting
Lorna; Mrs. Hale	Alda Cortese
Sven Hanson; Private Detective	Peter Delaurier
Jessica Hurstwood; Sanderson	Serena Ebhardt
Gaslight Director; Chorus Master	Leonard Haas
Policeman; Mr. Vance	David Ingram
Factory Worker; William	Mark Kenward
Eileen; Mrs. Vance	Joyce Lee
George Hurstwood Jr.; Poker Player	John Lumia
Political Agitator; Coal Man	Paul Meshejian
Mary; Maitland	Kathyrn Petersen
Minnie Hanson; Irish Striker	Ceal Phelan
Factory Girl; Julia Hurstwood	Marcia Saunders
Sally; Lola Osborne	Demetra Tseckares
Mr. Bamberger; Ames	Frank Wood
Factory Foreman; Strike Leader	Rozwill Young

Time and Place: Columbia City, Wisconsin; Chicago, Montreal and New York City, from 1889 to mid-1890s. One intermission.

Miami: *Coconut Grove Playhouse*

(Producing artistic director, Arnold Mittelman)

ONCE UPON A SONG. Conceived by Anthony Newley and Arnold Mittelman. February 19, 1991. Director, Arnold Mittelman; scenery, Kevin Rupnik; lighting, Pat Collins; costumes, Ellis Tillman.

Father	Anthony Newley
Mother	Bertilla Baker
Daughter	Tracy Venner
Son	Sean Dooley

JUST DESERTS. By Tom Dulack. April 9, 1991. Director, Arnold Mittelman; scenery, Stephen Lambert; lighting, Todd Wren; costumes, Ellis Tillman; sound, Steve Shapiro.

Tyrone Cross	Lewis J. Stadlen
Whitney Van Loon	Steve Arlen
News Anchor	Lynne Peyser

Place: A basement apartment in a run-down neighborhood in New York City. One intermission.

Milford, N.H.: *American Stage Festival*

(Producing director, Richard Rose)

Early Stages Readings:
PRANK. By Richard Kalinoski.
THE JEREMIAH. By Diane Ney.
ENOLA. By Charles Henrich.

TAINTED BLOOD. By Tom Jacobson.
HUMBLE SERVANT. By Donald Steele.
SENIOR DISCRETION. Book, music and lyrics by Frank Loesser.

Millburn, N.J.: *Paper Mill Playhouse*

(Artistic director, Robert Johanson; executive producer, Angelo Del Rossi)

THE MERRY WIDOW. Book by Robert Johanson, music by Franz Lehar, lyrics by Albert Evans, based on the operetta by Victor Leon, Leo Stein and Franz Lehar. April 3, 1991. Director, Robert Johanson; choreography, Sharon Halley; musical direction, Jim Coleman; scenery Michael Anania; lighting, Mark Stanley; costumes, Gregg Barnes; sound, David R. Paterson.

Hanna	Judy Kaye
Count Danilo	Richard White
Baron Zeta	Merwin Goldsmith
Valencienne	Hallie Neill
Camille de Rosillion	Mark Janicello
Njegus	Peter Bartlett
Bogdanovich	Grant Walden
Sylvanie	Georgia Bibeau
Kromov	Donald Norris
Olga	Sarah Rice
Cascada	Joseph Mahowald
St. Brioche	John Clonts

Ensemble: Robert Ashford, Brett Barsky, Jeffrey Lee Broadhurst, Diana Brownstone, Randy Charleville, Erik Chechak, Marcos Dinnerstein, Alyssa Epstein, Ashley Freiberger, Debbi Fuhrman, Mai Goda, Randall Graham, Alan Gray, Kristin Hennessy, Sean Hennessy, Grace Hyndman, Peter Kapetan, Julietta Marcelli, Marty McDonough, Joan Mirabella, Todd Murray, Joel Newman, Wendy Piper, Robert Randle, Catherine Ruivivar, Barbara Scanlon, Marguerite Shannon, Cynthia Thole, Blythe Turner, Gib Twitchell.

Two intermissions.

Milwaukee Repertory Theater

(Artistic director, John Dillon; managing director, Sara O'Connor)

4 AM AMERICA. By Ping Chong and Company. December 2, 1990. Director, Ping Chong; scenery, Ping Chong, Pat Dony; lighting, Thomas Hase; costumes, Dawn Gregory; sound and original music, Brian Hallas.

With Jawn Fleming, Jeannie Hutchins, Larry G. Malvern, Johanna Melamed, Ric Oquita, Louise Smith.

No intermission.

HOMEBOUND. By Tom Williams. April 14, 1991. Director, Kenneth Albers; scenery, Constanza Romero; lighting, Dan Kotlowitz; costumes, Judy Dearing.

Ernie Crepshaw . . . . . . Larry Dean Birkett
Franklin Chase . . . . Benny S. Cannon
Julie Schoen . . . . Catherine Lynn Davis
Reverend Crepshaw . . . . . Richard Halverson
Time: Scene 1: An afternoon in June. Scene 2: The next morning. Scene 3: A few hours later. Place: The living room of a small house on a tiny island north of Seattle. Two intermissions.

Work-in-Progress:

GOING FORWARD BACKWARD. By Daniel A. Stein. Director, Daniel A. Stein.

Minneapolis: Illusion Theater

(Executive producing director, Michael Robins; producing director, Bonnie Morris)

WOMEN WHO DRINK. By Leslye Orr. July 29, 1990. Directors, Myron Johnson, Leslye Orr; lighting, David Vogel; sound, Tony Gorzycki.

MISS EVERS' BOYS. By David Feldshuh. May 3, 1991. Directors, D. Scott Glasser, Michael Robins; scenery, Dean Holzman; lighting, Barry Browning; costumes, Katherine Maurer.

Eunice Evers . . . . . Denise Burse-Mickelbury

Hodman Bryan . . . . Mark M. Cryer
Ben Washington . . . . T. Michael Rambo
Willie Johnson. . . . . Lester Purry
Caleb Humphries. . . . . Dion Graham
Dr. John Douglas . . . . Peter Moore
Dr. Eugene Brodus. . . . . Brent S. Hendon
Place: In and around Macon County, Alabama. Act I: 1932, contagion. Act II: 1946, progression and 1972, endpoint. One intermission.

Nashville: Tennessee Repertory Theater

(Artistic director, Mac Pirkle; managing director, Brian J. Laczko)

A HOUSE DIVIDED. Book by Mac Pirkle, music by Mike Reid, lyrics by Mike Reid and Mac Pirkle. Director, Mac Pirkle; scenery, Craig Spain; lighting, Brian J. Laczko; costumes, Martha H. Cooper; sound, Eric Swartz.
Taylor; Union Officer . . . . Mark Cabus
Jasper . . . . Matthew Carlton
Mule . . . . Mark DeLaBarre
Elijah. . . . . Troy Ensley
Sarah . . . . Kimberly D. Fleming
Benjamin Montgomery . . . . Bob Frisch
Buckshot; Minister. . . . . Timothy Orr Fudge
Virginia Montgomery . . . . Nan Gurley
William Montgomery . . . . Christopher Harrod
Joshua. . . . . Gary Lowery
Jeb Montgomery . . . . Jonathan A. Lutz
Sergeant . . . . Myke Mueller
Priscilla Montgomery . . . . . Shelean Newman
Wedding Guests;
   Hospital Workers . . . . . . Jennifer S. Orth,
                          Maria V.S. Siegenthaler
Lewis. . . . . Ricky Russell
Moses. . . . . Barry Scott

Union Soldier . . . . Christopher Simonsen
Newspaperman . . . . Sam Wallace
Mozart . . . . Robert S. Whorton
One intermission.

SOME SWEET DAY. Book by Don Jones and Mac Pirkle, music and lyrics by Si Kahn. May 9, 1991. Director, Steven Kent; scenery, Brian J. Laczko; lighting, Brian J. Laczko; costumes, Jennifer S. Orth; sound, Eric Swartz.
Buddy Bolton . . . . Christopher Harrod
Sarah Jane Biggs . . . . Mary Jane Harvill
Emma Ingram . . . . Denice E. Hicks
Maxwell Blodgett . . . . Ron J. Hutchins
Isaac Ingram. . . . . Myke Mueller
Fob Lewis. . . . . Barry Scott
Virgil Jessup . . . . Ken Dale Thompson
Clea Bullock . . . . Shirley Tripp
Willetha Lewis . . . . Jackie Welch
Ensemble: Melva Boyd, Lattie Brown, Kimberly D. Fleming, Kimberly Jajuan, Maria V.S. Siegenthaler, Christopher Simonsen, Alex Stadaker, Lawrence D. Thomison, Marc Van Sickle.

New Brunswick, N.J.: Crossroads Theater Company

(Associate producer, Kenneth Johnson; literary manager, Sydné Mahone)

BONGI'S JOURNEY. By Thuli Dumakude and Welcome Msomi. December 9, 1990. Directors, Welcome Msomi, Ricardo Khan; scenery, Felix E. Cochren; lighting, William H. Grant III; costumes, Beth Ribblett.

Bongi	Thuli Dumakude
Mazibi	Debbi Blackwell-Cook
Siso	Kyra Hider
Mazondo	Jannie Jones
Sanusi	Terry Burrell

BUSES. By Denise Nicholas. February 5, 1991. Director, Shirley Jo Finney; scenery, Peter Harrison; lighting, Sandra Ross; costumes, Celia Bryant; sound, G. Thomas Clark.

Mary Ellen Pleasant	Iris Little
Rosa Parks	Petronia Paley

Time: Out of time. Place: A bus stop in a dream.

SANGOMA: THE MOTHER PROJECT. A collective creation by The Women of Sangoma, the Women's Company at Crossroads. April 23, 1991. Director, Sydné Mahone; scenery, Gary Kechely, Alice Baldwin; lighting, Robin Miller; costumes, Anita Ellis; sound, Carmen Whiip.

Mary	Evelyn Ayana Bateman
India	Gwendolen Hardwick
Renee	Alicia Rene Washington
Qwyn	Djanet Sears
Mamaya	Lynda Gravatt
Shadow	Janiera Warren
Storm	Stephanie Berry

Time: Now. Place. WomanSpace.

GEORGE STREET PLAYHOUSE, NEW BRUNSWICK, N.J.—
Eli Wallach and Anne Jackson in *Sparky and the Fitz* by Craig Volk

New Brunswick, N.J.: George Street Playhouse

(Producing artistic director, Gregory S. Hurst)

GREETINGS. By Tom Dudzick. October 2, 1990. Director, Gregory S. Hurst; scenery, Atkin Pace; lighting, Donald Holder; costumes, Barbara Forbes.

Andy Gorski	Mark Shannon
Randi Stein	Barbara Gulan
Emily Gorski	Beth Fowler
Phil Gorski	John Ramsey
Mickey Gorski	Patrick Kerr

Place: An American Airlines jetliner and the Gorski household, Pittsburgh. One intermission.

PENDRAGON. By Laurie H. Hutzler. January 18, 1991. Director, Wendy Liscow; scenery, Deborah Jasien; lighting, David Neville; costumes, Barbara Forbes.

Morganna	Socorro Santiago
Arthur	Ernest Abuba
Lancelot	Luis A. Ramos
Guinevere	Catherine Christianson
Garth; Gareth	Michael O'Shea
Mordred	Enrique Munoz
Page	Jay Duckworth

Time and Place: The mythic realm of Camelot and the forest surrounding King Arthur's domain.

SPARKY AND THE FITZ. By Craig Volk. February 21, 1991. Director, Stephen Rothman; scenery, Deborah Jasien; lighting, Donald Holder; costumes, Barbara Forbes.

Sparky	Eli Wallach
Fitz	Anne Jackson
Rudy	Ben Hammer

Time: Halloween and the day after. Place: A kitchen in a suburb. One intermission.

FORGIVING TYPHOID MARY. By Mark St.

Germain. March 12, 1991. Director, Gregory S. Hurst; scenery, Atkin Pace; lighting, Donald Holder; costumes, Barbara Forbes.

Mary Mallon	Estelle Parsons
Sarah	Meghan Andrews
Dr. William Mills	Jack Davidson
Dr. Ann Saltzer	Harriet Harris
Father Michael McKuen	Michael Louden
Intern; Martin Frazier	James Morgan

Time and Place: A small cottage on North Brother Island, New York, property of Riverside Hospital, July 1909 to February 1910, and in Mary's memory. One intermission.

THE ROOT. By Gary Richards. April 9, 1991. Director, Matthew Penn; scenery, Deborah Jasien; lighting, Donald Holder; costumes, Barbara Forbes.

Willie	Jesse Moore
Vinnie	John Shepard
Jerry	Jude Ciccolella
Chick	Larry Block

Place: a garage in the Williamsburg section of Brooklyn. One intermission.

Staged Readings:

REUNION. By Allen Crossett. November 1, 1990. Director, Wendy Liscow.
SAVING THE EAGLES. By Jacklyn Maddux. November 14, 1990. Director, Wendy Liscow.
DROP EVERYTHING. By Phyllis Purscel. December 12, 1990. Director, Wendy Liscow.
THE SUPERHETERODYN GIRL. By John Porter. December 20, 1990. Director, Wendy Liscow.
HEART OF STONE. By Laurie H. Hutzler. January 30, 1991. Director, Wendy Liscow.

New Haven, Conn.: Long Wharf Theater

(Artistic director, Arvin Brown)

THE VOYSEY INHERITANCE. By Harley Granville Barker; revised by James Luse. September 25, 1990 (American premiere). Director, Arvin Brown; scenery, John Lee Beatty; lighting, Arden Fingerhut; costumes, David Murin.

Peacey	Ralph Williams
Voysey Sr.	James Noble
Edward Voysey	Boyd Gaines
Major Booth Voysey	Doug Stender
Evans Colpus	William Swetland
George Booth	William Prince
Denis Tregoning	T. Scott Cunningham
Ethel Voysey	Louise Roberts
Alice Maitland	Caris Corfman

Honor Voysey	Jeanne Ruskin
Beatrice Voysey	Ann McDonough
Phoebe	Jody Rowell
Mary	Ashley Voos
Mrs. Voysey	Joyce Ebert
Emily Voysey	Rebecca Nelson
Trenchard Voysey	Tom Hewitt
Hugh Voysey	Michel R. Gill

Time: The first decade of the 20th century. Place: Boston. One intermission.

VALUED FRIENDS. By Stephen Jeffreys. November 20, 1990. Director, Robin Lefevre; scenery, Sue Plummer; lighting, Marc B. Weiss;

costumes, Sue Plummer.

Sherry	Jill Tasker
Howard	Bill Camp
Paul	John Benjamin Hickey
Marion	Liann Pattison
Scott	Mark Vietor
Stewart	Ian Trigger

Time: Early June 1984-May 1987. Place: The basement flat of a large late Victorian house in Earl's Court. One intermission.

The Workshops:
TEMPORARY HELP. By David Wiltse.

January 2, 1991. Director, Gordon Edelstein.
OUT THERE WITHOUT A PRAYER. By Reno. February 12, 1991. Director, Gordon Edelstein.
DEARLY DEPARTED. By David Bottrell and Jessie Jones. March 19, 1991. Director, Gloria Muzio.
HOW DO YOU LIKE YOUR MEAT? Program of four one-act plays by Joyce Carol Oates: *The Anatomy Lesson, Friday Night, Darling I'm Telling You* and the title play. April 12, 1991. Director, Gordon Edelstein.

Palo Alto, Calif.: TheaterWorks

(Artistic director, Robert Kelly)

GO DOWN GARVEY. Book, music and lyrics by Danny Duncan. May 30, 1991. Director, Anthony J. Haney; scenery, Joe Ragey; lighting, Barbara DuBois; costumes, Pamela Lampkin.

Amy Jacques	Sharon Leal
W.E.B. DuBois	Michael Le Roy Brown
Marcus Garvey	Jason Booker
Mama Garvey;	
Madame Morgan	Margarette Robinson
Amy Ashwood	Michelle E. Jordan
Duse Mohammed Ali	Rob Robinson

Tyler; Archbishop	Gary L. Rowland
Capt. Soul	Keith Jackson
Savannah	Andrea Brembry
One intermission.	

Staged Readings:
DANCING THE BOX STEP. By Kent Brown.
JUGGER'S RAIN. By Ron Mark.
HEADSET. By Bill Streib.
TIERRA DEL FUEGO. By Louis Phillips.
TALK-STORY. By Jeannie Barroga.
RAPPACCINI'S DAUGHTER. By Robert Mitchell.

Pasadena: California Music Theater

(Artistic director, Gary Davis)

CLOTHESPINS AND DREAMS. Book and lyrics by Ron Miller, music by Ken Hirsch, based on the play *Suds* by Tom Harris. August 8, 1990. Director, Gary Davis; musical direction, Jeff Rizzo; choreography, Nicole Barth; scenery, Terry Gates; lighting, Ward Carlisle;

costumes, Al Lehman.
   With Barney Martin, Eloise Laws, Tony Floyd, Ren Woods, Jordan Bennett, Valerie Washington, Sheila Grenham, Jewel Tompkins, Marilyn Rising, Whitney Rydbeck, Desiree Dargan.

Pasadena: Pasadena Playhouse

(Artistic director, Paul Lazarus)

THE WONDERFUL ICE CREAM SUIT. Book by Ray Bradbury, music by Jose Feliciano, lyrics by Jose Feliciano and Susan Feliciano. September 16, 1990. Director, Charles Rome Smith; choreography, Nancy Gregory; scenery, Deborah Raymond; lighting, Martin Aronstein; costumes, Zoe DuFour; sound, Bill Hewlett, Jack Allaway.

   With Christopher Aponte, Geoffrey Cascio, Linda Cevallos, Al Checco, Kay Cole, Joey Cuevas, Danna D'Amore, James Dybas, Nathan

Holland, Tito Larriva, Paul Lyday, Armelia McQueen, Patrick Montes, Tony Plana, Jim Raposa, Maia Winters.

DOUBLE CROSS. By Gary Bohlke. January 11, 1991. Director, A.J. Antoon; scenery, Andrew Jackness; lighting, Martin Aronstein; costumes, Lindsay W. Davis. With Sam Groom, Alyson Reed, John Benjamin Hickey, Ron Richardson, Betty Miller, Gary Swanson.
   One intermission.

Philadelphia: Philadelphia Festival Theater for New Plays

(Artistic and producing director, Carol Rocamora)

THREE SISTERS. By Anton Chekhov; adapted by David Mamet from a literal translation by Vlada Chemomordik. January 15, 1991. Director, W.H. Macy; scenery, James Wolk; lighting, Howard Werner; costumes, Laura Cunningham.

Olga Sergeyevna . . . . Melissa Bruder
Irini Sergeyevna. . . . . Mary McCann
Masha Sergeyevna . . . . Felicity Huffman
Ivan Romanovich
  Chebutykin. . . . . William Duff-Griffin
Nikolai Lvovich Tuzenbach. . . . . Todd Weeks
Vassily Vassilyevich Solyony. . . . Clark Gregg
Anfisa . . . . Barbara Winters Pinto
Ferapont . . . . Andrew B. McCosker
Alexandr Ignatyevich Vershinin. . . Jordan Lage
Andrei Sergevevich Prozoroff . . . . Neil Pepe
Fyodor Ilych Kulygin. . . . . Steven Goldstein
Natalya Ivanovna. . . . . Sarah Eckhardt
Alexei Petrovich Fedotik . . . . . . Robert Bella
Vladimir Karlovich Rode . . . . . . Scott Zigler
Maid . . . . Robin Spielberg
  Act I: The Prozoroff's house, a parlor. Act II: The same, 2 years later. Act III: Olga's and Irina's room, 1 year later. Act IV: The old garden of the Prozoroff house, a few months later. One intermission.

TOP OF THE WORLD. By Bruce Graham. April 16, 1991. Director, James J. Christy; scenery, James Wolk; lighting, Curt Senie; costumes, Vickie Esposito; sound, Conny M. Lockwood.

Gilbert Crawley . . . . Ben Siegler
Katherine McKinley. . . . . Janis Dardaris
Steve Kennedy. . . . . Paul Bernardo
Bob. . . . . Paul Lemos
Government Expert 1; Samovar;
  Senator Despot; The Pope;

Ed McMahon. . . . . Charles S. Roney
Government Expert 2; Agent Orange;
The President;
Johnny Carson . . . . Christopher Cline
Steve's Boss; Agent Garfield;
  A Typical American; Oil Company
  Spokesperson . . . . Beth Dannenfelser
Katherine's Boss;
  Anchorperson . . . . Deborah Stern
  Time: The present and the past. Place: Lubbock, Alaska and elsewhere. One intermission.

MOONSHADOW. By Richard Hellesen. May 7, 1991. Director, Carol Rocamora; scenery, Phillip A. Graneto; lighting, James L. Leitner; costumes, Vickie Esposito; sound, Conny M. Lockwood.

Jeff . . . . Joshua Reid Gordon
Ellen. . . . . Karen MacDonald
Jack . . . . Paul O'Brien
Laurel . . . . Dana Barron
Mark . . . . Stephen Mailer
  Time: Sunday, July 20, 1969. Place: A house in Castalia, Illinois. One intermission.

Previewers Reading Series:

A SMALL DELEGATION by Janet Nebris.
THE KID'S GONE KOSHER by Ernest Joselovitz.
THE FAN LETTER by Cassi Harris.
MOONSHADOW by Richard Hellesen.
THINGS BEING WHAT THEY ARE by Wendy MacLeod.
TOP OF THE WORLD by Bruce Graham.
THE LEARNED LADIES by Freyda Thomas.
EMPATHY by Ned Eisenberg.
DREAMS OF BABY by Mary Lathrop.
BREAKING UP by Michael Cristofer.
SIX EASY PIECES by Howard Korder.

Philadelphia: Society Hill Playhouse

(Artistic director, Jay Kogan)

SHOWDOWN AT ODDERNOOTS' DOUBLE CUPP DINER. By Giulietta Racciatti. Director, Susan Turlish; lighting, Neil Tomlinson. With the Philadelphia Youth Theater Company.

ALBERTA K. JOHNSON AMONG OTHERS.

By Joe Hall-Hoxter. Director Susan Turlish. With Tyra L. Davis.

THE UNKNOWN SOLDIER. By Michael P. Toner. Director, Susan Turlish. With Michael P. Toner.

Philadelphia: Walnut Street Theater

(Executive director, Bernard Havard)

A FAMILY AFFAIR. By Nick Dear; adapted from Alexander Ostrovsky. October 10, 1990 (American premiere). Director, Eugene Lazarev;

scenery and lighting, Paul Wonsek; costumes, Gail Cooper-Hecht; sound, Adam Wernick.

Lipochka . . . . Talia Paul
Agrafena . . . . Penny Larsen
Fominishna . . . . Billie Brenan
Ustinya . . . . Sheila Smith
Rispolozhensky. . . . . William Metzo
Bolshov . . . . Gerald Roberts
Lazar . . . . Ray Virta
Tishka . . . . Patrick Rose
   One intermission.

HOW IT WAS DONE IN ODESSA. Book and lyrics by Eric Haagensen, music by Alexander Zhurbin, based on the musical *Sunset* in the Russian language, by Asar Eppel and Alexander

Zhurbin, from a fable by Isaac Babel. April 10, 1991 (American premiere). Director, Robert Kalfin; dances and musical staging, Dania Krupska; musical direction and dance arrangements, Henry Aronson; scenery and lighting, Paul Wonsek; costumes, Gail Cooper-Hecht.
   With Mary Ellen Ashley, Jack Dabdoub, Carl Don, Paul Gallagher, Viola Harris, Jeff Hasler, Colleen Heffernan, Judith Moore, Gabor Morea, Grace Napier, Ronnie Newman, Michael Oberlander, Adam Rubin, Lorraine Serabian, Paul Anthony Stewart, Ted Thurston, Denise Whelan.
   One intermission.

Philadelphia: Wilma Theater

(Artistic directors, Jiri Zizka, Blanka Zizka)

THE PRESIDENT. By Thomas Bernhard, translated by Gitta Honegger. December 11, 1990 (American premiere). Director, Blanka Zizka; scenery, Andrei Efremoff; lighting, Jerold R. Forsyth; costumes, Maxine Hartswick; sound, Adam Wernick.
First Lady . . . . Lola Pashalinski

President . . . . Howard Witt
Mrs. Frolick. . . . . Jacqueline Wade
Actress . . . . Sharon Hope Nordlinger
   With James McCrane, Robert MacCallum, Barry Brait, W. Scott Roberts, Cheryl Gilbert.
   One intermission.

Phoenix: Arizona Theater Company

(Artistic director, Gary Gisselman; managing director, Robert Alpaugh)

THE HOLY TERROR. By Simon Gray. Director, Simon Gray; scenery, David Jenkins; lighting, Dennis Parichy; costumes, David Murin; sound, Brian Jerome Peterson.
Mark Melon . . . . Daniel Gerroll
Gladstone . . . . George Hall
Samantha . . . . Tracy Sallows
Michael; Jacob; Rupert;
   Graeme . . . . Anthony Fusco
Josh Melon . . . . Noel Derecki
Gladys Powers. . . . . Julie Boyd
Kate Melon . . . . Rebecca Nelson
   Time: The action moves between the present

and the last 15 years. Place: The memory: One intermission.

New Play Reading Series:

RIGS AND RED WINE. By Patrick Baliani. May 7, 1991. Director, Walter Schoen.
ALBATROSS. By Velina Hasu Houston. May 14, 1991. Director, Patricia Yasutake.
MOTORCADE. By Bill Corbett. May 21, 1991. Director, Howard Allen.
ATHENE. By Mike Fenlason. May 28, 1991. Director, Judy Rollings.

Pittsburgh: Pittsburgh Public Theater

(Producing director, William T. Gardner; managing director, Dan Fallon)

THE LAY OF THE LAND. By Mel Shapiro. April 10, 1991. Director, Lee Grant; scenery, Karl Eigsti; lighting, Dennis Parichy; costumes, Laura Crow; sound, James Capenos.
Husband . . . . Greg Mullavey
Wife . . . . Lisa Richards
   Time: The present.

A SUNBEAM. By John Henry Redwood. May 30, 1991. Director, Claude Purdy; scenery, James D. Sandefur; lighting, Phil Monat; costumes,

Felix E. Cochren; sound, James Capenos.
Maceo Gilchrist . . . . . Thomas Martell Brimm
Celia Gilchrist . . . . Mary Alice
Melvin McDaniels . . . . Noble Lee Lester
Sol Gilchrist . . . . Paul Bates
Dr. Sylvia Lefcourt . . . . Dorothy Holland
Lynda Knox . . . . Rosalyn Coleman
   Time: The present. Place: In and around Brooklyn, at the Gilchrist apartment, the Briberry Institute of Mental Hygiene and the Burning Bush Baptist Church. One intermission.

Pittsburgh: Three Rivers Shakespeare Festival

(Producing director, Attilio Favorini)

GOODNIGHT DESDEMONA (GOOD MORNING JULIET). By Ann-Marie MacDonald. Director, Peter Harrigan; scenery, Diane Melchitzky; lighting, Jean-Pierre Nutini.

Othello; Tybalt; Professor Claude Night; Juliet's Nurse—Brent Jefferson Lowe. Desdemona; Ramona; Mercutio; Capulet Servant—Bryn Bennett. Juliet; Student; Soldier of Cyprus—Carrie Tracy. Romeo; Chorus; Iago; Ghost—Greg Longenhagen. Constance Ledbelly—Patricia Grace Miles.

Time. The present. Place: Constance's office at Queens University, Kingston, Ontario, and other places in the zone of the conscious mind. One intermission.

Pittsfield, Mass.: The Berkshire Public Theater

(Director, Frank Bessell)

GULLIVER. By Lonnie Carter. Director, Neel Keller; scenery and lighting, Richard Meyer; costumes, Michelle Blancpain; sound, Frank Kennedy. With Bruce MacDonald, Khushi Ponter, Riene McDonell, Jay Whalen, Michael Wartella, Michelle Blancpain, Glenn Barrett, Kim Conley, George Bergen, Dina Cohan, Diedra Bollinger, Hillaire Lockwood, Tracy Campoli, Erika Ackerman, Jo Wartella.

Time: The future. Place: Regions of Jonathan Swift's Gulliver's Travels.

Staged Readings:

CARNIVAL ROUND THE CENTRAL FIGURE. By Diane Amsterdam. October 20, 1990. EMMA IN HER MACINTOSH. By Vincent Sessa. November 17, 1990.

Portland, Me.: Portland Stage Company

(Artistic director, Richard Hamburger)

WOLF AT THE DOOR. By Eric Ehn. April 11, 1991. Director, Richard Hamburger; scenery, Christopher Barreca; lighting, Christopher Akerlind; costumes, Susan Brown; sound, David Budries.

Holly. . . . . Arabella Field
Taylor . . . . Brad Newman
Mel . . . . Geraldine Librandi
Dad . . . . Stephen C. Bradbury
Charlie Bear . . . . Jay Patterson
Jac . . . . Carol Schultz
Collection Agent; Grandfather;
    Editor. . . . . Larry Golden
No intermission.

Princeton, N.J.: McCarter Theater

(Artistic director, Emily Mann; managing director, John Herochik)

THOSE THE RIVER KEEPS. By David Rabe. February 12, 1991. Director, David Rabe; scenery, Loren Sherman; lighting, Michael Lincoln; costumes, Sharon Sprague.
Susie . . . . Marcia Gay Harden
Phil . . . . Anthony La Paglia
Sal . . . . Burt Young
Janice . . . . Debra Cole
One intermission.

BETSEY BROWN. Book by Ntozake Shange and Emily Mann, based on an original idea by Ntozake Shange, music by Baikida Carroll, lyrics by Ntozake Shange. April 2, 1991. Director, Emily Mann; musical staging and choreography, George Faison; scenery, David Mitchell; lighting,

Pat Collins; costumes, Jennifer Von Mayrhauser.
Eugene. . . . . Harold Perrineau Jr.
Regina . . . . Tichina Arnold
Roscoe . . . . Ted Levy
Charlie. . . . . Marc Joseph
Carrie. . . . . Kecia Lewis-Evans
Mr. Jeff . . . . Eugene Fleming
Jane . . . . Pamela Isaacs
Greer . . . . Tommy Hollis
Margot. . . . . Mesha Millington
Allard . . . . Amir Jamal Williams
Vida . . . . Ann Duquesnay
Betsey Brown . . . . Raquel Herring
    Ensemble: Phillip Gilmore, Angel Jemmott, Melodee Savage.
One intermission.

Rochester, N.Y.: GeVa Theater

(Producing director, Howard J. Millman)

JANE EYRE. Conceived by Ted Davis, music by David Clark, lyrics by Ted Davis, based on the novel by Charlotte Bronte. September 4, 1990. Director, Ted Davis; scenery, Bob Barnett; lighting, F. Mitchell Dana; costumes, Pamela Schofield; sound, Dan Roach.
Jane Eyre . . . . Maryann Plunkett

Edward Rochester . . . . Charles Pistone
Ensemble: Melissa Gallagher, Jayne Houdyshell, Matthew Kimbrough, Rebecca Lamb, Joel Leffert, Cecile Mann, David Pursley, Maureen Sadusk, Peter Samuel, Jean Tafler.
One intermission.

St. Louis: Repertory Theater of St. Louis

(Artistic director, Steven Woolf; managing director, Mark D. Bernstein)

THE LAST SONG OF JOHN PROFFIT. By Tommy Thompson. October 24, 1990. Director, Susan Gregg; scenery and lighting, Dale F. Jordan; costumes, Carole Tucker.

John Proffit . . . . Tommy Thompson
Fiddler . . . . Clay Buckner
Time: A late September afternoon, 1990. Place: Point Pleasant, West Virginia.

Salt Lake City: Salt Lake City Acting Company

(Producing artistic director, Edward J. Gryska; managing director, Victoria M. Panella)

WHITE MONEY. By Julie Jensen. March, 1991. Director, Robert Graham Small; scenery, Cory Dangerfield; lighting, Megan McCormick; costumes, Christine Murdoch Becz; sound, Bob Cox.
Ella . . . . Garrison Burrell

Nervene; Seattle . . . . Jayne Luke
Snakes; Guy; Killer Bovine . . . . Russ McGinn
Mother; India Indian . . . . Jean Roberts
Time: Present and past. One intermission.

San Diego: Old Globe Theatre

(Artistic director, Jack O'Brien)

WHITE MAN DANCING. By Stephen Metcalfe. July 3, 1990. Director, Thomas Allan Bullard; scenery and lighting, Kent Dorsey; costumes, Robert Wojewodski; sound, Jeff Ladman.
Dell . . . . Dave Florek
Stuart . . . . Peter Zapp

THE WHITE ROSE. By Lillian Garrett. January 17, 1991. Director, Craig Noel; scenery, Ralph Funicello, lighting, David F. Segal; costumes, Steven Rubin; sound, Jeff Ladman.
Robert Mohr . . . . Jonathan McMurtry
Anton Mahler. . . . . J. Kenneth Campbell
Hans Scholl . . . . John K. Linton
Sophie Scholl . . . . Natalija Nogulich
Bauer . . . . Tim Donoghue
Alexander Schmorell . . . . Steven Culp
Christoph Probst . . . . Bray Poor
Wilhelm Graf . . . . Will Crawford
Nurse; Matron. . . . . Sandra Lindberg
Guards. . . . . Jesus Ontiveros, Triney Sandoval
Time: 1942-43. Place: Munich. One intermission

SUN BEARING DOWN. By Larry Ketron. March 9, 1991. Director, Stephen Metcalfe; scenery, Robert Brill; lighting, Ashley York Kennedy; costumes, Robert Wojewodski; sound, Jeff Ladman.
Forester. . . . . Bill Geisslinger
Price . . . . Annette O'Toole
Mallory . . . . Adam Philipson
Cawhill . . . . James Harper
Place: A small resort town on the South Carolina Coast. One intermission.

Play Discovery Program:

SCARLET MACAW. By Bernardo Solano. January 14, 1991. Director, Raul Moncada.
NECESSITIES. By Velina Hasu Houston. February 11, 1991. Director, Julianne Boyd.
BARGAINS. By Jack Heifner. March 11, 1991. Director, Mark Hofflund.
LOST CAUSES AND IMPOSSIBLE LOYALTIES. By Brent London. April 8, 1991. Director, Mark Hofflund.
GO TO GROUND. By Stuart Spencer. May 6, 1991. Director, Jack O'Brien.

OLD GLOBE THEATER, SAN DIEGO—Bill Geisslinger and Annette
O'Toole in the world premiere of Larry Ketron's *Sun Bearing Down*

San Diego: San Diego Repertory Theater

(Artistic director, Douglas Jacobs)

THE LIFE AND LIFE OF BUMPY JOHNSON.
By Amiri Baraka (a.k.a. LeRoi Jones). January
30, 1991. Director, George Ferencz; scenery, Bill
Stabile; lighting, Ashley York Kennedy; cos-
tumes, Sally J. Lesser; original music by Max
Roach, lyrics by Amiri Baraka.

With Babidiye Abernathy, Osayande Baruti,
Ronnell Bey, Jason Booker, Damon Bryant,
Robert Duncan, Damon Eskridge, Tracy Hughes,
Antonio Johnson, David Kirkwood, Carol
Maillard, Bruce McKenzie, Lance Roberts, Louis
Seitchik, Drew Tombrello.

San Francisco: American Conservatory Theater

(Artistic director, Edward Hastings; managing director, John Sullivan)

FOOD AND SHELTER. By Jane Anderson.
December 12, 1990. Director, Joy Carlin;
scenery, Gerard Howland; lighting, Derek Duarte;
costumes, Gerard Howland, music and sound,
Stephen LeGrand.
Earl . . . . Ed Hodson
Lois. . . . . Cathy Thomas-Grant
Chrissie . . . . . Alden Fletcher, Jennifer Lorch
Lamar . . . . Michael McFall
Disneyland Cop . . . . Richard Butterfield,
James Patrick Kennedy
Librarian. . . . . Judith Moreland

Clerk . . . . Tim Lord
Time: The present. Act I: Disneyland. Act II:
Various parts of East Los Angeles. One inter-
mission.

DARK SUN. By Lisette Lecat Ross. April 19,
1991. Director, Edward Hastings; scenery, Joel
Fontaine; lighting, Derek Duarte; costumes, Karin
Simonson Kopischke; sound, Stephen LeGrand;
produced in association with Lorraine Hansberry
Theater.
Simon Kgoathe . . . . Seth Sibanda

Lydia de Jager . . . . Joy Carlin
Sipho . . . . Michael Chinyamurindi
Policemen . . . . Dumile Sadiqa Vokwana,
James Patrick Kennedy
Time: Winter, between mid-afternoon and dawn of the following day. Place: A house in the poorer section of the South African township of Soweto. One intermission.

Plays-in-Progress Series:
BABYLON GARDENS by Timothy Mason.
RUSHMORE by Anna Theresa Cascio.
PIGEON EGGHEAD by Dan Zellner.
AVAILABLE LIGHT by Ellen Moore.
RAISING CAEN by Irene Mecchi.

San Francisco: Magic Theater

(Artistic director, John Lion; managing director, Harvey Seifter)

Springfest:
THE HOUSE OF YES. By Wendy MacLeod. Director, Andrew Doe.
Marty Pascel . . . . Art Manke
Anthony Pascal . . . . . Kenneth R. Jerckx Jr.
Lesly . . . . Amy Resnick
Mrs. Pascal. . . . . Nancy Shelby
Jackie-O . . . . Celia Shuman
Time and Place: McLean, Virginia on Thanksgiving, during a hurricane, some 25 years after JFK's assassination. One intermission.

THE RED ADDRESS. By David Ives. Director, Kenn Watt; scenery, Jeff Rowlings; lighting, David Welle; costumes, Ann Tree Newson; sound, Andrew Murdock.
Dick . . . . Michael Girardin
Driver . . . . Ron Kaell
Soldier; Maitre' D . . . . Ron Knapp
Prostitute; Anne . . . . Erin McCulla
E.G. . . . . C.W. Morgan
Time and Place: The present, a mid-sized city in America.

THE SOILED EYES OF A GHOST. By Erin Cressida Wilson. Director, Clay Snider; scenery, Jeff Rowlings; lighting, David Welle; costumes, Ann Tree Newson; sound, Andrew Murdock.
Kendall. . . . . Sean Blackman
Nellie. . . . . Erin Cressida Wilson
Hal . . . . Dennis Ludlow
Clara . . . . Kathleen Turco-Lyon
Time and Place: Past, present and dream, beginning in Nellie's bedroom.

THE LAST FRONTIER. By David Barth. April 10, 1991. Director, R.A. White; scenery, Jeff Rowlings; lighting, David Welle; costumes, Ann Tree Newson; sound, Andrew Murdock.
Russ . . . . Jack Black
Rich . . . . C.W. Morgan
Jeff. . . . . Patrick Morris
Mike . . . . Michael Rivkin
Greta . . . . Cintra Wilson
Place: A campsite in Alaska.

San Jose, Calif.: San Jose Repertory Theater

(Artistic director, Timothy Near; managing director, Shannon Leskin)

FIRE IN THE RAIN. . .SINGER IN THE STORM: A MUSICAL DOCUDRAMA. By Holly Near. May 10, 1991. Director, Timothy Near; scenery, Kate Edmunds; lighting, Robert Peterson; costumes, Sigrid Insull; sound, Kim Foscato.

Sarasota: Florida Studio Theater

(Artistic director, Richard Hopkins)

HI-HAT HATTIE. By Larry Parr. Director, Richard Hopkins; scenery, Jeffrey W. Dean; lighting, Paul D. Romance; costumes, Marcella Beckwith.
Hattie McDaniel. . . . . Sharon Scott
Time and Place: An old theater and in Hattie's memory. Act I: Hattie's life from 1895 to 1938. Act II: Hattie's life from 1938 to 1952.

DYNAMIC PRODUCTS. By Ron House. Director, Stephen Rothman; scenery, Jeffrey W. Dean; lighting, Paul D. Romance; costumes, Marcella Beckwith, Thomas Preziosi.
Jules Mercier. . . . . Bradford Wallace
Roger Gallais . . . . Tony Papenfuss
Lola Montezuma . . . . Gloria Hayes
Nobby Carlysle. . . . . Doug Jones
Wanda Harrington . . . . Julia Flood
Shelly Levine. . . . . Lisa Kay Powers
Harvey Martin . . . . Doug Jones
Time: The present. Place: West Hollywood, California. One intermission.

DEATH BY MISADVENTURE. By Michael Shaffer. Director, Richard Hopkins; scenery, Jeffrey W. Dean; lighting, Paul D. Romance; costumes, Marcella Beckwith.

1st Collector;
   Nicholas Skeres. . . . . . . David Paul Wilson
2d Collector;
   William Shakespeare . . . . . . Douglas Jones
Guard; Edward Blount . . . . . . Stephen Ivester
Maidservant. . . . . . Elizabeth Anne Margolius
Audrey Walsingham . . . . Julia Flood
Christopher Marlowe. . . . . Rob Gomes
Ingram Frizer. . . . . Joseph Butler
1st Constable. . . . . Michael Hodgson
2d Constable; Scrivener;
   Robert Poley . . . . Roy Sorenson
3d Constable;
   William Danby . . . . Steve Mountan
Thomas Walsingham. . . . . . Martin LaPlatney
Magistrate . . . . Robert B. Dorsen
Eleanor Bull. . . . . Debbie Richards

Fall New Play Series, 1990:

MASQUERADE. By John Ulmer and David Brunetti. November 18, 1990.

PICK UP AX. By Anthony Clarvoe. November 25, 1990.

TWO GOOD BOYS. By Bary Jay Kaplan. November 28, 1990.

NEBRASKA. By Keith Reddin. December 2, 1990.

ONE FOOT IN SCARSDALE/AT WIT'S END. By Jack Fournier. December 5, 1990.

BLOOD RELATIVE. By Kevin Ottem. December 9, 1990.

MUD PEOPLE. By Keith Huff. December 12, 1990.

DOWN THE ROAD. By Lee Blessing. December 16, 1990.

NANO AND NICKI IN BOCA RATON. By Sherry Kramer. December 16, 1990.

LOVERS' MASQUE. By Michael Yeager. December 19, 1990.

Seattle: A Contemporary Theater

(Artistic director, Jeff Steitzer)

A NORMAL LIFE. By Eric Brogger. July 12, 1990. Director, Mary B. Robinson; scenery and lighting, Kent Dorsey; costumes, Mimi Maxmen; sound, Steven M. Klein.
Ruth Hart . . . . Jane Hoffman
Rebecca Hart . . . . Jeanne Paulsen
Seymour Hart . . . . Randy Hoffmeyer
Sarah Hart Merwin. . . . . . . Cheri Sorenson
Jasper Merwin . . . . Jonathan Hochberg
Lenny Hart. . . . . Mark Chamberlin
Michael Merwin . . . . Will McGarrahan
Jacob Baumann . . . . Peter Silbert
James Mannheim. . . . . . . Laurence Ballard
William Schorr . . . . Ivar Brogger
Thelma Poole . . . . Jane Fleiss
One intermission.

Seattle: The Empty Space Theater

(Artistic director, M. Burke Walker; managing director, Melissa Hines)

SMOKEY JOE'S CAFE: A NEW RHYTHM 'N' BLUES REVUE. By M. Burke Walker. Director, M. Burke Walker; musical direction, Sam Smith; choreographer, Steve Tomkins; scenery, Bill Forrester; lighting, Darren McCroom; costumes, Jazmin Mercer.
Lulu Belle Jenkins . . . . Korla Wygal
Tiny Joe Turner . . . . James Caddell
Miles Long . . . . Benny S. Cannon
Silky Stan Wilkins . . . . . . Alexander Jenkins
Reba Mae Wolcott . . . . Mari-Lynn
Orpheus Shaw. . . . . Sam Smith
   Time: The recent past. Place: Smokey Joe's, a nightclub. Act I: Saturday night, final set. Act II: After hours.

VIRTUS. By Gregg Loughridge. November, 1990. Director, Gregg Loughridge; scenery, Michael Olich; lighting, Meg Fox; costumes, Frances Kenny.
A Guy . . . . Kevin C. Loomis
That Guy . . . . Benny S. Cannon
The New Guy. . . . . Todd Jamieson
This Other Guy . . . . David P. Whitehead
The Same Old Guy . . . . . . Gregg Loughridge

UNKLE TOMM'S KABIN: A DECONSTRUCTION OF THE NOVEL BY HARRIET BEECHER STOWE. By Rick Rankin; additional text by J.T. Stewart and the Ensemble. Director, Susan Finque; scenery, Karen Gjelsteen; lighting, Patty Matthieu; sound, Steven M. Klein.
Liza . . . . Tawnya Pettiford-Wates
George . . . . Timothy McCuen Piggee
Arthur . . . . Kurt Beattie
Emily . . . . Laurie Thomas
Eva . . . . . . Rachel Street, Claudine Wallace
Lizbeth . . . . Ambra Nykol-Wates
Harry . . Marcus Khalfani Rolland, Sean Connor
Tommy . . . . Frankie Trevino

Soviet Theater: New Translations
THE BODY SHOP by Alexander Buravsky.

THE BATHTUB by Vladimir Mayakovsky.
LITTLE EGOR by Oleg Antonov.

Seattle: Intiman Theater Company

(Artistic director, Elizabeth Huddle; associate artistic director, Susan Fenichell)

THE KENTUCKY CYCLE. By Robert Schenkkan. June 1, 1991. Director, Warner Shook; scenery, Michael Olich; lighting, Peter Maradudin; costumes, Frances Kenny; sound, Jim Ragland. With Patrick Broemeling, Demene Hall, Ronald Hippe, Anthony Lee, Tuck Milligan, Jeanne Paulsen, Lillian Garrett-Groag, Charles Hallahan, Gregory Itzin, Scott MacDonald, Randy Oglesby, Jillayne Sorenson, Michael Winters.

Play in Progress:
IN THE TURRET ROOM by Ki Gottberg.

Seattle: Seattle Group Theater

(Founding artistic director, Ruben Sierra; producing director, Paul O'Connell)

THE INDEPENDENCE OF EDDIE ROSE. By William S. Yellow Robe Jr. Director, Tim Bond; scenery, Yuri Degtjar; lighting Darren McCroom; costumes, Kathleen Maki; sound, Steven M. Klein.
Eddie Rose. . . . . M. Cochise Anderson
Thelma . . . . Phyllis Brisson
Katherine Rose. . . . . Sheri Foster
Mike Horse . . . . Jose Gonzales
Lenny Sharb . . . . Mitch Hale
Sam Jacobs . . . . Winston-Jose Rocha-Castillo
Theia Rose. . . . . Ah-Bead Soot
One intermission.

6th Annual Multi-Cultural Playwrights' Festival August 5-19, 1990:

INTERRACIAL RELATIONS. By Perry Miyake. August 6, 1990.
BAYCHESTER AVE./THE BRONX. By Dominic Taylor. August 11, 1990.
CANAL ZONE. By Roger Arturo Durling. August 13, 1990.
THE WAITING. By Mabel Jackson. August 16 & 18, 1990.
THE GOONG HAY KID. By Alvin Eng. August 17 & 19, 1990.
THE LIFE OF A WORM. By K.J. Warren. August 18, 1990.

Seattle: Seattle Repertory Theater

(Artistic director, Daniel Sullivan)

CONVERSATIONS WITH MY FATHER. By Herb Gardner. April 17, 1991. Director, Daniel Sullivan; scenery, Tony Walton; lighting, Pat Collins; costumes, Robert Wodjewodski; sound, Michael Holten.
Eddie. . . . . Judd Hirsch
Charlie . . . . Tony Shalhoub
Gusta. . . . . Gordana Rashovich
Zaretsky . . . . Lee Richardson
Young Joey. . . . . Jason M. Biggs
Hannah Di Blindeh . . . . June Gable
Nick. . . . . William Biff McGuire
Finney the Book . . . . Sean G. Griffin
Jimmy Scalso . . . . John Procaccino
Blue. . . . . Jack Wallace
Young Charlie. . . . . Benny Grant
Joey . . . . Rick Schatz
One intermission.

Springfield, Mass.: StageWest

(Artistic director, Eric Hill; managing director, Martha Richards)

SWEET 'N HOT IN HARLEM. Music by Harold Arlen, lyrics by Harold Arlen, Truman Capote, Ira Gershwin, E.Y. Harburg, Ted Koehler, Johnny Mercer, Billy Rose and Jack Yellen. Director, Clinton Turner Davis; scenery, Keith Henry; lighting, William H. Grant III; costumes, Kristin Yungkurth; sound, David A. Strang. With Mary Denise Bentley, Keith Davis, Julia Lema-Jackson, Andre Montgomery.
One intermission.

Stockbridge, Mass.: Berkshire Theater Festival

(Artistic director, Richard Dunlap)

SINCERITY FOREVER. By Mac Wellman. July 25, 1990. Director, Richard Caliban. Scenery, James Youmans; lighting, Kenneth Posner; costumes, Mary Myers; sound, Scott David Sanders.

Jesus H. Christ . . . . Ntare Mwine
Furball #1 . . . . Lu'Ann Adams

Furball #2 . . . . Tom Simpson

Sincere Young Persons; Members of the Invisible Empire: Angie Phillips, Kate Forbes, Jason Duchin, Tom Hildreth, Mark Singale, Ariane Brandt.

An ATCA selection; see introduction to this section.

SEATTLE GROUP THEATER—Sheri Foster and M. Chochise Anderson in the world premiere of *The Independence of Eddie Rose* by William S. Yellow Robe Jr.

Sunnyvale, Calif.: California Theater Center

(Resident director, Will Huddleston)

UNDINE. Music by Andras Ranki, lyrics by James Keller. November 10, 1990. Director, Albert Takazauckas; scenery, John Bonard Wilson; lighting, Kurt Landisman; costumes, Jane Lambert.

Undine	Alison Gleason
Hans von Ringstetten	Larry Henderson
Bertalda	Linnea D. Pyne
Uncle Coolspring	Will Huddleston
Fisherman	Robert Emmett Greene
Ilsebill	Mary Gibboney
Father Heilmann	Will Huddleston
Storm; Duke; Duchess;	
Water-spirits; Mourners	David Kelly,
	Veronique Jeanmarie,
	Dirk Leatherman

THE ELVES AND THE SHOEMAKER. Adapted by Gayle Cornelison. December 1, 1990. Director, Lynne A. Pace; scenery and lighting, Paul G. Vallerga; costumes, Jane Lambert.

Hans	Dirk Leatherman
Claudia	Linnea D. Pyne
Wolfgang	Charlie Shoemaker
The Elves:	
Alison	Alison Gleason
Jonathan	Jonathan Rider

THE UGLY DUCKLING. Adapted by Gayle Cornelison from Hans Christian Andersen. January 5, 1991. Director, Will Huddleston; scenery, Michael Cook; lighting, Bill M. Rupel; costumes, Colleen Troy Lewis. With Conrad Cimarra, Julianne Crofts, Veronique Jeanmarie, Kiira Jepson.

THE TIME MACHINE. Adapted by Gayle Cornelison from H.G. Wells. February 2, 1991. Director, Will Huddleston; scenery, Paul G. Vallerga; lighting, Bill M. Rupel; costumes, Jane Lambert.

Time Traveler	Alex Fernandez
Filby	Charlie Shoemaker
Mrs. Watchett	Kiira Jepson
Mayor	Dirk Leatherman
Doctor	Robert Emmett Greene
Psychologist	Jonathan Rider
Weena	Linnea D. Pyne
Cyclopede	Conrad Cimarra

KING OF THE GOLDEN RIVER. Adapted by James Still from the story by John Ruskin. April 13, 1991. Director, Will Huddleston; scenery, Paul G. Vallerga; lighting, Bill M. Rupel; costumes, Colleen Troy Lewis; sound, Dirk Leatherman.

Old Man	Alex Fernandez
Hans	Jonathan Rider
Schwartz	Charlie Shoemaker
Gluck	Alison Gleason
Southwest Wind	Xiao Yan Lu
King of the Golden River	Linnea D. Pyne

Washington, D.C.: Arena Stage

(Producing director, Zelda Fichandler; artistic director, Douglas C. Wager)

CERCEAU. By Viktor Slavkin. October 12, 1990. Director, Liviu Ciulei; lighting, Nancy Schertler; scenery, Liviu Ciulei; costumes, Marjorie Slaiman; sound, Susan R. White.

Petushok	Charles Geyer
Valyusha	Randy Danson
Vladimir Ivanovich	Jed Diamond
Lars	John Leonard Thompson
Nadya	Pamela Nyberg
Pasha	David Marks
Koka	Richard Bauer

   Time and Place: Late Summer, 1983, a summerhouse on the outskirts of Moscow.

BEFORE IT HITS HOME. By Cheryl West. January 18, 1991. Director, Tazewell Thompson; scenery, Douglas Stein; lighting, Nancy Schertler; costumes, Helen Qizhi Huang; sound, Susan R. White.

Wendal	Michael Jayce
Simone	Cynthia Martells
Douglass	Keith Randolph Smith
Reba	Trazana Beverly
Mrs. Peterson	Cynthia Martells
Nurse	Mercedes Herrero
Maybelle	Sandra Reaves-Phillips
Doctor	Jurian Hughes
Bailey	Wally Taylor
Dwayne	Ryan Richmond
Junior	Lee Simon Jr.

BORN GUILTY. Adapted by Ari Roth, based on the book by Peter Sichrovsky. January 20, 1991. Director, Zelda Fichandler; scenery, Douglas Stein; lighting, Nancy Schertler; costumes, Noel Borden; sound, Susan R. White.

Helen Carey	Pamela Nyberg
Marissa Copeland	Harold Perrineau Jr.
Ralph Cosham	Henry Strozier
Jed Diamond	John Leonard Thompson
David Marks	Halo Wines

   Time and Place: 1988-1990, Germany.

SOURCE THEATER COMPANY. WASHINGTON,
D.C.—Carlos Juan Gonzalez and Scott Morgan in a scene
from Roy Barber's *Children With Stones*

VIVISECTIONS FROM THE BLOWN MIND.
By Alonzo D. Lamont Jr. April 26, 1991.
Director, Clinton Turner Davis; scenery, Michael
Franklin-White; lighting, Christopher V. Lewton;
costumes, Betty Seigel; sound, Celeste A-Re.

Castro . . . . Lee Simon Jr.
Angelique . . . . Katrina Van Duyn
Dusty . . . . M.E. Hart
Goliath Ardsberry . . . . Vincent Brown

Washington, D.C.: Source Theater Company

(Producing artistic director, Pat Murphy Sheehy)

CHILDREN WITH STONES. By Roy Barber.
Director, Janet Wallis; scenery, Elizabeth
Jenkins; lighting, David Zemmels; costumes,
Janet Wallis.
Eli . . . . Carlos Juan Gonzalez
Ruth . . . . Barbara Rappaport
Isaac . . . . Scott Morgan
Beth . . . . Bari Biern

Ruben . . . . Richard Rohan
Dov . . . . Sheldon S. Gilbert
Esther Spiegel . . . . Karen Eriksen
UnAmin . . . . Louise Reynolds
Nadya . . . . Lisette LeCompte
Tasir . . . . Scott Sedar
Emil . . . . R. Daniel Luna
Muhammed . . . . George Fulginiti-Shakar

Daoud. . . . . Wayne Henson
Fawaz . . . . Jim Cantrell

Place: Various locations in Israel, the West Bank and Gaza. One intermission.

Waterford, Conn.: Eugene O'Neill Theater Center

(Artistic director, Lloyd Richards)

National Playwrights Conference
July 2-July 28, 1990

TIES THAT BIND. By Walter Allen Bennett Jr.
PART II: BUSTER COMES THROUGH. By Phil Bosakowski.
BRICKLAYERS. By Elvira DiPaolo.
DOWN THE SHORE. By Tom Donaghy.
EMPATHY. By Ned Eisenberg.
THE WIZARDS OF QUIZ. By Steve Feffer.
BOBBY, CAN YOU HEAR ME? By Judith GeBauer.
COYOTE HANGIN' ON A BARBED WIRE FENCE. By Percy Granger.
THE ENCHANTED MAZE. By Murphy Guyer.
JUMP AT THE SUN! By Kathleen McGhee-Anderson.
SONS OF DON JUAN. By John PiRoman.
OFF THE METER. By Peter Zablotsky.

EXODUS. By M. Mekhanoshin (U.S.S.R. exchange playwright).

National Music Theater Conference

CAPTAINS COURAGEOUS. Book and lyrics by Patrick Cook, music by Frederick Freyer.
IL MUSICA. Libretto by Ian Strasfogel, music by Larry Grossman.
SWAMP GAS AND SHALLOW FEELINGS. Book by Shirlee Strother, Williams Buck and Randy Buck, music and lyrics by Jack Eric Williams.
THE MASTER AND MARGARITA. Book by Sherry Kramer, music by Margaret R. Pine, lyrics by Sherry Kramer and Margaret R. Pine.

Directors and music directors: Barbara Damashek, Clay Fullum, Stephen Milbank, Will Roberson, Kelly Robinson.

Williamstown, Mass.: Williamstown Theater Festival

(Artistic director, Peter Hunt)

NO ORCHIDS FOR MISS BLANDISH. By Robert David MacDonald, adapted from the novel by James Hadley Chase. June 26, 1990 (American premiere). Director Rosey Hay; scenery, Craig Clipper; costumes, Eric Hansen; lighting, Christina Giannelli.

Miss Blandish. . . . . Margaret Klenek
Anna Morgenstern . . . . Kate Burton
Mr. Lucie . . . . Rudy Caporaso
Doyle . . . . Doug Harmsen
Riley . . . . Roberto Fente
Johnny . . . . Patrick Boll
Eddie Schultz . . . . Tom Tammi
Chunk . . . . Michael Johnson
Doc Williams . . . . Steve Lawson
Slim Grisson. . . . . John Hickey
Ma Grisson . . . . Molly Regan
Fenner . . . . Steve Ryan
One intermission.

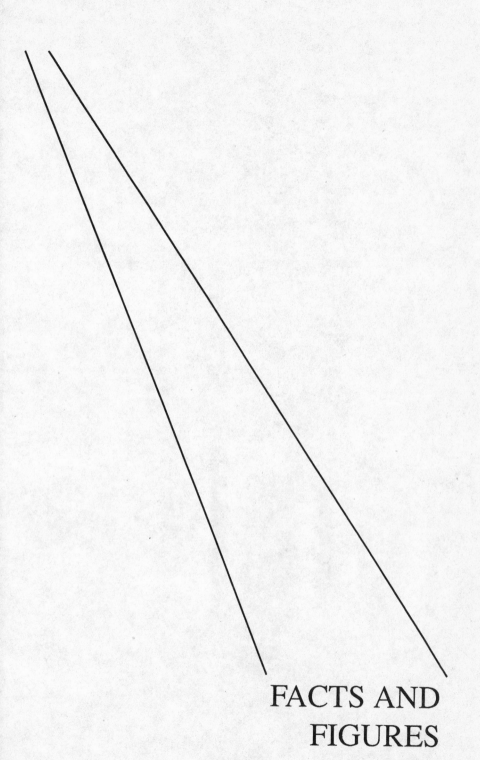

FACTS AND
FIGURES

LONG RUNS ON BROADWAY

The following shows have run 500 or more continuous performances in a single production, usually the first, not including previews or extra non-profit performances, allowing for vacation layoffs and special one-booking engagements, but not including return engagements after a show has gone on tour. In all cases, the numbers were obtained directly from the show's production offices. Where there are title similarities, the production is identified as follows: (p) straight play versions, (m) musical version, (r) revival.

THROUGH MAY 31, 1991

(PLAYS MARKED WITH ASTERISK WERE STILL PLAYING JUNE 1, 1991)

Plays	Number Performances	Plays	Number Performances
A Chorus Line.	6,137	Mary, Mary	1,572
Oh! Calcutta! (r).	5,959	Evita.	1,567
*Cats	3,610	The Voice of the Turtle	1,557
42nd Street	3,486	Barefoot in the Park.	1,530
Grease.	3,388	Brighton Beach Memoirs	1,530
Fiddler on the Roof	3,242	Dreamgirls	1,522
Life With Father.	3,224	Mame (m).	1,508
Tobacco Road.	3,182	Same Time, Next Year	1,453
Hello, Dolly!	2,844	Arsenic and Old Lace.	1,444
My Fair Lady	2,717	The Sound of Music.	1,443
Annie	2,377	My and My Girl.	1,420
Man of La Mancha	2,328	How to Succeed in Business	
Abie's Irish Rose	2,327	Without Really Trying	1,417
Oklahoma!	2,212	Hellzapoppin	1,404
Pippin.	1,944	*The Phantom of the Opera.	1,398
South Pacific	1,925	The Music Man	1,375
The Magic Show	1,920	Funny Girl.	1,348
Deathtrap	1,793	Mummenschanz.	1,326
Gemini	1,788	Angel Street.	1,295
Harvey.	1,775	Lightnin'	1,291
Dancin'	1,774	Promises, Promises	1,281
La Cage aux Folles	1,761	The King and I	1,246
Hair	1,750	Cactus Flower.	1,234
*Les Misérables.	1,696	Sleuth	1,222
The Wiz.	1,672	Torch Song Trilogy	1,222
Born Yesterday	1,642	1776.	1,217
The Best Little Whorehouse in		Equus	1,209
Texas.	1,639	Sugar Babies	1,208
Ain't Misbehavin'.	1,604	Guys and Dolls	1,200

Plays	Number Performances	Plays	Number Performances
Amadeus	1,181	Chapter Two	857
Cabaret	1,165	A Streetcar Named Desire	855
Mister Roberts	1,157	Barnum	854
Annie Get Your Gun	1,147	Comedy in Music	849
The Seven Year Itch	1,141	Raisin	847
Butterflies Are Free	1,128	You Can't Take It With You	837
Pins and Needles	1,108	La Plume de Ma Tante	835
Plaza Suite	1,097	Three Men on a Horse	835
They're Playing Our Song	1,082	The Subject Was Roses	832
Kiss Me, Kate	1,070	Black and Blue	824
Don't Bother Me, I Can't Cope	1,065	Inherit the Wind	806
The Pajama Game	1,063	Anything Goes (r)	804
Shenandoah	1,050	No Time for Sergeants	796
The Teahouse of the August Moon	1,027	Fiorello!	795
Damn Yankees	1,019	Where's Charley?	792
Never Too Late	1,007	The Ladder	789
Big River	1,005	Forty Carats	780
Any Wednesday	982	The Prisoner of Second Avenue	780
A Funny Thing Happened on the Way to the Forum	964	M. Butterfly	777
The Odd Couple	964	Oliver!	774
Anna Lucasta	957	The Pirates of Penzance (1980 r)	772
Kiss and Tell	956	Woman of the Year	770
Dracula (r)	925	My One and Only	767
Bells Are Ringing	924	Sophisticated Ladies	767
The Moon Is Blue	924	Bubbling Brown Sugar	766
Beatlemania	920	Into the Woods	765
The Elephant Man	916	State of the Union	765
Luv	901	Starlight Express	761
Chicago (m)	898	The First Year	760
Applause	896	Broadway Bound	756
Can-Can	892	You Know I Can't Hear You When the Water's Running	755
Carousel	890	Two for the Seesaw	750
I'm Not Rappaport	890	Joseph and the Amazing Technicolor Dreamcoat (r)	747
Hats Off to Ice	889	Death of a Salesman	742
Fanny	888	For Colored Girls, etc.	742
Children of a Lesser God	887	Sons o' Fun	742
Follow the Girls	882	Candide (m,r)	740
Camelot	873	Gentlemen Prefer Blondes	740
I Love My Wife	872	The Man Who Came to Dinner	739
The Bat	867	Nine	739
My Sister Eileen	864	Call Me Mister	734
No, No, Nanette (r)	861	West Side Story	732
Song of Norway	860	High Button Shoes	727

Plays	Number Performances	Plays	Number Performances
Finian's Rainbow	725	The Green Pastures	640
Claudia	722	Auntie Mame (p)	639
The Gold Diggers	720	A Man for All Seasons	637
Jesus Christ Superstar	720	Jerome Robbins' Broadway	634
Carnival	719	The Fourposter	632
The Diary of Anne Frank	717	The Music Master	627
I Remember Mama	714	Two Gentlemen of Verona (m)	627
Tea and Sympathy	712	The Tenth Man	623
Junior Miss	710	The Heidi Chronicles	621
Last of the Red Hot Lovers	706	Is Zat So?	618
Company	705	Anniversary Waltz	615
Seventh Heaven	704	The Happy Time (p)	614
Gypsy (m)	702	Separate Rooms	613
The Miracle Worker	700	*City of Angels	611
That Championship Season	700	Affairs of State	610
Da	697	Oh! Calcutta!	610
The King and I (r)	696	Star and Garter	609
Cat on a Hot Tin Roof	694	The Mystery of Edwin Drood	608
Li'l Abner	693	The Student Prince	608
The Children's Hour	691	Sweet Charity	608
Purlie	688	Bye Bye Birdie	607
Dead End	687	Irene (r)	604
The Lion and the Mouse	686	Sunday in the Park With George	604
White Cargo	686	Adonis	603
Dear Ruth	683	Broadway	603
East Is West	680	Peg o' My Heart	603
Come Blow Your Horn	677	Street Scene (p)	601
The Most Happy Fella	676	Flower Drum Song	600
The Doughgirls	671	Kiki	600
The Impossible Years	670	A Little Night Music	600
Irene	670	Agnes of God	599
Boy Meets Girl	669	Don't Drink the Water	598
The Tap Dance Kid	669	Wish You Were Here	598
Beyond the Fringe	667	Sarafina	597
Who's Afraid of Virginia Woolf?	664	A Society Circus	596
Blithe Spirit	657	Absurd Person Singular	592
A Trip to Chinatown	657	A Day in Hollywood/	
The Women	657	A Night in the Ukraine	588
Bloomer Girl	654	The Me Nobody Knows	586
The Fifth Season	654	The Two Mrs. Carrolls	585
Rain	648	Kismet (m)	583
*Grand Hotel	647	Brigadoon	581
Witness for the Prosecution	645	Detective Story	581
Call Me Madam	644	No Strings	580
Janie	642	Brother Rat	577

Plays	*Number Performances*	*Plays*	*Number Performances*
Blossom Time	576	Crimes of the Heart	535
Pump Boys and Dinettes	573	The Unsinkable Molly Brown	532
Show Boat	572	The Red Mill (r)	531
The Show-Off	571	Rumors	531
Sally	570	A Raisin in the Sun	530
Golden Boy (m)	568	Godspell	527
One Touch of Venus	567	Fences	526
The Real Thing	566	The Solid Gold Cadillac	526
Happy Birthday	564	Biloxi Blues	524
Look Homeward, Angel	564	Irma La Douce	524
Morning's at Seven (r)	564	The Boomerang	522
The Glass Menagerie	561	Follies	521
I Do! I Do!	560	Rosalinda	521
Wonderful Town	559	The Best Man	520
Rose Marie	557	Chauve-Souris	520
Strictly Dishonorable	557	Blackbirds of 1928	518
Sweeney Todd, the Demon Barber of Fleet Street	557	The Gin Game	517
The Great White Hope	556	Sunny	517
A Majority of One	556	Victoria Regina	517
Sunrise at Campobello	556	Fifth of July	511
Toys in the Attic	556	Half a Sixpence	511
Jamaica	555	The Vagabond King	511
Stop the World—I Want to Get Off	555	The New Moon	509
Florodora	553	The World of Suzie Wong	508
Noises Off	553	The Rothschilds	507
Ziegfeld Follies (1943)	553	On Your Toes (r)	505
Dial "M" for Murder	552	Sugar	505
Good News	551	Shuffle Along	504
Peter Pan (r)	551	Up in Central Park	504
Let's Face It	547	Carmen Jones	503
Milk and Honey	543	The Member of the Wedding	501
Within the Law	541	Panama Hattie	501
Pal Joey (r)	540	Personal Appearance	501
What Makes Sammy Run?	540	Bird in Hand	500
The Sunshine Boys	538	Room Service	500
What a Life	538	Sailor, Beware!	500
		Tomorrow the World	500

LONG RUNS OFF BROADWAY

Plays	Number Performances	Plays	Number Performances
*The Fantasticks	12,898	True West	762
The Threepenny Opera	2,611	Isn't It Romantic	733
Forbidden Broadway 1982-87	2,332	Dime a Dozen	728
*Nunsense	2,261	The Pocket Watch	725
Little Shop of Horrors	2,209	The Connection	722
Godspell	2,124	The Passion of Dracula	714
Vampire Lesbians of Sodom	2,024	Adaptation & Next	707
Jacques Brel	1,847	Oh! Calcutta!	704
Vanities	1,785	Scuba Duba	692
*Perfect Crime	1,677	The Foreigner	686
You're a Good Man Charlie Brown	1,597	The Knack	685
The Blacks	1,408	The Club	674
One Mo' Time	1,372	The Balcony	672
Let My People Come	1,327	Penn & Teller	666
Driving Miss Daisy	1,195	America Hurrah	634
The Hot l Baltimore	1,166	Oil City Symphony	626
I'm Getting My Act Together and Taking It on the Road	1,165	Hogan's Goat	607
Little Mary Sunshine	1,143	Beehive	600
Steel Magnolias	1,126	The Trojan Women	600
El Grande de Coca-Cola	1,114	The Dining Room	583
Tamara	1,036	Krapp's Last Tape & The Zoo Story	582
One Flew Over the Cuckoo's Nest (r)	1,025	The Dumbwaiter & The Collection	578
The Boys in the Band	1,000	Forbidden Broadway 1990-91	576
Fool for Love	1,000	Dames at Sea	575
Cloud 9	971	The Crucible (r)	571
*Other People's Money	954	The Iceman Cometh (r)	565
Sister Mary Ignatius Explains It All for You & The Actor's Nightmare	947	The Hostage (r)	545
Your Own Thing	933	What's a Nice Country Like You Doing in a State Like This?	543
Curley McDimple	931	Forbidden Broadway 1988-89	534
Leave It to Jane (r)	928	Frankie and Johnny in the Clair de Lune	533
The Mad Show	871	Six Characters in Search of an Author (r)	529
Scrambled Feet	831	The Dirtiest Show in Town	509
The Effect of Gamma Rays on Man-in-the-Moon Marigolds	819	Happy Ending & Day of Absence	504
A View From the Bridge (r)	780	Greater Tuna	501
The Boy Friend (r)	763	A Shayna Maidel	501
		The Boys From Syracuse (r)	500

NEW YORK DRAMA CRITICS CIRCLE AWARDS, 1935-36 to 1990-91

Listed below are the New York Drama Critics Circle Awards from 1935-36 through 1990-91 classsified as follows: (1) Best American Play, (2) Best Foreign Play, (3) Best Musical, (4) Best, regardless of category (this category was established by new voting rules in 1962-63 and did not exist prior to that year).

1935-36—(1) Winterset

1936-37—(1) High Tor

1937-38—(1) Of Mice and Men, (2) Shadow and Substance

1938-39—(1) No award, (2) The White Steed

1939-40—(1) The Time of Your Life

1940-41—(1) Watch on the Rhine, (2) The Corn Is Green

1941-42—(1) No award, (2) Blithe Spirit

1942-43—(2) The Patriots

1943-44—(2) Jacobowsky and the Colonel

1944-45—(1) The Glass Menagerie

1945-46—(3) Carousel

1946-47—(1) All My Sons, (2) No Exit, (3) Brigadoon

1947-48—(1) A Streetcar Named Desire, (2) The Winslow Boy

1948-49—(1) Death of a Salesman, (2) The Madwoman of Chaillot, (3) South Pacific

1949-50—(1) The Member of the Wedding, (2) The Cocktail Party, (3) The Consul

1950-51—(1) Darkness at Noon, (2) The Lady's Not for Burning, (3) Guys and Dolls

1951-52—(1) I Am a Camera, (2) Venus Observed, (3) Pal Joey (Special citation to Don Juan in Hell)

1952-53—(1) Picnic, (2) The Love of Four Colonels, (3) Wonderful Town

1953-54—(1) Teahouse of the August Moon, (2) Ondine, (3) The Golden Apple

1954-55—(1) Cat on a Hot Tin Roof, (2) Witness for the Prosecution, (3) The Saint of Bleecker Street

1955-56—(1) The Diary of Anne Frank, (2) Tiger at the Gates, (3) My Fair Lady

1956-57—(1) Long Day's Journey Into Night, (2) The Waltz of the Toreadors, (3) The Most Happy Fella

1957-58—(1) Look Homeward, Angel, (2) Look Back in Anger, (3) The Music Man

1958-59—(1) A Raisin in the Sun, (2) The Visit, (3) La Plume de Ma Tante

1959-60—(1) Toys in the Attic, (2) Five Finger Exercise, (3) Fiorello!

1960-61—(1) All the Way Home, (2) A Taste of Honey, (3) Carnival

1961-62—(1) The Night of the Iguana, (2) A Man for All Seasons, (3) How to Succeed in Business Without Really Trying

1962-63—(4) Who's Afraid of Virginia Woolf? (Special citation to Beyond the Fringe)

1963-64—(4) Luther, (3) Hello, Dolly! (Special citation to The Trojan Women)

1964-65—(4) The Subject Was Roses, (3) Fiddler on the Roof

1965-66—(1) The Persecution and Assassination of Marat as Performed by the Inmates of the Asylum of Charenton Under the Direction of the Marquis de Sade, (3) Man of La Mancha

1966-67—(4) The Homecoming, (3) Cabaret

1967-68—(4) Rosencrantz and Guildenstern Are Dead, (3) Your Own Thing

1968-69—(4) The Great White Hope, (3) 1776

1969-70—(4) Borstal Boy, (1) The Effect of Gamma Rays on Man-in-the-Moon Marigolds, (3) Company

1970-71—(4) Home, (1) The House of Blue Leaves, (3) Follies

1971-72—(4) That Championship Season, (2) The Screens, (3) Two Gentlemen of Verona (Special citation to Sticks and Bones and Old Times)

1972-73—(4) The Changing Room, (1) The Hot l Baltimore, (3) A Little Night Music

1973-74—(4) The Contractor, (1) Short Eyes, (3) Candide

1974-75—(4) Equus, (1) The Taking of Miss Janie, (3) A Chorus Line

1975-76—(4) Travesties, (1) Streamers, (3) Pacific Overtures

1976-77—(4) Otherwise Engaged, (1) American Buffalo, (3) Annie

1977-78—(4) Da, (3) Ain't Misbehavin'

1978-79—(4) The Elephant Man, (3) Sweeney Todd, the Demon Barber of Fleet Street

1979-80—(4) Talley's Folly, (2) Betrayal, (3) Evita (Special Citation to Peter Brook's Le Center International de Créations Théâtrales for its repertory)

1980-81—(4) A Lesson From Aloes, (1) Crimes of the Heart (Special citations to Lena Horne: The Lady and Her Music and the New York Shakespeare Festival production of The Pirates of Penzance)

1981-82—(4) The Life & Adventures of Nicholas Nickleby, (1) A Soldier's Play

1982-83—(4) Brighton Beach Memoirs, (2) Plenty, (3) Little Shop of Horrors (Special citation to Young Playwrights Festival)

1983-84—(4) The Real Thing; (1) Glengarry Glen Ross, (3) Sunday in the Park With George (Special citation to Samuel Beckett for the body of his work)

1984-85—(4) Ma Rainey's Black Bottom

1985-86—(4) A Lie of the Mind, (2) Benefactors (Special citation to The Search for Signs of Intelligent Life in the Universe)

1986-87—(4) Fences, (2) Les Liaisons Danger-

euses, (3) Les Misérables

1987-88—(4) Joe Turner's Come and Gone, (2) The Road to Mecca, (3) Into the Woods

1988-89—(4) The Heidi Chronicles, (2) Aristocrats (Special citation to Bill Irwin for Largely New York)

1989-90—(4) The Piano Lesson, (2) Privates on Parade, (3) City of Angels

1990-91—(4) Six Degrees of Separation, (2) Our Country's Good, (3) The Will Rogers Follies (Special citation to Eileen Atkins for her portrayal of Virginia Woolf in A Room of One's Own)

NEW YORK DRAMA CRITICS CIRCLE VOTING, 1990-91

The New York Drama Critics Circle voted John Guare's *Six Degrees of Separation* the best play of the season by a first-ballot majority of 13 votes (Michael Feingold, Melanie Kirkpatrick, Howard Kissel, Mimi Kramer, Jack Kroll, Michael Kuchwara, Don Nelsen, Julius Novick, Edith Oliver, William Raidy, Jerry Tallmer, Edwin Wilson, Linda Winer) to 5 votes for Neil Simon's *Lost in Yonkers* (Clive Barnes, John Beaufort, William A. Henry III, Jacques le Sourd, Douglas Watt) and 1 vote for David Hirson's *La Bête* (Jan Stuart). Of the three other Circle members, John Simon of *New York* did not attend the meeting nor submit a proxy, and Frank Rich and Mel Gussow of the New York *Times* are non-voting members, per their paper's policy against having its critics participate in such award-giving.

The Critics having selected an American play as best regardless of category, the Circle then proceeded to select a best foreign play. None having received a majority on the first ballot, under their rules the Circle then proceeded to a second weighted ballot (3 points for first choice, 2 for second and 1 for third), considering only those plays which had already received first-ballot first-choice votes. Timberlake Wertenbaker's *Our Country's Good* won with 32 points against Patrick Garland's adaptation of Virginia Woolf's book *A Room of One's Own* (20), Alan Ayckbourn's *Absent Friends* (17), William Nicholson's *Shadowlands* (15) and David Stevens's *The Sum of Us* (12)—see summary of this balloting below. Julius Novick of the New York *Observer* was absent and voting by proxy for *Absent Friends* in this category (and *Falsettoland* as best musical) on the first-choice ballot, but the Circle does not count proxies on weighted ballots, Michael Feingold of the *Village Voice* and Jerry Tallmer of the New York *Post* abstained.

In the voting for the season's best musical, no show received a first-ballot majority. On the second, weighted ballot, *The Will Rogers Follies* by Peter Stone, Cy Coleman, Betty Comden and Adolph Green won with 26 points (more than the requisite plurality of three times the number of members voting in the category— 15—divided by two, plus one—i.e., 24 in this case— see summary of the balloting below). *The Secret Garden* by Marsha Norman and Lucy Simon was a close second with 21 points, followed by *Assassins* by John Weidman and Stephen Sondheim (18), *Miss Saigon* by Alain Boublil, Claude-Michel Schönberg and

Richard Maltby Jr. (17) and *Falsettoland* by William Finn and James Lapine (8). Edith Oliver, William Raidy and Linda Winer abstained.

The 18 members of the circle present and voting at this meeting then voted a special award to Eileen Atkins for her portrayal of Virginia Woolf in *A Room of One's Own.*

SECOND BALLOT FOR BEST FOREIGN PLAY

Critic	1st Choice (3 pts.)	2d Choice (2 pts.)	3d Choice (1 pt.)
Clive Barnes *Post*	Our Country's Good	Shadowlands	Absent Friends
John Beaufort *Monitor*	Shadowlands	Our Country's Good	Absent Friends
William A. Henry III *Time*	Shadowlands	Absent Friends	The Sum of Us
Melanie Kirkpatrick *Wall St. Journal*	Our Country's Good	Shadowlands	A Room of One's Own
Howard Kissel *Daily News*	Our Country's Good	A Room of One's Own	Absent Friends
Mimi Kramer *The New Yorker*	The Sum of Us	A Room of One's Own	Absent Friends
Jack Kroll *Newsweek*	Our Country's Good	A Room of One's Own	Absent Friends
Michael Kuchwara Associated Press	Our Country's Good	A Room of One's Own	Absent Friends
Jacques le Sourd Gannett Newspapers	The Sum of Us	A Room of One's Own	Shadowlands
Don Nelsen *Daily News*	Our Country's Good	The Sum of Us	A Room of One's Own
Edith Oliver *The New Yorker*	Absent Friends	Our Country's Good	Shadowlands
William Raidy Newhouse Papers	A Room of One's Own	Absent Friends	Our Country's Good
Jan Stuart *Newsday*	Our Country's Good	The Sum of Us	Shadowlands
Douglas Watt *Daily News*	Absent Friends	A Room of One's Own	Our Country's Good
Edwin Wilson *Wall St. Journal*	Our Country's Good	Shadowlands	Absent Friends
Linda Winer *Newsday*	A Room of One's Own	Our Country's Good	The Sum of Us

SECOND BALLOT FOR BEST MUSICAL

Critic	1st Choice (3 pts.)	2d Choice (2 pts.)	3d Choice (1 pt.)
Clive Barnes	The Will Rogers Follies	The Secret Garden	Assassins
John Beaufort	The Will Rogers Follies	The Secret Garden	Miss Saigon
Michael Feingold	The Secret Garden	Falsettoland	The Will Rogers Follies
William A. Henry III	Falsettoland	The Secret Garden	Miss Saigon
Melanie Kirkpatrick	Miss Saigon	The Will Rogers Follies	Assassins
Howard Kissell	The Will Rogers Follies	Assassins	Miss Saigon
Mimi Kramer	The Secret Garden	Assassins	Falsettoland
Jack Kroll	The Will Rogers Follies	Assassins	The Secret Garden
Michael Kuchwara	Assassins	Miss Saigon	Falsettoland
Jacques le Sourd	Miss Saigon	The Will Rogers Follies	Assassins
Don Nelsen	Assassins	The Will Rogers Follies	The Secret Garden
Jan Stuart	The Secret Garden	Assassins	Falsettoland
Jerry Tallmer	The Will Rogers Follies	Miss Saigon	Assassins
Douglas Watt	The Will Rogers Follies	The Secret Garden	Miss Saigon
Edwin Wilson	Miss Saigon	The Secret Garden	The Will Rogers Follies

CHOICES OF SOME OTHER CRITICS

Critic	Best Play	Best Musical
Alvin Klein New York Times Regional, WNYC	Absent Friends	Falsettoland
Stewart Klein WNYW-TV	Six Degrees of Separation	"Chorus Girl" segment of The Will Rogers Follies
Jeffrey Lyons WPIX-TV, WCBS Radio	Six Degrees of Separation	The Will Rogers Follies
Neal Rosen WNCN Radio	Lost in Yonkers	Miss Saigon
Richard S. Scholem Greater N.Y. Radio	Lost in Yonkers	Miss Saigon
Leida Snow WINS Radio	Lost in Yonkers	The Secret Garden
Allan Wallach Newsday	Lost in Yonkers	Falsettoland

PULITZER PRIZE WINNERS, 1916-17 TO 1990-91

1916-17—No award
1917-18—Why Marry?, by Jesse Lynch Williams
1918-19—No award
1919-20—Beyond the Horizon, by Eugene O'Neill
1920-21—Miss Lulu Bett, by Zona Gale
1921-22—Anna Christie, by Eugene O'Neill
1922-23—Icebound, by Owen Davis
1923-24—Hell-Bent fer Heaven, by Hatcher Hughes
1924-25—They Knew What They Wanted, by Sidney Howard
1925-26—Craig's Wife, by George Kelly
1926-27—In Abraham's Bosom, by Paul Green
1927-28—Strange Interlude, by Eugene O'Neill
1928-29—Street Scene, by Elmer Rice
1929-30—The Green Pastures, by Marc Connelly
1930-31—Alison's House, by Susan Glaspell
1931-32—Of Thee I Sing, by George S. Kaufman, Morrie Ryskind, Ira and George Gershwin
1932-33—Both Your Houses, by Maxwell Anderson
1933-34—Men in White, by Sidney Kingsley
1934-35—The Old Maid, by Zoë Akins
1935-36—Idiot's Delight, by Robert E. Sherwood
1936-37—You Can't Take It With You, by Moss Hart and George S. Kaufman
1937-38—Our Town, by Thornton Wilder
1938-39—Abe Lincoln in Illinois, by Robert E. Sherwood
1939-40—The Time of Your Life, by William Saroyan
1940-41—There Shall Be No Night, by Robert E. Sherwood
1941-42—No award
1942-43—The Skin of Our Teeth, by Thornton Wilder
1943-44—No award
1944-45—Harvey, by Mary Chase
1945-46—State of the Union, by Howard Lindsay and Russel Crouse
1946-47—No award
1947-48—A Streetcar Named Desire, by Tennessee Williams
1948-49—Death of a Salesman, by Arthur Miller
1949-50—South Pacific, by Richard Rodgers, Oscar Hammerstein II and Joshua Logan
1950-51—No award
1951-52—The Shrike, by Joseph Kramm
1952-53—Picnic, by William Inge
1953-54—The Teahouse of the August Moon, by John Patrick
1954-55—Cat on a Hot Tin Roof, by Tennessee Williams

1955-56—The Diary of Anne Frank, by Frances Goodrich and Albert Hackett
1956-57—Long Day's Journey Into Night, by Eugene O'Neill
1957-58—Look Homeward, Angel, by Ketti Frings
1958-59—J.B., by Archibald MacLeish
1959-60—Fiorello!, by Jerome Weidman, George Abbott, Sheldon Harnick and Jerry Bock
1960-61—All the Way Home, by Tad Mosel
1961-62—How to Succeed in Business Without Really Trying, by Abe Burrows, Willie Gilbert, Jack Weinstock and Frank Loesser
1962-63—No award
1963-64—No award
1964-65—The Subject Was Roses, by Frank D. Gilroy
1965-66—No award
1966-67—A Delicate Balance, by Edward Albee
1967-68—No award
1968-69—The Great White Hope, by Howard Sackler
1969-70—No Place To Be Somebody, by Charles Gordone
1970-71—The Effect of Gamma Rays on Man-in-the-Moon Marigolds, by Paul Zindel
1971-72—No award
1972-73—That Championship Season, by Jason Miller
1973-74—No award
1974-75—Seascape, by Edward Albee
1975-76—A Chorus Line, by Michael Bennett, James Kirkwood, Nicholas Dante, Marvin Hamlisch and Edward Kleban
1976-77—The Shadow Box, by Michael Cristofer
1977-78—The Gin Game, by D.L. Coburn
1978-79—Buried Child, by Sam Shepard
1979-80—Talley's Folly, by Lanford Wilson
1980-81—Crimes of the Heart, by Beth Henley
1981-82—A Soldier's Play, by Charles Fuller
1982-83—'night, Mother, by Marsha Norman
1983-84—Glengarry Glen Ross, by David Mamet
1984-85—Sunday in the Park With George, by James Lapine and Stephen Sondheim
1985-86—No award
1986-87—Fences, by August Wilson
1987-88—Driving Miss Daisy, by Alfred Uhry
1988-89—The Heidi Chronicles, by Wendy Wasserstein
1989-90—The Piano Lesson, by August Wilson
1990-91—Lost in Yonkers, by Neil Simon

THE TONY AWARDS, 1990-91

The American Theater Wing's Antoinette Perry (Tony) Awards are presented annually in recognition of distinguished artistic achievement in the Broadway theater. The League of American Theaters and Producers and the American Theater Wing present the Tony Awards, founded by the Wing in 1947. Legitimate theater productions opening in eligible Broadway theaters during the Tony eligibility season of the current year—May 3, 1990 to May 1, 1991—are considered for Tony nominations.

The Tony Awards Administration Committee appoints the Tony Awards Nominating Committee which makes the actual nominations. The 1990-91 Nominating Committee consisted of Alvin Colt, costume designer; Jean Dalrymple, producer; Leonard Fleischer, manager of cultural contributions for the Exxon Corporation; Leonard Harris, writer-critic; Mary Henderson, theater historian and writer; Rosetta LeNoire, actress and founder/artistic director of Amas Musical Theater; Maurice Levine, musical director; Robert Marx, chief of the Performing Arts Research Center of the New York Public Library at Lincoln Center; Eve Merriam, playwright; Carole Rothman, director and co-artistic director of the Second Stage Theater; Suzanne Sato, arts executive with the Rockefeller Foundation; and Jeffrey Sweet, playwright-critic and associate editor of *Best Plays*.

The Tony awards are voted from the list of nominees by the members of the governing boards of the five theater artists' organizations: Actors' Equity Association, the Dramatists Guild, the Society of Stage Directors and Choreographers, the United Scenic Artists and the Casting Society of America, plus the members of the designated first night theater press, the board of directors of the American Theater Wing and the membership of the League of American Theaters and Producers. Because of fluctuation within these boards, the size of the Tony electorate varies from year to year. In the 1990-91 season, there were 624 qualified Tony voters.

The list of 1990-91 nominees follows, with winners in each category listed in **bold face type.**

BEST PLAY (award goes to both author and producer). *Lost in Yonkers* by Neil Simon, produced by **Emanuel Azenberg**; *Our Country's Good* by Timberlake Wertenbaker, produced by Frank and Woji Gero, Karl Sydow, Raymond L. Gaspard, Frederick Zollo, Diana Bliss, Hartford Stage Company; *Shadowlands* by William Nicholson, produced by Elliot Martin, James M. Nederlander, Brian Eastman, Terry Allen Kramer, Roger L. Stevens; *Six Degrees of Separation* by John Guare, produced by Lincoln Center Theater, Gregory Mosher, Bernard Gersten.

BEST MUSICAL (award goes to the producer). *Miss Saigon* produced by Cameron Mackintosh; *Once on This Island* produced by The Shubert Organization, Capital Cities/ABC Inc., Suntory International Corp., James Walsh, Playwrights Horizons; *The Secret Garden* produced by Heidi Landesman, Rick Steiner, Frederic H. Mayerson, Elizabeth Williams, Jujamcyn Theaters, TV ASAHI, Dodger Productions; *The Will Rogers Follies* produced by **Pierre Cossette, Martin Richards, Sam Crothers, James M. Nederlander, Stewart F. Lane, Max Weitzenhoffer, Japan Satellite Broadcasting, Inc.**

BEST BOOK OF A MUSICAL: *Miss Saigon* by Alain Boublil and Claude-Michel Schönberg; *Once on This Island* by Lynn Ahrens; *The Secret Garden* by Marsha Norman; *The Will Rogers Follies* by Peter Stone.

BEST ORIGINAL SCORE (music and lyrics) WRITTEN FOR THE THEATER: *Miss Saigon*, music by Claude-Michel Schönberg, lyrics by Richard Maltby Jr. and Alain Boublil; *Once on This Island*, music by Stephen Flaherty, lyrics by Lynn Ahrens; *The Secret Garden*, music by Lucy Simon, lyrics by Marsha Norman; *The Will Rogers Follies*, music by Cy Coleman, lyrics by Betty Comden and Adolph Green.

BEST LEADING ACTOR IN A PLAY. Peter Frechette in *Our Country's Good*, **Nigel Hawthorne** in *Shadowlands*, Tom McGowan in *La Bête*, Courtney B. Vance in *Six Degrees of Separation*.

BEST LEADING ACTRESS IN A PLAY. Stockard Channing in *Six Degrees of Separation*, Julie Harris in *Lucifer's Child*, Cherry Jones in *Our Country's Good*, **Mercedes Ruehl** in *Lost in Yonkers*.

BEST LEADING ACTOR IN A MUSICAL. Keith Carradine in *The Will Rogers Follies*, Paul Hipp in *Buddy: The Buddy Holly Story*, **Jonathan Pryce** in *Miss Saigon*, Topol in *Fiddler on the Roof*.

BEST LEADING ACTRESS IN A MUSICAL. June Angela in *Shogun: The Musical*, Dee Hoty in *The Will Rogers Follies*, Cathy Rigby in *Peter Pan*, **Lea Salonga** in *Miss Saigon*.

BEST FEATURED ACTOR IN A PLAY. Adam Arkin in *I Hate Hamlet*, Dylan Baker in *La Bête*, Stephen Lang in *The Speed of Darkness*, Kevin Spacey in **Lost in Yonkers**.

FIDDLER ON THE ROOF—Marcia Lewis as Golde and Topol as Tevye in the 25th anniversary revival production of the Joseph Stein-Jerry Bock-Sheldon Harnick musical, winner of the 1991 Tony Award as best revival

BEST FEATURED ACTRESS IN A PLAY.
Amelia Campbell in *Our Country's Good*,
Kathryn Erbe in *The Speed of Darkness*, J. Smith-
Cameron in *Our Country's Good*, **Irene Worth**
in *Lost in Yonkers*.

BEST FEATURED ACTOR IN A MUSICAL.
Bruce Adler in *Those Were the Days*, **Hinton
Battle** in *Miss Saigon*, Gregg Burge in *Oh, Kay!*,
Willy Falk in *Miss Saigon*.

BEST FEATURED ACTRESS IN A MUSICAL.
Daisy Eagan in *The Secret Garden*, Alison Fraser
in *The Secret Garden*, Cady Huffman in *The Will
Rogers Follies*, La Chanze in *Once on This
Island*.

BEST DIRECTION OF A PLAY. Richard Jones
for *La Bête*, Mark Lamos for *Our Country's
Good*, Gene Saks for *Lost in Yonkers*, **Jerry Zaks**
for *Six Degrees of Separation*.

BEST DIRECTION OF A MUSICAL. Graciela
Daniele for *Once on This Island*, Nicholas Hytner
for *Miss Saigon*, Eleanor Reissa for *Those Were
the Days*, **Tommy Tune** for *The Will Rogers
Follies*.

BEST SCENIC DESIGN. Richard Hudson for
La Bête, **Heidi Landesman** for *The Secret
Garden*, John Napier for *Miss Saigon*, Tony
Walton for *The Will Rogers Follies*.

BEST LIGHTING DESIGN. **Jules Fisher** for
The Will Rogers Follies, David Hersey for *Miss
Saigon*, Allen Lee Hughes for *Once on This
Island*, Jennifer Tipton for *La Bête*.

BEST COSTUME DESIGN.   Theoni V.
Aldredge for *The Secret Garden*, Judy Dearing
for *Once on This Island*, **Willa Kim** for *The Will
Rogers Follies*, Patricia Zipprodt for *Shogun: The
Musical*.

BEST CHOREOGRAPHY. Bob Avian for *Miss
Saigon*, Graciela Daniele for *Once on This Island*,
Dan Siretta for *Oh, Kay!*, **Tommy Tune** for *The
Will Rogers Follies*.

BEST REVIVAL OF A PLAY OR MUSICAL
(award goes to the producer). *Fiddler on the
Roof* produced by **Barry** and **Fran Weissler**,
Pace Theatrical Group; *The Miser* produced
by Circle in the Square Theater, Theodore
Mann, Paul Libin; *Peter Pan* produced by James
M. Nederlander, Arthur Rubin, Thomas P.
McCoy, Keith Stava, P.P. Investments, Inc.,
Jon B. Platt.

TONY HONOR. Posthumously to **Father
George Moore**, pastor of St. Malachy's Church,
the Actor's Chapel.

REGIONAL THEATER TONY. **Yale Repertory
Theater**, New Haven, Conn.

TONY AWARD WINNERS, 1947-1991

Listed below are the Antoinette Perry (Tony) Award winners in the categories of
Best Play and Best Musical from the time these awards were established until the present.

1947— No play or musical award
1948— Mister Roberts; no musical award
1949— Death of a Salesman; Kiss Me, Kate
1950— The Cocktail Party; South Pacific
1951— The Rose Tattoo; Guys and Dolls
1952— The Fourposter; The King and I
1953— The Crucible; Wonderful Town
1954— The Teahouse of the August Moon;
Kismet
1955— The Desperate Hours; The Pajama Game
1956— The Diary of Anne Frank; Damn Yan-
kees
1957— Long Day's Journey Into Night; My Fair
Lady
1958— Sunrise at Campobello; The Music Man
1959— J.B.; Redhead
1960— The Miracle Worker; Fiorello! and The
Sound of Music (tie)
1961— Beckett; Bye Bye Birdie
1962— A Man for All Seasons; How to Succeed

in Business Without Really Trying
1963— Who's Afraid of Virginia Woolf?; A
Funny Thing Happened on the Way to
the Forum
1964— Luther; Hello, Dolly!
1965— The Subject Was Roses; Fiddler on the
Roof
1966— The Persecution and Assassination of
Marat Performed by the Inmates of the
Asylum of Charenton Under the Direction of the Marquis de Sade; Man of La
Mancha
1967— The Homecoming; Cabaret
1968— Rosencrantz and Guildenstern Are Dead;
Hallelujah, Baby!
1969— The Great White Hope; 1776
1970— Borstal Boy; Applause
1971— Sleuth; Company
1972— Sticks and Bones; Two Gentlemen of
Verona

1973— That Championship Season; A Little Night Music
1974— The River Niger; Raisin
1975— Equus; The Wiz
1976— Travesties; A Chorus Line
1977— The Shadow Box; Annie
1978— Da; Ain't Misbehavin'
1979— The Elephant Man; Sweeney Todd, the Demon Barber of Fleet Street
1980— Children of a Lesser God; Evita
1981— Amadeus; 42nd Street
1982— The Life & Adventures of Nicholas Nickleby; Nine

1983— Torch Song Trilogy; Cats
1984— The Real Thing; La Cage aux Folles
1985— Biloxi Blues; Big River
1986— I'm Not Rappaport; The Mystery of Edwin Drood
1987— Fences; Les Misérables
1988— M. Butterfly; The Phantom of the Opera
1989— The Heidi Chronicles; Jerome Robbins' Broadway
1990— The Grapes of Wrath; City of Angels
1991— Lost in Yonkers; The Will Rogers Follies

THE OBIE AWARDS

The *Village Voice* Off-Broadway (Obie) Awards are given each year for excellence in various categories of off-Broadway (and frequently off-off-Broadway) shows, with close distinctions between these two areas ignored. The 36th annual Obies for the 1990-91 season, listed below, were chosen by a panel of judges chaired by Ross Wetzsteon and comprising *Village Voice* critics Michael Feingold, Robert Massa, Gordon Rogoff and Alisa Solomon and guest judges Margo Jefferson and Joan MacIntosh.

BEST NEW PLAY. *The Fever* by Wallace Shawn.

PLAYWRITING: **John Guare** for *Six Degrees of Separation,* **Mac Wellman** for *Sincerity Forever.*

SUSTAINED ACHIEVEMENT. *The Wooster Group.*

PERFORMANCE. **Eileen Atkins** in *A Room of One's Own,* **Stockard Channing** in *Six Degrees of Separation,* **Joan Copeland** in *The American Plan,* **Angela Goethals** in *The Good Times Are Killing Me,* **Tony Goldwyn** in *The Sum of Us,* **Jan Leslie Harding** in *Sincerity Forever,* **Jodie Markell** in *Machinal,* **Anne Pitoniak** in *Pygmalion,* **John Leguizamo** in *Mambo Mouth,* **Michael Lombard** in *What's Wrong With This Picture,* **Ron Rifkin** in *The Substance of Fire,* **Kathleen Widdoes** in *Tower of Evil,* **Bette Bourne, Precious Pearl, Peggy Shaw, Lois Weaver** (ensemble) in *Belle Reprieve.*

DIRECTION. **Michael Greif** for *Machinal,* **Lisa Peterson** our *Light Shining in Buckinghamshire.*

DESIGN. **Frances Aronson** for sustained excellence of lighting design, **Mark Beard** for sustained excellence of set design, **William Ivey Long** for sustained excellence of costume design, **John Gromada** for the sound design of *Machinal.*

SPECIAL CITATIONS. **Blue Man Group,** John Kelly for *Love of a Poet,* BACA Downtown, New York Theater Workshop, New York Shakespeare Festival 1990-91 season, Lori E. Seid for stage management, Theater for the New City for *Stop the War: A Festival for Peace in the Middle East.*

VILLAGE VOICE OFF-BROADWAY GRANTS. En Garde Arts, Hearts and Voices, Mettawee River Theater Company.

ADDITIONAL PRIZES AND AWARDS, 1990-91

The following is a list of major prizes and awards for achievement in the theater this season. In all cases the names and/or titles of the winners appear in **bold face type**.

1990 ELIZABETH HULL-KATE WARRINER AWARD. To the playwright whose work dealt with controversial subjects involving the fields of political, religious or social mores of the time, selected by the Dramatists Guild Council. **John Guare** for *Six Degrees of Separation*.

7th ANNUAL GEORGE AND ELISABETH MARTON AWARD. To an American playwright selected by a committee of the Foundation of the Dramatists Guild. **Jules Feiffer** for *Elliot Loves*.

6th ANNUAL ATCA NEW-PLAY AWARD. For an outstanding new play in cross-country theater, voted by a committee of the American Theater Critics Association. *Two Trains Running* by August Wilson.

THEATER HALL OF FAME. Annual election by members of the profession of nominees selected by vote of the American Theater Critics Association. **Robert Lewis, Pearl Bailey, Leland Hayward, Tony Walton, Paddy Chayefsky, Earl Blackwell, Tommy Tune, Chita Rivera, John Kander** and **Fred Ebb.** Arnold Weissberger Award for lifetime achievement to **Radie Harris.**

13th ANNUAL KENNEDY CENTER HONORS. For distinguished achievement by individuals who have made significant contributions to American culture through the arts. **Dizzy Gillespie, Katharine Hepburn, Risë Stevens, Jule Styne, Billy Wilder.**

1991 COMMON WEALTH AWARD. For excellence of achievment and high potential for future contributions to the dramatic arts. **James Earl Jones.**

1990 JUJAMCYN THEATERS AWARDS. Honoring an American regional theater that has made an outstanding contribution to the development of creative talent for the theater. **The Tyrone Guthrie Theater.**

7th ANNUAL ASSSOCATION OF ASIAN/ PACIFIC AMERICAN ARTISTS MEDIA AWARD. For sustained excellence in theater. **Pan Asian Repertory Theater.** Special awards: **David Henry Hwang** and **B.D. Wong** for advocacy on behalf of Asian-American theater artists.

5th ANNUAL LUCILLE LORTEL AWARDS. For outstanding achievement in off-Broadway theater, voted by a committee comprising Clive Barnes, Jeremy Gerard, Howard Kissel, Alvin Klein, Edith Oliver, Allan Wallach, Willard Swire and Lucille Lortel. Play: *Aristocrats* by **Brian Friel.** Musical: *Falsettoland* by **William Finn** and **James Lapine.** Revival: *Measure for Measure* produced by New York Shakespeare Festival. Director: **John Tillinger** for *The Lisbon Traviata.* Performer: **Nathan Lane** in *The Lisbon Traviata.* Body of work: **Circle Repertory Company.** Special lifetime achievement award: **Rosetta LeNoire.**

47th ANNUAL CLARENCE DERWENT A-WARDS. For the most promising male and female actors on the metropolitan scene during the 1990-91 season, overseen by the Actors' Equity Foundation. **Jane Adams** of *I Hate Hamlet,* **Danny Gerard** of *Lost in Yonkers,* **James Mc-Daniel** of *Six Degrees of Separation.*

1991 AMERICAN THEATER WING DESIGN AWARDS. For designs originating in the U.S., voted by a committee comprising Tish Dace, Henry Hewes, Michael Sommers and Julius Novick. Scenic and costume design, **Richard Hudson** for *La Bête.* Costume design, **Patricia Zipprodt** for *Shogun.* Lighting design, **Robert Wierzel** for *Hydrogen Jukebox.* Noteworthy unusual effects, **Paul Zaloom** for complete design, including puppets and found objects, in *My Civilization.*

1991 ALAN SCHNEIDER AWARD. For a director who has exhibited exceptional talent through work in a specific community or region, selected by a panel comprising Robert Falls, Carole Rothman and Mary B. Robinson. **David Saint.**

9th ANNUAL ELLIOT NORTON AWARD. To an individual who has made a distinguished contribution to the theater in Boston during the preceding years. **Julie Harris** for *Lucifer's Child* and *Love Letters.*

1st ANNUAL GILMAN & GONZALEZ-FALLA MUSICAL THEATER AWARD. For excellence in the American musical theater. **Craig Carnelia.**

10th ANNUAL WILLIAM INGE AWARD. For lifetime achievement in the American theater, administered by Independence, Kan. Community College. **Edward Albee.**

1991 THEATER WORLD AWARDS. 47th annual citations of outstanding new talent in Broadway and off-Broadway productions during the 1990-91 season, selected by a committee comprising Clive Barnes, Douglas Watt and John Willis. Jane Adams and Adam Arkin of *I Hate Hamlet*, Gillian Anderson and Brenda Blethyn of *Absent Friends*, Marcus Chong of *Stand-Up Tragedy*, Paul Hipp of *Buddy: The Buddy Holly Story*, La Chanze of *Once on This Island*, Kenny Neal of *Mule Bone*, Kevin Ramsey of *Oh, Kay!*, Francis Ruivivar of *Shogun*, Lea Salonga of *Miss Saigon*, Chandra Wilson of *The Good Times Are Killing Me*.

Special awards: Tracey Ullman for her New York debut; Ellen Stewart as founder and artistic director of La Mama.

41st ANNUAL OUTER CRITICS CIRCLE AWARDS. For outstanding achievement in the 1990-91 New York theater season, voted by an organization of critics on out-of-town periodicals and media. Broadway play: *Lost in Yonkers*. Performance by an actor: Nigel Hawthorne in *Shadowlands*. Performance by an actress: Mercedes Ruehl in *Lost in Yonkers*. Broadway musical: *Miss Saigon*. Actor in a musical: Jonathan Pryce in *Miss Saigon*. Actress in a musical: Lea Salonga in *Miss Saigon*. Off-Broadway play: *The Sum of Us*. Off-Broadway musical: *Falsettoland*. Off-Broadway musical revue: *And the World Goes 'Round*. Revival of a play or musical: *Fiddler on the Roof*. Director: Gene Saks for *Lost in Yonkers*. Choreography: Susan Stroman for *And the World Goes 'Round*. Design: scenery, Heidi Landesman; costumes, Theoni V. Aldredge; lighting, Tharon Musser (all for *The Secret Garden*). Debut of an actor: Tom McGowan in *La Bête*. Debut of an actress: Jane Adams in *I Hate Hamlet*. Achievement: John Leguizamo for *Mambo Mouth*.

John Gassner Playwriting Award: David Hirson for *La Bête*. Special Awards: Jackie Mason for his one-man show that demonstrates his remarkable brand of comedy and satire; the cast of *And the World Goes 'Round* for their brilliant ensemble performance; Broadway Cares, the AIDS resource organization for the theatrical community, for its dedication and commitment.

7th ANNUAL NEW YORK DANCE AND PERFORMANCE (BESSIE) AWARDS. For choreographers, performance artists, designers and others in the dance field who presented new work in New York. Choreographer/creator award: Ulysses Dove, Eiko and Koma, Karen Finley, Margarita Guergue and Hahn Rowe, Robbie McCauley, Mark Morris, Wim Vandekeybus. Sustained creative achievement: Garth Fagan, Pat Oleszko. Performers: Arthur Armijo, Victoria Finlayson, Penny Hutchinson, Jonathan Riseling, Louise Smith, Gail Turner. Visual design: Roma Flowers and Suzanne Poulin (lighting), Liz Prince and Matthew Yokobosky (costumes). Composers: Max Roach, Hans Peter Kuhn, A. Leroy and Mimi Goese. Special citations: Annabelle Gamson for revival of dances by Isadora Duncan and Mary Wigman, Beate Gordon for support and presentation of Asian arts in New York, Martha Wilson for continuous support of provocative performing artists.

7TH ANNUAL HELEN HAYES AWARDS. In recognition of excellence in Washington, D.C. theater. Production of a play, *Stand-Up Tragedy* by Bill Cain at *Arena Stage*. Production of a musical, *The Rocky Horror Show* by Richard O'Brien at the Woolly Mammoth Theater. Charles MacArthur Award for outstanding new play, *Mixed Babies* by Oni Faida Lampley. Director, Max Mayer for *Stand-Up Tragedy*. Lead actor in a play, Luis Ramos, in *Stand-Up Tragedy*. Lead actress in a play, Pat Carroll as Falstaff in *The Merry Wives of Windsor*. Lead actor in a musical, Scott Morgan in *Children With Stones*. Lead actress in a musical, Nanna Ingvarsson in *The Rocky Horror Show*. Design: scenery, F. Hallinan Flood for *Juno and the Paycock*; costumes, Martin Pakledinaz for *Mary Stuart*; lighting, Howard Binkley for *Richard III*; sound, Susan R. White for *Stand-Up Tragedy*.

1990 JOSEPH JEFFERSON AWARDS. 22nd annual citations for achievement in Chicago theater. Plays—Production: *The Tale of Cymbeline* produced by Shakespeare Repertory. New work/adaptation: *Marvin's Room* by Scott McPherson. *Pecong* by Steve Carter. Director: Barbara Gaines for *The Tale of Cymbeline*. Actor and actress in principal roles: Larry Yando in *Kiss of the Spider Woman*, Laura Esterman in *Marvin's Room*. Ensemble: *From the Mississippi Delta*. Actor and actress in supporting roles: B.J. Jones in *Peacekeeper*, Linda Emond in *The Winter's Tale*.

Musicals—Production: *Into the Woods* at Marriott's Lincolnshire Theater and Candlelight Dinner Playhouse. Original music: Willy Steele for *Pecong*. Director: William Pullinski for *Into the Woods*. Actor and actress in principal roles: James Harms in *Me and My Girl*, Hollis Resnik in *Into the Woods*. Actor and actress in supporting roles: William Akey in *Singin' in the Rain*, Mary Ernster in *Me and My Girl*. Choreography: Jim Corti in *Singin' in the Rain*. Musical direction: Kevin Stites for *Chess*.

Design—Scenery, Michael Merritt for *The*

Tale of Cymbeline. Costumes: **Nancy Missimi** for *Into the Woods*. Lighting: **Robert Shook** for *The Tale of Cymbeline*. Sound: **Rob Milburn** for *Peacekeeper*.

Special Award—Rev. **John C. Richardson**, president of DePaul University, for his outstanding leadership in the rescue and refurbishing of both the Theater School and the Blackstone Theater.

17th annual awards of the Joseph Jefferson Citations Wing for excellence in non-Equity Chicago theater, April 1, 1989-March 31, 1990. Production: *The Good Times Are Killing Me* produced by **City Lit Theater Company**. New work: *Incorruptible* by **Christopher Cartmill**. Adaptation: *The Good Times Are Killing Me* by **Arnold Aprill**. Original music: **Joseph Cerqua** for *The Sound of a Voice*. Ensemble: *The Good Times Are Killing Me*, *Teechers*. Direction: **Arnold Aprill** for *The Good Times Are Killing Me*, **John Cusack** for *Methusalem*. Actors and actresses in leading roles: **Charles Pike** and **Tony Fitzpatrick** in *Mass Murder*; **Patti Hannon** in *Ask for the Moon*, **Lorell J. Wyatt** in *The Good Times Are Killing Me*, **Kate Goehring** in *Laughing Wild*. Actors and actress in supporting roles: **Lawrence E. Bull** in *Of Mice and Men*, **Peter Mohawk** in *Vampire Lesbians of Sodom*; **Glenda Starr Kelley** in *The Good Times Are Killing Me*. Scenery: **David Lee Csicsko** and **Thomas Myron Bachtell** for *The Good Times Are Killing Me*, **Rob Hamilton** for *Hotel Universe*, **Richard** and **Jacqueline Penrod** for *Of Mice and Men*. Costumes: **Margaret Fitzsimmons Morettini** for *Incorruptible*, **Nanette Acosta** for *Methusalem*. Lighting: **Carl Forsberg** for *Ask for the Moon*, **Tom Fleming** for *Incorruptible*. Sound: **Joseph Cerqua** for *Chaos*, **Judy Myers** for *Incorruptible*. Musical direction: **Steve Rashid** for *The Good Times Are Killing Me*, **Jef Bek** for *Methusalem*. Special Award: **The Saints** for ten years of voluntary service in support of Chicago theater.

22d ANNUAL LOS ANGELES DRAMA CRITICS CIRCLE AWARDS. For distinguished achievement in Los Angeles theater during 1990. Production: *The Beggar's Opera* produced by **Mary Seward-McKeon** for Pacific Theater Ensemble; *The Illusion* produced by **Bill Bushnell, Diane White** and **Robert Lear** for Los Angeles Theater Center; *Present Laughter* produced by **Bill Haller** and **Sandra Kline**. Direction: **Martin Benson** for *Holy Days*, **Lisa James** for

Palladium Is Moving, **Richard Kline** for *Present Laughter*, **Stephanie Shroyer** for *The Beggar's Opera*. Writing: **Athol Fugard** for *My Children! My Africa!*. Lead performance: **Richard Doyle** and **Jeanne Paulsen** in *Holy Days*, **Charles S. Dutton** in *The Piano Lesson*, **Ian Ogilvy** in *Present Laughter*, **Brock Peters** in *My Children! My Africa!*, **Gordana Rashovich** in *A Shayna Maidel*. Featured performance: **John Fleck** in *The Illusion*, **Nathan Lane** in *The Lisbon Traviata*. Ensemble performance: *The Beggar's Opera*. Creation performance: **Sheri Glaser** in *Family Secrets*. Scenic design: **D. Martyn Bookwalter** for *The Crucible*; **Steve Markus, Kevin McKeon** and **Kurt Wahiner** for *The Beggar's Opera*; **Douglas D. Smith** for *The Illusion*. Lighting design: **Tom Ruzika** for *Holy Days*, **Douglas D. Smith** for *The Illusion*. Costume design: **John Brandt, Lori Martin, Sarah Zinsser** and **Betsy Berenson** for *The Beggar's Opera*; **Marianna Elliott** for *The Illusion*; **Shigeru Yaji** for *Man and Superman*. Mask design: **Xander Berkeley** for *The Good Woman of Setzuan*. Sound design: **Jon Gottlieb** for *The Illusion*. Music and lyrics: **Brian Shucker** for *Babes*. Makeup design: **Elene Meluchin Breckenridge** for *The Hip-Hop Waltz of Eurydice*. Margaret Harford Award: Colony Studio Theater. Ted Schmitt Award: *Search and Destroy* by Howard Korder. Special awards: **Peter Sellars** and the **L.A. Festival**; Mark Taper Forum for *50/60 Vision*.

BAY AREA THEATER CRITICS CIRCLE AWARDS. In recognition of outstanding San Francisco area theater. Productions of plays: *Man and Superman* by George Bernard Shaw at Berkeley Repertory Theater, *East* by Steven Berkoff at Industrial Strength Productions. Productions of musicals: *The Curse of the Werewolf* at Theater on the Square, *Into the Woods* by James Lapine and Stephen Sondheim at TheaterWorks. Original scripts: *Pick Up Ax* by Anthony Clarvoe, *House of Yes* by Wendy MacLeod. Direction of plays: **Irene Lewis** for *Man and Superman*, **Paul Hellyer** for *East*. Direction of musicals: **Michael Smuin** for *The Curse of the Werewolf*, **Robert Kelly** for *Into the Woods*, **Dianna Shuster** for *Jesus Christ Superstar*. Principal actors: **Michael J. Flynn** and **Joan McMurtrey** in *Man and Superman*, **Dennis Matthews** and **Delia MacDougall** in *East*, **Daniel Reichert** in *Burn This*, **Michael Learned** for *Hapgood*, **Celia Shuman** for *House of Yes*..

1990-91 PUBLICATION OF
RECENTLY-PRODUCED PLAYS

Beirut. Alan Bowne. Broadway Play Publishing (paperback).
Beside Herself. Joe Pintauro. Broadway Play Publishing (paperback).
City of Angels. Larry Gelbart, Cy Coleman and David Zippel. Applause (also paperback).
Fever, The. Wallace Shawn. Farrar, Straus and Giroux (also paperback).
Have You Seen Zandile? Goina Mhlophe, Maralin Venrenen and Thembi Mtshali. Heinemann/Methuen (paperback).
Heidi Chronicles, The, and Other Plays. Wendy Wasserstein. Harcourt Brace Jovanovich (also paperback).
Hidden Laughter. Simon Gray. Faber & Faber (paperback).
Hunting Cockroaches and Other Plays. Janusz Glowacki. Northwestern (paperback).
Hyde in Hollywood. Peter Parnell. Broadway Play Publishing (paperback).
Killing the Cat. David Spencer. Methuen (paperback).
Love Letters and Two Other Plays. A.R. Gurney. Plume/New American Library (paperback).
Man of the Moment. Alan Ayckbourn. Faber & Faber (paperback).
Moscow Gold. Tari Ali. Nick Hern Books (paperback).
Mountain Language. Harold Pinter. Grove Press (also paperback).
Mule Bone: A Comedy of Negro Life. Langston Hughes and Zora Neale Hurston. Harper Collins (also paperback).
Nebraska. Keith Reddin. Broadway Play Publishing (paperback).
Other People's Money. Jerry Sterner. Applause (also paperback).
Our Country's Good. Timberlake Wertenbaker. Methuen (paperback).
Piano Lesson, The. August Wilson. Dutton and New American Library (paperback).
Prelude to a Kiss. Craig Lucas. Broadway Play Publishing (paperback).
Search for Signs of Intelligent Life in the Universe, The. Jane Wagner. Harper & Row (paperback).
Secret Rapture, The. David Hare. Grove Press (paperback).
Sex, Drugs, Rock & Roll. Eric Bogosian. Harper Collins.
Shape of the Table, The. David Edgar. Nick Hern Books (paperback).
Six Degrees of Separation. John Guare. Random House (also paperback).
Square One. Steve Tesich. Applause (paperback).
Tales of the Lost Formicans. Constance Congdon. Broadway Play Publishing (paperback).

A SELECTED LIST OF OTHER PLAYS
PUBLISHED IN 1990-91

Andromache. Racine. Faber & Faber (paperback).
Australian Plays. Introduced by Katharine Brisbane. Nick Hern Books (paperback).
Best Plays of Albert Innaurato. Gay Press of New York (paperback).
Blood Knot, The, and Other Plays. Athol Fugard. Theater Communications Group (also paperback).
Contemporary Plays by Women. Emilie S. Kilgore, editor. Prentice-Hall (also paperback).
Elektra. Sophocles; version by Ezra Pound and Rudd Fleming. Princeton.
Fantasticks, The: 30th Anniversary Edition. Tom Jones and Harvey Schmidt. Applause.
Fefu and Her Friends. Maria Irene Fornes. PAJ Publications (paperback).
Four Plays. Lee Blessing. Heinemann/Methuen (paperback).
Four Puppet Plays/Play Without a Title/Prose Poems and Dramatic Pieces/Divan Poems and Other Poems. Federico Garcia Lorca. Sheep Meadow Press (paperback).
Funny Thing Happened on the Way to the Forum, A. Burt Shevelove, Larry Gelbart and Stephen Sondheim. Applause (also paperback).
Game at Chess, A. Thomas Middleton. Malone Society, Oxford.
Golden Years, The/The Man Who Had All the Luck. Arthur Miller. Methuen (also paperback).
Little Night Music, A. Stephen Sondheim and Hugh Wheeler. Applause (also paperback).

Loom of Time, The. Kalidasa. Penguin (paperback).
Lulu Plays, The/The Marquis of Keith. Frank Wedekind. Absolute Press (paperback).
Major Plays of Chikamatsu. Columbia University Press (paperback).
Pacific Overtures. Stephen Sondheim and John Weidman. Theater Communications Group (also paperback).
Peace Plays: Two. Stephen Lowe, editor. Methuen (paperback).
Plautus: Three Comedies. Peter L. Smith, translator. Cornell University (paperback).
Plays: Three. Arthur Miller. Methuen (paperback).
Plays: Two. Caryl Churchill. Methuen (paperback).
Plays: Two. David Edgar. Methuen (paperback).
Redevelopment or Slum Clearance. Vaclav Havel; James Saunders, translator. Faber & Faber (paperback).
Roots of African American Drama, The: An Anthology of Early Plays, 1858-1938. Leo Hamalian and James V. Hatch, editors. Wayne State University.
Salome. Oscar Wilde, illustrations by David Shenton (cartoon-strip version). Quartet Books.
Six Plays. Mikhail Bulgakov. Methuen (paperback).
Slab Boys Trilogy, The. John Byrne. Penguin (paperback).
Slant Six: New Theater. Morgan Jennes, John Richardson and Mac Wellman, editors. New Rivers Press (paperback).
Sunday in the Park With George. Stephen Sondheim and James Lapine. Applause (also paperback).
Sweeney Todd, the Demon Barber of Fleet Street. Stephen Sondheim and Hugh Wheeler. Applause (also paperback).
Texas Plays. William B. Martin, editor. Southern Methodist University (also paperback).
Theater of Tennessee Williams, Volume 1 and *Volume 2*. New Directions (paperbacks).
Three Plays by Terrence McNally. Plume/Penguin (paperback).
Three Vanek Plays. Vaclac Havel. Faber & Faber (paperback).

NECROLOGY

MAY 1990—MAY 1991

PERFORMERS

Acquavella, Demian (32)—June 2, 1990
Alex, Robert (30)—August 6, 1990
Alexander, John (67)—December 8, 1990
Alford, Lamar (46)—March 29, 1991
Alinder, Dallas (58)—July 14, 1990
Appleby, Dorothy (84)—August 9, 1990
Applewhite, Charles (39)—May 13, 1990
Arden, Eve (83)—November 12, 1990
Arkin, David (49)—January 14, 1991
Arnt, Charles (83)—August 6, 1990
Attles, Joseph E. (88)—October 29, 1990
Bailey, Pearl (72)—August 17, 1990
Bailey, William H. (72)—August 7, 1990
Balin, Ina (52)—June 20, 1990
Baney, Joan Blazer (55)—April 28, 1990
Bara, Nina (66)—August 15, 1990
Barnett, Darrell (41)—January 16, 1991
Bartell, Eddie (83)—February 13, 1991
Bates, Ralph (50)—March 27, 1991
Baxley, Barbara (63)—June 7, 1990
Beagle, Edward H. (46)—April 24, 1990
Bell, Hal (65)—May 2, 1991
Bennett, Jill (59)—October 4, 1990
Bennett, Joan (80)—December 7, 1990
Bennett, Matt (52)—March 29, 1991
Berghof, Herbert (81)—November 5, 1990
Beverly, Helen (81)—April 28, 1991
Bingo, Joe (65)—November 27, 1990
Binns, Edward (74)—December 4, 1990
Blake, Katharine (62)—March 1, 1991
Bloch, Walter (74)—June 8, 1990
Block, Eva Sully (88)—August 7, 1990
Bodendork, Robert Edward (73)—February 23, 1991
Boncoeur, Michael (41)—March 17, 1991
Bond, Lillian (83)—January 18, 1991
Booth, Edwina (86)—May 19, 1991
Bottcher, Ron (50)—April 18, 1991
Boulet, Gerry (44)—July 18, 1990
Bowne, Richard L. (40)—May 19, 1990
Bray, Stephen (33)—June 10, 1990
Briggs, Richard R. (71)—July 12, 1990
Brock, Stanley (59)—January 25, 1991
Brockmeyer, John (50)—December 16, 1990
Brodenova, Lida (88)—February 11, 1991
Brown, Ralph (76)—November 19, 1990
Brown, Tom (77)—June 3, 1990
Bunnage, Avis (67)—October 29, 1990
Burke, Paul (68)—October 29, 1990
Burns, Jimmy (90)—February 10, 1991

Campbell, Edward 4th (33)—June 8, 1990
Carlin, Thomas A. (62)—May 6, 1990
Carman, Charles (79)—August 29, 1990
Carol, Lynne (76)—Summer 1990
Carpenter, Charles (77)—November 13, 1990
Casper, Richard (41)—August 3, 1990
Catá, Alfonso (53)—September 15, 1990
Chabeau, Ray Edgar (49)—December 7, 1990
Chamberlin, Billye (82)—October 6, 1990
Champlin, Irene—July 10, 1990
Chernichaw, Irma—January 17, 1991
Christmas, Jason (49)—January 11, 1991
Christy, June (64)—June 12, 1990
Cieslak, Ryszard (53)—June 15, 1990
Clibanoff, Louis (79)—October 20, 1990
Clinton, Julia Rooney (102)—October 20, 1990
Colvig, Vance (72)—March 4, 1991
Coates, Odia (49)—May 19, 1991
Condos, Steve (71)—September 16, 1990
Connors, Marc (40)—March 25, 1991
Cook, Roderick (58)—August 17, 1990
Cossman, Ian (80)—November 8, 1990
Crandall, Brad (mid-60s)—March 14, 1991
Craven, Edward (83)—May 14, 1990
Crosby, Dennis M. (56)—May 4, 1991
Cummings, Bob (80)—December 2, 1990
Curtis, Ken (74)—April 27, 1991
Dale, Rex (69)—July 14, 1990
Dashiell, Jackie (60)—February 21, 1991
Dathey, Dalton (44)—December 31, 1990
Davis, Patrick (87)—November 18, 1990
Day, Bobby (60)—July 27, 1990
DeAcutis, William (33)—May 5, 1991
Decroux, Etienne (92)—March 12, 1991
Dempster, Carol (89)—February 1, 1991
de Treaux, Tamara (31)—November 28, 1990
DeWitt, Lew (53)—August 15, 1990
Diovanni, Paul (58)—June 17, 1990
Dixon, Troy (22)—July 14, 1990
Doll, Eugenia (79)—December 13, 1990
Donn, Lee (96)—March 25, 1991
Doyle, Jay (59)—June 2, 1990
Draper, Don (62)—December 17, 1990
Duff, Howard (76)—July 8, 1990
Dunne, Irene (91)—September 4, 1990
Dux, Pierre (82)—December 1, 1990
Dwornek, Edward L. Jr. (41)—July 18, 1990
Dyson, Ronnie (40)—November 10, 1990
Earwood, Robert N. (40)—May 30, 1990
Easterling, Gary Lamont (38)—October 11, 1990
Eckhardt, John (82)—January 5, 1991
Edwards, Florida (79)—August 3, 1990
Erenstein, Evelyn (72)—May 29, 1990

Esmond, Jill (82)—July 28, 1990
Farren, Vivian—May 3, 1990
Farwell, Jo (55)—August 18, 1990
Flamant, Georges (86)—July 23, 1990
Fonteyn, Margot (71)—February 21, 1991
Ford, Lloyd (79)—May 8, 1991
Foreman, Steve (39)—May 31, 1990
Frank, Ben (56)—September 11, 1990
French, Valerie (59)—November 3, 1990
Gatliff, Frank (62)—Summer 1990
George, Alma Urquhart (87)—July 5, 1990
Gibson, March (51)—April 30, 1991
Gilford, Jack (81)—June 2, 1990
Gobel, George (71)—February 24, 1991
Green, Del—October 8, 1990
Guard, Dave (56)—March 22, 1991
Guariglia, William (86)—June 7, 1990
Gurewich, Mrinka (88)—December 23, 1990
Hagerty, Michael (39)—April 30, 1991
Haimsohn, Michael Anthony (34)—June 14, 1990
Hall, Kevin Peter (35)—April 10, 1991
Hall, Stuart (86)—June 2, 1990
Hamilton, Frank (66)—April 25, 1991
Hardy, Joseph (71)—May 28, 1990
Harrison, Rex (82)—June 2, 1990
Harvout, Clifford (77)—July 22, 1990
Harwood, Elizabeth (52)—June 22, 1990
Hayden, Vernon (76)—Summer 1990
Hayes, Dorsha (93)—November 27, 1990
Henson, Basil (71)—December 19, 1990
Herrick, Landon (85)—January 10, 1991
Hicks, Joe (64)—January 7, 1991
Hillary, Lucy (67)—March 13, 1991
Hobart, Sebastian (30)—March 28, 1991
Hoffa, Portland—December 25, 1990
Holden, Gloria (82)—March 22, 1991
Hughes, Don (72)—May 2, 1990
Hugo, Ludi Claire (70)—July 3, 1990
Hunter, George Jager (80)—June 28, 1990
Huntley, Raymond (86)—Spring 1990
Hyde-White, Wilfrid (87)—May 6, 1991
Iden, Rosalind (79)—November 5, 1990
Irwin, Dotti (67)—June 28, 1990
Jackson, Freda (82)—October 20, 1990
Jackson, Joe Jr. (78)—January 10, 1991
Jagger, Dean (87)—February 5, 1991
Jasinski, Roman (83)—April 16, 1991
Johnston, Robert (93)—January 2, 1991
Kalil, Margaret (66)—March 14, 1991
Katcharoff, Michel (82)—October 25, 1990
King, Harry (87)—September 7, 1990
Kirk, Lisa (62)—November 11, 1990
Kramer, Joan Whitney (76)—July 12, 1990
Krebs, Nita (85)—January 18, 1991
Kriner, William (84)—May 13, 1990
Kroeger, Berry (78)—January 4, 1991
Kulp, Nancy (69)—February 3, 1991
Kuluva, Will (73)—November 6, 1990
Lamont, Estelle (82)—June 28, 1990

Langan, Glenn (73)—January 19, 1991
Lanham, Roy (68)—February 14, 1991
Lanson, Snooky (76)—July 2, 1990
Lauter, Harry (76)—October 30, 1990
LaVere, June (87)—February 7, 1991
Lawrence, Keith (39)—July 25, 1990
Lehmann, Carla (73)—Winter 1991
Leigh, Megan (26)—June 16, 1990
Lensky, Leib (82)—May 2, 1991
Leon, Geoffrey (44)—August 11, 1990
Leslie, Bob (64)—February 4, 1991
Le Vere, Florrie (93)—June 12, 1990
Lewis, Elliott (73)—May 20, 1990
Linden, Marta (87)—December 13, 1990
Lipstone, Ruth (88)—November 10, 1990
Lloyd-Jones, Jane (69)—March 11, 1991
Lockwood, Margaret (73)—July 15, 1990
Lott, Lawrence (40)—January 24, 1991
Luke, Keye (86)—January 12, 1991
Lund, Art (75)—May 31, 1990
Maass, Margit (88)—Winter 1990
Mack, Jess (85)—October 29, 1990
Mackaill, Dorothy (87)—August 12, 1990
Man Ray, Juliet (79)—January 17, 1991
Markham, Marcella (68)—February 24, 1991
Maroff, Robert (57)—March 14, 1991
Marr, Alice (89)—June 7, 1990
Marston, Merlin (45)—August 22, 1990
Martin, Kiel (46)—December 28, 1990
Martin, Mary (76)—November 4, 1990
Mazurki, Mike (82)—December 9, 1990
McConnell, Emma J. (59)—July 6, 1990
McCrea, Joel (84)—October 20, 1990
McIntire, John (83)—January 30, 1991
McLaughlin, Emily (61)—April 26, 1991
McLoughlin, Maurice (82)—September 13, 1990
McPhillips, Hugh (70)—October 31, 1990
Meisels, Saul (93)—September 7, 1990
Metcalf, Pony Sherrell—December 8, 1990
Minotis, Alexis (90)—October 10, 1990
Mitchell, Frank—January 21, 1991
Mondo, Peggy (50)—February 19, 1991
Montalban, Carlos (87)—March 28, 1991
Moore, Ada (64)—January 6, 1991
Murdoch, Richard B. (83)—October 9, 1990
Nelson, Herbert (76)—July 19, 1990
Noble, Clarence Lancelot (77)—July 15, 1990
O'Brien, Christopher J. (30)—January 8, 1991
Oliver, Susan (58)—May 16, 1990
Page, Jean (95)—December 15, 1990
Palk, Anna (48)—July 1, 1990
Palmer, Maree (84)—November 29, 1990
Parks, Mama Lu (61)—September 23, 1990
Pippin, Nick (35)—July 27, 1990
Pond, Barbara—June 16, 1990
Price, Gilbert (48)—January 2, 1991
Quattropani, Maria A. (42)—July 22, 1990
Quidd, Jimmi (36)—August 26, 1990
Quillan, Eddie (83)—July 19, 1990

Rabold, Rex (39)—July 26, 1990
Raffetto, Michael (91)—May 31, 1990
Rascel, Renato (78)—January 2, 1991
Ray, Aldo (64)—March 27, 1991
Raymonde, George (76)—Fall 1990
Reachi, Ramon (87)—June 25, 1990
Reed, Gavin (59)—December 3, 1990
Reeve, Scott (38)—December 15, 1990
Revere, Anne (87)—December 18, 1990
Reynolds, Helene Fortescu (65)—March 28, 1991
Rice, Feliz (46)—October 19, 1990
Ripepi, Nino (74)—August 3, 1990
Robinson, Meghan (35)—November 18, 1990
Roderick, William (80s)—April 13, 1991
Rogers, Jean (74)—February 24, 1991
Rosqui, Tom (62)—April 11, 1991
Russell, Craig (42)—October 30, 1990
Russell, John (70)—January 19, 1991
Russell, Paul (49)—February 15, 1991
Sachs, Leonard (82)—June 15, 1990
St. Jacques, Raymond (60)—August 27, 1990
Salcido, Michael A. (39)—October 10, 1990
Sansberry, Hope (94)—December 14, 1990
Sauer, Bernard (67)—February 13, 1991
Schafer, Natalie (90)—April 10, 1991
Scopino, Tony (33)—March 13, 1991
Sedgwick, Eileen (93)—March 15, 1991
Seeger, Sara (76)—August 12, 1990
Seigner, Louis (87)—January 20, 1991
Servent, Arthur (86)—April 30, 1991
Seville, Pauline (65)—December 6, 1990
Seyler, Athene (101)—September 12, 1990
Seyrig, Delphine (58)—October 15, 1990
Sharbutt, Meri Bell (78)—February 15, 1991
Shaw, Beverly (81)—May 26, 1990
Shaw, Steve (25)—December 5, 1990
Shawley, Robert (63)—May 9, 1990
Shimabuku, Norris M. (44)—April 10, 1991
Siletti, Mario (65)—January 7, 1991
Smathers, Ben (61)—September 13, 1990
Smith, William Henry (51)—July 23, 1990
Solari, Rudy (56)—April 23, 1991
Soler, Francisco Gabilondo (83)—December 14, 1990
Sommer, Bert (42)—July 23, 1990
Stanley, Jack (87)—August 15, 1990
Steber, Eleanor (76)—October 3, 1990
Stephens, Robert (35)—October 4, 1990
Sterling, Jack (75)—October 31, 1990
Stierle, Edward (23)—March 8, 1991
Stuart, Muriel (90)—January 29, 1991
Sullivan, Marie Madeline (80)—January 5, 1991
Taylor, Burton (47)—February 13, 1991
Tennyson, Jean (86)—March 15, 1991
Tessier, Robert (56)—October 11, 1990
Thomas, Danny (79)—February 6, 1991
Thorpe, Richard (95)—May 1, 1990
Tognazzi, Ugo (68)—October 27, 1990
Tupper, Loretta Clemens (84)—September 18,
1990
Turnage, Wayne J. (47)—July 9, 1990
Turner, Eva (98)—June 16, 1990
Ventura, Clyde (54)—November 2, 1990
Vrooman, Richard C. (54)—December 31, 1990
Walters, Marrian (67)—August 4, 1990
Warfield, Marjorie (88)—April 15, 1991
Warren, Betty (83)—December 15, 1990
Watts, Leroy Jr. (72)—September 22, 1990
Wayne, Johnny (72)—July 18, 1990
Willock, David (81)—November 12, 1990
Wilshin, Sunday (86)—March 19, 1991
Winslow, Dick (75)—February 7, 1991
Winters, Bernie (58)—May 4, 1991
Winton, Violet (90)—February 8, 1991
Wittenberg, Marguerite N. (77)—December 25,
1990
Wood, George (56)—July 22, 1990
Workman, Martin (71)—May 10,1990
Wyler, Margaret Tallichet (77)—May 3, 1991
Young, Karen (39)—January 26,1991

PLAYWRIGHTS

Bannerman, Kay (71)—March 11, 1991
Bass, George Houston (52)—August 14, 1990
Blaney, Harry Clay (86)—October 3, 1990
Caristi, Vincent (42)—September 20, 1990
Chandler, David (78)—October 19, 1990
Chesley, Robert (47)—December 5, 1990
Dante, Nicholas (49)—May 21, 1991
Duerrenmatt, Friedrich (69)—December 14, 1990
Eichelberger, James R. (Ethyl) (45)—August 12,
1990
Eyen, Tom (50)—May 26, 1991
Frisch, Max (79)—April 4, 1991
Fuller, John (76)—November 7, 1990
Gallu, Samuel G. (73)—March 27, 1991
Greene, Graham (86)—April 3, 1991
Kerman, Sheppard (62)—April 15, 1991
Markle, Fletcher (70)—May 23, 1991
Metcalfe, Gordon (43)—August 6, 1990
Miller, Harold (71)—June 16, 1990
Pertwee, Michael (74)—April 17, 1991
Scott, Dennis (51)—February 21, 1991
Turner, David (63)—Winter 1990
Wolfson, Victor—Summer 1990
Wood, Raymond (43)—July 20, 1990

COMPOSERS, LYRICISTS, SONGWRITERS

Ackerman, Jack (59)—April 27, 1991
Arel, Bulent (71)—November 24, 1990
Ashman, Howard (40)—March 14, 1991

Bernstein, Leonard (72)—October 14, 1990
Brown, Ralph H. (55)—January 9, 1991
Butler, BIlly (66)—March 20, 1991
Carter, John (61)—March 31, 1991
Cleveland, James (59)— February 9, 1991
Copeland, Aaron (90)— December 2, 1990
Coppola, Carmine (80)—April 26, 1991
Effinger, Cecil (76)—December 22, 1990
Fran, Paul (56)—March 14, 1991
Gaillard, Slim (74)—February 26, 1991
Gorney, Jay (93)—June 14, 1990
Graham, Willis S. (71)—July 23, 1990
Huston, Scott S. (74)—March 1, 1991
Janowski, Max (79)—April 8, 1991
Johansen, Gunnar (85)—May 25, 1991
Kreutz, Arthur R. (84)—March 11, 1991
Lake, Sol (79)—March 2, 1991
Langlais, Jean (84)—May 8, 1991
Loose, William (80)—February 22, 1991
Manning, Dick (79)—April 11, 1991
Marriott, Steve (44)—April 20, 1991
Mercer, Wallace (82)—June 24, 1990
Moss, Earle (91)—May 19, 1991
Mossman, Bina (97)—May 13, 1990
Mydland, Brent (38)—July 26, 1990
Nevins, Morty (73)—July 20, 1990
Noveilli, Santo A. (73)—October 28, 1990
Ott, Joseph H. (60)—May 16, 1990
Paul, Charles F. (88)—September 19, 1990
Pleis, Jack K. (73)—December 6, 1990
Pomus, Doc (65)—March 14, 1991
Ram, Samuel (83)—January 1, 1991
Rose, David (80)—August 23, 1990
Saunders, John (76)—June 6, 1990
Sharp, Carol (90)—June 9, 1990
Siegmeister, Elie (82)—March 10, 1991
Starobin, Daniel (43)—January 13, 1991
Thunders, Johnny (38)—April 23, 1991
Vallon, Paul (63)—March 21, 1991
Walberg, Betty (69)—October 3, 1990
Warren, Elinor Remick (91)—April 27, 1991
Winters, John (81)—August 24, 1990
Yellen, Jack (98)—April 17, 1991

CONDUCTORS

Adler, Peter Herman (91)—October 2, 1990
Ainsworth, Alyn (66)—October 4, 1990
Boskovsky, Willi (81)—April 21, 1991
Carl, Elwood Stanley (73)—January 13, 1991
Crawford, Hector William (77)—March 11, 1991
Cugat, Xavier (90)—October 27, 1990
Dorian, Frederick (89)—January 24, 1991
Epstein, Max (39)—December 14, 1990
Fardink, Michael (36)—March 31, 1991
Flood, Joseph W. (77)—December 15, 1990
Follett, Warren (56)—June 27, 1990
Gayten, Paul (71)—March 26, 1991

Haasemann, Frauke (68)—April 12, 1991
Hill, Lawrence W. (41)—April 12, 1991
Holden, Charlie (mid-70s)—May 26, 1990
Janssen, Werner (91)—September 19, 1990
Kaplan, Sol (71)—November 14, 1991
Kohlman, Freddie (72)—September 29, 1990
Koller, William (60)—July 26, 1990
Lanin, Howard (93)—April 26, 1991
Marx, Walter Burle (88)—December 28, 1990
McCoy, Clyde (83)—June 11, 1990
McPherson, Hugh (77)—February 3, 1991
Nesco, John T. (80)—July 10, 1990
Pancoast, Ace (86)—March 15, 1991
Paterson, John Y. (86)—June 26, 1990
Riley, Luke (82)—September 29, 1990
Rozsnyai, Zoltan (64)—September 10, 1990
Sack, Victor (74)—December 18, 1990
Schandler, Hyman (90)—September 9, 1990
Scott, Bobby (53)—November 5, 1990
Wills, Billy Jack (65)—March 2, 1991

CRITICS

Audry, Colette (84)—October 20, 1990
Briggs, John Jr. (74)—August 10, 1990
Calta, Louis (77)—September 23, 1990
Dash, Thomas R. (93)—May 21, 1991
Feder, Edgar (81)—July 22, 1990
Ferreira, Carlos (78)—September 25, 1990
Fox, Charles (70)—May 9, 1991
Galkin, Elliott W. (69)—May 24, 1990
Glanville-Hicks, Peggy (77)—June 25, 1990
Grilli, Marcel F. (83)—September 20, 1990
Hildebrand, Harold (67)—November 28, 1990
Hummler, Richard J. (47)—October 16, 1990
Kihlman, Marten (48)—May 28, 1990
Kovner, Leo (71)—October 16, 1990
Lorente, Joan (47)—September 11, 1990
MacDonald, Iain (62)—February 2, 1991
Mahoney, John C. (55)—December 23, 1990
Mitropoulou, Aglaia (64)—January 12, 1991
Pennington, Bob (68)—November 14, 1990
Standish, Myles (83)—January 10, 1991

MUSICIANS

Barefield, Eddie (81)—January 3, 1991
Bargen, Karl (38)—December 8, 1990
Bators, Stiv (30s)—June 3, 1990
Biro, Sari (78)—September 2, 1990
Blakey, Art (71)—October 16, 1990
Bossi, Dott (85)—January 29, 1991
Campoli, Alfredo (84)—March 27, 1991
Castle, Lee (75)—November 15, 1990
Castleberry, Kelly L. II (43)—December 10, 1990
Clark, Steve (30)—January 8, 1991

Davis Walter Jr. (57)—June 2, 1990
Diamond, Eddie (69)—June 10, 1990
Dudero, Gordon (74)—December 21, 1990
Eisner, Leonard (70)—April 15, 1991
Fleece, Marianne (67)—July 21, 1990
Flessig, Camen (81)—August 24, 1990
Fogerty, Tom (48)—September 6, 1990
Freeman, Bud (84)—March 15, 1991
Gendron, Emilia J. (69)—May 7, 1990
Gordon, Steven R. (45)—June 23, 1990
Grady, John (56)—September 27, 1990
Grey, John L. (64)—July 24, 1990
Hardman, Bill (57)—December 6, 1990
Harris, H. Alfred Jr. (79)—June 24, 1990
Hodder, Jimmy (42)—June 5, 1990
Holley, Major (66)—October 25, 1990
Jacob, Otto (99)—May 28, 1990
Kempff, Wilhelm (95)—May 23, 1991
Kievman, Louis (80)—December 4, 1990
Kirk, Mary (90)— November 20, 1990
Klink, Al (75)—March 7, 1991
Kushner, Sylvia Deutscher (65)—August 17, 1990
Kuziak, Stanley (82)—May 9, 1990
Ladish, Josephine (77)—July 31, 1990
Lahr, Mary (80)—December 17, 1990
Leahy, Harry (54)—August 12, 1990
Lowenthal, Ronit Amir (56)—August 9, 1990
Margliss, Frances (76)—April 21, 1991
Mayes, Samuel (73)—August 24, 1990
McPartland, Jimmy (83)—March 13, 1991
Napolean, Phil (89)—Fall 1990
Norwood, Idell (78)—February 8, 1991
Pierce, Webb (69)—February 24, 1991
Potter, Irene (82)—July 14, 1990
Przybcin, Edward A. (59)—June 26, 1990
Pukwana, Dudu (52)—June 29, 1990
Purcell, Joseph (41)—June 29, 1990
Remler, Emily (32)—May 4, 1990
Rhodes, Walter (50)—July 4, 1990
Rice, Raymond G. (64)—July 24, 1990
Ruden, Sol (87)—May 5, 1990
Rudewicz, Kasmeir W. (85)—May 7, 1990
Russianoff, Leon (73)—September 16, 1990
Sadowski, Ed (69)—October 30, 1990
Serkin, Rudolf (88)—May 8, 1991
Smith, Jabbo (82)—January 16, 1991
Spitalny, Evelyn Klein (79)—July 13, 1990.
Stephens, Arthur (56)—May 11, 1990
Szelest, Stan (48)—January 20, 1991
Tedeschi, Anthony A. (88)—July 4, 1990
Thomas, Jerry (49)—August 31, 1990
Turner, Joe (82)—July 21, 1990
Valenti, Fernando (63)—September 6, 1990
VanDeMark, Edward C. (79)—July 17, 1990
Vaughan, Stevie Ray (35)—August 27, 1990
Ventrilli, George J. (62)—June 30, 1990
Veyron-Lacroix, Robert (68)—April 2, 1991
Vola, Louis (88)—August 1990

Walters, Howard Duke (72)—March 31, 1991
Weakley, Harold (60)—July 25, 1990
Weinrich, Carl (86)—May 13, 1991
Whitney, Herman W. (50)—May 19, 1990
Young, Robert (89)—June 2, 1990
Zardis, Chester (90)—July 16, 1990

DESIGNERS

Anderson, William (45)—July 9, 1990
Carter, Paul D. (33)—August 9, 1990
de Rosier, Philippe (72)—March 12, 1991
Franklin, Robert E. (46)—November 16, 1990
Guzman, Pato (57)—January 2, 1991
Karatzas, Steven G. (44)—April 14, 1991
Lesser, Gilbert (55)—August 28, 1990
Morley, Ruth (65)— February 12, 1991
Rampino, Lewis D. (47)—October 30, 1990
Tirelli, Umberto (62)—December 26, 1990
Travilla, Bill (69)—November 2, 1990
Wein, Albert (75)—March 30, 1991

PRODUCERS, DIRECTORS, CHOREOGRAPHERS

Ackerman, Harry (78)—February 3, 1991
Allison, Karl Jr. (42)—July 4, 1990
Alper, Jonathan (40)—December 3, 1990
Bakman, Patrick T. (46)—December 16, 1990
Bales, William (80)—September 8, 1990
Batcheller, Ruth (74)—July 15, 1990
Bavar, Michael (50)—December 25, 1990
Blatt, Edward A. (88)—February 12, 1991
Brodkin, Herbert (77)—October 29, 1990
Brooks, Norman J. (64)—January 3, 1991
Bryant, Ken (35)—October 2, 1990
Bunch, Jack (61)—May 7, 1990
Burton, Bernard (92)—February 26, 1991
Bush, Warren V. (65)—April 16, 1991
Campion, Clifford (40)—December 24, 1990
Chaffey, Don (72)—November 13, 1990
Clarke, Alan (54)—July 24, 1990
Cowan, Lester (83)—October 21, 1990
Davis, Barry (54)—September 15, 1990
Delakova, Katya (76)—April 10, 1991
Demy, Jacques (59)—October 27, 1990
Dozier, William (83)—April 23, 1991
Duncan, Virginia (61)—January 14, 1991
Englund, Richard (59)—February 15, 1991
Epstein, Jon (62)—November 24, 1990
Erickson, Carey (40)—December 13, 1990
Forde, Larry (57)—August 23, 1990
Franck, Edward A. (70)—July 12, 1990
Graeme, Joyce (71)—February 26, 1991
Graham, Martha (96)—April 1, 1991

Haas, Tom (53)—February 21, 1991
Haeseler, John A. (90)—September 4, 1990
Haizlip, Ellis (61)—January 25, 1991
Herndon, William F. (54)—November 12, 1990
Hill, Lawrence W. (41)—April 12, 1991
Hurwitz, Stan (46)—January 5, 1991
Irving, Richard (73)—December 30, 1990
Kantor, Tadeusz (75)—December 2, 1990
Kasha, Lawrence (57)—September 29, 1990
King, Eleanor (85)—February 27, 1991
Kochno, Boris (86)—December 9, 1990
Kovich, Robert (40)—April 21, 1991
Kowalski, Rob (37)—May 15, 1990
Lean, David (83)—April 16, 1991
Levin, Herman (83)—December 27, 1990
Levy, Edwin Lewis (73)—April 3, 1991
Lias, Bernard (44)—May 9, 1990
LoBianco, Robert (44)—April 11, 1991
Lucas, Jonathan (70)—February 5, 1991
Marmelstein, Linda (55)—February 18, 1991
Marriott, B. Rodney (52)—September 9, 1990
McInerney, Timothy C. (39)—August 24, 1990
McRae, Edna (88)—June 7, 1990
Mendenhall, Jim (62)—December 1, 1990
Mendes, Antonio (41)—February 7, 1991
Miller, Tod (46)—December 14, 1990
Minor, Philip (63)—April 9, 1991
Morgan, George J. (77)—March 28, 1991
Moscow, Robert (69)—August 10, 1990
Nichols, George III (70)—April 25, 1991
Nusbaum, Jane C.—July 13, 1990
Page, Ruth (92)—April 1991
Pan, Hermes (80)—September 19, 1990
Perrotti, Joseph A. (45)—September 7, 1990
Ritt, Martin (76)—December 8, 1990
Robinson, Thelma (66)—October 27, 1990
Romano, Jack (53)—March 21, 1991
Rudolph, Oscar (79)—February 1, 1991
Rusinow, Irving (75)—August 2, 1990
Sabinson, Lee (79)—April 14, 1991
Sagan, Gene Hill (59)—March 1, 1991
Schepard, Eric (66)—February 27, 1991
Schmitt, Ted (50)—May 30, 1990
Scott, Gordon (71)—April 3, 1991
Sebastian, Stuart (40)—January 16, 1991
Selznick, Irene Mayer (83)—October 10, 1990
Sheehan, John J. (68)—December 15, 1990
Sherman, George (82)—March 15, 1991
Smith, Fran (69)—September 26, 1990
Soares, George—July 22, 1990
Sugarman, Howard L. (34)—April 20, 1991
Tamber, Selma (84)—January 14, 1990
Thompson, David (40)—July 22, 1990
Trauberg, Leonid Z. (89)—November 14, 1990
Upshaw, Vic (50)—November 5, 1990
Vanoff, Nick (61)—March 20, 1991
Vesak, Norbert (53)—October 2, 1990
Wolshonak, Derek (44)—January 4, 1991
Zwickler, Phil (36)—May 7, 1991

OTHERS

Alexander, Hal (87)—June 20, 1990
  Actors' Equity of Australia
Antonello, John (74)—November 1, 1990
  Promoter
Baker, Charles Adams (70)— March 15, 1991
  Agent
Baker, Terence (52)—May 20, 1991
  Agent
Baron, Ron (42)—April 13, 1991
  Publicist
Batchelor, Bill—September 23, 1990
  Publicist
Beck, Mike (81)—January 10, 1991
  Publicist
Berwick, Ray (75)—July 2, 1990
  Animal trainer
Blowers, J. Garrett (48)—September 3, 1990
  Publicist
Braddell, Maurice (89)—July 28, 1990
  Noel Coward understudy
Bright, Charles Randall (51)—June 5, 1990
  Disneyland
Brooks, Robert H. (34)—August 27, 1990
  Booking Agent
Browning, John (44)—July 6, 1990
  Publicist
Buckley, Peter (52)—May 21, 1991
  Writer
Burns, Stan Z. (63)—November 16, 1990
  Broadcaster
Carroll, Carroll (88)—February 5, 1991
  Variety
Casado, Frank (66)—July 5, 1990
  Restaurateur
Clark, Kenneth W. (91)—August 17, 1990
  Publicist
Cooper, Elliot (59)—October 5, 1990
  Norwalk Youth Symphony
Corcoran, Tom (41)—October 14, 1990
  San Diego Dance Alliance
Cox, Edna (75)—March 2, 1990
  Variety
Cullen, Bill (70)—July 7, 1990
  Gameshow host
Dahl, Roald (74)—November 23, 1990
  Writer
Daly, John (77)—February 25, 1991
  Moderator, *What's My Line*
Daniels, Pearl (84)—February 10, 1991
  Booking agent
DeCourcy, Dayson (69)—July 4, 1990
  Mark Twain Masquers
Delacorte, George T. (97)—May 4, 1991
  Dell Publishing
Devlin, Virginia (80)—May 5, 1990
  Aerialist

Donovan, Hedley (76)—August 13, 1990
Time, Inc.
Edington, Priscilla (69)—July 27, 1990
Stage manager
Edwards, A.J. (37)—July 27, 1990
Acrobat
Edwards, Douglas (73)—October 13, 1990
TV reporter
Emmet, Alfred (82)—January 16, 1991
Questors Theater
Forester, Dr. Stuart W. (44)—January 11, 1991
House physician
Gaxton, Madeline (early 80s)—May 23, 1990
Widow of William Gaxton
Geick, Fred S. (81)—May 22, 1990
Ticket taker
Glackens, Ira (83)—November 26, 1990
Writer
Goldwurm, Jean (97)—October 25, 1990
Film distributor
Goren, Charles (90)—April 3, 1991
Bridge player
Grant, Hank (77)—July 19, 1990
Columnist
Green, Stanley (67)—December 12, 1990
Historian
Grossman, Michael Jay (48)—April 6, 1991
Ahmanson Theater
Habeeb, Tony (64)—April 14, 1991
Publicist
Hale, Alan L. (41)—January 22, 1991
Publicist
Halperin, Jonas (60)—May 23, 1991
Publicist
Haynes, Wallace (84)—May 22, 1990
Sound effects editor
Hays, Ron—April 16, 1991
Multimedia artist
Hoenig, Joe (65)—February 13, 1991
Publicist
Hohner, Frank (81)—October 3, 1990
Harmonica manufacturer
Hurst, Walter (60)—January 24, 1991
Publisher
John, Yango (74)—June 26, 1990
Impresario
Jones, Steven (29)—April 28, 1991
Costume designer
Kieffer, Townsend T. (51)—August 28, 1990
Publicist
Kirchner, Dietmar (47)—July 5, 1990
Photographer
Kook, Edward F. (87)—September 29, 1990
Century Lighting Co.
Kramer, Edith (78)—January 4, 1991
Rehearsal studio
Kummer, Martin (64)—July 8, 1990
Agent
Landry, Robert John (87)—May 23, 1991
Variety

Larrabee, Eric (68)—December 4, 1990
Arts administrator
Leavitt, Joseph (74)—September 21, 1990
Wolf Trap
Leonard, Robert (49)—Fall 1990
Voice teacher
Lester, Edwin (95)—December 13, 1990
L.A. Civic Light Opera
Liebhart, David (39)—July 5, 1990
Agent
Little, Francis J. (56)—July 30, 1990
New York Philharmonic
Love, Edmund G. (78)—August 30, 1990
Writer
Macdonald, James (84)—February 1, 1991
Voice of Mickey Mouse
MacDougall, Maggie—February 22, 1991
Friars Club
Markert, Russell (91)—December 1, 1990
Radio City Music Hall
Martindale, Stephen (47)—June 13, 1990
Publicist
McBean, Angus (86)—June 9, 1990
Photographer
McKenzie, Helen Sherman (92)—July 24, 1990
Publicist
McNeely, Dick (72)—February 4, 1991
Publicist
Miler, Millicent (81)—May 29, 1990
Vivian Leigh's stand-in *GWTW*
Milstein, Murray (75)—May 19, 1990
Agent
Moore, George W. (64)—May 3, 1991
St. Malachy's
Moran, Jay (45)—October 28, 1990
Actors' Equity
Murray, Arthur (95)—March 3, 1991
Dance instructor
Natwick, Grim (100)—October 7, 1990
Animator
Oberreich, Robert L. (80)—March 5, 1991
Stage manager
Okubo, Michi (81)—April 30, 1991
Costumer
Paley, William S. (89)—October 26, 1990
CBS
Parker, Kenneth R. (61)—March 29, 1991
Publicist
Parker, Lida-Virginia (77)—July 8, 1990
Neighborhood Playhouse
Paul, Harry (81)—December 17, 1990
Publicist
Peresson, Sergio (78)—April 16, 1991
Violin maker
Pickard, Lillian (66)—August 30, 1990
Publicist
Pine, Edward Seth (42)—September 21, 1990
Publicist
Pitluck, Sherman (78)—July 15, 1990
Booking agent

Preston, Joel (66)—October 29, 1990
   Publicist
Puig, Manuel (57)—July 22, 1990
   Writer
Remer, Jay (63)—April 14, 1991
   Publicist
Roberts, Cecil (76)—May 29, 1990
   Alabama Arts Council
Rogers, Kipp Alan (32)—May 26, 1990
   Lawyer
Sandy (16)—August 29, 1990
   Annie's dog
Sarnoff, Pam Martin (61)—May 4, 1991
   Opera Guild
Schang, Frederick (96)—August 26, 1990
   Columbia Artists
Scharper, Marie (86)—July 22, 1990
   Publicist
Schoenhut, George W. (83)—September 13, 1990
   Drama professor
Scofield, Elizabeth (65)—August 11, 1990
   Publicist
Shikanai, Nobutaka (78)—October 20, 1990
   Fujisankei Communications
Silden, Isobel Katleman (69)—December 16,
   1990
   Publicist
Souttar, Fred C. (86)—July 2, 1990
   National General Theaters
Spangler, David H. (37)—June 28, 1990
   Publicist
Spofford, Charles M. (88)—March 24, 1991
   Metropolitan Opera

Starr, Jimmy (86)—August 13, 1990
   Columnist
Stern, Miriam Rose (76)—December 9, 1990
   Agent
Stout-Kerr, Barbara Zinn (55)—May 31, 1990
   Theater tours
Thompson, Johnny (73)—April 2, 1991
   Arranger
Tishman, Max (91)—June 7, 1990
   Booking agent
Trethowan, Ian (68)—December 12, 1990
   Thames Television
Tucker, Lem (52)—March 2, 1991
   Reporter
Unkefer, Linn (84)—June 24, 1990
   Publicist
Varnell, Lon S. (77)—February 17, 1991
   Promoter
Waiss, George C. (83)—July 17, 1990
   Animator
Wallace, Irving (74)—June 29, 1990
   Writer
Wilson, Josphine (86)—November 7, 1990
   Mermaid Theater, London
Wise, Jeffrey L. (41)—May 26, 1990
   Publicist
Young, Gary M. (48)—April 28, 1990
   Conn. Arts Commission
Zolotow, Maurice (77)—March 14, 1991
   Biographer

THE BEST PLAYS, 1894-1990

Listed in alphabetical order below are all those works selected as Best Plays in previous volumes of the *Best Plays* series. Opposite each title is given the volume in which the play appears, its opening date and its total number of performances. Two separate opening-date and performance-number entries signify two separate engagements off Broadway and on Broadway when the original production was transferred from one area to the other, usually in an off-to-on direction. Those plays marked with an asterisk (*) were still playing on June 1, 1991 and their number of performances was figured through May 31, 1991. Adaptors and translators are indicated by (ad) and (tr), the symbols (b), (m) and (l) stand for the author of the book, music and lyrics in the case of musicals and (c) signifies the credit for the show's conception.

PLAY	VOLUME	OPENED	PERFS
ABE LINCOLN IN ILLINOIS—Robert E. Sherwood	38-39	Oct. 15, 1938	472
ABRAHAM LINCOLN—John Drinkwater	19-20	Dec. 15, 1919	193
ACCENT ON YOUTH—Samson Raphaelson	34-35	Dec. 25, 1934	229
ADAM AND EVA—Guy Bolton, George Middleton	19-20	Sept. 13, 1919	312
ADAPTATION—Elaine May; and NEXT—Terrence McNally	68-69	Feb. 10, 1969	707
AFFAIRS OF STATE—Louis Verneuil	50-51	Sept. 25, 1950	610
AFTER THE FALL—Arthur Miller	63-64	Jan. 23, 1964	208
AFTER THE RAIN—John Bowen	67-68	Oct. 9, 1967	64
AGNES OF GOD—John Pielmeier	81-82	Mar. 30, 1982	486
AH, WILDERNESS!—Eugene O'Neill	33-34	Oct. 2, 1933	289
AIN'T SUPPOSED TO DIE A NATURAL DEATH—(b, m, l) Melvin Van Peebles	71-72	Oct. 7, 1971	325
ALIEN CORN—Sidney Howard	32-33	Feb. 20, 1933	98
ALISON'S HOUSE—Susan Glaspell	30-31	Dec. 1, 1930	41
ALL MY SONS—Arthur Miller	46-47	Jan. 29, 1947	328
ALL OVER TOWN—Murray Schisgal	74-75	Dec. 12, 1974	233
ALL THE WAY HOME—Tad Mosel, based on James Agee's novel *A Death in the Family*	60-61	Nov. 30, 1960	333
ALLEGRO—(b, l) Oscar Hammerstein II, (m) Richard Rodgers	47-48	Oct. 10, 1947	315
AMADEUS—Peter Shaffer	80-81	Dec. 17, 1980	1,181
AMBUSH—Arthur Richman	21-22	Oct. 10, 1921	98
AMERICA HURRAH—Jean-Claude van Itallie	66-67	Nov. 6, 1966	634
AMERICAN BUFFALO—David Mamet	76-77	Feb. 16, 1977	135
AMERICAN WAY, THE—George S. Kaufman, Moss Hart	38-39	Jan. 21, 1939	164
AMPHITRYON 38—Jean Giraudoux, (ad) S.N. Behrman	37-38	Nov. 1, 1937	153
AND A NIGHTINGALE SANG—C.P. Taylor	83-84	Nov. 27, 1983	177
ANDERSONVILLE TRIAL, THE—Saul Levitt	59-60	Dec. 29, 1959	179
ANDORRA—Max Frisch, (ad) George Tabori	62-63	Feb. 9, 1963	9
ANGEL STREET—Patrick Hamilton	41-42	Dec. 5, 1941	1,295
ANGELS FALL—Lanford Wilson	82-83	Oct. 17, 1982	65
ANIMAL KINGDOM, The—Philip Barry	31-32	Jan.12, 1932	183
ANNA CHRISTIE—Eugene O'Neill	21-22	Nov. 2, 1921	177
ANNA LUCASTA—Philip Yordan	44-45	Aug. 30, 1944	957
ANNE OF THE THOUSAND DAYS—Maxwell Anderson	48-49	Dec. 8, 1948	286
ANNIE—(b) Thomas Meehan, (m) Charles Strouse, (l) Martin Charnin, based on Harold Gray's comic strip "Little Orphan Annie"	76-77	Apr. 21, 1977	2,377

PLAY   VOLUME OPENED   PERFS

PLAY   VOLUME OPENED   PERFS

CLARENCE—Booth Tarkington 19-20   Sept. 20, 1919   306
CLAUDIA—Rose Franken 40-41   Feb. 12, 1941   722
CLEARING IN THE WOODS, A—Arthur Laurents 56-57   Jan. 10, 1957   36
CLIMATE OF EDEN, THE—Moss Hart, based on
    Edgar Mittleholzer's novel *Shadows Move Among Them* . . 52-53   Nov. 13, 1952   20
CLIMBERS, THE—Clyde Fitch 99-09   Jan. 21, 1901   163
CLOUD 9—Caryl Churchill 80-81   May 18, 1981   971
CLUTTERBUCK—Benn W. Levy 49-50   Dec. 3, 1949   218
COCKTAIL HOUR, THE—A.R. Gurney 88-89   Aug. 10, 1989   351
COCKTAIL PARTY, THE—T.S. Eliot 49-50   Jan. 21, 1950   409
COLD WIND AND THE WARM, THE—S.N. Behrman 58-59   Dec. 8, 1958   120
COLLECTION, THE—Harold Pinter 62-63   Nov. 26, 1962   578
COME BACK, LITTLE SHEBA—William Inge 49-50   Feb. 15, 1950   191
COMEDIANS—Trevor Griffiths 76-77   Nov. 28, 1976   145
COMMAND DECISION—William Wister Haines 47-48   Oct. 1, 1947   408
COMPANY—(b) George Furth, (m, l) Stephen Sondheim 69-70   Apr. 26, 1970   705
COMPLAISANT LOVER, THE—Graham Greene 61-62   Nov. 1, 1961   101
CONDUCT UNBECOMING—Barry England 70-71   Oct. 12, 1970   144
CONFIDENTIAL CLERK, THE—T.S. Eliot 53-54   Feb. 11, 1954   117
CONNECTION, THE—Jack Gelber (picked as a supplement
    to the Best Plays) 60-61   Feb. 22, 1961   722
CONSTANT WIFE, THE—W. Somerset Maugham 26-27   Nov. 20, 1926   295
CONTRACTOR, THE—David Storey 73-74   Oct. 17, 1973   72
COQUETTE—George Abbott, Ann Preston Bridgers 27-28   Nov. 8, 1927   366
CORN IS GREEN, THE—Emlyn Williams 40-41   Nov. 26, 1940   477
COUNTRY GIRL, THE—Clifford Odets 50-51   Nov. 10, 1950   235
COUNTY CHAIRMAN, THE—George Ade 99-09   Nov. 24, 1903   222
CRADLE SONG, THE—Gregorio & Maria Martinez Sierra,
    (tr) John Garrett Underhill 26-27   Jan. 24, 1927   57
CRAIG'S WIFE—George Kelly 25-26   Oct. 12, 1925   360
CREATION OF THE WORLD AND OTHER BUSINESS,
    THE—Arthur Miller 72-73   Nov. 30, 1972   20
CREEPS—David E. Freeman 73-74   Dec. 4, 1973   15
CRIMES OF THE HEART—Beth Henley 80-81   Dec. 9, 1980   35
                                               81-82   Nov. 4, 1981   535
CRIMINAL CODE, THE—Martin Flavin 29-30   Oct. 2, 1929   173
CRUCIBLE, THE—Arthur Miller 52-53   Jan. 22, 1953   197
CYNARA—H.M. Harwood, R.F. Gore-Browne 31-32   Nov. 2, 1931   210

DA—Hugh Leonard 77-78   May 1, 1978   697
DAISY MAYME—George Kelly 26-27   Oct. 25, 1926   112
DAMASK CHEEK, THE—John van Druten, Lloyd Morris 42-43   Oct. 22, 1942   93
DANCE AND THE RAILROAD, THE—David Henry Hwang 81-82   July 16, 1981   181
DANCING MOTHERS—Edgar Selwyn, Edmund Goulding 24-25   Aug. 11, 1924   312
DARK AT THE TOP OF THE STAIRS, THE—William Inge 57-58   Dec. 5, 1957   468
DARK IS LIGHT ENOUGH, THE—Christopher Fry 54-55   Feb. 23, 1955   69
DARKNESS AT NOON—Sidney Kingsley, based on
    Arthur Koestler's novel 50-51   Jan. 13, 1951   186
DARLING OF THE GODS, THE—David Belasco,
    John Luther Long 99-09   Dec. 3, 1902   182
DAUGHTERS OF ATREUS—Robert Turney 36-37   Oct. 14, 1936   13
DAY IN THE DEATH OF JOE EGG, A—Peter Nichols 67-68   Feb. 1, 1968   154
DEAD END—Sidney Kingsley 35-36   Oct. 28, 1935   687
DEADLY GAME, THE—James Yaffe, based on
    Friedrich Duerrenmatt's novel 59-60   Feb. 2, 1960   39
DEAR RUTH—Norman Krasna 44-45   Dec. 13, 1944   683
DEATH OF A SALESMAN—Arthur Miller 48-49   Feb. 10, 1949   742

PLAY   VOLUME OPENED PERFS

END OF SUMMER—S.N. Behrman 35-36   Feb. 17, 1936   153
ENEMY, THE—Channing Pollock 25-26   Oct. 20, 1925   203
ENOUGH, FOOTFALLS and ROCKABY—Samuel Beckett 83-84   Feb. 16, 1984   78
ENTER MADAME—Gilda Varesi, Dolly Byrne............. 20-21   Aug. 16, 1920   350
ENTERTAINER, THE—John Osborne..................... 57-58   Feb. 12, 1958   97
EPITAPH FOR GEORGE DILLON—John Osborne,
    Anthony Creighton 58-59   Nov. 4, 1958   23
EQUUS—Peter Shaffer.............................. 74-75   Oct. 24, 1974 1,209
ESCAPE—John Galsworthy 27-28   Oct. 26, 1927   173
ETHAN FROME—Owen and Donald Davis, based on
    Edith Wharton's novel........................ 35-36   Jan. 21, 1936   120
EVE OF ST. MARK, THE—Maxwell Anderson 42-43   Oct. 7, 1942   `307
EXCURSION—Victor Wolfson.......................... 36-37   Apr. 9, 1937   116
EXECUTION OF JUSTICE—Emily Mann 85-86   Mar. 13, 1986   12
EXTREMITIES—William Mastrosimone 82-83   Dec. 22, 1982   325

FALL GUY, THE—James Gleason, George Abbott.......... 24-25   Mar. 10, 1925   176
FAMILY BUSINESS—Dick Goldberg 77-78   Apr. 12, 1978   438
FAMILY PORTRAIT—Lenore Coffee, William Joyce Cowen 38-39   May 8, 1939   111
FAMOUS MRS. FAIR, THE—James Forbes................. 19-20   Dec. 22, 1919   344
FAR COUNTRY, A—Henry Denker...................... 60-61   Apr. 4, 1961   271
FARMER TAKES A WIFE, THE—Frank B. Elser,
    Marc Connelly, based on Walter D. Edmonds's
    novel Rome Haul 34-35   Oct. 30, 1934   104
FATAL WEAKNESS, THE—George Kelly................. 46-47   Nov. 19, 1946   119
FENCES—August Wilson 86-87   Mar. 26, 1987   526
FIDDLER ON THE ROOF—(b) Joseph Stein, (l) Sheldon
    Harnick, (m) Jerry Bock, based on
    Sholom Aleichem's stories..................... 64-65   Sept. 22, 1964 3,242
5TH OF JULY, THE—Lanford Wilson
    (also called Fifth of July)..................... 77-78   Apr. 27, 1978   159
FIND YOUR WAY HOME—John Hopkins.................. 73-74   Jan. 2, 1974   135
FINISHING TOUCHES—Jean Kerr..................... 72-73   Feb. 8, 1973   164
FIORELLO!—(b) Jerome Weidman, George Abbott,
    (l) Sheldon Harnick, (m) Jerry Bock 59-60   Nov. 23, 1959   795
FIREBRAND, THE—Edwin Justus Mayer................. 24-25   Oct. 15, 1924   269
FIRST LADY—Katherine Dayton, George S. Kaufman........ 35-36   Nov. 26, 1935   246
FIRST MONDAY IN OCTOBER —Jerome Lawrence,
    Robert E. Lee 78-79   Oct. 3, 1978   79
FIRST MRS. FRASER, THE—St. John Ervine 29-30   Dec. 28, 1929   352
FIRST YEAR, THE—Frank Craven 20-21   Oct. 20, 1920   760
FIVE FINGER EXERCISE—Peter Shaffer................. 59-60   Dec. 2, 1959   337
FIVE-STAR FINAL—Louis Weitzenkorn 30-31   Dec. 30, 1930   175
FLIGHT TO THE WEST—Elmer Rice 40-41   Dec. 30, 1940   136
FLOATING LIGHT BULB, THE—Woody Allen.............. 80-81   Apr. 27, 1981   65
FLOWERING PEACH, THE—Clifford Odets................ 54-55   Dec. 28, 1954   135
FOLLIES—(b) James Goldman, (m, l) Stephen Sondheim...... 70-71   Apr. 4, 1971   521
FOOL, THE—Channing Pollock...................... 22-23   Oct. 23, 1922   373
FOOL FOR LOVE—Sam Shepard 83-84   May 26, 1983   1,000
FOOLISH NOTION—Philip Barry 44-45   Mar. 3, 1945   104
FOREIGNER, THE—Larry Shue 84-85   Nov. 1, 1984   686
FORTY CARATS—Pierre Barillet and Jean-Pierre Gredy,
    (ad) Jay Allen.............................. 68-69   Dec. 26, 1968   780
FOXFIRE—Susan Cooper, Hume Cronyn, (m) Jonathan
    Holtzman; based on materials from the Foxfire books.... 82-83   Nov. 11, 1982   213
42ND STREET—(b) Michael Stewart, Mark Bramble,
    (m, l) Harry Warren, Al Dubin, (add'l l) Johnny Mercer,
    Mort Dixon, based on the novel by Bradford Ropes 80-81   Aug. 25, 1980 3,486

PLAY	VOLUME	OPENED	PERFS
FOURPOSTER, THE—Jan de Hartog	51-52	Oct. 24, 1951	632
FRONT PAGE, THE—Ben Hecht, Charles MacArthur	28-29	Aug. 14, 1928	276
GENERATION—William Goodhart	65-66	Oct. 6, 1965	299
GEORGE WASHINGTON SLEPT HERE—George S. Kaufman, Moss Hart	40-41	Oct. 18, 1940	173
GETTING OUT—Marsha Norman	78-79	Oct. 19, 1978	259
GIDEON—Paddy Chayefsky	61-62	Nov. 9, 1961	236
GIGI—Anita Loos, based on Colette's novel	51-52	Nov. 24, 1951	219
GIMME SHELTER—Barrie Keefe (*Gem, Gotcha* and *Getaway*)	78-79	Dec. 10, 1978	17
GIN GAME, THE—D.L. Coburn	77-78	Oct. 6, 1977	517
GINGERBREAD LADY, THE—Neil Simon	70-71	Dec. 13, 1970	193
GIRL ON THE VIA FLAMINIA, THE—Alfred Hayes, based on his novel	53-54	Feb. 9, 1954	111
GLASS MENAGERIE, THE—Tennessee Williams	44-45	Mar. 31,1945	561
GLENGARRY GLEN ROSS—David Mamet	83-84	Mar. 25, 1984	378
GOBLIN MARKET—(ad) Peggy Harmon and Polly Pen from the poem by Christina Rosetti, (m) Polly Pen (special citation)	85-86	Apr. 13, 1986	89
GOLDEN APPLE , THE—(b, l), John Latouche, (m) Jerome Moross	53-54	Apr. 20, 1954	125
GOLDEN BOY—Clifford Odets	37-38	Nov. 4, 1937	250
GOOD—C. P. Taylor	82-83	Oct. 13, 1982	125
GOOD DOCTOR, THE—Neil Simon; adapted from and suggested by stories by Anton Chekhov	73-74	Nov. 27, 1973	208
GOOD GRACIOUS ANNABELLE—Clare Kummer	09-19	Oct. 31, 1916	111
GOODBYE, MY FANCY—Fay Kanin	48-49	Nov. 17, 1948	446
GOOSE HANGS HIGH—Lewis Beach	23-24	Jan. 29, 1924	183
GRAND HOTEL—Vicki Baum, (ad) W. A. Drake	30-31	Nov. 13, 1930	459
*GRAND HOTEL: THE MUSICAL—(b) Luther Davis, (m, l) Robert Wright, George Forrest, (add'l m, l) Maury Yeston, based on Vicki Baum's *Grand Hotel*	89-90	Nov. 12, 1989	647
GRAPES OF WRATH, THE—(ad) Frank Galati from the novel by John Steinbeck	89-90	Mar. 21, 1990	188
GREAT DIVIDE, THE—William Vaughn Moody	99-09	Oct. 3, 1906	238
GREAT GOD BROWN, THE—Eugene O'Neill	25-26	Jan. 23,1926	271
GREAT WHITE HOPE, THE—Howard Sackler	68-69	Oct. 3, 1968	556
GREEN BAY TREE, THE—Mordaunt Shairp	33-34	Oct. 20, 1933	166
GREEN GODDESS, THE—William Archer	20-21	Jan. 18, 1921	440
GREEN GROW THE LILACS—Lynn Riggs	30-31	Jan. 26, 1931	64
GREEN HAT, THE—Michael Arlen	25-26	Sept. 15, 1925	231
GREEN JULIA—Paul Abelman	72-73	Nov. 16, 1972	147
GREEN PASTURES, THE—Marc Connelly, based on Roark Bradford's *Ol Man Adam and His Chillun*	29-30	Feb. 26, 1930	640
GUS AND AL—Albert Innaurato	88-89	Feb. 27, 1989	25
GUYS AND DOLLS—(b) Jo Swerling, Abe Burrows, based on a story and characters by Damon Runyon, (l, m) Frank Loesser	50-51	Nov. 24, 1950	1,200
GYPSY—Maxwell Anderson	28-29	Jan. 14, 1929	64
HADRIAN VII—Peter Luke, based on works by Fr. Rolfe	68-69	Jan. 8, 1969	359
HAMP—John Wilson, based on an episode from a novel by J.L. Hodson	66-67	Mar. 9, 1967	101
HAPPY TIME, THE—Samuel Taylor, based on Robert Fontaine's book	49-50	Jan. 24, 1950	614
HARRIET—Florence Ryerson, Colin Clements	42-43	Mar. 3, 1943	377

PLAY	VOLUME	OPENED	PERFS
HARVEY—Mary Chase	44-45	Nov. 1, 1944	1,775
HASTY HEART, THE—John Patrick	44-45	Jan. 3, 1945	207
HE WHO GETS SLAPPED—Leonid Andreyev, (ad) Gregory Zilboorg	21-22	Jan. 9, 1922	308
HEART OF MARYLAND, THE—David Belasco	94-99	Oct. 22, 1895	240
HEIDI CHRONICLES, THE—Wendy Wasserstein	88-89	Dec. 11, 1988	81
	88-89	Mar. 9, 1989	621
HEIRESS, THE—Ruth and Augustus Goetz, suggested by Henry James's novel *Washington Square*	47-48	Sept. 29, 1947	410
HELL-BENT FER HEAVEN—Hatcher Hughes	23-24	Jan. 4, 1924	122
HELLO, DOLLY!—(b) Michael Stewart, (m, l) Jerry Herman, based on Thornton Wilder's *The Matchmaker*	63-64	Jan. 16, 1964	2,844
HER MASTER'S VOICE—Clare Kummer	33-34	Oct. 23, 1933	224
HERE COME THE CLOWNS—Philip Barry	38-39	Dec. 7, 1938	88
HERO, THE—Gilbert Emery	21-22	Sept. 5, 1921	80
HIGH TOR—Maxwell Anderson	36-37	Jan. 9, 1937	171
HOGAN'S GOAT—William Alfred	65-66	Nov. 11, 1965	607
HOLIDAY—Philip Barry	28-29	Nov. 26, 1928	229
HOME—David Storey	70-71	Nov. 17, 1970	110
HOME—Samm-Art Williams	79-80	Dec. 14, 1979	82
	79-80	May 7, 1980	279
HOMECOMING, THE—Harold Pinter	66-67	Jan. 5, 1967	324
HOME OF THE BRAVE—Arthur Laurents	45-46	Dec. 27, 1945	69
HOPE FOR A HARVEST—Sophie Treadwell	41-42	Nov. 26, 1941	38
HOSTAGE, THE—Brendan Behan	60-61	Sept. 20, 1960	127
HOT L BALTIMORE, The—Lanford Wilson	72-73	Mar. 22, 1973	1,166
HOUSE OF BLUE LEAVES, THE—John Guare	70-71	Feb. 10, 1971	337
HOUSE OF CONNELLY, THE—Paul Green	31-32	Sept. 28, 1931	91
HOW TO SUCCEED IN BUSINESS WITHOUT REALLY TRYING— (b) Abe Burrows, Jack Weinstock, Willie Gilbert, based on Shepherd Mead's novel, (l, m) Frank Loesser	61-62	Oct. 14, 1961	1,417
HURLYBURLY—David Rabe	84-85	June 21, 1984	45
	84-85	Aug. 7, 1984	343
I AM A CAMERA—John van Druten, based on Christopher Isherwood's Berlin stories	51-52	Nov. 28, 1951	214
I KNOW MY LOVE—S.N. Behrman, based on Marcel Achard's *Auprès de Ma Blonde*	49-50	Nov. 2, 1949	246
I NEVER SANG FOR MY FATHER—Robert Anderson	67-68	Jan. 25, 1968	124
I OUGHT TO BE IN PICTURES—Neil Simon	79-80	Apr. 3, 1980	324
I REMEMBER MAMA—John van Druten, based on Kathryn Forbes's book *Mama's Bank Account*	44-45	Oct. 19, 1944	714
ICEBOUND—Owen Davis	22-23	Feb. 10, 1923	171
ICEMAN COMETH, THE—Eugene O'Neill	46-47	Oct. 9, 1946	136
IDIOT'S DELIGHT—Robert E. Sherwood	35-36	Mar. 24, 1936	300
IF I WERE KING—Justin Huntly McCarthy	99-09	Oct. 14, 1901	56
I'M NOT RAPPAPORT—Herb Gardner	85-86	June 6, 1985	101
	85-86	Nov. 18, 1985	890
IMMORALIST, THE—Ruth and Augustus Goetz, based on André Gide's novel	53-54	Feb. 8, 1954	96
IN ABRAHAM'S BOSOM—Paul Green	26-27	Dec. 30, 1926	116
IN THE MATTER OF J. ROBERT OPPENHEIMER—Heinar Kipphardt, (tr) Ruth Speirs	68-69	Mar. 6, 1969	64
IN THE SUMMER HOUSE—Jane Bowles	53-54	Dec. 29, 1953	55
IN TIME TO COME—Howard Koch, John Huston	41-42	Dec. 28, 1941	40
INADMISSABLE EVIDENCE—John Osborne	65-66	Nov. 30, 1965	166
INCIDENT AT VICHY—Arthur Miller	64-65	Dec. 3, 1964	99

PLAY	VOLUME	OPENED	PERFS
MOTHER COURAGE AND HER CHILDREN—Bertolt Brecht,			
(ad) Eric Bentley	62-63	Mar. 28, 1963	52
MOURNING BECOMES ELECTRA—Eugene O'Neill	31-32	Oct. 26, 1931	150
MR. AND MRS. NORTH—Owen Davis, based on			
Frances and Richard Lockridge's stories	40-41	Jan. 12, 1941	163
MRS. BUMSTEAD-LEIGH—Harry James Smith	09-19	Apr. 3, 1911	64
MRS. MCTHING—Mary Chase	51-52	Feb. 20, 1952	350
MRS. PARTRIDGE PRESENTS—Mary Kennedy,			
Ruth Hawthorne	24-25	Jan. 5, 1925	144
MY CHILDREN! MY AFRICA!—Athol Fugard	89-90	Dec. 18, 1989	28
MY FAIR LADY—(b, l) Alan Jay Lerner, based on			
George Bernard Shaw's *Pygmalion*,			
(m) Frederick Loewe	55-56	Mar. 15, 1956	2,717
MY ONE AND ONLY—(b) Peter Stone, Timothy S. Mayer,			
(m) George Gershwin from *Funny Face* and other			
shows, (l) Ira Gershwin	82-83	May 1, 1983	767
MY SISTER EILEEN—Joseph Fields, Jerome Chodorov,			
based on Ruth McKenney's stories	40-41	Dec. 26, 1940	864
MY 3 ANGELS—Samuel and Bella Spewack, based on			
Albert Huston's play *La Cuisine des Anges*	52-53	Mar. 11, 1953	344
MYSTERY OF EDWIN DROOD, THE—(b, m, l)			
Rupert Holmes (also called *Drood*)	85-86	Aug. 4, 1985	25
	85-86	Dec. 12, 1985	608
NATIONAL HEALTH, THE—Peter Nichols	74-75	Oct. 10, 1974	53
NATIVE SON—Paul Green, Richard Wright, based on			
Mr. Wright's novel	40-41	Mar. 24, 1941	114
NEST, THE—(ad) Grace George, from Paul Geraldy's			
Les Noces d'Argent	21-22	Jan. 28, 1922	152
NEVIS MOUNTAIN DEW—Steve Carter	78-79	Dec. 7, 1978	61
NEXT (see *Adaptation*)			
NEXT TIME I'LL SING TO YOU—James Saunders	63-64	Nov. 27, 1963	23
NICE PEOPLE—Rachel Crothers	20-21	Mar. 2, 1921	247
NICHOLAS NICKLEBY (see *The Life & Adventures of Nicholas*			
Nickleby)			
NIGHT OF THE IGUANA, The—Tennessee Williams	61-62	Dec. 28, 1961	316
'NIGHT, MOTHER—Marsha Norman	82-83	Mar. 31, 1983	380
	83-84	Apr. 18, 1984	54
NINE—(b) Arthur L. Kopit, (m, l) Maury Yeston,			
(ad) Mario Fratti from the Italian	81-82	May 9, 1982	739
NO MORE LADIES—A. E. Thomas	33-34	Jan. 23, 1934	162
NO PLACE TO BE SOMEBODY—Charles Gordone	68-69	May 4, 1969	250
NO TIME FOR COMEDY—S. N. Behrman	38-39	Apr. 17, 1939	185
NO TIME FOR SERGEANTS—Ira Levin, based on			
Mac Hyman's novel	55-56	Oct. 20, 1955	796
NOEL COWARD IN TWO KEYS—Noel Coward (*Come			
Into the Garden Maud* and *A Song at Twilight*)	73-74	Feb. 28, 1974	140
NOISES OFF—Michael Frayn	83-84	Dec. 11, 1983	553
NORMAN CONQUESTS, THE—(see *Living Together*,			
Round and Round the Garden and *Table Manners*)			
NUTS—Tom Topor	79-80	Apr. 28, 1980	96
O MISTRESS MINE—Terence Rattigan	45-46	Jan. 23, 1946	452
ODD COUPLE, THE—Neil Simon	64-65	Mar. 10, 1965	964
OF MICE AND MEN—John Steinbeck	37-38	Nov. 23, 1937	207
OF THEE I SING—George S. Kaufman, Morrie Ryskind,			
(l) Ira Gershwin, (m) George Gershwin	31-32	Dec. 26, 1931	441

PLAY	VOLUME	OPENED	PERFS
OH DAD, POOR DAD, MAMA'S HUNG YOU IN THE CLOSET			
AND I'M FEELIN' SO SAD—Arthur L. Kopit..............	61-62	Feb. 26, 1962	454
OHIO IMPROMPTU, CATASTROPHE and WHAT WHERE—			
Samuel Beckett................................	83-84	June 15, 1983	350
OKLAHOMA!—(b, l) Oscar Hammerstien II, based on			
Lynn Riggs's play *Green Grow the Lilacs,*			
(m) Richard Rodgers	42-43	Mar. 31, 1943	2,212
OLD MAID, THE—Zoë Akins, based on			
Edith Wharton's novel.........................	34-35	Jan. 7, 1935	305
OLD SOAK, THE—Don Marquis	22-23	Aug. 22, 1922	423
OLD TIMES—Harold Pinter	71-72	Nov. 16, 1971	119
OLDEST LIVING GRADUATE, THE—Preston Jones	76-77	Sept. 23, 1976	20
ON BORROWED TIME—Paul Osborn, based on Lawrence			
Edward Watkins's novel	37-38	Feb. 3, 1938	321
ON GOLDEN POND—Ernest Thompson	78-79	Sept. 13, 1978	30
	78-79	Feb. 28, 1979	126
ON TRIAL—Elmer Rice............................	09-19	Aug. 19, 1914	365
ONCE IN A LIFETIME—Moss Hart, George S. Kaufman	30-31	Sept. 24, 1930	406
*ONCE ON THIS ISLAND— (b, l) Lynn Ahrens, (m) Stephen			
Flaherty, based on the novel *My Love My Love*			
by Rosa Guy.................................	89-90	May 6, 1990	24
	90-91	Oct. 18, 1990	258
ONE SUNDAY AFTERNOON—James Hagan	32-33	Feb. 15, 1933	322
ORPHEUS DESCENDING—Tennessee Williams.............	56-57	Mar. 1, 1957	68
*OTHER PEOPLE'S MONEY—Jerry Sterner	88-89	Feb. 16, 1989	954
OTHERWISE ENGAGED—Simon Gray	76-77	Feb. 2, 1977	309
OUTRAGEOUS FORTUNE—Rose Franken	43-44	Nov. 3, 1943	77
OUR TOWN—Thornton Wilder	37-38	Feb. 4, 1938	336
OUTWARD BOUND—Sutton Vane.....................	23-24	Jan. 7, 1924	144
OVER 21—Ruth Gordon	43-44	Jan. 3, 1944	221
OVERTURE—William Bolitho.......................	30-31	Dec. 5, 1930	41
P.S. 193—David Rayfiel...........................	62-63	Oct. 30, 1962	48
PACIFIC OVERTURES—(b) John Weidman, (m, l)			
Stephen Sondheim, (add'l material) Hugh Wheeler	75-76	Jan. 11, 1976	193
PACK OF LIES—Hugh Whitemore	84-85	Feb. 11, 1985	120
PAINTING CHURCHES—Tina Howe....................	83-84	Nov. 22, 1983	206
PARIS BOUND—Philip Barry	27-28	Dec. 27, 1927	234
PASSION OF JOSEPH D., THE—Paddy Chayevsky..........	63-64	Feb. 11, 1964	15
PATRIOTS, THE—Sidney Kingsley.....................	42-43	Jan. 29, 1943	173
PERFECT PARTY, THE—A. R. Gurney	85-86	Apr. 2, 1986	238
PERIOD OF ADJUSTMENT—Tennessee Williams............	60-61	Nov. 10, 1960	132
PERSECUTION AND ASSASSSINATION OF MARAT AS			
PERFORMED BY THE INMATES OF THE ASYLUM OF			
CHARENTON UNDER THE DIRECTION OF THE			
MARQUIS DE SADE, THE—Peter Weiss, English version			
by Geoffrey Skelton, verse (ad) Adrian Mitchell	65-66	Dec. 27, 1965	144
PETRIFIED FOREST, THE—Robert E. Sherwood	34-35	Jan. 7, 1935	197
*PHANTOM OF THE OPERA, THE—(b) Richard Stilgoe,			
Andrew Lloyd Webber, (m) Andrew Lloyd Webber,			
(l) Charles Hart, (add'l l) Richard Stilgoe, adapted from			
the novel by Gaston Leroux (special citation)	87-88	Jan. 26, 1988	1,398
PHILADELPHIA, HERE I COME!—Brian Friel	65-66	Feb. 16, 1966	326
PHILADELPHIA STORY, THE—Philip Barry	38-39	Mar. 28, 1939	417
PHILANTHROPIST, THE—Christopher Hampton	70-71	Mar. 15, 1971	72
PHYSICISTS, THE—Friedrich Duerrenmatt,			
(ad) James Kirkup............................	64-65	Oct. 13, 1964	55

PLAY   VOLUME OPENED PERFS

PLAY	VOLUME	OPENED	PERFS
RUGGED PATH, THE—Robert E. Sherwood	45-46	Nov. 10, 1945	81
RUNNER STUMBLES, THE—Milan Stitt	75-76	May 18, 1976	191
ST. HELENA—R.C. Sheriff, Jeanne de Casalis	36-37	Oct. 6, 1936	63
SAME TIME, NEXT YEAR—Bernard Slade	74-75	Mar. 13, 1975	1,453
SATURDAY'S CHILDREN—Maxwell Anderson	26-27	Jan. 26, 1927	310
SCREENS, THE—Jean Genet, (tr) Minos Volanakis	71-72	Nov. 30, 1971	28
SCUBA DUBA—Bruce Jay Friedman	67-68	Oct. 10, 1967	692
SEA HORSE, THE—Edward J. Moore (James Irwin)	73-74	Apr. 15, 1974	128
SEARCHING WIND, THE—Lillian Hellman	43-44	Apr. 12, 1944	318
SEASCAPE—Edward Albee	74-75	Jan. 26, 1975	65
SEASON IN THE SUN—Wolcott Gibbs	50-51	Sept. 28, 1950	367
SEASON'S GREETINGS—Alan Ayckbourn	85-86	July 11, 1985	20
SECOND THRESHOLD—Philip Barry	50-51	Jan. 2, 1951	126
SECRET SERVICE—William Gillette	94-99	Oct. 5, 1896	176
SEPARATE TABLES—Terence Rattigan	56-57	Oct. 25, 1956	332
SERENADING LOUIE—Lanford Wilson	75-76	May 2, 1976	33
SERPENT, THE—Jean-Claude van Itallie	69-70	May 29, 1973	3
SEVEN KEYS TO BALDPATE—(ad) George M. Cohan, from the novel by Earl Derr Biggers	09-19	Sept. 22, 1913	320
1776—(b) Peter Stone, (m, l) Sherman Edwards, based on a conception by Sherman Edwards	68-69	Mar. 16, 1969	1,217
SEX, DRUGS, ROCK & ROLL—Eric Bogosian	89-90	Feb. 8, 1990	103
SHADOW AND SUBSTANCE—Paul Vincent Carroll	37-38	Jan. 26, 1938	274
SHADOW BOX, THE—Michael Christofer	76-77	Mar. 31, 1977	315
SHADOW OF HEROES—(see *Stone and Star*)			
SHE LOVES ME—(b) Joe Masteroff, based on Miklos Laszlo's play *Parfumerie*, (l) Sheldon Harnick, (m) Jerry Bock	62-63	Apr. 23, 1963	301
SHINING HOUR, THE—Keith Winter	33-34	Feb. 13, 1934	121
SHIRLEY VALENTINE—Willy Russell	88-89	Feb. 16, 1989	324
SHORT EYES—Miguel Piñero	73-74	Feb. 28, 1974	54
	73-74	May 23, 1974	102
SHOW-OFF, THE—George Kelly	23-24	Feb. 5, 1924	571
SHRIKE, THE—Joseph Kramm	51-52	Jan. 15, 1952	161
SILVER CORD, THE—Sidney Howard	26-27	Dec. 20, 1926	112
SILVER WHISTLE, THE—Robert McEnroe	48-49	Nov. 24, 1948	219
SIX CYLINDER LOVE—William Anthony McGuire	21-22	Aug. 25, 1921	430
6 RMS RIV VU—Bob Randall	72-73	Oct. 17, 1972	247
SKIN GAME, THE—John Galsworthy	20-21	Oct. 20, 1920	176
SKIN OF OUR TEETH, THE—Thornton Wilder	42-43	Nov. 18, 1942	359
SKIPPER NEXT TO GOD—Jan de Hartog	47-48	Jan. 4, 1948	93
SKYLARK—Samson Raphaelson	39-40	Oct. 11, 1939	256
SLEUTH—Anthony Shaffer	70-71	Nov. 12, 1970	1,222
SLOW DANCE ON THE KILLING GROUND—William Hanley	64-65	Nov. 30, 1964	88
SLY FOX—Larry Gelbart, based on *Volpone* by Ben Jonson	76-77	Dec. 14, 1976	495
SMALL CRAFT WARNINGS—Tennessee Williams	71-72	Apr. 2, 1972	192
SOLDIER'S PLAY, A—Charles Fuller	81-82	Nov. 20, 1981	468
SOLDIER'S WIFE—Rose Franken	44-45	Oct. 4, 1944	253
SPEED-THE-PLOW—David Mamet	87-88	May 3, 1988	278
SPLIT SECOND—Dennis McIntyre	84-85	June 7, 1984	147
SQUAW MAN, THE—Edward Milton Royle	99-09	Oct. 23, 1905	222
STAGE DOOR—George S. Kaufman, Edna Ferber	36-37	Oct. 22, 1936	169
STAIRCASE—Charles Dyer	67-68	Jan. 10, 1968	61
STAR-WAGON, THE—Maxwell Anderson	37-38	Sept. 29, 1937	223
STATE OF THE UNION—Howard Lindsay, Russel Crouse	45-46	Nov. 14, 1945	765
STEAMBATH—Bruce Jay Friedman	70-71	June 30, 1970	128

PLAY	VOLUME	OPENED	PERFS
TIME OF THE CUCKOO, THE—Arthur Laurents.	52-53	Oct. 15, 1952	263
TIME OF YOUR LIFE, THE—William Saroyan	39-40	Oct. 25, 1939	185
TIME REMEMBERED—Jean Anouilh's *Léocadia*,			
(ad) Patricia Moyes.	57-58	Nov. 12, 1957	248
TINY ALICE—Edward Albee	64-65	Dec. 29, 1964	167
TOILET, THE—LeRoi Jones (a.k.a. Amiri Baraka)	64-65	Dec. 29, 1964	151
TOMORROW AND TOMORROW—Philip Barry	30-31	Jan. 13, 1931	206
TOMORROW THE WORLD—James Gow, Arnaud d'Usseau.	42-43	Apr. 14, 1943	500
TORCH SONG TRILOGY—Harvey Fierstein (*The*			
International Stud, Fugue in a Nursery,			
Widows and Children First)	81-82	Jan. 15, 1982	117
	82-83	June 10, 1982	1,222
TOUCH OF THE POET, A—Eugene O'Neill	58-59	Oct. 2, 1958	284
TOVARICH—Jacques Deval, (tr) Robert E. Sherwood	36-37	Oct. 15, 1936	356
TOYS IN THE ATTIC—Lillian Hellman	59-60	Feb. 25, 1960	556
TRACERS—John DiFusco (c); Vincent Caristi, Richard Chaves.			
John DiFusco, Eric E. Emerson, Rick Gallavan,			
Merlin Marston, Harry Stephens with Sheldon Lettich . . .	84-85	Jan. 21, 1985	186
TRAGÉDIE DE CARMEN, LA—(see *La Tragédie de Carmen*)			
TRANSLATONS—Brian Friel	80-81	Apr. 7, 1981	48
TRAVESTIES—Tom Stoppard	75-76	Oct. 30, 1975	155
TRELAWNY OF THE WELLS—Arthur Wing Pinero	94-99	Nov. 22, 1898	131
TRIAL OF THE CATONSVILLE NINE, THE—Daniel Berrigan,			
Saul Levitt	70-71	Feb. 7, 1971	159
TRIBUTE—Bernard Slade.	77-78	June 1, 1978	212
TWO BLIND MICE—Samuel Spewack	48-49	Mar. 2, 1949	157
UNCHASTENED WOMAN, THE—Louis Kaufman Anspacher.	09-19	Oct. 9, 1915	193
UNCLE HARRY—Thomas Job	41-42	May 20, 1942	430
UNDER MILK WOOD—Dylan Thomas	57-58	Oct. 15, 1957	39
VALLEY FORGE—Maxwell Anderson.	34-35	Dec. 10, 1934	58
VENUS OBSERVED—Christopher Fry	51-52	Feb 13, 1952	86
VERY SPECIAL BABY, A—Robert Alan Aurthur	56-57	Nov. 14, 1956	5
VICTORIA REGINA—Laurence Housman.	35-36	Dec. 26, 1935	517
VIEW FROM THE BRIDGE, A—Arthur Miller	55-56	Sept. 29, 1955	149
VISIT, THE—Friedrich Duerrenmatt, (ad) Maurice Valency. . . .	57-58	May 5, 1958	189
VISIT TO A SMALL PLANET—Gore Vidal	56-57	Feb. 7, 1957	388
VIVAT! VIVAT REGINA!—Robert Bolt	71-72	Jan. 20, 1972	116
VOICE OF THE TURTLE, THE—John van Druten	43-44	Dec. 8, 1943	1,557
WAGER, THE—Mark Medoff	74-75	Oct. 21, 1974	104
WAITING FOR GODOT—Samuel Beckett	55-56	Apr. 19, 1956	59
WALK IN THE WOODS, A—Lee Blessing	87-88	Feb. 28, 1988	136
WALTZ OF THE TOREADORS, THE—Jean Anouilh,			
(tr) Lucienne Hill	56-57	Jan. 17, 1957	132
WATCH ON THE RHINE—Lillian Hellman.	40-41	Apr. 1, 1941	378
WE, THE PEOPLE—Elmer Rice	32-33	Jan. 21, 1933	49
WEDDING BELLS—Salisbury Field	19-20	Nov. 12, 1919	168
WEDNESDAY'S CHILD—Leopold Atlas	33-34	Jan. 16, 1934	56
WENCESLAS SQUARE—Larry Shue.	87-88	Mar. 2, 1988	55
WHAT A LIFE—Clifford Goldsmith.	37-38	Apr. 13, 1938	538
WHAT PRICE GLORY?— Maxwell Anderson,			
Laurence Stallings	24-25	Sept. 3, 1924	433
WHAT THE BUTLER SAW—Joe Orton	69-70	May 4, 1970	224
WHEN YOU COMIN' BACK, RED RYDER?—Mark Medoff	73-74	Dec. 6, 1974	302

INDEX

INDEX

Play titles appear in bold face. *Bold face italic* page numbers refer to those pages where complete cast and credit listings for New York productions may be found.